OWJC

April, 1967

In the Atlantic Channel

In the Atlantic channel space meets time;
    Within these waters continents touch and grow.

    The blood of Europe, flowing to the sea,
Swelled the thin veins of the Americas.

I think of those long drowned in deeps of time
    Who yet distill through me their ancient blood:

    Their only space is time, whose time in me
Is writ in blood, as continents in water.

The unity of life is writ in water,
    Or writ in blood that makes a watery round.

    It is not merely that the earth is one;
By watery nets and bloody we are bound.

Kenneth Scholes

ROBERT BELOOF

University of California, Berkeley

The Performing Voice in Literature

Little, Brown and Company   BOSTON, TORONTO

Frontispoem: "In the Atlantic Channel" by Kenneth Scholes is reprinted with the author's permission.

page 3: (Whitehead) from *The Aims of Education and Other Essays* by Alfred North Whitehead (The Macmillan Co., N.Y., 1929), pp. 78 and 91.

page 27: (Thomas) from *Quite Early One Morning* by Dylan Thomas (New Directions, N.Y., 1954), p. 161.

page 67: (Whitehead) from *The Aims of Education and Other Essays* by Alfred North Whitehead (The Macmillan Co., N.Y., 1929), p. 91.

page 107: (Lewis) from *Experiment in Criticism* by C. S. Lewis (Cambridge University Press, 1961), p. 29.

page 202: (Forster) from *Aspects of the Novel* by E. M. Forster (Harcourt, Brace & World, Inc., N.Y., 1927), p. 67.

page 239: (Conrad) from Preface to *The Nigger of the Narcissus* by Joseph Conrad (Doubleday & Co., Inc., N.Y., 1926), p. xiii.

page 239: (Stevens) from the poem "Theory" by Wallace Stevens. Reprinted from *Collected Poems* by Wallace Stevens, by permission of the publishers, Alfred A. Knopf Co.

page 314: (Lubbock) from *The Craft of Fiction* by Percy Lubbock (Harrison Smith and Jonathan Cape, 1931), p. 251.

page 381: (Yeats) from *Essays* by William Butler Yeats (The Macmillan Co., N.Y., 1924), pp. 195–196. Reprinted by permission of The Macmillan Company and The Macmillan Company of Canada Ltd.

page 417: (Tolstoi) from *The Diaries of Leo Tolstoi*, translated by Hogarth and Sirnis, and reprinted by permission of the publishers, E. P. Dutton & Co., Inc.

page 489: (Frost) from *A Way Out* by Robert Frost. All rights reserved. Reprinted by permission of the Estate of Robert Frost and Holt, Rinehart & Winston, Inc.

TO THE MEMORY OF

Juliet Reeve

friend — Friend — representative
of all true teachers

Preface

Interpretation is a technique of criticism and pedagogy. It has been developed primarily in Speech departments as a means of ensuring that the breath of life remains in a poem or story during the process of analysis. *Interpretation* is also designed to provide a means of exposing the power of those works of literary art which by their aesthetic bases do not fully reveal their force to a purely abstract intellectualization. Moving on from the New Criticism, or *explication de texte,* interpretation adds to the usual page-oriented critical techniques the act of reading aloud as a central means of becoming aware of total passionate meaning (which we take to include a work's dramatic as well as its thematic, grammatic, lexicographic qualities). Therefore, this book takes as its first assumption that inflection, pace, volume, melodic pattern, neural stimuli are all essential to expressing, and comprehending the expression of, emotion through English. The title we have chosen, then, has a double meaning. First this book is background for and introduction to the oral reading of literature by college students in a classroom situation; second, literature itself performs. It is a temporal art that acts out its symbolic fate, and is akin to the musical score in being capable of a certain comprehension on the page (though probably only because of prior experience in the living relationship of voice and body), but is most deeply realized as its possibilities in performance are realized.

Another assumption underlying the book is that fictive prose and poetry, at least initially, might well be viewed as variants of the same art. When one comes to think how many problems they have in common — diction, rhythm, character, imagery, time, narrator — it would really appear only a matter of convenience to discuss these things together. One might, even, see the poet and the fictionalist as two kinds of personalities practicing the same art. I have as yet found no more satisfactory formulation of the problem of "what is poetry and what is prose" than that by Tolstoy, which is quoted at the beginning of Chapter Thirteen. No doubt on the subtler levels the development of a figure or character in a narrative poem is affected by its larger form, and so is somehow an achievement different from a figure or character in a prose story. But these are matters that may well await a later course, where the modes may more happily be separated. For in my experience there are certain unfortunate

vii

tendencies where prose fiction and poetry are introduced in separate semesters. In the poetry course, the whole narrative aspect of poetry tends to be overlooked. Characterization, the development of time, the nature of the voice(s) heard in the poem, even the scene or setting, as such, are often minimized. The student is too often left with the impression that to understand figurative language, prosodic structure, rhythm, and sound devices, will suffice. The opposite condition will often be found in the prose fiction semester. In such cases, it is usual for characterization, the character of the narrator, narrative structure, to be emphasized; figurative language (except, usually, for some attention to the symbol), rhythms of syllable, or event, or place, or figure, are often as good as ignored.

Not every type of writing is included in this book, however. First, factual essays and reportage were eliminated, in order to concentrate on the forms most obviously imaginative (fictional). Further, drama, one of the main forms of imaginative writing, is represented by but one small excerpt, since it requires, in my opinion, to be studied in relation to its medium and the dramatic conventions of the period. Still, the imaginative essays by Melville and Swift should serve as sharp reminders of the indeterminate quality of the line which separates the (from a distance) neatly categorized genres. Melville's essay could have been reportage. In fact, it could have been part of a standard travel book. Instead, the external appearance of the Galapagos Islands and the tortoises that inhabit them are fictionalized into a symbolic vision of man's world and man's nature. Similarly, the Swift essay could have been a statistical, or a polemic, essay on Ireland's poverty. Instead it is a fictive satirization of the eternal, and contemporary, ability of man to abstract someone else's misery. If these borderline works are here partly to remind that genres blend into one another, so are the portions of Austen's novel and *Tristram Shandy* suggestive of the problems that await a further, later, study of the larger fictive forms. For various reasons, then, this book centers on the chief shorter fictive forms — lyric poetry, narrative poetry, the tale, the short story — with other directions hinted at in the essays by Melville and Swift, the excerpt from Hawthorne's notebooks, small parts of two novels, and one short scene from a play.

All this points to a rather curious void in critical terminology (at least in English). So far as I know, there is no clear word which names that body of writing concerned primarily with imaginative constructions. I hope the reader, then, will forgive me if I use the word "fiction" as sometimes meaning, narrowly, prose fiction and at other times, more broadly, all writing, prose or poetry, whose chief aim is the construction of a described rather than a reflected reality. One is already accustomed to this double duty with many words. "Metaphor," for instance, names a very specific kind of figure of speech, but the word is also used in a broadly categorizing manner, meaning simply "figurative." Other words besides this will be found doing service both as narrow, technical, and as broad, inclusive, terms. Thus, "tone," will be used, now to describe the effect of a single phrase, and at other times to refer to a collection of smaller tones which, at some distance, blend into a larger tone. "Description," too, is a word used, broadly, to define the aim of literature and, narrowly, to distinguish the main purpose of one passage from the main purpose of another. Perhaps with greater effort and learning, these semantic difficulties would have yielded to a more sensible solution. But the proliferation of jargon was decidedly *not* one of the aims of this book. As with these and other inevitable terminological difficulties met by anyone who would speak at length of literature, I shall try, no doubt sometimes unsuccessfully, to make the local context resolve local ambiguities.

Another aim of this book is to depart frequently from the usual textbook custom of discussing a poem or story in only one of its aspects. As I have assigned students the task of writing essays, comprehensively discussing a piece in its various elements, it has been borne in upon me that the texts available have not generally offered integrated, coherent examples. Rather, after they have discussed, say, the figurative language of a poem, the reader hears no more about it. Therefore, although many of the works referred to are used only once, others are again discussed in other relationships. In this way it is hoped the student will become accustomed to returning to a work for further exploration to illuminate new problems. Certainly interpretation as critical and tutorial technique underlines that humane, never-ending exploration of the human spirit which is the ideal literary masterpiece-reader relationship.

It may be felt that the chapters on rhythm and meter are of excessive length. Obviously, any book which places the oral aspects of literature in a central position must treat rhythm and meter with great care. Beyond this simple fact, I was driven to summarizing historical background because in my own teaching experience I have found it almost impossible to get the problems of meter clear to the students without placing them in historical perspective. I have been driven to elaborate the problem of determining *stress* by the fact that it *is* a difficult problem, and unless it is so treated, intelligent students are left unsatisfied. But beyond these and other matters derived directly from years of trying to make metrics a meaningful study in the classroom, I found it of first importance to break from the tradition which most texts have followed of making metrics and rhythm unimportant by treating it as if a few simple Latin terms and rules would do the job. Rhythm and metrics are vital to the comprehension of a work, and nowhere is it more clear that the oral dimension must be mastered for total comprehension. In short, it is a complicated, vital problem; and, in my opinion, it cannot be simplified beyond a certain point without loss of essential insight.

And finally, a word about the style of the book. I realize that there is a safe and sane text style, in which the author, by pretending to deal only with objective truths, actually places himself in an unreachable, anonymous position. It seems to me that at this time and place a book of literary "facts" would be a triviality, that some personal insights into fictive visions are decidedly more true than others, but, true or false, they should nonetheless never be so disguised as to appear to be of the same aspect of truth as Ohm's law. The tone I tried to achieve for this book was a rather personal one, in which my judgments would obviously be out of my personal capacity for insight, inviting other judgments out of other capacities. When one person who read the manuscript of this book wrote: ". . . the personal tone often leaves me feeling that I am listening to Mr. Beloof talking *today*, and that if I were to talk back, he might talk rather differently tomorrow," I knew that I had succeeded at least in certain stylistic aims. Perhaps I have succeeded too well. For just as many want that impossible (and to my way of thinking, undesirable) thing, "scientific," totally objective history, so do some people not like to recall that their feelings about *Hamlet* and their ability to perceive its meaning, have not been static. It has been my observation that those students who take literature into their lives *talk* about it. For others literature is too remote and forbidding for discussion. (One may argue about a movie, enriching one's insight by other visions, but literature has a capital "L" and is too grand for the grubby hands of the layman.) Thus I wanted a book that, while dealing with objective fact, such as the definition of hyperbole, used an appropriate tone. But also I wanted one that *talked* about literature, with all that implies both of necessary commitment of the moment and the implied growth in the endless dialogue looking behind and beyond itself.

My debts to friends and colleagues are many and deep. Those colleagues selected by my publisher to criticize this book are unknown to me but their comments were very valuable. Those known to me I have thanked more personally than can be done here. The flaws that remain in what follows merely show that I am a recalcitrant pupil and do not reflect on their tutorship. I owe an especial debt to Mrs. Pearlanna Briggs for her close stylistic scrutiny, persevered in against all hope of intrinsic reward. I must thank Mrs. Eleanor McGuffey for her devoted support as well as for secretarial aid. For her perceptive work on table of contents, indexes, and other vital matters I thank Mrs. Miriam Ostroff. And finally, of course, homage to my wife, Ruth LaBarre Beloof, who in so many ways kept the ship on course.

Contents

The Performing Voice
in Literature

Yet vanity inclines us to find faults anywhere rather than in ourselves. He that reads and grows no wiser, seldom suspects his own deficiency, but complains of hard words and obscure sentences, and asks why books are written which cannot be understood.

SAMUEL JOHNSON

PART ONE

*The Why and How
of Literature's Third Dimension*

CHAPTER ONE

A Case for Oral
Presentation of Literature

Above all the art of reading aloud should be
cultivated.

I lay it down as an educational axiom that in
teaching you will come to grief as soon as you
forget that your pupils have bodies.

ALFRED NORTH WHITEHEAD

Increasing numbers of students over the country are finding oral reading a valuable approach to literature. The simple purpose of this book is to show others why, and to encourage them to similar explorations.

Therefore, before more detailed matters arise, this would seem the appropriate place to state as briefly as possible a justification for an oral approach to literature as well as to summarize what some of its general benefits might be. I can then move on to specific professional problems of its general relevance as a part of the literary discipline.

There are certain pragmatic, tutorial advantages in the use of reading aloud so far as the teaching of literature is concerned, advantages which may be discovered by any teacher who cares to take the time to discipline his own ear and voice. I should like to suggest further that there is evidence that the tuning of body and voice to the text as part of this process is not in its absence simply one pleasure missing, but might rather be considered an irremediable loss, permanently limiting the possibility for full comprehension.

The nature of this loss might be defined most simply by recalling the absolutely essential role that oral imitation plays (not only in vocabulary, but also in pitch, volume, pause, and timbre) in the process of a child's mastering the first levels of his parents' expressive language. Imagine then that the average person's reservoir of expressive patterns levels off (as does his vocabulary) as he approaches and achieves adulthood. This leveling off will obviously be limited by such factors as geography, class, profession. Imagine, then, this same person faced with an array of literary minds with a *genius* for expressive language. Does it not seem logical that new and more complex oral disciplines, consisting of hearing new patterns and of repetitive and experimental speech, might play an important role in making that further leap into comprehension of a higher expressiveness? And, more speculatively, could it not be possible that the general public's increasing disinterest in fine prose and fine poetry may be laid in part at the door of an educative system that generally keeps this obviously auditory art mute?

But one need not speculate so broadly. Sufficient evidence has already been gathered by psychologists and physiologists to indicate that in the workings of imaginative man (and with what else is literature dealing?) the body and the mind are inseparable, that they feast together and starve together, that they are ignorant, or knowledgeable, together.

I shall not press this obvious point. We have all been made increasingly familiar during the last half century with the idea that emotional factors affect our physical condition; indeed the word "psychosomatic" has almost become another witching word, like those phrases of an earlier age, "blood disorder," "consumption," or "catarrh." We are perhaps less familiar with the opposite theory, that the body may *create* emotional conditions and may, at least to some extent, control them. The theory has served as the basis of some fruitful work by physiologists, especially in the area of controlling such symptoms as the *globus hystericus* (commonly experienced as "lump in the throat") by training the body in techniques of relaxation.[1] Certainly there have been for some time theories that, in a non-psychopathic personality, at least some emotions cannot arise until glandular, vascular, and certain other physiological changes take place. For example, these theories indicate that panic does not arise without prior glandular and other bodily alterations. Faced by a lion, the hunter controls his nerves, muscles, heartbeats, probably at least partly by concentrating on his hunting technique, and this concentration limits, disciplines, and utilizes his fear. Sometimes a simple experiment will illustrate this point. Very often it is possible to create a change in one's inner feeling simply by balling up the hands into fists, clenching the teeth, and tensing the body. These acts often prove sufficient, even in the absence of any external stimuli, to alter the heartbeat and bloodpressure. It is well known that some actors can cause tears to flow by screwing up the face, and that emotions follow, which make a further flow of tears spontaneous.

These two approaches, the psychological and the physiological, to the understanding of the essential unity of a human being do not really contradict one another, but rather intermingle in ways we cannot yet, and may never, untangle. Meanwhile they serve to redirect our attention to the inseparability of psyche and body. A good deal of the research on the conditions of peripheral muscle-responses to reading has given results which are particularly pertinent to the problem of reading aloud as it affects comprehension of literature. The research seems to suggest a very interesting dichotomy. If the material read is prosaic, routine material, the measuring devices of scientists register an insignificant degree of bodily response. But if one reads new, unfamiliar, difficult, or emotionally charged material, the body responds significantly in muscular and neural ways, including responses of nerve impulses in the tongue. Interestingly enough, for deaf people these reactions may include finger movements.[2] Certainly no competent teacher of literature would like to think that his students are approaching stories and poems as dull, routine material.

But the evidence given above raises a question. Is the silent reader, responding as he is in subliminal ways with his body and his ear to the work, responding accurately? Here again experimental evidence has shown

---

[1] Edmund Jacobson, *Progressive Relaxation*, University of Chicago Press, 1938.

[2] See, for instance, studies by A. N. Sokolov, "A Psychological Analysis of the Understanding of a foreign text," *Izvestia* A P N RSFSR (1947), #7; "Investigations into the Problems of the Speech Mechanisms of Thinking," *Psikol. Nauka* V SSSR 1959, vol. 1; "Silent Speech in the Study of Foreign Languages," *Vop. Psik.* (1960), #5.

that when people listen, they remember what they have heard by re-creating it to themselves. This process explains why foreigners hear people speak with the accent they themselves use. In short, the material comes in and is converted into the listener's system of signs and signals, and the understanding of the communication is based on his own system. This series of psychological events must also indicate what happens to reading and hearing of difficult and complex literary material. The material comes in and is converted to physical signals within the bodily vocabulary of the hearer, and it is that which determines the hearer's or reader's degree of understanding.[3]

Some implications should be immediately clear. If a person has not in his head the vocal intonation, the proper bodily response as well as the vocabulary for

> O for a beaker full of the warm south!
> Full of the true, the blushful Hippocrene,
> With beaded bubbles winking at the brim,
>   And purple-stained mouth;

then he *cannot* understand its tonal meaning. He can look the words up in a dictionary, but the yearning toward the Pagan, toward the clear Mediterranean, toward the southern mind, toward a delicious irresponsibility, the particular tonal combination — its exact depth and power — will be beyond him. The evidence would seem to indicate that it can only fully and exactly live for him as he learns to bring it alive in the voice and body.

It is of little comfort to the student of literature that many, in fact most, of the best writers read aloud abominably, yet obviously write good stories and poetry. The intonations in nearly all writers' heads are limited and may very well account for the unique style which marks each writer from his fellows. Many Hemingway characters, really, talk alike. That is, they have the same intonations, sentence structures, and, usually, the same vocabulary. (Is it any accident that Shakespeare, an actor and hence accustomed to adopting in his own body a variety of vocal intonations, has perhaps the broadest, most varied style in literature?) All Herrick poems, for an older example, all Eliot for a modern one, bear the same kind of imprint from the limited patterns of their makers' minds.[4] Such a writer obviously, then, is exploring a relatively limited range of human passion-

---

[3] See, for instance, studies by Alvin M. Liberman, *et al.*, "The Discrimination of Speech Sounds Within and Across Phoneme Boundaries," *Journal of Experimental Psychology*, 54 (1957), 358–368; "The Discrimination of Relative Onset-Time of the Components of Certain Speech and Nonspeech Patterns," *Journal of Experimental Psychology*, 61 (1961), 379–388.

[4] A book by a British critic has explored this relationship of the writer's own voice to the voices in his work. Francis Berry, *Poetry and The Physical Voice*, Oxford University Press, 1962.

ate utterance, and it is logical that his performing voice has to bear out a *general* relationship to the subtleties he holds in his head. No matter how poorly the poet reads his own work, I have always been able to hear in it the source of his own poetry. Yet reading someone else's work, the poet is simply in the same boat as any other intelligent and untrained oral reader — and his reading, and his tastes, show it. The writer, of course, is under chief obligation to his own voice and vision, not to "literature" in general. The oral reader — in sum, he who would have a living comprehension of the world of literature — has a different obligation.

Another implication: if the reader has *learned wrongly* the vocal and bodily experience, the poem is beyond him. If he reads with a singsong rhythm or some other ironbound vocal pattern, this limitation will not merely impair his reading aloud; it will impair his silent reading, for surely the evidence points out that one needs to know the proper vocal patterns even to read silently — providing that one is reaching for the profound rather than the superficial level. Not so many years ago a book called *Practical Criticism* by I. A. Richards revolutionized attitudes toward teaching literature by the simple device of demonstrating that university students, in their readings of literature, were missing a good deal of the tonal subtlety. This rather elementary discovery has been the foundation of a widespread — one might almost say universal — acceptance of close criticism as an essential part of the undergraduate university curriculum. The gain has been admirable, yet it is necessary to heed such cautionary advice as that expressed by Professor Don Geiger: ". . . we have some cause to fear that an inordinate stress on critical activity simply produces people who become interested in critical activity." After quoting Miss Mona Van Duyn, the editor of *Perspective,* a literary magazine, as saying that in her experience there are "at least five times as many people who are interested in reading what someone has to say about certain novels, stories, and poems than there are people who are interested in reading novels, stories, and poems," Mr. Geiger goes on to point out that he does not "really attribute this deplorable lack of balance in the reading diet simply to the introduction of critical analysis in the classroom. It is sufficient, I think, to note that a very great emphasis on 'close' reading has not yet perceptibly increased the affection of the public for fiction and poetry."[5]

The point of all this goes back, in my estimation, to the kind of tonal qualities which Richards found students were not hearing. These students seemed to have little trouble with what one might call the basic, biologically oriented tones — hate, greed, love, pain, those tones whose lingual signals they would adequately have developed in their own bodies by

[5] Don Geiger, *The Sound, Sense, and Performance of Literature,* Scott, Foresman & Co., 1963, p. 29.

imitation of the normal bodily, vocal, and verbal signals of their everyday environment. What was escaping them was precisely those tones arising out of a more complex, more sophisticated level of verbal signals than they were likely to have encountered during their openly imitative period: tones of irony, ambiguity, and other complicated balances of attitudes. And how were they to learn this new and subtle language? So far the effort has been made almost entirely through a careful definition of the types of irony and ambiguity — through a purely book-bound, purely intellectual effort. Valuable as this approach may be, excellent as many of these books have been, and successful as they have no doubt been with many individual students, the evidence points to it as falling short of the optimum tutorial technique.

For there are yet further implications of the evidence concerning language learning and the relation of the body and voice to total emotional comprehension. One is that people can be forced out of routine and superficial reading by making them read aloud, by making them hear the thinness of their own perception, and by having them listen to richer, more subtle vocal experiences. Another facet of this evidence is that, once past the open, imitative stage of childhood, adults tend to penetrate directly *through* the sound, rhythm, and vocal patterning of language to the denotative meaning of words, a habit which is, of course, deadly to the comprehension of the subtleties of fine prose and poetry, and which ties in with what has already been said about the fact that many people seem to stop short of comprehending in any living way the more subtle tones. How can one get the adult to revert to the child's fascination with sound, rhythm, and vocal pattern, a reversion that is necessary to start the surge toward absorbing new and more complicated lingual — one might say biological — insights? It would seem obvious that, along with close reading and careful, imaginative discussion, reading aloud may well be a vital element in the process of coming to terms with writing which is structured to achieve aesthetic ends more subtle than ordinary expository prose, ends of emotional, rather than of merely logical, accuracy. Yet other evidence points to the relation of bodily involvement to sympathetic understanding. Opinion-changing experiments indicate that people who read silently the opinions of others were not much affected, but that people who played a role, who orally presented the arguments appropriate to a position different from their own were definitely swayed.[6] Having actively become involved with their bodies and voices, they found themselves with new knowledge of, I suspect, the most valuable kind. Obviously, in our culture, most reading is going to continue to be silent reading. But the great question I hope I have raised is whether or not the quality,

[6] See, for instance, Irving Janis and Bert King, "The influence of role playing on opinion change," *J. Abnorm. Soc. Psych.*, 49 (1954), 211–218.

depth, and excitement of that silent reading is not profoundly affected by the ability of the body and mind to give proper biological signals,[7] an ability which can best be learned in the same way a child learns to express his needs and reactions, through overt bodily and vocal involvement and through a close relationship with a teacher of trained, responsive voice and sensitive mind.

What is the relevance of all this for the validation of oral interpretation? There is every indication, regarding understanding of a literary work of art, that full comprehension can come only through the participation of our bodies — that even the rational process itself is a special kind of emotional set which must be learned through a certain control of the body. And one explanation for that not uncommon phenomenon, the person who has read all the past masterpieces and yet cannot, faced with a new work, come to any sense of its quality, power, importance, or even, all too often, meaning, may well be that a mere training of the historical or analytical faculty may be insufficient. Perhaps a training of the *whole man* would fill a lack.

Thus I think one can point to the sanction of oral interpretation in this more and more widely realized fact: that whether, as the psychiatrists say, the body responds to the emotions or, as the physiologists say, the emotions respond to the body, neither can exist without the other; that in fact they are inseparable in creating and controlling the human psyche. Further, we would comprehend nothing important of a literary text without our whole history of bodily responses giving us its reactions to the symbolic gestures of the language. Thus, the value of oral interpretation in the classroom centers around its power to force the teacher and the student consciously to discover and, through symbolic language interacting with representational action (gesture, expression, intonation), to project and outwardly define these subtle and otherwise subliminal reactions. In other words, oral interpretation can force the reader and his audience to a *realization* of his and their reactions to the work of art. Or, and this is equally educative, the reader can force his hearers to recognize disagreements in interpretation of which they might not otherwise have been aware.

This discussion is, I hope, straightforward, and one might well ask where then does the feeling against oral interpretation as a legitimate part of the curriculum arise. I should like to suggest that it arises in precisely those moments in the classroom when the subliminal bodily responses are required to be bodied forth in a series of such physical manifestations as gestures, expressions, and vocal tones, in a tight relationship

[7] For a study of the limitations on communication skills that can rise from the situation of the total person, see Edith Buxbaum, "The role of a second language in the formation of ego and superego," *Psych. Q.*, (1949), 18:279–89.

with the language of the text. Obviously, to accomplish one of those transliterations requires training, either conscious or cultural; since the advent of printing fewer and fewer people have disciplined themselves to achieve such transliterations with any degree of success.

In general, the public has lost its ear, and young people's auditory responses are not being retrained in the schools; there are no academic rewards for the teacher who goes beyond the present call of duty to learn the discipline of reading aloud. As a result, when one does hear literature read aloud, poetry especially, he almost always hears one of two main kinds of stylistic error. Robert Breen has described them quite succinctly. "The reader may characteristically use a conversational mode for his readings and thereby do disservice to the lyrical" [and one would add — dramatic] "quality of the verse. Or he may employ a singing mode for poetry because he feels that poetry and conversation do not mix."[8] In the latter case he is usually afraid that the listeners won't recognize the "poetry" in it. In either case both readers, in their respective ways, make all the poems they read sound alike, no matter how various the passionate meanings. Some teachers and, though they should know better, even some poets make a programmatic assertion in favor of such "sound alike" readings. The usual argument is that the text should be read in a neutral voice so as not to confuse the reader's personality with the text. It should be clear that such an attitude *inevitably achieves precisely the result it would avoid*. For example, to read Gerard Manley Hopkins' poem, "God's Grandeur," in a calm, neutral voice would constitute a violation of the tone of the text and would therefore call attention to the personality of the reader as someone who was in some way withholding himself, and consequently us, from the text. Even worse, what such persons usually *really* mean by this argument is, "I have an untrained voice and body but, after all, that is the best way to be when reading literature, for that will ensure my being natural." If a voice that is monotonously repeating the same melodic patterns, going on at the same rate and volume no matter what is happening in the poem, is natural, then naturalness is a value which we must seriously rethink.

Not too many years ago I went to hear a famous poet read. A thousand people were assembled. He read with his eyes on the book, his voice directed at the rostrum and fixed in a monotonous hum that left one quite certain that an article was of the same quality as a verb, that each poem had no beginning or end, and that one poem had exactly the same weight and quality of passion as the next. Whatever that person's contribution to letters at the writing table, I am quite clear in my mind that that evening his disservice to letters was real, and that he accepted his fee under false

---

[8] Robert Breen, "Some Difficulties in Reading Modern Poetry Publicly," *Western Speech* (Oct. 1955), 249.

pretenses. And the result was *not* that his personality withdrew from between the poems and the audience. On the contrary, the attention and discomfort of the audience was directed at the reader.

If a poor pianist ventures a Mozart sonata, his miserable mistakes do not call our attention *from* him, but *to* him. The truth is that the only way for a reader to efface himself in favor of the text is to have so trained himself that he can exactly reflect the movement and passion of the piece: that he can become precisely, according to the potential of his own instrument, his voice and body, the voice or voices that emerge from the text or, rather, that are the text.

Recently a young professor, who knew all there was to know in a scholarly and critical way about a poem (and its poet) which he was trying to read aloud, came up with a reading completely missing the tone of the poem. Finally, after several weeks more of oral exploration of the text, he had worked out a revealing reading. Puzzling over the reason why his critical labors had still left him short of a comprehension of the tone, a comprehension which he achieved only after a further extensive exploration through voice and body, he said that perhaps it was like the difference between reading a map and trying to find one's way over the actual terrain. This is one of the most satisfying figures I have heard to describe the insight of those who have actually gone through the experience. For those who have not, it is, like love in the abstract, a very difficult thing to comprehend.

If there is, then, a particular kind of literary activity with which oral interpretation in its simpler undergraduate application is most closely tied, it is, I suggest, textual explication. The analysis of the text is the prior, if not, indeed, the concurrent condition to the oral reading; and it is therefore in classes concentrating in an intense deliberation on a relatively few texts that oral interpretation in its introductory courses has some of its most useful moments. Though this abstract analysis is requisite to a lifting of any study of vocal technique above the mechanical, at the same time a body and voice unable to translate the abstract meaning into some kind of biological reality belongs to a person suffering from a fatal literary schizophrenia, from which not cleverness, learning, or native brilliance can save him. Most of this book is concerned with developing a technique of rhetorical analysis especially suited to classes devoted to this reciprocity, this unity, of body and mind. That this technique arises principally out of an attempt to learn exactly the central tonal elements, I take as some possible contribution to the field of close criticism.

We hear much these days of the sterility of close criticism, of its having painted itself into some kind of dusty corner which has turned out to be strangely anti-poetic. To the extent that this unhappy situation has occurred, is it not possibly because our critics have not carried their theories

to their logical conclusion, namely, that language really *is* gesture and that
perhaps the truest close reading might be in an oral, a living, expression
of the text or, at least, that such a reading might be the best proof of the
close criticism?

An oral approach to literature is not a panacea for the enormous problem of involving students in a creative way with a work of literature.
Philological, historical, biographical, and critical considerations must all
play their part in that process. Nonetheless, it should not be ignored, for
no other technique offers so creative a potential for unifying the critically
discovered parts of the work of art in the psychosomatic whole which is
the student's sensibility.

SELECTIONS

Sense and Sensibility

JANE AUSTEN

I

The family of Dashwood had been long settled in Sussex. Their estate
was large, and their residence was at Norland Park, in the centre of their
property, where, for many generations, they had lived in so respectable a
manner as to engage the general good opinion of their surrounding acquaintance. The late owner of this estate was a single man, who lived to a
very advanced age, and who for many years of his life had a constant
companion and housekeeper in his sister. But her death, which happened
ten years before his own, produced a great alteration in his home; for to
supply her loss he invited and received into his house the family of his
nephew Mr. Henry Dashwood, the legal inheritor of the Norland estate,
and the person to whom he intended to bequeath it. In the society of his
nephew and niece, and their children, the old gentleman's days were
comfortably spent. His attachment to them all increased. The constant
attention of Mr. and Mrs. Henry Dashwood to his wishes, which proceeded not merely from interest, but from goodness of heart, gave him
every degree of solid comfort which his age could receive; and the cheerfulness of the children added a relish to his existence.

By a former marriage, Mr. Henry Dashwood had one son; by his
present lady, three daughters. The son, a steady, respectable young man,
was amply provided for by the fortune of his mother, which had been
large, and half of which devolved on him on his coming of age. By his
own marriage, likewise, which happened soon afterwards, he added to his

wealth. To him, therefore, the succession to the Norland estate was not so really important as to his sisters; for their fortune, independent of what might arise to them from their father's inheriting that property, could be but small. Their mother had nothing, and their father only seven thousand pounds in his own disposal; for the remaining moiety of his first wife's fortune was also secured to her child, and he had only a life-interest in it.

The old gentleman died: his will was read; and, like almost every other will, gave as much disappointment as pleasure. He was neither so unjust, nor so ungrateful, as to leave his estate from his nephew; but he left it to him on such terms as destroyed half the value of the bequest. Mr. Dashwood had wished for it more for the sake of his wife and daughters than for himself or his son; but to his son, and his son's son, a child of four years old, it was secured, in such a way as to leave to himself no power of providing for those who were most dear to him, and who most needed a provision, by any charge on the estate, or by any sale of its valuable woods. The whole was tied up for the benefit of this child, who, in occasional visits with his father and mother at Norland, had so far gained on the affections of his uncle, by such attractions as are by no means unusual in children of two or three years old, — an imperfect articulation, an earnest desire of having his own way, many cunning tricks, and a great deal of noise, — as to outweigh all the value of all the attention which for years he had received from his niece and her daughters. He meant not to be unkind, however, and, as a mark of his affection for the three girls, he left them a thousand pounds apiece.

Mr. Dashwood's disappointment was at first severe; but his temper was cheerful and sanguine; and he might reasonably hope to live many years, and by living economically, lay by a considerable sum from the produce of an estate already large, and capable of almost immediate improvement. But the fortune, which had been so tardy in coming, was his only one twelvemonth. He survived his uncle no longer; and ten thousand pounds, including the late legacies, was all that remained for his widow and daughters.

His son was sent for as soon as his danger was known; and to him Mr. Dashwood recommended, with all the strength and urgency which illness could command, the interest of his mother-in-law and sisters.

Mr. John Dashwood had not the strong feelings of the rest of the family; but he was affected by a recommendation of such a nature at such a time, and he promised to do everything in his power to make them comfortable. His father was rendered easy by such an assurance, and Mr. John Dashwood had then leisure to consider how much there might prudently be in his power to do for them.

He was not an ill-disposed young man, unless to be rather cold-hearted and rather selfish is to be ill-disposed; but he was, in general, well respected, for he conducted himself with propriety in the discharge of his ordinary duties. Had he married a more amiable woman, he might have been made still more respectable than he was; he might even have been made amiable himself, for he was very young when he married, and very fond of his wife. But Mrs. John Dashwood was a strong caricature of himself, — more narrow-minded and selfish.

When he gave his promise to his father, he meditated within himself to increase the fortunes of his sisters by the present of a thousand pounds apiece. He then really thought himself equal to it. The prospect of four thousand a year, in addition to his present income, besides the remaining half of his own mother's fortune, warmed his heart, and made him feel capable of generosity. "Yes, he would give them three thousand pounds; it would be liberal and handsome! It would be enough to make them completely easy. Three thousand pounds! he could spare so considerable a sum with little inconvenience." He thought of it all day long, and for many days successively, and he did not repent.

No sooner was his father's funeral over than Mrs. John Dashwood, without sending any notice of her intention to her mother-in-law, arrived with her child and their attendants. No one could dispute her right to come; the house was her husband's from the moment of his father's decease; but the indelicacy of her conduct was so much the greater, and to a woman in Mrs. Dashwood's situation, with only common feelings, must have been highly unpleasing; but in *her* mind there was a sense of honor so keen, a generosity so romantic, that any offence of the kind, by whomsoever given or received, was to her a source of immovable disgust. Mrs. John Dashwood had never been a favorite with any of her husband's family; but she had had no opportunity, till the present, of showing them with how little attention to the comfort of other people she could act when occasion required it.

So acutely did Mrs. Dashwood feel this ungracious behavior, and so earnestly did she despise her daughter-in-law for it, that, on the arrival of the latter, she would have quitted the house forever, had not the entreaty of her eldest girl induced her first to reflect on the propriety of going, and her own tender love for all her three children determined her afterwards to stay, and for their sakes avoid a breach with their brother.

Elinor, this eldest daughter whose advice was so effectual, possessed a strength of understanding and coolness of judgment which qualified her, though only nineteen, to be the counsellor of her mother, and enabled her frequently to counteract, to the advantage of them all, that eagerness of mind in Mrs. Dashwood which must generally have led to imprudence. She had an excellent heart; her disposition was affectionate, and her feelings were strong, but she knew how to govern them. It was a knowledge which her mother had yet to learn, and which one of her sisters had resolved never to be taught.

Marianne's abilities were, in many respects, quite equal to Elinor's. She was sensible and clever, but eager in everything: her sorrows, her joys, could have no moderation. She was generous, amiable, interesting; she was everything but prudent. The resemblance between her and her mother was strikingly great.

Elinor saw, with concern, the excess of her sister's sensibility; but by Mrs. Dashwood it was valued and cherished. They encouraged each other now in the violence of their affliction. The agony of grief which overpowered them at first was voluntarily renewed, was sought for, was created again and again. They gave themselves up wholly to their sorrow, seeking increase of wretchedness in every reflection that could afford it, and resolved against ever admitting consolation in future. Elinor, too, was deeply afflicted; but still she could struggle, she could exert herself. She could consult with her brother; could receive her sister-in-law on her arrival, and treat her with proper attention; and could strive to rouse her mother to similar exertion, and encourage her to similar forbearance.

Margaret, the other sister, was a good-humored, well-disposed girl; but as she had already imbibed a good deal of Marianne's romance without having much of her sense, she did not, at thirteen, bid fair to equal her sisters at a more advanced period of life.

II

Mrs. John Dashwood now installed herself mistress of Norland; and her mother and sisters in law were degraded to the condition of visitors. As such, however, they were treated by her with quiet civility; and by her husband with as much kindness as he could feel towards anybody beyond himself, his wife, and their child. He really pressed them, with some earnestness, to consider Norland as their home; and, as no plan appeared so eligible to Mrs. Dashwood as remaining there till she could accommodate herself with a house in the neighborhood, his invitation was accepted.

A continuance in a place where everything reminded her of former delight was exactly what suited her mind. In seasons of cheerfulness no temper could be more cheerful than hers, or possess in a greater degree that sanguine expectation of happiness which is happiness itself. But in sorrow she must be equally carried away by her fancy, and as far beyond consolation as in pleasure she was beyond alloy.

Mrs. John Dashwood did not at all approve of what her husband intended to do for his sisters. To take three thousand pounds from the fortune of their dear little boy would be impoverishing him to the most dreadful degree. She begged him to think again on the subject. How could he answer it to himself to rob his child, and his only child too, of so large a sum? And what possible claim could the Miss Dashwoods, who were related to him only by half blood, which she considered as no relationship at all, have on his generosity to so large an amount? It was very well known that no affection was ever supposed to exist between the children of any man by different marriages; and why was he to ruin himself and their poor little Harry by giving away all his money to his half-sisters?

"It was my father's last request to me," replied her husband, "that I should assist his widow and daughters."

"He did not know what he was talking of, I dare say; ten to one but he was light-headed at the time. Had he been in his right senses, he could not have thought of such a thing as begging you to give away half your fortune from your own child."

"He did not stipulate for any particular sum, my dear Fanny; he only requested me, in general terms, to assist them, and make their situation more comfortable than it was in his power to do. Perhaps it would have been as well if he had left it wholly to myself. He could hardly suppose I should neglect them. But as he required the promise, I could not do less than give it; at least, I thought so at the time. The promise therefore was given, and must be performed. Something must be done for them whenever they leave Norland and settle in a new home."

"Well, then, *let* something be done for them; but *that* something need not be three thousand pounds. Consider," she added, "that when the money is once parted with, it never can return. Your sisters will marry, and it will be gone forever. If, indeed, it could ever be restored to our poor little boy — "

"Why, to be sure," said her husband, very gravely, "that would make a great difference. The time may come when Harry will regret that so large a sum was parted with. If he should have a numerous family, for instance, it would be a very convenient addition."

"To be sure it would."

"Perhaps, then, it would be better for all parties if the sum were diminished one half. Five hundred pounds would be a prodigious increase to their fortunes!"

"Oh! beyond anything great! What brother on earth would do half so much for his sisters, even if *really* his sisters! And as it is, — only half-blood! But you have such a generous spirit!"

"I would not wish to do anything mean," he replied. "One had rather, on such occasions, do too much than too little. No one, at least, can think

I have not done enough for them; even themselves, they can hardly expect more."

"There is no knowing what *they* may expect," said the lady, "but we are not to think of their expectations: the question is, what you can afford to do."

"Certainly; and I think I may afford to give them five hundred pounds apiece. As it is, without any addition of mine, they will each have above three thousand pounds on their mother's death, — a very comfortable fortune for any young woman."

"To be sure it is; and, indeed, it strikes me that they can want no addition at all. They will have ten thousand pounds divided amongst them. If they marry, they will be sure of doing well; and if they do not, they may all live very comfortably together on the interest of ten thousand pounds."

"That is very true, and therefore I do not know whether, upon the whole, it would not be more advisable to do something for their mother while she lives, rather than for them, — something of the annuity kind, I mean. My sisters would feel the good effects of it as well as herself. A hundred a year would make them all perfectly comfortable."

His wife hesitated a little, however, in giving her consent to this plan.

"To be sure," said she, "it is better than parting with fifteen hundred pounds at once. But then, if Mrs. Dashwood should live fifteen years, we shall be completely taken in."

"Fifteen years! my dear Fanny; her life cannot be worth half that purchase."

"Certainly not; but if you observe, people always live forever when there is an annuity to be paid them; and she is very stout and healthy, and hardly forty. An annuity is a very serious business; it comes over and over every year, and there is no getting rid of it. You are not aware of what you are doing. I have known a great deal of the trouble of annuities; for my mother was clogged with the payment of three to old superannuated servants by my father's will, and it is amazing how disagreeable she found it. Twice every year these annuities were to be paid; and then there was the trouble of getting it to them; and then one of them was said to have died, and afterwards it turned out to be no such thing. My mother was quite sick of it. Her income was not her own, she said, with such perpetual claims on it; and it was the more unkind in my father, because, otherwise, the money would have been entirely at my mother's disposal, without any restriction whatever. It has given me such an abhorrence of annuities, that I am sure I would not pin myself down to the payment of one for all the world."

"It is certainly an unpleasant thing," replied Mr. Dashwood, "to have those kind of yearly drains on one's income. One's fortune, as your mother justly says, is *not* one's own. To be tied down to the regular payment of such a sum on every rent-day is by no means desirable; it takes away one's independence."

"Undoubtedly; and, after all, you have no thanks for it. They think themselves secure; you do no more than what is expected, and it raises no gratitude at all. If I were you, whatever I did should be done at my own discretion entirely. I would not bind myself to allow them anything yearly. It may be very inconvenient some years to spare a hundred or even fifty pounds from our own expenses."

"I believe you are right, my love; it will be better that there should be no annuity in the case: whatever I may give them occasionally will be of far greater assistance than a yearly allowance, because they would only enlarge their style of living if they felt sure of a larger income, and would not be sixpence the richer for it at the end of the year. It will certainly be much the best way. A present of fifty pounds now and then will prevent their ever being distressed for money, and will, I think, be amply discharging my promise to my father."

"To be sure it will. Indeed, to say the truth, I am convinced within myself that your father had no idea of your giving them any money at all. The assistance he thought of, I dare say, was only such as might be reasonably expected of you; for instance, such as looking out for a comfortable small house for them, helping them to move their things, and sending them presents of fish and game, and so forth, whenever they are in season. I'll lay my life that he meant nothing farther; indeed, it would be very strange and unreasonable if he did. Do but consider, my dear Mr. Dashwood, how excessively comfortable your mother-in-law and her daughters may live on the interest of seven thousand pounds, besides the thousand pounds belonging to each of the girls, which brings them in fifty pounds a year apiece, and of course they will pay their mother for their board out of it. Altogether, they will have five hundred a year amongst them, and what on earth can four women want for more than that? — They will live so cheap! Their housekeeping will be nothing at all. They will have no carriage, no horses, and hardly any servants; they will keep no company, and can have no expenses of any kind! Only conceive how comfortable they will be! Five hundred a year! I am sure I cannot imagine how they will spend half of it; and as to your giving them more, it is quite absurd to think of it. They will be much more able to give *you* something."

"Upon my word," said Mr. Dashwood, "I believe you are perfectly right. My father certainly could mean nothing more by his request to me than what you say. I clearly understand it now, and I will strictly fulfil my engagement by such acts of assistance and kindness to them as you have described. When my mother removes into another house, my services shall be readily given to accommodate her as far as I can. Some little present of furniture, too, may be acceptable then."

"Certainly," returned Mrs. John Dashwood. "But, however, *one* thing must be considered. When your father and mother moved to Norland, though the furniture of Stanhill was sold, all the china, plate, and linen was saved, and is now left to your mother. Her house will therefore be almost completely fitted up as soon as she takes it."

"That is a material consideration undoubtedly. A valuable legacy indeed! And yet some of the plate would have been a very pleasant addition to our own stock here."

"Yes; and the set of breakfast china is twice as handsome as what belongs to this house; a great deal too handsome, in my opinion, for any place *they* can ever afford to live in. But, however, so it is. Your father thought only of *them*. And I must say this, that you owe no particular gratitude to him, nor attention to his wishes; for we very well know that if he could he would have left almost everything in the world to *them*."

This argument was irresistible. It gave to his intentions whatever of decision was wanting before; and he finally resolved that it would be absolutely unnecessary, if not highly indecorous, to do more for the widow and children of his father than such kind of neighborly acts as his own wife pointed out.

Three Deaths

(last two paragraphs)

LEO TOLSTOY*

The axe sounded duller and duller at the base of the trunk, the juicy, white chips were flying on the dew-covered grass, and the strokes made a light crackling to the ear. The tree shuddered through all its body, bent down and swiftly straightened, swaying frightfully on its root. For a moment everything came to a standstill, but once again the tree bent down, a crack was heard in its trunk, and breaking boughs and lowering branches, it crashed with its top on the damp soil. The sounds of the axe and of the steps died down. The warbler whistled and darted up higher. The small branch which the bird snagged with its wings wavered for a moment, and swiftly became immobile with the other branches and all their leaves. In the newly opened spaciousness the trees, through their motionless branches, yet more joyously revealed their beauty.

The first rays of the sun, having pierced the translucent cloud, glittered in the air and raced over the earth and sky. The mist began to roll

* Translated by Norair N. Taschian.

in waves in the dells; the dew, shining, began to play on the verdure; translucent, whitened cloudlets scudded over the vault, which gradually grew more blue. Birds fluttered in the thicket and, as though lost, twittered something happy; the juice-filled leaves whispered to each other joyfully and calmly on the treetops, and the branches of the living trees slowly, majestically, began to move over the dead and fallen tree.

In Memory of W. B. Yeats*

(d. Jan. 1939)

I

He disappeared in the dead of winter:
The brooks were frozen, the airports almost deserted,
And snow disfigured the public statues;
The mercury sank in the mouth of the dying day.
O all the instruments agree
The day of his death was a dark cold day.

Far from his illness
The wolves ran on through the evergreen forests,
The peasant river was untempted by the fashionable quays;
By mourning tongues
The death of the poet was kept from his poems.

But for him it was his last afternoon as himself,
An afternoon of nurses and rumours;
The provinces of his body revolted,
The squares of his mind were empty,
Silence invaded the suburbs,
The current of his feeling failed: he became his admirers.

Now he is scattered among a hundred cities
And wholly given over to unfamiliar affections;
To find his happiness in another kind of wood
And be punished under a foreign code of conscience.
The words of a dead man
Are modified in the guts of the living.

But in the importance and noise of tomorrow
When the brokers are roaring like beasts on the floor of the Bourse,
And the poor have the sufferings to which they are fairly accustomed,
And each in the cell of himself is almost convinced of his freedom;
A few thousand will think of this day
As one thinks of a day when one did something slightly unusual.

O all the instruments agree
The day of his death was a dark cold day.

II

You were silly like us: your gift survived it all;
The parish of rich women, physical decay,
Yourself; mad Ireland hurt you into poetry.
Now Ireland has her madness and her weather still,
For poetry makes nothing happen: it survives
In the valley of its saying where executives
Would never want to tamper; it flows south
From ranches of isolation and the busy griefs,
Raw towns that we believe and die in; it survives,
A way of happening, a mouth.

III

Earth, receive an honoured guest;
William Yeats is laid to rest:
Let the Irish vessel lie
Emptied of its poetry.

Time that is intolerant
Of the brave and innocent,
And indifferent in a week
To a beautiful physique,

Worships language and forgives
Everyone by whom it lives;
Pardons cowardice, conceit,
Lays its honours at their feet.

Time that with this strange excuse
Pardoned Kipling and his views,
And will pardon Paul Claudel,
Pardons him for writing well.

In the nightmare of the dark
All the dogs of Europe bark,
And the living nations wait,
Each sequestered in its hate;

Intellectual disgrace
Stares from every human face,
And the seas of pity lie
Locked and frozen in each eye.

Follow, poet, follow right
To the bottom of the night,
With your unconstraining voice
Still persuade us to rejoice;

With the farming of a verse
Make a vineyard of the curse,
Sing of human unsuccess
In a rapture of distress;

In the deserts of the heart
Let the healing fountain start,
In the prison of his days
Teach the free man how to praise.

                    W. H. AUDEN

Epitaph on Salomon Pavy
A Child of Queen Elizabeth's Chapel

Weep with me all you that read
    This little story:
And know, for whom a tear you shed,
    Death's self is sorry.
'Twas a child, that so did thrive
    In grace, and feature,
As *Heaven* and *Nature* seem'd to strive
    Which own'd the creature.
Years he numb'red scarce thirteen
    When *Fates* turn'd cruel,
Yet three fill'd zodiacs had he been
    The stage's jewel;

And did act (what now we moan)
    Old men so duly,
As, sooth, the Parcae thought him one,
    He play'd so truly.
So, by error, to his fate
    They all consented:
But viewing him since (alas, too late)
    They have repented.
And have sought (to give new birth)
    In baths to steep him;
But being so much too good for earth,
    Heaven vows to keep him.

BEN JONSON

Bells for John Whiteside's Daughter*

There was such speed in her little body,
And such lightness in her footfall,
It is no wonder her brown study
Astonishes us all.

Her wars were bruited in our high window.
We looked among orchard trees and beyond,
Where she took arms against her shadow,
Or harried unto the pond

The lazy geese, like a snow cloud
Dripping their snow on the green grass,
Tricking and stopping, sleepy and proud,
Who cried in goose, Alas,

For the tireless heart within the little
Lady with rod that made them rise
From their noon apple-dreams and scuttle
Goose-fashion under the skies!

But now go the bells, and we are ready,
In one house we are sternly stopped
To say we are vexed at her brown study,
Lying so primly propped.

JOHN CROWE RANSOM

Cymbeline

Second Song, Guiderius and Arviragus,
Act IV, Scene II

Guiderius:
Feare no more the heate o' th' Sun,
Nor the furious Winters rages,
Thou thy worldly task hast don,
Home art gone, and tane thy wages.
Golden Lads, and Girles all must,
As Chimney-Sweepers come to dust.

Arviragus:
Feare no more the frowne o' th' Great,
Thou art past the Tirants stroake,
Care no more to cloath and eate,
To thee the Reede is as the Oake:
    The Scepter, Learning, Physicke must,
    All follow this and come to dust.

Guid: Feare no more the Lightning flash.
Arvi: Nor th' all-dreaded Thunder stone.
Guid: Feare not Slander, Censure rash.
Arvi: Thou hast finish'd joy and mone.
Both: All Lovers young, all Lovers must,
        Consigne to thee and come to dust.

Guid: No Exorcisor harme thee,
Arvi: Nor no witch-craft charme thee.
Guid: Ghost unlaid forbeare thee.
Arvi: Nothing ill come neere thee.
Both: Quiet consumation have,
        And renowned be thy grave.

WILLIAM SHAKESPEARE

XIX

*To an Athlete Dying Young**

The time you won your town the race
We chaired you through the market-place;
Man and boy stood cheering by,
And home we brought you shoulder-high.

Today, the road all runners come,
Shoulder-high we bring you home,
And set you at your threshold down,
Townsman of a stiller town.

Smart lad, to slip betimes away
From fields where glory does not stay
And early though the laurel grows
It withers quicker than the rose.

Eyes the shady night has shut
Cannot see the record cut,
And silence sounds no worse than cheers
After earth has stopped the ears:

Now you will not swell the rout
Of lads that wore their honours out,
Runners whom renown outran
And the name died before the man.

So set, before its echoes fade,
The fleet foot on the sill of shade,
And hold to the low lintel up
The still-defended challenge-cup,

And round that early-laurelled head
Will flock to gaze the strengthless dead,
And find unwithered on its curls
The garland briefer than a girl's.

A. E. HOUSMAN

* From "A Shropshire Lad" — Authorized Edition — from *The Collected Poems of A. E. Housman.* Copyright 1940 by Holt, Rinehart and Winston, Inc. Reprinted by permission of Holt, Rinehart and Winston, Inc., and The Society of Authors as the literary representative of the Estate of the late A. E. Housman and Messrs. Jonathan Cape Ltd., publishers of A. E. Housman's *Collected Poems.*

At Melville's Tomb*

Often beneath the wave, wide from this ledge
The dice of drowned men's bones he saw bequeath
An embassy. Their numbers as he watched,
Beat on the dusty shore and were obscured.

And wrecks passed without sound of bells,
The calyx of death's bounty giving back
A scattered chapter, livid hieroglyph,
The portent wound in corridors of shells.

Then in the circuit calm of one vast coil,
Its lashings charmed and malice reconciled,
Frosted eyes there were that lifted altars;
And silent answers crept across the stars.

Compass, quadrant and sextant contrive
No farther tides . . . High in the azure steeps
Monody shall not wake the mariner.
This fabulous shadow only the sea keeps.

                                        HART CRANE

CHAPTER TWO

The Instruments
of Expression: The Voice

. . . the voice discovers the poet's ear . . .
DYLAN THOMAS

THE PLATFORM PROBLEM

Three ideas that emerged in the last chapter will serve to start this one. First, a history of learned oral speech lies behind every successful silent reading of emotive literature. What one has learned to do and express can be recreated in the mind by written symbols. I doubt that anyone will question that premise.

Second, many things are best clarified and comprehended by direct recourse to oral re-creation.[1] Fewer persons will automatically accept this as a truism, but I will give two brief examples to show the kind of problem I have in mind. In the first scene of James Thurber's story (p. 184) "A Box to Hide In," it is possible, indeed probable, that a silent reader will fail to make a commitment in his own mind about certain tones of voice.

"Whatta ya mean you want to hide in this box?" one grocer asked me.

"It's a form of escape," I told him, "hiding in a box. It circumscribes your worries and the range of your anguish. You don't see people either."

"How in the hell do you eat when you're in this box?" asked the grocer. "How in the hell do you get anything to eat?" I said I had never been in a box and didn't know, but that that would take care of itself.

"Well," he said, finally, "I haven't got any boxes, only some pasteboard cartons that cans come in."

There are many possibilities in this passage that a silent reader is not likely to recognize, let alone decide upon. One of them is the pause that follows the word "anguish," and precedes the sentence, "You don't see people either." There are two possibilities here; and deciding between them will control one's interpretation of the personality and condition of the narrator. Is the sentence uttered out of a general despair of, and a desire to escape from, man? Or is the speaker, now annoyed at the grocer's questioning, directing this sentence at the grocer ironically, implying, in effect, "If I were in a box I wouldn't have to look at *you*"? Obviously, to choose between these readings is to make a major decision on just how far out of touch with his immediate surroundings the speaker is. In short, an essentially *oral* distinction forces one to clarify his sense of the narrator and, hence, of the whole story.

[1] It has been found that judges are able to distinguish aggressiveness reliably from the voices of speakers, but not from content alone in typescript. J. A. Starkweather, "Content-free speech as a source of information about the speaker," *Journal of Abnorm. Psychology* (1956), 52:394–402. Further, producing vocal cues which are inappropriate to meaning causes judges to disagree significantly concerning the message. P. E. Kaufman, *An Investigation of Some Psychological Stimulus Properties of Speech Behavior*, Ph.D. Diss., Univ. of Chicago, 1954.

The second instance of the value of oral re-creation involves a very common misreading of a famous poem. In fact, so common is the misreading that I cannot recall a critic or scholar who did not make this error. I refer to the end of Keats' "Ode on a Grecian Urn" (p. 228). Keats, addressing the urn and the exquisite decorations on it, finds himself tormented by the tug between the eternal, static beauty of art and the mortal, unorganized beauty of life. He concludes the poem

> . . . Cold Pastoral!
>   When old age shall this generation waste,
>   Thou shalt remain, in midst of other woe
>   Than ours, a friend to man, to whom thou say'st,
>   "Beauty is truth, truth beauty," — that is all
>   Ye know on earth and all ye need to know.

Critics and scholars have made many efforts to reconcile the easy ending — the platitude that suddenly concludes this merciless probing. But whatever answers they have come to have been predicated on the assumption that in the last line and a half Keats turns to his reader immediately following "Beauty is truth, truth beauty" and says to him, "That is all / Ye know on earth and all ye need to know." In this case, the line is given the following rhythm: **that** is **all** / Ye **know** on **earth,** and **all** ye **need** to **know.** Notice that not only is the rhetorical purpose of the line to approve of, emphasize, or recommend a maxim, but the very rhythm is quite regular, reflecting certainty and an end to struggle.

But suppose one gives the line the following rhythm, "**that** is **all /** **YE know** on **earth,** and all **ye NEED** to **know.**" Then one must ask, why is the pronoun suddenly of importance? The answer comes from a fresh look at the *dramatic* and *vocal* situation. Keats has all this time been addressing the urn. Then the urn, in Keats' imagination, speaks the maxim, "Beauty is truth, truth beauty." Why should we think that Keats suddenly turns to speak to the reader? Isn't it more likely that he would retain the dramatic structure and continue to address the urn? And doesn't that realization bring the further realization that the pronouns must be stressed, because Keats is *not* agreeing with the urn, but is instead making a distinction between himself (and consequently humanity) and the urn? Thus the last line ironically (and here one sees the importance of the double stress on "need") implies that the maxim no doubt satisfies the urn's earthly needs, but that humans, and notably he himself, have other, less easily answered questions and needs. It is amazing how this simple shift in stress and rhythm illuminates the true dramatic situation of the poem and converts what has always admittedly been a weak and disappointing ending of a magnificent composition into one perfectly controlling and bringing to a final stasis the ambivalent agony of the poem. It not only explains, it magnificently justifies what would otherwise be, as T. S. Eliot says, "a serious blemish on a beautiful poem." It is interesting that a glance at Keats scholarship gives us some inference that Keats himself worked toward a *grammatic* way of making this *dramatic* situation clear to the reader. The manuscript of the poem (1819), as well as copies made by Keats's friends, reads in this way,

> Beauty is truth, truth beauty, — that is all
> Ye know on earth, and all ye need to know.

But when the text was first printed in *Annals of The Fine Arts* (January 1820), it read:

> Beauty is truth, truth beauty. That is all
> Ye know on earth and all ye need to know.

But, again, when the poem appeared in the volume which Keats published later in 1820, the text read as follows:

> 'Beauty is truth, truth beauty,' — That is all
> Ye know on earth, and all ye need to know.

Thus it would seem that Keats was trying to find some way of making clear that the maxim is the urn's, not his, and such a careful distinction would seem pointless if he is simply about to make the urn's maxim his own.

Yet another problem concerning the ending of this poem is raised and solved by the oral reader's necessity to know *who* is speaking and *to whom*. The problem is raised by the shift of pronoun from the singular to the plural. That Keats intended to use "ye" as a plural is shown, not only by earlier usage in this poem (". . . therefore ye soft pipes, play on . . ."), but by usage in other poems ("Bards of Passion and of Mirth, / Ye have left your souls on earth"). Thus the oral reader, for proper tonality, finds that he must explain how Keats changed from addressing the urn as "thou," to addressing it as "ye." Again the answer is no doubt to be found in the total structure of the poem. The poem begins by seeing the urn as a whole ("Thou still unravish'd bride of quietness"), then turns to seeing it, no longer as a whole, but as the sum of parts, of the maidens, trees, lovers, of, in fact, a whole village procession and religious festival. Surely this movement is repeated in the last stanza. At its beginning he again addresses the urn as a whole, so he calls it "thou," singular. But finally, it is the *people* of the urn's world he addresses (the lovers, the melodist, the priest); and the simple truth they need in their static world, contrasted to the truths living people live with, is the means by which Keats makes his final irony direct and powerful.

Of course, once this view of the final stanza emerges, all oral details are both subtly or not so subtly altered. "Cold pastoral" must appear a more ambiguous epithet than before; and, perhaps most important, the phrase "friend to man," cannot now be uttered with a simple, direct conviction. Friend it is, but limited and distant. The voice, with this phrase, must seek an irony distant from sarcasm, gentle, perhaps a bit nostalgic, perhaps a bit envious, never denying the truth of the friendship, but placing it, limiting it.

The third point derived from the last chapter, and the one that leads directly on to what follows in this chapter, is that training of the voice in conjunction with the study of texts is a necessity for optimum oral reading of the text and is highly valuable for silent reading in that it increases the expressive vocabulary of sound-gestures which the reader can bring to mind. It is on this point that many readers may feel I have gone farther than they care to go. I have already spoken at some length about the usefulness of platform experience and vocal training for the enrichment of silent reading. Here the concern primarily is with the proposition that vocal training is an essential to good oral reading of literature, a proposition surely based on several easily perceivable truths.

In addition to an adequate historical and critical background combined with a sympathetic imagination, two personal elements lie behind every successful oral reading of literature: (1) in order to be responsive to the passionate variety presented by literature, the voice and body must be trained; and (2) every reading situation, whether on a platform, in the home, or before a microphone, is artificial, requiring the acceptance of certain conventions both by the reader and the audience. No grasp — no matter how thorough — of literary history, no gift for writing poetry or fiction or criticism, not even any combination of these or other abilities will automatically qualify one for reading aloud. In music, such an idea is seen instantly for the nonsense it is. But in literature it has come to be widely accepted as perfectly sound, since the whole culture, and especially the schools upon which the culture grows increasingly dependent, has emasculated the tradition of reading aloud (except for the narrow field of drama, where this folly is exposed regularly by certain amateur productions). To what extent this idea arises from an instinct to minimize the significance of their own deficiency or from a desire to denigrate abilities they have not themselves taken time to develop, I shall not venture a guess. But I have heard poets and professors, grown famous (or notorious) enough to receive the occasional invitation to read aloud, speak at great length on the proper reading of a work of literary art, when their voices were monotonous, if not unpleasant, and their bodies caught in what often appeared a perfectly spastic series of compulsive gestures, absurd, meaningless, and distracting.

Suppose we were all forced to learn musical notation to the point that we could read a musical score as fluently as words. How long would it be before we dismissed the performer as unnecessary, as interfering with *our* understanding of the piece? How soon before we became impatient with the recreated and living musical sound because it impinged upon our private world and forced us into a more widely cultural, less private, relationship with the score? How long before we concluded that playing a musical instrument well was not an essential act of artistic achievement, but something about which we really could learn all we needed in ten easy lessons? How long before we ceased to regard a performance of the score as the ultimate critical act, the most perfectly humane criticism available, and started to regard it as of secondary importance even to the publication of historical minutiae and clever, if cranky, critical studies, to the tracing of the faintest influences, or to the attack or support of the piece as a move in the game of musical fashion and politics?

Many questions — and perhaps best left unanswered. Abandoning such speculations, we can say that certain simple insights should be accessible to anybody. It is good manners to read *to* the audience; it is poor manners, indicating a contempt or, at best, a disregard for the audience, to read with one's eyes primarily on the book. It is good manners to stand relatively still without body sway or head jiggling or other distracting bodily movements; it is poor manners to call attention to oneself and away from the text by idiosyncratic vocal, facial, or bodily gestures. It is good manners to read in a voice audible, various, well-modulated, and responsive to the passionate demands of the material read; it is poor manners, it is downright boorish, to mumble, to read monotonously, to read as if the text had no more variety or intensity or accuracy of passion (and as if you cared no more for that text and its passion) than a casual conversation in the classroom, club, or on the street corner. It would seem obvious that the reader should honor the material and its audience by bringing to the reading a command of his body, his voice, and the text. For what other legitimate purpose can a reading occur than as an occasion wherein a trained and sensitive instrument can create a living complex of tones coherent with the abstract symbols of the text and, in so doing, reveal, enrich, define some of the possibilities of man's passionate existence?

So much would seem obvious. Yet how many readers of this book can command on a platform to the service of a *comprehended* text, their bodies and their voices? To achieve control over the speaking voice requires a training, perhaps not so extensive as that of a singer, yet not unlike it. To control the body requires at least a rudimentary understanding of the development of gesture, of an awareness of the expressiveness, or lack of it, of the body. In each case most persons may be sure that a collection of *bad* habits will have to be eliminated before control can be achieved.

I have suggested that there are three areas to this problem of reading aloud: (1) a grasp of the text, (2) control of the body, (3) control of the voice. By far the bulk of this book is dedicated to exposing possibilities which will, I hope, assist the student in mastering the subtleties of a fictive text through a cooperative effort of the voice, body, and mind meeting in a unified, humane experience. Without sensitive insight into the text and without a judgment and taste earned in the knowledge of the craft of fiction, all that can be produced by the finest training of body and voice is mechanical dross, and the weight placed on textual criticism in this work should state my conviction more eloquently than a simple axiom. Nonetheless, the training of the voice and body is an essential task, a long, arduous one not to be mastered in this or any other beginning class. Particularly the training of the voice is a special and continuous labor. Sometimes indeed it is initially so complicated as to require a grasp of the relationship of the voice to human psychology, calling in extreme cases for the services of a psychiatrist[2] and/or the speech therapist. Even when the student's voice problems are symptomatic not primarily of psychological problems, but simply of a severe case of poor vocal habits, I should recommend use of a book specifically devoted to training the voice.[3]

What I can do here is to start the student on a useful road with some simple clarifications and suggestions. Where the problems are not severe, this book should, with a good teacher, prove sufficient. What I am about to delineate are by no means rules. They are practical suggestions, a passing on of techniques drawn partly from fine teachers and readers with whom I have worked, partly from extensive platform and recording experience, and partly from teaching students, in my turn, the art of reading aloud. Even here I must accept the self-imposed limit of most books on the art of reading aloud and exclude the techniques of informal group reading and of reading for radio, tape, and record, for these demand special approaches and variant techniques. I shall rather confine myself to the classroom situation, i.e., reading before a specific live audience.

[2] See, for example, Paul J. Moses, *The Voice of Neurosis*, Gryne & Stratton, N.Y., 1954, and Erving Goffman, *The Presentation of the Self in Everyday Life*, Doubleday, 1959.

[3] See, for example, Hahn, Lomas, Hargis, Vandraegen, *Basic Voice Training for Speech*, 2nd ed. McGraw-Hill, N.Y., 1957.

DISCOVERING YOUR VOICE

That humans are creatures of habit is as true in the use of the voice as elsewhere. Each person has what is usually called an *habitual pitch level*. This may be defined as that level of pitch around which the speaker clusters most of his vocal activity. As he goes up or down the pitch scale, he returns to this pitch area as the most comfortable. The trouble sometimes is that with a given individual this habitual speech level does not always coincide with the *optimum pitch level*. The optimum pitch may be defined as the level best suited to the individual's physical instrument, the pitch level at which there is a minimum of muscular involvement, meaning a maximum of muscular relaxation, producing the richest and purest tone. Obviously, a person who habitually uses a pitch level other than his optimum level, is handicapping himself in the expressive capacity of his voice. How does it happen that a person may begin habitually to use a pitch level other than that most favorable to him? A person who speaks tensely and who has forgotten how to relax his vocal mechanism differentially from the rest of his body may have an habitually higher, thinner pitch and tone than his optimum. Conversely, a person who speaks lazily, indifferently, without much muscular involvement, may have a lower and fuzzier pitch and tone than his optimum. These are two of the many speaking habits which can cause a speaker to deviate from his optimum pitch. The remedy lies in discovering your optimum pitch and your habitual pitch, and in making them one and the same. To find your habitual pitch, read a passage of prose or listen to yourself in conversation until you come to know where your habitual pitch is and can prolong it on a held vowel sound. Then, with the aid of a musical instrument, locate this pitch on the musical scale. Finding the optimum pitch is more difficult. One suggested method is to start singing at the lowest note you can comfortably produce, sing upward five notes, and that should be your optimum level. The note thus reached will not always be precisely the optimum level; in fact it may change as one learns to relax the voice in general and hence widen the melodic capacity upward and downward. But keep experimenting up and down the range of your voice till you find the level that seems to produce the most pleasant tone with the least effort. Usually this tone will be found noticeably below the middle of your range. One must then work to make the optimum and the habitual pitch level the same.

You should by now have come to some awareness of the present *range* of your voice. This may not be very happy knowledge, for many people are comfortable on only three or four notes, instead of the octave or octave and a half which the normal, trained voice is capable of. Even a wide range will not really be utilized if the habitual tone is too near the top or the bottom, for then all speaking patterns will tend in one direction. Thus, although it is important to develop as usefully wide a range as you can, it is imperative to develop a relaxed habitual tone which coincides with the optimum tone.

It is also valuable to assess the volume habits of your voice. In discovering the normal volume of your voice in relation to those of other people recording devices are of little help, since the volume is determined electronically. Your teacher, classmates, friends are necessary to tell you whether or not you read too softly or too loudly, on the average. However a tape recorder *will* help in giving you a sense of the *range* of volume, and it, as well as your teacher, can assist you in determining to what extent you need to be able to exploit this dimension further.

In the above manner, you should have come to some understanding of the range and *tone* of your voice and of its pattern of volume. Now you must determine your normal rate, your range of rate, and the normal *quality* of your voice. For all of this, a recording of your voice is really invaluable; and now that tape machines are so widely available, it should be possible for you to arrange to record a sampling of your voice. And if you have never heard your voice before, prepare for a surprise. For of all the illusions man clings to, none does he regard more fondly than his own image of what his voice sounds like. Actually, it takes a long time for singers to be able to tell, from what they hear internally, whether or not they are in good voice. And until high-fidelity recording no speaker or singer ever heard his voice as others heard it.

When you make this recording, read a passage as slowly as you can — to the limit of what "sounds right" to you. Then read a passage at what seems to you the most comfortable rate, then another passage as fast as still feels "natural." Now listen to the tape. Does there seem much variety to you? Is the slow appreciably slower than the fast? Is your "normal" rate clipped and hurried, or slow and drawly, or somewhere in between? Figure out about how many words a minute you are speaking in your "fast rate," your "slow rate," and your "normal rate." Now take some recordings by great actors reading — Laughton, Gielgud, Olivier — and find out how many words per minute they speak in their slow passages, how many in their fast, and what is their normal rate. You should now have a fairly clear notion of what you have to correct. For instance, many people who speak quite crisply and rapidly feel very uncomfortable, as if they were "dragging," when they read at a rate which other people would call only a normal rate. Obviously, such a person reading the famous "To be or not to be" soliloquy would be unable truly to reflect the passionate thought of the passage because of a habit of rate. For such persons work on elongating the vowels and of giving more vocalization and tone coloration to certain consonants is essential. The opposite sort of problem can, of course, occur. And having a truly "average" rate does not mean that one is necessarily able to increase or decrease speed effectively. Such a person may have as much habit-enlarging to do as persons with other problems.

Having listened to your recording for rate, now listen to your voice for timbre and quality. Is yours a tenor voice, a contralto? Is it thin, tense, piercing, devoid of overtones? Is it thick and fuzzy with overtones — foggy? There is a certain point beyond which one cannot change the quality. A tenor voice, except for a *very* exceptional voice, cannot encompass the bass span of tones; a light lyric quality can seldom also be rich and vibrant. But one need not be too concerned about his lacks, for each *natural* quality has its virtues as well as its limitations. What *should* concern one are the unpleasant tones, the flaws of quality and timbre which come from poor habits in breathing, from tension, and from a combination of other possible bad habits, for these are *never* virtues, but are simple roadblocks in the way of expressive re-creation of a fictive text.

Now that you have discovered what your voice *is really like,* it is necessary to check the foundations of the structure; and the foundation of the voice is breath — the habits and control of the process of inhaling and exhaling.

Below is a simple diagram of an experiment frequently done in early physics classes to illustrate the nature of a vacuum. In the neck of a bell jar is placed a stopper with a glass tube running through a hole in it. On the end of the glass tube inside the jar a balloon is placed. The open bottom of the bell jar is covered with a rubber diaphragm.

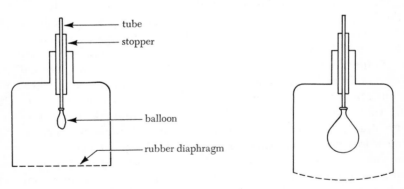

If you pull down on the diaphragm, a partial vacuum is created. Air will rush through the tube, filling the balloon until the internal and external pressures are stabilized and the vacuum is eliminated. Contrariwise, if you put your finger over the tube so that air will not rush in, you will find it very difficult to distend the diaphragm downward by very much, because of the rapid disequilibrium of pressure on the diaphragm.

Actually, one inhales in much this way. The ribs form a cage not dissimilar to the bell jar. (Of course, the ribs are somewhat flexible and the bell jar is not.) Below the lungs and above the stomach cavity is a flexible membrane called the *diaphragm*. Thus, *and this is important to remember,* one does not actually pull the air in to the lungs. Rather, as with the bell jar, the diaphragm is lowered and distended, the lower ribs are somewhat extended, thus creating a vacuum around the lungs, and the air rushes into the lungs to equalize this pressure. If you want a vivid demonstration of this process, perform the following experiment. At the bottom of exhalation, close your lips tightly, clamp your nostrils closed. Now try to lift or enlarge your chest. You will find that once air cannot reach the lungs to equalize pressure, the chest is frozen into immobility. Thus energy is used in inhaling, since the lower chest must be somewhat expanded and the diaphragm lowered and pushed outward.

Exhaling, on the other hand, when one is breathing normally without speech, requires little or no energy, since the weight of relaxation of the muscular expansion is adequate to force out the used air.

Now it is necessary to note your own breathing habits. Place one hand high on your chest, just under the neck. Place the other hand on the "bread-basket" or solar plexus region, palm inward, the thumb just resting on the point where the ribs divide away from the sternum. If, in your normal breathing, the upper hand moves up and down strongly, and the lower hand moves vaguely or not more strongly than the top hand, then you may be sure that you have developed habits of breathing which will have to be corrected, for reasons that will be made clear. If you think that you may become self-conscious in this process and may change your breathing habits while you are, so to speak, thinking about it or watching yourself, get a roommate or friend or a member of your family to watch, when you are not aware of it, the movement of your upper and lower chest and abdomen in breathing and to tell you what they have observed. For a good example of proper breathing, observe a baby at rest, for babies have not yet had time to develop improper breathing habits.

TRAINING THE VOICE

I have said that proper breathing is the basis of voice control. If we carry this idea further we can say that control of the breath is the basis of all successful reading. If you cannot sustain your breath, you will be required, by simple biological need, to break long phrases with pauses where none are needed or wanted. If you cannot control the volume of air, you will be unable to make the changes in volume, subtle or great, required by the text. These are but two basic examples of the dependence of the performance of literature on vocal training.

Obviously, most of the problems of achieving breath control lie in the phase of exhalation, for it is in exhalation that the air, passing over the vocal chords and vibrating them, produces speech. The inhalation pattern is usually altered only in depth and rate. In normal breathing, one breathes in rhythm. The phases of exhalation and inhalation are about equal in length, and the breath is not usually drawn in deeply. But in a speech situation, the breath is brought in sharply and, if done properly, usually deeply, since speech requires a lengthy and controlled flow in exhalation.

If one goes back to the bell-jar analogy, it becomes apparent that one controls the rate by which air is emptied from the balloon by controlling the diaphragm at the bottom of the jar. Similarly the speaker must master at all times the rate and force of the air leaving his lungs by control of the diaphragm and lower ribs. The seat of this control lies in the powerful flat muscles in the front of the abdomen. Some of these muscles are attached to the lower thorax. They act, in contraction, together with muscles inside the rib cage to press against the abdomen. This action in turn forces the viscera up against the diaphragm which, moving upward in the chest, reduces the vacuum, and by that much reduces the air in the lungs. This pressure, in speech, must at all times be under control; and a firm balance must be created between the controlled relaxation of the diaphragm-rib muscle complex and the pressure exerted by the stomach muscles at the command of the oral reader, who is in turn taking his command from the text.

It should now be clear why breathing by expanding principally the top of the chest must be corrected if control of the voice is to be gained. First of all, you will not be able to take in much air, since you are filling only the top of the lungs. Second, you will not, in exhaling, establish control of the column of air extending from the stomach muscles upward. In correcting this habit, three simple procedures may help. Put your hands on your chest as previously described. (1) Press the top hand against the chest while leaving the lower one resting easily over the abdomen, encouraging expansion there. (2) Sit upright on a stool and grasp its rear legs as far down as you can reach without bending your back, so that when you breathe, your shoulders cannot rise. Practice controlling breath from the diaphragm. (3) Lie down on the floor. Put a couple of books on the top part of your chest, and a couple of books over the abdomen–solar plexus region. While breathing, concentrate on keeping the top books motionless and the lower books rising and falling regularly with your breathing.

Once the habit of proper breathing is established, then one has gained the possibility of speech controlled from the stomach and diaphragm. Here it is necessary to learn the process of differential relaxation, for while the stomach muscles must be tensed and constantly engaged, the speaker must learn to keep that constant tension localized so that it does not transmit itself to tensions of the body elsewhere that might mar expressiveness. Most especially it is necessary to keep the vocal chords and the general throat area relaxed, for unnecessary tension in this area will lead to squeakiness, thinness of tone, and tired, raw throats. Many persons, as a matter of habit, speak with the throat too tense. Others begin to tense their throats in the process of mastering the chain of control from the stomach muscles. Two exercises may help to counteract this tendency. (1) Stand erect. With the left hand, put the thumb along one side of the jaw line, the fingers along the other. Now press the jaw backward till it aches a little and the mouth is slightly open. Now, controlling the breathing from the diaphragm, exhale the air slowly, and vocalize letters (A, B, C) slowly, with a minimum of muscular involvement of jaw and tongue, in such a way that the sound seems to dribble over and down the chin. Allow the jaw to move only slightly. The object of this procedure is to acquire the *feel* of the relaxed throat. Increase slowly the pressure from the abdomen and the muscular involvement of the jaw. When you feel the throat getting tense, go back to the beginning. (2) Lie on the floor with books placed as described above. Now make the jaw respond earthward with the force of gravity. Use gravity to force the jaw to relax. Proceed with vocalization as above.

With proper breathing control on the way toward being established, attention can be shifted back to the voice itself. In discovering the qualities of your voice as it exists, you will have noticed that the voice is a three-dimensional instrument. It has (1) melodic pattern (the movement of the voice up and down the scale), (2) volume, and (3) rate. There are two principle methods of altering rate: (1) by increasing or decreasing the length of pause, and (2) by increasing or decreasing the length of vowel (certain consonants — *m* and *l* for instance — can also be elongated within rather strict limits).

For the person who is beginning to learn to read aloud, the first goal after attaining sufficient sophistication in criticism to master a text must be the mastery of the voice. The ideal is complete flexibility, i.e., a voice that can move through any of the infinite combinations of melody, volume, and rate without effort, at the command of the mind. This is an ideal that takes several years of intelligent effort to approach, and then most of us reach inborn limitations — of range and timbre primarily — which no amount of work can overcome.

As has been said, humans are creatures of habit, and most beginners find their voices trapped in a web of meaninglessly repeated patterns which must be worked out before the voice can respond to the particular tone and movements of tones in a complex work of art. Very few persons can, in the beginning, get much variety of volume or of rate while in the reading situation. Most persons will use about three or at most four "notes" in the melodic movement of their voices, but what is worse, the movement within this limited range is usually predictable; that is, the voice will go up and down in monotonously similar movement. And of all that is predictable with beginners, the most predictable is that above 80 per cent of American students will have a deadly dropping pattern at the end of each important word or phrase, a way of curving the final word downward which remains, no matter what the tonal demands of the material, always the same. Though it is true that in a very broad sense the accepted intonational pattern for the English declarative sentence is downward at the end, there are hundreds of possible permutations of that downward pattern. And since no two phrases are quite identical (this is true even of poems in which a phrase is repeated [see "Edward" p. 135], for even though the words are the same, the emotional impact alters with the repetition) it should be clear that, except when done quite deliberately for an appropriate effect, a repeated vocal pattern is not expressing the unique tonal quality of each phrase.

In conquering this dropping pattern and all other melodic habits, it is useful to think of the voice moving up and down on a scale, as when singing. There should be two basic aims in all work done in this area: (1) an attempt to increase range both in the upper and the lower ends of the scale, and (2) an effort to achieve perfect flexibility within that range. (Improving quality or timbre is a technical and often complex physical and psychological problem that cannot be dealt with in such a limited treatment as is here presented.) It is precisely at this point that one must not scorn mechanical exercises any more than the singer scorns his scales or the pianist his finger exercises. For the layman who simply wishes to overcome the worst of his habitual limitations and to discover and speak a melodic pattern roughly appropriate to a given phrase, a few simple exercises faithfully and *consciously* worked at fifteen minutes a day will generally achieve substantial results.

First of all, by saying practice phrases as described earlier in this chapter, discover the present range of your speaking voice — the highest you can comfortably speak a word and the lowest you can comfortably speak a word. For some persons this will be a surprisingly narrow gap. However narrow, until the range is widened, it is within these limitations that all melodic variety must be achieved. Those persons with a relatively narrow range must cultivate all the more assiduously the greatest possible subtleties in shifts of tone within their restricted potential. The key to all effective practice of this sort is to try *consciously* to direct your voice to follow a *predetermined* pattern. Beginners often find it useful literally to draw a rough pattern and to follow it through a series of gently increasing complexity.

```
top of range    I—                    home—                        stay—
                                                                     to—
          go—          go—                     home—       home—
                                                 go—          go—
bottom of range    home—   I—                I—           I—
```

```
top of range    I—          stay—      I—                 —I
                                        go—              —go
          go—        to—              home—            —home
                                       to—              —to
                home—                  stay—            —sit
                                                        —and
bottom of range                                         —read
```

If the voice insists on following its habitual pattern rather than the one desired, either while the student is working on a specific phrase in a text or while exercising, I have found that that habit is often peculiarly attached to the *words* and that if the speaker substitutes letters or numbers for the words, it is frequently easier to get the voice to follow the conceived pattern. Something about the abstraction of numbers or letters frees the voice from its habitual reaction to certain concepts. As soon as the proper pattern is achieved with numbers or letters, switch back to words while the pattern is in the mind. If the pattern escapes achievement again, go back to letters. Continue until successful.

Curiously, one of the hardest things for most beginners to learn is to make the voice pattern a level one when that is appropriate. As an exercise, not necessarily as the optimum in effective patterns for the phrase, try this.

```
top —    tomorrow and to mor row and to mor row creeps in its petty
         ___   ____  ___  __  ___            last
         pace from day to day   to the    syllable
                                             of
                                             re   ____
                                            corded
                                             time
bottom —
```

Control of the voice during the utterance of a word is essential to this sort of thing, and exercises on individual words are very valuable.

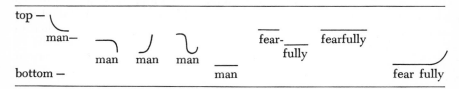

The reader may develop his own exercises from this point. In my experience, students find it helpful, at least in the beginning, literally to write their patterns down, as suggested, then with that visualization before them, to try to make the voice conform to them.

After some control of the melodic pattern is achieved, variation in rate should be added to the preconceived pattern; and finally, for exercises in the full three-dimensional control of the voice, volume shifts should be added.

Despite the fact that the general problem of the pause will be touched upon in following chapters, I think some comments are in order at this time, as the pause relates specifically to the platform problem. In general, the beginning reader has two chief faults in his use of pause: (1) being afraid of pauses, he tends to reduce them to a minimum and to give them very little extension when they occur, and (2) the extension of time, or quantity, given to pauses is usually very regular — mechanically so. It is a curious anomaly in all these vocal matters that we fear that exercises to master the voice will lead to mechanical readings, when the truth is that nothing is more ironbound, more incapable of charm, grace, force — in sum, of aptness — than a voice in the grip of its unadulterated habit patterns. The first requirement toward using *pause* correctly is a psychological one which consists of overcoming one's fears of a silence when on the platform. Far from being weaknesses in the fabric of a reading, pauses are perhaps the most powerful non-denotative technique at the command of the reader. All the more reason why they should be consciously controlled by an understanding of the text. I have found it a useful device to think of a poem or story as containing a range of pauses, from almost imperceptible ones to longer ones, and I make it my job to use my analysis of the piece to discover the range of pause appropriate and where the longest and shortest might be.

A pause is no more empty or useless than space in a painting or enclosed air in a statue. Something must happen in a pause, and what that something is can be either (1) principally a grammatical pause (that is, a pause during which what principally occurs is a shift in ideational content), or (2) a pause in which not only an idea-group terminates but a discernible change in emotion must also take place. Of course, in a fictive piece, the idea never changes without some slight change of emotion; and I have no desire to flounder again into the old and futile attempt at separating the mind from the body, especially when this technique of teaching literature has as its chief aim and advantage the elimination of precisely that destructive schism. Perhaps it would be more accurate to say that some pauses contain *primarily the emotion of a shift in idea,* whereas others engage in a more complex pattern of emotional changes.

Two things are essential to the effective performance of a pause: (1) a crystal-clear understanding of what occurs grammatically and dramatically in the pause, and (2) effective command of the face and body so that what occurs in the pause may absolutely reflect what occurs in the text and may be projected to the audience. All this leads to a consideration of some of the particular problems concerning effective use of the body in reading aloud to an audience.

SELECTIONS

Eveline*

James Joyce

She sat at the window watching the evening invade the avenue. Her head was leaned against the window curtains and in her nostrils was the odour of dusty cretonne. She was tired.

Few people passed. The man out of the last house passed on his way home; she heard his footsteps clacking along the concrete pavement and afterwards crunching on the cinder path before the new red houses. One time there used to be a field there in which they used to play every evening with other people's children. Then a man from Belfast bought the field and built houses in it — not like their little brown houses but bright brick houses with shining roofs. The children of the avenue used to play together in that field — the Devines, the Waters, the Dunns, little Keogh the cripple, she and her brothers and sisters. Ernest, however, never played: he was too grown up. Her father used often to hunt them in out of the field with his blackthorn stick; but usually little Keogh used to keep *nix* and call out when he saw her father coming. Still they seemed to have been rather happy then. Her father was not so bad then; and besides, her

* From *Dubliners* by James Joyce. Originally published by B. W. Huebsch in 1916. Reprinted by permission of The Viking Press, Inc.

mother was alive. That was a long time ago; she and her brothers and
sisters were all grown up; her mother was dead. Tizzie Dunn was dead,
too, and the Waters had gone back to England. Everything changes. Now
she was going to go away like the others, to leave her home.

Home! She looked round the room, reviewing all its familiar objects which she had dusted once a week for so many years, wondering
where on earth all the dust came from. Perhaps she would never see again
those familiar objects from which she had never dreamed of being divided. And yet during all those years she had never found out the name of
the priest whose yellowing photograph hung on the wall above the broken
harmonium beside the coloured print of the promises made to Blessed
Margaret Mary Alacoque. He had been a school friend of her father.
Whenever he showed the photograph to a visitor her father used to pass
it with a casual word:

"He is in Melbourne now."

She had consented to go away, to leave her home. Was that wise? She
tried to weigh each side of the question. In her home anyway she had shelter and food; she had those whom she had known all her life about her.
Of course she had to work hard, both in the house and at business. What
would they say of her in the Stores when they found out that she had run
away with a fellow? Say she was a fool, perhaps; and her place would be
filled up by advertisement. Miss Gavan would be glad. She had always
had an edge on her, especially whenever there were people listening.

"Miss Hill, don't you see these ladies are waiting?"

"Look lively, Miss Hill, please."

She would not cry many tears at leaving the Stores.

But in her new home, in a distant unknown country, it would not be
like that. Then she would be married — she, Eveline. People would treat
her with respect then. She would not be treated as her mother had been.
Even now, though she was over nineteen, she sometimes felt herself in
danger of her father's violence. She knew it was that that had given her the
palpitations. When they were growing up he had never gone for her, like he
used to go for Harry and Ernest, because she was a girl; but latterly
he had begun to threaten her and say what he would do to her only for her
dead mother's sake. And now she had nobody to protect her. Ernest was
dead and Harry, who was in the church decorating business, was nearly
always down somewhere in the country. Besides, the invariable squabble
for money on Saturday nights had begun to weary her unspeakably. She
always gave her entire wages — seven shillings — and Harry always sent
up what he could but the trouble was to get any money from her father.
He said she used to squander the money, that she had no head, that he
wasn't going to give her his hard-earned money to throw about the streets,

and much more, for he was usually fairly bad on Saturday night. In the end he would give her the money and ask her had she any intention of buying Sunday's dinner. Then she had to rush out as quickly as she could and do her marketing, holding her black leather purse tightly in her hand as she elbowed her way through the crowds and returning home late under her load of provisions. She had hard work to keep the house together and to see that the two young children who had been left to her charge went to school regularly and got their meals regularly. It was hard work — a hard life — but now that she was about to leave it she did not find it a wholly undesirable life.

She was about to explore another life with Frank. Frank was very kind, manly, open-hearted. She was to go away with him by the night-boat to be his wife and to live with him in Buenos Ayres where he had a home waiting for her. How well she remembered the first time she had seen him; he was lodging in a house on the main road where she used to visit. It seemed a few weeks ago. He was standing at the gate, his peaked cap pushed back on his head and his hair tumbled forward over a face of bronze. Then they had come to know each other. He used to meet her outside the Stores every evening and see her home. He took her to see *The Bohemian Girl* and she felt elated as she sat in an unaccustomed part of the theatre with him. He was awfully fond of music and sang a little. People knew that they were courting and, when he sang about the lass that loves a sailor, she always felt pleasantly confused. He used to call her Poppens out of fun. First of all it had been an excitement for her to have a fellow and then she had begun to like him. He had tales of distant countries. He had started as a deck boy at a pound a month on a ship of the Allan Line going out to Canada. He told her the names of the ships he had been on and the names of the different services. He had sailed through the Straits of Magellan and he told her stories of the terrible Patagonians. He had fallen on his feet in Buenos Ayres, he said, and had come over to the old country just for a holiday. Of course, her father had found out the affair and had forbidden her to have anything to say to him.

"I know these sailor chaps," he said.

One day he had quarrelled with Frank and after that she had to meet her lover secretly.

The evening deepened in the avenue. The white of two letters in her lap grew indistinct. One was to Harry; the other was to her father. Ernest had been her favourite but she liked Harry too. Her father was becoming old lately, she noticed; he would miss her. Sometimes he could be very nice. Not long before, when she had been laid up for a day, he had read her out a ghost story and made toast for her at the fire. Another day, when their mother was alive, they had all gone for a picnic to the Hill of

Howth. She remembered her father putting on her mother's bonnet to make the children laugh.

Her time was running out but she continued to sit by the window, leaning her head against the window curtain, inhaling the odour of dusty cretonne. Down far in the avenue she could hear a street organ playing. She knew the air. Strange that it should come that very night to remind her of the promise to her mother, her promise to keep the home together as long as she could. She remembered the last night of her mother's illness; she was again in the close dark room at the other side of the hall and outside she heard a melancholy air of Italy. The organ-player had been ordered to go away and given sixpence. She remembered her father strutting back into the sickroom saying:

"Damned Italians! coming over here!"

As she mused the pitiful vision of her mother's life laid its spell on the very quick of her being — that life of commonplace sacrifices closing in final craziness. She trembled as she heard again her mother's voice saying constantly with foolish insistence:

"Derevaun Seraun! Derevaun Seraun!"

She stood up in a sudden impulse of terror. Escape! She must escape! Frank would save her. He would give her life, perhaps love, too. But she wanted to live. Why should she be unhappy? She had a right to happiness. Frank would take her in his arms, fold her in his arms. He would save her.

* * *

She stood among the swaying crowd in the station at the North Wall. He held her hand and she knew that he was speaking to her, saying something about the passage over and over again. The station was full of soldiers with brown baggages. Through the wide doors of the sheds she caught a glimpse of the black mass of the boat, lying in beside the quay wall, with illumined portholes. She answered nothing. She felt her cheek pale and cold and, out of a maze of distress, she prayed to God to direct her, to show her what was her duty. The boat blew a long mournful whistle into the mist. If she went, tomorrow she would be on the sea with Frank, steaming towards Buenos Ayres. Their passage had been booked. Could she still draw back after all he had done for her? Her distress awoke a nausea in her body and she kept moving her lips in silent fervent prayer.

A bell clanged upon her heart. She felt him seize her hand:

"Come!"

All the seas of the world tumbled about her heart. He was drawing her into them: he would drown her. She gripped with both hands at the iron railing.

"Come!"

No! No! No! It was impossible. Her hands clutched the iron in frenzy. Amid the seas she sent a cry of anguish!

"Eveline! Evvy!?"

He rushed beyond the barrier and called to her to follow. He was shouted at to go on but he still called to her. She set her white face to him, passive, like a helpless animal. Her eyes gave him no sign of love or farewell or recognition.

The Lagoon*

JOSEPH CONRAD

The white man, leaning with both arms over the roof of the little house in the stern of the boat, said to the steersman —

"We will pass the night in Arsat's clearing. It is late."

The Malay only grunted, and went on looking fixedly at the river. The white man rested his chin on his crossed arms and gazed at the wake of the boat. At the end of the straight avenue of forests cut by the intense glitter of the river, the sun appeared unclouded and dazzling, poised low over the water that shone smoothly like a band of metal. The forests, sombre and dull, stood motionless and silent on each side of the broad stream. At the foot of big, towering trees, trunkless nipa palms rose from the mud of the bank, in bunches of leaves enormous and heavy, that hung unstirring over the brown swirl of eddies. In the stillness of the air every tree, every leaf, every bough, every tendril of creeper and every petal of minute blossoms seemed to have been bewitched into an immobility perfect and final. Nothing moved on the river but the eight paddles that rose flashing regularly, dipped together with a single splash; while the steersman swept right and left with a periodic and sudden flourish of his blade describing a glinting semicircle above his head. The churned-up water frothed alongside with a confused murmur. And the white man's canoe, advancing up stream in the short-lived disturbance of its own making, seemed to enter the portals of a land from which the very memory of motion had forever departed.

The white man, turning his back upon the setting sun, looked along the empty and broad expanse of the sea-reach. For the last three miles of its course the wandering, hesitating river, as if enticed irresistibly by the freedom of an open horizon, flows straight into the sea, flows straight to the east — to the east that harbours both light and darkness. Astern of the boat the repeated call of some bird, a cry discordant and feeble, skipped

* Reprinted from *Tales of Unrest* by Joseph Conrad, by permission of J. M. Dent & Sons Ltd.

along over the smooth water and lost itself, before it could reach the
other shore, in the breathless silence of the world.

The steersman dug his paddle into the stream, and held hard with
stiffened arms, his body thrown forward. The water gurgled aloud; and
suddenly the long straight reach seemed to pivot on its centre, the forests
swung in a semicircle, and the slanting beams of sunset touched the
broadside of the canoe with a fiery glow, throwing the slender and distorted shadows of its crew upon the streaked glitter of the river. The
white man turned to look ahead. The course of the boat had been altered
at right-angles to the stream, and the carved dragonhead of its prow was
pointing now at a gap in the fringing bushes of the bank. It glided
through, brushing the overhanging twigs, and disappeared from the
river like some slim and amphibious creature leaving the water for its
lair in the forests.

The narrow creek was like a ditch: tortuous, fabulously deep; filled
with gloom under the thin strip of pure and shining blue of the heaven.
Immense trees soared up, invisible behind the festooned draperies of
creepers. Here and there, near the glistening blackness of the water, a
twisted root of some tall tree showed amongst the tracery of small ferns,
black and dull, writhing and motionless, like an arrested snake. The short
words of the paddlers reverberated loudly between the thick and sombre
walls of vegetation. Darkness oozed out from between the trees, through
the tangled maze of the creepers, from behind the great fantastic and
unstirring leaves; the darkness, mysterious and invincible; the darkness
scented and poisonous of impenetrable forests.

The men poled in the shoaling water. The creek broadened, opening
out into a wide sweep of a stagnant lagoon. The forests receded from the
marshy bank, leaving a level strip of bright green, reedy grass to frame
the reflected blueness of the sky. A fleecy pink cloud drifted high above,
trailing the delicate colouring of its image under the floating leaves and
the silvery blossoms of the lotus. A little house, perched on high piles,
appeared black in the distance. Near it, two tall nibong palms, that seemed
to have come out of the forests in the background, leaned slightly over the
ragged roof, with a suggestion of sad tenderness and care in the droop of
their leafy and soaring heads.

The steersman, pointing with his paddle, said, "Arsat is there. I see
his canoe fast between the piles."

The polers ran along the sides of the boat glancing over their shoulders at the end of the day's journey. They would have preferred to spend
the night somewhere else than on this lagoon of weird aspect and ghostly
reputation. Moreover, they disliked Arsat, first as a stranger, and also because he who repairs a ruined house, and dwells in it, proclaims that he is
not afraid to live amongst the spirits that haunt the places abandoned by

mankind. Such a man can disturb the course of fate by glances or words; while his familiar ghosts are not easy to propitiate by casual wayfarers upon whom they long to wreak the malice of their human master. White men care not for such things, being unbelievers and in league with the Father of Evil, who leads them unharmed through the invisible dangers of this world. To the warnings of the righteous they oppose an offensive pretence of disbelief. What is there to be done?

So they thought, throwing their weight on the end of their long poles. The big canoe glided on swiftly, noiselessly, and smoothly, towards Arsat's clearing, till, in a great rattling of poles thrown down, and the loud murmurs of "Allah be praised!" it came with a gentle knock against the crooked piles below the house.

The boatmen with uplifted faces shouted discordantly, "Arsat! O Arsat!" Nobody came. The white man began to climb the rude ladder giving access to the bamboo platform before the house. The juragan of the boat said sulkily, "We will cook in the sampan, and sleep on the water."

"Pass my blankets and the basket," said the white man curtly.

He knelt on the edge of the platform to receive the bundle. Then the boat shoved off, and the white man, standing up, confronted Arsat, who had come out through the low door of his hut. He was a man young, powerful, with a broad chest and muscular arms. He had nothing on but his sarong. His head was bare. His big, soft eyes stared eagerly at the white man, but his voice and demeanour were composed as he asked, without any words of greeting —

"Have you medicine, Tuan?"

"No," said the visitor in a startled tone. "No. Why? Is there sickness in the house?"

"Enter and see," replied Arsat, in the same calm manner, and turning short round, passed again through the small doorway. The white man, dropping his bundles, followed.

In the dim light of the dwelling he made out on a couch of bamboos a woman stretched on her back under a broad sheet of red cotton cloth. She lay still, as if dead; but her big eyes, wide open, glittered in the gloom, staring upwards at the slender rafters, motionless and unseeing. She was in a high fever, and evidently unconscious. Her cheeks were sunk slightly, her lips were partly open, and on the young face there was the ominous and fixed expression — the absorbed, contemplating expression of the unconscious who are going to die. The two men stood looking down at her in silence.

"Has she been long ill?" asked the traveller.

"I have not slept for five nights," answered the Malay, in a deliberate tone. "At first she heard voices calling her from the water and struggled

against me who held her. But since the sun of today rose she hears nothing — she hears not me. She sees nothing. She sees not me — me!"

He remained silent for a minute, then asked softly —

"Tuan, will she die?"

"I fear so," said the white man sorrowfully. He had known Arsat
years ago, in a far country in times of trouble and danger, when no friendship is to be despised. And since his Malay friend had come unexpectedly
to dwell in the hut on the lagoon with a strange woman, he had slept many
times there, in his journeys up and down the river. He liked the man who
knew how to keep faith in council and how to fight without fear by the
side of his white friend. He liked him — not so much perhaps as a man
likes his favourite dog — but still he liked him well enough to help and
ask no questions, to think sometimes vaguely and hazily in the midst of
his own pursuits, about the lonely man and the long-haired woman with
audacious face and triumphant eyes, who lived together hidden by the
forests — alone and feared.

The white man came out of the hut in time to see the enormous conflagration of sunset put out by the swift and stealthy shadows that, rising
like a black and impalpable vapour above the treetops, spread over the
heaven, extinguishing the crimson glow of floating clouds and the red
brilliance of departing daylight. In a few moments all the stars came out
above the intense blackness of the earth, and the great lagoon gleaming
suddenly with reflected lights resembled an oval patch of night sky flung
down into the hopeless and abysmal night of the wilderness. The white
man had some supper out of the basket, then collecting a few sticks that
lay about the platform, made up a small fire, not for warmth, but for the
sake of the smoke, which would keep off the mosquitoes. He wrapped
himself in his blankets and sat with his back against the reed wall of the
house, smoking thoughtfully.

Arsat came through the doorway with noiseless steps and squatted
down by the fire. The white man moved his outstretched legs a little.

"She breathes," said Arsat in a low voice, anticipating the expected
question. "She breathes and burns as if with a great fire. She speaks not;
she hears not — and burns!"

He paused for a moment, then asked in a quiet, incurious tone —

"Tuan . . . will she die?"

The white man moved his shoulders uneasily, and muttered in a
hesitating manner —

"If such is her fate."

"No, Tuan," said Arsat calmly. "If such is my fate. I hear, I see, I
wait. I remember . . . Tuan, do you remember the old days? Do you
remember my brother?"

"Yes," said the white man. The Malay rose suddenly and went in.

The other, sitting still outside, could hear the voice in the hut. Arsat said: "Hear me! Speak!" His words were succeeded by a complete silence. "O Diamelen!" he cried suddenly. After that cry there was a deep sigh. Arsat came out and sank down again in his old place.

They sat in silence before the fire. There was no sound within the house, there was no sound near them; but far away on the lagoon they could hear the voices of the boatmen ringing fitful and distinct on the calm water. The fire in the bows of the sampan shone faintly in the distance with a hazy red glow. Then it died out. The voices ceased. The land and the water slept invisible, unstirring and mute. It was as though there had been nothing left in the world but the glitter of stars streaming, ceaseless and vain, through the black stillness of the night.

The white man gazed straight before him into the darkness with wide-open eyes. The fear and fascination, the inspiration and the wonder of death — of death near, unavoidable, and unseen, soothed the unrest of his race and stirred the most indistinct, the most intimate of his thoughts. The ever-ready suspicion of evil, the gnawing suspicion that lurks in our hearts, flowed out into the stillness round him — into the stillness profound and dumb, and made it appear untrustworthy and infamous, like the placid and impenetrable mask of an unjustifiable violence. In that fleeting and powerful disturbance of his being the earth enfolded in the starlight peace became a shadowy country of inhuman strife, a battlefield of phantoms terrible and charming, august or ignoble, struggling ardently for the possession of our helpless hearts. An unquiet and mysterious country of inextinguishable desires and fears.

A plaintive murmur rose in the night; a murmur saddening and startling, as if the great solitudes of surrounding woods had tried to whisper into his ear the wisdom of their immense and lofty indifference. Sounds hesitating and vague floated in the air round him, shaped themselves slowly into words; and at last flowed on gently in a murmuring stream of soft and monotonous sentences. He stirred like a man waking up and changed his position slightly. Arsat, motionless and shadowy, sitting with bowed head under the stars, was speaking in a low and dreamy tone —

". . . for where can we lay down the heaviness of our trouble but in a friend's heart? A man must speak of war and of love. You, Tuan, know what war is, and you have seen me in time of danger seek death as other men seek life! A writing may be lost; a lie may be written; but what the eye has seen is truth and remains in the mind!"

"I remember," said the white man quietly. Arsat went on with mournful composure —

"Therefore I shall speak to you of love. Speak in the night. Speak before both night and love are gone — and the eye of day looks upon my sorrow and my shame; upon my blackened face; upon my burnt-up heart."

A sigh, short and faint, marked an almost imperceptible pause, and then his words flowed on, without a stir, without a gesture.

"After the time of trouble and war was over and you went away from my country in the pursuit of your desires, which we, men of the islands, cannot understand, I and my brother became again, as we had been before, the sword-bearers of the Ruler. You know we were men of family, belonging to a ruling race, and more fit than any to carry on our right shoulder the emblem of power. And in the time of prosperity Si Dendring showed us favour, as we, in time of sorrow, had showed to him the faithfulness of our courage. It was a time of peace. A time of deer-hunts and cock-fights; of idle talks and foolish squabbles between men whose bellies are full and weapons are rusty. But the sower watched the young rice-shoots grow up without fear, and the traders came and went, departed lean and returned fat into the river of peace. They brought news too. Brought lies and truth mixed together, so that no man knew when to rejoice and when to be sorry. We heard from them about you also. They had seen you here and had seen you there. And I was glad to hear, for I remembered the stirring times, and I always remembered you, Tuan, till the time came when my eyes could see nothing in the past, because they had looked upon the one who is dying there — in the house."

He stopped to exclaim in an intense whisper, "O Mara bahia! O Calamity!" then went on speaking a little louder.

"There's no worse enemy and no better friend than a brother, Tuan, for one brother knows another, and in perfect knowledge is strength for good or evil. I loved my brother. I went to him and told him that I could see nothing but one face, hear nothing but one voice. He told me: 'Open your heart so that she can see what is in it — and wait. Patience is wisdom. Inchi Midah may die or our Ruler may throw off his fear of a woman!' . . . I waited! . . . You remember the lady with the veiled face, Tuan, and the fear of our Ruler before her cunning and temper. And if she wanted her servant, what could I do? But I fed the hunger of my heart on short glances and stealthy words. I loitered on the path to the bath-houses in the daytime, and when the sun had fallen behind the forest I crept along the jasmine hedges of the women's courtyard. Unseeing, we spoke to one another through the scent of flowers, through the veil of leaves, through the blades of long grass that stood still before our lips; so great was our prudence, so faint was the murmur of our great longing. The time passed swiftly . . . and there were whispers amongst women — and our enemies watched — my brother was gloomy, and I began to think of killing and of a fierce death. . . . We are of a people who take what they want — like you whites. There is a time when a man should forget loyalty and respect. Might and authority are given to rulers, but to all men is given love and strength and courage. My brother said, 'You shall take her from their midst. We are two who are like one.' And I answered, 'Let it be soon, for I find no warmth in sunlight that does not shine upon her.' Our time came when the Ruler and all the great people went to the mouth of the river to fish by torchlight. There were hundreds of boats, and on the white sand, between the water and the forests, dwellings of leaves were built for the households of the Rajahs. The smoke of cooking-fires was like a blue mist of the evening, and many voices rang in it joyfully. While they were making the boats ready to beat up the fish, my brother came to me and said, 'To-night!' I looked to my weapons, and when the time came our canoe took its place in the circle of boats there was darkness. When the shouting began and the excitement made them like mad we dropped out. The water swallowed our fire, and we floated back to the shore that was dark with only here and there the glimmer of embers. We could hear the talk of slave-girls amongst the sheds. Then we found a place deserted and silent. We waited there. She came. She came running along the shore, rapid and leaving no trace, like a leaf driven by the wind into the sea. My brother said gloomily, 'Go and take her; carry her into our boat.' I lifted her in my arms. She panted. Her heart was beating against my breast. I said, 'I take you from those people. You came to the cry of my heart, but my arms take you into my boat against the will of the great!' 'It is right,' said my brother. 'We are men who take what we want and can hold it against many. We should have taken her in daylight.' I said, 'Let us be off'; for since she was in my boat I began to think of our Ruler's many men. 'Yes. Let us be off,' said my brother. 'We are cast out and this boat is our country now — and the sea is our refuge.' He lingered with his foot on the shore, and I entreated him to hasten, for I remembered the strokes of her heart against my breast and thought that two men cannot withstand a hundred. We left, paddling downstream close to the bank; and as we passed by the creek where they were fishing, the great shouting had ceased, but the murmur of voices was loud like the humming of insects flying at noonday. The boats floated, clustered together, in the red light of torches, under a black roof of smoke; and men talked of their sport. Men that boasted, and praised, and jeered — men that would have been our friends in the morning, but on that night were already our enemies. We paddled swiftly past. We had no more friends in the country of our birth. She sat in the middle of the canoe with covered face; silent as she is now; unseeing as she is now — and I had no regret at what I was leaving because I could hear her breathing close to me — as I can hear her now."

He paused, listened with his ear turned to the doorway, then shook his head and went on.

"My brother wanted to shout the cry of challenge — one cry only — to

let the people know we were freeborn robbers who trusted our arms and
the great sea. And again I begged him in the name of our love to be silent.
Could I not hear her breathing close to me? I knew the pursuit would
come quick enough. My brother loved me. He dipped his paddle without
a splash. He only said, 'There is half a man in you now — the other half is
in that woman. I can wait. When you are a whole man again, you will
come back with me here to shout defiance. We are sons of the same
mother.' I made no answer. All my strength and all my spirit were in my
hands that held the paddle — for I longed to be with her in a safe place
beyond the reach of men's anger and of women's spite. My love was so
great, that I thought it could guide me to a country where death was unknown, if I could only escape from Inchi Midah's fury and from our
Ruler's sword. We paddled with haste, breathing through our teeth. The
blades bit deep into the smooth water. We passed out of the river; we flew
in clear channels amongst the shallows. We skirted the black coast; we
skirted the sand beaches where the sea speaks in whispers to the land; and
the gleam of white sand flashed back past our boat, so swiftly she ran upon
the water. We spoke not. Only once I said, 'Sleep, Diamelen, for soon you
may want all your strength.' I heard the sweetness of her voice, but I never
turned my head. The sun rose and still we went on. Water fell from my
face like rain from a cloud. We flew in the light and heat. I never looked
back, but I knew that my brother's eyes, behind me, were looking steadily
ahead, for the boat went as straight as a bushman's dart, when it leaves the
end of the sumpitan. There was no better paddler, or better steersman
than my brother. Many times, together, we had won races in that canoe.
But we never had put out our strength as we did then — then, when for
the last time we paddled together! There was no braver or stronger man
in our country than my brother. I could not spare the strength to turn my
head and look at him, but every moment I heard the hiss of his breath
getting louder behind me. Still he did not speak. The sun was high. The
heat clung to my back like a flame of fire. My ribs were ready to burst, but
I could no longer get enough air into my chest. And then I felt I must cry
out with my last breath, 'Let us rest!' . . . 'Good!' he answered; and his
voice was firm. He was strong. He was brave. He knew not fear and no
fatigue . . . My brother!"

A murmur powerful and gentle, a murmur vast and faint; the murmur
of trembling leaves, of stirring boughs, ran through the tangled depths of
the forests, ran over the starry smoothness of the lagoon, and the water between the piles lapped the slimy timber once with a sudden splash. A
breath of warm air touched the two men's faces and passed on with a
mournful sound — a breath loud and short like an uneasy sigh of the
dreaming earth.

Arsat went on in an even, low voice:

"We ran our canoe on the white beach of a little bay close to a long tongue of land that seemed to bar our road; a long wooded cape going far into the sea. My brother knew that place. Beyond the cape a river has its entrance, and through the jungle of that land there is a narrow path. We made a fire and cooked rice. Then we lay down to sleep on the soft sand in the shade of our canoe, while she watched. No sooner had I closed my eyes than I heard her cry of alarm. We leaped up. The sun was halfway down the sky already, and coming in sight in the opening of the bay we saw a prau manned by many paddlers. We knew it at once; it was one of our Rajah's praus. They were watching the shore, and saw us. They beat the gong, and turned the head of the prau into the bay. I felt my heart become weak within my breast. Diamelen sat on the sand and covered her face. There was no escape by sea. My brother laughed. He had the gun you had given him, Tuan, before you went away, but there was only a handful of powder. He spoke to me quickly: 'Run with her along the path. I shall keep them back, for they had no firearms, and landing in the face of a man with a gun is certain death for some. Run with her. On the other side of that wood there is a fisherman's house — and a canoe. When I have fired all the shots I will follow. I am a great runner, and before they can come up we shall be gone. I will hold out as long as I can, for she is but a woman — that can neither run nor fight, but she has your heart in her weak hands.' He dropped behind the canoe. The prau was coming. She and I ran, and as we rushed along the path I heard shots. My brother fired — once — twice — and the booming of the gong ceased. There was silence behind us. That neck of land is narrow. Before I heard my brother fire the third shot I saw the shelving shore, and I saw the water again: the mouth of a broad river. We crossed a grassy glade. We ran down to the water. I saw a low hut above the black mud, and a small canoe hauled up. I heard another shot behind me. I thought, 'That is his last charge.' We rushed down to the canoe; a man came running from the hut, but I leaped on him, and we rolled together in the mud. Then I got up, and he lay still at my feet. I don't know whether I had killed him or not. I and Diamelen pushed the canoe afloat. I heard yells behind me, and I saw my brother run across the glade. Many men were bounding after him. I took her in my arms and threw her into the boat, then leaped in myself. When I looked back I saw that my brother had fallen. He fell and was up again, but the men were closing round him. He shouted, 'I am coming!' The men were close to him. I looked. Many men. Then I looked at her. Tuan, I pushed the canoe! I pushed it into deep water. She was kneeling forward looking at me, and I said, 'Take your paddle,' while I struck the water with mine. Tuan, I heard him cry. I heard him cry my name twice; and I

heard voices shouting, 'Kill! Strike!' I never turned back. I heard him calling my name again with a great shriek, as when life is going out together
with the voice — and I never turned my head. My own name! . . . My
brother! Three times he called — but I was not afraid of life. Was she not
there in that canoe? And could I not with her find a country where death is
forgotten — where death is unknown!"

The white man sat up. Arsat rose and stood, an indistinct and silent
figure above the dying embers of the fire. Over the lagoon a mist drifting
and low had crept, erasing slowly the glittering images of the stars. And
now a great expanse of white vapour covered the land: it flowed cold and
grey in the darkness, eddied in noiseless whirls round the tree-trunks and
about the platform of the house, which seemed to float upon a restless and
impalpable illusion of a sea. Only far away the tops of the trees stood outlined on the twinkle of heaven, like a sombre and forbidding shore — a
coast deceptive, pitiless and black.

Arsat's voice vibrated loudly in the profound peace.

"I had her there! I had her! To get her I would have faced all mankind. But I had her — and —"

His words went out ringing into the empty distances. He paused, and
seemed to listen to them dying away very far — beyond help and beyond
recall. Then he said quietly —

"We all love our brothers."

Arsat burst out with an intense whispering violence —

"What did I care who died? I wanted peace in my own heart."

He seemed to hear a stir in the house — listened — then stepped in
noiselessly. The white man stood up. A breeze was coming in fitful puffs.
The stars shone paler as if they had retreated into the frozen depths of
immense space. After a chill gust of wind there were a few seconds of perfect calm and absolute silence. Then from behind the black and wavy line
of the forests a column of golden light shot up into the heavens and spread
over the semicircle of the eastern horizon. The sun had risen. The mist
lifted, broke into drifting patches, vanished into thin flying wreaths; and
the unveiled lagoon lay, polished and black, in the heavy shadows at the
foot of the wall of trees. A white eagle rose over it with a slanting and ponderous flight, reached the clear sunshine and appeared dazzlingly brilliant
for a moment, then soaring higher, became a dark and motionless speck
before it vanished into the blue as if it had left the earth for ever. The
white man, standing gazing upwards before the doorway, heard in the hut
a confused and broken murmur of distracted words ending with a loud
groan. Suddenly Arsat stumbled out with outstretched hands, shivered,
and stood still for some time with fixed eyes. Then he said —

"She burns no more."

Before his face the sun showed its edge above the tree-tops, rising steadily. The breeze freshened; a great brilliance burst upon the lagoon, sparkled on the rippling water. The forests came out of the clear shadows of the morning, became distinct, as if they had rushed nearer — to stop short in a great stir of leaves, of nodding boughs, of swaying branches. In the merciless sunshine the whisper of unconscious life grew louder, speaking in an incomprehensible voice round the dumb darkness of that human sorrow. Arsat's eyes wandered slowly, then stared at the rising sun.

"I can see nothing," he said half aloud to himself.

"There is nothing," said the white man, moving to the edge of the platform and waving his hand to his boat. A shout came faintly over the lagoon and the sampan began to glide towards the abode of the friend of ghosts.

"If you want to come with me, I will wait all the morning," said the white man, looking away upon the water.

"No, Tuan," said Arsat softly. "I shall not eat or sleep in this house, but I must first see my road. Now I can see nothing — see nothing! There is no light and no peace in the world; but there is death — death for many. We were sons of the same mother — and I left him in the midst of enemies; but I am going back now."

He drew a long breath and went on in a dreamy tone:

"In a little while I shall see clear enough to strike — to strike. But she has died, and . . . now . . . darkness."

He flung his arms wide open, let them fall along his body, then stood still with unmoved face and stony eyes, staring at the sun. The white man got down into his canoe. The polers ran smartly along the sides of the boat, looking over their shoulders at the beginning of a weary journey. High in the stern, his head muffled up in white rags, the juragan sat moody, letting his paddle trail in the water. The white man, leaning with both arms over the grass roof of the little cabin, looked back at the shining ripple of the boat's wake. Before the sampan passed out of the lagoon into the creek he lifted his eyes. Arsat had not moved. He stood lonely in the searching sunshine; and he looked beyond the great light of a cloudless day into the darkness of a world of illusions.

To His Coy Mistress

Had we but world enough, and time,
This coyness, lady, were no crime.
We would sit down, and think which way
To walk, and pass our long loves day.
Thou by the Indian Ganges side
Should'st rubies find; I by the tide
Of Humber would complain. I would
Love you ten years before the flood:
And you should, if you please, refuse
Till the conversion of the Jews.
My vegetable love should grow
Vaster than empires, and more slow.
An hundred years should go to praise
Thine eyes, and on thy forehead gaze.
Two hundred to adore each breast;
But thirty thousand to the rest.
An age at least to every part,
And the last age should show your heart.
For, lady, you deserve this state;
Nor would I love at lower rate.

    But at my back I alwaies hear
Times wingéd charriot hurrying near;
And yonder all before us lye
Deserts of vast eternity.
Thy beauty shall no more be found;
Nor in thy marble vault shall sound
My echoing song; then worms shall try
That long preserv'd virginity;
And your quaint honour turn to dust;
And into ashes all my lust.
The grave's a fine and private place,
But none I think do there embrace.

    Now therefore, while the youthful hew
Sits on thy skin like morning dew,
And while thy willing soul transpires
At every pore with instant fires,
Now let us sport us while we may;
And now, like am'rous birds of prey,
Rather at once our time devour,
Than languish in his slow-chapt pow'r.

Let us roll all our strength, and all
Our sweetness, up into one ball;
And tear our pleasures with rough strife,
Through the iron gates of life.
Thus, though we cannot make our sun
Stand still, yet we will make him run.

ANDREW MARVELL

A Valediction: Forbidding Mourning[4]

As virtuous men passe mildly away,
    And whisper to their soules, to goe,
Whilst some of their sad friends doe say,
    The breath goes now, and some say, no:

So let us melt, and make no noise,
    No teare-floods, nor sigh-tempests move,
T'were prophanation of our joyes
    To tell the layetie our love.

Moving of th'earth brings harmes and feares;
    Men reckon what it did and meant,
But trepidation of the spheares,
    Though greater farre, is innocent.

Dull sublunary lovers love
    (Whose soule is sense) cannot admit
Absence, because it doth remove
    Those things which elemented it.

But we by a love so much refin'd,
    That our selves know not what it is,
Inter-assuréd of the mind,
    Care lesse, eyes, lips, and hands to misse.

Our two soules therefore, which are one,
    Though I must goe, endure not yet
A breach, but an expansion,
    Like gold to ayery thinnesse beate.

[4] Written when Donne parted from his wife to go into France in 1612.

If they be two, they are two so
   As stiffe twin compasses are two,
Thy soule the fixt foot, makes no show
   To move, but doth, if th'other doe.

And though it in the center sit,
   Yet when the other far doth rome,
It leanes, and hearkens after it,
   And growes erect, as that comes home.

Such wilt thou be to mee, who must
   Like th'other foot, obliquely runne;
Thy firmnes makes my circle just,
   And makes me end, where I begunne.

JOHN DONNE

The Equilibrists*

Full of her long white arms and milky skin
He had a thousand times remembered sin.
Alone in the press of people traveled he,
Minding her jacinth, and myrrh, and ivory.

Mouth he remembered: the quaint orifice
From which came heat that flamed upon the kiss,
Till cold words came down spiral from the head,
Grey doves from the officious tower illsped.

Body: it was a white field ready for love,
On her body's field, with the gaunt tower above,
The lilies grew, beseeching him to take,
If he would pluck and wear them, bruise and break.

Eyes talking: Never mind the cruel words,
Embrace my flowers, but not embrace the swords.
But what they said, the doves came straightway flying
And unsaid: Honor, Honor, they came crying.

Importunate her doves. Too pure, too wise,
Clambering on his shoulder, saying, Arise,
Leave me now, and never let us meet,
Eternal distance now command thy feet.

Predicament indeed, which thus discovers
Honor among thieves, Honor between lovers.
O such a little word is Honor, they feel!
But the grey word is between them cold as steel.

At length I saw these lovers fully were come
Into their torture of equilibrium;
Dreadfully had forsworn each other, and yet
They were bound each to each, and they did not forget.

And rigid as two painful stars, and twirled
About the clustered night their prison world,
They burned with fierce love always to come near,
But Honor beat them back and kept them clear.

Ah, the strict lovers, they are ruined now!
I cried in anger. But with puddled brow
Devising for those gibbeted and brave
Came I descanting: Man, what would you have?

For spin your period out, and draw your breath,
A kinder saeculum begins with Death.
Would you ascend to Heaven and bodiless dwell?
Or take your bodies honorless to Hell?

In Heaven you have heard no marriage is,
No white flesh tinder to your lecheries,
Your male and female tissue sweetly shaped
Sublimed away, and furious blood escaped.

Great lovers lie in Hell, the stubborn ones
Infatuate of the flesh upon the bones;
Stuprate, they rend each other when they kiss,
The pieces kiss again, no end to this.

But still I watched them spinning, orbited nice.
Their flames were not more radiant than their ice.
I dug in the quiet earth and wrought the tomb
And made these lines to memorize their doom: —

Epitaph

Equilibrists lie here; stranger, tread light;
Close, but untouching in each other's sight;
Mouldered the lips and ashy the tall skull,
Let them lie perilous and beautiful.

JOHN CROWE RANSOM

A Song
(from *Aglaura,* Act IV, Scene I)

No, no, fair heretic, it needs must be
          But an ill love in me,
          And worse for thee:

For were it in my power
To love thee now this hour,
          More than I did the last;

'Twould then so fall,
I might not love at all;

Love that can flow, and can admit increase,
Admits as well an ebb, and may grow less.

True love is still the same; the torrid zones,
          And those more frigid ones,
          It must not know:

For love, grown cold or hot,
Is lust or friendship, not
          The thing we have;

For that's a flame would die,
Held down, or up too high:
          Then think I love more than I can express,
          And would love more, could I but love thee less.

SIR JOHN SUCKLING

The Zoo*

The elephant never forgets.
Africa sailed away,
The forests burned,
And all the streams went dry.
But as his great bulk turns
Within his tiny eye,
As if those wrinkles smiled,
The lowing song is heard.

The polar bear never forgets.
The arctic thawed apart,
The water warmed,
And all the cold fish died.
But as he roars alarm
And turns within his cage
His huge paws form
Their great, applauding heart.

Even the turtledove
Whose sky has lost its air
Does not forget,
And from his wire bar,
Perched for that old wit
Of green and sun, stares out
On flying doves, and yet
Sings yet again of love.

ANTHONY OSTROFF

Song of Myself
(Leaves of Grass)

5

I believe in you my soul, the other I am must not abase itself to you,
And you must not be abased to the other.

Loafe with me on the grass, loose the stop from your throat,
Not words, not music or rhyme I want, not custom or lecture, not even the
    best,
Only the lull I like, the hum of your valvéd voice.

* © 1956, by Anthony Ostroff. Reprinted from his volume, *Imperatives*, by permission of Harcourt, Brace & World, Inc.

I mind how once we lay such a transparent summer morning,
How you settled your head athwart my hips and gently turn'd over upon
    me,
And parted the shirt from my bosom-bone, and plunged your tongue to my
    bare-stript heart,
And reach'd till you felt my beard, and reach'd till you held my feet.

Swiftly arose and spread around me the peace and knowledge that pass
    all the argument of the earth,
And I know that the hand of God is the promise of my own,
And I know that the spirit of God is the brother of my own,
And that all the men ever born are also my brothers, and the women my
    sisters and lovers,
And that a kelson of the creation is love,
And limitless are leaves stiff or drooping in the fields,
And brown ants in the little wells beneath them,
And mossy scabs of the worm fence, heap'd stones, elder, mullein and
    poke-weed.

WALT WHITMAN

LXI

Since there's no helpe, come let us kisse and part;
Nay, I have done: you get no more of me,
And I am glad, yea glad withall my heart,
That thus so cleanly, I myselfe can free;
Shake hands forever, cancel all our vows,
And when we meet at any time againe,
Be it not seene in either of our browes
That we one jot of former love reteyne.
Now at the last gaspe of Love's latest breath,
When his pulse fayling, Passion speechlesse lies,
When Faith is kneeling by his bed of death,
And Innocence is closing up his eyes,
    Now if thou wouldst, when all have given him over,
    From death to life, thou might'st him yet recover.

MICHAEL DRAYTON

All My Senses

All my senses, like Beacons flame,
Gave Alarum to desire
To take armes in Cynthia's name,
And set all my thoughts on fire:
Furies wit perswaded me,
Happy love was hazards heire,
Cupid did best shoot and see
In the night where smooth is faire;
Up I start beleeving well
To see if Cynthia were awake;
Wonders I saw, who can tell?
And thus unto my selfe I spake;
Sweet God Cupid where am I,
That pale Diana's light:
Such rich beauties doe espie,
As harme our senses with delight?
Am I borne up to the skyes?
See where Jove and Venus shine,
Shewing in her heavenly eyes
That desire is divine:
Looke where lyes the Milken way,
Way unto that dainty throne,
Where while all the Gods would play,
Vulcan thinkes to dwell alone.
I gave reynes to this conceipt,
Hope went on the wheele of lust:
Phansies scales are false of weight,
Thoughts take thought that goe of trust,
I stept forth to touch the skye,
I a God by Cupid dreames,
Cynthia who did naked lye,
Runnes away like silver streames;
Leaving hollow banks behind,
Who can neither forward move,
Nor if rivers be unkind,
Turne away or leave to love.
There stand I, like Articke pole,
Where Sol passeth o're the line,
Mourning my benighted soule,

Which so loseth light divine.
There stand I like Men that preach
From the Execution place,
At their death content to teach
All the world with their disgrace:
He that lets his Cynthia lye,
Naked on a bed of play,
To say prayers ere she dye,
Teacheth time to runne away:
Let no Love-desiring heart,
In the Starres goe seeke his fate,
Love is onely Natures art,
Wonder hinders Love and Hate.
   None can well behold with eyes,
   But what underneath him lies.

BROOKE, FULKE GREVILLE, BARON

CHAPTER THREE

The Instruments
of Expression: The Body

The connections between intellectual activity
and the body, though diffused in every bodily
feeling, are focused in the eyes, the ears, the
voice, and the hands.

A. N. WHITEHEAD

GENERAL CONSIDERATIONS

Of all the aspects of reading aloud, perhaps the problem of the proper handling of the body is most controversial. For this immediately involves questions of *taste* and of *style*, two highly variable, in fact, two inevitably variable, aspects of any appreciation or practice of art. Perhaps one of the most difficult insights is for a person of a given time or culture to realize that, while much in the art he admires is universal, much is, quite crudely, the inevitable bodying forth of that art in the time-and-space limiting elements of a culturally accepted *mode*. Nothing, seemingly, can more easily become the basis for major aesthetic misunderstandings than the odd *means* of an exotic art. Even in a relatively close time and place, the leap may be too much.

A clear example of this difficulty may be seen by looking at styles of acting. The grand gesture of the era just preceding ours spells only one thing to us, "ham." Yet there must have been, in fact we know there were, great actors in that period. Will not some day the present style of acting, with its concentration on an illusion of *realism*, on its mumblings, its jerks, its total lack of the pleasures of grace, line, and movement, will not this one day seem as artificial? Yet it works very well in modern plays, because the author has designed the total play, the language, the stage movement, the decor, to make an aesthetic unity with this kind of acting. But try it with Shakespeare, or even more revealing, with the Restoration drama, and one sees a vivid illustration of the *inevitable close relationship of the human body to the literary text*. For the people of William Congreve's society, the whole theory behind the modern actor's attempt to act "naturally" and the modern author's desire to write "naturally" would have seemed grotesque. The author's and the actor's desire to expose the naked neurotic man would have seemed to them not merely indecent, but laughable in its philosophic absurdity. Everybody knew man was basically a mewling, puking beast. What was interesting was his ability to be mannered, to direct that raw meat into clever, graceful, and sometimes diabolical, *manners*. I'm not sure but that they had as much of the truth as Tennessee Williams.

Surely we are brought to a primary fact: that the act of reading aloud is not merely, as is by far the prevailing present sentiment, a problem of "reading naturally" (which generally means "conversationally"). At the very beginning we see that what must be achieved is an extremely sophisticated knowledge of style and of the psychology behind the various literary styles, hence, inevitably of the bodily attitudes involved in that style. For words in fictions are gestures; they are essentially based on an imagination which sees human beings in certain biologically and conventionally meaningful attitudes.

In a later chapter I shall be talking about time, both as a stream down which the work of literature drifts from its original point of creation and as a flow that must be ordered in a certain way *within* the work by the author. If that discussion seems in some way remote from the problem of comprehending literature through reading it aloud, remember this first generalization that we have come to concerning the role of the body in reading. A work of literature in its style, mode of feeling, and method of thought implies the human body in real attitudes toward the world around it. These attitudes are inevitably conventional to a large degree, and are betrayed if bodied forth in too alien a system of gesture. Therefore a knowledge of the literature *in time* is important because of the necessity for the imaginative recreation of the world of gesture that makes the words live. And a knowledge of *time in* the work is essential because the gestures will be ordered and disciplined by the way time is expanded or compressed within the work. Robert Graves, the poet and novelist, said somewhere that all poetry should be read in a conversational manner. Certainly this is how *his* excellent poetry should be read and, perhaps, how most modern British poetry (to its loss?) should be read. But to read Keats in this way would be to deny the romantic mode. To read Hopkins in this way would be to deny the religious agony or exaltation. To read Shakespeare in this way is to deny the dramatic voice and the elevation of the style. Unfortunately for those who consider reading aloud an easy art, the corpus of literature is too alive, presents too much variety in its human image, for any such simple solution. It is an *art,* and is therefore complex. It is an art performing another art, and therefore twice as complex. I doubt if most persons in the Anglo-American culture have any notion how thoroughly the genteel tradition has strangled the humane art of sharing literature aloud.

Before going on to some practical discussion of gesture in reading aloud, certain further generalizations need to be made about gesture; and as is so often the case, their implications can best be grasped in some historical perspective.

I have already alluded to the style of reading aloud that preceded our era — that of the so-called "elocutionists." It is difficult now to give them their due, yet they did not exist in isolation; they participated in the conventions of the time, and their style was, no less than the then-accepted styles of acting, one that if well-done held meaning for at least some of their contemporaries. Certainly, the man taken as the most original teacher of the period, a Frenchman named François Delsarte, has been very much maligned by history. A brief discussion of this man's work and its virtues and limitations is made all the more meaningful by a recent book by Ted Shawn,[1] in which that noted pioneer of modern dance declares that Del-

[1] Ted Shawn, *Every Little Movement* (privately printed), 1954.

sarte's theories of gesture are the undoubted base of modern dance and are to this day handed down from teacher to pupil. How is it that Delsarte's influence in the oral reading of literature has dwindled to insignificance, whereas in the *Dance* it can retain such vitality? I think the answer to this question will offer the simplest path to certain distinctions about gesture.

Delsarte (b. 1811) must, I think, be taken as a pioneer in what is now being called the science of kinesics. So far as the ultimate use of his theories is concerned, his aim was certainly not, as some have claimed, the creation of those horribly mechanical children of all ages who not many years back delighted some and bored others through the given precision of the gesture that accompanied "give me liberty or give me death." As one of his disciples says, "The only way Delsarte sought is Nature's way." And Delsarte sought to learn Nature's way, not hit or miss, but by the scientific method of actual observation. Over the years he collected an enormous amount of data, even dissecting corpses and observing inmates of insane asylums. He tried, as Mr. Shawn says, to observe "human beings in every aspect and condition of life and death, normal and abnormal." Yet the view of Delsarte as a leader of the "mechanical" school of reading aloud was not simple fabrication. It was Delsarte's adoption of what he took to be the scientific method of observation and classification that made it possible for his untalented followers to make something mechanical out of the system.

And ironically, it was a strange thread of mysticism, together with an inability to distinguish between metaphoric and factual language, that minimized the usefulness of his observations to science. He said, "The principle of my system lies in the statement that there is in the world a universal formula which may be applied to all sciences, to all things possible. This formula is the trinity . . . thus the three principles of our being, life, mind and soul, form a trinity." And again, Mr. Shawn tells us that one of Delsarte's principal laws derived from his seeing life as an "unfolding process," and it is not surprising that, given the vegetative quality of the figure, a fern is given as an example (but couldn't it be as truthfully said that children grow by accretion, or by combustion, or by multiplication, or by any of many other metaphors?). Although we have ample evidence that Delsarte was a performing musician and an orator of first rank, he can hardly be taken seriously either as a philosopher or scientist, and his system cannot be called, as Mr. Shawn would like to have it, "an exact science." What it is, and this is perhaps no less important (certainly *more* important to a dancer), is a system of emblematic gestures, potentially quite powerful because based on observation of western man in the French subculture and, at the least, not denying actuality in that sense.

I say "emblematic gesture," for it was the distinction between "symbolic gesture,"[2] which can be as precise as language in its connotation, and the emblematic, or more natural, gesture, with its inevitable ambiguities when removed from a larger Gestalt, that Delsarte never saw. Thus, in Delsarte and his followers one runs again and again upon the word "universal" in referring to this system of gesture; that is, "scientific," hence, like physical laws, "universal." Thus Shawn himself distinguishes between the Delsarte gesture and what I call symbolic gesture, by saying it differs from the "arbitrary and stylized positions of the Hindu dance" with its "57,000 catalogued hand positions, each having the specific value of a word as explicit and distinct meaning." Yet what is *not* clearly seen by Delsarte and his followers is that (1) often a given "universal" gesture turns out to be cultural; (2) even when truly "universal," the gesture is often so devoid of denotation that, out of context, it is unsatisfactorily ambiguous; and (3) that even where denotation is sufficiently firm for some accurate communication, that which is communicated must, once out of sophisticated context, lack any depth or range. I will expound briefly on these three points, as they are central to an understanding of the function of gesture in reading aloud.

As to point (1) Shawn himself notes a curious cultural exception to the "universal" gesture of waving the hand toward oneself to beckon someone to come nearer. He says the Japanese take this gesture to mean goodbye. And I can testify by my own experience that this cultural difference is not an East-West matter — the Italians agree with the Japanese. What would seem to be the universal truth is that man has a tendency to create hand-symbols for "goodbye" and "come here," but that the form and shape of these, although obviously likely to involve a sense of direction, are not predictable. A recent edition of *Expression of the Emotions in Man and Animals* by Charles Darwin[3] offers a variety of interesting evidence along this line. In the back of this new edition there are some recent photos from *Balinese Character* by Gregory Bateson and Margaret Mead, which show two thieves being tried for having committed a murder. Their bodily reaction to the fear and tension of the situation is typical among the Balinese — they fell asleep right in the midst of the trial. This reaction to fear is certainly listed nowhere, in my knowledge, among the Delsartian "universal" bodily poses.

Now, as to point (2) some gestures certainly are universal, yet they may still be ambiguous. Take for example the frown. Assume it is a uni-

---

[2] A symbolic gesture is a gesture with a precise denotation. Thus, when an American makes a circle with thumb and forefinger, fingers pointing upward, he is saying "it's ok." An emblematic gesture on the other hand depends for its denotation on a larger context; thus a shrug of the shoulders might mean "I'm in despair," or "let's get on with it," or "you've got me beat."

[3] Charles Darwin, *Expression of the Emotions in Man and Animals*, Philosophical Library, N.Y., 1955.

versal gesture. Say one sees a face or, better yet, a picture of a forehead, frowning. I would guess that it would be very difficult to say whether the frown was one of anxiety, or of disapproval, or of puzzlement. Darwin tells of having presented certain photographs of expression reproduced on a large scale to twenty persons of various ages and both sexes. "Several of the expressions were instantly recognized by almost everyone, though described in not exactly the same terms . . . on the other hand, the most widely different judgments were pronounced in regard to some of them. This exhibition was of use in another way, by convincing me how easily we may be misguided by our imagination; for when I first looked through Mr. Duchenne's photographs, reading at the same time the text, and thus learning what was intended, I was struck with admiration at the truthfulness of all, with only a few exceptions. Nevertheless, if I had examined them without any explanation, no doubt I should have been so much perplexed, in some cases, as other persons have been." Another kind of ambiguity arises from certain emotions which are complex or abstract enough that one doubts if they could yield their meaning through a single, simple gesture, or even a single, isolated bodily attitude. Darwin has the following to say concerning certain of these emotions: "*Jealousy, Envy, Avarice, Revenge, Suspicion, Deceit, Slyness, Guilt, Vanity, Conceit, Ambition, Pride, Humility, etc.* — It is doubtful whether the greater number of the above complex states of mind are revealed by any fixed expression, sufficiently distinct to be described or delineated. When Shakespeare speaks of envy as *lean-faced,* or *black,* or *pale,* and Jealousy as 'the green-eyed monster,' and when Spenser describes suspicion as 'Foul, ill-favoured, and grim,' they must have felt this difficulty. Nevertheless, the above feelings — at least many of them — can be detected by the eye; for instance, conceit; but we are guided in a much greater degree than we suppose by our previous knowledge of the persons or circumstances." This ambiguity of meaning, in short, calls (as does point (3) above) for a larger context.

In regard to (3), let us assume that the frown already mentioned can be determined to be a frown of disapproval. But of what, of whom, of what duration, depth, and degree? Only a larger, more sophisticated context can give these answers to aroused curiosity.

Dance has, essentially, two methods of constructing this larger context. It can create a *language* of gesture, gaining specific denotation by taking steps away from the emblematic stage toward the symbolic, or further toward the sign. On the other hand, it can accept the ambiguities of the emblematic, or natural, gesture and make communication accurate and complex through context of scenery, props, makeup, interaction with other bodies, program notes, titles, and other means of delineating a story or emotive line.

Oral interpretation as an art has no such simple choice. It is the handmaid of a verbal art, an enormous and subtle system of available signs, already existing at the other extreme from the emblematic. The interpreter's task is to bring those abstract signs to life. He must illuminate or intensify in the imagination of the listener, by means of vocal and bodily gestures, the reality which the author's imagination saw. The author tried to recreate that reality in the reader through the medium of a highly controlled and conventionalized system of signs, symbols, and signals. The oral reader must transform this frozen system into a convincing world of living sounds and movements. Of course, in the process of gaining this immediacy, this illumination and intensity, another element is added, the interpreter, just as the musical performer is added in order to bring the abstract score to life.

And here is where, I think, one finds the great resistance to gesture among our contemporaries. With music we are still willing to accept poor performances for the sake of the illuminating ones or are still willing to say, "Well, I didn't read the score quite that way, but the performance I have just heard was nonetheless a coherent conceptualization from which I have learned of certain potentials in the score," or to feel rewarded if certain passages in a performance were illuminating and the rest offered no new insight. But in literature the act of silent reading has become so much the *only* act, we have been so much driven into isolation of our own insights and imaginations, that we have become narcissistic. Too many adults are willing to accept only a *performance* of literature which leaves their own private view of the work of art untroubled. This attitude must inevitably lead to castrated readings, readings so devoid of emotional commitment in the voice and body of the reader that each member of the audience is left quite undisturbed in his own emotional relationship to the work of art. The sterility, the antihumanistic quality of such a situation should be obvious. I have heard much complaint lately among musicians of a comparable problem brought on by the phonograph. Listeners, hearing a certain interpretation of a piece flawlessly played over and over on the machine, become petrified and are uneasy with, or unwilling to listen to, any other interpretation. This mechanical perfection has even had its effect on young performers. I heard recently of a master performer called in to hear the final performance examination of young musicians at one of our leading schools of music. He came away depressed, saying they all played perfectly, flawlessly, more so perhaps than he himself would have done, yet they were all lifeless, passionless.

Nonetheless, important as I think gesture is in the vivification of living literature, it takes its cues from words. We may now see why Delsarte's system may be at once very valuable to the dancer and of dubious merit to the interpreter. For he believed "Gesture is more than speech. It is not what we say that persuades, but the manner of saying it. Speech is in-

ferior to gesture because it corresponds to the phenomena of the mind.
Gesture is the agent of the heart, the persuasive agent. That which demands a volume is uttered by a single gesture." It is this belief in the
superiority of gesture over language that leads, in oral interpretation, to
elocution in the worst sense. It leads to lack of literary taste, for clearly
the quality of the text is unimportant so long as the gesture is effective
and moving. And it leads to a betrayal of good texts, because good texts
do not very often lend themselves to the full and uncomplicated gesture.
If it were really true that "That which demands a volume is uttered by a
single gesture," all art would become the art of the single gesture. But
truthfully we know that no gesture can convey the fullness of *Moby Dick*
or *Hamlet*, although a series of gestures, controlled by the physical situation and the text, may illuminate or extend the meaning of these works for
the audience.

With these distinctions and generalizations concerning the nature of
gesture, it is time for the more practical questions concerning the body in
the situation of the oral interpreter and of the limitations and possibilities
for gesture within that environment.

The use of the body in reading aloud is severely restricted by the
physical fact of the platform and lectern and by the aesthetic necessity
to assume, very often in rapid succession, a variety of points of view or
fictive voices in a dramatic dialogue, as well as to range easily from
describing an action, to describing a setting, to philosophic comment on
the action or setting. In its aesthetic demands on the use of the body,
reading aloud is to acting what the sketch is to the painting. The aim of
reading aloud is, like that of acting, the creation of an illusion — the illusion that the reader is not in fact "reciting," but is spontaneously bringing
forth in exactly their proper intensities, degrees, and subordination the
movement of passionate thought and action to be found in the text from
which he is reading. Yet compared with the actor, who may roam freely,
use his whole body, react to other actors, and exploit the physical properties on the stage, the oral interpreter in the beginning classroom must
achieve his illusion without aid of person or prop and with very restricted
attitudes and movements of the body.

If the student becomes the professional performer and begins to read
to a variety of audiences in a variety of circumstances, he will find, thanks
to his own nature conjoined with the nature of the physical surroundings,
that there is a broad range of acceptable conventions for reading aloud.
Some of these possibilities eliminate the lectern, and some (chamber
theater, for instance) involve reading in concert with others. If the student
becomes, in regard to literature, simply the average citizen, reading from
an easy chair to his family or sharing some work with a few friends, the
lectern is gone, and he is left with the book in his hand. However, the

classroom is the medium in which most people will start reading aloud, and there the single person reading to a rowed, facing audience is the almost unexceptioned physical situation and the one with which we shall concern ourselves.

The neutral attitude is the position of the body from which all expressions, gestures, and characterizations begin and to which they return. It is in contrast to this neutrality that they acquire meaning. Standing a short step behind the lectern the reader puts his feet comfortably apart, with one foot a bit farther forward than the other. Speakers or readers who sway excessively often trace the cause to the fact that their feet are too close together and too exactly in line to give them a solid base. The width of this stance can probably be increased to as much as a foot without becoming expressive, but if it becomes much wider, the audience will begin to take it as an expressive attitude. The torso is easily erect, the hands loosely at the sides or resting easily on the sides of the lectern. Of all the suggestions in this chapter this one may seem the most ridiculously mechanical, and yet nothing is at first so hypnotic and finally so boring as a reader whose body sways meaninglessly or who develops his expressions out of an already distorted pose. It is like trying to arrive at logical sense from a shifting or a false premise.

Normally the aesthetic convention of the lectern limits the movement of the feet. A short step or two away from the neutral position is generally about the extent acceptable to the audience. (There are exceptions; introductory remarks or the comments between pieces in a program of short works offers a much more informal situation and greater opportunity for movement than the readings themselves). Yet though the upper torso and the face carry most of the expressive burden in reading aloud, the legs and feet must not contradict those focal areas. An attitude of eager anticipation — the slight forward thrust of the shoulders carried on through the head, the open eyes, the slightly parted lips, all are reinforced by a slight step forward of one foot, the increased muscular involvement of the legs, an involvement as necessary for oral readers as it is for athletes, dancers, and actors.

Some students will automatically find themselves using hand gestures. Others will find such gestures terribly difficult. Yet others will find that, thanks to an unusually expressive voice and face, these gestures are not frequently needed. Sometimes a teacher will advise a student to make exaggerated gestures, so that more normal-sized gestures will soon come more naturally. In any case, planning pays. The elimination, in practice, of meaningless, compulsive gestures, the noting and exploiting of illuminating ones, requires an integration with the rest of the body which will be but erratically seen in the beginning student.

It is not my purpose to set down here any kind of systematic vocabulary of gesture (I include in the word "gesture" facial expression as well as bodily movement). These should arise naturally out of a person's own knowledge, though there is no doubt in my mind that such a personal range of gesture can in all cases be profitably enlarged by conscious observation of people in everyday life and of actors and other readers and by training with competent teachers. However, if the reading is to appear as an *experience* rather than as a "recitation," it is useful to remember that normally the action or gesture will precede the word.

That is to say, people normally feel the movement of emotion within them, they respond to it by some expression or gesture, then formulate their feelings into language. (In fact the emotion *is* a bodily gesture, always having as a necessary part of its coming into being a change, however invisible, in the body's structure.) A little common sense confirms this sequence. If someone asks you, "Do you want to come along?" you think about it, then shake your head, then reply in words. In extreme emotion — great certainty, eagerness, rage — the word often can seem to come simultaneously with the gesture. On the other extreme, it can sometimes happen that time enough must be given for several emotions, or for considerable progress or alteration through several emotions, to take place before words are uttered. Of course there are exceptions to this order. For instance, sometimes comic affects are based on a disruption of the normal sequence. When the hero in the melodrama cries to the villain, "go!" and then follows the word with a grand gesture pointing to the wings, the audience sees this use of gesture as a logical part of the whole comic style. Another example of a convincing use of an unusual sequence might be a person talking himself into an emotion he does not yet feel, perhaps whipping himself into feeling angry at someone he really loves.

The problem of reading from a manuscript is a vexing one and there is no doubt much truth to the theory that a performance should probably be practiced often enough to achieve memorization. Charles Laughton told a charming story which casts a good deal of light on how professionals solve this problem. The story concerns a time when Laughton and several other actors, including Charles Boyer, were touring in a highly successful dramatic reading from Shaw. One evening in full flight of speech, Boyer blanked out on his line, simply froze up. Later when the others asked what happened to him, he replied that his eye had actually caught the line he was speaking in the texts they carried more or less as props, and that this strange occurrence had distracted him completely.

However, since this book is aimed at a more general usefulness than the purely professional platform (primarily for classroom courses in literature) and since it is seldom practicable to memorize completely a text of any length for more or less informal reading aloud, some general suggestions for effective reading from a text can be given.

Reading from a text is part of the general group of problems which center around the use of the eyes. The eyes, as the center of expressiveness, are a key to (1) proper development and flow of emotions, (2) clear and unobstructed control of and communication with the audience. It should be clear beyond argument that both these necessary goals of the oral reader are impossible for the person whose eyes cannot leave the page. Thus, although it may not be possible to memorize *completely* the material to be read, it is a matter of real importance to have a great familiarity with it. Beyond this requirement, however, a way of minimizing the loss of audience contact caused by looking down at the text appears with the realization that a glance at the text *while one is speaking* is scarcely noticeable to the audience, while a look at the text during a pause is almost certain to be distracting and to break the mood. Why this difference should be is made clear by recalling what was said earlier about the importance of the pause in the shifting of emotions. Obviously, words are a verbal exploration of a general emotion which is already expressed in the face and body. This general emotion is unlikely to undergo major change until a pause or series of pauses, signaling new emotional directions, leads to new verbal possibilities. In sum, if, as stated, emotions, expressions, gestures precede the word and do not ordinarily begin during the word, it is in the pause that the nonfunctional, nonexpressive glance at the book is most likely to damage the convincing flow of one emotion into another. It is for this reason that the following method, though a bit disturbing to work with at first, offers a possibility for results leading to a greater naturalness of audience contact. Simply, one should try to learn to look at the text, not during the pause, but just prior to the pause, catching enough of the phrase following the pause to leave the eyes quite free of the text during appropriate duration of the silence. Thus

↓↑
↓↑ The family of Dashwood had been long
    settled in Sussex. Their estate was large,
   ↓↑
  and their residence was at Norland Park, . . .

or

↓↑ There was a weasel lived in the sun
   ↓↑
  With all his family,
       ↓↑
  Till a keeper shot him with his gun
     ↓↑
  And hung him up on a tree,
  Where he swings . . .

These markings are, of course, not prescriptive, but are meant only to suggest the general technique.

But the problem of effective management of the eyes when reading from a text is only one aspect of the general study of their use.

The eyes are our chief means of bringing the audience into the story or poem. Let a reader stand before a group of people, reading from a page with his eyes fixed on the sheet, and soon, no matter how interesting the material, the audience's attention will tend to drift away. But it is not enough to look up vaguely from the page. The reader must know what to do with his eyes.

AUDIENCE AND AUDITORIUM

In general, apart from glancing at the book, the eyes should be looking at individuals in the audience. Among the exceptions are when two or more characters are engaged in dialogue and when the reader is using his eyes to create a visual scene for himself in order to make a descriptive passage more vivid. In some cases there is a possible choice as to the use of the eyes. Richard Wilbur's poem "Driftwood" (see p. 208) might be read in the ordinary way directly at the audience. Or the reader might choose subtly to dramatize the setting for his audience. The poem is an internal monologue said to himself by the poet upon the occasion of finding some driftwood while walking along the beach. The reader might suggest the introspective nature of the poem tactfully by starting his reading looking intently at the driftwood. And here we come to a matter wherein a personal sense of propriety, together with a recognition of the necessity for convention, is invaluable to the reader. He cannot imagine this driftwood to be right at his feet, as it would be in reality, for then the audience would be looking at the remarkably inexpressive top of his head and his voice would be directed downward at the stage rather than outward at the audience. On the other hand, the eyes cannot place the driftwood above the heads of the audience, floating somewhere in space. The only solution is a *conventional* one, and that is to place the driftwood out sufficiently from the reader to leave at once the possibility of creating an *illusion* of looking at the driftwood, while thus raising the face and eyes enough so that the audience can read their expressions. Naturally, the reader need not continue to keep his eyes riveted on the driftwood throughout the reading. On the contrary, as soon as he has sufficiently established the imaginative reality of the driftwood and is fairly launched into the imaginative reconstruction of the driftwood's spiritual history, he would quite logically move his eyes from place to place in the audience as he imagines new details and episodes from the past. Other methods or approaches might be used to make this scene real, but *neither the pro-cedures I have suggested nor any other mechanical gesture of head or eye will work without the inner vision.* The reader must *see* that driftwood, and he must *understand* the complex comparison and the subsequent complex moral meaning with which the poet has endowed it. If he has this comprehension and if he *sees* and *believes in* the reality of that driftwood, the audience will see that reality in his face and body and will believe it too.

We are brought now to the whole problem of the reading of descriptive passages. The beginner always wants to rush through description. Action, speech, yes that is *something*, but description? Well, he says, anybody can see it is static. He is wrong. Motionless, yes. Static, no. The great descriptive passage is as dramatic as the fall of an axe. But it must be respected; it must be given a chance to open up its meaning at its proper rate, and this opening can be achieved only by *a loving attention to its detail.* Let the reader try a little experiment. Read the following aloud to yourself, "The moon is snow. The sky is frosted with clouds. The birch is a bare bone. My eyes are numb and have no tears." Now look up to a specific spot slightly above your eye level to your left, and say "The moon is snow." Now let the eyes drift across space slowly until you are looking to your right, then say "The sky is frosted with clouds." Now lower the eyes a bit and let them drift toward a spot still somewhat to your right. When you have your eyes fixed on this spot, say "The birch is a bare bone." Now let the eyes drift to a spot yet lower and directly in front of you, and say, when you are looking at that specific spot, "My eyes are numb and have no tears." At each step try to visualize, at the spot where you are looking, the thing you are about to describe.

Did you feel *in* you the greater reality of the second reading experience? If so, it was because you were respecting the detail, giving each detail time to add its full power to the build toward insight. In short, the reason for visualizing descriptions, the value in the reader's actually placing the objects from his scene in the area before him, lies in the fact that as a result he himself will respond *accurately* and hence more *profoundly.* Not only his *intellect,* but his *nerves,* his subliminal responses, will know how to react to a moon of snow, if his imagination bodies it forth before him with sufficient vividness. And those subliminal clues are what capture an audience; they are what make an audience enter into the writer's imaginative world through the reader.

Another problem which must often be solved to the best of the reader's ability is the performance of dialogue — how to keep two or more characters who are speaking to each other straight in the minds of the audience and how to make them emotionally effective. Much, of course, can be done with the voice. Without the reader's going to such ludicrous and distracting extremes as speaking in a falsetto for women and a muddy bass for men, it should be clear that the speech of a child is likely to have a different pace, volume, and rhythm from that of an adult. A full analysis of the story or poem should leave one with a clear sense of the degree of complexity of a character, of his purpose in the work, and how his personality would express itself through the voice. Thus, in the little Scots poem about the rivers Tweed and Till (see p. 150), it would be appropriate to personify Till, the slow stream, and Tweed, the fast stream, with appropriate rates of voice, though it would be wrong to indicate vocally very much complexity of personality in so simple a personification.

The eyes and head and body can also be used to aid in characterizations. As far as the body is concerned, it should be obvious that the convention of one person reading several characters aloud makes it impossible for anything like a complete characterization. For instance, in a dialogue between a very old man and a young boy, only a ridiculous effect would be created by an attempt to shift the body into a completely characterized pose from speech to speech. Rather, some slight shift of pose must serve to symbolize the two persons.

The eyes can help in keeping characters clear by looking in different spots as different characters speak. Thus, the reader might place character A by looking at a spot to the back of the room on a level with his own eyes and slightly to the right, while character B is slightly to the left. Obviously, they must not be placed too far apart, lest the reader give the appearance of watching a tennis match. Certainly there is a limit to the number of characters in a scene which can be handled in this manner without becoming ludicrous. Once the character's positions are fixed, their relationship clarified, and the illusion well established, the reader can often gently drop this focusing. But as long as the scene is going on, the spot spoken to must not shift or waver, unless the character who is being spoken to is actually moving while being addressed. And unless he has moved between speeches, the reader must always look at the same spot when speaking to him. Below is a diagram of a speaker and an auditorium or room seen from side elevation, top elevation, and rear elevation. The back corners of the room are generally good guides as to the limits of normal head movement for placing characters or visualizing scenes. That is, with the eyes looking straight ahead, the head should not be turned farther than a position in which the eyes are looking at the back corners of the room. Only the need to create an extraordinary effect should lead the reader to turn his head farther to the side, or higher or lower. And he should certainly *not* get caught in a situation in which he has to switch repeatedly into such very strong, and distorting, head positions. The line of X's shows the usual area for placing characters or for visualizing scenes, i.e., just over the heads of the last row of the floor level. (Of course, in reading directly to the audience, the reader should establish eye contact with all parts of his audience wherever seated, if at all possible.) But all these conventions for using the eyes are acceptable and effective only when the pause is handled properly.

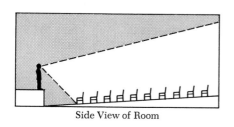
Side View of Room

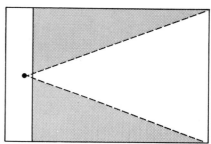
Looking Down on the Room

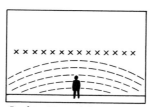
Looking Toward the Audience

There are no doubt many ways of learning how to handle dialogue, but one of the best is to watch people, especially in crowds, at restaurants, concerts, etc., where you cannot hear the content of the words, but can watch the pattern of gesture and the rhythm of response, where, in short, you can become aware of the interaction of the two people, of the interplay of their pauses, gestures, and words. From this observation you will quickly become aware of the point at which the beginning reader inevitably fails to give realism to his dialogue. In his tension and uncertainty, he has speech follow speech with mechanical regularity. Character A speaks. He is immediately followed by B, who speaks as if what he says were a virgin birth and had no relation to what A said. In reality, character B may look doubtful, bite his nail, twiddle his thumbs, hitch up his trousers, and finally, with a look of decision, respond to what A has said. As an example, let us look at what might occur in the scene in Austen's

Sense And Sensibility (p. 12). John Dashwood insists to his wife that "It was my father's last request to me, that I should assist his widow and daughters." Mrs. Dashwood shrugs her shoulders, or perhaps makes a gesture of dismissal with the hand, then says, "He did not know what he was talking of, I dare say . . . he could not have thought of such a thing as begging you to give away half your fortune from your own child." Now the reader must decide on Dashwood's response to that. He does not at once surrender his position, but starts out as if explaining a fact. Still, his statement "He did not stipulate for any particular sums . . ." is the basis for his whole later rationalization, so a touch of thoughtfulness, of inner reassessment might begin in the look that comes on his face before he replies. Other qualities might be appropriate to this pause — the patience of the husband with the little woman, an attitude modified by the secret knowledge that he knows he is ultimately going to lose the argument, and perhaps further qualified by the unconscious *desire* to lose the argument.

"Just a Little One" is a story in which the necessity of pauses that take a living part in the development is particularly clear. At the end of paragraph three, the woman's chatter is obviously interrupted by the man, Fred, who apparently asks her what she wants to drink. Therefore, if the monologue is to be convincing to the audience, before he reads her reply the reader must pause, focus on the question, then develop the emotion appropriate to the character before saying, "Why I don't know, Fred . . . what are you going to have?" Here is another obvious pause during which she absorbs the answer, then perhaps with a shrug of the shoulders, she says, "Then I guess I'll have a highball too. . . ."

In this matter of developing emotion, of actually expressing in gesture (including facial expression) the passionate thought of the selection, one of the most frequent and pernicious fears of the beginning student is that he will overact. Would that word had never been invented, for in my opinion it is a term with slight usefulness but with an infinite capacity for damage. A particular poem or story has a certain range of passion. To miss that depth and quality is simply to miss it. Obviously it can be missed in all sorts of ways. It can be missed by mumbling the words unintelligibly, to name one frequent result of the fear of "overacting." Look for a moment at the elegy by W. H. Auden, "In Memory of W. B. Yeats." Structurally and tonally, the poem has three parts. Part I has what may be called a public-conversation tone. The section speaks of Yeats as "he" — an impersonality that is enhanced by the very rapid identification of the dead poet's body with the urban elements of modern civilization. However, the dead Yeats is spoken of with a special type of objectivity, and the tone, for all it is conversational, is tinged with the elegiac element, largely through the repetition of certain phrases, as well as the repetition of certain unobtrusive rhythms and the obviously coherent figurative development. In sum, when the oral reader comes to the rendering of the last lines of this stanza, there has accrued a weight of foreboding, a degree of solemnity which he must discover in his voice and share honestly with his inner as well as his outer audience. These lines are slow, portentous. The vocal patterns are probably descending. The face and body must reflect this tone of quiet premonition and quiet decay.

In the next section, the tone is obviously more personal. Here the speaker turns to speak directly to the ghost, or memory, of the poet. The figures change from urban ones to pastoral ones, emphasizing the single-ness, the inevitable individuality, the animality even, of the spirit's lonely journey. The tone changes with these figures to a fond, somewhat intimate one: intimate, that is, to the memory of the poet, not to the listener who is more in the background as the speaker draws closer to the memory of the poet. Here the conventional tone, although continued, must be im-portantly modified away from general conversation to a private one. The voice is less obviously solemn, more lively, with more small vocal playful-ness. The face, too, is less abstractly serious, more taken up with such slighter expressions as wryness and assurance. The body, too, is less erect, more pliant, more intimate in its slight movement and gestures.

But now a great change occurs in the third section. Having said his personal farewell, the speaker then turns to make his formal statement on the meaning of this death. The tone is set by the very first line. The earth is addressed with complete formality and solemnity, and appropriately the rhythm becomes metrical and much more regular, and the poet turns to the greater formality of rhyme. But why is the line short, when most elegies choose the long, sonorous line? The answer, I believe, is to be found in a new element in the tone. Added to the complete change from any conversational element to a greater formality is the overt use of biting irony, which rises in the middle stanzas, to contain a strong tone of disgust and grim condemnation. The voice emphasizes the metrical, strong rhythms and the greater speed of the short, frequently run-on lines. This speed points to the less subtle, less involuted thought–feeling. In expressing its disgust the voice no more disdains to use and exploit the harsh sound of "dogs," than it did the intimate, loose rhythm and sibillance of "you were silly like us." The body of the oral reader cannot deny the voice. It too must reflect in its stance the formality of the address — no, more, it too must explore and expose the weight and power of the ironies, the disgust. It is erect, reserved, tense, the expression centering in the face. Gone is the intimacy of the second section. The face, in its expression of serious-ness, irony, condemnation, is impersonal, at one with the power and force which the voice, in its own way, is creating.

Why go into this matter in such detail? Among other reasons, so as to demonstrate how much beside the point the whole question of overacting or underacting is. Broad, formal gestures of voice and body would not be *over*acting in relation to Part Two. They would simply prove that the person didn't, in the deepest sense, understand the poem.

There is the tone of the phrase, of the stanza, of the poem, each made up of ever more subtle combinations of tones of the smaller elements. *But these tones are three dimensional.* As the oral reader explores the many threads making up the fabric of this book, all of which he will be testing and illuminating through that grand and synthesizing power of the body for exploring the realities of thought–emotion, he will have but one aim: the achievement of the tone of the work of art as it can exist with most reality in a given moment of time in his responding body. The oral reader must discover the *performance* of the work; that is, he must *perform* the work; otherwise he knows it with but part of his being — the abstract, less humane part, and otherwise the work remains largely where it was, on the page. It is not a question of overacting or underacting. It is simply a question of ignorance or misunderstanding.

SELECTIONS

Just a Little One*

DOROTHY PARKER

I like this place, Fred. This is a nice place. How did you ever find it? I think you're perfectly marvelous, discovering a speakeasy in the year 1928. And they let you right in, without asking you a single question. I bet you could get into the subway without using anybody's name. Couldn't you, Fred?

Oh, I like this place better and better, now that my eyes are getting accustomed to it. You mustn't let them tell you this lighting system is original with them, Fred; they got the idea from the Mammoth Cave. This is you sitting next to me, isn't it? Oh, you can't fool me. I'd know that knee anywhere.

* From *The Portable Dorothy Parker*. Copyright 1928, © 1956 by Dorothy Parker. Reprinted by permission of The Viking Press, Inc.

You know what I like about this place? It's got atmosphere. That's what it's got. If you would ask the waiter to bring a fairly sharp knife, I could cut off a nice little block of the atmosphere, to take home with me. It would be interesting to have for my memory book. I'm going to start keeping a memory book tomorrow. Don't let me forget.

Why, I don't know, Fred — what are you going to have? Then I guess I'll have a highball, too; please, just a little one. Is it really real Scotch? Well, that will be a new experience for me. You ought to see the Scotch I've got home in my cupboard; at least it was in the cupboard this morning — it's probably eaten its way out by now. I got it for my birthday. Well, it was something. The birthday before, all I got was a year older.

This is a nice highball, isn't it? Well, well, well, to think of me having real Scotch; I'm out of the bush leagues at last. Are you going to have another one? Well, I shouldn't like to see you drink all by yourself, Fred. Solitary drinking is what causes half the crime in the country. That's what's responsible for the failure of prohibition. But please, Fred, tell him to make mine just a little one. Make it awfully weak; just cambric Scotch.

It will be nice to see the effect of veritable whisky upon one who has been accustomed only to the simpler forms of entertainment. You'll like that, Fred. You'll stay by me if anything happens, won't you? I don't think there will be anything spectacular, but I want to ask you one thing, just in case. Don't let me take any horses home with me. It doesn't matter so much about stray dogs and kittens, but elevator boys get awfully stuffy when you try to bring in a horse. You might just as well know that about me now, Fred. You can always tell that the crash is coming when I start getting tender about Our Dumb Friends. Three highballs, and I think I'm St. Francis of Assisi.

But I don't believe anything is going to happen to me on these. That's because they're made of real stuff. That's what the difference is. This just makes you feel fine. Oh, I feel swell, Fred. You do too, don't you? I knew you did, because you look better. I love that tie you have on. Oh, did Edith give it to you? Ah, wasn't that nice of her? You know, Fred, most people are really awfully nice. There are darn few that aren't pretty fine at heart. You've got a beautiful heart, Fred. You'd be the first person I'd go to if I were in trouble. I guess you are just about the best friend I've got in the world. But I worry about you, Fred. I do so, too. I don't think you take enough care of yourself. You oughtn't to drink all this terrible stuff that's around; you owe it to your friends to be careful. You don't mind my talking to you like this, do you? You see, dear, it's because I'm your friend that I hate to see you not taking care of yourself. It hurts me to see you batting around the way you've been doing. You ought to stick to this place, where they have real Scotch that can't do you any harm. Oh, darling, do you really think I ought to? Well, you tell him just a little bit of a one. Tell him, sweet.

Do you come here often, Fred? I shouldn't worry about you so much if I knew you were in a safe place like this. Oh, is this where you were Thursday night? I see. Why, no, it didn't make a bit of difference, only you told me to call you up, and like a fool I broke a date I had, just because I thought I was going to see you. I just sort of naturally thought so, when you said to call you up. Oh, good Lord, don't make all that fuss about it. It really didn't make the slightest difference. It just didn't seem a very friendly way to behave, that's all. I don't know — I'd been believing we were such good friends. I'm an awful idiot about people, Fred. There aren't many who are really your friend at heart. Practically anybody would play you dirt for a nickel. Oh, yes, they would.

Was Edith here with you, Thursday night? This place must be very becoming to her. Next to being in a coal mine, I can't think of anywhere she could go that the light would be more flattering to that pan of hers. Do you really know a lot of people that say she's good-looking? You must have a wide acquaintance among the astigmatic, haven't you, Freddie, dear? Why, I'm not being any way at all — it's simply one of those things, either you can see it or you can't. Now to me, Edith looks like something that would eat her young. Dresses well? Edith dress well? Are you trying to kid me, Fred, at my age? You mean you mean it? Oh, my God. You mean those clothes of hers are intentional? My heavens, I always thought she was on her way out of a burning building.

Well, we live and learn. Edith dresses well! Edith's got good taste! Yes, she's got sweet taste in neckties. I don't suppose I ought to say it about such a dear friend of yours, Fred, but she is the lousiest necktie-picker-out I ever saw. I never saw anything could touch that thing you have around your neck. All right, suppose I did say I liked it. I just said that because I felt sorry for you. I'd feel sorry for anybody with a thing like that on. I just wanted to try to make you feel good, because I thought you were my friend. My friend! I haven't got a friend in the world. Do you know that, Fred? Not one single friend in this world.

All right, what do you care if I'm crying? I can cry if I want to, can't I? I guess you'd cry, too, if you didn't have a friend in the world. Is my face very bad? I suppose that damned mascara has run all over it. I've got to give up using mascara, Fred; life's too sad. Isn't life terrible? Oh, my God, isn't life awful? Ah, don't cry, Fred. Please don't. Don't you care, baby. Life's terrible, but don't you care. You've got friends. I'm the one that hasn't got any friends. I am so. No, it's me. I'm the one.

I don't think another drink would make me feel any better. I don't know whether I want to feel any better. What's the sense of feeling good, when life's so terrible? Oh, all right, then. But please tell him just a little one, if it isn't too much trouble. I don't want to stay here much longer. I don't like this place. It's all dark and stuffy. It's the kind of place Edith would be crazy about — that's all I can say about this place. I know I oughtn't to talk about your best friend, Fred, but that's a terrible woman. That woman is the louse of this world. It makes me feel just awful that you trust that woman, Fred. I hate to see anybody play you dirt. I'd hate to see you get hurt. That's what makes me feel so terrible. That's why I'm getting mascara all over my face. No, please don't, Fred. You mustn't hold my hand. It wouldn't be fair to Edith. We've got to play fair with the big louse. After all, she's your best friend, isn't she?

Honestly? Do you honestly mean it, Fred? Yes, but how could I help thinking so, when you're with her all the time — when you bring her here every night in the week? Really, only Thursday? Oh, I know — I know how those things are. You simply can't help it, when you get stuck with a person that way. Lord, I'm glad you realize what an awful thing that woman is. I was worried about it, Fred. It's because I'm your friend. Why, of course I am, darling. You know I am. Oh, that's just silly, Freddie. You've got heaps of friends. Only you'll never find a better friend than I am. No, I know that. I know I'll never find a better friend than you are to me. Just give me back my hand a second, till I get this damned mascara out of my eye.

Yes, I think we ought to, honey. I think we ought to have a little drink, on account of our being friends. Just a little one, because it's real Scotch, and we're real friends. After all, friends are the greatest things in the world, aren't they, Fred? Gee, it makes you feel good to know you have a friend. I feel great, don't you, dear? And you look great, too. I'm proud to have you for a friend. Do you realize, Fred, what a rare thing a friend is, when you think of all the terrible people there are in this world? Animals are much better than people. God, I love animals. That's what I like about you, Fred. You're so fond of animals.

Look, I'll tell you what let's do, after we've had just a little highball. Let's go out and pick up a lot of stray dogs. I never had enough dogs in my life, did you? We ought to have more dogs. And maybe there'd be some cats around, if we looked. And a horse, I've never had one single horse, Fred. Isn't that rotten? Not one single horse. Ah, I'd like a nice old cab-horse, Fred. Wouldn't you? I'd like to take care of it and comb its hair and everything. Ah, don't be stuffy about it, Fred, please don't. I need a horse, honestly I do. Wouldn't you like one? It would be so sweet and kind. Let's have a drink and then let's you and I go out and get a horsie, Freddie — just a little one, darling, just a little one.

A Painful Case[*]

JAMES JOYCE

Mr. James Duffy lived in Chapelizod because he wished to live as far as possible from the city of which he was a citizen and because he found all the other suburbs of Dublin mean, modern and pretentious. He lived in an old sombre house and from his windows he could look into the disused distillery or upwards along the shallow river on which Dublin is built. The lofty walls of his uncarpeted room were free from pictures. He had himself bought every article of furniture in the room: a black iron bedstead, an iron washstand, four cane chairs, a clothes-rack, a coal-scuttle, a fender and irons and a square table on which lay a double desk. A bookcase had been made in an alcove by means of shelves of white wood. The bed was clothed with white bedclothes and a black and scarlet rug covered the foot. A little hand-mirror hung above the washstand and during the day a white-shaded lamp stood as the sole ornament of the mantelpiece. The books on the white wooden shelves were arranged from below upwards according to bulk. A complete Wordsworth stood at one end of the lowest shelf and a copy of the *Maynooth Catechism*, sewn into the cloth cover of a notebook, stood at one end of the top shelf. Writing materials were always on the desk. In the desk lay a manuscript translation of Hauptmann's *Michael Kramer*, the stage directions of which were written in purple ink, and a little sheaf of papers held together by a brass pin. In these sheets a sentence was inscribed from time to time and, in an ironical moment, the headline of an advertisement for *Bile Beans* had been pasted on to the first sheet. On lifting the lid of the desk a faint fragrance escaped — the fragrance of new cedarwood pencils or of a bottle of gum or of an overripe apple which might have been left there and forgotten.

Mr. Duffy abhorred anything which betokened physical or mental disorder. A mediæval doctor would have called him saturnine. His face, which carried the entire tale of his years, was of the brown tint of Dublin streets. On his long and rather large head grew dry black hair and a tawny moustache did not quite cover an unamiable mouth. His cheekbones also gave his face a harsh character; but there was no harshness in the eyes which, looking at the world from under their tawny eyebrows, gave the impression of a man ever alert to greet a redeeming instinct in others but often disappointed. He lived at a little distance from his body, regarding his own acts with doubtful side-glances. He had an odd autobiographical habit which led him to compose in his mind from time to time a short sentence about himself containing a subject in the third person and a

[*] From *Dubliners* by James Joyce. Originally published by B. W. Huebsch in 1916. Reprinted by permission of The Viking Press, Inc.

predicate in the past tense. He never gave alms to beggars and walked firmly, carrying a stout hazel.

He had been for many years cashier of a private bank in Baggot Street. Every morning he came in from Chapelizod by tram. At midday he went to Dan Burke's and took his lunch — a bottle of lager beer and a small trayful of arrowroot biscuits. At four o'clock he was set free. He dined in an eating-house in George's Street where he felt himself safe from the society of Dublin's gilded youth and where there was a certain plain honesty in the bill of fare. His evenings were spent either before his landlady's piano or roaming about the outskirts of the city. His liking for Mozart's music brought him sometimes to an opera or a concert: these were the only dissipations of his life.

He had neither companions nor friends, church nor creed. He lived his spiritual life without any communion with others, visiting his relatives at Christmas and escorting them to the cemetery when they died. He performed these two social duties for old dignity's sake but conceded nothing further to the conventions, which regulate the civic life. He allowed himself to think that in certain circumstances he would rob his bank but, as these circumstances never arose, his life rolled out evenly — an adventureless tale.

One evening he found himself sitting beside two ladies in the Rotunda. The house, thinly peopled and silent, gave distressing prophecy of failure. The lady who sat next him looked round at the deserted house once or twice and then said:

"What a pity there is such a poor house tonight! It's so hard on people to have to sing to empty benches."

He took the remark as an invitation to talk. He was surprised that she seemed so little awkward. While they talked he tried to fix her permanently in his memory. When he learned that the young girl beside her was her daughter he judged her to be a year or so younger than himself. Her face, which must have been handsome, had remained intelligent. It was an oval face with strongly marked features. The eyes were very dark blue and steady. Their gaze began with a defiant note but was confused by what seemed a deliberate swoon of the pupil into the iris, revealing for an instant a temperament of great sensibility. The pupil reasserted itself quickly, this half-disclosed nature fell again under the reign of prudence, and her astrakhan jacket, moulding a bosom of a certain fullness, struck the note of defiance more definitely.

He met her again a few weeks afterwards at a concert in Earlsfort Terrace and seized the moments when her daughter's attention was diverted to become intimate. She alluded once or twice to her husband but her tone was not such as to make the allusion a warning. Her name was

Mrs. Sinico. Her husband's great-great-grandfather had come from Leghorn. Her husband was captain of a mercantile boat plying between Dublin and Holland; and they had one child.

Meeting her a third time by accident he found courage to make an appointment. She came. This was the first of many meetings; they met always in the evening and chose the most quiet quarters for their walks together. Mr. Duffy, however, had a distaste for underhand ways and, finding that they were compelled to meet stealthily, he forced her to ask him to her house. Captain Sinico encouraged his visits, thinking that his daughter's hand was in question. He had dismissed his wife so sincerely from his gallery of pleasures that he did not suspect that anyone else would take an interest in her. As the husband was often away and the daughter out giving music lessons Mr. Duffy had many opportunities of enjoying the lady's society. Neither he nor she had had any such adventure before and neither was conscious of any incongruity. Little by little he entangled his thoughts with hers. He lent her books, provided her with ideas, shared his intellectual life with her. She listened to all.

Sometimes in return for his theories she gave out some fact of her own life. With almost maternal solicitude she urged him to let his nature open to the full: she became his confessor. He told her that for some time he had assisted at the meetings of an Irish Socialist Party where he had felt himself a unique figure amidst a score of sober workmen in a garret lit by an inefficient oil-lamp. When the party had divided into three sections, each under its own leader and in its own garret, he had discontinued his attendances. The workmen's discussions, he said, were too timorous; the interest they took in the question of wages was inordinate. He felt that they were hard-featured realists and that they resented an exactitude which was the produce of a leisure not within their reach. No social revolution, he told her, would be likely to strike Dublin for some centuries.

She asked him why did he not write out his thoughts. For what, he asked her, with careful scorn. To compete with phrasemongers, incapable of thinking consecutively for sixty seconds? To submit himself to the criticisms of an obtuse middle class which entrusted its morality to policemen and its fine arts to impresarios?

He went often to her little cottage outside Dublin; often they spent their evenings alone. Little by little, as their thoughts entangled, they spoke of subjects less remote. Her companionship was like a warm soil about an exotic. Many times she allowed the dark to fall upon them, refraining from lighting the lamp. The dark discreet room, their isolation, the music that still vibrated in their ears united them. This union exalted him, wore away the rough edges of his character, emotionalised his mental life. Sometimes he caught himself listening to the sound of his own voice.

He thought that in her eyes he would ascend to an angelical stature; and, as he attached the fervent nature of his companion more and more closely to him, he heard the strange impersonal voice which he recognised as his own, insisting on the soul's incurable loneliness. We cannot give ourselves, it said: we are our own. The end of these discourses was that one night during which she had shown every sign of unusual excitement, Mrs. Sinico caught up his hand passionately and pressed it to her cheek.

Mr. Duffy was very much surprised. Her interpretation of his words disillusioned him. He did not visit her for a week; then he wrote to her asking her to meet him. As he did not wish their last interview to be troubled by the influence of their ruined confessional they met in a little cakeshop near the Parkgate. It was cold autumn weather but in spite of the cold they wandered up and down the roads of the Park for nearly three hours. They agreed to break off their intercourse: every bond, he said, is a bond of sorrow. When they came out of the Park, they walked in silence towards the tram; but here she began to tremble so violently that, fearing another collapse on her part, he bade her good-bye quickly and left her. A few days later he received a parcel containing his books and music.

Four years passed. Mr. Duffy returned to his even way of life. His room still bore witness of the orderliness of his mind. Some new pieces of music encumbered the music-stand in the lower room and on his shelves stood two volumes by Nietzsche: *Thus Spake Zarathustra* and *The Gay Science*. He wrote seldom in the sheaf of papers which lay in his desk. One of his sentences, written two months after his last interview with Mrs. Sinico, read: Love between man and man is impossible because there must not be sexual intercourse and friendship between man and woman is impossible because there must be sexual intercourse. He kept away from concerts lest he should meet her. His father died; the junior partner of the bank retired. And still every morning he went into the city by tram and every evening walked home from the city after having dined moderately in George's Street and read the evening paper for dessert.

One evening as he was about to put a morsel of corned beef and cabbage into his mouth his hand stopped. His eyes fixed themselves on a paragraph in the evening paper which he had propped against the water-carafe. He replaced the morsel of food on his plate and read the paragraph attentively. Then he drank a glass of water, pushed his plate to one side, doubled the paper down before him between his elbows and read the paragraph over and over again. The cabbage began to deposit a cold white grease on his plate. The girl came over to him to ask was his dinner not properly cooked. He said it was very good and ate a few mouthfuls of it with difficulty. Then he paid his bill and went out.

He walked along quickly through the November twilight, his stout hazel stick striking the ground regularly, the fringe of the buff *Mail* peeping out of a side-pocket of his tight reefer overcoat. On the lonely road which leads from the Parkgate to Chapelizod he slackened his pace. His stick struck the ground less emphatically and his breath, issuing irregularly, almost with a sighing sound, condensed in the wintry air. When he reached his house he went up at once to his bedroom and, taking the paper from his pocket, read the paragraph again by the failing light of the window. He read it not aloud, but moving his lips as a priest does when he reads the prayers *Secreto*. This was the paragraph:

DEATH OF A LADY AT SYDNEY PARADE

A Painful Case

Today at the City of Dublin Hospital the Deputy Coroner (in the absence of Mr. Leverett) held an inquest on the body of Mrs. Emily Sinico, aged forty-three years, who was killed at Sydney Parade Station yesterday evening. The evidence showed that the deceased lady, while attempting to cross the line, was knocked down by the engine of the ten o'clock slow train from Kingstown, thereby sustaining injuries of the head and right side which led to her death.

James Lennon, driver of the engine, stated that he had been in the employment of the railway company for fifteen years. On hearing the guard's whistle he set the train in motion and a second or two afterwards brought it to rest in response to loud cries. The train was going slowly.

P. Dunne, railway porter, stated that as the train was about to start he observed a woman attempting to cross the lines. He ran towards her and shouted, but, before he could reach her, she was caught by the buffer of the engine and fell to the ground.

A JUROR. "You saw the lady fall?"

WITNESS. "Yes."

Police Sergeant Croly deposed that when he arrived he found the deceased lying on the platform apparently dead. He had the body taken to the waiting-room pending the arrival of the ambulance.

Constable 57E corroborated.

Dr. Halpin, assistant house surgeon of the City of Dublin Hospital, stated that the deceased had two lower ribs fractured and had sustained severe contusions of the right shoulder. The right side of the head had been injured in the fall. The injuries were not sufficient to have caused death in a normal person. Death, in his opinion, had been probably due to shock and sudden failure of the heart's action.

Mr. H. B. Patterson Finlay, on behalf of the railway company, expressed his deep regret at the accident. The company had always taken every precaution to prevent people crossing the lines except by the bridges, both by placing notices in every station and by the use of patent spring gates at level crossings. The deceased had been in the habit of crossing the lines late at night from platform to platform and, in view of certain other circumstances of the case, he did not think the railway officials were to blame.

Captain Sinico, of Leoville, Sydney Parade, husband of the deceased, also gave evidence. He stated that the deceased was his wife. He was not in Dublin at the time of the accident as he had arrived only that morning from Rotterdam. They had been married for twenty-two years and had lived happily until about two years ago when his wife began to be rather intemperate in her habits.

Miss Mary Sinico said that of late her mother had been in the habit of going out at night to buy spirits. She, witness, had often tried to reason with her mother and had induced her to join a League. She was not at home until an hour after the accident.

The jury returned a verdict in accordance with the medical evidence and exonerated Lennon from all blame.

The Deputy Coroner said it was a most painful case, and expressed great sympathy with Captain Sinico and his daughter. He urged on the railway company to take strong measures to prevent the possibility of similar accidents in the future. No blame attached to anyone.

Mr. Duffy raised his eyes from the paper and gazed out of his window on the cheerless evening landscape. The river lay quiet beside the empty distillery and from time to time a light appeared in some house on the Lucan road. What an end! The whole narrative of her death revolted him and it revolted him to think that he had ever spoken to her of what he held sacred. The threadbare phrases, the inane expressions of sympathy, the cautious words of a reporter won over to conceal the details of a commonplace vulgar death attacked his stomach. Not merely had she degraded herself; she had degraded him. He saw the squalid tract of her vice, miserable and malodorous. His soul's companion! He thought of the hobbling wretches whom he had seen carrying cans and bottles to be filled by the barman. Just God, what an end! Evidently she had been unfit to live, without any strength of purpose, an easy prey to habits, one of the wrecks on which civilisation had been reared. But that she could have sunk so low! Was it possible he had deceived himself so utterly about her? He remembered her outburst of that night and interpreted it in a harsher sense than he had ever done. He had no difficulty now in approving of the course he had taken.

As the light failed and his memory began to wander he thought her hand touched his. The shock which had first attacked his stomach was now attacking his nerves. He put on his overcoat and hat quickly and went out. The cold air met him on the threshold; it crept into the sleeves of his coat. When he came to the public-house at Chapelizod Bridge he went in and ordered a hot punch.

The proprietor served him obsequiously but did not venture to talk. There were five or six workingmen in the shop discussing the value of a gentleman's estate in County Kildare. They drank at intervals from their huge pint tumblers and smoked, spitting often on the floor and sometimes dragging the sawdust over their spits with their heavy boots. Mr. Duffy sat on his stool and gazed at them, without seeing or hearing them. After a while they went out and he called for another punch. He sat a long time over it. The shop was very quiet. The proprietor sprawled on the counter reading the *Herald* and yawning. Now and again a tram was heard swishing along the lonely road outside.

As he sat there, living over his life with her and evoking alternately the two images in which he now conceived her, he realised that she was dead, that she had ceased to exist, that she had become a memory. He began to feel ill at ease. He asked himself what else could he have done. He could not have carried on a comedy of deception with her; he could not have lived with her openly. He had done what seemed to him best. How was he to blame? Now that she was gone he understood how lonely her life must have been, sitting night after night alone in that room. His life would be lonely too until he, too, died, ceased to exist, became a memory — if anyone remembered him.

It was after nine o'clock when he left the shop. The night was cold and gloomy. He entered the Park by the first gate and walked along under the gaunt trees. He walked through the bleak alleys where they had walked four years before. She seemed to be near him in the darkness. At moments he seemed to feel her voice touch his ear, her hand touch his. He stood still to listen. Why had he withheld life from her? Why had he sentenced her to death? He felt his moral nature falling to pieces.

When he gained the crest of the Magazine Hill he halted and looked along the river towards Dublin, the lights of which burned redly and hospitably in the cold night. He looked down the slope and, at the base, in the shadow of the wall of the Park, he saw some human figures lying. Those venal and furtive loves filled him with despair. He gnawed the rectitude of his life; he felt that he had been outcast from life's feast. One human being had seemed to love him and he had denied her life and happiness: he had sentenced her to ignominy, a death of shame. He knew that the prostrate creatures down by the wall were watching him and wished him gone. No one wanted him; he was outcast from life's feast. He turned his eyes to the grey gleaming river, winding along towards Dublin. Beyond the river he saw a goods train winding out of Kingsbridge Station, like a worm with a fiery head winding through the darkness, obstinately and laboriously. It passed slowly out of sight; but still he heard in his ears the laborious drone of the engine reiterating the syllables of her name.

He turned back the way he had come, the rhythm of the engine pounding in his ears. He began to doubt the reality of what memory told him. He halted under a tree and allowed the rhythm to die away. He could not feel her near him in the darkness nor her voice touch his ear. He waited for some minutes listening. He could hear nothing: the night was perfectly silent. He listened again: perfectly silent. He felt that he was alone.

They Fle from Me

They fle from me that sometyme did me seke
  With naked fote stalking in my chambre.
I have sene theim gentill tame and meke
  That nowe are wyld and do not remember
  That sometyme they put theimself in daunger
To take bred at my hand; and nowe they raunge
Besely[4] seking with a continuell chaunge.

Thancked be fortune, it hath ben othrewise
  Twenty tymes better; but ons in speciall,
In thyn arraye after a pleasaunt gyse,
  When her lose gowne from her shoulders did fall,
  And she me caught in her armes long and small;
Therewithall swetely did me kysse,
And softely saide, dere hert, howe like you this?

It was no dreme: I lay brode waking
  But all is torned thorough my gentilnes
Into a straunge fasshion of forsaking;
  And I have leve to goo of her goodenes,
  And she also to use new fangilnes.
But syns that I so kyndely ame served,
I would fain knowe what she hath deserved.

SIR THOMAS WYATT

4 busily

Song

Out upon it! I have loved
    Three whole days together;
And am like to love three more,
    If it prove fair weather!

Time shall moult away his wings,
    Ere he shall discover
In the whole wide world again
    Such a constant lover.

But the spite on't is, no praise
    Is due at all to me:
Love with me had made no stays,
    Had it any been but she.

Had it any been but she,
    And that very face,
There had been at least ere this
    A dozen dozen in her place!

                    SIR JOHN SUCKLING

As I Walked Out One Evening*

As I walked out one evening,
    Walking down Bristol Street,
The crowds upon the pavement
    Were fields of harvest wheat.

And down by the brimming river
    I heard a lover sing
Under an arch of the railway:
    "Love has no ending.

I'll love you, dear, I'll love you
    Till China and Africa meet,
And the river jumps over the mountain
    And the salmon sing in the street.

I'll love you till the ocean
  Is folded and hung up to dry,
And the seven stars go squawking
  Like geese about the sky.

The years shall run like rabbits
  For in my arms I hold
The Flower of the Ages
  And the first love of the world."

But all the clocks in the city
  Begin to whirr and chime:
"O let not Time deceive you,
  You cannot conquer Time.

In the burrows of the Nightmare
  Where Justice naked is,
Time watches from the shadow
  And coughs when you would kiss.

In headaches and in worry
  Vaguely life leaks away,
And Time will have his fancy
  To-morrow or to-day.

Into many a green valley
  Drifts the appalling snow;
Time breaks the threaded dances
  And the diver's brilliant bow.

O plunge your hands in water,
  Plunge them in up to the wrist;
Stare, stare in the basin
  And wonder what you've missed.

The glacier knocks in the cupboard,
  The desert sighs in the bed,
And the crack in the tea-cup opens
  A lane to the land of the dead.

Where the beggars raffle the banknotes
  And the Giant is enchanting to Jack,
And the Lily-white Boy is a Roarer
  And Jill goes down on her back.

O look, look in the mirror,
  O look in your distress;
Life remains a blessing
  Although you cannot bless.

O stand, stand at the window
  As the tears scald and start;
You shall love your crooked neighbour
  With your crooked heart."

It was late, late in the evening,
  The lovers they were gone;
The clocks had ceased their chiming
  And the deep river ran on.

                              W. H. Auden

Cirque d'Hiver*

Across the floor flits the mechanical toy,
fit for a king of several centuries back.
A little circus horse with real white hair.
His eyes are glossy black.
He bears a little dancer on his back.

She stands upon her toes and turns and turns.
A slanting spray of artificial roses
is stitched across her skirt and tinsel bodice.
Above her head she poses
another spray of artificial roses.

His mane and tail are straight from Chirico.
He has a formal, melancholy soul.
He feels her pink toes dangle toward his back
along the little pole
that pierces both her body and her soul

and goes through his, and reappears below,
under his belly, as a big tin key.
He canters three steps, then he makes a bow,
canters again, bows on one knee,
canters, then clicks and stops, and looks at me.

    * Reprinted from *North and South* by Elizabeth Bishop, by permission of Houghton Mifflin Company.

The dancer, by this time, has turned her back.
He is the more intelligent by far.
Facing each other rather desperately —
his eye is like a star —
we stare and say, "Well, we have come this far."

ELIZABETH BISHOP

Song

Goe, and catche a falling starre,
   Get with child a mandrake[5] roote,
Tell me, where all past yeares are,
   Or who cleft the Divels foot,
Teach me to heare mermaides singing,
   Or to keep off envies stinging,
         And finde
         What winde
Serves to advance an honest minde.

If thou beest borne to strange sights,
   Things invisible to see,
Ride ten thousand daies and nights,
   Till age snow white haires on thee,
Thou, when thou retorn'st, wilt tell mee
All strange wonders that befell thee,
         And sweare
         No where
Lives a woman true, and faire.

If thou finds't one, let mee know,
   Such a pilgrimage were sweet;
Yet doe not, I would not goe,
   Though at next doore wee might meet,
Though shee were true, when you met her,
And last, till you write your letter,
         Yet shee
         Will bee
False, ere I come, to two, or three.

JOHN DONNE

[5] The root of the mandrake suggests the shape of the human body.

*Men and Women**
(From her *Journal*)

"I get on best with women,"
   She laughed and crumbled her cake.
"Men are such unknown country.
   I never know how to take
What they say, nor how they mean it
   And — oh, well they *are* so queer,
So — don't you know! — *so* — this and that.
   You know what I mean, my dear!

"With women it's so much simpler,"
   She laughed and cuddled her muff.
"One doesn't have to keep smiling —
   Now what have I said? — It's enough
To chat over nothing important.
   That is such a rest, I find,
In these strenuous days, don't you know, dear?
   They put *such* a strain on the mind."

                      KATHERINE MANSFIELD

The Love Song of J. Alfred Prufrock†

S'io credesse che mia risposta fosse
A persona che mai tornasse al mondo,
Questa fiamma staria senza piu scosse.
Ma perciocche giammai di questo fondo
Non torno vivo alcun, s'i'odo il vero,
Senza tema d'infamia ti rispondo.

Let us go then, you and I,
When the evening is spread out against the sky
Like a patient etherised upon a table;
Let us go, through certain half-deserted streets,

The muttering retreats
Of restless nights in one-night cheap hotels
And sawdust restaurants with oyster-shells:
Streets that follow like a tedious argument
Of insidious intent
To lead you to an overwhelming question . . .
Oh, do not ask, "What is it?"
Let us go and make our visit.

In the room the women come and go
Talking of Michelangelo.

The yellow fog that rubs its back upon the window-panes,
The yellow smoke that rubs its muzzle on the window-panes
Licked its tongue into the corners of the evening,
Lingered upon the pools that stand in drains,
Let fall upon its back the soot that falls from chimneys,
Slipped by the terrace, made a sudden leap,
And seeing that it was a soft October night,
Curled once about the house, and fell asleep.

And indeed there will be time
For the yellow smoke that slides along the street,
Rubbing its back upon the window-panes;
There will be time, there will be time
To prepare a face to meet the faces that you meet;
There will be time to murder and create,
And time for all the works and days of hands
That lift and drop a question on your plate;
Time for you and time for me,
And time yet for a hundred indecisions,
And for a hundred visions and revisions,
Before the taking of a toast and tea.

In the room the women come and go
Talking of Michelangelo.

And indeed there will be time
To wonder, "Do I dare?" and, "Do I dare?"
Time to turn back and descend the stair,
With a bald spot in the middle of my hair —
(They will say: "How his hair is growing thin!")

My morning coat, my collar mounting firmly to the chin,
My necktie rich and modest, but asserted by a simple pin —
(They will say: "But how his arms and legs are thin!")
Do I dare
Disturb the universe?
In a minute there is time
For decisions and revisions which a minute will reverse.

For I have known them all already, known them all: —
Have known the evenings, mornings, afternoons,
I have measured out my life with coffee spoons;
I know the voices dying with a dying fall
Beneath the music from a farther room.
    So how should I presume?

And I have known the eyes already, known them all —
The eyes that fix you in a formulated phrase,
And when I am formulated, sprawling on a pin,
When I am pinned and wriggling on the wall,
Then how should I begin
To spit out all the butt-ends of my days and ways?
    And how should I presume?

And I have known the arms already, known them all —
Arms that are braceleted and white and bare
(But in the lamplight, downed with light brown hair!)
Is it perfume from a dress
That makes me so digress?
Arms that lie along a table, or wrap about a shawl.
    And should I then presume?
    And how should I begin?

✻   ✻   ✻

Shall I say, I have gone at dusk through narrow streets
And watched the smoke that rises from the pipes
Of lonely men in shirt-sleeves, leaning out of windows? . . .
I should have been a pair of ragged claws
Scuttling across the floors of silent seas.

✻   ✻   ✻

And the afternoon, the evening, sleeps so peacefully!
Smoothed by long fingers,

Asleep . . . tired . . . or it malingers,
Stretched on the floor, here beside you and me.
Should I, after tea and cakes and ices,
Have the strength to force the moment to its crisis?
But though I have wept and fasted, wept and prayed,
Though I have seen my head (grown slightly bald) brought in
    upon a platter,
I am no prophet — and here's no great matter;
I have seen the moment of my greatness flicker,
And I have seen the eternal Footman hold my coat, and
    snicker,
And in short, I was afraid.

And would it have been worth it, after all,
After the cups, the marmalade, the tea,
Among the porcelain, among some talk of you and me,
Would it have been worth while,
To have bitten off the matter with a smile,
To have squeezed the universe into a ball
To roll it toward some overwhelming question,
To say: "I am Lazarus, come from the dead,
Come back to tell you all, I shall tell you all" —
If one, settling a pillow by her head,
    Should say: "That is not what I meant at all.
    That is not it, at all."

And would it have been worth it, after all,
Would it have been worth while,
After the sunsets and the dooryards and the sprinkled streets,
After the novels, after the teacups, after the skirts that trail
    along the floor —
And this, and so much more? —
It is impossible to say just what I mean!
But as if a magic lantern threw the nerves in patterns on a
    screen:
Would it have been worth while
If one, settling a pillow or throwing off a shawl,
And turning toward the window, should say:
    "That is not it at all,
    That is not what I meant, at all."

          ❋   ❋   ❋

No! I am not Prince Hamlet, nor was meant to be;
Am an attendant lord, one that will do
To swell a progress, start a scene or two,
Advise the prince; no doubt, an easy tool,
Deferential, glad to be of use,
Politic, cautious, and meticulous;
Full of high sentence, but a bit obtuse;
At times, indeed, almost ridiculous —
Almost, at times, the Fool.
I grow old . . . I grow old . . .
I shall wear the bottoms of my trousers rolled.

Shall I part my hair behind? Do I dare to eat a peach?
I shall wear white flannel trousers, and walk upon the beach.
I have heard the mermaids singing, each to each.

I do not think that they will sing to me.

I have seen them riding seaward on the waves
Combing the white hair of the waves blown back
When the wind blows the water white and black.

We have lingered in the chambers of the sea
By sea-girls wreathed with seaweed red and brown
Till human voices wake us, and we drown.

                                        T. S. ELIOT

*Eros Turannos**

She fears him, and will always ask
    What fated her to choose him;
She meets in his engaging mask
    All reasons to refuse him;
But what she meets and what she fears
Are less than are the downward years,
Drawn slowly to the foamless weirs
    Of age, were she to lose him.

Between a blurred sagacity
    That once had power to sound him,

And Love, that will not let him be
 The Judas that she found him,
Her pride assuages her almost,
 As if it were alone the cost, —
He sees that he will not be lost,
 And waits and looks around him.

A sense of ocean and old trees
 Envelops and allures him;
Tradition, touching all he sees,
 Beguiles and reassures him;
And all her doubts of what he says
Are dimmed with what she knows of days —
Till even prejudice delays
 And fades, and she secures him.

The falling leaf inaugurates
 The reign of her confusion;
The pounding wave reverberates
 The dirge of her illusion;
And home, where passion lived and died,
Becomes a place where she can hide,
While all the town and harbor side
 Vibrate with her seclusion.

We tell you, tapping on our brows,
 The story as it should be, —
As if the story of a house
 Were told, or ever could be;
We'll have no kindly veil between
Her visions and those we have seen, —
As if we guessed what hers have been,
 Or what they are or would be.

Meanwhile we do no harm; for they
 That with a god have striven,
Not hearing much of what we say,
 Take what the god has given;
Though like waves breaking it may be
Or like a changed familiar tree,
Or like a stairway to the sea
 Where down the blind are driven.

E. A. ROBINSON

The maidens came

The maidens came
When I was in my mothers bower.
I hade all that I wolde.
The baily berith the bell away,[6]
The lilly, the rose, the rose I lay,
The silver is whit, red is the golde,
The robes thay lay in fold;
The baily berith the bell away,
The lilly, the rose, the rose I lay;
And through the glasse window
Shines the sone.
How shuld I love and I so young?
The baily berith the bell away,
The lilly, the rose, the rose I lay.

For to report it were now tedius:
We will therfor now sing no more
Of the games joyus.
Right mighty and famus
    Elizabeth, our quen princis,
    Prepotent and eke victorius,
    Vertuos and bening,[7]
    Lett us pray all
    To Christ Eternall,
    Which is the hevenly King,
    After ther liff grant them
    A place eternally to sing. Amen.

ANONYMOUS

[6] the bailiff carries the prize away
[7] benign

CHAPTER FOUR

The Audience

They have no ears. They read exclusively by eye. The most horrible cacophonies and the most perfect specimens of rhythm and vocalic melody are to them exactly equal. It is by this that we discover some highly educated people to be unliterary.

C. S. LEWIS

IN THE CLASSROOM

Everyone knows what an audience is. Still, it might be safer to define that perfectly obvious animal, at least for the purpose of this book. An audience is one or more persons who for various reasons, usually of their own free will, accept for a certain time a common convention for receiving communication from a common source.

There are two audiences which the oral reader must consider in preparing for his interpretation of the work. First is the audience to which he must read and of which (particularly in the classroom) he is an intimate part. Second is the audience which existed consciously or unconsciously in the author's mind at the time of composition. Therefore, after an examination of the more obvious problems of the student-reader and his classroom-audience, the discussion will move on to a more general and theoretical consideration of the nature of the audience which the artist has had in his mind, and of how that audience, in the broadest sense, has changed through the ages. We shall then conclude with some examination of aesthetic complexities that arise out of the writer-audience relationship, and their effect on selection of an appropriate work and its oral performance.

In the classroom the oral reader is that small part through which the writer (the source) reaches the larger part of his audience. What the oral reader himself is able to understand with his whole being — his voice, his body, his mind — he has a chance to communicate to other people, provided they comprehend enough of his systems of communication to close the gap between their past experience and the new experience offered to them. Ideally, of course, every silent reader should have experience as an oral reader, as every silent reader of drama should have in himself some actual experience of the stage. But were this ideal possible, we should still need, even if we are now largely ignorant of that need, professional oral readers to enlarge our more limited horizons by means of their naturally greater gifts and out of their more intense study of literature and the art of its presentation, just as the presence of a wide and healthy amateur theater makes more important, rather than less, the existence of a Laurence Olivier. Few students in any class in which this book is used will be likely, however, to choose this sort of professional career.

One can see, then, why such students accept the "common convention for receiving communication" of the classroom, becoming audiences for their teacher and for each other. The students in a classroom in which literature is being absorbed with the aid, among other techniques, of oral performance, are in a mutual conspiracy to become part of an audience for literature, to help to realize Walt Whitman's dream of a country in which many private citizens, beyond the special role of scholars and critics, exercise a wise and loving judgment out of a knowing heart. In this conspiracy all are stumbling toward knowledge and enlightenment with ever surer feet but with an ever-receding goal; or rather, with no other goal than the ever enriched and enriching experiences which each person is capable of living and at times sharing.

It is well that, in the beginning, the oral reader has his classmates for his audience. Understanding variant audiences and reading to them is a rather sophisticated affair, and should the student wish to go beyond these initial skills of reading to people near to himself, he will no doubt gain such knowledge in later classes from his experienced teachers, building upon this simple but suitable beginning. But beyond that the classroom presents a situation wherein the fact that the reader is also part of the audience is particularly clear. It presents a situation in which the student, out of the evidence of himself, can best discover what it is the rest of the audience, to which he is performer, requires for a satisfactory aesthetic experience. For just as he is clearly there to present to his classmates works of literature in such a way as mutually to enhance the success of that conspiracy mentioned above, so will he in turn sit as audience, perceiving the extent to which another can assist him toward wisdom. Thus, an alert examination by the student of his own need, as reader-audience, should provide him with the basic information he requires in dealing with the rest of the audience.

Since he must at various times separate himself from his fellows in order to stand, one might say, as their paraclete in relation to the work of art, he has an opportunity to see that audience in a somewhat objective light. Out of the process of his growth in understanding and rapport with the work, he comes to realize very strongly that being an audience to that work cannot be a passive role. This impression is much strengthened when his time comes to stand before his fellows and act as a bridge — to perform for them in his own being the fate of the story or poem.

There he finds that the last things he and his work require are so many nonresponding stones. He wants to feel that the audience is sympathetic, ready for the rewarding labor that is wisdom. He hopes that they will not refuse to listen to his sonnet by Donne because of some prior attitude, "It's too hard," or "It's old stuff," or "Who cares about a religious poem by an Anglican minister?" or "We studied that in high school." He himself, perhaps had entertained some of these attitudes before the poem became his, and he found in the process of his labors that the poem began to move him with a strange power.

He thinks that, if they will but give the poem a chance, they will also find something meaningful. "Too hard," "dull," "remote," there are many reasons why a member of an audience may refuse the active role required of him to reach for understanding, but that part of the audience presently standing before his fellows is aware of something basically unfair and self-limiting in such prejudgments. For just as people may be too complex, or too simple, or too dull, or too remote, yet be very much worth the effort required to understand them, so the work of art has a potential which deserves more than a prior dismissal.

As he stands before the rest of the audience with the poem that is now a part of him, that he wishes to share, he knows how easy it is to feign attention. He knows that minor distractions can be allowed to build into major blocks between the listener and the poem. He sees that both of these attitudes ruin any chance which the audience might have had for growth.

Further, he knows that he is far from a professional reader, that he is going to make mistakes. He knows that his audience will note these errors since part of their function is to help him improve as an interpreter. Nonetheless he hopes his listeners will give the poem its chance, will pay attention to it, and will try to become aware of its values despite his weaknesses. So it is that when he resumes his role as listening audience, his role as oral reader will have made him more sharply aware than he might otherwise be of what is required of him if he is truly to be a listener and not a lump.

But I have perhaps leaped ahead of the order of events as they will in fact occur. Sooner or later, the student will receive his first assignment to read something aloud to the class. Perhaps, for a beginning, the teacher has restricted the student in some way — to poetry, or to selections from the text, or whatever. In any case, the student is faced with looking over a number of pieces in a process of selection. If things are really grim, he hopes to find a work he can "just understand." But granted there are a number available to him above that level, what guides his choice? Well, he is likely to say simply, "I like this one best." But if he stops to consider what lies behind this really uninformative commonplace, he may realize that somehow this work moved him. He was able to "feel with" the event of the work; he seemed to have some insight beyond rational explanation.

This intuitive response is recognized every day in many ways. One hears the question, "Which is your favorite author?" If anything reasonable is implied in this question, it is that the reader (audience) has a limited range of abilities to "feel with," and that certain authors or certain works, no matter how powerful, how universally acclaimed, simply do not have the subject matter, themes, feeling for the world, to move certain readers. This limitation is an inevitable fact. By wide reading, by exposing himself to authors he has little immediate response to, but whom other judges he respects consider meaningful, by the whole process of education and growth, a reader can and should come to recognize fine writing even when it does not move him deeply. He will also undoubtedly vastly extend the range of authors who *do* so move him. But there will inevitably remain a body of writing which the reader recognizes as superb, but which does not in his case call forth that excitement which is the reader's (audience's) primary reward. These voids are not anything to boast about, but neither are they anything to be ashamed of, so long as one has made an honest effort to assess the writing for himself.

Empathy is the word given to this "feeling with." There are no doubt as many kinds of empathy as there are experiences of it. However, it should not be confused with that sort of emotional response evoked, for instance, by watching a movie in which a car is speeding toward a child. When one finds his hand reaching out to avert the danger, this is a feeling *toward*, not a feeling *with*. But when one sees a movie in which a car is gracefully swooping over a countryside, and one finds oneself leaning into the curves, lifting and sinking with the rises, in short, when one is experiencing to some degree in one's own body the action or emotion presented, then one is trying to identify, to feel *with*, and that is empathy.

Through empathy, then, the reader to some extent identifies himself with the literary event. But the emotions are tricky things, and identification is a two-way road. Sometimes it happens that instead of the reader identifying with the literary event, the reader makes the literary event identify with himself. We might call this kind of aesthetic identification *projection*. It is, of course, a denial of the true nature of the work of art and can lead to nothing good. The person who reads *Hamlet* and concludes "Hamlet was just like me, my mother didn't understand me either," has not gone very far in his understanding of Hamlet, of himself, or of the proper uses of literature.

Having made these distinctions, we can go on to say that if the student when in his role as audience recognizes his own empathic participation, this recognition should give him some confidence that he can move his audience when he is in his role as oral reader. Put briefly, what he finds is that his own lack of empathy is almost always lack of understanding *in his own physical being* of the flex and flow of the work's passionate movement as it works out the fate of its central passionate concern. There are many aspects to this lack of physical (mind and body) comprehension of a work's passionate structure. As the reader works through these ignorances and develops his oral reading in the light of the growing comprehension of his whole being, he discovers in himself a degree of empathic response so strong that, if he forgets his initial coldness (as commonly occurs), he thinks of his response to the piece as natural, even instinctive, rather than as of something learned. So usual is this growth-into-empathy that beginning students might well be advised that the worst way they can spend their limited time is in a search for a work they "like" on first sight. Picked from a qualitatively reliable, limited anthology, time spent *with* any piece will reward much more than time spent jumping from work to work looking for the "right" one. The value of oral reading as a means of empathic discovery has already been touched on in the first chapter. The point is repeated here, since the student's personal discovery that he actually *does* grow in empathic response as his oral reading becomes a reality should encourage him to think that what he can do *without* any assistance, his audience can do with his help.

And the audience has yet another aid that he, as solitary reader, did not have. Each single member of the audience is part of a dynamic process which includes not only the effect the author is creating on him but also the effect which the author, through the interpreter, is creating on the auditors surrounding him. Watch the crowd at a football game. Watch the bodies twist with the runner. Hear the people grunt with the tackler. Get out of the way as they leap and shout. Theirs is empathy of the most immediate sort. Yet the fact is this conduct is licensed by the group *around* them. A Brazilian, in whose country it is necessary to put an enormous dry moat around the soccer field to protect the players from *aficionados,* a Brazilian behaving as a Brazilian at a British soccer game would be visibly inappropriate in his empathic response and presumably would become subdued under the general weight of disapproval.

Fortunately for the reader, the group dynamic can move its members *toward* greater empathy. A skilful reader, building from the empathy of the sympathetic faces of the audience, can gradually, through them, establish a sympathetic climate generally. Further, by carefully watching his audience to make sure he is getting an appropriate response, by keeping calm and concentrating on the passionate core of his work in the face of any disturbingly noisy or inattentive members, he usually can convince such disturbing elements of his faith in the importance of the piece he is reading and of his own unselfish interest in the act of communicating the work of art. By so facing difficulties with unselfconscious calm, he can create a general feeling of confidence and security which will go far toward opening the way for the audience to pay attention only to the work being read to them and to its directions.

Of course, there are inappropriate responses from the audience other than noisiness or inattention, and they may be caused by the reader. I have mentioned that a skilful reader, starting with the most obviously alert and sympathetic members of his audience, can establish a generally warm give and take. This feedback can intensify as the emotional direction of the work unfolds, the audience following the reader's emotion and the reader intensifying his own at-oneness with the work by his sense that the audience is with him. But there is no guarantee that the reader is going to take the audience in the right direction. Though they are connected and overlap, there are at least four general ways in which readers may debase their empathic interplay with the audience.

Exhibitionism is perhaps what occurs to most people when they think of a situation where an oral reader wrongly directs an audience. Their minds go back to the performances they have seen by children, or on back to elocution days. They think of the studied gesture, the obviously planned burst of anger, all designed to give pleasure, not by illuminating the work of art, but by demonstrating the skill which the reader has achieved in controlling his voice and body.

Closely related to exhibitionism are two other ways of misusing and misguiding the audience's empathy: basing a reading on a misguided theoretical approach to reading aloud, and settling for the easy response. Misguided theories are of many kinds. I have already mentioned the dreary and betraying effect of readings arising from the theory that all works should be read in the same set of tones. Usually a part of this theory is that the readers should be "natural," i.e., totally untrained. There are others: the theory that reading literature is exactly the same skill as acting; the theory that reading aloud is an inferior kind of silent reading. You can no doubt think of others, or of variations of these.

Not quite the same thing is the reader who settles for the easy response. Preparing and executing an interpretation from a wrong theory can arise from ignorance on the part of the reader. But the person who, as they say of actors, "plays it for the laughs" or is "a tear-jerker" is insecure, to give him the benefit of the doubt. He is afraid he can't bring the audience all the way into the work. So out of his fear that he will have a total loss he settles for that half-success which is so much worse than honest failure because it embodies a contempt both for the work and for the audience.

But the most common cause in the classroom of erroneous empathic direction is the reader's simple lack of understanding, or his misunderstanding, of the work's true depth and direction. It is for this reason that so much of this book is concerned with developing methods by which the reader may identify himself with the work's true character.

I have been talking about the establishment of an empathic rapport between the reader and the rest of the audience, by means of which rapport the reader innocently or with malice aforethought takes his classmates in directions other than those indicated by the work of art he is reading. But in other cases the reader is himself unhappily aware that he is receiving an inappropriate reaction, and may find himself unable to discover the proper corrective. He may wish to attribute such an unwelcome response to some basic lack of sympathy in the audience, but the cause is seldom so reassuringly outside the reader.

In fact, in nearly all cases the reader has a basically sympathetic audience. People *want* to empathize, to be engrossed, if for no other reason than that they hate being bored. True, this is an initial sympathy which can be lost in many ways, including lack of skill. However, here we come to another reason why the reader is lucky to be part of a classroom audience. For though another audience looks for achieved skill and is usually (quite uncritically) bored without it, the classroom contains about the only kind of audience to which the weak elements of an interpretation are as interesting as the strong. For this audience is, as has been said, gathered for the common purpose, not of being entertained, but of becoming a *greater* audience. And since to become a greater audience involves, in this classroom, becoming better oral readers, it follows that the audience should be as creatively alert for (and should find as significant) what was not conveyed to them as they are appreciative of a successfully shared portion of the text.

Some of the causes of inappropriate responses are irremediable once the person is on the platform. Reading a totally inappropriate selection is one of these doomed-from-the-start errors, such as reading an Edgar Guest poem to your college classmates who are there for the purpose of becoming intimate with fine literature. The reader's clothes, or his pronunciation, or meaningless compulsive movements (empathy is truly a double-edged sword — an audience will fidget with a fidgety reader), or any other such element which cannot be remedied from the platform, can so distract the audience that it never listens to the work appropriately. Fortunately, these are matters which prior care and experience can prevent. But there are mistakes which can be corrected from the platform, and the causes of most of these are to be found in errors of *clarity* and *appropriateness*.

Obviously, if an audience at a live reading is to hope to empathize with the work, the reader must be both *audible* and *visible*. By audible, I do not mean simply that the voice must be heard. That much should go without saying. What I mean is that the *expressive patterns* of the voice must be broad enough in their effects to carry to the last row of the audience. Similarly, by visible I do not mean simply that the reader must not duck his face down and present the top of his head to the audience. I mean rather that any facial or bodily gesture which cannot be seen by the back rows is simply lost and might as well, in fact, should better, not have been. It is more frequent than not for a beginning oral reader to hear in his own head that he is reading with tremendous vocal variation — melodic range, rate, and volume — when to his classmates little is audible but two or three pitches on the melodic scale and virtually no change in volume or rate. The same is true of facial expressions and gestures. And the problem grows as the room or audience gets larger. Not so many years ago Laurence Olivier and Vivien Leigh co-starred in a production of Shakespeare's *Antony and Cleopatra*. It was in one of New York's largest theaters, and the sad truth was that Miss Leigh's small voice and small, delicate gestures, so effective in the close-up of the movie camera or in an intimate theater, were simply lost to most of the audience. The lifting of an eyebrow a fraction of an inch, which may convey meaning to someone two feet away, vanishes in four or five more feet and the reader is required to substitute what may seem a cruder gesture, but which may very well convey to the audience just the delicate effect he desires. Audibility and visibility taken in this sense are the foundations of clarity.

Certain problems of clarity can be solved in an introduction, and, despite later references to this question, it might be well to comment briefly on the functions and limitations of the introduction. The student should always state the title of the work and the author before reading it. But beyond this a simple explanation of any unusual words or allusions, a suggestion as to the direction the work will take, if that is appropriate, a comment on any knotty relationships or incongruities in the work, and, if only part of a work is read, a preparation of setting, incident and theme, are all ways in which a well-conceived introduction can assist in the achievement of clarity. But one must always remember, in making introductory remarks, not to say too much. Again, the oral reader should recall his experience as audience for works of literature. Has he ever been discouraged rather then encouraged by an introduction to a book? Has he ever found the writers of some introductions more interested in showing off their own wit and style than in genuinely assisting the reader into the works that follow? Has he ever found such introductions supercilious? condescending? beside the point? long-winded? If so, then he may well conclude that these are faults into which he himself, unless he takes care, might fall.

In preparing the introduction, it is of especial importance for the oral reader to remember that he is, like the pianist, an interpreter, an instrument for the revelation of a meaningful work of art. The listening audience is not interested in displays of modesty, false or otherwise, or in unnecessary displays of erudition, however quaint and curious. The purpose of the introduction is to permit the work of art to be read with greater clarity of communication. In such a case true grace consists in saying effectively no more or less than is necessary. In the classroom, it is possible that the student will be reading material the whole class is acquainted with or material of an extremely clear, direct quality. In such cases no introduction may at times be the best introduction. Often I have known a student to prepare the class better by what he did in the considerable pause that follows the naming of title and author than he could have done with unnecessary words. A subtle shift of body, a firming of facial expression, a general moving into a characterizing, expressive bearing of body, head, and eyes, should give a strong clue to much that is to follow. Certainly there is always the question of propriety. A Shakespeare sonnet which may take less than a minute to read — how could one really justify overbearing this with an introduction several times as long? On the other hand, an introduction of some length might seem quite appropriate for a long work, rich in difficulties for a modern audience, such as Milton's *Lycidas*.

Granted that the reader is coming through clearly to the audience, then what the audience hears and sees must be appropriate. I do not mean simply that a sad work must be said in a sad voice. The qualities of sadness are infinite, as varied as there are individual experiences of sadness. As preparation for projecting the appropriate tones to this larger audience, the oral reader, as audience, must understand the style of the work, the nature of its verbal gestures and of the physical gestures made explicit or implicit by the verbal gestures. (Since the achievement of this understanding is the primary problem, this book, which is for the first course, concentrates on it.) He must, for instance, understand the faith in rationality that underlies the rationalisms of Mr. and Mrs. Dashwood, and how this faith affects the choice of words, the sentence structure, the use of figure. Once he is able to achieve such insight, there remain the problems of manifesting these gestures in actual vocal and bodily gestures that will be accepted by a modern audience, without betraying the gestures of the work.

If there are no two audiences alike, nonetheless there will be, in any given age in any given culture, a style of performance, whether of acting or oral reading, within which the audience finds its appropriate gestures. The problem that confronts an oral reader again and again is how to modify the contemporary style of performance to convey a style of writing which is suited to other mores. Sadness, in short, its development and qualification, must be given a local habitation and a name which the auditors will accept both as real (as they would put it) and as nonetheless faithful to a style of writing which is now to some extent unreal. There is a style which is appropriate, let us say, to the modern realistic drama or to the reading of a modern novel. But if that style is attempted unmodified when one is reading *Antony and Cleopatra*, for instance, or Homer, the audience will (perhaps unconsciously) sense a fatal gap between the audience as implied in the work and the audience as it actually is. The oral reader's task is to create, among all the other illusions of art, the illusion that no such gap exists.

But beyond these large problems of style, the oral reader will find that such simple physical alterations as merely sitting down to read will obviously make certain tones and gestures inappropriate which were quite effective standing up; that, in fact, any change of the reader-audience situation will subtly affect the possibilities for appropriate vocal or bodily gestures.

BACKGROUND OF THE WRITER-AUDIENCE RELATIONSHIP

So far I have been talking about the audience as it is to be met in the classroom, a living audience in which each auditor in turn is also interpreter, to the enrichment in understanding of each role. It is common for oral readers, when they think of the "audience," to limit their thoughts in some such way to this audience before them. Surely the whole problem of the audience-reader relationship begins far back of that, in another, less concrete audience's effect on the *writer* and on the work he has produced. Insight into that influence should prove of value to the interpreter. It is easy enough for a handbook on public speaking to talk about "pitching the speech to the audience," but the oral reader already has his texts written, a whole range of great and near-great works of literary art. In a public speech there is almost always a straightforward audience-speaker relationship. But in the interpreter's texts the situation is very different. There, sometimes the speaker-audience situation (the fictive dramatic situation) within the work is almost identical with the writer-audience relationship, but in other cases these two diverge radically. The numberless situations that lie between these positions offer endless complexity to the interpreter. Thus, in John Donne's *Holy Sonnets*, the speaker-audience situation is that of an individual addressing God directly, and with little consideration for any other listener. It would appear that this is very near to the actual writer-audience situation, i.e., that John Donne was in fact addressing God in a private sense. On the other hand, Defoe's novel *Moll Flanders* was written for the English reading masses, with both the narrative voice, Moll Flanders, and the author addressing themselves to somewhat similar audiences, though from different viewpoints. Both the *Holy Sonnets* and *Moll Flanders* are obviously great works, but they would not necessarily be appropriate to the same occasions and only partially to the same techniques. But before becoming involved in analysis of the writer-audience situation within a work, or a comparison in this regard between several works, there is a gross historical development which we must touch upon. It should be obvious that the audience which existed in Homer's mind is not the same audience as that which existed in Hemingway's. It would be wise to see, however sketchily, the nature and background of such large shifts in the aesthetic direction of a work.

Let us start by repeating the definition of an audience with which the chapter began. An audience is one or more persons who, for various reasons, usually of their own free will, accept for a certain time a common convention for receiving communication from a common source. What, then, have been the grosser changes in the nature of that audience for literature over the centuries?

One of the first things to be noted about this creature is that its individual parts need not share the same general time or space. This is a highly significant fact for the interpreter. One is at present very much aware that an audience is not so confined, thanks to records, tapes, films, and other methods for preserving aesthetic events for presentation at disparate times and places. And one is also aware, or should be, that reading for a tape, for instance, because of the changed audience situation, requires techniques quite different from those used in reading to a live audience. These techniques, along with those required for other non-live audience situations, will not be dealt with in this book, which is concerned with the achievement and sharing of literary insight with a present audience through the discipline of integrated voice and gesture.

But of course long before the electronic age, ever since the advent of writing and, earlier, with the advent of painting, there have been methods for reaching people not gathered together. There is in Africa, painted relatively recently on a cave wall, an amusing story of several Bushmen surprised by a lion. Any other Bushman chancing that way has been that Bushman's audience. But since this painting was reproduced in a national magazine with an enormous circulation, the number of viewers of that painting has enormously increased.

Are these later viewers, these millions of car-owning, movie-going TV lovers, a part of the audience of that work? Well, certainly not in the same sense that an itinerant Bushman is an audience. In their inner beings they know nothing about South Africa, nothing about lions, nothing about spears. They know how amusing it is to see someone take a pratfall, as one of these surprised hunters evidently did. Certainly it was not for such shallow viewers that the *painter* painted. Except for the broad (and for some people, constantly surprising) fact that we are all human, and that consequently we all find certain physical degradations (in others) funny, the Bushman painter would hardly have had the average American in mind as one of those persons who might gather around his painting in a "common convention for receiving common communication." In fact, insofar as many of these New World viewers would deprecate his work with such condescending judgments as "charming" or "quaint" or "primitive," I suspect the Bushman painter would strongly reject that audience. Yet who can deny that for most American viewers of the picture such secondary aesthetic pleasures as we often derive from the exotic were very largely substituted for any direct empathy with the art in its organization of reality by its own conventions. Would it be possible then to speculate that to the degree that the audience seeing or hearing the work of art is different from the audience that existed consciously or unconsciously in the artist's mind, just so much more unlikely will be an achievement of a primary aesthetic communication, with a subsequent growth in importance for the audience of such secondary aesthetic satisfactions as those just suggested?

However that may be, there is little doubt that painting and certain kinds of statuary were the first kinds of aesthetic events capable of influencing an audience not present at their making or performance. There is also considerable evidence that this absent audience was not immediately thought of as central in the execution of the work either by the artist or by the people who were with him at the time of its creation. Tentatively, anthropologists generally conclude that the actual act of painting on a given day with a given group of people in a particular circumstance was the important aesthetic aspect of the act of painting for the painter and for his audience. Thereafter, they (the paintings) were apparently considered to have lost their value, for later painters paid little attention to earlier works, painting over them at will.

The purposes for which the works were created, in fact, were almost surely magical rather than aesthetic. For instance, by creating an image of hunters successfully killing game, the painter and his audience hoped magically to absorb some of the prowess of the painted images in the forthcoming hunt. Their attention was not, so far as we can determine, turned toward the creation of beauty or other aesthetic considerations, except as such might serve to make the magic stronger. In a certain sense, prehistoric painters painted to the gods as a kind of magic-prayer. The people who happened to see the painting executed were not the object for which these early painters worked, that is in any aesthetic sense.

No doubt a long time passed before anything like the modern artist-audience relationship developed and hence before the audience shaped in any conscious way the construct of the work of art in the mind of the artist. When the artist shapes his statue in privacy, with no immediate observers, for the express purpose of creating a form in such manner as to affect the minds of viewers of many sorts through many generations, there can be little question that he is carrying his audience in his mind in a very sophisticated way and that his aims and purposes are a far cry from those of the prehistoric painter.

Compared to these early modes of reaching absent audiences, writing was a latecomer. By the time writing was invented, fiction was an art orally composed by such typical artists as bards, story-tellers, and priests.

Writing as applied to literature, therefore, came as a means of fixing the text and extending the audience for an art that could exist, and had existed, without spatial habitation other than the minds of those whose memories encompassed or whose inventive powers created its being. This temporal existence is in direct contrast to a sculpture or a painting which exists in only one place as an original. Writing is a spatial manifestation of a basically temporal art and there is not, strictly speaking, an "original." Rather the poem or story exists wherever there are true copies on paper or in the mind. Yet despite this extensibility of writing, the bards, the rhapsodes, in short the oral readers, were not really shoved off center stage (and their kind of audience was not ignored) until the advent of relatively cheap printing.

In the beginning there were the memorizers and composers of poems and tales, and they were often also the reciters of poetry and tales, highly trained in a specific if relatively limited tradition. With the spread of writing, these jobs tended to be more often divided, since the two gifts may occur in unequal degrees in a given person. Still, copying was done by hand, and so scarce were copies that the first part of his audience reached by the writer was likely the rhapsode, and the rest of the audience was the larger number of people to whom the interpreter could recite or read the work. (There are descriptions from Roman times of audiences gathering for several successive days to hear a new history read aloud.) This relationship is still basically the modern oral reader's with the text and the people he is reading to, as it is still in music basically the performer's with his score and his audience.

Cheap printing, however, changed these old relationships — writer, interpreter, audience — completely. For the first time the writer could entirely overleap the oral reader and reach directly an audience whose size was hitherto unimagined. True, this wider audience would be a silent one whose individual member was now rendered both solitary and more and more incapable of recreating oral effects in his own mind. Still, here placed in the writer's hand was the first true mass medium, a tremendous accession of power and influence such as man, whether he should or not, has seldom been able to resist. Some of the technical compositional effects which the invention of writing and later of cheap printing has had on fiction will be discussed briefly in a later chapter. It is probably impossible to trace the broader formal effects completely, but among the prominent results was the reduction or elimination of various kinds of repetitions or formulas such as inevitably made up a vital part of any oral tradition.

As might be expected, forms were developed, such as the novel, which were not only broadly "public" in subject matter and theme, but which also increased their mass appeal by eliminating the implicit formal demand made by such ancestor forms as the epic for an aurally sophisticated audience. On the other hand, there has been time for a kind of counterprocess away from mass-oriented writing to take place — though this has generally confirmed the increasing reduction of the oral as opposed to the visual in literature — I refer as an example to the development of the tight short-story form from the looser forms of earlier tales.

So much, however briefly, for a summary of the movement of fiction from oral (composed and communicated orally), to written (composed in writing and usually communicated orally), to printed (composed in writing and communicated in print) literature. Why sketch this historical movement here? To lay a background for distinctions which might prove important to the oral reader, distinctions to be touched upon while underlining the fact that the audience for which the writer composes affects profoundly the work of art and that the nature of that audience should not be taken for granted by the oral interpreter.

THE AUDIENCE IN THE WORK OF ART

Occasional remarks have been made concerning the selection of a work appropriate to an audience; and before going on to discuss the problem of the audience in the work, I should like to mention selection as a specific problem for the interpreter. It is not a problem that is likely to be of great significance in the classroom. A highly selective process has taken place to bring the students there, and their aims are, as already suggested, such aims as should make them welcome any work of sufficient artistic weight so long as it fulfills their instructor's assignment. The student may postpone for a later course the problem of audience analysis, but what he must face to some degree from the start is the problem of the audience in the work of art. He must face it early because a proper understanding of this aspect of a work of literary art is very much involved in a revealing oral interpretation of that work.

I should like to discuss three problems whose solution should prove useful in determining the aesthetic nature of the author-audience relationship, and hence useful in the achieving of realistically based tones of voice and body: (1) the degree to which the work was written for oral communication; (2) the degree of intimacy with which the author approaches his audience; and (3) the degree to which the audience is excluded from the author's direct attention. The last two are not redundant as they may seem to be at first glance. An author may not treat his audience very intimately, yet he may nonetheless include it very forcefully.

But before going on to the three problems mentioned, an initial distinction is necessary for the sake of clarity: the narrator of the work may well be addressing one audience, whereas the writer is addressing another. Thus, in Marvell's "To His Coy Mistress," the speaker in the dramatic situation of the poem is addressing a woman. Yet we sense, however vaguely, that the poet is including an audience beyond this woman. Certainly the poet invites the audience's attention in one way which was, I suspect, very important to him. The poem's *carpe diem* theme was a favorite with ancient authors a well as with the English poets of the fifteenth, sixteenth and seventeenth centuries, and it was often developed in just this dramatic situation — a young man wooing a young woman. There is little doubt that Marvell expected the cultivated audience for which the poem was written to know those previous attempts and to measure Marvell's achievement against that of earlier master poets using the same theme and dramatic situation.

In Austen's *Sense and Sensibility*, on the other hand, the narrator addresses the same audience which the author wishes to reach — one which is outside the dramatic framework and clearly of the same social class as the author or at least capable of profoundly appreciating the values of that class.

The oral reader will find that this split or union of what one might call the fictive audience and the reading audience occurs in varying degrees and with subtle permutations which, as a few examples will later show, can be a significant element in his interpretation. Meanwhile, let us return to the more direct questions concerning that audience which, existing perhaps unconsciously in the author's mind, exerts its powerful shaping influence.

In the process of discovering to what degree a specific work was conceived for oral communication, two useful possibilities may be considered: (1) that the oral reader was a certain part of the audience which the author had in mind, and (2) that in some significant degree the work demands an educated attention to such auditory elements as rhythm, vowel-and-consonant music, rhyme, and phrasal balance.

A work may well have been written with the second possibility and not the first as part of the aesthetic aim. On the other hand, the obvious presence of the first would lead one to expect the second (though one may not always find it). This distinction is by no means trivial for it is, within limits, one of the touchstones of genre. That is, a drama obviously is always written with an oral delivery in mind. And in the second possibility undoubtedly lies one of the core differences between poetry and prose, however many exceptions on either side may be found. Certainly it is true that over the long haul as the silent reader grew in importance in the author's mind, so did prose more and more dominate the literary scene.

The broad but basic distinction suggested by the second possibility is of especial significance to the oral reader and will affect his selection for his audience. A highly educated audience will not necessarily possess a discerning literary ear. As C. S. Lewis states in a quotation used at the opening of this chapter, highly educated people may be oral-aural illiterates. On the other hand, a working man brought up on a rich tradition of folk song, folk tale, and the Bible may have a discriminating, if limited, ear.

If a work was composed orally for oral dissemination, it will be clear at once that the interpreter's delivery is involved. Homer is not to be read in the same way as Milton, if for no other reason than that Homer's epics are works with a profound oral tradition, passed from bard to bard and based on oral compositional techniques which were until quite recently (and may still be) alive in remote parts of Europe. Milton, on the other hand, though obviously demanding an audience of great aural sophistication, composed for the person who will read the poem silently more often than he will hear it. Thus in the first instance the oral reader will find all sorts of the formulas, the repetitions, the set-pieces which were part of the tradition of oral composition, and which were aids to the composer as well as the auditor.

When a certain character in the *Iliad* is always brought on scene with the same descriptive phrase, three conditions are met which are of great importance in oral composition: (1) the composer is not required to think of some original descriptive term each time he comes to the character; (2) although the phrase has an echo effect, like a refrain, it is not necessarily static in meaning since it may be used with various degrees of irony, approbation, or any other attitude which the changing environment may each time cast over the repeated formula; and (3) the listening audience (which cannot reread something it did not at first hearing understand) is aided in keeping character straight, is aided in keeping the salient traits of the characters in mind, and is aided in grasping the changing ironies and fates that surround the character as the story goes forward.

Milton's *Samson*, on the other hand, written for the act of silent reading, nonetheless demands a highly active and trained ear in that silent reader. Thus there are great oral riches here for the interpreter, but they require great care in reading aloud since few of the audience aids which Homer used are built into the work. In fact, I suspect it is partly this demand for a highly "poetic" ear which makes Milton's longer works a dubious choice for reading to many modern audiences; so much of the delight lies in that aural realm which is virtually inaccessible to them.

To take a work at the other extreme from Homer, we find in Swift's "A Modest Proposal" both a masterpiece of prose and a work clearly and firmly written for the silent reader. One could even go so far as to say that, in reading aloud certain works, particularly certain novels, one is doing something the writer hardly had in mind at all. Compare Dickens' novels, for instance, which are orally oriented, to those of George Eliot. But back to "A Modest Proposal," its implied audience and its interpreter.

"A Modest Proposal" and "Two Sides to a Tortoise" are the prose pieces in this collection farthest from full-blown fiction. Each would be classed unhesitatingly as an essay — one a descriptive-travel essay, the other an essay of social protest. Yet beyond doubt each has certain elements heightened to the realm of fiction — at least such is their scope and impact. In "Two Sides to a Tortoise," this heightening is achieved by the intensely imaginative use of figurative language. In "A Modest Proposal," the fictionalization lies in the creation of a fictive speaker and a fictive audience for that speaker.

Swift's irony, of course, lies in the fact that both the speaker and audience were recognizable in their day as common enough types, fictionalized only by the device of their carrying their arguments and attitudes to the ultimate, horrible absurdity. It was the Age of Reason. Men prided themselves on their ability to rule emotions off the scene when it came to solving problems, even poetic problems. And while poets (eventually Swift among them) went mad in unprecedented numbers, emotion became a dirty word. Worse, it was considered a furiously flourishing cancer from man's savage past which had to be continually sought after and cut out by the cool knife of reason. By an enormous irony of fate, Swift was just such a man of reason, and the apelike Yahoo and the horselike Houyhnhnm were the polar villain and hero in the highly symbolic world of his fiction. But as he observed the starving multitudes of Ireland, this rationalist was overcome with compassion, and the result was "A Modest Proposal."

One can imagine that this compassion was not suspect to Swift himself because it was well mixed with hatred and scorn. (For some reason, even as with some persons today, the emotions of hatred, scorn, and their close companions were not nearly so suspect to the Rational Man as were love and compassion.) At any rate the men of that age, which was also the age of the first mass use of printing, very dearly loved to demonstrate their rational minds by exercising them on various problems in pamphlets or broadcast newsheets. And they very often did this (witness the Addison and Steele essays) in the guise of a fictive, though usually sympathetic, speaker. These letters, pamphlets, essays, poems were then much and vehemently discussed by other men, who prided themselves on their powers of reasoning, in coffee-houses and studies and parlors throughout Great Britain.

It was this audience which shaped "A Modest Proposal" as it formed in Swift's mind, and it was not an audience likely to be interested in hearing such an essay read aloud with proper passion. What those men looked for were arguments they could chew, facts they could digest, wit they could appreciate — the pleasures of the mind when brought to bear on current social manifestations. They obviously wanted plain but clear prose and the sense of a mind at work. They wanted figures and incisive turns of phrase they could come back to when the going got hot over their coffee tables. This was Swift's audience as he saw it and as he fictionalized it and as it will affect oral performance.

The response in this case to our two early possibilities will be: "The oral reader was *not* a part of the audience which the author had in mind," and "The ear is evoked in the audience minimally compared to the rational element." Thus the oral reader will seek to make his effect most appropriately by bringing the audience to perceive the rich interplay between the rational tones of the speaker and the ironic tones which arise from the author's intent. Anything which would point to this rational prosiness would be useful in a reading. For instance, I should think a deliberate sense of *reading* rather than interpreting the manuscript — quite contrary to what was urged in Chapter three — would be very helpful in the submerged task of explicating Swift's audience to the modern audience of the interpreter, of joining the two in the living audience's mind.

The degree to which an audience is included or excluded from the work and the degree to which it is treated distantly or intimately are related, but not identical, problems. If an audience is excluded, then obviously it is simply not there, to be treated intimately or otherwise. But if the audience is a presence in the work, then all shades and degrees of intimacy can be registered, whether that presence is prominent or merely suggested.

I have mentioned earlier that there is an audience to which Marvell is addressing his poem. We can deduce that the audience must be of strong wit, sensitive to the music and image of language, and very much aware of the profound and eternal pagan view of man's destiny as opposed to the Hebraic-Christian view. We can also deduce, as I have said earlier, that the audience should be aware of the history of this pagan theme through western literature and should be able to appreciate Marvell's triumphant re-creation. Having become aware of this greater audience the reader should nonetheless clearly see that the *fictive* audience, the girl, need share only some of these qualities, and then only to a degree, with the wider audience to which Marvell is directing his poem.

The Marvell poem brings us to the fact that the fictive audience addressed by the narrator in the poem, like the larger audience to which the poet addresses his work, may exist anywhere in a continuum between a vague and amorphous existence to a concrete, specific, well-defined one. Thus the girl in "To His Coy Mistress" becomes what might be called an *ostensible fictive audience.** The oral reader of this poem might be free, therefore, to make his audience into Marvell's larger audience; and when comment seems less directly addressed ("But at my back I always hear . . ."), he might feel free to turn from addressing the girl to addressing the audience. On the other hand, there is nothing ostensible about the envoy in Browning's "My Last Duchess." He is a very concrete fictive audience, and the oral reader, as the Duke's voice, would address himself exclusively to the envoy.

"To His Coy Mistress" presents a problem of a rather indirectly addressed author-audience. This audience (the one toward which the poet directs his poem) must be created in the mind of the interpreter's audience only by indirect means. Perhaps a few judicious remarks in an introduction might help. But the great weapon the interpreter has in this indirect creation is the interplay of rich sound, the vivid, highly contrasting figures, and the tone which is urgent, powerfully masculine and at the same time elegant — in short, that elevation of language which constantly points beyond the immediate persuasive-dramatic situation to great issues.

Austen's *Sense and Sensibility*, on the other hand, includes the audience firmly, affectionately one might almost say. As has been said, there is no split between the author and the speaker, hence no split in their audience. This audience is quite different from Marvell's indirect one. It is much more prosaic, much more everyday — it need be neither so intellectual, so rawly passionate, nor so aurally oriented. This middle-class audience, in short, is being told a tale of its own class, and the nuances that lead to larger human themes are very much those of their own world. What is the degree of intimacy? I should think some such degree as one would feel sitting in Miss Austen's drawing room and listening to her tell the tale. The interpreter is free to treat his own audience as directly. The more he can suggest the manners, gestures, and attitudes of the period as they might have been evident in the narrator, the easier it should be for his audience to become part of the upper middle-class audience which was Miss Austen's.

"A Modest Proposal" is unlike the Austen selection in having a split between the speaker and the author, but no split in audience. Both the fictive writer with his "wife past child-bearing" and Swift are addressing the same men — the coffee-house rationalists briefly described above. Their difference arises in what they want to do to the audience and what they want from it. The speaker wants its usual serious attention and, if not its approval, at least its discussion of his idea. Swift wants to expose it to itself.

* I am indebted to Professor Thomas Sloan, University of Illinois, for this distinction.

The gap between the audience for which Swift wrote and the modern interpreter's is great in some ways and not so great in others. The whole social situation of the essay has passed on, both the readers of the essay and their surroundings, and the particular subject matter — the wholesale starvation of people in Ireland. So the oral reader is aware that his material, however brilliantly written, is going to be somewhat cold and distant to the members of his audience, who are likely to enjoy the skill of Swift's prose, but are likely to be left feeling how fortunate we are that babies are no longer starving in Ireland. There is going to be quite a difference, in other words, between the aesthetic reactions which Swift and the present day interpreter could expect from their respective audiences.

How to bridge the gap, how to bring the two audiences into some kind of communion, is one of the interpreter's first aesthetic requirements as he begins preparing for the interpretation. And the first step lies in his own mind. Penetrating beyond the material which was current then and is dead now, he must seek that which is still alive — and he will soon see that man has not really changed. Well-fed men are still able, in cold round figures and rational tones, to decry public aid to human misery, both domestic and foreign, and do so in journals every day. Indeed, issues from hydrogen deaths to impoverished old age and hungry children are discussed constantly as dispassionately as Swift's proposer discusses boiling year-old infants, and with the same high-minded "no other motive than the public good of my country." Since all of us share to a greater or lesser degree this ability to reason calmly on others' misery, so must any likely audience that a reader might have. And here, I should think, is where the two audiences might be brought into close enough relationship for something of Swift's savage irony to move the modern heart to self-knowledge.

How is the audience to be made to feel this identity? I think an introduction might help, provided it became neither fantastical nor too dogged, to make some of this relationship clear. Certainly the interpreter must feel a burning inner conviction of the contemporary validity of Swift's attack. Unless he can feel in himself at least a portion of Swift's horror and rage, he will probably be unable to find the technical means of uniting the two audiences with his reading. For in this reading the interpreter must create in his mind not only a fictive character, but a fictive audience as well. He must create the fictive character in such a way that Swift's personal vision will shine through and beyond it. In the same way he must create in his mind an audience which can talk about the price of stuffed child as objectively as it would read its math book. For the oral reader, "A Modest Proposal" must become a good deal more than a literary masterpiece. If he can see Swift's audience in the audience before him, then he has a chance to create that vision of itself in the audience's mind, as he calmly, doggedly, and oh! so sincerely! presents his modest proposal. He is blind to their boredom, shock, or laughter. He is reading his proposal. His very reasonableness declares, "But listen, this is *you* speaking! I know because I'm one of you. Don't you see that I'm one of you?" His every tone and gesture force them to add to their role as present audience this fictive role. If the reader cannot, in the process of his analysis and oral preparation, come to see Swift's audience as somehow a part of the audience he is to read to, then he should select another work, for he will fail of the aesthetic aim which Swift has riveted to "A Modest Proposal."

What this chapter has suggested is that the classroom situation offers a rich possibility for the student to enlarge his capacities as audience and performer-audience. These roles, as the student assumes them alternately, will be found to produce a mutual enrichment. And it is the role of performer which serves as catalyst to transform the otherwise too-often passive role of the reading audience and the listening audience into a positive working activity, transforming the reading or listening audience into a participating creator. This chapter has further suggested that there was an audience for which the artist wrote and perhaps a specific fictive audience within the work as well. A realization of those audiences on the part of the interpreter will be an important part of becoming an effective reader of that work.

SELECTIONS

Knoxville: Summer of 1915*

JAMES AGEE

We are talking now of summer evenings in Knoxville, Tennessee in the time that I lived there so successfully disguised to myself as a child. It was a little bit mixed sort of block, fairly solidly lower middle class, with one or two juts apiece on either side of that. The houses corresponded: middle-sized gracefully fretted wood houses built in the late nineties and early nineteen hundreds, with small front and side and more spacious back yards, and trees in the yards, and porches. These were soft-wooded trees, poplars, tulip trees, cottonwoods. There were fences around one or two of the houses, but mainly the yards ran into each other with only now and then a low hedge that wasn't doing very well. There were few good friends among the grown people, and they were not poor enough for the other sort of intimate acquaintance, but everyone nodded and spoke, and even might talk short times, trivially, and at the two extremes of the general or the particular, and ordinarily nextdoor neighbors talked quite a bit when they happened to run into each other, and never paid calls. The men were mostly small businessmen, one or two very modestly executives, one or two worked with their hands, most of them clerical, and most of them between thirty and forty-five.

But it is of these evenings, I speak.

Supper was at six and was over by half past. There was still daylight, shining softly and with a tarnish, like the lining of a shell; and the carbon lamps lifted at the corners were on in the light, and the locusts were started, and the fireflies were out, and a few frogs were flopping in the dewy grass, by the time the fathers and the children came out. The children ran out first hell bent and yelling those names by which they were known; then the fathers sank out leisurely in crossed suspenders, their collars removed and their necks looking tall and shy. The mothers stayed back in the kitchen washing and drying, putting things away, recrossing their traceless footsteps like the lifetime journeys of bees, measuring out the dry cocoa for breakfast. When they came out they had taken off their aprons and their skirts were dampened and they sat in rockers on their porches quietly.

It is not of the games children play in the evening that I want to speak now, it is of a contemporaneous atmosphere that has little to do with them: that of the fathers of families, each in his space of lawn, his shirt fishlike pale in the unnatural light and his face nearly anonymous, hosing his lawn. The hoses were attached at spigots that stood out of the brick foundations of the houses. The nozzles were variously set but usually so there was a long sweet stream of spray, the nozzle wet in the hand, the water trickling the right forearm and the peeled-back cuff, and the water whishing out a long loose and low-curved cone, and so gentle a sound. First an insane noise of violence in the nozzle, then the still irregular sound of adjustment, then the smoothing into steadiness and a pitch as accurately tuned to the size and style of stream as any violin. So many qualities of sound out of one hose: so many choral differences out of those several hoses that were in earshot. Out of any one hose, the almost dead silence of the release, and the short still arch of the separate big drops, silent as a held breath, and the only noise the fluttering noise on leaves and the slapped grass at the fall of each big drop. That, and the intense hiss with the intense stream; that, and that same intensity not growing less but growing more quiet and delicate with the turn of the nozzle, up to that extreme tender whisper when the water was just a wide bell of film. Chiefly, though, the hoses were set much alike, in a compromise between distance and tenderness of spray (and quite surely a sense of art behind this compromise, and a quiet, deep joy, too real to recognize itself) and the sounds therefore were pitched much alike; pointed by the snorting start of a new hose; decorated by some man playful with the nozzle; left empty, like God by the sparrow's fall, when any single one of them desists: and all, though near alike, of various pitch; and in this unison. These sweet pale streamings in the light lift out their pallors and their voices all together, mothers hushing their children, the hushing unnaturally prolonged, the men gentle and silent and each snail-like withdrawn into the quietude of what he singly is doing, the urination of huge children stood loosely military against an invisible wall, and gently happy and peaceful, tasting the mean goodness of their living like the last of their suppers in their mouths; while the locusts carry on this noise of hoses on their much higher and sharper key. The noise of the locust is dry, and it seems not to be rasped or vibrated but urged from him as if through a small orifice by a breath that can never give out. Also there is never one locust but an illusion of at least a thousand. The noise of each locust is pitched in some classic locust range out of which none of them varies more than two full tones: and yet you seem to hear each locust discrete from all the rest, and there is a long, slow, pulse in their noise, like the scarcely defined arch of a long and high set bridge. They are all around in every tree, so that the noise seems to come from nowhere and everywhere at once, from the whole shell heaven, shivering in your flesh and teasing your eardrums, the boldest of all the sounds of night. And yet it is habitual to summer nights, and is of the great order of noises, like the noises of the sea and of the blood of her precocious grandchild, which you realize you are hearing only when you catch yourself listening. Meantime from low in the dark, just outside the swaying horizons of the hoses, conveying always grass in the damp of dew and its strong green-black smear of smell, the regular yet spaced noises of the crickets, each a sweet cold silver noise three-noted, like the slipping each time of three matched links of a small chain.

But the men by now, one by one, have silenced their hoses and drained and coiled them. Now only two, and now only one, is left, and you see only ghostlike shirt with the sleeve garters, and sober mystery of his mild face like the lifted face of large cattle enquiring of your presence in a pitch-dark pool of meadow; and now he too is gone; and it has become that time of evening when people sit on their porches, rocking gently and talking gently and watching the street and the standing up into their sphere of possession of the trees, of birds' hung havens, hangars. People go by; things go by. A horse, drawing a buggy, breaking his hollow iron music on the asphalt; a loud auto; a quiet auto; people in pairs, not in a hurry, scuffling, switching their weight of aestival body, talking casually, the taste hovering over them of vanilla, strawberry, pasteboard, and starched milk, the image upon them of lovers and horsemen, squared with clowns in hueless amber. A streetcar raising its iron moan; stopping; belling and starting, stertorous; rousing and raising again its iron increasing moan and swimming its gold windows and straw seats on past and past and past, the bleak spark crackling and cursing above it like a small malignant spirit set to dog its tracks; the iron whine rises on rising speed; still risen, faints; halts; the faint stinging bell; rises again, still fainter; fainting, lifting, lifts, faints foregone: forgotten. Now is the night one blue dew.

Now is the night one blue dew, my father has drained, he has coiled the hose.
Low on the length of lawns, a frailing of fire who breathes.
Content, silver, like peeps of light, each cricket makes his comment over and over in the drowned grass.
A cold toad thumpily flounders.
Within the edges of damp shadows of side yards are hovering children nearly sick with joy of fear, who watch the unguarding of a telephone pole.
Around white carbon corner lamps bugs of all sizes are lifted elliptic, solar systems. Big hardshells bruise themselves, assailant: he is fallen on his back, legs squiggling.
Parents on porches: rock and rock. From damp strings morning glories hang their ancient faces.
The dry and exalted noise of the locusts from all the air at once enchants my eardrums.

On the rough wet grass of the back yard my father and mother have spread quilts. We all lie there, my mother, my father, my uncle, my aunt, and I too am lying there. First we were sitting up, then one of us lay down, and then we all lay down, on our stomachs, or on our sides, or on our backs, and they have kept on talking. They are not talking much, and the talk is quiet, of nothing in particular, of nothing at all in particular, of nothing at all. The stars are wide and alive, they seem each like a smile of great sweetness, and they seem very clear. All my people are larger bodies than mine, quiet, with voices gentle and meaningless like the voices of sleeping birds. One is an artist, he is living at home. One is a musician, she is living at home. One is my mother who is good to me. One is my father who is good to me. By some chance, here they are, all on this earth; and who shall ever tell the sorrow of being on this earth, lying, on quilts,

on the grass, in a summer evening, among the sounds of the night. May
God bless my people, my uncle, my aunt, my mother, my good father, oh,
remember them kindly in their time of trouble; and in the hour of their
taking away.

After a little I am taken in and put to bed. Sleep, soft smiling, draws
me unto her: and those receive me, who quietly treat me, as one familiar
and well-beloved in that home: but will not, oh, will not, not now, not
ever; but will not ever tell me who I am.

1938

The Bishop Orders His Tomb At Saint Praxed's Church[1]

[Rome, 15—.]

Vanity, saith the preacher, vanity![2]
Draw round my bed: is Anselm keeping back?
Nephews — sons mine . . . ah God, I know not! Well —
She, men would have to be your mother once,
Old Gandolf envied me, so fair she was!
What's done is done, and she is dead beside,
Dead long ago, and I am Bishop since,
And as she died so must we die ourselves,
And thence ye may perceive the world's a dream.
Life, how and what is it? As here I lie
In this state-chamber, dying by degrees,
Hours and long hours in the dead night, I ask
"Do I live, am I dead?" Peace, peace seems all.
Saint Praxed's ever was the church for peace;
And so, about this tomb of mine. I fought
With tooth and nail to save my niche, ye know:
— Old Gandolf cozened me, despite my care;
Shrewd was that snatch from out the corner South
He graced his carrion with, God curse the same!
Yet still my niche is not so cramped but thence
One sees the pulpit o' the epistle-side,
And somewhat of the choir, those silent seats,
And up into the aery dome where live
The angels, and a sunbeam's sure to lurk:
And I shall fill my slab of basalt there,

---

[1] The church in Rome was named after St. Praxed, or Praxedes, a Christian
virgin and saint of the first century who gave her wealth to the poor and to the
persecuted Christians.
[2] *Ecclesiastes*, i, 2.

And 'neath my tabernacle take my rest,
With those nine columns round me, two and two,
The odd one at my feet where Anselm stands:
Peach-blossom marble all, the rare, the ripe
As fresh-poured red wine of a mighty pulse.
— Old Gandolf with his paltry onion-stone,[3]
Put me where I may look at him! True peach,
Rosy and flawless: how I earned the prize!
Draw close: that conflagration of my church
— What then? So much was saved if aught were missed!
My sons, ye would not be my death? Go dig
The white-grape vineyard where the oil-press stood,
Drop water gently till the surface sink,
And if ye find . . . Ah God, I know not, I! . . .
Bedded in store of rotten fig-leaves soft,
And corded up in a tight olive-frail,[4]
Some lump, ah God, of *lapis lazuli*,
Big as a Jew's head cut off at the nape,
Blue as a vein o'er the Madonna's breast . . .
Sons, all have I bequeathed you, villas, all,
That brave Frascati villa with its bath,
So, let the blue lump poise between my knees,
Like God the Father's globe on both His hands
Ye worship in the Jesu Church[5] so gay,
For Gandolf shall not choose but see and burst!
Swift as a weaver's shuttle fleet our years:[6]
Man goeth to the grave, and where is he?
Did I say basalt for my slab, sons? Black —
'Twas ever antique-black I meant! How else
Shall ye contrast my frieze to come beneath?
The bas-relief in bronze ye promised me,
Those Pans and Nymphs ye wot of, and perchance
Some tripod,[7] thyrsus,[8] with a vase or so,
The Saviour at his sermon on the mount,
Saint Praxed in a glory, and one Pan
Ready to twitch the Nymph's last garment off,

---

[3] An inferior marble, subject to splitting.
[4] A basket for olives.
[5] Il Gesu, the Jesuit church in Rome.
[6] *Job*, vii, 6.
[7] The three-legged stool used by the priestess of Apollo.
[8] A staff used by Bacchus' followers.

And Moses with the tables . . . but I know
Ye mark me not! What do they whisper thee,
Child of my bowels, Anselm? Ah, ye hope
To revel down my villas while I gasp
Bricked o'er with beggar's mouldy travertine[9]
Which Gandolf from his tomb-top chuckles at!
Nay, boys, ye love me — all of jasper, then!
'Tis jasper ye stand pledged to, lest I grieve.
My bath must needs be left behind, alas!
One block, pure green as a pistachio-nut,
There's plenty jasper somewhere in the world —
And have I not Saint Praxed's ear to pray
Horses for ye, and brown Greek manuscripts,
And mistresses with great smooth marbly limbs?
— That's if ye carve my epitaph aright,
Choice Latin, picked phrase, Tully's[10] every word,
No gaudy ware like Gandolf's second line —
Tully, my masters? Ulpian serves his need!
And then how I shall lie through centuries,
And hear the blessed mutter of the mass,
And see God made and eaten all day long,
And feel the steady candle-flame, and taste
Good strong thick stupefying incense-smoke!
For as I lie here, hours of the dead night,
Dying in state and by such slow degrees,
I fold my arms as if they clasped a crook,
And stretch my feet forth straight as stone can point,
And let the bedclothes, for a mortcloth, drop
Into great laps and folds of sculptor's-work:
And as yon tapers dwindle, and strange thoughts
Grow, with a certain humming in my ears,
About the life before I lived this life,
And this life too, popes, cardinals and priests,
Saint Praxed at his sermon on the mount,
Your tall pale mother with her talking eyes,
And new-found agate urns as fresh as day,
And marble's language, Latin pure, discreet,
— Aha, ELUCESCEBAT[11] quoth our friend?
No Tully, said I, Ulpian at the best!

[9] A cheap white limestone.
[10] Cicero's.
[11] "He was famous"; the classic form was *Elucebat*.

Evil and brief hath been my pilgrimage.
All *lapis,* all, sons! Else I give the Pope
My villas! Will ye ever eat my heart?
Ever your eyes were as a lizard's quick,
They glitter like your mother's for my soul,
Or ye would heighten my impoverished frieze,
Piece out its starved design, and fill my vase
With grapes, and add a vizor and a Term,[12]
And to the tripod ye would tie a lynx
That in his struggle throws the thyrsus down,
To comfort me on my entablature
Whereon I am to lie till I must ask
"Do I live, am I dead?" There, leave me, there!
For ye have stabbed me with ingratitude
To death — ye wish it — God, ye wish it! Stone —
Gritstone, a-crumble! Clammy squares which sweat
As if the corpse they keep were oozing through —
And no more *lapis* to delight the world!
Well, go! I bless ye. Fewer tapers there,
But in a row: and, going, turn your backs
— Ay, like departing altar-ministrants,
And leave me in my church, the church for peace,
That I may watch at leisure if he leers —
Old Gandolf, at me, from his onion-stone,
As still he envied me, so fair she was!

ROBERT BROWNING

Edward

"Why dois your brand sae drap wi bluid,
    Edward, Edward,
Why dois your brand sae drap wi bluid,
  And why sae sad gang yee O?"
"O I hae killed my hauke[13] sae guid,
    Mither, mither,
O I hae killed my hauke sae guid,
  And I had nae mair bot hee O."

[12] A type of bust and pedestal.
[13] hawk

"Your haukis bluid was nevir sae reid,
      Edward, Edward,
Your haukis bluid was nevir sae reid,
  My deir son I tell thee O."
"O I hae killed my reid-roan steid,
      Mither, mither,
O I hae killed my reid-roan steid,
  That erst was sae fair and frie O."

"Your steid was auld, and ye hae gat mair,
      Edward, Edward,
Your steid was auld, and ye hae gat mair,
  Sum other dule ye drie[14] O."
"O I hae killed my fadir deir,
      Mither, mither,
O I hae killed my fadir deir,
  Alas, and wae is mee O!"

"And whatten penance wul ye drie for that,
      Edward, Edward?
And whatten penance will ye drie for that?
  My deir son, now tell me O."
"Ile set my feit in yonder boat,
      Mither, mither,
Ile set my feit in yonder boat,
  And Ile fare ovir the sea O."

"And what wul ye doe wi your towirs and your ha,
      Edward, Edward?
And what wul ye doe wi your towirs and your ha,
  That were sae fair to see O?"
"Ile let thame stand tul they doun fa,
      Mither, mither,
Ile let thame stand tul they doun fa,
  For here nevir mair maun I bee O."

"And what wul ye leive to your bairns and your wife,
      Edward, Edward?
And what wul ye leive to your bairns and your wife,
  Whan ye gang ovir the sea O?"

[14] grief you suffer

"The warldis room, late them beg thrae life,
    Mither, mither,
The warldis room, late them beg thrae life,
    For thame nevir mair wul I see O."

"And what wul ye leive to your ain mither deir,
    Edward, Edward?
And what wul ye leive to your ain mither deir?
    My deir son, now tell me O."
"The curse of hell frae me sall ye beir,
    Mither, mither,
The curse of hell frae me sall ye beir,
    Sic counseils ye gave to me O."

ANONYMOUS

Vacation*

Rapidly, down our way from the park,
grains of darkness are filling the light.
Our daughter is skipping
the cracks on the walk;
our son, intent in his cart,
is amazed at the sight:
my wife and I, arm-in-arm swaying,
continue our talk.
    And nothing to do with life but ease it;
    nothing to do with love but link it.

Out of the shadows, rusty and black,
a grinning dog leaps,
to knit our raveled procession
until he retreats.
Then he comes, but waved back
to the dark, still he follows;
and larger by one, we depart,
all amazing our son, intent in his cart.
    And nothing to do with life but ease it;
    nothing to do with love but link it.

---

* From *Unexpected Truce* (Round Table Books, Los Altos, California: 1956). Reprinted by permission of the author.

Beside the bowl we've given,
wondering when he'll be gone,
he wags, and curls up with a yawn.
Our children in bed, our talk continues to wander,
until, speechless, we stop in wonder
at their breathing's rise and fall.
Clasping, we soar on the marvelous swing
which gently descends into dark with us all.
    And nothing to do with life but link it;
    nothing to do with love but ease it.

DON GEIGER

On My First Sonne

Farewell, thou child of my right hand, and joy;
    My sinne was too much hope of thee, lov'd boy,
Seven yeeres tho'wert lent to me, and I thee pay,
    Exacted by thy fate, on the just day.
O, could I lose all father, now. For why
    Will man lament the state he should envie?
To have so soone scap'd worlds, and fleshes rage,
    And, if no other miserie, yet age?
Rest in soft peace, and, ask'd, say, here doth lye
    Ben: Jonson his best piece of *poetrie*.
For whose sake, hence-forth, all his vowes be such,
    As what he loves may never like too much.

BEN JONSON

Devil, Maggot and Son*

(translated from the Irish)

Three things seek my death,
    Hard at my heels they run —
Hang them, sweet Christ, all three, —
    Devil, maggot and son.

So much does each of them crave
    The morsel that falls to his share,
He cares not a thrauneen what
    Falls to the other pair.

* Reprinted by permission of A. D. Peters, on behalf of the author.

If the devil, that crafty one,
   Can capture my soul in sin
He'll leave my flesh to the worm,
   My money to my kin.

My sons think more of the money
   That will come to them when I die
Than a soul that they could not spend,
   A body that none would buy.

And how would the maggots fare
   On a soul too thin to eat
And money too tough to chew?
   The maggots must have meat.

Christ, speared by the blind man,
   Christ, nailed to a naked tree,
The three that are seeking my end
   Hang them, sweet Christ, all three!

FRANK O'CONNOR

My Last Duchess

Ferrara

That's my last Duchess painted on the wall,
Looking as if she were alive. I call
That piece a wonder, now: Frà Pandolf's hands
Worked busily a day, and there she stands.
Will't please you sit and look at her? I said
"Frà Pandolf" by design, for never read
Strangers like you that pictured countenance,
The depth and passion of its earnest glance,
But to myself they turned (since none puts by
The curtain I have drawn for you, but I)
And seemed as they would ask me, if they durst,
How such a glance came there; so, not the first
Are you to turn and ask thus. Sir, 'twas not
Her husband's presence only, called that spot
Of joy into the Duchess' cheek: perhaps
Frà Pandolf chanced to say "Her mantle laps
Over my lady's wrist too much," or "Paint

Must never hope to reproduce the faint
Half-flush that dies along her throat:" such stuff
Was courtesy, she thought, and cause enough
For calling up that spot of joy. She had
A heart — how shall I say? — too soon made glad,
Too easily impressed; she liked whate'er
She looked on, and her looks went everywhere.
Sir, 'twas all one! My favour at her breast,
The dropping of the daylight in the West,
The bough of cherries some officious fool
Broke in the orchard for her, the white mule
She rode with round the terrace — all and each
Would draw from her alike the approving speech,
Or blush, at least. She thanked men, — good! but thanked
Somehow — I know not how — as if she ranked
My gift of a nine-hundred-years-old name
With anybody's gift. Who'd stoop to blame
This sort of trifling? Even had you skill
In speech — (which I have not) — to make your will
Quite clear to such an one, and say, "Just this
Or that in you disgusts me; here you miss,
Or there exceed the mark" — and if she let
Herself be lessoned so, nor plainly set
Her wits to yours, forsooth, and made excuse,
— E'en then would be some stooping; and I choose
Never to stoop. Oh sir, she smiled, no doubt,
Whene'er I passed her; but who passed without
Much the same smile? This grew; I gave commands;
Then all smiles stopped together. There she stands
As if alive. Will't please you rise? We'll meet
The company below, then. I repeat,
The Count your master's known munificence
Is ample warrant that no just pretence
Of mine for dowry will be disallowed;
Though his fair daughter's self, as I avowed
At starting, is my object. Nay, we'll go
Together down, sir! Notice Neptune, though,
Taming a sea-horse, thought a rarity,
Which Claus of Innsbruck cast in bronze for me!

ROBERT BROWNING

PART TWO

The Critical Aspects of Performance

CHAPTER FIVE

Tone

A word is not a crystal, transparent and unchanged, it is the skin of a living thought . . .
MR. JUSTICE HOLMES

The eye reader is a barbarian.
ROBERT FROST

THE WRITER AND THE READER

The word *tone* has many meanings, and in this book it is used in several ways. "Tone of voice" is a usage that has earlier appeared in this book and will occur again. In this chapter, however, (and at appropriate subsequent places) I should like to use it as a term for a much larger concept. I should like to consider tone as the total impression and meaning of a desired communication. Sometimes I will talk about the tone of a small phrase. At other times I will use the word in describing the tone reflected by a whole work, a general tone made up of many small tones. In either case I will be thinking of tone as the sum of all factors that go into the given communication: inflection, quality and tone of voice, lexical meaning and bodily gesture.

The written words "I am going downtown" are a factual statement, a simple exposition. They reflect the most impersonal kind of communicable tones short of scientific formulas. But if the words are spoken loudly, accompanied by some such gesture as beating the fist in the palm of the hand, there is a more complicated tonal situation. The same words are used, but the tone of voice and the gesture, really functioning as units of communication as much as do words, add their new meaning. We recognize the tone of anger, the enrichment of the emotional texture, and questing curiosity is brought to life; why is he angry, what has made him so? In life, gestures are thus constantly enriching and shading our tonal communication. We run on the bright beach shouting. Can words ever communicate that particular experience of joy more eloquently than our bodily gestures and our irrational cries? But how fleeting! That very evening we are at a loss to describe even to ourselves that ecstasy of air and sea and body.

Here lies at least part of the challenge, the impossible challenge, for the creative writer. His gestures are words alone. He must convey a sense of the immediacy and meaning of life by those lingual gestures, and they are standardized and abstract. He must convey the three-dimensional tone (implying the living tones of voice and body) through manipulations of the symbols and signs of a written language. Yet the loss of freshness and directness which he must accept when he exchanges the living gesture for the word gesture is not without some gain. He gains an expressive means which, if not quite eternal, is at least durable, an expressive system of gesture which can create and illustrate values in sufficiently permanent form that civilizations may be raised upon them.

Start, then, with a word. First of all, though we are not too conscious of the fact, a word must signal to the reader its *function* in the total system of signs. It must signal, for instance, whether it is a sign of a thing (a noun), a sign of an action (a verb), a sign of an attribute (an adjective), or, simply, a sign of a relationship between other signs. (A period, a comma, a semicolon, the word "and," the word "an" are all among those signs whose principle function is to point to a relationship between other signs. Such signs are essentially different from such words as "rain" or "run" which point to some thing or idea which they represent, as well as implying a function. The meaning of a comma *is its function with relation to other signs.*)

But take "(the) *gang*" as a specific example. This word is saying, "I am a naming word of the kind that names things or concepts and you must use me in your language system where such kinds of words are appropriate." Note there are many things this naming word (noun) does not tell; for instance it does not tell whether it is the-thing-named which is doing the act or whether it is the-thing-named which is being acted upon. In many languages, including Latin, the naming-words are required to signify some of these other functions. (By looking at the word *porta,* the reader knows that it is a thing-naming-word which is doing the action, whereas by looking at the word *portam* he knows that this is the naming word which is acted upon.) We usually experience a degree of shock when a word is used in such a way that it must signal a function other than its usual, conventional one. In the poem by E. E. Cummings, for instance (p. 294), the first line contains two such switches in functions. "Anyone" is normally a *pronoun* (a generalized thing-naming word used in place of a more specific thing-naming word, or *noun*). This pronoun signals that it has become a *proper noun,* naming an allegorical character. Likewise, the word "how," whose modern uses are as an adverb (a word which signals that its function is to denote manner or means, as in "How do I read this?") or as a noun (a thing-naming-word, as in "you must learn the when as well as the how"), signals that it has become an adjective (a sign used to limit or qualify a noun or other substantive). "How," in this instance, signals its new function mostly because of its *new position in the word order,* a fact which would not necessarily bear on its meaning in some languages. This is one reason why *syntax (word order)* is always a significant element to study in the comprehension of literary art as it is practiced in English.

If the first task of the oral reader is to comprehend the functional signals of words, then certainly the second task is to achieve a clear reading of the central meaning, or denotation, of the word. Thus we know that the word "gang" *designates a group, usually of people;* that it can also denote other kinds of groups, as, for instance, a gang of switches. Sometimes this problem of discovering the denotation is made somewhat difficult by the necessity to find out which of several meanings, all commonly accepted, best fits the circumstance. The word "table" has almost an automatic denotation, yet if someone says, "That motion is on the table," it is clear that the *context,* or the surrounding environment, has altered the denotation of the word.

We now come to the third of the reader's responsibilities with a written word. He must determine as accurately as he can to what area of sensibility the word's *overtones,* or *connotations,* relate and, perhaps yet more difficult, what limit the context places on those connotations. The word "gang," for instance, denotes a group, but it also has connotations in several directions. It can be used with affection, if one speaks of a circle of friends, or it might be used as carrying certain other social overtones, as with a gang of criminals. For instance, because of those criminal associations, it may be used as a term of contempt, "Hitler and his gang." Denotation, then, and even to a greater extent connotation, though in a real way fired off by the word itself, are not usually very accurately defined and delimited by the word alone, any more than a gun without a barrel can direct a fired bullet. The blank sheet presents its infinite choice, which the appearance of a word relatively restricts. But there is a long way to go from there to the creation of that subtle interplay of hundreds of denotations and connotations which one might call a fine poem or story.

To read "gang" aloud, *by itself,* is to understand its lack of tonal depth very clearly, for, without some hint as to the proper tone, one is forced to read the word in a neutral way, without color or life. The word, as a sign designating something, does not satisfy any complex expectation of communication.

And so the reader arrives at his fourth and most complex task, which is to understand the word in its *dramatic environment.* Much of what follows in subsequent chapters in this book is a systematic attempt to strengthen the reader's ability to evaluate this dramatic environment as a means of deepening his understanding. And as an essential tool in achieving this understanding I think of re-creations of the poem through the voice and body as a means of exposing relationships not firmly understood, of hearing tones not really imagined in the mind, and finally of returning to its living medium the abstraction which is committed to the page only for convenience, preservation, and distribution.

But before exposing the over-all dramatic patterns by means of which words fit together to achieve those fuller meanings of works of literary art, I should like to suggest certain constant qualities of individual words toward which the reader must always direct his awareness. Words usually have some *temporal quality;* that is, they are archaic, or contemporary standard, or very new and relatively unfamiliar. Sometimes a word may be very old, but may have changed its meaning and still be in use, like the word *suffer* which will appear later in a poem. Sometimes words have histories which are in themselves interesting and which serve to sensitize us to the modern usages. For instance, the word *mob* comes from the Latin word *mobile,* which meant "easily moved, fickle." In addition to this temporal quality, a word usually may be placed somewhere on a scale from the totally abstract ("thinking" "soul") to the totally concrete ("running" "rock"). The sentence "God moves in a mysterious way his wonders to perform" is all abstraction, while "Give us each day our daily bread" is, curiously, more figurative, yet more concrete. The source of words sometimes has a bearing on this matter of the degree of concreteness of a word. When the French-speaking Normans conquered England, they left the native Anglo-Saxon language to be carried on by the lower classes. As a result, our common everyday articles and actions still have Anglo-Saxon words, whereas our more elevated or less common actions have Latinate words, or words from yet other languages. It is no accident, for instance, that "Give us each day our daily bread," which is simple and concrete, consists entirely of words from the Anglo-Saxon, whereas in the other quote *moves* and *perform* and *mysterious* derive, ultimately, from Latin.

In addition to a word's *temporal quality* and its *degree of concreteness,* many words are at home on some *level of language.* Though words like *the, and,* and *above* are spoken by everybody in every situation, by no means would the technical word *legatee* be used commonly nor would *sweat* be used by someone who was trying to be genteel. We can often tell a person's age, or profession, or class, or education, by his use of certain words. Thus, *elegant* is a word used by women of good taste and education, but *just elegant* is a phrase used only by school girls, or the naive or uneducated. A word may be technical, slang, vulgar, common, learned, professional, or colloquial, or it may have usages in two or more of these. Thus the word *gang* may be slang, "a gang of guys," or technical, "a gang plow."

If we are sufficiently aware of the individual qualities of the word, of its function (grammatical), of its possible denotations and its possible connotations, of its temporal qualities, its degree of concreteness, and its possible level of usage, then we are ready to see how the word functions in its environment. Until we know who is speaking, who is being addressed, and under what conditions, we cannot know that the connotations selected by the author, and their attendant tones, are congruous with the over-all tone or meaning of the poem.

"The gang wanted to give Oedipus Rex a going away present." In this usage of *gang* the reader is faced with an incongruity in the denotation of the words. It would be congruous to say, "The gang wanted to give the boss a going-away present," because the overtones, or connotations, are all those of a modern office or business, where the personal relationships are of a friendly, informal quality. But Oedipus Rex was a Greek king who, unbeknown to himself, murdered his father (the former king) then married his mother, and sired his own siblings. Upon the discovery of these things he put out his eyes and exiled himself from his city in order to free it from the plague visited on it as a result of his crimes. The working out in meaningful language of this incongruity between, on the one hand, the trivial tone of the words connected with a trivial modern business custom, and, on the other, the myth and Sophoclean drama with their tale of enormous suffering and final exile is the key to the discovery of the technique and meaning of the poem. And this meaning must be resolved as a *living voice*, a Persona, a fictive character who could logically speak all the words in this poem in the order and circumstance of their occurrence.

Oedipus*

The gang wanted to give Oedipus Rex a going away present.
He had been a good hard-working father and king.
And besides it is the custom in this country
To give gifts on departure.

But we didn't know what to give Oedipus; he had everything.
Even in his loss, he had more than average.
So we gave him a travelling case, fitted, which we personally
Should have liked to receive.

JOSEPHINE MILES

So it is that such words as congruity, precision, brevity, all key terms in judging the value of the use of a word and of a literary work, seldom aid in real insight if used too simplemindedly. What at first appears verbose may really be economical; what first appears incongruous may in the end prove the essence of congruity. A great poem is largely lost if the reader is inadequate. Reading fine literature well is a process of skilful, intelligent participation. Literature is for those who are prepared for a strenuous interplay with the spirits of great humans, *and the comprehension of its tone, in the detail and in the whole, is the final proof that the reader has the full, living grasp of the poem or story.*

This final task for the reader, this energetic reconstruction of the community of words that is a poem or story, requires more imagination and good taste than the other tasks, for it is more elusive. Dictionaries

* Reprinted by permission of the Indiana University Press.

will not help, only the real grasp of a living language yields this three-dimensional vision. In English a great deal of meaning is carried by the emphasis, pacing, and melodic pattern of the voice. If a young lady says to a young man, "No-o-o, I'm not going to go with you," we realize that for some reason she is reluctant. But if she says, "No, I'm not going with YOU," then we know a bit more about the source of her reluctance. We further imagine that the first is said slowly to emphasize the doubt. The second could be said either slowly or rapidly, depending on the quality of the dislike expressed, and this we could only determine from a fuller context. I have recently read a most interesting example of criticism in which the *tone of voice* becomes crucial. In a symposium[1] edited by Mr. Anthony Ostroff, three poet-critics write a criticism of Theodore Roethke's poem, "In a Dark Time" (p. 453) and Mr. Roethke concludes with a comment from the author's point of view. Two of these critics comment on the *tone* of the third line in stanza IV as being crucial. Babette Deutsch says of it: "The fight for identity is sharpened as the poem proceeds. In this last stanza it takes shape in the shrilling cry, 'Which I is *I?*' But relief comes at the close: . . . " On the other hand Stanley Kunitz says, "Roethke succeeds, for me, in effecting this illusion through three complete stanzas of mounting intensity and almost halfway through the fourth, where I stumble on his rhetorical question. The fussy grammar of 'Which I is *I?*' is only a part of the trouble; I am more concerned with the clinically analytic tone, which jars on the ear that has been listening to strange music. Furthermore, I am not wholly persuaded by the final couplet, superbly turned as it is. It may be my own deficiency that leads me to resist whatever seems to smack of conventional piety, but I cannot agree that anything in the poem prepares me for so pat a resolution." To which Mr. Roethke responds in his final essay, "And this is where the turn comes. It seems to me that Mr. Kunitz ignores the intensity of the identification with the fly: Am I this many-eyed, mad filthy thing, or am I human? 'Which I is *I?*' The cry comes shrilly, says Miss Deutsch. I am with her in this. If this is not understood, the poem does indeed falter."

It is not for me to make any final judgment as to the critical question. I should merely like to point out that a *tone of voice,* an *oral dimension,* becomes critical at the crucial moment of the poem, and the poet himself says that if this tone is not really there, or if it is not comprehended by the reader, the whole ending of the poem will not be accurately comprehended. The reader is required to engage in this kind of imaginative reconstruction, in this kind of filling out of the skeletal meaning to a comprehension of the full meaning, using the nuances of the common history,

---

[1] Anthony Ostroff, ed., *The Contemporary Poet As Artist And Critic,* Little, Brown and Co., 1964, p. 36.

personal relationships and attitudes which we share with the poet, (being human and of the same culture).

And now perhaps we are ready to begin a survey of those larger elements governing the tonal usage of words.

THE INSUFFICIENCY OF MOOD OR THEME

Some readers seek mood in a story or poem: is it happy, mysterious, somber? Others read works of literature to find themes, messages, "truths" (usually "truths" that confirm their own limited view of existence). Neither of these approaches is rewarding to the mature reader. Only the cross-fertilization of incident, theme, mood, to the living whole of the *total meaning* in the mind of a perceptive, imaginative reader will accomplish the miracle of artistic communication. This is the bodied gesture, the full emotional intellectuality.

> Says Tweed to Till
> "What gars ye rin sae still?"
> Says Till to Tweed,
> "Though ye rin with speed
> And I rin slaw,
> For ae man that ye droon
> I droon twa."
>
> ANONYMOUS

It is neither sufficient to say of this poem that its mood is argumentative, nor to say that its theme could be expressed by the old saying, "still waters run deep," though it is necessary to comprehend both facts. The tone is arrived at only when, in the reader's mind, certain other facts are assimilated. First of all, there is a dialogue. Now dialogues bring a special sort of complexity, for there are separate personalities to understand, in addition to the quality of their relationship in the story or poem. In this case, one sees from the dialect that the speakers are Scots, that furthermore they are not real people, but personifications, that is, non-human things (in this case, rivers of Scotland) imaginatively given human qualities. Immediately, then, it seems likely the the broadly human applications of this poem may take some of their particular flavor and reality from a Scots locale.

The poem begins with a rather standard, widely familiar tone; the impatient contempt of the fast-moving and quick-witted for the slow. But the ending is not conventional, for the slow river, which might have replied with boasts about its greater usefulness or its more calm beauty, chooses to prove its superiority by pointing to its destructive power, a point made so much more effective by its deceptive civility. But beyond what is said, one must *hear* the rhetorical and rhythmic structure of the poem: the short, contemptuous question, so characterizing of the first speaker, and the slower, more ponderously involved, but devastating reply. In short the very structure of the sentences reflects the character of the speakers. And if the poem conveys something of the profound skepticism bred in a tough people by a hard land, then we respond to it because all of us in some ambivalent way share this dubious view of man's and nature's mercy.

Alexander Pope wrote the following couplet for the collar of King Charles II's dog.

> I am His Highness' dog at Kew.
> Pray tell me, sir, whose dog are you?

Is it enough to be able to say that this poem's theme is "all men have their masters" and that the mood is one of satiric subservience? No, the fun, the liveliness, is gone. For to evaluate *satire*, to get that final qualification of its tone, we must know what is satirized and how it is satirized. The poem depends, as do all good poems, on a high degree of reader participation. There is, no doubt, a general truth about all societies in this poem, but the satire is sharpened if one knows enough history to set the scene. Kew Gardens, where the dog "says" he walks, was the promenade for the lords and ladies of the dissolute court and "Town" of Charles II's reign. In our imaginations, then, we see a nobleman, haughtily dressed in the silks and ribbons of the highborn, bending down to read the inscription on the King's dog's collar. The direct address to the "Sir," the anger of the nobleman at finding himself mocked in the poem, the inviolability of the King's dog from the nobleman's boot, all these elements are added together to give us that final totality, certainly more than the bare bones of theme and nerves of mood, which is the embodied tone of the poem.

Many tones have their basis in some kind of biological adjustment. For instance, the feelings of happiness, sadness, illness, discomfort, all seem in origin nonlingual, because they have such obvious and inevitable bodily correlations. But certain tones are primarily intellectual and, because they are less instinctive and more literary in their construction and comprehension, are more difficult to recognize. A sad person does not bounce along, smile, and talk crisply (unless he is dissembling), but what exactly is the bodily attitude which expresses paradox or irony? No doubt a dancer could execute a *series* of movements which would express these concepts, but no simple physical pose is likely to spring to the reader's mind that is very expressive. It would be well to get clearly in our minds these more conceptual, lingual, literary tones.

IRONY

There are many tones of *Irony*, but common to them all is a sense of discrepancy — always we notice a gap between what is said and what is meant, between what we see in the present and what we know of the past or future, between appearance and reality. In a line like,

> Pity all the mighty Caesars

the adjective "mighty" brings to our mind the ineffable power and grandeur of Imperial Rome, and the word "pity" prepares us in some way for, perhaps, the tragic isolation of power or for the downfall of the great. The reader's emotional reaction is all the more certain because the *epithet* is an often used one, a cliché. But the whole poem is:

> Pity all the mighty Caesars
> They pulled each whisker out with tweezers.

This verse, which appeared many years ago along the country's roads as one of the ubiquitous Burma Shave signs, says, if we will take it a little seriously, a great deal about the value and limitation of the concept of progress, a subject much considered during the last century. The technique is irony, of course. There is a great discrepancy between our expectations, as aroused by the first line, and the quality of pity, as spelled out in the last line. Note that the rhyming words "Caesars" and "tweezers" in themselves create the sharp focus of the discrepancy between the classical, the noble and the everyday, the comic. No doubt any adequate reading of this poem would take its tonal cue from the first line, reading the whole in the clichéd, noble tones evoked by that line, letting the irony illustrate itself in the discrepancy between the tone of voice and the commonplace image evoked by the last line.

> If all be true that I do think
> There are five reasons we should drink:
> Good wine, a friend, or being dry,
> Or lest we should be by and by;
> Or any other reason why.

The ironic tone of this little poem depends upon the disparity between the first two lines, so rational, so logical, and the progressive disintegration of logic through the next three lines. Another level to the irony is that the last line, with its total surrender of any pretense of rationality, is much nearer the *truth* than the first, more reasonable lines. In short, the poem is comical about the drinker's attempt at rationality, but, in a larger sense, it makes an ironic comment on the limitations of rational explanations of human behavior.

Some of the possible "other reasons why" are touched on still more powerfully in the following poem whose irony depends not only on a disintegration of an expectation, but on a contrast of irreconcilables.

> Hey nonny no!
> Men are fools that wish to die!
> Is't not fine to dance and sing
> When the bells of death do ring?
> Is't not fine to swim in wine,
> And turn upon the toe
> And sing hey nonny no,
> When the winds do blow,
> And the seas do flow?
> Hey nonny no!

In Elizabethan towns it was customary for the bells of the church to toll when someone died. Thus the dramatic situation in the poem concerns a group of people making merry as the bells of death ring. But the two events are disparate, with no relation to each other. We know this because the song (and the poem is in song-lyric form) is sung by one of the revelers, and the two juxtaposed facts are held in his mind in a kind of grim balance. The awareness of death lends the reveling a note of hysteria ("Swim in wine"), and the nervous repetitions of "Is't not fine," do not in this case convince us by their repetition, but make us rather doubt the singer, especially when we are aware that the final images are of those eternal natural manifestations, the sea and the wind. These massive images rise up in his mind, uncontrollably one imagines, to make the final "hey nonny no" ring with the tenuousness of bombast. The initial "hey nonny no," which at first reading we must unironically take in its traditional usage of leading off a song of uncomplicated revelry, is thus modified in tone through its successive repetitions.

The meaning of death to those left alive is treated in quite another way by Tolstoy in the closing paragraphs of his story "Three Deaths." It should be remembered that the final death of the story, the death of a tree, provides the climactic action to the two earlier human deaths. (See prose selection, p. 19.) In the song "Hey nonny no," the irony is felt by the survivors and serves to modify and complicate their emotional reaction.

In contrast, the death of the tree does not create a complex situation for the surviving trees but, simply, a happier one. In the struggle for survival "In the newly opened spaciousness the trees, through their motionless branches, yet more joyously revealed their beauty."

The irony, then, has shifted from the perception of the participants (as in "hey nonny no") and has become an emotional perception by a narrator totally removed from the drama being enacted. This distance of the ironic viewpoint has its effect on the tone. The irony is the very opposite of frenetic; it is, rather, calm, detached. Certainly it is tonally important that the death is that of a tree, for if trees experience this reaching out, this release, upon the death of a neighbor, aren't we led to accept this evaluation as true of humans, who are so much more various in their needs and so much more competitive?

These tones of irony have their vocal tones and their related bodily tones; otherwise when we read them silently, they could not communicate their purpose to us. It is clear that the Tolstoy passage, compared with "If all be true," would be slower, clearer, altogether more stately in vocal gesture, just as its serenity gives an altogether different, more deliberate irony than that urgent, swift, frantic irony of "Hey nonny no."

But in human relations death is not always so simple a release or triumph for the living as in the case of the trees. In the third paragraph of her novel *Sense and Sensibility*, Jane Austen almost casually begins to explore the whole wreckage of insecurity and injustice which a foolish man with too little "sense" and too much "sensibility" can leave behind. The old man, we are told, has been lovingly looked after for ten years by his nephew, his nephew's second wife, and their three daughters. These women have no significant financial resources but such as he wills to them. He chooses to entail his property through his nephew to his nephew's only other child, a son by the first marriage. This young man is already wealthy in his own right through inheritance from his mother and through a rich marriage. Austen describes the reason for this act of injustice: the child "by such attractions as are by no means unusual in children of two or three — an imperfect articulation, an earnest desire of having his own way, many cunning tricks, and a great deal of noise, — as to outweigh all the value of all the attention which for years he had received from his niece and her daughters." The irony, of course, lies in the disparity between what is deserved and what is rewarded, between the world truly and intelligently seen and the world seen through the momentary enchantments of one's sensibility. To grasp the depth of statement of this irony, however, one must understand that the whole long novel — the whole complex action of human tears, treachery, and wisdom gained through agony — is an exceedingly complex and ironic exploration of exactly this question,

"Should one live by rational judgment or by the excitement of one's momentary emotional commitments?" and that the whole series of nearly disastrous events is precipitated because one old man was foolishly enchanted by the gurgles of a child. Austen, however, is not quite through with the paragraph; and lest one miss the irony, she comments with the faintest praise that he left the girls a thousand pounds each because "he meant not to be unkind." So much for kind *intentions*.

But Austen's book returns often to ironies of kind intentions. Her theme is, "Intentions are cheap, the action is what counts." Shortly after the old man dies, the nephew also dies, not having lived long enough to provide for his daughters' dowry, without which a suitable match is most unlikely. On his deathbed he has asked his wealthy son to provide for his stepmother and half sisters, and the son, "affected by such a recommendation at such a time," promises to "do everything in his power to make them comfortable." All this is very well, but we notice no hard figures have been named; the foolish father (his temper, as we have been told, is "cheerful and sanguine,") asks merely for a general promise, and he gets what he asks for.

The second chapter, a masterpiece of ironic prose, details how fragile such general, easily given promises, often are. The son's determination to give each half sister three thousand pounds turns, in a few minutes, to an agreement with his wife that "I am convinced within myself that your father had no idea of your giving them any money at all," and in a final determination agrees, because his father left his stepmother some plate and china, that his "father thought only of *them*." And so Miss Austen completes the second turn of a convoluted pattern of ironies in her exploration of her theme. From the ironies of a disordered death and inheritance, we immediately contemplated another ironically foolish deathbed illusion, and then we turned to a thematic irony we have met before in "If all be true that I do think" — the discrepancy between the power of the human mind in rationalization and its lack of power in rationality.

In the selection from Austen we have an example of a special kind of irony called *satire*, a kind we have already met in Pope's little couplet for the dog. Satire usually concerns itself with exposing the social and characteristic vices and foibles of humankind. An interesting fact about good satire is that always, wherever it is a major element in a story or poem, there is a *satiric norm*; that is, there is a set of values of which the author approves and which the lives of people do not achieve. Thus, in *Sense and Sensibility*, Jane Austen's norm might be stated as "sensibility guided by sense." She has no cheers for either alone. Thus she is careful to point to the fact that the nephew's second wife and their daughters do not take care of the old man out of some romantic ideal of pure devotion. Their care ". . . proceeded not merely from interest, but from goodness of heart . . ." The key word here is *merely,* and the admission which it makes is vital to the establishment of the author's satiric norm. It tells us that Miss Austen is not on the one hand simpleminded enough to believe that, with a fortune involved, people's motives are likely to be unmixed. But she indicates that she knows there *is* such a thing as a good heart and that it is a very important ingredient in the evaluation of a person. However, for Miss Austen a good heart is proved only through action, as by these women's cheerful devotion over the years to the old man. The good *intentions* of the old man, of their stepfather, and of their half brother, are, in the crucial moment, no more than mere *sentimentalities,* because never effectually acted upon, and as such are examples of that human folly which is her chief object of satire throughout the novel.

We have said that the basis of all irony is a sense of discrepancy. If the discrepancy resides in the words themselves ("Caesars–tweezers"), then we have a *verbal irony.* If the discrepancy is in character or in situation, between, for instance, what the reveler in the poem insists his condition is and what we know it to be, then we have *dramatic irony.* And if we have a discrepancy between, for instance, the fact that Mr. Henry Dashwood is "rendered easy" by his son's promise to look after his half sisters and what we learn of the shallowness of that commitment, then we have a dramatic irony used for satiric purpose. But always in all irony there is the tug between what is real and what is illusion.

AMBIGUITY

Ambiguity is, in all its developments, a duality or plurality of perception. A pun is a verbal duality which may be used for quite lovely as well as quite dismaying effects. It is no accident that both Shakespeare and your neighbor, who is incapable of any verbal subtlety at all, are fond of the pun. For the truth is that nothing can be more subtle, and few things more tedious, than the perception of ambiguity, whether verbal or emotional. Well used, the verbal ambiguity can be simply a detail. Thus, when Keats addressed the Grecian Urn as "O Attic Shape! Fair attitude! with brede / Of marble men and maidens overwrought," he means both brede — a border, an embroidery — and, if we will, breed — a race of men. So the pun makes the phrase mean both an *embroidery* or *border* of marble men and women and a *race* of marble men and women. Similarly, overwrought means "wrought over," that is, a border worked onto the vase. It also means "over-excited," and on this level reminds us that the people on the vase, who are portrayed as taking part in a ceremony are in an emotionally heightened condition. Puns used so are marvelously economical means of achieving at once richness of statement and syntactic simplicity. Notice

how unobtrusive they are here, how, in a sense, it is not necessary to see
the two levels of meaning for basic communication to take place. Yet how
much more rewarding the lines are if we are aware of these possibilities.
On the other hand a pun may stand as a keystone in a poem.

> Go, lovely Rose!
> Tell her that wastes her time and me,
> That now she knows,
> When I resemble her to thee,
> How sweet, and fair, she seems to be.
>
> Tell her that's young,
> And shuns to have her graces spied,
> That hadst thou sprung
> In deserts, where no men abide,
> Thou must have uncommended died.
>
> Small is the worth
> Of beauty from the light retired:
> Bid her come forth,
> Suffer herself to be desired,
> And not blush so to be admired.
>
> Then die! that she
> The common fate of all things rare
> May read in thee:
> How small a part of time they share,
> That are so wondrous sweet, and fair!
>
> EDMUND WALLER

In this poem the word "suffer" is ambiguous. In Waller's day it carried not only our sense of "to endure hardship," but perhaps most frequently then meant simply "to permit, to allow." So Waller is saying, "Tell
her to permit herself to be desired." But he also implies, by choosing this
word, that he is aware that such an action on her part will not be easy,
will be painful, will be something to endure. Many things contribute toward making this a fine poem, but the poem's poignancy, its depth of
humanity, spreads outward from this pun, wherein the poet delicately
makes clear his awareness of the price of what he asks and of his care for
her. In a poem deliberately conventional in its artifice, it is this word more
than any other that strikes the deeper resonances of reality.

Paradox is a particular kind of ambiguity presenting two apparently
impossibly conflicting possibilities which are yet somehow resolved. The
purposes of a paradox is usually to force us to synthesize the problem on a
higher level of experience. Thus the mystical paradox that one must lose

one's life to gain it can only be resolved if one defines "life" in two ways at the same time. Thus, W. H. Auden ends his poem "In Memory of W. B. Yeats,"

> In the deserts of the heart
> Let the healing fountain start,
> In the prison of his days
> Teach the free man how to praise.

The gift he asks of the great poet is described in two paradoxes, a fountain in a desert and freedom in a prison. The paradoxes force us to face the difficulty of the task, force us to face the intransigence of the will, its resistance to its own salvation.

But such purely lingual aspects of ambiguity are probably less important than those massive ambiguities of the human situation that are so often a part of the larger insights with which great writers concern themselves. In this same poem of W. H. Auden's, for instance, the many details of ambiguity are probably gathered around a central one which is emphasized by the date, given as a subtitle, January, 1939, and the fact that the constantly recurring images of the poem (airports, parks, public statues, squares, suburbs) are images of urban life. For in fact, Auden is writing not only of the death of the great poet, but also of the death of a civilization, of the death of peace, and of the death of trust and love; and the interweaving ambiguous relationship of all these deaths makes up the stuff of the poem.

In his story *Eveline,* James Joyce has made an emotional ambiguity the central crisis of his story. Eveline is a young girl left by her dead mother to work in a store all day and to look after a bullying father and two younger children. Clearly she has been thrust into a responsibility which is beyond her years, not of her making, and deadly to her. Now, with the children grown up, she has fallen in love with Frank, a "kind, open-hearted" young sailor, who wants to take her to Buenos Aires, "where he had a home waiting for her." It appears impossible that the freer, greener prospect that opens before her should not triumph. But the negative, deathly gesture has powerful allies too, in this case her promise to the dead, her guilt, her sense of duty. But where does duty lie? With the dead or with the living? She is at the dock with Frank. The ship is there, they are pressed by the mob of travelers, Frank says something to her, the crowd moves him on. She grips the iron railing, torn between her duty to the past and the call of the future, between the certainty of the known dead and the wide venture of living. The ambiguity is too great for her to bear, and "all the seas of the world tumbled about her heart." Her nature is split in the dual and equal strife, her emotional center is drowned in the ambiguity of her feelings. Her humanity dies in the chaos of the struggle with "a cry of anguish," and when Frank, beyond the iron barrier, looks back at her, he sees only a face in which conflict has killed any "sign of love or farewell or recognition."

PREPARATION FOR PERFORMANCE – "The Windhover"

Gerard Manley Hopkins' lyric "The Windhover" (p. 233) will be examined at the conclusion of each appropriate chapter in Part II. This device will permit the student to observe how the oral elements of one work of art reveal, and are revealed by, each particular critical insight, and how this mutual revelation will affect the whole performance. Such connections from the page to the speaker can seldom be made too explicit in literal vocal or bodily gesture. A gesture that would be effective in a certain spot for a tall man might look ludicrous if used by a short woman. Similar limitations arise out of difference in vocal quality between individuals. The attempt will be, rather, to see what tones and attitudes are implicit in the work and in what direction the revealing gestures lie.

There is of necessity a disquieting, piecemeal quality about these brief forays into a most moving lyric. However, the tutorial aid to the student will, I trust, somewhat offset an otherwise distressing departure from the basic truth that one should try to see the whole poem. The last chapter in the book, in any case, consists of just such a whole approach to a narrative poem and to a short story.

Tone

Thematically the poem is a plea for Christ to make the sacrifice necessary to take possession of the speaker's heart, and the general mood is one of exaltation achieved through intense visual excitement. However, the specific modifications of this theme and of this general mood are all-important and will be exposed as the details of the poem are discussed.

As one tries to bring the poem alive in one's vision, an important aesthetic problem immediately emerges; namely, the long and complicated sentence which takes the first seven and one-half lines of the poem. The sentence starts with three exactly parallel object phrases.

> morning's *minion*
> kingdom of daylight's *dauphin*
> dapple-dawn-drawn *Falcon*

That is to say, each of the three italicized words is another way of naming the object of the main clause of this long sentence. Though a full discussion of the implications for the oral reader of these specific words must await the chapter on figurative language, it should be clear at a glance that the words are not simply equal, but constitute the creation of the first minor climax of the poem. The suspense, which has been sustained through the figurative epithets, is used to heighten the portentousness of the naming of the Falcon. It may aid vocal realization to suggest that this sequence of phrases partakes to some degree of the heralding of an arriving prince, but with intensely personal, rather than general and public, titles and honorifics. In any case, the climactic structure of these two lines makes an initial oral demand which cannot be ignored.

At the very end of the second line and on through the third begins the description of the Falcon's condition when the speaker "caught" him. The remainder of the long sentence modifies what the Falcon did "in his riding" and provides the gross clue for the vocal patterns. The end of the long sentence marks a moving back in perspective in order to include the poet's heart in the picture of the bird's flight, as the poet describes the immediate effect on himself and summarizes what it was of the Falcon that so moved him. This summary completes the direct experience of the soaring Falcon, and the reader comes to the turning point of the poem. This turning point, as will be seen at the appropriate times, is marked in many ways. But not the least important is the change in the frequency of verbs. In a poem fourteen lines in length (a sonnet) one discovers, either as predicate or in such variations as the gerund and the participle, twenty uses of verbs. Of these, fourteen are in the first eight lines, and only six are in the final six lines. The more frequent usage is no doubt accounted for by the necessity to describe the flight scene vividly. The oral reader must therefore expect to realize a greater sense of motion in the octet.

Beyond the fact of the *frequency* of the verbs, it should be noted that all but three are (in their infinitive form) one-syllable words and that the three exceptions are but two-syllable words. Some of these one-syllable verbs, in the form used here (participial), are of two syllables. But none of the verbs as they appear in the poem are more than two syllables in length. Further, all but a few are Anglo-Saxon in origin and retain the direct, concrete impact of most words from that original source. This is part of the poem's straightforward emotion. Certain words are ambiguous, but these ambiguities are not used for purposes of irony or satire. The oral reader, then, is free to follow both the Falcon and the excitement of the speaker's stirring heart without those long pauses and edges of tones usually used to convey the innuendos of irony. Such interpretative devices would in any case be inappropriate since the poem contains elements of an appeal — a prayer — to Christ. All these broad emotional elements indicate that the speaker's body is intensely alert, with a general sense of release from constraint and retreat which is part and parcel with the recurrence of exclamation marks. Yet this excitement and release, for reasons that will be clear later, are expressed with minimal gesture and are complicated by other attitudes which will have their subtle effect on the body's gesture.

SELECTIONS

Petrified Man*

EUDORA WELTY

"Reach in my purse and git me a cigarette without no powder in it if you kin, Mrs. Fletcher, honey," said Leota to her ten o'clock shampoo-and-set customer. "I don't like no perfumed cigarettes."

Mrs. Fletcher gladly reached over to the lavender shelf under the lavender-framed mirror, shook a hair net loose from the clasp of the patent-leather bag, and slapped her hand down quickly on a powder puff which burst out when the purse was opened.

"Why, look at the peanuts, Leota!" said Mrs. Fletcher in her marveling voice.

"Honey, them goobers has been in my purse a week if they's been in it a day. Mrs. Pike bought them peanuts."

"Who's Mrs. Pike?" asked Mrs. Fletcher, settling back. Hidden in this den of curling fluid and henna packs, separated by a lavender swing door from the other customers, who were being gratified in other booths, she could give her curiosity its freedom. She looked expectantly at the black part in Leota's yellow curls as she bent to light the cigarette.

"Mrs. Pike is this lady from New Orleans," said Leota, puffing, and pressing into Mrs. Fletcher's scalp with strong red-nailed fingers. "A friend, not a customer. You see, like maybe I told you last time, me and Fred and Sal and Joe all had us a fuss, so Sal and Joe up and moved out, so we didn't do a thing but rent out their room. So we rented it to Mrs. Pike. And Mr. Pike." She flicked an ash into the basket of dirty towels. "Mrs. Pike is a very decided blonde. She bought me the peanuts."

"She must be cute," said Mrs. Fletcher.

"Honey, 'cute' ain't the word for what she is. I'm tellin' you, Mrs. Pike is attractive. She has her a good time. She's got a sharp eye out, Mrs. Pike has."

She dashed the comb through the air, and paused dramatically as a cloud of Mrs. Fletcher's hennaed hair floated out of the lavender teeth like a small storm cloud.

"Hair fallin'."

"Ah, Leota."

"Uh-huh, commencin' to fall out," said Leota, combing again, and letting fall another cloud.

"Is it any dandruff in it?" Mrs. Fletcher was frowning, her hair-line eyebrows diving down toward her nose, and her wrinkled, beady-lashed eyelids batting with concentration.

"Nope." She combed again. "Just fallin' out."

"Bet it was that last perm'nent you gave me that did it," Mrs. Fletcher said cruelly. "Remember you cooked me fourteen minutes."

"You had fourteen minutes comin' to you," said Leota with finality.

"Bound to be somethin'," persisted Mrs. Fletcher. "Dandruff, dandruff. I couldn't of caught a thing like that from Mr. Fletcher, could I?"

"Well," Leota answered at last, "you know what I heard in here yestiddy, one of Thelma's ladies was settin' over yonder in Thelma's booth gittin' a machineless, and I don't mean to insist or insinuate or anything, Mrs. Fletcher, but Thelma's lady just happ'med to throw out — I forgotten what she was talkin' about at the time — that you was p-r-e-g., and lots of times that'll make your hair do awful funny, fall out and God knows what all. It just ain't our fault, is the way I look at it."

There was a pause. The women stared at each other in the mirror.

"Who was it?" demanded Mrs. Fletcher.

"Honey, I really couldn't say," said Leota. "Not that you look it."

"Where's Thelma? I'll get it out of her," said Mrs. Fletcher.

"Now, honey, I wouldn't go and git mad over a little thing like that," Leota said, combing hastily, as though to hold Mrs. Fletcher down by the hair. "I'm sure it was somebody didn't mean no harm in the world. How far gone are you?"

"Just wait," said Mrs. Fletcher, and shrieked for Thelma, who came in and took a drag from Leota's cigarette.

"Thelma, honey, throw your mind back to yestiddy if you kin," said Leota, drenching Mrs. Fletcher's hair with a thick fluid and catching the overflow in a cold wet towel at her neck.

"Well, I got my lady half wound for a spiral," said Thelma doubtfully.

"This won't take but a minute," said Leota. "Who is it you got in there, old Horse Face? Just cast your mind back and try to remember who your lady was yestiddy who happ'm to mention that my customer was pregnant, that's all. She's dead to know."

Thelma drooped her blood-red lips and looked over Mrs. Fletcher's head into the mirror. "Why, honey, I ain't got the faintest," she breathed. "I really don't recollect the faintest. But I'm sure she meant no harm. I declare, I forgot my hair finally got combed and thought it was a stranger behind me."

"Was it that Mrs. Hutchinson?" Mrs. Fletcher was tensely polite.

"Mrs. Hutchinson? Oh, Mrs. Hutchinson." Thelma batted her eyes.

"Naw, precious, she come on Thursday and didn't ev'm mention your name. I doubt if she ev'm knows you're on the way."

"Thelma!" cried Leota staunchly.

"All I know is, whoever it is 'll be sorry some day. Why, I just barely knew it myself!" cried Mrs. Fletcher. "Just let her wait!"

"Why? What're you gonna do to her?"

It was a child's voice, and the women looked down. A little boy was making tents with aluminum wave pinchers on the floor under the sink.

"Billy Boy, hon, mustn't bother nice ladies," Leota smiled. She slapped him brightly and behind her back waved Thelma out of the booth. "Ain't Billy Boy a sight? Only three years old and already just nuts about the beauty-parlor business."

"I never saw him here before," said Mrs. Fletcher, still unmollified.

"He ain't been here before, that's how come," said Leota. "He belongs to Mrs. Pike. She got her a job but it was Fay's Millinery. He oughtn't to try on those ladies' hats, they come down over his eyes like I don't know what. They just git to look ridiculous, that's what, an' of course he's gonna put 'em on: hats. They tole Mrs. Pike they didn't appreciate him hangin' around there. Here, he couldn't hurt a thing."

"Well! I don't like children that much," said Mrs. Fletcher.

"Well!" said Leota moodily.

"Well! I'm almost tempted not to have this one," said Mrs. Fletcher. "That Mrs. Hutchinson! Just looks straight through you when she sees you on the street and then spits at you behind your back."

"Mr. Fletcher would beat you on the head if you didn't have it now," said Leota reasonably. "After going this far."

Mrs. Fletcher sat up straight. "Mr. Fletcher can't do a thing with me."

"He can't!" Leota winked at herself in the mirror.

"No siree, he can't. If he so much as raises his voice against me, he knows good and well I'll have one of my sick headaches, and then I'm just not fit to live with. And if I really look that pregnant already — "

"Well, now, honey, I just want you to know — I habm't told any of my ladies and I ain't goin' to tell 'em — even that you're losin' your hair. You just get you one of those Stork-a-Lure dresses and stop worryin'. What people don't know don't hurt nobody, as Mrs. Pike says."

"Did you tell Mrs. Pike?" asked Mrs. Fletcher sulkily.

"Well, Mrs. Fletcher, look, you ain't ever goin' to lay eyes on Mrs. Pike or her lay eyes on you, so what diffunce does it make in the long run?"

"I knew it!" Mrs. Fletcher deliberately nodded her head so as to destroy a ringlet Leota was working on behind her ear. "Mrs. Pike!"

Leota sighed. "I reckon I might as well tell you. It wasn't any more Thelma's lady tole me you was pregnant than a bat."

"Not Mrs. Hutchinson?"

"Naw, Lord! It was Mrs. Pike."

"Mrs. Pike!" Mrs. Fletcher could only sputter and let curling fluid roll into her ear. "How could Mrs. Pike possibly know I was pregnant or otherwise, when she doesn't even know me? The nerve of some people!"

"Well, here's how it was. Remember Sunday?"

"Yes," said Mrs. Fletcher.

"Sunday, Mrs. Pike an' me was all by ourself. Mr. Pike and Fred had gone over to Eagle Lake, sayin' they was goin' to catch 'em some fish, but they didn't, a course. So we was settin' in Mrs. Pike's car, it's a 1939 Dodge — "

"1939, eh," said Mrs. Fletcher.

" — An' we was gettin' us a Jax beer apiece — that's the beer that Mrs. Pike says is made right in N.O., so she won't drink no other kind. So I seen you drive up to the drugstore an' run in for just a secont, leavin' I reckon Mr. Fletcher in the car, an' come runnin' out with looked like a perscription. So I says to Mrs. Pike, just to be makin' talk, 'Right yonder's Mrs. Fletcher, and I reckon that's Mr. Fletcher — she's one of my regular customers,' I says."

"I had on a figured print," said Mrs. Fletcher tentatively.

"You sure did," agreed Leota. "So Mrs. Pike, she give you a good look — she's very observant, a good judge of character, cute as a minute, you know — and she says, 'I bet you another Jax that lady's three months on the way.' "

"What gall!" said Mrs. Fletcher. "Mrs. Pike!"

"Mrs. Pike ain't goin' to bite you," said Leota. "Mrs. Pike is a lovely girl, you'd be crazy about her, Mrs. Fletcher. But she can't sit still a minute. We went to the travelin' freak show yestiddy after work. I got through early — nine o'clock. In the vacant store next door? What, you ain't been?"

"No, I despise freaks," declared Mrs. Fletcher.

"Aw. Well, honey, talkin' about bein' pregnant an' all, you ought to see those twins in a bottle, you really owe it to yourself."

"What twins?" asked Mrs. Fletcher out of the side of her mouth.

"Well, honey, they got these two twins in a bottle, see? Born joined plumb together — dead a course." Leota dropped her voice into a soft lyrical hum. "They was about this long — pardon — must of been full time, all right, wouldn't you say? — an' they had these two heads an' two faces an' four arms an' four legs, all kind of joined here. See, this face looked this-a-way, and the other face looked that-a-way, over their shoulder, see. Kinda pathetic."

"Glah!" said Mrs. Fletcher disapprovingly.

"Well, ugly? Honey, I mean to tell you — their parents was first cousins and all like that. Billy Boy, git me a fresh towel from off Teeny's stack — this 'n's wringin' wet—an' quit ticklin' my ankles with that curler. I declare! He don't miss nothin'."

"Me and Mr. Fletcher aren't one speck of kin, or he could never of had me," said Mrs. Fletcher placidly.

"O course not!" protested Leota. "Neither is me an' Fred, not that we know of. Well, honey, what Mrs. Pike liked was the pygmies. They've got these pygmies down there, too, an' Mrs. Pike was just wild about 'em. You know, the tee-niniest men in the universe? Well honey, they can just rest back on their little bohunkus an' roll around an' you can't hardly tell if they're sittin' or standin'. That'll give you some idea. They're about forty-two years old. Just suppose it was your husband!"

"Well, Mr. Fletcher is five foot nine and one half," said Mrs. Fletcher quickly.

"Fred's five foot ten," said Leota, "but I tell him he's still a shrimp, account of I'm so tall." She made a deep wave over Mrs. Fletcher's other temple with the comb. "Well, these pygmies are a kind of a dark brown, Mrs. Fletcher. Not bad lookin' for what they are, you know."

"I wouldn't care for them," said Mrs. Fletcher. "What does that Mrs. Pike see in them?"

"Aw, I don't know," said Leota. "She's just cute, that's all. But they got this man, this petrified man, that ever' thing ever since he was nine years old, when it goes through his digestion, see, somehow Mrs. Pike says it goes to his joints and has been turning to stone."

"How awful!" said Mrs. Fletcher.

"He's forty-two too. That looks like a bad age."

"Who said so, that Mrs. Pike? I bet she's forty-two," said Mrs. Fletcher.

"Naw," said Leota, "Mrs. Pike's thirty-three, born in January, an Aquarian. He could move his head — like this. A course his head and mind ain't a joint, so to speak, and I guess his stomach ain't, either — not yet anyways. But see — his food, he eats it, and it goes down, see, and then he digests it" — Leota rose on her toes for an instant — "and it goes out to his joints and before you can say 'Jack Robinson,' it's stone — pure stone. He's turning to stone. How'd you like to be married to a guy like that? All he can do, he can move his head just a quarter of an inch. A course he looks just terrible."

"I should think he would," said Mrs. Fletcher frostily. "Mr. Fletcher takes bending exercises every night of the world. I make him."

"All Fred does is lay around the house like a rug. I wouldn't be surprised if he woke up some day and couldn't move. The petrified man just sat there moving his quarter of an inch though," said Leota reminiscently.

"Did Mrs. Pike like the petrified man?" asked Mrs. Fletcher.

"Not as much as she did the others," said Leota deprecatingly. "And then she likes a man to be a good dresser, and all that."

"Is Mr. Pike a good dresser?" asked Mrs. Fletcher skeptically.

"Oh, well, yeah," said Leota, "but he's twelve- fourteen years older 'n her. She ast Lady Evangeline about him."

"Who's Lady Evangeline?" asked Mrs. Fletcher.

"Well, it's this mind reader they got in the freak show," said Leota. "Was real good. Lady Evangeline is her name, and if I had another dollar I wouldn't do a thing but have my other palm read. She had what Mrs. Pike said was the 'sixth mind' but she had the worst manicure I ever saw on a living person."

"What did she tell Mrs. Pike?" asked Mrs. Fletcher.

"She told her Mr. Pike was as true to her as he could be and besides, would come into some money."

"Humph!" said Mrs. Fletcher. "What does he do?"

"I can't tell," said Leota, "because he don't work. Lady Evangeline didn't tell me near enough about my nature or anything. And I would like to go back and find out some more about this boy. Used to go with this boy got married to this girl. Oh, shoot, that was about three and a half years ago, when you was still goin' to the Robert E. Lee Beauty Shop in Jackson. He married her for her money. Another fortune teller tole me that at the time. So I'm not in love with him any more, anyway, besides being married to Fred, but Mrs. Pike thought, just for the hell of it, see, to ask Lady Evangeline was he happy."

"Does Mrs. Pike know everything about you already?" asked Mrs. Fletcher unbelievingly. "Mercy!"

"Oh yeah, I tole her ever'thing about ever'thing, from now on back to I don't know when — to when I first started goin' out," said Leota. "So I ast Lady Evangeline for one of my questions, was he happily married, and she says, just like she was glad I ask her, 'Honey,' she says, 'naw, he idn't. You write down this day, March 8, 1941,' she says, 'and mock it down: three years from today him and her won't be occupyin' the same bed.' There it is, up on the wall with them other dates — see, Mrs. Fletcher? And she says, 'Child, you ought to be glad you didn't git him, because he's so mercenary.' So I'm glad I married Fred. He sure ain't mercenary, money don't mean a thing to him. But I sure would like to go back and have my other palm read."

"Did Mrs. Pike believe in what the fortune teller said?" asked Mrs. Fletcher in a superior tone of voice.

"Lord, yes, she's from New Orleans. Ever'body in New Orleans believes ever'thing spooky. One of 'em in New Orleans before it was raided says to Mrs. Pike one summer she was goin' to go from state to state and meet some gray-headed men, and, sure enough, she says she went on a beautician convention up to Chicago . . ."

"Oh!" said Mrs. Fletcher. "Oh, is Mrs. Pike a beautician too?"

"Sure she is," protested Leota. "She's a beautician. I'm goin' to git her in here if I can. Before she married. But it don't leave you. She says sure enough, there was three men who was a very large part of making her trip what it was, and they all three had gray in their hair and they went in six states. Got Christmas cards from 'em. Billy Boy, go see if Thelma's got any dry cotton. Look how Mrs. Fletcher's a-drippin'."

"Where did Mrs. Pike meet Mr. Pike?" asked Mrs. Fletcher primly.

"On another train," said Leota.

"I met Mr. Fletcher, or rather he met me, in a rental library," said Mrs. Fletcher with dignity, as she watched the net come down over her head.

"Honey, me an' Fred, we met in a rumble seat eight months ago and we was practically on what you might call the way to the altar inside of a half an hour," said Leota in a guttural voice, and bit a bobby pin open. "Course it don't last. Mrs. Pike says nothin' like that ever lasts."

"Mr. Fletcher and myself are as much in love as the day we married," said Mrs. Fletcher belligerently as Leota stuffed cotton into her ears.

"Mrs. Pike says it don't last," repeated Leota in a louder voice. "Now go git under the dryer. You can turn yourself on, can't you? I'll be back to comb you out. Durin' lunch I promised to give Mrs. Pike a facial. You know — free. Her bein' in the business, so to speak."

"I bet she needs one," said Mrs. Fletcher, letting the swing door fly back against Leota. "Oh, pardon me."

A week later, on time for her appointment, Mrs. Fletcher sank heavily into Leota's chair after first removing a drugstore rental book, called *Life Is Like That*, from the seat. She stared in a discouraged way into the mirror.

"You can tell it when I'm sitting down, all right," she said.

Leota seemed preoccupied and stood shaking out a lavender cloth. She began to pin it around Mrs. Fletcher's neck in silence.

"I said you sure can tell it when I'm sitting straight on and coming at you this way," Mrs. Fletcher said.

"Why, honey, naw you can't," said Leota gloomily. "Why, I'd never know. If somebody was to come up to me on the street and say, 'Mrs. Fletcher is pregnant!' I'd say, 'Heck, she don't look it to me.' "

"If a certain party hadn't found it out and spread it around, it wouldn't be too late even now," said Mrs. Fletcher frostily, but Leota was almost choking her with the cloth, pinning it so tight, and she couldn't speak clearly. She paddled her hands in the air until Leota wearily loosened her.

"Listen, honey, you're just a virgin compared to Mrs. Montjoy," Leota was going on, still absent-minded. She bent Mrs. Fletcher back in the chair and, sighing, tossed liquid from a teacup onto her head and dug both hands into her scalp. "You know Mrs. Montjoy — her husband's that premature-gray-headed fella?"

"She's in the Trojan Garden Club, is all I know," said Mrs. Fletcher.

"Well, honey," said Leota, but in a weary voice, "she come in here not the week before and not the day before she had her baby — she come in here the very selfsame day, I mean to tell you. Child, we was all plumb scared to death. There she was! Come for her shampoo an' set. Why, Mrs. Fletcher, in a hour an' twenty minutes she was layin' up there in the Babtist Hospital with a seb'm-pound son. It was that close a shave. I declare, if I hadn't been so tired I would of drank up a bottle of gin that night."

"What gall," said Mrs. Fletcher. "I never knew her at all well."

"See, her husband was waitin' outside in the car, and her bags was all packed an' in the back seat, an' she was all ready, 'cept she wanted her shampoo an' set. An' havin' one pain right after another. Her husband kep' comin' in here, scared-like, but couldn't do nothin' with her a course. She yelled bloody murder, too, but she always yelled her head off when I give her a perm'nent."

"She must of been crazy," said Mrs. Fletcher. "How did she look?"

"Shoot!" said Leota.

"Well, I can guess," said Mrs. Fletcher. "Awful."

"Just wanted to look pretty while she was havin' her baby, is all," said Leota airily. "Course, we was glad to give the lady what she was after — that's our motto — but I bet a hour later she wasn't payin' no mind to them little end curls. I bet she wasn't thinkin' about she ought to have on a net. It wouldn't of done her no good if she had."

"No, I don't suppose it would," said Mrs. Fletcher.

"Yeah man! She was a-yellin'. Just like when I give her her perm'nent."

"Her husband ought to make her behave. Don't it seem that way to you?" asked Mrs. Fletcher. "He ought to put his foot down."

"Ha," said Leota. "A lot he could do. Maybe some women is soft."

"Oh, you mistake me, I don't mean for her to get soft — far from it! Women have to stand up for themselves, or there's just no telling. But now you take me — I ask Mr. Fletcher's advice now and then, and he appreciates it, especially on something important, like is it time for a permanent — not that I've told him about the baby. He says, 'Why dear, go ahead!' Just ask their *advice.*"

"Huh! If I ever ast Fred's advice we'd be floatin' down the Yazoo River on a houseboat or somethin' by this time," said Leota. "I'm sick of Fred. I tole him to go over to Vicksburg."

"Is he going?" demanded Mrs. Fletcher.

"Sure. See, the fortune teller — I went back and had my other palm read, since we've got to rent the room agin — said my lover was goin' to work in Vicksburg, so I don't know who she could mean, unless she meant Fred. And Fred ain't workin' here — that much is so."

"Is he going to work in Vicksburg?" asked Mrs. Fletcher. "And —"

"Sure, Lady Evangeline said so. Said the future is going to be brighter than the present. He don't want to go, but I ain't gonna put up with nothin' like that. Lays around the house an' bulls — did bull — with that good-for-nothin' Mr. Pike. He says if he goes who'll cook, but I says I never get to eat anyway — not meals. Billy Boy, take Mrs. Grover that *Screen Secrets* and leg it."

Mrs. Fletcher heard stamping feet go out the door.

"Is that that Mrs. Pike's little boy here again?" she asked, sitting up gingerly.

"Yeah, that's still him." Leota stuck out her tongue.

Mrs. Fletcher could hardly believe her eyes. "Well! How's Mrs. Pike, your attractive new friend with the sharp eyes who spreads it around town that perfect strangers are pregnant?" she asked in a sweetened tone.

"Oh, Mizziz Pike." Leota combed Mrs. Fletcher's hair with heavy strokes.

"You act like you're tired," said Mrs. Fletcher.

"Tired? Feel like it's four o'clock in the afternoon already," said Leota. "I ain't told you the awful luck we had, me and Fred? It's the worst thing you ever heard of. Maybe *you* think Mrs. Pike's got sharp eyes. Shoot, there's a limit! Well, you know, we rented out our room to this Mr. and Mrs. Pike from New Orleans when Sal an' Joe Fentress got mad at us 'cause they drank up some home-brew we had in the closet — Sal an' Joe did. So, a week ago Sat'day Mr. and Mrs. Pike moved in. Well, I kinda fixed up the room, you know — put a sofa pillow on the couch and picked some ragged robbins and put in a vase, but they never did say they appreciated it. Anyway, then I put some old magazines on the table."

"I think that was lovely," said Mrs. Fletcher.

"Wait. So, come night 'fore last, Fred and this Mr. Pike, who Fred just took up with, was back from they said they was fishin', bein' as neither one of 'em has got a job to his name, and we was all settin' around in their room. So Mrs. Pike was settin' there, readin' a old *Startling G-Man Tales* that was mine, mind you, I'd bought it myself, and all of a sudden she jumps! — into the air — you'd 'a' thought she'd set on a spider — an' says, 'Canfield' — ain't that silly, that's Mr. Pike — 'Canfield, my God A'mighty,' she says, 'honey,' she says, 'we're rich, and you won't have to work.' Not that he turned one hand anyway. Well, me and Fred rushes over to her, and Mr. Pike, too, and there she sets, pointin' her finger at a photo in my copy of *Startling G-Man.* 'See that man?' yells Mrs. Pike. 'Remember him, Canfield?' 'Never forget a face,' says Mr. Pike. 'It's Mr. Petrie, that we stayed with him in the apartment next to ours in Toulouse Street in N.O. for six weeks. Mr. Petrie.' 'Well,' says Mrs. Pike, like she can't hold out one secont longer, 'Mr. Petrie is wanted for five hundred dollars cash, for rapin' four women in California, and I know where he is.'"

"Mercy!" said Mrs. Fletcher. "Where was he?"

At some time Leota had washed her hair and now she yanked her up by the back locks and sat her up.

"Know where he was?"

"I certainly don't," Mrs. Fletcher said. Her scalp hurt all over.

Leota flung a towel around the top of her customer's head. "Nowhere else but in that freak show! I saw him just as plain as Mrs. Pike. *He* was the petrified man!"

"Who would ever have thought that!" cried Mrs. Fletcher sympathetically.

"So Mr. Pike says, 'Well whatta you know about that,' an' he looks real hard at the photo and whistles. And she starts dancin' and singin' about their good luck. She meant our bad luck! I made a point of tellin' that fortune teller the next time I saw her. I said, 'Listen, that magazine was layin' around the house for a month, and there was five hundred dollars in it for somebody. An' there was the freak show runnin' night an' day, not two steps away from my own beauty parlor, with Mr. Petrie just settin' there waitin'. An' it had to be Mr. and Mrs. Pike, almost perfect strangers.'"

"What gall," said Mrs. Fletcher. She was only sitting there, wrapped in a turban, but she did not mind.

"Fortune tellers don't care. And Mrs. Pike, she goes around actin' like she thinks she was Mrs. God," said Leota. "So they're goin' to leave tomorrow, Mr. and Mrs. Pike. And in the meantime I got to keep that mean, bad little ole kid here, gettin' under my feet ever' minute of the day an' talkin' back too."

"Have they gotten the five hundred dollars' reward already?" asked Mrs. Fletcher.

"Well," said Leota, "at first Mr. Pike didn't want to do anything about it. Can you feature that? Said he kinda liked that ole bird and said he was real nice to 'em, lent 'em money or somethin'. But Mrs. Pike simply tole him he could just go to hell, and I can see her point. She says, 'You ain't worked a lick in six months, and here I make five hundred dollars in two seconts, and what thanks do I get for it? You go to hell, Canfield,' she says. So," Leota went on in a despondent voice, "they called up the cops and they caught the old bird, all right, right there in the freak show where I saw him with my own eyes, thinkin' he was petrified. He's the one. Did it under his real name — Mr. Petrie. Four women in California, all in the month of August. So Mrs. Pike gits five hundred dollars. And my magazine, and right next door to my beauty parlor. I cried all night, but Fred said it wasn't a bit of use and to go to sleep, because the whole thing was just a sort of coincidence — you know: can't do nothin' about it. He says it put him clean out of the notion of goin' to Vicksburg for a few days till we rent out the room agin — no tellin' who we'll git this time."

"But can you imagine anybody knowing this old man, that's raped four women?" persisted Mrs. Fletcher, and she shuddered audibly. "Did Mrs. Pike *speak* to him when she met him in the freak show?"

Leota had begun to comb Mrs. Fletcher's hair. "I says to her, I says, 'I didn't notice you fallin' on his neck when he was the petrified man — don't tell me you didn't recognize your fine friend?' And she says, 'I didn't recognize him with that white powder all over his face. He just looked familiar,' Mrs. Pike says, 'and lots of people look familiar.' But she says that ole petrified man did put her in mind of somebody. She wondered who it was! Kep' her awake, which man she'd ever knew it reminded her of. So when she seen the photo, it all come to her. Like a flash. Mr. Petrie. The way he'd turn his head and look at her when she took him in his breakfast."

"Took him in his breakfast!" shrieked Mrs. Fletcher. "Listen — don't tell me. I'd 'a' felt something."

"Four women. I guess those women didn't have the faintest notion at the time they'd be worth a hundred an' twenty-five bucks apiece someday to Mrs. Pike. We ast her how old the fella was then, an' she says he musta had one foot in the grave, at least. Can you beat it?"

"Not really petrified at all, of course," said Mrs. Fletcher meditatively. She drew herself up. "I'd 'a' felt something," she said proudly.

"Shoot! I did feel somethin'," said Leota. "I tole Fred when I got home I felt so funny. I said, 'Fred, that ole petrified man sure did leave me with a funny feelin'.' He says, 'Funny-haha or funny-peculiar?' and I says, 'Funny-peculiar.'" She pointed her comb into the air emphatically.

"I'll bet you did," said Mrs. Fletcher.

They both heard a crackling noise.

Leota screamed, "Billy Boy! What you doin' in my purse?"

"Aw, I'm just eatin' these ole stale peanuts up," said Billy Boy.

"You come here to me!" screamed Leota, recklessly flinging down the comb, which scattered a whole ash tray full of bobby pins and knocked down a row of Coca-Cola bottles. "This is the last straw!"

"I caught him! I caught him!" giggled Mrs. Fletcher. "I'll hold him on my lap. You bad, bad boy, you! I guess I better learn how to spank little old bad boys," she said.

Leota's eleven o'clock customer pushed open the swing door upon Leota paddling him heartily with the brush, while he gave angry but belittling screams which penetrated beyond the booth and filled the whole curious beauty parlor. From everywhere ladies began to gather round to watch the paddling. Billy Boy kicked both Leota and Mrs. Fletcher as hard as he could, Mrs. Fletcher with her new fixed smile.

"There, my little man!" gasped Leota. "You won't be able to set down for a week if I knew what I was doin'."

Billy Boy stomped through the group of wild-haired ladies and went out the door, but flung back the words, "If you're so smart, why ain't you rich?"

Where the Rainbow Ends*

I saw the sky descending, black and white,
Not blue, on Boston where the winters wore
The skulls to jack-o'-lanterns on the slates,
And Hunger's skin-and-bone retrievers tore
The chickadee and shrike. The thorn tree waits
Its victim and tonight
The worms will eat the deadwood to the foot
Of Ararat: the scythers, Time and Death,
Helmed locusts, move upon the tree of breath;
The wild ingrafted olive and the root

Are withered, and a winter drifts to where
The Pepperpot,[2] ironic rainbow, spans
Charles River and its scales of scorched-earth miles,
I saw my city in the Scales, the pans
Of judgment rising and descending. Piles
Of dead leaves char the air —
And I am a red arrow on this graph
Of Revelations. Every dove is sold.
The Chapel's sharp-shinned eagle shifts its hold
On Serpent-Time, the rainbow's epitaph.

* From *Lord Weary's Castle*, copyright, 1944, 1946, by Robert Lowell. Reprinted by permission of Harcourt, Brace & World, Inc.

[2] A local name for a certain bridge.

In Boston serpents whistle at the cold.
The victim climbs the altar steps and sings:
"Hosannah to the lion, lamb, and beast
Who fans the furnace-face of IS with wings:
I breathe the ether of my marriage feast."
At the high altar, gold
And a fair cloth. I kneel and the wings beat
My cheek. What can the dove of Jesus give
You now but wisdom, exile? Stand and live,
The dove has brought an olive branch to eat.

ROBERT LOWELL

London, 1802

Milton! thou shouldst be living at this hour:
England hath need of thee: she is a fen
Of stagnant waters: altar, sword, and pen,
Fireside, the heroic wealth of hall and bower,
Have forfeited their ancient English dower
Of inward happiness. We are selfish men;
Oh! raise us up, return to us again;
And give us manners, virtue, freedom, power.
Thy soul was like a Star, and dwelt apart;
Thou hadst a voice whose sound was like the sea:
Pure as the naked heavens, majestic, free,
So didst thou travel on life's common way,
In cheerful godliness; and yet thy heart
The lowliest duties on herself did lay.

WILLIAM WORDSWORTH

from the Book of Micah

VI

1. Hear what the Lord says:
   Arise, plead your case before the mountains,
   and let the hills hear your voice.

2. Hear, you mountains, the controversy of the Lord,
   and you enduring foundations of the earth;
   for the Lord has a controversy with his people,
   and he will contend with Israel.

3. "O my people, what have I done to you?
 In what have I wearied you?
  Answer me!

4. For I brought you up from the land of Egypt,
 and redeemed you from the house of bondage;
 and I sent before you Moses, Aaron and Miriam.

5. O my people, remember what Balak king of Moab devised,
 and what Balaam the son of Beor answered him,
 and what happened from Sittim to Silgal,
  that you may know the saving act of the Lord."

6. "With what shall I come before the Lord,
 and bow myself before God on high?
 Shall I come before him with burnt offerings,
  with calves a year old?

7. Will the Lord be pleased with thousands of rams,
 with ten thousands of rivers of oil?
 Shall I give my first-born for my transgression,
  the fruit of my body for the sin of my soul?"

8. He has showed you, O man, what is good;
 and what does the Lord require of you
 but to do justice, and to love kindness,
  and to walk humbly with your God?

9. The voice of the Lord cries to the city —
 and it is sound wisdom to fear thy name:
 "Hear, O tribe and assembly of the city!

10. Can I forget the treasures of wickedness in the house of the wicked,
 and the scant measure that is accursed?

11. Shall I acquit the man with wicked scales
 and with a bag of deceitful weights?

12. Your rich men are full of violence;
 your inhabitants speak lies,
 and their tongue is deceitful in their mouth.

13. Therefore I have begun to smite you,
 making you desolate because of your sins."

Sonnet: England in 1819

An old, mad, blind, despised, and dying king, —
Princes, the dregs of their dull race, who flow
Through public scorn, — mud from a muddy spring, —
Rulers who neither see, nor feel, nor know,
But leech-like to their fainting country cling,
Till they drop, blind in blood, without a blow, —
A people starved and stabbed in the untilled field, —
An army, which liberticide and prey
Makes as a two-edged sword to all who wield, —
Golden and sanguine laws which tempt and slay;
Religion Christless, Godless — a book sealed;
A Senate, — Time's worst statute unrepealed, —
Are graves, from which a glorious Phantom may
Burst, to illumine our tempestuous day.

PERCY BYSSHE SHELLEY

The Lie

Go soul the body's guest
Upon a thankless arrant:[3]
Fear not to touch the best
The truth shall be thy warrant.
  Go since I needs must die,
  And give the world the lie.

Say to the court it glows
And shines like rotten wood,
Say to the Church it shows
What's good, and doth no good.
  If church and court reply,
  Then give them both the lie.

Tell potentates they live
Acting by others' action,
Not loved unless they give,
Not strong but by a faction:
  If potentates reply,
  Give potentates the lie.

[3] errand

Tell men of high condition,
That manage the Estate,
Their purpose is ambition,
Their practice only hate:
   And if they once reply,
   Then give them all the lie.

Tell them that brave it most,
They beg for more by spending
Who in their greatest cost
Seek nothing but commending.
   And if they make reply,
   Then give them all the lie.

Tell zeal it wants devotion
Tell love it is but lust.
Tell time it meets but motion
Tell flesh it is but dust:
   And wish them not reply,
   For thou must give the lie.

Tell age it daily wasteth,
Tell honour how it alters.
Tell beauty how she blasteth
Tell favour how it falters
   And as they shall reply,
   Give every one the lie.

Tell wit how much it wrangles
In tickle point of niceness,
Tell wisdom she entangles
Herself in over-wiseness.
   And when they do reply
   Straight give them both the lie.

Tell physic of her boldness,
Tell skill it is pretension
Tell charity of coldness,
Tell law it is contention,
   And as they do reply
   So give them still the lie.

Tell fortune of her blindness,
Tell nature of decay,
Tell friendship of unkindness,
Tell justice of delay.
　And if they will reply,
　Then give them all the lie.

Tell arts they have no soundness,
But vary by esteeming;
Tell school they want profoundness
And stand too much on seeming.
　If arts and schools reply,
　Give arts and schools the lie.

Tell faith it's fled the city,
Tell how the country erreth
Tell manhood shakes off pity,
Tell virtue least preferréd,
　And if they do reply,
　Spare not to give the lie.

So when thou hast, as I
Commanded thee, done blabbing,
Because to give the lie,
Deserves no less than stabbing,
　Stab at thee he that will,
　No stab the soul can kill.

SIR WALTER RALEIGH

CHAPTER SIX

The Work of Art in Time

. . . Nothing of him that doth fade,
But doth suffer a Sea-change
Into something rich, and strange . . .

W. SHAKESPEARE

THE PASSING CENTURIES

A work of literary art may, in a sense, be immortal. There it is on the page or, as it may be, on the stone. And let us suppose (a supposition not usually justified) that it is transferred truly from page to succeeding page through the years. But humanity and humanity's civilizations are not immortal. The poem's words grow quaint, then archaic, as they move with the rest of their language to the silent land of unspoken tongues. The poem sooner or later becomes frozen in a kind of glacial country of its own immortality, where nothing rusts or rots, but where few people have the stamina or will to journey.

How long will a slang phrase like "he fed her a line" be recognized? Some poor reader two hundred years from now, encountering that in a story and searching his dictionaries of archaic phrases, will perhaps wonder by what stretch of chance a ship's rope or a telephone connection has made a sudden appearance. But more important, a person reading a twentieth century poem 500 years from now will have to reconstruct whole attitudes and values whose shapes and forms will have mutated drastically. We find it hard to accept that in an ancient Greek play a Greek princess would defy the King's edict, on pain of death, in order to sprinkle a handful of dust over her brother's body. We can only accept Antigone's attitude as a fact and one that was perfectly comprehensible to the ancient Greeks. We take to ourselves as best we may in a "suspension of disbelief" the conviction that the soul of one whose body was not in this way ceremoniously buried was condemned to wander restless and homeless over the earth. And why do we accept it? Why bother trying to put ourselves in the place of persons whose beliefs we find mere superstition? Partly, at least, because by so doing we see that men in all ages share certain problems. As Antigone found blood loyalty greater than tribe loyalty and died for her defiance of the King, so we too in different guises find ourselves at times plagued by the stress between the individual conscience and the demands of the state. It is not simply that thus we feel ourselves a part of a human community that goes back to the cave dwellers, though that recognition is an exciting and important feeling. It is that we *learn* from each of these highly refined recitations of human behavior. We come to know, we discover, potentials in ourselves and in humanity that a lifetime in one man's necessarily restricted experience could not begin to reveal to him.

That a story or poem alters as its environment alters and that labor is required for each generation to refocus is true. But that is not the whole story. Not even, perhaps, the important part of it. Compared with the momentary life of the casual gesture, a work of literary art may have a kind of immortality. Perhaps this is the place to recall something said in an earlier chapter; namely, that the writer, through the non-living verbal gesture, "gains an expressive means which, if not quite eternal, is at least more durable, an expressive system of gesture which can create and illustrate values in permanent enough form that civilizations may be raised upon them." If, as Auden says in "In Memory of W. B. Yeats," "the words of a dead man are modified in the guts of the living," it is also true that, in return, the words of dead men modify the living guts. Indeed, to pursue Auden's biological metaphor, scientific biology tells us that in the long run the food modifies the animal more than the animal modifies the food. And this effect of the past on the present is why it is still essential that as large a segment of our present society as is practicable should relive, as best it may with the crutches of footnotes and annotations, such receding worlds as that of Shakespeare.

Although the general public may have an option as to whether it does or does not wish to make the scholarly effort to reconstruct the values of a past era, the oral interpreter really has no option in the matter. If he is to read *Antigone* with the proper passion, he must understand the local cultural quality of the symbolic action through which Antigone's confrontation projects its universal, timeless meanings. Why? Because in literature this "local quality" means the *pattern* of gesture, the *manner* of gesture (vocal and bodily) out of which the audience's conviction of the depth, the reality of the symbol arises. And this evocation of gesture is not a trivial matter, for a passionate attitude, a passionate belief or thought, cannot be abstracted from its manner of bodying forth, any more than man can separate his soul from his body. It seems to me obvious that a person reading *Antigone* aloud can do so adequately only when he knows something of the mores, costumes, religion, philosophy, and science of the period, and beyond that, since *Antigone* is a play, something of the bodily stance, the gestures, and in short the medium of communication of which the play was a central part.

I do not mean that the best reading of *Antigone* will consist of a literal imitation of Greek gesture and costumes. That sort of intellectual preciosity is of very little use. It only attracts attention to the exotic *mechanics* of the performance. But a proper reading of *Antigone will* make an imaginative re-creation of that Greek attitude in modern vocal intonations and gestures, which the modern audience is prepared to evaluate properly. Obviously such a re-creation, such a transliteration, of the Greek gestures into a modern vocabulary requires, beyond the intellectual knowledge mentioned above, an imaginative grasp of style in language which is at once the ultimate achievement of the interpreter and his great gift to literature. For this re-creation is no peripheral matter. It begins with the process of gaining an imaginative, three-dimensional understanding of the text and ends with an appropriate bodying forth of that imaginative understanding in illuminating bodily and vocal gestures. In the poem "Evening Quatrains" (p. 212), a general understanding of the English social structure and rural scene is necessary in order to make an accurate assessment of the relationship of the speaker to the scene and of the character and nature of the Persona speaking the poem. Both these insights are basic to a competent oral interpretation. A firm understanding of the speaker's position in the scene will determine the effectiveness and appropriateness of the visualization of the scene on the part of the reader, while the nature of the Persona, and his attitudes, mentality, will combine in the oral reader to make a convincing re-creation of a certain kind of person reacting to a certain scene.

We have been supposing all this while that the work of art itself remains unchanged. But of course it does not. Very often what happens to the work of art through the course of time may lend it a special meaning which it did not have to its contemporary observers. It is foolish of us to take a purist view and ignore or deny the working of history on the poem. William Butler Yeats understood this very clearly, and in his poem "Lapis Lazuli" (see p. 369), in which he is looking at such a stone carved long ago by some Chinese artist, he speaks of "every accidental crack or dent," and these are part of the meaning of the stone to him, part of what moves him. Very often of course what happens to the work of art is not accidental at all. An interesting comparison was once made between the text of a Shakespeare sonnet as found printed in the Oxford Anthology of English Verse (it is the standard text used by most modern editors), and in the first printing of that poem, which occurred while Shakespeare was alive. It is a deeply perceptive poem, almost impossible to ruin, but the two versions are quite different in important ways.

Oxford Anthology Version
#129

Th' expense of Spirit in a waste of shame
Is lust in action; and till action, lust
Is perjured, murderous, bloody, full of blame,
Savage, extreme, rude, cruel, not to trust;
Enjoy'd no sooner but despised straight;
Past reason hunted; and, no sooner had,
Past reason hated, as a swallow'd bait
On purpose laid to make the taker mad:
Mad in pursuit and in possession so;
Had, having, and in quest to have, extreme;
A bliss in proof, and proved, a very woe;
Before, a joy proposed; behind, a dream.
  All this the world well knows; yet none knows well
  To shun the heaven that leads men to this hell.

Quarto Version

Th' expence of Spirit in a waste of shame
Is lust in action, and till action, lust
Is periurd, murdrous, blouddy full of blame,
Sauage, extreame, rude, cruell, not to trust,
Injoyd no sooner but dispised straight,
Past reason hunted, and no sooner had
Past reason hated as a swollowed bayt,
On purpose layd to make the taker mad.
Made in pursut and in possession so,
Had, hauing, and in quest, to have extreame,
A blisse in proofe and proud and very wo,
Before a joy proposed behind a dreame,
    All this the world well knowes yet none knowes well,
    To shun the heauen that leads men to this hell.

Take, for instance, the substitution of a semicolon for a comma after the word "action." The semicolon has the effect of making it very clear that the phrase "and till action" belongs to what follows. But in the Quarto version this phrase is ambiguous. One may read the lines as the Oxford editor has them, or one may read them, "Is lust in action, and till action, lust. . . ." The effects of the removal of this ambiguity on the total structure of the poem are interesting, but for the moment it is enough for our purpose to see that editors, coming several hundred years after the fact, choose to correct Shakespeare (or, as one would imagine these editors would say, Shakespeare's printer and the chaotic condition of Elizabethan punctuation).

There are further examples. Observe how the semi-colon after the word "trust" eliminates the effect of the early punctuation, which was to list all the attributes of lust that follow as equal, whether a single word or a phrase. Contrast the line

    Had, hauing, and in quest, to have extreame,

with

    Had, having, and in quest to have, extreme;

Certainly the phrase "and in quest to have" is in a sense redundant, for the word "quest" in itself includes the notion of pursuing something for the purpose of possession, whereas the original punctuation makes "to have extreame" refer to the past, present, as well as the future, which would seem not only to freshen the phrasing, but to make much more sense. The line, "A blisse in proof and proud and very wo," besides containing a greater emotional value in the seemingly parallel phrases which actually contain an anticlimax, would seem to have a meaning different from the editor's; it says that "in proof and proved" lust is both a "blisse" and a "very wo." It presents, in short, a paradox. The modern editor neatly removes the paradox by his punctuation, so the line reads that "Lust is a bliss in proof," but once proved, is a "very woe." I will leave it to the reader to decide which version penetrates to the deeper truth.

For a final example, consider the phrase as printed in the Quarto version, "Is periured, murdrous, blouddy full of blame," as opposed to "Is perjured, murderous, bloody, full of blame." Surely in the later version, "full of blame" is comically anticlimactic after such savage words as "perjured," "murderous," and "bloody," whereas "bloudy full of blame" is not only climactic, but is to this day good, idiomatic British English, since the usual way one hears an Englishman use the word "bloody" is as part of some such phrase as "bloody awful."

These and other highly dubious changes which alter the meaning of the poem might well cause one to ask how all this came about, given the respected editors who have used this version. They would no doubt say, as suggested above, that Elizabethan printers weren't reliable and that Elizabethan spelling and punctuation weren't regularized. But could any professional printer of any age make that many mistakes? And must punctuation be regularized to be expressive? Let us get to the point. Shall one ever know of a certain certainty how the text left Shakespeare's hand? No. Very well, then, there are two poems here. One was written by Shakespeare-Elizabethan printer; the other was written Shakespeare-Elizabethan printer-modern scholar. One is stripped of ambiguity and paradox; the other is compounded of them. If both versions are distorted, which is more humanely, profoundly true? The oral reader cannot dodge such a decision, but, while arriving at his conclusion, he might profitably consider that the words of a dead man are subject to mutilation and debasement by the self-righteous, the greedy, the procrustean, the lazy, and the clever, and these hazards are added to those of fire, rot, neglect and other natural wastage.

The obvious point of this specific comparison for the oral interpreter is that he may not, unfortunately, accept without question whatever text comes to hand. A degree of scholarly and aesthetic sophistication is certainly a requisite. The style and sensibility of each literary period and their relationship to the beauties derived from patina are also temporal matters that concern the performer. In the case of this sonnet, the reader's sense of textual appropriateness tells him at once that the person who "cleared up" the punctuation has eliminated not a printer's carelessness, but an aesthetic attitude on the part of the poet which delights in and utilizes ambiguities and complexities. With this insight, the only clear alternative is to shift one's attitude toward the poem from one which says "I can change the punctuation wherever ambiguities or complexities make the meaning difficult or eliptical" to one which says, "I must accept the ambiguities and complexities wherever they exist, as a part of the aesthetic means of the poet, and I can only safely assume a printing error where the meaning is unintelligible." Such a decision would probably not be appropriate to, say, most eighteenth-century poetry, but with Shakespeare it certainly is; and one can again see the necessity on the part of the oral interpreter for some awareness of the interaction of time and the text. Obviously, such a decision in relation to the Shakespeare sonnet is crucial, since the whole nature of the oral reading will change with the acceptance of the older punctuation, not simply in the displacing of pauses and inflections, but in the necessity to integrate and reconcile a far greater range of ambiguity and complexity when creating the poem in the living voice and body.

SELECTIONS

A Box to Hide In*

JAMES THURBER

I waited till the large woman with the awful hat took up her sack of groceries and went out, peering at the tomatoes and lettuce on her way. The clerk asked me what mine was.

"Have you got a box," I asked, "a large box? I want a box to hide in."

"You want a box?" he asked.

"I want a box to hide in," I said.

"Whatta you mean?" he said. "You mean a big box?"

I said I meant a big box, big enough to hold me.

"I haven't got any boxes," he said. "Only cartons that cans come in."

I tried several other groceries and none of them had a box big enough for me to hide in. There was nothing for it but to face life out. I didn't feel strong, and I'd had this overpowering desire to hide in a box for a long time.

"Whatta you mean you want to hide in this box?" one grocer asked me.

"It's a form of escape," I told him, "hiding in a box. It circumscribes your worries and the range of your anguish. You don't see people either."

"How in the hell do you eat when you're in this box?" asked the grocer. "How in the hell do you get anything to eat?" I said I had never been in a box and didn't know, but that that would take care of itself.

"Well," he said, finally, "I haven't got any boxes, only some pasteboard cartons that cans come in."

It was the same every place. I gave up when it got dark and the groceries closed, and hid in my room again. I turned out the light and lay on the bed. You feel better when it gets dark. I could have hid in a closet, I suppose, but people are always opening doors. Somebody would find you in a closet. They would be startled and you'd have to tell them why you were in the closet. Nobody pays any attention to a big box lying on the floor. You could stay in it for days and nobody'd think to look in it, not even the cleaning-woman.

My cleaning-woman came the next morning and woke me up. I was still feeling bad. I asked her if she knew where I could get a large box.

"How big a box you want?" she asked.

"I want a box big enough for me to get inside of," I said. She looked at me with big, dim eyes. There's something wrong with her glands. She's awful but she has a big heart, which makes it worse. She's unbearable, her husband is sick and her children are sick and she is sick too. I got to thinking how pleasant it would be if I were in a box now, and didn't have to see her. I would be in a box right there in the room and she wouldn't know. I wondered if you have a desire to bark or laugh when someone who doesn't know walks by the box you are in. Maybe she would have a spell with her heart, if I did that, and would die right there. The officers and the elevatorman and Mr. Gramadge would find us. "Funny doggone thing happened at the building last night," the doorman would say to his wife. "I let in this woman to clean up 10-F and she never come out, see? She's never there more'n an hour, but she never come out, see? So when it got to be time for me to go off duty, why I says to Crennick, who was on the elevator, I says what the hell you suppose has happened to that woman cleans 10-F.' He says he didn't know; he says he never seen her after he took her up. So I spoke to Mr. Gramadge about it. 'I'm sorry to bother you, Mr. Gramadge,' I says 'but there's something funny about that woman cleans 10-F.' So I told him. So he said we better have a look and we all three goes up and knocks on the door and rings the bell, see, and nobody answers so he said we'd have to walk in so Crennick opened the door and we walked in and here was this woman cleans the apartment dead as a herring on the floor and the gentleman that lives there was in a box." . . .

The cleaning-woman kept looking at me. It was hard to realize she wasn't dead. "It's a form of escape," I murmured. "What say?" she asked, dully.

"You don't know of any large packing boxes, do you?" I asked.

"No, I don't," she said.

I haven't found one yet, but I still have this overpowering urge to hide in a box. Maybe it will go away, maybe I'll be all right. Maybe it will get worse. It's hard to say.

An Experiment in Misery[*]

STEPHEN CRANE

It was late at night, and a fine rain was swirling softly down, causing the pavements to glisten with hue of steel and blue and yellow in the rays of the innumerable lights. A youth was trudging slowly, without enthusiasm, with his hands buried deep in his trousers' pockets, toward the downtown places where beds can be hired for coppers. He was clothed in an aged and tattered suit, and his derby was a marvel of dust-covered crown and torn rim. He was going forth to eat as the wanderer may eat, and sleep as the homeless sleep. By the time he had reached City Hall Park he was so completely plastered with yells of "bum" and "hobo," and with various unholy epithets that small boys had applied to him at intervals, that he was in a state of the most profound dejection. The sifting rain saturated the old velvet collar of his overcoat, and as the wet cloth pressed against his neck, he felt that there no longer could be pleasure in life. He looked about him searching for an outcast of highest degree that they too might share miseries, but the lights threw a quivering glare over rows and circles of deserted benches that glistened damply, showing patches of wet sod behind them. It seemed that their usual freights had fled on this night to better things. There were only squads of well-dressed Brooklyn people who swarmed towards the bridge.

The young man loitered about for a time and then went shuffling off down Park Row. In the sudden descent in style of the dress of the crowd he felt relief, and as if he were at last in his own country. He began to see tatters that matched his tatters. In Chatham Square there were aimless men strewn in front of saloons and lodging-houses, standing sadly, patiently, reminding one vaguely of the attitudes of chickens in a storm. He

    [*] Published 1930 by Alfred A. Knopf, Inc. Reprinted from *Stephen Crane: An Omnibus*, edited by Robert Wooster Stallman, by permission of Alfred A. Knopf, Inc.

aligned himself with these men, and turned slowly to occupy himself with the flowing life of the great street.

Through the mists of the cold and storming night, the cable cars went in silent procession, great affairs shining with red and brass, moving with formidable power, calm and irresistible, dangerful and gloomy, breaking silence only by the loud fierce cry of the gong. Two rivers of people swarmed along the sidewalks, spattered with black mud, which made each shoe leave a scarlike impression. Overhead elevated trains with a shrill grinding of the wheels stopped at the station, which upon its leglike pillars seemed to resemble some monstrous kind of crab squatting over the street. The quick fat puffings of the engines could be heard. Down an alley there were somber curtains of purple and black, on which street lamps dully glittered like embroidered flowers.

A saloon stood with a voracious air on a corner. A sign leaning against the front of the door-post announced "Free hot soup to-night!" The swing door, snapping to and fro gorged itself with plump men, eating with astounding and endless appetite, smiling in some indescribable manner as the men came from all directions like sacrifices to a heathenish superstition.

Caught by the delectable sign the young man allowed himself to be swallowed. A bartender placed a schooner of dark and portentous beer on the bar. Its monumental form upreared until the froth a-top was above the crown of the young man's brown derby.

"Soup over there, gents," said the bartender affably. A little yellow man in rags and the youth grasped their schooners and went with speed toward a lunch counter, where a man with oily but imposing whiskers ladled genially from a kettle until he had furnished his mendicants with a soup that was steaming hot, and in which there were little floating suggestions of chicken. The young man, sipping his broth, felt the cordiality expressed by the warmth of the mixture, and he beamed at the man with oily but imposing whiskers, who was presiding like a priest behind an altar. "Have some more, gents?" he inquired of the two sorry figures before him. The little yellow man accepted with a swift gesture, but the youth shook his head and went out, following a man whose wondrous seediness promised that he would have a knowledge of cheap lodging-houses.

On the sidewalk he accosted the seedy man. "Say, do you know a cheap place to sleep?"

The other hesitated for a time, gazing sideways. Finally he nodded in the direction of the street, "I sleep up there," he said, "when I've got the price."

"How much?"

"Ten cents."

The young man shook his head dolefully. "That's too rich for me."

At that moment there approached the two a reeling man in strange garments. His head was a fuddle of bushy hair and whiskers, from which his eyes peered with a guilty slant. In a close scrutiny it was possible to distinguish the cruel lines of a mouth which looked as if its lips had just closed with satisfaction over some tender and piteous morsel. He appeared like an assassin steeped in crimes performed awkwardly.

But at this time his voice was tuned to the coaxing key of an affectionate puppy. He looked at the men with wheedling eyes, and began to sing a little melody for charity.

"Say, gents, can't yeh give a poor feller a couple of cents t' git a bed? I got five, and I gets anudder two I gits me a bed. Now, on th' square, gents, can't yeh jest gimme two cents t' git a bed? Now, yeh know how a respecter'ble gentem'n feels when he's down on his luck, an' I — "

The seedy man, staring with imperturbable countenance at a train which clattered overhead, interrupted in an expressionless voice — "Ah, go t' h—!"

But the youth spoke to the prayerful assassin in tones of astonishment and inquiry. "Say, you must be crazy! Why don't yeh strike somebody that looks as if they had money?"

The assassin, tottering about on his uncertain legs, and at intervals brushing imaginary obstacles from before his nose, entered into a long explanation of the psychology of the situation. It was so profound that it was unintelligible.

When he had exhausted the subject, the young man said to him:

"Let's see th' five cents."

The assassin wore an expression of drunken woe at this sentence, filled with suspicion of him. With a deeply pained air he began to fumble in his clothing, his red hands trembling. Presently he announced in a voice of bitter grief, as if he had been betrayed — "There's on'y four."

"Four," said the young man thoughtfully. "Well, look here, I'm a stranger here, an' if ye'll steer me to your cheap joint I'll find the other three."

The assassin's countenance became instantly radiant with joy. His whiskers quivered with the wealth of his alleged emotions. He seized the young man's hand in a transport of delight and friendliness.

"B' Gawd," he cried, "if ye'll do that, b' Gawd, I'd say yeh was a damned good fellow, I would, an' I'd remember yeh all m' life I would, b' Gawd, an' if I ever got a chance I'd return the compliment" — he spoke with drunken dignity — "b' Gawd, I'd treat yeh white, I would, an' I'd allus remember yeh."

The young man drew back, looking at the assassin coldly. "Oh, that's all right," he said. "You show me th' joint — that's all you've got t' do."

The assassin, gesticulating gratitude, led the young man along a dark street. Finally he stopped before a little dusty door. He raised his hand impressively. "Look-a-here," he said, and there was a thrill of deep and ancient wisdom upon his face, "I've brought yeh here, an' that's my part, ain't it? If th' place don't suit yeh, yeh needn't git mad at me, need yeh? There won't be no bad feelin', will there?"

"No," said the young man.

The assassin waved his arm tragically, and led the march up the steep stairway. On the way the young man furnished the assassin with three pennies. At the top a man with benevolent spectacles looked at them through a hole in a board. He collected their money, wrote some names on a register, and speedily was leading the two men along a gloom-shrouded corridor.

Shortly after the beginning of this journey the young man felt his liver turn white, for from the dark and secret places of the building there suddenly came to his nostrils strange and unspeakable odors, that assailed him like malignant diseases with wings. They seemed to be from human bodies closely packed in dens; the exhalations from a hundred pairs of reeking lips; the fumes from a thousand bygone debauches; the expression of a thousand present miseries.

A man, naked save for a little snuff-colored undershirt, was parading sleepily along the corridor. He rubbed his eyes, and, giving vent to a prodigious yawn, demanded to be told the time.

"Half-past one."

The man yawned again. He opened a door, and for a moment his form was outlined against a black, opaque interior. To this door came the three men, and as it was again opened the unholy odors rushed out like fiends, so that the young man was obliged to struggle as against an overpowering wind.

It was some time before the youth's eyes were good in the intense gloom within, but the man with benevolent spectacles led him skilfully, pausing but a moment to deposit the limp assassin upon a cot. He took the youth to a cot that lay tranquilly by the window, and showing him a tall locker for clothes that stood near the head with the ominous air of a tombstone, left him.

The youth sat on his cot and peered about him. There was a gas-jet in a distant part of the room, that burned a small flickering orange-hued flame. It caused vast masses of tumbled shadows in all parts of the place, save where, immediately about it, there was a little grey haze. As the young man's eyes became used to the darkness, he could see upon the cots that thickly littered the floor the forms of men sprawled out, lying in deathlike silence, or heaving and snoring with tremendous effort, like stabbed fish.

The youth locked his derby and his shoes in the mummy case near him, and then lay down with an old and familiar coat around his shoulders. A blanket he handled gingerly, drawing it over part of the coat. The cot was covered with leather, and as cold as melting snow. The youth was obliged to shiver for some time on this affair, which was like a slab. Presently, however, his chill gave him peace, and during this period of leisure from it he turned his head to stare at his friend the assassin, whom he could dimly discern where he lay sprawled on a cot in the abandon of a man filled with drink. He was snoring with incredible vigor. His wet hair and beard dimly glistened, and his inflamed nose shone with subdued lustre like a red light in a fog.

Within reach of the youth's hand was one who lay with yellow breast and shoulders bare to the cold drafts. One arm hung over the side of the cot, and the fingers lay full length upon the wet cement floor of the room. Beneath the inky brows could be seen the eyes of the man exposed by the partly opened lids. To the youth it seemed that he and this corpselike being were exchanging a prolonged stare, and that the other threatened with his eyes. He drew back, watching his neighbor from the shadows of his blanket edge. The man did not move once through the night, but lay in this stillness as of death like a body stretched out expectant of the surgeon's knife.

And all through the room could be seen the tawny hues of naked flesh, limbs thrust into the darkness, projecting beyond the cots; upreared knees, arms hanging long and thin over the cot edges. For the most part they were statuesque, carven, dead. With the curious lockers standing all about like tombstones, there was a strange effect of a graveyard where bodies were merely flung.

Yet occasionally could be seen limbs wildly tossing in fantastic nightmare gestures, accompanied by guttural cries, grunts, oaths. And there was one fellow off in a gloomy corner, who in his dreams was oppressed by some frightful calamity, for of a sudden he began to utter long wails that went almost like yells from a hound, echoing wailfully and weird through this chill place of tombstones where men lay like the dead.

The sound in its high piercing beginnings, that dwindled to final melancholy moans, expressed a red and grim tragedy of the unfathomable possibilities of the man's dreams. But to the youth these were not merely the shrieks of a vision-pierced man: they were an utterance of the meaning of the room and its occupants. It was to him the protest of the wretch who feels the touch of the imperturbable granite wheels, and who then cries with an impersonal eloquence, with a strength not from him, giving voice to the wail of a whole section, a class, a people. This, weaving into the young man's brain, and mingling with his views of the vast and sombre shadows that, like mighty black fingers, curled around the naked bodies, made the young man so that he did not sleep, but lay carving the biographies for these men from his meagre experience. At times the fellow in the corner howled in a writhing agony of his imaginations.

Finally a long lance-point of grey light shot through the dusty panes of the window. Without, the young man could see roofs drearily white in the dawning. The point of light yellowed and grew brighter, until the golden rays of the morning sun came in bravely and strong. They touched with radiant color the form of a small fat man, who snored in stuttering fashion. His round and shiny bald head glowed suddenly with the valor of a decoration. He sat up, blinked at the sun, swore fretfully, and pulled his blanket over the ornamental splendors of his head.

The youth contentedly watched this rout of the shadows before the bright spears of the sun, and presently he slumbered. When he awoke he heard the voice of the assassin raised in valiant curses. Putting up his head, he perceived his comrade seated on the side of the cot engaged in scratching his neck with long finger-nails that rasped like files.

"Hully Jee, dis is a new breed. They've got can-openers on their feet." He continued in a violent tirade.

The young man hastily unlocked his closet and took out his shoes and hat. As he sat on the side of the cot lacing his shoes, he glanced about and saw that daylight had made the room comparatively commonplace and uninteresting. The men, whose faces seemed stolid, serene or absent, were engaged in dressing, while a great crackle of bantering conversation arose.

A few were parading in unconcerned nakedness. Here and there were men of brawn, whose skins shone clear and ruddy. They took splendid poses, standing massively like chiefs. When they had dressed in their ungainly garments there was an extraordinary change. They then showed bumps and deficiencies of all kinds.

There were others who exhibited many deformities. Shoulders were slanting, humped, pulled this way and pulled that way. And notable among these latter men was the little fat man who had refused to allow his head to be glorified. His pudgy form, builded like a pear, bustled to and fro, while he swore in fishwife fashion. It appeared that some article of his apparel had vanished.

The young man attired speedily, and went to his friend the assassin. At first the latter looked dazed at the sight of the youth. This face seemed to be appealing to him through the cloud wastes of his memory. He scratched his neck and reflected. At last he grinned, a broad smile gradually spreading until his countenance was a round illumination. "Hello, Willie," he cried cheerily.

"Hello," said the young man. "Are yeh ready t' fly?"

"Sure." The assassin tied his shoe carefully with some twine and came ambling.

When he reached the street the young man experienced no sudden relief from unholy atmospheres. He had forgotten all about them, and had been breathing naturally, and with no sensation of discomfort or distress.

He was thinking of these things as he walked along the street, when he was suddenly startled by feeling the assassin's hand, trembling with excitement, clutching his arm, and when the assassin spoke, his voice went into quavers from a supreme agitation.

"I'll be hully, bloomin' blowed if there wasn't a feller with a nightshirt on up there in that joint."

The youth was bewildered for a moment, but presently he turned to smile indulgently at the assassin's humor.

"Oh, you're a d—d liar," he merely said.

Whereupon the assassin began to gesture extravagantly, and take oath by strange gods. He frantically placed himself at the mercy of re-markable fates if his tale were not true.

"Yes, he did! I cross m' heart thousan' times!" he protested, and at the moment his eyes were large with amazement, his mouth wrinkled in un-natural glee.

"Yessir! A nightshirt! A hully white nightshirt! A hully white night-shirt!"

"You lie!"

"No, sir! I hope ter die b'fore I kin get anudder ball if there wasn't a jay wid a hully, bloomin' white nightshirt!"

His face was filled with the infinite wonder of it. "A hully white night-shirt," he continually repeated.

The young man saw the dark entrance to a basement restaurant. There was a sign which read "No mystery about our hash!" and there were other age-stained and world-battered legends which told him that the place was within his means. He stopped before it and spoke to the assassin. "I guess I'll git somethin' t' eat."

At this the assassin, for some reason, appeared to be quite embar-rassed. He gazed at the seductive front of the eating place for a moment. Then he started slowly up the street. "Well, good-bye, Willie," he said bravely.

For an instant the youth studied the departing figure. Then he called out, "Hol' on a minnet." As they came together he spoke in a certain fierce way, as if he feared that the other would think him to be charitable. "Look-a-here, if yeh wanta git some breakfas' I'll lend yeh three cents t' do it with. But say, look-a-here, you've gota git out an' hustle. I ain't goin' t' support yeh, or I'll go broke b'fore night. I ain't no millionaire."

"I take me oath, Willie," said the assassin earnestly, "th' on'y thing I really needs is a ball. Me t'roat feels like a fryin'-pan. But as I can't get a ball, why, th' next bes' thing is breakfast, an' if yeh do that for me, b' Gawd, I say yeh was th' whitest lad I ever see."

They spent a few moments in dexterous exchanges of phrases, in which they each protested that the other was, as the assassin had originally said, "a respecter'ble gentlem'n." And they concluded with mutual assurances that they were the souls of intelligence and virtue. Then they went into the restaurant.

There was a long counter, dimly lighted from hidden sources. Two or three men in soiled white aprons rushed here and there.

The youth bought a bowl of coffee for two cents and a roll for one cent. The assassin purchased the same. The bowls were webbed with brown seams, and the tin spoons wore an air of having emerged from the first pyramid. Upon them were black mosslike encrustations of age, and they were bent and scarred from the attacks of long-forgotten teeth. But over their repast the wanderers waxed warm and mellow. The assassin grew affable as the hot mixture went soothingly down his parched throat, and the young man felt courage flow in his veins.

Memories began to throng in on the assassin, and he brought forth long tales, intricate, incoherent, delivered with a chattering swiftness as from an old woman. " — great job out'n Orange. Boss keep yeh hustlin' though all time. I was there three days, and then I went an' ask 'im t' lend me a dollar. 'G-g-go ter the devil,' he ses, an' I lose me job."

"South no good. Damn niggers work for twenty-five an' thirty cents a day. Run white man out. Good grub, though. Easy livin'."

"Yas; useter work little in Toledo, raftin' logs. Make two or three dollars er day in the spring. Lived high. Cold as ice, though, in the winter."

"I was raised in northern N'York. O-a-ah, yeh just oughto live there. No beer ner whisky, though, way off in the woods. But all th' good hot grub yeh can eat. B'Gawd, I hung around there long as I could till th' ol' man fired me. 'Git t' hell outa here, yeh wuthless skunk, git t' hell outa here, an' go die,' he ses. 'You're a hell of a father,' I ses, 'you are,' an' I quit 'im."

As they were passing from the dim eating place, they encountered an old man who was trying to steal forth with a tiny package of food, but a tall man with an indomitable moustache stood dragon fashion, barring the way of escape. They heard the old man raise a plaintive protest. "Ah, you always want to know what I take out, and you never see that I usually bring a package in here from my place of business."

As the wanderers trudged slowly along Park Row, the assassin began to expand and grow blithe. "B'Gawd, we've been livin' like kings," he said, smacking appreciative lips.

"Look out, or we'll have t' pay fer it t'night," said the youth with gloomy warning.

But the assassin refused to turn his gaze toward the future. He went with a limping step, into which he injected a suggestion of lamblike gambols. His mouth was wreathed in a red grin.

In the City Hall Park the two wanderers sat down in the little circle of benches sanctified by traditions of their class. They huddled in their old garments, slumbrously conscious of the march of the hours which for them had no meaning.

The people of the street hurrying hither and thither made a blend of black figures changing yet frieze-like. They walked in their good clothes as upon important missions, giving no gaze to the two wanderers seated upon the benches. They expressed to the young man his infinite distance from all that he valued. Social position, comfort, the pleasures of living, were unconquerable kingdoms. He felt a sudden awe.

And in the background a multitude of buildings, of pitiless hues and sternly high, were to him emblematic of a nation forcing its regal head into the clouds, throwing no downward glances; in the sublimity of its aspirations ignoring the wretches who may flounder at its feet. The roar of the city in his ear was to him the confusion of strange tongues, babbling heedlessly; it was the clink of coin, the voice of the city's hopes which were to him no hopes.

He confessed himself an outcast, and his eyes from under the lowered rim of his hat began to glance guiltily, wearing the criminal expression that comes with certain convictions.

The Lachrymae Pavan

Flow, my tears, fall from your springs!
Exiled for ever let me mourne,
Where night's black-bird her sad infamy sings,
There let me live forlorne.

Down vain lights, shine you no more!
No nights are dark enough for those
That in dispaire, their lost fortunes deplore,
Light doth but shame disclose.

Never may my woes be relievèd
Since pitie is fled,
And teares, and sighs, and groanes, my weary dayes
All joys have deprived.

From the highest spire of contentment,
My fortune is throwne,
And feare, and grief, and paine for my deserts
Are my hopes, since hope is gone.

Hark you shadowes that in darkness dwell,
Learn to contemne light.
Happy, happy they that in hell
Feel not the world's despite.

JOHN DOWLAND

Design*

I found a dimpled spider, fat and white,
On a white heal-all, holding up a moth
Like a white piece of rigid satin cloth —
Assorted characters of death and blight
Mixed ready to begin the morning right,
Like the ingredients of a witches' broth —
A snow-drop spider, a flower like a froth,
And dead wings carried like a paper kite.

What had that flower to do with being white,
The wayside blue and innocent heal-all?
What brought the kindred spider to that height,
Then steered the white moth thither in the night?
What but design of darkness to appall? —
If design govern in a thing so small.

ROBERT FROST

Ode on Melancholy

I

No, no, go not to Lethe, neither twist
  Wolf's-bane, tight-rooted, for its poisonous wine;
Nor suffer thy pale forehead to be kiss'd
  By nightshade, ruby grape of Proserpine;
Make not your rosary of yew-berries,
  Nor let the beetle, nor the death-moth be
    Your mournful Psyche, nor the downy owl
A partner in your sorrow's mysteries;
  For shade to shade will come too drowsily,
    And drown the wakeful anguish of the soul.

II

But when the melancholy fit shall fall
  Sudden from heaven like a weeping cloud,
That fosters the droop-headed flowers all,
  And hides the green hill in an April shroud;
Then glut thy sorrow on a morning rose,
  Or on the rainbow of the salt sand-wave,
    Or on the wealth of globed peonies;
Or if thy mistress some rich anger shows,
  Emprison her soft hand, and let her rave,
    And feed deep, deep upon her peerless eyes.

III

She dwells with Beauty — Beauty that must die;
  And Joy, whose hand is ever at his lips
Bidding adieu; and aching Pleasure nigh,
  Turning to poison while the bee-mouth sips:
Ay, in the very temple of Delight
  Veil'd Melancholy has her sovran shrine,
    Though seen of none save him whose strenuous tongue
Can burst Joy's grape against his palate fine;
His soul shall taste the sadness of her might,
  And be among her cloudy trophies hung.

JOHN KEATS

The Man-Moth*

Here, above,
cracks in the buildings are filled with battered moonlight.
The whole shadow of Man is only as big as his hat.
It lies at his feet like a circle for a doll to stand on,
and he makes an inverted pin, the point magnetized to the moon.
He does not see the moon; he observes only her vast properties,
feeling the queer light on his hands, neither warm nor cold,
of a temperature impossible to record in thermometers.

But when the Man-Moth[1]
pays his rare, although occasional, visits to the surface,
the moon looks rather different to him. He emerges
from an opening under the edge of one of the sidewalks
and nervously begins to scale the faces of buildings.
He thinks the moon is a small hole at the top of the sky,
proving the sky quite useless for protection.
He trembles, but must investigate as high as he can climb.

Up the façades,
his shadow dragging like a photographer's cloth behind him,
he climbs fearfully, thinking that this time he will manage
to push his small head through that round clean opening
and be forced through, as from a tube, in black scrolls on the light.
(Man, standing below him, has no such illusions.)
But what the Man-Moth fears most he must do, although
he fails, of course, and falls back scared but quite unhurt.

Then he returns
to the pale subways of cement he calls his home. He flits,
he flutters, and cannot get aboard the silent trains
fast enough to suit him. The doors close swiftly.
The Man-Moth always seats himself facing the wrong way
and the train starts at once at its full, terrible speed,
without a shift in gears or a gradation of any sort.
He cannot tell the rate at which he travels backwards.

* Reprinted from *North and South* by Elizabeth Bishop, by permission of
Houghton Mifflin Company.

[1] Newspaper misprint for "mammoth."

Each night he must
be carried through artificial tunnels and dream recurrent dreams.
Just as the ties recur beneath his train, these underlie
his rushing brain. He does not dare look out the window,
for the third rail, the unbroken draught of poison,
runs there beside him. He regards it as a disease
he has inherited the susceptibility to. He has to keep
his hands in pockets, as others must wear mufflers.

If you catch him,
hold up a flashlight to his eye. It's all dark pupil,
an entire night itself, whose haired horizon tightens
as he stares back, and closes up the eye. Then from the lids
one tear, his only possession, like the bee's sting, slips.
Slyly he palms it, and if you're not paying attention
he'll swallow it. However, if you watch, he'll hand it over,
cool as from underground springs and pure enough to drink.

ELIZABETH BISHOP

The Convergence of the Twain*
(Lines on the loss of the "Titanic")

I

In a solitude of the sea
Deep from human vanity,
And the Pride of Life that planned her, stilly couches she.

II

Steel chambers, late the pyres
Of her salamandrine fires,
Cold currents thrid, and turn to rhythmic tidal lyres.

III

Over the mirrors meant
To glass the opulent
The sea-worm crawls — grotesque, slimed, dumb, indifferent.

* Reprinted from *Collected Poems of Thomas Hardy* by permission of The
Macmillan Company (New York); the Executors of the Hardy Estate, Macmillan
& Co. Ltd. (London), The Macmillan Company of Canada Limited. Copyright
1925 by The Macmillan Company.

IV

Jewels in joy designed
To ravish the sensuous mind
Lie lightless, all their sparkles bleared and black and blind.

V

Dim moon-eyed fishes near
Gaze at the gilded gear
And query: "What does this vaingloriousness down here?" . . .

VI

Well: while was fashioning
This creature of cleaving wing,
The Immanent Will that stirs and urges everything

VII

Prepared a sinister mate
For her — so gaily great —
A Shape of Ice, for the time far and dissociate.

VIII

And as the smart ship grew
In stature, grace, and hue,
In shadowy silent distance grew the Iceberg too.

IX

Alien they seemed to be:
No mortal eye could see
The intimate welding of their later history.

X

Or sign that they were bent
By paths coincident
On being anon twin halves of one august event,

XI

Till the Spinner of the Years
Said "Now!" And each one hears,
And consummation comes, and jars two hemispheres.

THOMAS HARDY

In Time of Pestilence

1593

Adieu, farewell earth's bliss!
This world uncertain is:
Fond are life's lustful joys,
Death proves them all but toys.
None from his darts can fly;
I am sick, I must die —
    Lord, have mercy on us!

Rich men, trust not in wealth,
Gold cannot buy you health;
Physic himself must fade;
All things to end are made;
The plague full swift goes by;
I am sick, I must die —
    Lord, have mercy on us!

Beauty is but a flower
Which wrinkles will devour;
Brightness falls from the air;
Queens have died young and fair;
Dust hath closed Helen's eye;
I am sick, I must die —
    Lord, have mercy on us!

Strength stoops unto the grave,
Worms feed on Hector brave;
Swords may not fight with fate;
Earth still holds ope her gate;
Come, come! the bells do cry;
I am sick, I must die —
    Lord, have mercy on us!

Wit with his wantonness
Tasteth death's bitterness;
Hell's executioner
Hath no ears for to hear
What vain art can reply;
I am sick, I must die —
    Lord, have mercy on us!

Haste therefore each degree
To welcome destiny;
Heaven is our heritage,
Earth but a player's stage.
Mount we unto the sky;
I am sick, I must die —
    Lord, have mercy on us!

THOMAS NASHE

CHAPTER SEVEN

Time in the Work of Art

. . . as soon as fiction is completely delivered
from time it cannot express anything at all . . .

E. M. FORSTER

Since all events move in time, or themselves create time, and since a work of art is a selection of events, whether physical or psychological, that have an especially meaningful relationship, it follows that the ordering of time is one of the most significant aspects of the writer's job. For the student to see more clearly the peculiarity of that ordering, it is well for him to make the common distinction between the temporal work of literary art and the spatial arts, that is, those arts which occupy primarily the spatial dimension of the space-time continuum. We can only read, as it were, one word or phrase at a time. What we read the minute before is already being forgotten, what we shall read next minute is merely something half-guessed at in anticipation, or if we have read the work before, half-remembered from another state of being. Further, we read with a certain anticipation that a story or poem will be told within a certain time, as one might calculate approximately where a golf ball might land from seeing its initial direction and arc. In creating the over-all structure, and in giving allotments of time to the various details, the writer must face these facts about the temporal nature of the mind of his reader.

The novel *Tristram Shandy* by Laurence Sterne is, in part at least, one of the most profound and most hilarious examinations to be found anywhere of the problems time creates for the artist. The hero of the book, Tristram Shandy, has as his main purpose the telling of the story of his life or, more particularly, of the one long disaster which he sees as being his life, and of the causes of that disaster. As he finally gets around to telling us, he adopts as his approach to the structuring of time a happy *laissez faire* method, which he describes in Chapter 22 of Book I:

I was just going, for example, to have given you the great outlines of my uncle Toby's most whimsical character; — when my aunt Dinah and the coachman came across us, and led us a vagary some millions of miles into the very heart of the planetary system: Notwithstanding all this, you perceive that the drawing of my uncle Toby's character went on gently all the time; — not the great contours of it, — that was impossible, — but some familiar strokes and faint designations of it, were here and there touch'd on, as we went along, so that you are much better acquainted with my uncle Toby now than you was before.

By this contrivance, the machinery of my work is of a species by itself; two contrary motions are introduced into it, and reconciled, which were thought to be at variance with each other. In a word, my work is digressive, and it is progressive too, — and at the same time.

This, Sir, is a very different story from that of the earth's moving round her axis in her diurnal rotation, with her progress in her elliptic orbit, which brings about the year, and constitutes that variety and vicissitude of seasons we enjoy; — though I own it suggested the thought, — as I believe the greatest of our boasted improvements and discoveries have come from such trifling hints.

Digressions, incontestably, are the sunshine; — they are the life, the soul of reading! — take them out of this book, for instance, — you might as well take the book along with them; — one cold eternal winter would reign in every page of it; restore them to the writer; — he steps forth like a bridegroom, — bids All-hail; brings in variety, and forbids the appetite to fail.

All the dexterity is in the good cookery and management of them, so as to be not only for the advantage of the reader, but also of the author, whose distress in this matter is truly pitiable: For, if he begins a digression, — from that moment, I observe, his whole work stands stock still; — and if he goes on with his main work, — then there is an end of his digression.

— This is vile work. — For which reason, from the beginning of this, you see, I have constructed the main work, and the adventitious parts of it, with such intersections, and have so complicated and involved the digressive and progressive movements, one wheel within another, that the whole machine, in general, has been kept a-going; — and, what's more, it shall be kept a-going these forty years, if it pleases the fountain of health to bless me so long with life and good spirits.

Chapter 23

I have a strong propensity in me to begin this chapter very nonsensically, and I will not baulk my fancy. — Accordingly I set off thus:
Excerpts from Chapters 22 & 23
Book I

Let us, in short, start with the fact that everything in life must in some way or other relate to every other thing. "Well, then," says Tristram, "why can't I put anything I want in my book anywhere? Further, why doesn't this constant relationship of things have its psychological counterpart, in that anything which interests me ought to interest the reader also." This sanguine faith in his method and in his ability to maintain it is shaken later on, when he finds an extraordinary fact: that it has taken him 256 pages and one year of writing to arrive at his Christening, an event which occurred the day he was born.

I will not finish that sentence till I have made an observation upon the strange state of affairs between the reader and myself, just as things stand at present — an observation never applicable before to any one biographical writer since the creation of the world, but to myself — and I believe, will never hold good to any other, until its final destruction — and therefore, for the very novelty of it alone, it must be worth your worships attending to.

I am this month one whole year older than I was this time twelve-month; and having got, as you perceive, almost into the middle of my fourth volume — and no farther than to my first day's life — 'tis demonstrative that I have three hundred and sixty-four days more life to write just now, than when I first set out; so that instead of advancing, as a common writer, in my work with what I have been doing at it — on the contrary, I am just thrown so many volumes back — was every day of my life to be as busy a day as this — And why not? — and the transactions and opinions of it to take up as much description — And for what reason should they be cut short? as at this rate I should just live 364 times faster than I should write — It must follow, an' please your worships, that the more I write, the more I shall have to write — and consequently, the more your worships will have to read.

Will this be good for your worships' eyes?

Book IV, Chapter 13

By Book V, he is seeking ways to avoid some of the commitments he made so blithely in his more carefree beginning.

Stay — I have a small account to settle with the reader before Trim can go on with his harangue. — It shall be done in two minutes.

Amongst many other book-debts, all of which I shall discharge in due time, — I own myself a debtor to the world for two items, — a chapter upon chamber-maids and button-holes, which, the former part of my work, I promised and fully intended to pay off this year; but some of your worships and reverences telling me, that the two subjects, especially so connected together, might endanger the morals of the world, — I pray the chapter upon chamber-maids and button-holes may be forgiven me, — and that they will accept of the last chapter in lieu of it; which is nothing, an't please your reverences, but a chapter of chamber-maids, green gowns, and old hats.

Trim took his off the ground, — put it upon his head, — and then went on with his oration upon death, in manner and form following.

Book V, Chapter 8

And by Book VI the problem bears in upon him to the point that he comes to compliment himself on some straightening of his narrative line (over-optimistically we would imagine, knowing Tristram).

I am now beginning to get fairly into my work; and by the help of a vegetable diet, with a few of the cold seeds, I make no doubt but I shall be able to go on with my uncle Toby's story and my own in a tolerable straight line. Now,

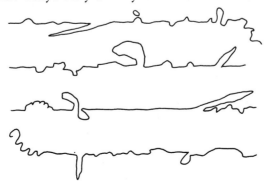

These were the four lines I moved in through my first, second, third, and fourth volumes. — In the fifth volume I have been very good, — the precise line I have described in it being this:

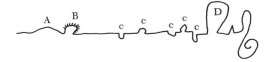

By which it appears, that except at the curve, marked A, where I took a trip to Navarre, — and the indented curve B, which is the short airing when I was there with the Lady Baussiere and her page, — I have not taken the least frisk of a digression, till John de la Casse's devils led me the round you see marked D. — for as for c c c c c they are nothing but parentheses, and the common ins and outs incident to the lives of the greatest ministers of state; and when compared with what men have done, — or with my own transgressions at the letters A B D — they vanish into nothing.

In this last volume I have done better still — for from the end of LeFever's episode, to the beginning of my uncle Toby's campaigns, — I have scarce stepped a yard out of my way.

If I mend at this rate, it is not impossible — by the good leave of his grace of Benevento's devils — but I may arrive hereafter at the excellency of going on even thus:

———————————————————————————————————

which is a line drawn as straight as I could draw it, by a writing-master's ruler (borrowed for that purpose), turning neither to the right hand nor to the left.

This right line, — the path-way for Christians to walk in! say divines —

— The emblem of moral rectitude! says Cicero —

— The best line! say cabbage planters — is the shortest line, says Archimedes, which can be drawn from one given point to another. —

I wish your ladyships would lay this matter to heart, in your next birth-day suits!

— What a journey!

Pray can you tell me, — that is, without anger, before I write my chapter upon straight lines — by what mistake — who told them so — or how it has come to pass, that your men of wit and genius have all along confounded this line, with the line of Gravitation?

Book VI, Chapter 40

This ingenious discussion by Sterne (via Tristram) gives a clue to the distractions, temptations, experimentations, and subsequent wisdom and discipline of any successful creative writer. But they also offer clues to the oral interpreter of central significance. Action (and a shift of inner feeling is action) is ordered in *some* way in every piece of fiction. Its compressions, its extensions, those things which are elaborated and those things only implied, must all enter into the preparatory calculations and must play a significant role in the revelations, of a successful reading. *Tristram Shandy* itself is an excellent example. How does one read it aloud? A prior question must surely be, what does it say? In other words, in what direction are its meanings pointed? Thematically, one comes very quickly to see the similarity to the novel of Jane Austen, *Sense and Sensibility*, two chapters of which have already been touched upon; namely, that both are concerned with the problem of sensibility vs. sense, of whether or not it is better to let the heart rule than the head. Attempting to read *Tristram* aloud will bring one's attention forcefully to the problem of sentence construction (perhaps one should speak about phrase construction, since Tristram's sentences are seldom other than a shattered series of phrases), and from there one is forced to the nature of the psychological linkage from phrase to phrase from thought to thought and to the larger linkage of action to action. And one soon comes to an understanding that these are all of a piece, one long series of concepts, thoughts, and actions in which logical progression may at any time be interrupted by whim. Thus one comes to see that whim is the ruling passion of Tristram, that this is the central emotional fact of his character. The above selections, though narrowly about the art of writing, are as good a paradigm of Tristram's character as his thoughts on anything, their very scatteredness demonstrating as clearly as the hyphenated fragments of any sentence you chose to pick, the painful, the hilarious nature of Tristram's malady. In short, while it is common enough to think of a sentence and its construction as giving significant clues to oral expression, it should be no less obvious that the larger patterns of temporal structure must give an equally significant if less immediate clue to oral performance. Put it in another way. It is possible to read Tristram silently and miss much helter-skelter quality of his action, to miss the sudden total digression, which by the sheer bravado of its juxtaposition creates humorous levels of satire. It is possible to read *Tristram* aloud in the same way, dully. But the betrayal of the text is obvious at once. Sterne is a kind of Charlie Chaplin in the movements of his mind and in his construction of action through time. An oral reading forces one to begin to follow in the living voice the vagaries of Tristram's phrases and the inconsequence of his sequence of actions. From this it is but a step to the understanding in some depth of how these qualities are in themselves the bodying forth of the passion and purpose of the novel.

STRUCTURAL TIME

Essentially, of course, there are only two ways of structuring time: to take the events in natural sequence of occurrence, or, alternatively, to catch the sequence at its end or in mid-career and to relate the beginning and development in flashback (narration of time past). And the total time it takes to relate these events, however ordered, is the *total structural time* of the poem or story.

For the oral interpreter, this is the time it takes him to read the work from beginning to end. It will help in all subsequent matters if the interpreter can form the habit of seeing a work thus in a temporal frame, within which all decisions of vocal production and gesture must be ordered to create an expressive and harmonious relationship.

The poem "Driftwood" by Richard Wilbur is 229 words. That total, with attendant rhythmic effects, is the *structural time* of the poem. Within that framework, which has seemed best to the poet, he must make all his temporal decisions — how much each part shall have of the whole, how they shall blend and contrast.

Driftwood*

In greenwoods once these relics must have known
A rapt, gradual growing,
That are cast here like slag of the old
Engine of grief;

Must have affirmed in annual increase
Their close selves, knowing
Their own nature only, and that
Bringing to leaf.

Say, for the seven cities or a war
Their solitude was taken,
They into masts shaven, or milled into
Oar and plank;

Afterward sailing long and to lost ends,
By groundless water shaken,
Well they availed their vessels till they
Smashed or sank.

Then on the great generality of waters
Floated their singleness,
And in all that deep subsumption they were
Never dissolved;

But shaped and flowingly fretted by the waves'
Ever surpassing stress,
With the gnarled swerve and tangle of tides
Finely involved.

* From *Ceremony and Other Poems*, copyright, 1948, 1949, 1950, by Richard Wilbur. Reprinted by permission of Harcourt, Brace & World, Inc.

Brought in the end where breakers dump and slew
On the glass verge of the land,
Silver they rang to the stones when the sea
Flung them and turned.

Curious crowns and scepters they look to me
Here on the gold sand,
Warped, wry, but having the beauty of
Excellence earned.

In a time of continual dry abdications
And of damp complicities,
They are fit to be taken for signs, these emblems
Royally sane,

Which have ridden to homeless wreck, and long revolved
In the lathe of all the seas,
But have saved in spite of it all their dense
Ingenerate grain.

RICHARD WILBUR

In this poem the structural time is used to relate the history of the drift-wood as the author imagines it and its present appearance as he sees it. In the first stanza we are given a sharp contrast between the present and the furthest past, almost like a thematic statement. The driftwood is seen to have had three periods in its history. The author touches each of these in a flashback in a frankly summational way, giving general evaluative images rather than specific events, all in keeping with his attempt to relate a history he did not witness, but is reconstructing from present evidences. It is interesting to note the careful balance in attention given to each age: two stanzas each, and each covering a number of years. The final development, in which the driftwood is cast up on the shore and the narrator finds it, is a matter of hours and finally, of minutes. Nevertheless this last brief time has the weight of four stanzas. Thus the use of structural time places heaviest emphasis on that which is, according to the real time it took for the events to occur, the least important by far. Yet because the present appearance of the driftwood represents in sum and symbol all that has gone before and because it is this that falls within the poet's literal experi-ence, we accept this temporal structure as aesthetically logical. Indeed, the ordering of time has in itself had a great deal to do with creating the necessary tone. The classic balance of the initial statement and of the first three sequences, and the distance the author keeps in his images of the driftwood from those experiences which he can only imagine are both im-portant elements in creating the tone of profound, yet unpresumptuous admiration. There is something tasteful and true in the poet's refusal to identify his own ego with the driftwood by inventing details of romantic adventure, in the refusal to intrude where he is not essential, that prepares for the final image and tone of quiet veneration of these emblems of spiritual royalty. That this tone in its complex development is essentially an auditory one, one that must exist in the mind of the silent reader from previous oral experiences, should go without saying. And if they do not exist in any *real* and *literal* sense in his mind, he may be helped to them by hearing an adequate oral projection of them, or he may struggle to that reality through progressive efforts to vocalize them himself.

FICTIVE   TIME

We have defined structural time as the vessel which contains the form of the work of art, limiting the number of pages, the extent of a character's development, the length of a stanza, and the balance of one incident with another. But within that volume which offers itself, time is also a running thing in the story. Time flows, in short, not only for the reader of the story, but also for the characters *in* the story and for each mental and verbal gesture in it. Along with Tristram Shandy, we soon learn that the time it takes a thing to happen in a story or a poem is seldom the same thing as real time. This time-in-the-story we shall call *fictive time*.

Now fictive time itself would seem to be essentially of three kinds: (1) that which is frankly distorted, either lengthened or shortened, (2) that which is an approximation of reality, and (3) that which attempts a *psychological* approximation of reality. In other words, an author can frankly distort time, either extend an event unrealistically or collapse it unrealistically; or he can give us the thoughts or events roughly at the rate at which they might occur in real time; or he can try to make us believe that a certain time has passed whereas in actuality (structurally) significantly less or more has passed.

We have just had, in the early stanzas of "Driftwood," an excellent example of the compression of time. Let us imagine for ourselves an example of time which is distorted by drawing-out. "I picked up the gun — it was an heirloom, elaborate with engravings and gloomy with the patina of generations — and as I picked it up I jarred the delicate hair-trigger and it fired." Clearly this takes longer than would the actual gesture of picking up a gun. What especially elongates the fictive time is the descriptive passage, the middle clause of the sentence, coming as it does to interrupt the action after it has begun for the reader. What are the purposes of such a distortion? As in everything else having to do with the supreme art of fiction, there is no simple answer. The reasons and their permutations are as various as are the occasions themselves. In this as always we would have to see the part in the whole, the relationship of this one distortion of time to the whole time scheme and purpose of the story or poem. In our example, we have a potentially dramatic action begun. When anyone handles a gun, even the dullest reader is likely to sense something important is happening. Then what better way to cause suspense than to interrupt the action with a descriptive passage? Let the reader anticipate, savor the moment, grow a little anxious even. . . . Then again, it is probably true to say that no great writer ever used such a structural device for the simple, crude purpose of suspense. He might, for instance, take advantage of the awareness of the reader, heightened by the drama of the pistol, to develop a description or symbol essential to the total meaning of the story. The relationship between the fact that the gun is an heirloom, that it is "elaborate and gloomy" might have a great deal to do, in the thematic development of the story, with the fact that it fired as soon as it was picked up. If only there were a larger context, we might find the author is trying to tell us something about our relationship with certain events of the past: that some events of the past are dangerous and better left alone, or that the age of an event does not render it harmless, or indeed any one of countless thematic possibilities.

As to the third means of handling time, that which attempts a psychological rather than a literal temporal reality, one of the most successful attempts to distort time in a deceptive way is to be found in the climactic speech by Dr. Faustus in Christopher Marlowe's play of the same name. Faustus has sold his soul to the devil for knowledge or, as we might put it, he has purchased his knowledge at the expense of virtue. The Devil has just come to tell Faustus that he has one hour to live, and then he must pay the price of his bargain — his immortal soul. The clock strikes eleven as the Bad Angel vanishes, leaving Faustus to his hour of anguish. Now, in a soliloquy that takes between five to ten minutes on stage, a precise hour is marked off by the striking of the clock; and so subtle and powerful the language, so deep the insight into Faustus' spiritual dilemma, as his mind twists between its agonized vision and its necessary, saving action (too late come to for execution) "I'll burn my books," that we accept the convention as a successful transcription of literal time.

THE INTERPLAY OF FICTIVE TIME
AND STRUCTURAL TIME

As became apparent in the discussion of "Driftwood," it is virtually impossible to separate structural time from fictive time, their interaction is so intimate. For the shape that fictive time takes, that is, the transformation of real time into the conventional time of fiction, is so disciplined by the total structural time, and vice versa, that the reader must forever refer

to the one to clarify the other. Let us illustrate this point further by looking at another poem and comparing it with "Driftwood."

Evening Quatrains

I

The day's grown old, the fainting sun
Has but a little way to run,
And yet his steeds, with all his skill,
Scarce lug the chariot down the hill,

II

With labor spent and thirst opprest,
Whilst they strain hard to gain the West,
From fetlocks hot drops melted light,
Which turn to meteors in the night.

III

The shadows now so long do grow
That brambles like tall cedars show,
Mole-hills seem mountains, and the ant
Appears a monstrous elephant.

IV

A very little, little flock
Shades thrice the ground that it would stock;
Whilst the small stripling following them
Appears a mighty Polypheme.

V

These being brought into the fold,
And by the thrifty master told,
He thinks his wages are well paid,
Since none are either lost, or stray'd.

VI

Now lowing herds are each-where heard,
Chains rattle in the villein's yard,
The cart's on tail set down to rest,
Bearing on high the Cuckold's crest.

VII

The hedge is stripped, the clothes brought in,
Nought's left without should be within;

The bees are hiv'd and hum their charm,
Whilst every house does seem a swarm.

VIII

The cock now to the roost is prest,
For he must call up all the rest;
The sow's fast pegg'd within the sty,
To still her squeaking progeny.

IX

Each one has had his supping mess,
The cheese is put into the press,
The pans and bowls clean scalded all,
Reared up against the milk-house wall.

X

And now on benches all are sat
In the cool air to sit and chat,
Till Phoebus, dipping in the West,
Shall lead the world the way to rest.

CHARLES COTTON

Both "Evening Quatrains" and "Driftwood" are poems ten quatrains in length, so that in structural time they are nearly identical. In fictive time, however, one covers hours, the other many years. This difference in fictive time is at bottom of many of these poems' differences. I have already mentioned that the descriptive figures in "Driftwood" are summational: "Afterward sailing long and to lost ends / By groundless water shaken." What are the lost ends? What are the particular shaking events? Not only do we not need to know, but telling us would disrupt the entire structure of the poem. One has, in these summary figures, what one needs: a sense of numerous events of a certain sort happening over a long stretch of time. In "Evening Quatrains" the events are much more specific, realistic occurrences. In fact, the author obviously wishes to people our minds with these images of a rural evening. And yet for all the specificity of the one poem and the generality of the other, we receive from both poems a sense of the author keeping his distance from his subject matter, with a resultant objectivity and coolness of tone that would lead, if the poem were read aloud, to a minimum of physical response on the part of the reader and to relatively calm vocal patterns and contrasts. Yet this sense of distance is achieved differently, and within this general tone there is certainly more minor variation in "Evening Quatrains."

In "Driftwood" the distance is, as we have said, primarily one of time, the author casting back in imagination to general events or epochs, for he finally comes to look at the driftwood closely. In Cotton's poem the distance is one of space, for although the events of the evening are realistic ones, some humorous, some quaint, some brutish, some beautiful, we nonetheless see none of them in detail. We do not see the individual sheep; we see the flock. We do not see the boy only; we see him, his shadow, and his relationship to the flock. We do not see the details of the cart, but at a distance we observe the humorous appearance of its skyward tongue as it is set off its wheels for the night. In short we see these elements of the scene from some point central to them all, yet not so near to any that we feel immediately involved. This sense of distance is enhanced by the fact that none of the events are given a great deal of structural time, but the central observing eye, after having noted a salient feature, moves on. The effect is one of a landscape full of life, a life in which the human and animal are completely interwoven and in which each is moving in his own ordered way to the close of the day.

Is there any other reason for this distance? Certainly it is difficult to see how a closer involvement would have permitted the classical allusions. In spite of its apparently simple texture, this poem involves certain complexities. The first indirect reference to Phoebus, the description of the weary horses and the chariot, is a metaphor of unusually disparate elements, especially the likening of the sweat falling from a horse's fetlocks to those bright streaks of light cast from the setting sun, which later, the poet says, turn into meteors. And all the way through the poem there is a bold effort to combine different levels of diction into a meaningful whole, from words like "steed" and "chariot" on the literary level, to "lug" on the colloquial level. There is a further effort to combine the strikingly beautiful and the strikingly common, from the densely musical "the bees are hived and hum their charm," to the flat "Each one has had his supping mess." But over all these unions of divergences is the great one (which can be only in the literate person's mind, in the mind of just such an observer as speaks in the poem) of the past with the present, of his contemporary rural England with Ancient Greece. So that finally with the image, not of a seventeenth-century English sun, but of Phoebus, leading the world to rest, these simple country acts are transformed into something immemorial, and the literal evening has become an archetype, a human scene which the observer sees repeating itself till the world shall follow the weakening sun to its final rest.

Thus in successful writing the problems raised by fictive and by structural time work to their mutual solution. Although there are obviously as many such solutions as there are poems and stories, certain patterns are so frequently encountered as to become recognizable.

One difficulty frequent in writing is the necessity to relate a past history in which a few details are essential to the story, but are not really *in* the story to be presented. It is essential that the oral interpreter be alert to this problem and to the variant solutions if he is to define his narrative task clearly. Each of these solutions presents its tonal difficulties, and an awareness both of the problems and how the author solves them will give the reader essential clues to adequate vocalization. A little thought concerning the following will show that each will hold its own special vocal difficulties and opportunities.

The most straightforward answer to this problem is the summary, an excellent example of which is the first chapter of Austen's *Sense and Sensibility*. The summary offers a quick, clear, simple method of presenting material whose relative structural unimportance forbids a more elaborate solution. Its difficulties are a part of its strengths. It is likely to be bare, abrupt, and colorless, and structurally is likely to leave the reader feeling glad it is out of the way. Drama, fun, heightened interest of any kind, are difficult to inject into a recitation of vital statistics. There are many ways of making the summary lively. Jane Austen has pointed in one direction: the interest of style and witty insight can provide an intellectual excitement which, in its ironies and perceptions, can serve as substitutes for richness of drama, or at least it can do so for a while. The early stanzas in "Driftwood" show another method, as Wilbur combines a lovely musicality with exciting new combinations of generality and sharp, specific images, for instance, "knowing / Their own nature only, and that / Bringing to leaf." Another kind of interest in summary is that to be found in Joyce's "Eveline," in which a character recalls the past. Here the recitation of history can be made absorbing by our interest in the character and by our participation in the mood of the past as seen through that character's eyes. The device is essential in this story, because it is only as we become emotionally convinced of Eveline's absorption with the past that we accept her final act of rejection of the future. We can see this close participation at once if we stop and think a moment of the difference in the tone of voice that would be appropriate were we asked to read both "Eveline" and *Sense and Sensibility* aloud. The first would be personal, no doubt, with the indication of those sighs and sudden spurts of recollection that might accompany such a reverie as this. The second would be clear, crisp, the humor intellectually projected through ironic voice patterns.

Sometimes the small but essential knowledge of the past is evoked bit by bit, thus keeping attention fresh, while adding other qualities of emotional intensification. We can, perhaps, see this technique operate in even so short a poem as this of Thomas Hardy, in which remembrance of the past brings sharp, momentary contrasts to the present.

In a Former Resort After Many Years*

Do I know these, slack-shaped and wan,
Whose substance, one time fresh and furrowless,
Is now a rag drawn over a skeleton,
    As in El Greco's canvases? —
Whose cheeks have slipped down, lips become indrawn,
    And statures shrunk to dwarfishness?

Do they know me, whose former mind
Was like an open plain where no foot falls,
But now is as a gallery portrait-lined,
    And scored with necrologic scrawls,
Where feeble voices rise, once full-defined,
    From underground in curious calls?

THOMAS HARDY

However it is done, the methods are usually one variety or another of what we may call the flashback: a picking up of certain necessary selected details of the past.

The other face of the coin is seen in certain situations where the past is more important than the present — the *main* story is in the past, but the present must be introduced in its own right. The simplest means of solving this problem is by using a variant of the frame story, so called because the present forms a sort of frame around the past. Joseph Conrad was fond of the frame story, and we see an example in "The Lagoon," in which the white man comes to Arsat's dwelling, Arsat relates a story of the past, then the white man leaves.

Another structural problem frequently encountered involving time is the necessity to keep track of actions occurring in different places at the same time, a problem the old melodramas used to solve with, "Meanwhile back on the farm. . . ." (Varieties of this phrase still represent the simplest and in many cases, therefore, the best solution to this problem.) Parallel time can present the writer with both great opportunities and dangers. Like the montage technique in the movies, it can bring some apparently quite disparate things into close dramatic relationship, and it can also seem meaningless or florid. (Montage is a movie device whereby a view of one scene or happening or object is shown on a split screen with, or is immediately followed without transition by, a quite different one. The viewer is left to draw the meaning of the relationship between the two scenes or

* Reprinted from *Collected Poems of Thomas Hardy* by permission of The Macmillan Company (New York); the Executors of the Hardy Estate, Macmillan & Co. Ltd. (London), the Macmillan Company of Canada Limited. Copyright 1925 by The Macmillan Company. Renewed 1953 by Lloyds Bank Ltd.

objects for himself. Montage seems likewise a valuable name for literary studies.)

In "A Painful Case," Joyce has solved a problem in parallel time by having Duffy read of Mrs. Sinico's death in a newspaper, so that there is no necessity to switch from our focus on Duffy's monotonous life. Both her death and Duffy may in this way be held in focus at the same time. The method is forceful here because it emphasizes the screen of impersonality through which all events of importance to Duffy came to him. Also, Mrs. Sinico's common, publicly sordid end is just the kind that would most shock Duffy, hence would be most psychologically likely to move him to some deeper insight.

As has been suggested, the straightforward device of saying, "While this was happening . . . ," is not necessarily the least effective technique, where structurally suitable. In Thomas Hardy's "The Convergence of the Twain," for instance, it is particularly appropriate because of the great distance from which we see the twin happenings. The structure itself creates the tone of a dispassionate view of the workings of fate. It is as if, now that time has passed, we are able to view the two contrasting scenes, drawn nearer to each other by distance, with a single, grim eye. The problem of moving from the present into the past is also exemplified here. Nearly half the poem structurally is used in describing the present. This proportion would seem out of balance considering the lack of action — that the purpose of the time-present scenes is to describe stillness and obscurity. Yet their purpose also is to make us sense eternality — and in addition each stanza is relieved by a preparatory flash into the past through a comparison. We might see this as a rather unusually ordered frame story, with the crux of action in the past and the tone largely deriving from the treatment of the present. Certainly the striking structure of this poem serves to indicate once more that each work of art requires its own peculiar solutions.

It would seem that up to now we have talked about the necessity of distorting time in the narrative perspective and have ignored those stories and poems told directly and simply from start to finish of the action. Such a poem is Waller's "Go Lovely Rose" (see p. 157): a person is addressing the flower and it takes just as long for the person to say his words as it takes for us to read the poem; the structural and fictive times are equal. We notice, however, that there is a good deal of distortion and summary in the handling of the future time about which the narrator is thinking. We have, in a sense, a kind of frame story, looking to the future rather than to the past. And so we often find that what looks like a simple, direct tale has, nonetheless, some subtlety in the handling of time.

In Dorothy Parker's "Just a Little One," we have a story told without any apparent temporal deviation, yet time is nonetheless a good deal distorted, compressed. As in Waller's poem, there is one speaker, but in this case, the speaker is addressing another person. Let us examine a few lines to see how time is shortened.

"Do you come here often, Fred? I shouldn't worry about you so much if I knew you were in a safe place like this." [We must infer that at this point Fred replies that he comes here often and was here Thursday night, for she goes on to say,] "Oh, is this where you were Thursday night?" [Fred responds.] "I see." [We must infer here that Fred asks her if she minds, or has forgiven him, or some such.] "Why, no, it didn't make a bit of difference. . . ." All the bracketed material is insisted upon, by what we are given, as having happened, so that the fictive time is moving much faster than the incident would have in real time. The technique is handled in structural time by concentrating on her speech and leaving the understanding of the total scene to the imagination of the reader. In short, none of her reactions is distorted in the structural pattern, but everything else is simply excised, as a means of compressing the fictive time.

In poetry this kind of economy of time is called a dramatic monologue: dramatic, because an action or rather interaction between two people is the basis of the structure; monologue, of course, because we hear only one of the persons speaking. A brief and amusing dramatic monologue is the following poem, in which we hear the protesting, but not too firmly protesting, voice of a lady to her importunate lover.

> Sweet, let me go! Sweet, let me go!
> What do you mean to vex me so?
> Cease, cease, cease your pleading force!
> Do you think thus to extort remorse?
> Now, now! alas you overbear me;
> And I would cry, but some would hear, I fear me.

ANONYMOUS

We must not make too much of these or other categories, for they are descriptions after the fact; we note a certain pattern recurring and it is enlightening to see why it does and how it is varied in each circumstance. The overriding awareness we *must* have is that the temporal demands of structure inevitably integrate with the handling of fictive time, and further that each new successful solution will seem at once familiar and quite new. As we read on in poetry and stories, there will be no end to what we will learn about the problems of selectivity imposed by time, and we will find that each author must build on what is in the past, but also we will discover that there are never really any secure precedents or models for the act of creation. In this sense the oral interpreter and the writer are like the woman in the old Polish Hassidic legend.

The Story of the Cape*

Eighteenth-century legend retold by

MARTIN BUBER

A woman came to Rabbi Israil, the maggid of Koznitz, and told him, with many tears, that she had been married a dozen years and still had not borne a son. "What are you willing to do about it?" he asked her. She did not know what to say.

"My mother," so the maggid told her, "was aging and still had no child. Then she heard that the holy Baal Shem, a Jewish mystic, inspirer of the Hassidic movement was stopping over in Apt in the course of a journey. She hurried to his inn and begged him to pray she might bear a son. 'What are you willing to do about it?' he asked. 'My husband is a poor book-binder' she replied, 'but I do have one fine thing that I shall give to the rabbi.' She went home as fast as she could and fetched her good cape, her 'Katinka,' which was carefully stowed away in a chest. But when she returned to the inn with it, she heard that the Baal Shem had already left for Mezbizh. She immediately set out after him and since she had no money to ride, she walked from town to town with her 'Katinka' until she came to Mezbizh. The Baal Shem took the cape and hung it on the wall. 'It is well,' he said. My mother walked all the way back, from town to town, until she reached Apt. A year later, I was born."

"I, too," cried the woman, "will bring you a good cape of mine so that I may get a son."

"That won't work," said the maggid. "You heard the story. My mother had no story to go by."

If it is true, then, that each story or poem must find its own solution to the temporal problem, it is also eternally true that, although variety is no doubt the spice of life, we all have nonetheless an inborn sense of structure, a desire for expectations to be fulfilled within the time that might reasonably be used for their development. As a result, the writer learns, like Shandy, that if *to select* is not the name of art, it is certainly its necessary verb.

Let us take a final look at an example of the interaction of structural demands on time with the process of temporal selectivity that leads to an appropriate development of fictive time.

We notice in the story "A Painful Case" that in a structural sense the time taken to tell the story is divided in two almost equal parts. The first half takes us down through Mr. Duffy's acquaintance with Mrs. Sinico, and ends with the sentence, "a few days later he received a parcel containing his books and music." The first half starts with a description of his life up to the time of his meeting with Mrs. Sinico and ends with the development and conclusion of their friendship. The second half starts with a de-

* Reprinted by permission of Schocken Books Inc. from *Tales of the Hasidim: The Later Masters* by Martin Buber, Copyright © 1948 by Schocken Books Inc., New York, translated by Olga Marx.

scription of his life during the next four years, and ends with a description of his feelings on reading of her death. These halves may be seen themselves to have each a division. A chart may clarify this pattern. There are in the story around 3,600 words, and the following chart will show how they are divided within the developmental pattern mentioned above.

		Approximate # of words	Approximate % structural time	Approximate fictive time
First half	1st part	700	20	40 years
	2nd part	1,120	31	not certain, perhaps ½ year to 1 year
Second half	3rd part	140	4	4 years
	4th part	1,640	45	one evening

Some interesting facts become clear here about the handling of time in this story. There is an almost perfect balance in structural time between that part which precedes the climactic action (the breaking of the friendship) and the development of the conclusive actions (the last half), yet in fictive time there is a striking imbalance. Actually, it needs no more than a glance at the chart to see that the final evening is of overpowering importance, taking 45 per cent of the structural time. We see how the handling of time both fictive and structural must itself reinforce the total meaning of the story. Why are only 140 words devoted to describing four years? Partly because it can be done in that time. After Duffy ends the friendship, there is nothing for him to do but return to his routine life, and his routine has already been described in the first part of the story. There is no reason to think that the author could not invent more incidents such as the one in which Mr. Duffy writes the sentence about "friendship" in his sheaf of papers. But the question remains, should he do so? And the answer is that there is a very real limit to the effective length of this section, since, by its very brevity as much as any other method, it indicates the sterility of Duffy's life. It does so especially as it contrasts with the living, almost minute-by-minute agony suffered by Duffy when that reality which he has kept so long at bay sweeps irresistibly over his defenses. All told, it takes 800 words to describe forty-four years of Duffy's life, as against 2,760 to describe his brief time with Mrs. Sinico and his one evening of truthful memory of that friendship. And this disbalance in itself describes the barren limitation of his fearfully, prudishly singular existence, as against its richness during the brief time he allows one other person into his life.

It is wrong, then, to think of the pressure to condense, to discipline time in a fictive way, as a thing to be regretted. Tristram Shandy's perplexities are the eternal ones of the author; but when the author has miraculously solved these problems, the result is pure gain for the reader. Do we really need the actions of the aggressive lover in the little dramatic monologue described for us? Do we really need a clinical analysis of what causes the lady to cry, "Now, now! No more!"? On the contrary, the fun is in not knowing everything, of knowing enough to both limit and set free the play of imagination. The joy is in seeing the chaotic happenings in time selected, rendered, turned into controlled flows of time that imply their significance. Learning to read great stories and poems is largely learning when to take, and when not to take, a hint.

Though these compositional problems of the author may seem remote from the task of one who would read the story or poem aloud, it is a fact, as has been said, that an awareness of the problems of structuring time will help enormously in arriving at the vocal and bodily cues which will make the work live for an audience. How will it help to see that in "Evening Quatrains" structural time represents a relatively slight compression of fictive time, whereas in "Driftwood" the fictive time covers a lifetime, though the structural time is roughly equivalent to that of "Evening Quatrains"? The reader can see at once that his tonal patterns and bodily attitudes in the one must work to create an illusion of standing in a scene and describing it. Thus, the speed will be the speed of natural attention as the eyes move realistically from one object to another. In "Driftwood," on the other hand, the summary part covers a great amount of time. The poet's eye is on his own imaginings as they recreate the ages of man, rather than on a static, vivid scene made up of sharp details. This introspection will affect the reader's use of his eyes and his quality of bodily tension and attitude. Thus the rate of delivery is slower, I think, than in "Evening Quatrains," with vocal tones at once more sonorous and contemplative. In all truth (reading the two poems silently), would one be sure of experiencing this significant element of rate? I think it is only through the oral discipline that the reader is forced into such subtle but vital discoveries.

The problems of reading aloud the poem "In a Former Resort After Many Years" will be made clearer if one sees that the phrases "one time fresh and furrowless," "whose former mind / Was like an open plain where no foot falls," and "once full-defined" are flashbacks and present a specific problem for the oral reader. These flashbacks must be differentiated *dramatically* from their surroundings. They must, however subtly in vocal intonation and facial expression and bodily attitude, be made to express the emotional, ironic contrast with the surrounding phrases. And finally, though separated from each other in the poem, theirs is not a vague technical similarity. The oral reader must see how they are related *expressively* in a structurally meaningful way.

In other words, structural time in reading aloud is profoundly affected by the way in which the fictive time is being handled. "Just a Little One" is a case in point. Once the interpreter sees the method of compressing the fictional time in this story, it becomes obvious that it will be necessary, in order to do a convincing interpretation, to create the illusion that the woman is responding to the man and to her surroundings. Thus, when she says, "Oh, is this where you were Thursday night? I see. Why, no, it didn't make a bit of difference . . . ," there must be a pause after "night," and a pause after "I see." But they will be of different length and quality. The pause after "night" will be very short, because all the woman needs is confirmation. As soon as the man nods his head or says simply "yes," she can go on with "I see." But the next pause is longer; we must imagine the man to make a speech of some duration, because the woman responds, as I have said, apparently to some question as to whether or not she minds. In creating this illusion obviously the interpreter does not need to wait *literally* the length of time it would take to make such a speech, but he must pause long enough to create the *illusion* and thus to justify the woman's reaction (and by the way, one learns a good deal about the proper tone of voice in which to read the sentence "I see," from the fact that the man asks her if she objects.) So it is clear that the compressions and distortions of fictive time practiced by the writer will affect in greater or lesser ways the interpreter's re-creation. It is his job to catch these temporal hints and to echo them precisely in the conventions of his performing art.

PREPARATION FOR PERFORMANCE — "The Windhover"

Time

The reader has before him a reliable text, concerning which no questions have been raised. The poem is a relatively modern one. The speaker and the situation, though they are based on the Christian tradition, are not rooted in the particular images or attitudes of a historic period. Thus, the oral reader need not look for styles of speech and bodily attitudes foreign to his classroom audience, styles which might require subtle reintegrations into gestures of voice and body which are more meaningful to that audience.

So far as the handling of time *in* the poem is concerned, there is a central fact which must inform any oral realization. The first stanza is told in the *past tense*. The oral reader, then, is not directly seeing the Falcon — his visualization of it is not an immediate experience taking place before the eyes of the audience. Rather, the description takes the form of a recollection, related sometime during the same day when the exalting spell of the vision is still strong, yet now modified by the poet's more mature sense of the significance of this vision for him.

For this reason the reader before the audience should not visualize the bird in the air, except as the reader's bodily attitude makes it perfectly clear that this is a *remembered* visualization, however vivid. Thus, temporally, the octet is a flashback, a remembrance of a vivid scene. The sestet (the last six lines) has its own peculiarity. For though it is in the present tense, the poet's attention is drawn to nothing in the present, but is still fixed to that image of the Falcon, now gone except in memory. Again the oral reader is not reflecting an environment that surrounds him in the present but is responding, and talking, to an internal image. Though it would therefore be appropriate to read to the audience, it is not, in the sestet, being directly addressed, and this distinction must be incorporated in oral performance.

SELECTIONS

Two Sides to a Tortoise

Most ugly shapes and horrible aspects,[1]
Such as Dame Nature selfe mote feare to see,
Or shame, that ever should so fowle defects
From her most cunning hand escaped bee;
All dreadfull pourtraicts of deformitee
Ne wonder, if these do a man appall;
For all that here at home we dreadfull hold
Be but as bugs to fearen babes withall
Compared to the creatures in these isles' entrall

  .   .   .   .

Feare naught, then saide the Palmer well aviz'd,
For these same monsters are not these in deed,
But are into these fearful shapes disguiz'd.

  .   .   .   .

And lifting up his vertuous staffe on hye,
Then all that dreadfull armie fast can flye
Into great Zethy's bosome, where they hidden lye.

In view of the description given, may one be gay upon the Encantadas? Yes: that is, find one the gaiety, and he will be gay. And, indeed, sackcloth and ashes as they are, the isles are not perhaps unmitigated gloom. For while no spectator can deny their claims to a most solemn

[1] From Fairie Queene, Book II, Canto XII, Stanzas XXIII, XXV; Book II, Canto XII, Stanza XXVI. (There are some changes.)

and superstitious consideration, no more than my firmest resolutions can decline to behold the spectre-tortoise when emerging from its shadowy recess; yet even the tortoise, dark and melancholy as it is upon the back, still possesses a bright side; its calipee or breast-plate being sometimes of a faint yellowish or golden tinge. Moreover, everyone knows that tortoises as well as turtles are of such a make, that if you but put them on their backs you thereby expose their bright sides without the possibility of their recovering themselves, and turning into view the other. But after you have done this, and because you have done this, you should not swear that the tortoise has no dark side. Enjoy the bright, keep it turned up perpetually if you can, but be honest, and don't deny the black. Neither should he, who cannot turn the tortoise from its natural position so as to hide the darker and expose his livelier aspect, like a great October pumpkin in the sun, for that cause declare the creature to be one total inky blot. The tortoise is both black and bright. But let us to particulars.

Some months before my first stepping ashore upon the group, my ship was cruising in its close vicinity. One noon we found ourselves off the South Head of Albemarle, and not very far from the land. Partly by way of freak, and partly by way of spying out so strange a country, a boat's crew was sent ashore, with orders to see all they could, and besides, bring back whatever tortoises they could conveniently transport.

It was after sunset, when the adventurers returned. I looked down over the ship's high side as if looking down over the curb of a well, and dimly saw the damp boat deep in the sea with some unwonted weight. Ropes were dropt over, and presently three huge antediluvian-looking tortoises, after much straining, were landed on deck. They seemed hardly of the seed of earth. We had been abroad upon the waters for five long months, a period amply sufficient to make all things of the land wear a fabulous hue to the dreamy mind. Had three Spanish custom-house officers boarded us then, it is not unlikely that I should have curiously stared at them, felt of them, and stroked them much as savages serve civilised guests. But instead of three custom-house officers, behold these really wondrous tortoises — none of your schoolboy mudturtles — but black as widower's weeds, heavy as chests of plate, with vast shells medallioned and orbed like shields, and dented and blistered like shields that have breasted a battle, shaggy, too, here and there, with dark green moss, and slimy with the spray of the sea. These mystic creatures, suddenly translated by night from unutterable solitudes to our peopled deck, affected me in a manner not easy to unfold. They seemed newly crawled forth from beneath the foundations of the world. Yea, they seemed the identical tortoises whereon the Hindoo plants this total sphere. With a lantern I inspected them more closely. Such worshipful venerableness of aspect! Such furry greenness mantling the rude peelings and healing the fissures

of their shattered shells. I no more saw three tortoises. They expanded —
became transfigured. I seemed to see three Roman Coliseums in magnificent decay.

Ye oldest inhabitants of this, or any other isle, said I, pray, give me
the freedom of your three walled towns.

The great feeling inspired by these creatures was that of age: — dateless, indefinite endurance. And, in fact, that any other creature can live
and breathe as long as the tortoise of the Encantadas, I will not readily
believe. Not to hint of their known capacity of sustaining life, while going
without food for an entire year, consider that impregnable armor of their
living mail. What other bodily being possesses such a citadel wherein to
resist the assaults of Time?

As, lantern in hand, I scraped among the moss and beheld the ancient
scars of bruises received in many a sullen fall among the marly mountains
of the isle — scars strangely widened, swollen, half obliterate, and yet distorted like those sometimes found in the bark of very hoary trees, I seemed
an antiquary of a geologist, studying the bird-tracks and ciphers upon the
exhumed slates trod by incredible creatures whose very ghosts are now
defunct.

As I lay in my hammock that night, overhead I heard the slow weary
draggings of the three ponderous strangers along the encumbered deck.
Their stupidity or their resolution was so great, that they never went aside
for any impediment. One ceased his movements altogether just before the
mid-watch. At sunrise I found him butted like a battering-ram against the
immovable foot of the foremast, and still striving, tooth and nail, to force
the impossible passage. That these tortoises are the victims of a penal, or
malignant, or perhaps a downright diabolical enchanter, seems in nothing
more likely than in that strange infatuation of hopeless toil which so often
possesses them. I have known them in their journeyings ram themselves
heroically against rocks, and long abide there, nudging, wriggling, wedging, in order to displace them, and so hold on their inflexible path. Their
crowning curse is their drudging impulse to straightforwardness in a belittered world.

Meeting with no such hinderance as their companion did, the other
tortoises merely fell foul of small stumbling-blocks — buckets, blocks, and
coils of rigging — and at times in the act of crawling over them would
slip with an astounding rattle to the deck. Listening to these draggings
and concussions, I thought me of the haunt from which they came; an
isle full of metallic ravines and gulches, sunk bottomlessly into the hearts
of splintered mountains, and covered for many miles with inextricable
thickets. I then pictured these three straightforward monsters, century
after century, writhing through the shades, grim as blacksmiths; crawling
so slowly and ponderously, that not only did toadstools and all fungous

things grow beneath their feet, but a sooty moss sprouted upon their backs. With them I lost myself in volcanic mazes; brushed away endless boughs of rotting thickets; till finally in a dream I found myself sitting cross-legged upon the foremost, a Brahmin similarly mounted upon either side, forming a tripod of foreheads which upheld the universal cope.

Such was the wild nightmare begot by my first impression of the Encantadas tortoise. But next evening, strange to say, I sat down with my shipmates, and made a merry repast from tortoise steaks and tortoise stews; and supper over, out knife, and helped convert the three mighty concave shells into three fanciful soup-tureens, and polished the three flat yellowish calipees into three gorgeous salvers.

HERMAN MELVILLE

American Note-Books

(excerpt)

NATHANIEL HAWTHORNE

September 7th. — In a wood, a heap or pile of logs and sticks, that had been cut for firewood, and piled up square, in order to be carted away to the house when convenience served, — or, rather, to be sledded in sleighing time. But the moss had accumulated on them, and leaves falling over them from year to year and decaying, a kind of soil had quite covered them, although the softened outline of the woodpile was perceptible in the green mound. It was perhaps fifty years — perhaps more — since the woodman had cut and piled those logs and sticks, intending them for his winter fires. But he probably needs no fire now. There was something strangely interesting in this simple circumstance. Imagine the long-dead woodman, and his long-dead wife and family, and the old man who was a little child when the wood was cut, coming back from their graves, and trying to make a fire with this mossy fuel.

The Wood-Pile*

Out walking in the frozen swamp one grey day,
I paused and said, 'I will turn back from here.
No, I will go on farther — and we shall see.'

The hard snow held me, save where now and then
One foot went through. The view was all in lines
Straight up and down of tall slim trees
Too much alike to mark or name a place by
So as to say for certain I was here
Or somewhere else: I was just far from home.
A small bird flew before me. He was careful
To put a tree between us when he lighted,
And say no word to tell me who he was
Who was so foolish as to think what *he* thought.
He thought that I was after him for a feather —
The white one in his tail; like one who takes
Everything said as personal to himself.
One flight out sideways would have undeceived him.
And then there was a pile of wood for which
I forgot him and let his little fear
Carry him off the way I might have gone,
Without so much as wishing him good-night.
He went behind it to make his last stand.
It was a cord of maple, cut and split
And piled — and measured, four by four by eight.
And not another like it could I see.
No runner tracks in this year's snow looped near it.
And it was older sure than this year's cutting,
Or even last year's or the year's before.
The wood was grey and the bark warping off it
And the pile somewhat sunken. Clematis
Had wound strings round and round it like a bundle.
What held it though on one side was a tree
Still growing, and on one a stake and prop,
These latter about to fall. I thought that only
Someone who lived in turning to fresh tasks
Could so forget his handiwork on which
He spent himself, the labour of his axe,
And leave it there far from a useful fireplace
To warm the frozen swamp as best it could
With the slow smokeless burning of decay.

ROBERT FROST

Ode on a Grecian Urn

I

Thou still unravish'd bride of quietness,
　Thou foster-child of silence and slow time,
Sylvan historian, who canst thus express
　A flowery tale more sweetly than our rhyme:
What leaf-fring'd legend haunts about thy shape
　Of deities or mortals, or of both,
　　In Tempe or the dales of Arcady?
　What men or gods are these? What maidens loth?
What mad pursuit? What struggle to escape?
　　What pipes and timbrels? What wild ecstasy?

II

Heard melodies are sweet, but those unheard
　Are sweeter; therefore, ye soft pipes, play on;
Not to the sensual ear, but, more endear'd,
　Pipe to the spirit ditties of no tone:
Fair youth, beneath the trees, thou canst not leave
　Thy song, nor ever can those trees be bare;
　　Bold Lover, never, never canst thou kiss,
Though winning near the goal — yet, do not grieve;
　She cannot fade, though thou hast not thy bliss,
　　For ever wilt thou love, and she be fair!

III

Ah, happy, happy boughs! that cannot shed
　Your leaves, nor ever bid the Spring adieu;
And, happy melodist, unwearied,
　For ever piping songs for ever new;
More happy love! more happy, happy love!
　For ever warm and still to be enjoy'd,
　　For ever panting, and for ever young;
All breathing human passion far above,
　That leaves a heart high-sorrowful and cloy'd,
　　A burning forehead, and a parching tongue.

IV

Who are these coming to the sacrifice?
  To what green altar, O mysterious priest,
Lead'st thou that heifer lowing at the skies,
  And all her silken flanks with garlands drest?
What little town by river or sea shore,
  Or mountain-built with peaceful citadel,
    Is emptied of this folk, this pious morn?
And, little town, thy streets for evermore
  Will silent be; and not a soul to tell
    Why thou art desolate, can e'er return.

V

O Attic shape! Fair attitude! with brede
  Of marble men and maidens overwrought,
With forest branches and the trodden weed;
  Thou, silent form, dost tease us out of thought
As doth eternity: Cold Pastoral!
  When old age shall this generation waste,
    Thou shalt remain, in midst of other woe
Than ours, a friend to man, to whom thou say'st,
  "Beauty is truth, truth beauty," — that is all
    Ye know on earth, and all ye need to know.

JOHN KEATS

To Autumn

I

Season of mists and mellow fruitfulness,
  Close bosom-friend of the maturing sun;
Conspiring with him how to load and bless
  With fruit the vines that round the thatch-eves run;
To bend with apples the moss'd cottage-trees,
  And fill all fruit with ripeness to the core;
    To swell the gourd, and plump the hazel shells
With a sweet kernel; to set budding more,
  And still more, later flowers for the bees,
  Until they think warm days will never cease,
    For Summer has o'er-brimm'd their clammy cells.

II

Who hath not seen thee oft amid thy store?
   Sometimes whoever seeks abroad may find
Thee sitting careless on a granary floor,
   Thy hair soft-lifted by the winnowing wind;
Or on a half-reap'd furrow sound asleep,
    Drows'd with the fume of poppies, while thy hook
      Spares the next swath and all its twined flowers:
And sometimes like a gleaner thou dost keep
    Steady thy laden head across a brook;
    Or by a cyder-press, with patient look,
      Thou watchest the last oozings hours by hours.

III

Where are the songs of Spring? Ay, where are they?
   Think not of them, thou hast thy music too, —
While barred clouds bloom the soft-dying day,
   And touch the stubble-plains with rosy hue;
Then in a wailful choir the small gnats mourn
    Among the river sallows,[2] born aloft
      Or sinking as the light wind lives or dies;
And full-grown lambs loud bleat from hilly bourn;
    Hedge-crickets sing; and now with treble soft
    The red-breast whistles from a garden-croft;
      And gathering swallows twitter in the skies.

JOHN KEATS

Musée des Beaux Arts*

About suffering they were never wrong,
The Old Masters: how well they understood
Its human position; how it takes place
While someone else is eating or opening a window or just walking dully
   along;
How, when the aged are reverently, passionately waiting
For the miraculous birth, there always must be

---

[2] willows

Children who did not specially want it to happen, skating
On a pond at the edge of the wood:
They never forgot
That even the dreadful martyrdom must run its course
Anyhow in a corner, some untidy spot
Where the dogs go on with their doggy life and the torturer's horse
Scratches its innocent behind on a tree.

In Brueghel's *Icarus*, for instance: how everything turns away
Quite leisurely from the disaster; the ploughman may
Have heard the splash, the forsaken cry,
But for him it was not an important failure; the sun shone
As it had to on the white legs disappearing into the green
Water; and the expensive delicate ship that must have seen
Something amazing, a boy falling out of the sky,
Had somewhere to get to and sailed calmly on.

W. H. AUDEN

Island Quarry*

Square sheets — they saw the marble into
Flat slabs there at the marble quarry
At the turning of the road around the roots of the mountain
Where the straight road would seem to ply below the stone, that fierce
Profile of marble spiked with yonder
Palms against the sunset's towering sea, and maybe
Against mankind. It is at times —

In dusk it is at times as though this island lifted, floated
In Indian baths. At Cuban dusk the eyes
Walking the straight road toward thunder —
This dry road silvering toward the shadow of the quarry
— It is at times as though the eyes burned hard and glad
And did not take the goat path quivering to the right,
Wide of the mountain — thence to tears and sleep —
But went on into marble that does not weep.

HART CRANE

The Waterfall at Powerscourt*

Looping off feline through the leisured air
    Water, a creature not at home in water,
Takes to the air. It comes down on its forepaws, changes
    Feet on the rockface and again extended
Bounds.   For it neither
    Pours nor is poured, but only here on its quarry
Falls at last, pours. No more the amphibious otter
    Than foundered ram can walk this water thrown
Catwalk across a further element.

Water itself is not at home in water
    But fails its creatures, as a fallen nature
Swerves from its course. And, less adaptable,
    Out of an element itself thrown out
The fallen creature cannot find itself
    Nor its own level, headlong.

Or else as a sealion, heavy and limber,
    Sedately slithers its short rock chute in the zoo
(Foolish and haughty as, propped on a stock, the Prince Regent),
    And over the water it takes to
Shoots,   so the water
    Lobs itself, immerses in rock and, rebounding,
Surfaces smoothly backwards into space,
    Swimming the air as for freshwater miles offshore
The Orinoco dyes the ocean cold.

What end it answers, over the Sabine country
    Of Mrs. Rafferty's Tusculum and Dublin's
Weekend hinterland, arching; or what use
    Insinuating underneath that ocean
Its chill of wit, who knows? The end it answers,
    The level it seeks, is its own.

Donald Davie

* Reprinted by permission of the author.

The Sheaves*

Where long the shadows of the wind had rolled,
Green wheat was yielding to the change assigned;
And as by some vast magic undivined
The world was turning slowly into gold.
Like nothing that was ever bought or sold
It waited there, the body and the mind;
And with a mighty meaning of a kind
That tells the more the more it is not told.
So in a land where all days are not fair,
Fair days went on till on another day
A thousand golden sheaves were lying there,
Shining and still, but not for long to stay —
As if a thousand girls with golden hair
Might rise from where they slept and go away.

                                        E. A. ROBINSON

The Windhover:†

To Christ Our Lord

I caught this morning morning's minion, king-
    dom of daylight's dauphin, dapple-dawn-drawn Falcon, in his riding
Of the rolling level underneath him steady air, and striding
High there, how he rung upon the rein of a wimpling wing
In his ecstasy! then off, off forth on swing,
    As a skate's heel sweeps smooth on a bow-bend: the hurl and gliding
Rebuffed the big wind. My heart in hiding
Stirred for a bird, — the achieve of, the mastery of the thing!

Brute beauty and valour and act, oh, air, pride, plume, here
    Buckle! *and* the fire that breaks from thee then, a billion
Times told lovelier, more dangerous, O my chevalier!

No wonder of it: shéer plód makes plough down sillion
Shine, and blue-bleak embers, ah my dear,
    Fall, gall themselves, and gash gold-vermilion.

                                GERARD MANLEY HOPKINS

*Wreck**

The hulk stranded in Scalpay bay,
Hung like a hall with seaweed, stuck
Its long snout through my holiday.
It lay foundered on its own bad luck.

Twice every day it took aboard
A cargo of the tide; its crew
Flitted with fins. And sand explored
What ever cranny it came to.

It should have carried deaths to give
To me stumbling across the stones;
It never spoke of what could live.
I saw no ghosts between its bones.

It had not learned that it had failed;
Its voyages would not let it be.
More slow than glacier it sailed
Into the bottom of the sea.

NORMAN MacCAIG

Mouse's Nest

I found a ball of grass among the hay
And progged it as I passed and went away;
And when I looked I fancied something stirred,
And turned agen and hoped to catch the bird —
When out an old mouse bolted in the wheats
With all her young ones hanging at her teats;
She looked so odd and so grotesque to me,
I ran and wondered what the thing could be,
And pushed the knapweed bunches where I stood;
Then the mouse hurried from the craking brood.
The young ones squeaked, and as I went away
She found her nest again among the hay.
The water o'er the pebbles scarce could run
And broad old cesspools glittered in the sun.

JOHN CLARE

* Reprinted from *Riding Lights* by Norman MacCaig, by permission of
The Hogarth Press Ltd. (London).

Composed Upon Westminster Bridge,
September 3, 1802

Earth has not anything to show more fair:
Dull would he be of soul who could pass by
A sight so touching in its majesty:
This City now doth, like a garment, wear
The beauty of the morning; silent, bare,
Ships, towers, domes, theatres, and temples lie
Open unto the fields, and to the sky;
All bright and glittering in the smokeless air.
Never did sun more beautifully steep
In his first splendour, valley, rock, or hill;
Ne'er saw I, never felt, a calm so deep!
The river glideth at his own sweet will:
Dear God! the very houses seem asleep;
And all that mighty heart is lying still!

WILLIAM WORDSWORTH

Walking in Mist*

At first the river Noe
Like a snake's belly gleamed below,
And then in mist was lost;
The hill too vanished like a ghost
And all the day was gone
Except the damp grey light that round me shone.

From Lose Hill to Mam Tor,
Darkness behind me and before,
I gave the track its head;
But as I followed where it led,
That light went all the way
As though I made and carried my own day.

ANDREW YOUNG

* Reprinted from *The Collected Poems of Andrew Young* by permission of Rupert Hart-Davis Limited (London).

The Dorm in Autumn*

Fistfuls of winter flung at our window
dignify our school: storm-remembered.
Before we were born these winds
looking for fur were here after our equals
    the wild creatures.

Neighbors, treetops, fieldmice — how dark it becomes!
Ours are weak signals up from the chimneys,
but richly inside our siege is mounded
by study, thought like incense. Allwise,
    we study upward.

WILLIAM STAFFORD

Juggler†

A ball will bounce, but less and less. It's not
A light-hearted thing, resents its own resilience.
Falling is what it loves, and the earth falls
So in our hearts from brilliance,
Settles and is forgot.
It takes a sky-blue juggler with five red balls

To shake our gravity up. Whee, in the air
The balls roll round, wheel on his wheeling hands,
Learning the ways of lightness, alter to spheres
Grazing his finger ends,
Cling to their courses there,
Swinging a small heaven about his ears.

But a heaven is easier made of nothing at all
Than the earth regained, and still and sole within
The spin of worlds, with a gesture sure and noble
He reels that heaven in,
Landing it ball by ball,
And trades it all for a broom, a plate, a table.

Oh, on his toe the table is turning, the broom's
Balancing up on his nose, and the plate whirls
On the tip of the broom! Damn, what a show, we cry:
The boys stamp, and the girls
Shriek, and the drum booms
And all comes down, and he bows and says good-bye.

If the juggler is tired now, if the broom stands
In the dust again, if the table starts to drop
Through the daily dark again, and though the plate
Lies flat on the table top,
For him we batter our hands
Who has won for once over the world's weight.

RICHARD WILBUR

There Was a Child Went Forth

(*Leaves of Grass*, Autumn Rivulets section)

There was a child went forth every day,
And the first object he look'd upon, that object he became,
And that object became part of him for the day or a certain part of the day,
Or for many years or stretching cycles of years.

The early lilacs became part of this child,
And grass and white and red morning-glories, and white and red clover,
    and the song of the phoebe-bird,
And the Third-month lambs and the sow's pink-faint litter, and the mare's
    foal and the cow's calf,
And the noisy brood of the barnyard or by the mire of the pond-side,
And the fish suspending themselves so curiously below there, and the
    beautiful curious liquid,
And the water-plants with their graceful flat heads, all became part of him.

The field-sprouts of Fourth-month and Fifth-month became part of him,
Winter-grain sprouts and those of the light-yellow corn, and the esculent
    roots of the garden,
And the apple-trees cover'd with blossoms and the fruit afterward, and
    wood-berries, and the commonest weeds by the road,
And the old drunkard staggering home from the outhouse of the tavern
    whence he had lately risen,

And the schoolmistress that pass'd on her way to the school,
And the friendly boys that pass'd, and the quarrelsome boys,
And the tidy and fresh-cheek'd girls, and the barefoot negro boy and girl,
And all the changes of city and country wherever he went.

His own parents, he that had father'd him and she that had conceiv'd him
   in her womb and birth'd him,
They gave this child more of themselves than that,
They gave him afterward every day, they became part of him.
The mother at home quietly placing the dishes on the supper-table,
The mother with mild words, clean her cap and gown, a wholesome odor
   falling off her person and clothes as she walks by,
The father, strong, self-sufficient, manly, mean, anger'd, unjust,
The blow, the quick loud word, the tight bargain, the crafty lure,
The family usages, the language, the company, the furniture, the yearning
   and swelling heart,
Affection that will not be gainsay'd, the sense of what is real, the thought
   if after all it should prove unreal,
The doubts of day-time and the doubts of night-time, the curious whether
   and how,
Whether that which appears so is so, or is it all flashes and specks?
Men and women crowding fast in the streets, if they are not flashes and
   specks what are they?
The streets themselves and the façades of houses, and goods in the
   windows,
Vehicles, teams, the heavy-plank'd wharves, the huge crossing at the ferries,
The village on the highland seen from afar at sunset, the river between,
Shadows, aureola and mist, the light falling on roofs and gables of white
   or brown two miles off,
The schooner near by sleepily dropping down the tide, the little boat
   slack-tow'd astern,
The hurrying tumbling waves, quick-broken crests, slapping,
The strata of color'd clouds, the long bar of maroon-tint away solitary by
   itself, the spread of purity it lies motionless in,
The horizon's edge, the flying sea-crow, the fragrance of salt marsh and
   shore mud,
These become part of that child who went forth every day, and who now
   goes, and will always go forth every day.

                                                  WALT WHITMAN

CHAPTER EIGHT

Description

All art, therefore, appeals primarily to the senses, and the artistic aim when expressing itself in written words must also make its appeal through the senses, if its high desire is to reach the secret spring of responsive emotions.

JOSEPH CONRAD

I am what is around me.

Women understand this.
One is not a duchess
A hundred yards from a carriage.

WALLACE STEVENS

To describe is the central purpose of fictive writing. The writer wants to tell how certain things seem to him. For our part, as readers, the growth into wisdom is also very much involved with coming to understand how the world *really* seems to us, with coming to recognize our submerged evaluations of the events of our world and their relationship to our surface reactions. We are greatly aided in this process by sharing with those who have a great skill in language their deepest experiences of reality. The price of continued growth for the individual is a deeper and deeper insight into the moral scope of life — its objects, attitudes, actions. A fine writer can help immeasurably by offering to us a coherent view of life from a perspective we could never otherwise have shared. For a writer to accomplish this incredibly difficult act of total description, he must have at his disposal many of the tools of literature. He will use quite abstract techniques, such as rhythm, and quite abstract concepts. But he will also use the primary sensory appeals upon which all else is constructed.

For the human sensibility is formed of an uncounted and ceaseless bombardment of the primary sensory channels, and if the writer would describe a condition of mind to someone else, he must in large part use the basic sensory experiences common to humans. In short, abstract concepts or feelings are complications and permutations of the simple sensory responses. As an example, the awareness excited in our minds by some such phrase as "the government of the United States" is the sum of many sensory experiences — pictures of the Capitol, the feel of a stamp, our knowledge of national history, our tension in a voting booth. Since these basic sensory responses are the foundation of the more complex or abstract experiences, this chapter will concern itself with a discussion of their nature and of their use in forming artistic patterns of description.

THE SENSES

Although the experience created by a literary sensory reference must not be confused with that created by a nonliterary object (to kiss a girl is quite a different experience from reading about kissing one), and although a memory evoked by literary reference is quite a different thing from a memory evoked by a repetition of the experience in reality (to hear a tune that brings on an old memory is a different thing from having the same thing happen to a character in a story), still the experience we have with literature is not "unreal." An experience aroused by a line of poetry is as real as that aroused by a flower. But it is wise that we do not confuse the two kinds of reality lest we come to value art more than life.

To make his sensory impression an author must work through the five primary channels of sensation: the eye (visual), the ear (auditory), the nose (olfactory), the tongue (taste, gustatory), and touch (tactile). Sometimes the author's purpose stops with the desire to create a visual or an auditory impression; but sometimes his aim is less to create an ordered primary sensual response than it is to make us *feel* something inside, to make us slightly nauseated, to make our blood race, to make us feel disequilibrium. When his purpose is such, then even more important than the primary sensory pattern is this secondary one, set up by our organic responses, which is called the *kinesthetic* response. Sometimes the simple absence of a kinesthetic response where one is expected can make an emotional and thematic point. In the narration of the death of the tree in Tolstoy's "Three Deaths," it is the cool, impersonal tone of the narrator toward the gladness of the other trees that makes, perhaps, the strongest element in the total tone. In any case it is interesting to watch the many ways in which these six modes of sensation, the five primary and the more difficult-to-define secondary one, are used to create and support the development of a total literary meaning.

It should be clear that for one who would read aloud, a convincing rendering of descriptive passages is based on a sensitivity to the sensory appeals the author makes — to their pattern through the piece. For this pattern will give the elementary clues to the oral reader's bodily reaction to the work, enabling him to avoid such an error as developing a strong response through the eyes to a passage essentially auditory in its appeal or, a more common error, ignoring all sensory appeal except the visual. And beyond the mere avoidance of error, a subtle and informative bodily response can be constructed once the sensory pattern of the piece is known.

DESCRIPTION OF OBJECTS

This chapter began with a very broad use of the word *description:* "to describe is the central purpose of fictive writing." But alas the word will have to do more than single duty. At the other extreme from this wide application, a specific *portion* of a work may be called a descriptive phrase or sentence or passage in order to distinguish its basic fictive technique from other passages which are primarily developed by methods other than pure description, such as dialogue. In a middle position between the application of the word to detail, and its use as somehow applicable to the whole aim and method of fiction, one also hears it used to describe a *type* of work. Thus, there are descriptive pieces and descriptive essays and descriptive poems. Keats' "To Autumn" is a successful attempt to get a fresh vision of a very old subject through description. Yet we note that Autumn is itself not an entity but an abstract term for a whole complex change of things in nature, and Keats' final purpose through his vivid definition of a variety of objects surrounding a female personification of the season is less to make us *see* Autumn, though we see vividly many of its details, than finally to reach some deeper emotional integration with its ease and richness. And so it would seem that with all fine writers, as soon as the descriptions begin, the hints begin; for to describe is to select that which seems significant, and to select that which seems significant is to evaluate, even though that evaluation may at times be a decision not to take sides for or against any of the elements in the work. In this sense no poem is purely descriptive, but is a reflection of an organization the author is imposing on the object and hence his evaluation of it. In Donald Davie's "The Waterfall at Powerscourt," even though, after describing the waterfall, the author seems deliberately to refuse a guess as to the mystery of its meaning, he has nonetheless given tantalizing hints in the insistence on its "fallen" nature, its unhappiness within itself, and its betrayal of itself and of those who live by it — its isolation and self-absorption (see p. 232).

In the following poem the hints are partly given by visual means. Following are a few of these effects. In the way the words are run together there is a sense of the flawlessness of the horse's gait and of the rapidity as well as accuracy of the shots. Something of a tone of boyish awe would seem to be involved here, a tone helped along by the spelling out of "Mister," yet this tone of innocent wonder is strongly qualified by the word "Defunct," which is not a boyish word, especially as it is used with such conscious irony. An oral reader would have to recognize this problem, and in seeking for his fully realized tone would no doubt be driven to see that this vision of the perfection of Buffalo Bill is in the past, and that the speaker of the poem is an adult. Certainly the question posed by the poem is an adult and very ancient one — what is the meaning of death in relation to beauty or perfection?

> Buffalo Bill's
> defunct
>
> Who used to
> ride a watersmooth-silver
>
> stallion
> and break onetwothreefourfive pigeonsjustlikethat
>
> Jesus
> he was a handsome man
> and what i want to know is
> how do you like your blueeyed boy
> Mister Death

E. E. CUMMINGS*

Thus, the dramatic situation is extremely important. These descriptive details are vividly remembered by an adult, but are not immediately before him. The symbol of perfection is supported by extreme accuracy in details, even to the fact that the old six-guns were carried with only five shells in them, it being necessary for safety that an empty chamber rest under the hammer. (The poet here would seem to be less "poetic" in the slang meaning of "vague" than the western movies one sees.) In short this tone of awe at a perfect thing is modified by a tone of reminiscence, and to this tone of reminiscence is added the ironic perceptions and question of the adult. Such is the subtlety of tone which a performance of this poem would have to achieve.

Robert Graves, in the following poem, chooses to describe a butterfly with great vividness and at the same time to make his hints rather explicit.

Flying Crooked*

The butterfly, a cabbage-white,
(His honest idiocy of flight)
Will never now, it is too late,
Master the art of flying straight,
Yet has — who knows so well as I? —
A just sense of how not to fly:
He lurches here and here by guess
And God and hope and hopelessness.
Even the aerobatic swift
Has not his flying-crooked gift.

ROBERT GRAVES

The poem makes use of visual imagery strictly appropriate to its central metaphor of flying, with perhaps some kinesthetic response from the word "lurches" as the reader begins to identify with the butterfly. First of all, one notices the poet has selected no multicolored butterfly but rather a plain looking, off-white one and has made it even plainer by comparing its color to a rather unglamorous vegetable. If white is the color of purity, this white is an everyday sort of purity. This unremarkable butterfly is made even less prepossessing by the author's telling us that its flight, though honest, is "idiocy" and that it is too late for bettering. So much for the initial tone, apparently merely descriptive, but really evaluative in its selectivity. Having said the worst, the poet seems to want to say something good, especially as he suddenly identifies himself with the butterfly's lack of grace, with its lack of certainty and skill. The sudden overt identity

* From *Collected Poems* by Robert Graves, published by Doubleday & Co., Ltd. Reprinted by permission of International Authors, N.V.

takes one, of course, a long way from mere objective description, yet the following lines are so accurate in the double-description, both of the way a butterfly flies and of a man's passage through the world, that we get no sense of a suddenly distorted or abruptly changed point of view. And when the end comes, with the butterfly's ability to fly crooked seen half-wryly as, after all, a gift, a kind of triumph, we are willing to take as applicable to the human both the description and the ambiguous half-comforting irony that goes with it.

Suggestiveness, duality, ambiguity, all those hints in art, are instruments of prose as well as poetry. Herman Melville wrote a series of sketches called "The Encantadas" (Enchanted Isles), which was one of the Spanish names for the Galapagos Islands. The second sketch of this series describes the huge and ancient tortoises that inhabit those islands (see p. 223). The first sketch has given a nighmarish description of the islands, a description to which he alludes again toward the end of the sketch, "an isle of metallic ravines and gulches, sunk bottomlessly into the hearts of splintered mountains, and covered for many miles with inextricable thickets."

The theme of this second sketch is stated in the first two lines: "In view of the description given, may one be gay upon the Encantadas? Yes: that is, find one the gaiety, and he will be gay." We are then given a description of the "two sides to a tortoise" (remember this is the title of the sketch), and are told that there is a dark upper shell and a bright under shell. There follows a bit of overt moralizing and generalizing upon this duality — to the effect that we must not deny the existence of either the dark or the bright. This much is explicit.

The sailors bring "three huge antediluvian-looking tortoises" to the ship and with the phrase, "they seemed hardly of the seed of the earth," the author begins a description magnificent in its richness and suggestiveness. First they are seen as creatures of suffering, of "infinite solitude," of "dateless, indefinite endurance," as if they were the very turtles which in Hindu mythology uphold the earth. To enhance the impression of endurance and suffering, the shells are likened to widower's weeds and to battle-battered shields, and these initial images of bravery and timelessness are finally transfigured till Melville sees "three Roman coliseums in magnificent decay." And so it is that the turtles seem to become emblems of man's history, his endless sorrow and endurance.

Having made his imaginative leap, Melville proceeds to describe what seems their chief characteristic, straightforwardness. (Yet even in simply stating the characteristic Melville leaves us with questions.) Is it indeed stupidity or is it resolution that they "never went aside for any impediment"? In any case it is their "crowning curse," this "drudging im-

pulse to straightforwardness in a belittered world." But straightforwardness is a characteristic we admire. Is it really stupidity? Is it noble
resolution? The ironies and overtones seem to reverberate endlessly. Then
in the next to last paragraph, Melville merges into this identification of the
tortoises with humanity till, in a dream, sharing with them their endless
travail, he himself seems joined with them in upholding "the universal
cope." Thus does he make manifest the reality of blackness, of pain, of
timeless efforts, in short, the dark shell of the world. And, of course, the
brightness is in the last paragraph where the very object of Melville's
veneration, the living symbol of timeless tragedy with which he has
identified himself the night before, is the substance of a "merry feast," and
raw material for creating artifacts of great beauty.

An interesting fact about the sensory pattern of this description is
that for all the wealth of visual excitement, it is only when he can no
longer see the tortoises that his imagination really soars. Lying in his
bunk at night, freed from visual exactitude, but exalted by their less
definite, more suggestive, *sounds* from the deck, he is able to achieve that
final sense of union with their fate. This sensory pattern might be compared to Keats' "Ode to a Nightingale." In that poem also, it is only when
the visual world is blotted out that the poet is able to achieve union with
the song of the invisible bird and all that it represents.

DESCRIPTION OF SCENE AND SETTING

Just as there are descriptive pieces that concentrate on an object to
the exclusion of all else, so there are descriptive pieces that in like manner
concentrate on a scene. We have already had one such example in Cotton's
"Evening Quatrains" (discussed in Chapter 3, p. 212). We saw then, as an
element of the descriptive means of the poem, that although a number of
things are described, all are kept at some distance and are highlighted
with only one or two details. The purpose is to fill a landscape, to make us
see not all the details of an English rural evening in the early 1600's but
the generality, the *tone* of the whole. In this poem, as might be expected
from the serenity and the distance from detail, there is neither kinesthetic sense nor touch nor smell nor taste in any primary sense. It is a
poem almost entirely of visual impressions. There are few auditory impressions and, perhaps because of their scarcity, they convey some of our
sharpest impressions. Yet each is a muted sound; even the chain's rattle is
at a distance "in the villein's yard." And it is interesting that the auditory
images are all in the latter part of the poem as the animals and humans
draw inward from the fields toward the houses where one feels the narrator to be.

Jonathan Swift's description of a London morning would seem to offer striking similarities and contrasts to the poem by Cotton. There is a similarity in artistic purpose. Both the morning and evening scenes are primarily collections of visual impressions meant to convert what must in reality be very generalized experiences into sharply focused ones. A few auditory impressions liven and give dimension to the scenes. We see this similarity of sensory technique despite the contrasting effort on the part of the one poet to depict a peaceful, morally and physically integrated rural community and on the part of the other poet to show us a noisy, individuated, morally disparate city.

A Description of the Morning

Now hardly here and there an hackney-coach
Appearing, show'd the ruddy morn's approach,
Now Betty from her master's bed had flown,
And softly stole to discompose her own.
The slip-shod 'prentice from his master's door
Had par'd the dirt, and sprinkled round the floor.
Now Moll had whirl'd her mop with dext'rous airs,
Prepar'd to scrub the entry and the stairs.
The youth with broomy stumps began to trace
The Kennel-edge, where wheels had worn the place.
The small-coal man was heard with cadence deep,
Till drown'd in shriller notes of chimney-sweep;
Duns at his lordship's gate began to meet,
And brickdust Moll had scream'd through half the street.
The turnkey now his flock returning sees,
Duly let out a-nights to steal for fees:
The watchful bailiffs take their silent stands,
And school-boys lag with satchels in their hands.

                                        JONATHAN SWIFT

Contrast this poem with the intense, almost kaleidoscopic, sensual imagery of Keats' "Ode to a Nightingale" (p. 375), in which the very first reference is to the kinesthetic sense. And the kinesthetic sense is not merely touched on but is elaborated over the length of four lines in an attempt to convey accurately the poet's inner sense of ache and numbness. In contrast to the objectivity of the evening and morning poems, the whole point and triumph of the Keats poem is its depiction of the transmutations of conflict, hope, and despair as we live with the poet his agonizing ambivalence toward art and toward mortality. Because it is the life of the senses that is the subject of the poem, there are repeated appeals to all the sensory responses. In fact, when through an act of the heightened imagination the poet succeeds in entering the realm of art, it is precisely the metaphor of the loss of sight that permits him to do so, yet the same metaphor makes him start the emotional pendulum-swing back from that immortal, blind land toward brief but visible mortality.

> But here there is no light . . .
> I cannot see what flowers are at my feet,
> Nor what soft incense hangs along the boughs . . .

But in this poem, with the poet's sensibility as a center of the poem, we have moved away from *scene* toward *setting*, toward, in short, the scene as *background for the object*. This importance of setting was true also, in spite of the concentration on the tortoise, in the Melville sketch. For a good deal of the tortoises' meaning for Melville came from the "belittered world" in which they moved.

THE INTERPLAY OF OBJECT AND SETTING

To place the object in a setting is to limit the imagination as it plays upon an object in the way an adjective limits a noun. But this limitation may be more than compensated for by the addition of rich possibilities for imaginative interaction between the two. Such interaction can be discovered in the following poem.

Anecdote of the Jar*

> I placed a jar in Tennessee,
> And round it was, upon a hill.
> It made the slovenly wilderness
> Surround that hill.
>
> The wilderness rose up to it,
> And sprawled around, no longer wild.
> The jar was round upon the ground
> And tall and of a port in air.
>
> It took dominion everywhere.
> The jar was gray and bare.
> It did not give of bird or bush,
> Like nothing else in Tennessee.

WALLACE STEVENS

Let us for the moment violate this poem by separating the description of
the jar from the description of its setting.

the jar	*the setting*
And round it was	in Tennessee
The jar was round upon the ground	upon a hill
And tall and of a port in air	the slovenly wilderness
It took dominion everywhere	Surround that hill
The jar was gray and bare	The wilderness rose up to it
	And sprawled around, no longer wild

concluding generalizing description
joining object and setting

It did not give of bird or bush
Like nothing else in Tennessee

First of all notice the roundness of the jar is mentioned twice, no doubt
to emphasize both that it is an artifact and that roundness, an abstract
perfection, is not a shape nature has frequent use for. We note that though
the jar seems to dominate all the scene around it, to be in fact a "port," a
place toward which all things tend, it is not beautiful, but is "gray and
bare." Here again we see the selectivity of the author at work. Note the
difference between this jar and the Grecian urn in Keats' poem, with its
beautiful border depicting an important event in an ancient community.
The dullness of Stevens' jar would seem selected to make more forceful
the irony that the artifact, by sole reason of its being an organized entity,
dominates the unorganized wilderness. When one turns to the setting, the
chief attribute of the wilderness seems its disorderliness in contrast to the
jar. The wilderness seems slightly personified in the second stanza, as
though it were a savage that tries to rise to a greater complexity of culture
but, failing, falls part way back into an undignified but tame attendance.

Let us now forget the artificial separation of the object and its setting,
for the tone of the poem arises from the switching of attention back and
forth between object and setting and from the consequent unfolding
insight into their relationship. We note that from the first there is a deliberate quality about the poem, as though the poet were conducting an experiment. There is a sense of a deliberate act in "I placed a jar in Tennessee."
The first impression is all favorable to the jar. It orders the "slovenly"
wilderness, gives it focus. The second impression, though, is of something
gone wrong. The wilderness has risen "up to it" but, unable to alter its
own nature, has fallen back into a halfway condition, not civilized, yet on
the other hand, "no longer wild." The dominance and centrality of the

jar is then developed, its imperious presence. Yet again something seems wrong. The jar is gray and bare, and the final ironic insight is that it is incapable of any act of creation. It is barren, dead. So Stevens develops in layers of irony the relationship as he sees it between nature and culture or, perhaps, the relationship between order and chaos, or even, perhaps, the drama of the loss of innocence. We are lucky in the Stevens poem in that his subject *and* his theme are the relationship between the object and its setting, so that in describing the first we are arriving at the second. His sensory technique is entirely visual, and the sense of firm objective analysis is no doubt a good deal reinforced by the immobility of his point of vision.

Of course all this interaction between object and setting is an oral, not simply an abstractly intellectual problem, and the poem should be rescued from the temporary dismemberment above, however useful its purpose. The tone starts as simply and firmly as the language, "I placed a jar in Tennessee." The action is forthright, and the first comment "slovenly" is read directly, with no irony and with clear disapproval. At this point the wilderness is just that and no more. It is, simply, slovenly. The anti-climax after the wilderness "rose up to it" is expressed in the pause, where the body, having reflected the preceding line (and the voice having taken an upward line), anticipates the next by a general relaxing, and the voice describes a vaguely downward pattern. This swing of the pendulum, with subtle changes in emphasis, occurs again. The next three lines are expressive of the power of the jar, built up again to the anticlimactic "the jar was gray and bare." But this time the downward swinging anticlimax neither reflects nor expresses weakness. For the subject is not the failure of the jar, but the anticlimax is rather a forceful series of negatives, making a positive, if unfavorable, judgment.

"An Experiment in Misery" is a story which offers a different pattern of relationship between the object and the setting. In the Stevens poem a duality is set up in which both setting and object suffer in value from the presence of the other. In Stephen Crane's story the subject is overwhelmed by his environment. The process is a gradual one. The first description is a sentence describing a fine rain falling in a city. Into this quickly drawn generalized setting, the central subject is immediately introduced. He is clothed both in the dress and in the small-boy taunts of "bum" and "hobo." He is described as "profoundly dejected." Reaching the area of the city where others of his class are, he feels more comfortable. He "aligned himself with these men." The most significant aspect of the lengthy description of the life of the city which comes next is that the detail, primarily visual, is so selected as to emphasize the fact that the young man is remote from it. The streams of life go by him, somehow at once distant yet menacing (we get such phrases as "formidable power," "dangerful and gloomy," "scarlike impression," "shrill grinding," "monstrous kind of crab"). Then follows paragraph after paragraph of detailed description of one evening, night, and morning as this young man moves through the life of extreme poverty in the company of an old bum referred to significantly as "the assassin." In this long description many fascinating insights are subtly suggested, such as the "men of brawn, whose skins shone clear and ruddy," and who stood "massively like chiefs," yet who, once dressed in their "ungainly garments," "showed bumps and deficiencies of all kinds." But one fact stands out as primary. When the young man woke up, the smells that had at first made his "liver turn white" had become so ordinary that when he left them he "experienced no sudden relief from unholy atmospheres. He had forgotten all about them, and had been breathing naturally, and with no sensation of discomfort or distress." It is this change in his awareness of the smells which leads to a climactic recapitulation of those very early images of the young man standing apart from the life of the city. But now in his changed state of feeling, this life from which he is excluded is no longer merely menacing, though it is still "pitiless." It is now also "regally high"; it ignores him in the "sublimity of its aspirations." And it is this sense that makes him feel not merely dejected, separated, menaced, as early in the story, but now somehow "guilty" and "wearing the criminal expression that comes with certain convictions." It is instructive to note that in the patterning of the sensual responses both the early and the final paragraphs detailing his sense of separation from the life of the city are almost entirely visual and are, naturally, chosen to enhance the sense of distance. On the other hand, in the pages detailing his supper, bed, and breakfast, all the senses are profusely appealed to, with the sense of smell, as has been mentioned above, used as key to the turning point of the story.

Of course in a good story or poem thematic development is always indivisible from the opening up of the subject matter. The meaning, for instance, of the whole final setting in "Eveline," the fact that it is a port, with the press of life around her pushing her on to the future, a pressure which requires her mortal strength to resist, is something we note particularly in the skilful introduction of the sense of obstruction, indicated by a flood of kinesthetic detail. First we see in her a kind of hysterical deafness to Frank's voice, then she sees through the "wide doors" the black mass of the boat, but she feels her cheeks "pale and cold," her torment grows and awakes a "nausea," and in a climax of kinesthetic feeling she feels herself drowning. She grips the "iron railing," then she clutches the "iron in frenzy," then Frank rushes "beyond the barrier." What all this careful mention of "iron" and "barrier" in the setting has been building up to is clear in the final terrible vision of the central person in the setting reduced to a "helpless animal." And it is interesting to observe how, after her involuntary "cry of anguish" which is the climax of the kinesthetic reactions, the author immediately abandons her mind and takes us outside her, and from then on we see her only externally. In this way Joyce emphasizes that inside she is dead or, like a "helpless animal," has no describable emotions.

PREPARATION FOR PERFORMANCE — "The Windhover"

Description

The descriptive elements in this poem are of central significance. First an object is described in its setting — a falcon in the sky. Then the speaker describes his emotional condition and his reaction to the falcon, in his heart. He must at the same time describe the falcon, since he tells *why* his heart responds as it does. Next, in the process of speaking to the falcon, he describes the bird yet again, first a general summary, and then a new action which the speaker desires to occur. This new action is then illustrated or illuminated by using figurative comparisons to describe two parallel actions. Obviously, in this poem it is difficult to separate the literal-descriptive elements from the figurative ones, for even the first stanza (the octet), which would seem descriptive of the flying falcon, is really creating a symbol of the falcon as Christ abroad in the world. One can see an example here of how oftentimes a series of "images" becomes, in its totality, figurative, for it is through description that this central symbol of the falcon is largely drawn. The first sentence sets the scene of the chief visual experience, which is now in the past (it is interesting that the setting of the speaker as he speaks is left quite undefined, both as to time — except that it is the same day — and as to place).

It was dawn, when birds are most active and the air has a special clarity and freshness. The falcon is described as "dapple-dawn-drawn." In its descriptive force, this phrase is ambiguous. It can mean on the one hand that the bird is drawn to his flight by the dappled dawn. On the other hand it can mean that the bird in his flight is drawn, that is, painted, in dapple colors by the dawn. These meanings are not contradictory, but rather reinforce each other. The oral reader, therefore, must be careful to read this epithet in such a vocal pattern as to leave both these possibilities viable. It is possible to do so, since the activating word "drawn" is the same in both cases, though the pause between "dapple" and "dawn" must in this case be left ambiguous in the emphasis that would point to its reference.

Now, having told us what we were watching, the poet goes on to describe the power and beauty of the bird's movements, his place in his setting. A meaning of the word "riding" which should be incorporated in the oral reader's sensibility along with the common one is "to seem to float," "to seem to move or become borne along by an intangible agency." The words "rolling level" would seem to smack of the paradoxical, till we realize that "roll" can mean "to flow in a continuous stream," "to be extended." Yet even if one takes the phrase as paradoxical, the paradox resolves itself in the meaning "to have an undulating contour; to display a gently rising and falling surface," where the surface may be undulating but still have a significant mean level. So the reader sees the bird as floating on a flowing if undulating air. This movement is majestic, as a "stride" is more measured and noble than a step. Now a new movement is described. "Rung" as the past tense of "ring" means both to wheel around and to rise in the air spirally, and is used both in falconry and the show-ring for horses. The word "to wimple" means "to cause to ripple," and also "to follow a curving course: meander, twist." The oral reader may respond to this phrase, then, as a further description of the bird's ringing or as a detailed observation of the fluttering of the wing itself. Next, the spiraling ring gives way to a long swooping curve. The movement ends in the powerful phrase "rebuffed the big wind," to which the rhythm and sound lend such climactic force that the "big wind" becomes almost of necessity a key to the setting around the bird — a summation of the physical world which Christ so masters. Essentially the above-described three movements are those which the oral reader must himself visualize in order to reach the appropriate vocal expression of the action.

After all the large, free movement, the next verb, concerning the poet's heart, delimits a terribly small, if portentous, action. "Stirred" has several connotations which are important besides the common one of "to impart movement to." It also means "to excite to activity or strong feeling" and "to bring a subject into notice or debate."

It should be noted again how important in description the verb forms are in this poem. After the turning point, at the end of the octet, the actions described by the verbs differ in nature. Whereas the octet was full of verbs reflective of free flight, the verbs of the second stanza (with the sole exception of "makes") center around the actions of falling or breaking up: "buckle," "break," "fall," "gall," "gash." However, the poem does not weaken in tone, though specific dropping intonations may be appropriate for certain of these phrases. This sustained tone is due to the fact that, according to the speaker, this falling is not a failure or defeat, but rather the cause of yet greater beauty. In short, the free-sweeping sense of the first stanza is in contrast to an intensity that increases, though evoked by quieter, more limited and concentrated action.

With so much of the poem consisting of description and so much of that description written of action, it is not surprising that no other senses are evoked than the visual and the kinesthetic, and it is through a reflection of these that the reader must seek his re-creation, if he is to be faithful to the original score.

SELECTIONS

A Resumed Identity

I

The Review as a Form of Welcome

One summer night a man stood on a low hill overlooking a wide expanse of forest and field. By the full moon hanging low in the west he knew what he might not have known otherwise: that it was near the hour of dawn. A light mist lay along the earth, partly veiling the lower features of the landscape, but above it the taller trees showed in well-defined masses against a clear sky. Two or three farmhouses were visible through the haze, but in none of them, naturally, was a light. Nowhere, indeed, was any sign or suggestion of life except the barking of a distant dog, which, repeated with mechanical iteration, served rather to accentuate than dispel the loneliness of the scene.

The man looked curiously about him on all sides, as one who among familiar surroundings is unable to determine his exact place and part in the scheme of things. It is so, perhaps, that we shall act when, risen from the dead, we await the call to judgment.

A hundred yards away was a straight road, showing white in the moonlight. Endeavouring to orient himself, as a surveyor or navigator might say, the man moved his eyes slowly along its visible length, and at a distance of a quarter-mile to the south of his station saw, dim and grey in the haze, a group of horsemen riding to the north. Behind them were men afoot, marching in column, with dimly gleaming rifles aslant above their shoulders. They moved slowly and in silence. Another group of horsemen, another regiment of infantry, another and another — all in unceasing motion toward the man's point of view, past it, and beyond. A battery of artillery followed, the cannoneers, riding with folded arms on limber and caisson. And still the interminable procession came out of the obscurity to south and passed into the obscurity to north, with never a sound of voice, nor hoof nor wheel.

The man could not rightly understand: he thought himself deaf; said so, and heard his own voice, although it had an unfamiliar quality that almost alarmed him; it disappointed his ear's expectancy in the matter of timbre and resonance. But he was not deaf, and that for the moment sufficed.

Then he remembered that there are natural phenomena to which some one has given the name "acoustic shadows." If you stand in an acoustic shadow there is one direction from which you will hear nothing. At the battle of Gaines's Mill, one of the fiercest conflicts of the Civil War, with a hundred guns in play, spectators a mile and a half away on the opposite side of the Chickahominy valley heard nothing of what they clearly saw. The bombardment of Port Royal, heard and felt at St. Augustine, a hundred and fifty miles to the south, was inaudible two miles to the north in a still atmosphere. A few days before the surrender at Appomattox a thunderous engagement between the commands of Sheridan and Pickett was unknown to the latter commander, a mile in the rear of his own line.

These instances were not known to the man of whom we write, but less striking ones of the same character had not escaped his observation. He was profoundly disquieted, but for another reason than the uncanny silence of that moonlight march.

"Good Lord!" he said to himself — and again it was as if another had spoken his thought — "if those people are what I take them to be we have lost the battle and they are moving on Nashville!"

Then came a thought of self — an apprehension — a strong sense of personal peril, such as in another we call fear. He stepped quickly into the shadow of a tree. And still the silent battalions moved slowly forward in the haze.

The chill of a sudden breeze upon the back of his neck drew his attention to the quarter whence it came, and turning to the east he saw a faint grey light along the horizon — the first sign of returning day. This increased his apprehension.

"I must get away from here," he thought, "or I shall be discovered and taken."

He moved out of the shadow, walking rapidly toward the greying east. From the safer seclusion of a clump of cedars he looked back. The entire column had passed out of sight: the straight white road lay bare and desolate in the moonlight!

Puzzled before, he was now inexpressibly astonished. So swift a passing of so slow an army! — he could not comprehend it. Minute after minute passed unnoted; he had lost his sense of time. He sought with a terrible earnestness a solution of the mystery, but sought in vain. When at last he roused himself from his abstraction the sun's rim was visible above the hills, but in the new conditions he found no other light than that of day; his understanding was involved as darkly in doubt as before.

On every side lay cultivated fields showing no sign of war and war's ravages. From the chimneys of the farmhouses thin ascensions of blue smoke signalled preparations for a day's peaceful toil. Having stilled its immemorial allocution to the moon, the watch-dog was assisting a negro who, prefixing a team of mules to the plough, was flatting and sharping contentedly at his task. The hero of this tale stared stupidly at the pastoral picture as if he had never seen such a thing in all his life; then he put his hand to his head, passed it through his hair and, withdrawing it, attentively considered the palm — a singular thing to do. Apparently reassured by the act, he walked confidently toward the road.

II

When You Have Lost Your Life Consult a Physician

Dr. Stilling Malson, of Murfreesboro, having visited a patient six or seven miles away, on the Nashville road, had remained with him all night. At daybreak he set out for home on horseback, as was the custom of doctors of the time and region. He had passed into the neighbourhood of Stone's River battlefield when a man approached him from the roadside and saluted in the military fashion, with a movement of the right hand to the hat brim. But the hat was not a military hat, the man was not in uniform and had not a martial bearing. The doctor nodded civilly, half thinking that the stranger's uncommon greeting was perhaps in deference to the historic surroundings. As the stranger evidently desired speech with him he courteously reined in his horse and waited.

"Sir," said the stranger, "although a civilian, you are perhaps an enemy."

"I am a physician," was the non-committal reply.

"Thank you," said the other. "I am a lieutenant of the staff of General Hazen." He paused a moment and looked sharply at the person whom he was addressing, then added, "Of the Federal army."

The physician merely nodded.

"Kindly tell me," continued the other, "what has happened here. Where are the armies? Which has won the battle?"

The physician regarded his questioner curiously with half-shut eyes. After a professional scrutiny, prolonged to the limit of politeness, "Pardon me," he said; "one asking information should be willing to impart it. Are you wounded?" he added, smiling.

"Not seriously — it seems."

The man removed the unmilitary hat, put his hand to his head, passed it through his hair, and, withdrawing it, attentively considered the palm.

"I was struck by a bullet and have been unconscious. It must have been a light, glancing blow: I find no blood and feel no pain. I will not trouble you for treatment, but will you kindly direct me to my command — to any part of the Federal army — if you know?"

Again the doctor did not immediately reply: he was recalling much that is recorded in the books of his profession — something about lost identity and the effect of familiar scenes in restoring it. At length he looked the man in the face, smiled, and said:

"Lieutenant, you are not wearing the uniform of your rank and service."

At this the man glanced down at his civilian attire, lifted his eyes, and said with hesitation:

"That is true. I — I don't quite understand."

Still regarding him sharply but not unsympathetically, the man of science bluntly inquired:

"How old are you?"

"Twenty-three — if that has anything to do with it."

"You don't look it; I should hardly have guessed you to be just that."

The man was growing impatient. "We need not discuss that," he said; "I want to know about the army. Not two hours ago I saw a column of troops moving northward on this road. You must have met them. Be good enough to tell me the colour of their clothing, which I was unable to make out, and I'll trouble you no more."

"You are quite sure that you saw them?"

"Sure? My God, sir, I could have counted them!"

"Why, really," said the physician, with an amusing consciousness of his own resemblance to the loquacious barber of the Arabian Nights, "this is very interesting. I met no troops."

The man looked at him coldly, as if he had himself observed the likeness to the barber. "It is plain," he said, "that you do not care to assist me. Sir, you may go to the devil!"

He turned and strode away, very much at random, across the dewy fields, his half-penitent tormentor quietly watching him from his point of vantage in the saddle till he disappeared beyond an array of trees.

III

The Danger of Looking into a Pool of Water

After leaving the road the man slackened his pace, and now went forward, rather deviously, with a distinct feeling of fatigue. He could not account for this, though truly the interminable loquacity of that country doctor offered itself in explanation. Seating himself upon a rock, he laid one hand upon his knee, back upward, and casually looked at it. It was lean and withered. He lifted both hands to his face. It was seamed and furrowed; he could trace the lines with the tips of his fingers. How strange! — a mere bullet-stroke and a brief unconsciousness should not make one a physical wreck.

"I must have been a long time in hospital," he said aloud. "Why, what a fool I am! The battle was in December, and it is now summer." He laughed. "No wonder that fellow thought me an escaped lunatic. He was wrong: I am only an escaped patient."

At a little distance a small plot of ground enclosed by a stone wall caught his attention. With no very definite intent he rose and went to it. In the centre was a square, solid monument of hewn stone. It was brown with age, weather-worn at the angles, spotted with moss and lichen. Between the massive blocks were strips of grass the leverage of whose challenge of this ambitious structure Time had laid his destroying hand upon, and it would soon be "one with Nineveh and Tyre." In an inscription on one side his eye caught a familiar name. Shaking with excitement, he craned his body across the wall and read:

HAZEN'S BRIGADE

TO

THE MEMORY OF ITS SOLDIERS

WHO FELL AT

STONE RIVER, DEC. 31, 1862

The man fell back from the wall, faint and sick. Almost within an arm's length was a little depression in the earth; it had been filled by a recent rain — a pool of clear water. He crept to it to revive himself, lifted the upper part of his body on his trembling arms, thrust forward his head and saw the reflection of his face, as in a mirror. He uttered a terrible cry. His arms gave way; he fell, face downward, into the pool and yielded up the life that had spanned another life.

AMBROSE BIERCE

Letter to the Patrol Twenty Years After*

Remember Ralph who ran so fast and far?
Remember Frank who found the way through dark?
Remember Leo who never missed the mark?
And Nick whose hands could bend an iron bar?

Lieutenant Smith — can't you just see him yet?
Always out front, a natural leader, he.
I followed him with you. Remember me?
I am the one who never could forget.

* Reprinted by permission of the author.

French girls we swore to marry as a whim
Come floating up to mind; it's age I guess;
And are you others having much success?
The prisoner we shot — remember him?

Not since the army have I held a gun.
I grow rare roses; that wouldn't interest you,
But men should have some different thing to do.
I'd like to hear what all the rest have done.

Lieutenant, still ahead? Nick, just as strong?
Leo, as steady? Frank, still on the track?
And Ralph, as quick? It's quite some distance back,
And who'd have thought one death could take so long?

LEONARD E. NATHAN

Apples and Water*

Dust in a cloud, blinding weather,
    Drums that rattle and roar!
A mother and daughter stood together
    By their cottage door.

"Mother, the heavens are bright like brass,
    The dust is shaken high,
With labouring breath the soldiers pass,
    Their lips are cracked and dry.

"Mother, I'll throw them apples down,
    I'll fetch them cups of water."
The mother turned with an angry frown,
    Holding back her daughter.

"But, mother, see, they faint with thirst,
    They march away to war."

* From *Collected Poems* by Robert Graves, published by Doubleday & Co.,
Inc., and Cassell & Co. Ltd. Reprinted by permission of International Authors
N.V.

"Ay, daughter, these are not the first
    And there will come yet more.

"There is no water can supply them
    In western streams that flow;
There is no fruit can satisfy them
    On orchard-trees that grow.

"Once in my youth I gave, poor fool,
    A soldier apples and water;
And may I die before you cool
    Such drouth as his, my daughter."

ROBERT GRAVES

In Distrust of Merits*

Strengthened to live, strengthened to die for
    medals and positioned victories?
They're fighting, fighting, fighting the blind
    man who thinks he sees, —
who cannot see that the enslaver is
enslaved; the hater, harmed. O shining O
        firm star, O tumultuous
            ocean lashed till small things go
        as they will, the mountainous
            wave makes us who look, know

depth. Lost at sea before they fought! O
    star of David, star of Bethlehem,
O black imperial lion
    of the Lord — emblem
of a risen world — be joined at last, be
joined. There is hate's crown beneath which all is
        death; there's love's without which none
            is king; the blessed deeds bless
        the halo. As contagion
            of sickness makes sickness,

* Reprinted with permission of The Macmillan Company from *Collected Poems* by Marianne Moore. Copyright 1944 by Marianne Moore.

contagion of trust can make trust. They're
    fighting in deserts and caves, one by
one, in battalions and squadrons;
    they're fighting that I
may yet recover from the disease, My
Self; some have it lightly; some will die. "Man
      wolf to man." And we devour
        ourselves. The enemy could not
      have made a greater breach in our
      defenses. One pilot-

ing a blind man can escape him, but
    Job disheartened by false comfort knew
that nothing is so defeating
    as a blind man who
can see. O alive who are dead, who are
proud not to see, O small dust of the earth
      that walks so arrogantly,
        trust begets power and faith is
      an affectionate thing. We
      vow, we make this promise

to the fighting — it's a promise — "We'll
    never hate black, white, red, yellow, Jew,
Gentile, Untouchable." We are
    not competent to
make our vows. With set jaw they are fighting,
fighting, fighting, — some we love whom we know,
      some we love but know not — that
        hearts may feel and not be numb.
      It cures me; or am I what
      I can't believe in? Some

in snow, some on crags, some in quicksands,
    little by little, much by much, they
are fighting fighting fighting that where
    there was death there may
be life. "When a man is prey to anger,
he is moved by outside things; when he holds
      his ground in patience patience
        patience, that is action or
      beauty," the soldier's defense
      and hardest armor for

the fight. The world's an orphans' home. Shall
  we never have peace without sorrow?
without pleas of the dying for
  help that won't come? O
quiet form upon the dust, I cannot
look and yet I must. If these great patient
    dyings — all these agonies
      and woundbearings and blood shed —
    can teach us how to live, these
      dyings were not wasted.

Hate-hardened heart, O heart of iron,
  iron is iron till it is rust.
There never was a war that was
  not inward; I must
fight till I have conquered in myself what
causes war, but I would not believe it.
    I inwardly did nothing.
      O Iscariotlike crime!
    Beauty is everlasting
      and dust is for a time.

MARIANNE MOORE

Eighth Air Force*

If, in an odd angle of the hutment,
A puppy laps the water from a can
Of flowers, and the drunk sergeant shaving
Whistles *O Paradiso!* — shall I say that man
Is not as men have said: a wolf to man?

The other murderers troop in yawning;
Three of them play Pitch, one sleeps, and one
Lies counting missions, lies there sweating
Till even his heart beats: One; One; One.
O murderers! . . . Still, this is how it's done:

* From *Losses* by Randall Jarrell, copyright, 1948, by Harcourt, Brace &
World, Inc. and reprinted with their permission.

This is a war. . . . But since these play, before they die,
Like puppies with their puppy; since, a man,
I did as these have done, but did not die —
I will content the people as I can
And give up these to them: Behold the man!

I have suffered, in a dream, because of him,
Many things; for this last saviour, man,
I have lied as I lie now. But what is lying?
Men wash their hands, in blood, as best they can:
I find no fault in this just man.

RANDALL JARRELL

Trench Raid Near Hooge*

At an hour before the rosy-fingered
        Morning should come
To wonder again what meant these sties,
These wailing shots, these glaring eyes,
        These moping mum,

Through the black reached strange long rosy fingers
        All at one aim
Protending and bending: down they swept,
Succession of similars after leapt
        And bore red flame

To one small ground of the eastern distance,
        And thunderous touched;
East then and west false dawns fan-flashed
And shut, and gaped; false thunders clashed.
        Who stood and watched

Caught needled horror from the desperate pit
        Which with ten men
Was center of this. The blood burnt, feeling
The fierce truth there and the last appealing,
        "Us? Us? Again?"

---

* Reprinted by permission of A. D. Peters (London) from *Undertones of War* by Edmund Blunden.

Nor rosy dawn at last appearing
　　Through the icy shade
Might mark without trembling the new deforming
Of earth that had seemed past human storming.
　　Her fingers played,

One thought, with something of human pity
　　On six or seven
Whose looks were hard to understand,
But that they ceased to care what hand
　　Lit earth and heaven.

EDMUND BLUNDEN

*Lessons of the War**

To Alan Michell

Vivi duellis nuper idoneus
Et militavi non sine gloria

I. Naming of Parts

To-day we have naming of parts. Yesterday,
We had daily cleaning. And to-morrow morning,
We shall have what to do after firing. But to-day,
To-day we have naming of parts. Japonica
Glistens like coral in all of the neighbouring gardens,
　　And to-day we have naming of parts.

This is the lower sling swivel. And this
Is the upper sling swivel, whose use you will see,
When you are given your slings. And this is the piling swivel,
Which in your case you have not got. The branches
Hold in the gardens their silent, eloquent gestures,
　　Which in our case we have not got.

This is the safety-catch, which is always released
With an easy flick of the thumb. And please do not let me
See anyone using his finger. You can do it quite easy
If you have any strength in your thumb. The blossoms
Are fragile and motionless, never letting anyone see
　　Any of them using their finger.

* From *A Map of Verona and Other Poems*, copyright, 1947, by Henry Reed. Reprinted by permission of Harcourt, Brace & World, Inc. and Jonathan Cape Limited.

And this you can see is the bolt. The purpose of this
Is to open the breech, as you see. We can slide it
Rapidly backwards and forwards: we call this
Easing the spring. And rapidly backwards and forwards
The early bees are assaulting and fumbling the flowers;
     They call it easing the Spring.

They call it easing the Spring: it is perfectly easy
If you have any strength in your thumb: like the bolt,
And the breech, and the cocking-piece, and the point of balance,
Which in our case we have not got; and the almond-blossom
Silent in all of the gardens and the bees going backwards and forwards,
     For to-day we have naming of parts.

II. Judging Distances

Not only how far away, but the way that you say it
Is very important. Perhaps you may never get
The knack of judging a distance, but at least you know
How to report on a landscape: the central sector,
The right of arc and that, which we had last Tuesday,
     And at least you know

That maps are of time, not place, so far as the army
Happens to be concerned — the reason being,
Is one which need not delay us. Again, you know
There are three kinds of tree, three only, the fir and the popular,
And those which have bushy tops to; and lastly
     That things only seem to be things.

A barn is not called a barn, to put it more plainly,
Or a field in the distance, where sheep may be safely grazing.
You must never be over-sure. You must say, when reporting:
At five o'clock in the central sector is a dozen
Of what appear to be animals; whatever you do,
     Don't call the bleeders *sheep.*

I am sure that's quite clear; and suppose, for the sake of example,
The one at the end, asleep, endeavours to tell us
What he sees over there to the west, and how far away,
After first having come to attention. There to the west,
On the fields of summer the sun and the shadows bestow
     Vestments of purple and gold.

The still white dwellings are like a mirage in the heat,
And under the swaying elms a man and a woman
Lie gently together. Which is, perhaps, only to say
That there is a row of houses to the left of arc,
And that under some poplars a pair of what appear to be humans
    Appear to be loving.

Well that, for an answer, is what we might rightly call
Moderately satisfactory only, the reason being,
Is that two things have been omitted, and those are important.
The human beings, now: in what direction are they,
And how far away, would you say? And do not forget
    There may be dead ground in between.

There may be dead ground in between; and I may not have got
The knack of judging a distance; I will only venture
A guess that perhaps between me and the apparent lovers,
(Who, incidentally, appear by now to have finished,)
At seven o'clock from the houses, is roughly a distance
    Of about one year and a half.

III. Unarmed Combat

In due course of course you will all be issued with
Your proper issue; but until to-morrow,
You can hardly be said to need it; and until that time,
We shall have unarmed combat. I shall teach you,
The various holds and rolls and throws and breakfalls
    Which you may sometimes meet.

And the various holds and rolls and throws and breakfalls
Do not depend on any sort of weapon,
But only on what I might coin a phrase and call
The ever-important question of human balance,
And the ever-important need to be in a strong
    Position at the start.

There are many kinds of weakness about the body,
Where you would least expect, like the ball of the foot.
But the various holds and rolls and throws and breakfalls
Will always come in useful. And never be frightened
To tackle from behind: it may not be clean to do so,
    But this is global war.

So give them all you have, and always give them
As good as you get; it will always get you somewhere.
(You may not know it, but you can tie a Jerry
Up without rope; it is one of the things I shall teach you.)
Nothing will matter if only you are ready for him.
      The readiness is all.

The readiness is all. How can I help but feel
I have been here before? But somehow then,
I was the tied-up one. How to get out
Was always then my problem. And even if I had
A piece of rope I was always the sort of person
      Who threw the rope aside.

And in my time I have given them all I had.
Which was never as good as I got, and it got me nowhere.
And the various holds and rolls and throws and breakfalls
Somehow or other I always seemed to put
In the wrong place. And as for war, my wars
      Were global from the start.

Perhaps I was never in a strong position,
Or the ball of my foot got hurt, or I had some weakness
Where I had least expected. But I think I see your point.
While awaiting a proper issue, we must learn the lesson
Of the ever-important question of human balance.
      It is courage that counts.

Things may be the same again; and we must fight
Not in the hope of winning but rather of keeping
Something alive: so that when we meet our end,
It may be said that we tackled wherever we could,
That battle-fit we lived, and though defeated,
      Not without glory fought.

HENRY REED

The Widow at Windsor*

'Ave you 'eard o' the Widow at Windsor
  With a hairy gold crown on 'er 'ead?
She 'as ships on the foam — she 'as millions at 'ome,
  An' she pays us poor beggers in red.[1]
    (Ow, poor beggars in red!)
There's 'er nick on the cavalry 'orses,
  There's 'er mark on the medical stores —
An' 'er troopers you'll find with a fair wind be'ind
  That takes us to various wars.
    (Poor beggars! — barbarious wars!)
      Then 'ere's to the Widow at Windsor,
        An' 'ere's to the stores an' the guns,
      The men an' the 'orses what makes up the forces
        O' Missis Victorier's sons.
    (Poor beggars! Victorier's sons!)

Walk wide o' the Widow at Windsor,
  For 'alf o' Creation she owns:
We 'ave bought 'er the same with the sword an' the flame,
  An' we've salted it down with our bones.
    (Poor beggars! — it's blue with our bones!)
Hands off o' the sons o' the Widow,
  Hands off o' the goods in 'er shop,
For the Kings must come down an' the Emperors frown
  When the Widow at Windsor says "Stop!"
    (Poor beggars! — we're sent to say "Stop!")
      Then 'ere's to the Lodge o' the Widow,
        From the Pole to the Tropics it runs —
      To the Lodge that we tile[2] with the rank an' the file,
        An' open in form with the guns.
    (Poor beggars! — it's always they guns!)

---

* Reprinted from *Barrack-Room Ballads* by Rudyard Kipling, by permission of Doubleday & Company, Inc., Mrs. George Bambridge, and the Macmillan Company of Canada.

[1] A "red" or a "red 'un" was slang for a coin, usually a sovereign. But because of the low pay of the enlisted man in the British Army and the numerous deductions often made from it, few were the months when the soldier was not in debt to the pay-master, that is, "in the red."

[2] Technically, to "tile" or "tyle" is to protect a Masonic lodge from intrusion.

We 'ave 'eard o' the Widow at Windsor,
  It's safest to leave 'er alone:
For 'er sentries we stand by the sea an' the land
  Wherever the bugles are blown.
    (Poor beggars! — an' don't we get blown!)
Take 'old o' the Wings o' the Mornin',
  An' flop round the earth till you're dead;
But you won't get away from the tune that they play
  To the bloomin' old rag over'ead.
    (Poor beggars! — it's 'ot over'ead!)
    Then 'ere's to the Sons o' the Widow,
      Wherever, 'owever they roam.
    'Ere's all they desire, an' if they require
      A speedy return to their 'ome.
    (Poor beggars! — they'll never see 'ome!)

RUDYARD KIPLING

Greater Love*

Red lips are not so red
  As the stained stones kissed by the English dead.
Kindness of wooed and wooer
Seems shame to their love pure.
O Love, your eyes lose lure
  When I behold eyes blinded in my stead!

Your slender attitude
  Trembles not exquisite like limbs knife-skewed,
Rolling and rolling there
Where God seems not to care;
Till the fierce Love they bear
  Cramps them in death's extreme decrepitude.

Your voice sings not so soft, —
  Though even as wind murmuring through raftered loft, —
Your dear voice is not dear,
Gentle, and evening clear,
As theirs whom none now hear,
  Now earth has stopped their piteous mouths that cough.

Heart, you were never hot,
   Nor large, nor full like hearts made great with shot;
And though your hand be pale,
Paler are all which trail
Your cross through flame and hail:
   Weep, you may weep, for you may touch them not.

WILFRED OWEN

Strange Meeting*

It seemed that out of the battle I escaped
Down some profound dull tunnel, long since scooped
Through granites which Titanic wars had groined.
Yet also there encumbered sleepers groaned,
Too fast in thought or death to be bestirred.
Then, as I probed them, one sprang up, and stared
With piteous recognition in fixed eyes,
Lifting distressful hands as if to bless.
And by his smile, I knew that sullen hall;
By his dead smile I knew we stood in Hell.
With a thousand pains that visions's face was grained;
Yet no blood reached there from the upper ground,
And no guns thumped, or down the flues made moan,
"Strange, friend," I said, "here is no cause to mourn."
"None," said the other, "save the undone years,
The hopelessness. Whatever hope is yours,
Was my life also; I went hunting wild
After the wildest beauty in the world,
Which lies not calm in eyes, or braided hair,
But mocks the steady running of the hour,
And if it grieves, grieves richlier than here.
For by my glee might many men have laughed,
And of my weeping something has been left,
Which must die now. I mean the truth untold,
The pity of war, the pity war distilled.
Now men will go content with what we spoiled,
Or, discontent, boil bloody, and be spilled.
They will be swift with swiftness of the tigress,
None will break ranks, though nations trek from progress.

Courage was mine, and I had mystery,
Wisdom was mine, and I had mastery;
To miss the march of this retreating world
Into vain citadels that are not walled.
Then when much blood had clogged their chariot-wheels
I would go up and wash them from sweet wells,
Even with truths that lie too deep for taint.
I would have poured my spirit without stint
But not through wounds; not on the cess of war.
Foreheads of men have bled where no wounds were.
I am the enemy you killed, my friend.
I knew you in this dark; for so you frowned
Yesterday through me as you jabbed and killed.
I parried; but my hands were loath and cold.
Let us sleep now. . . ."

                                             WILFRED OWEN

The Chances*

I mind as 'ow the night before that show
Us five got talking, — we was in the know, —
"Over the top to-morrer; boys, we're for it.
First wave we are, first ruddy wave; that's tore it."
"Ah well," says Jimmy, — an' 'e's seen some scrappin' —
"There ain't more nor five things as can 'appen; —
Ye get knocked out; else wounded — bad or cushy;
Scuppered; or nowt except yer feeling mushy."

One of us got the knock-out, blown to chops.
T'other was hurt like, losin' both 'is props.
An' one, to use the word of 'ypocrites,
'Ad the misfortoon to be took by Fritz.
Now me, I wasn't scratched, praise God Amighty
(Though next time please I'll thank 'im for a blighty),
But poor young Jim, 'e's livin' an' 'e's not;
'E reckoned 'e'd five chances, an 'e 'ad;
'E's wounded, killed, and pris'ner, all the lot,
The bloody lot all rolled in one. Jim's mad.

                                             WILFRED OWEN

Channel Firing*

That night your great guns, unawares,
Shook all our coffins as we lay,
And broke the chancel window-squares,
We thought it was the Judgment-day

And sat upright. While drearisome
Arose the howl of wakened hounds:
The mouse let fall the altar-crumb,
The worms drew back into the mounds,

The glebe cow drooled. Till God called, 'No;
It's gunnery practice out at sea
Just as before you went below;
The world is as it used to be:

"All nations striving strong to make
Red war yet redder. Mad as hatters
They do no more for Christés sake
Than you who are helpless in such matters.

"That this is not the judgment-hour
For some of them's a blessed thing,
For if it were they'd have to scour
Hell's floor for so much threatening. . . .

"Ha, ha. It will be warmer when
I blow the trumpet (if indeed
I ever do; for you are men,
And rest eternal sorely need)."

So down we lay again. "I wonder,
Will the world ever saner be,"
Said one, "than when He sent us under
In our indifferent century!"

And many a skeleton shook his head.
"Instead of preaching forty year,"

* Reprinted from *Collected Poems of Thomas Hardy* by permission of The Macmillan Company (New York); the Executors of the Hardy Estate, Macmillan & Co. Ltd. (London), The Macmillan Company of Canada Limited. Copyright 1925 by The Macmillan Company.

My neighbour Parson Thirdly said,
"I wish I had stuck to pipes and beer."

Again the guns disturbed the hour,
Roaring their readiness to avenge,
As far inland as Stourton Tower,
And Camelot, and starlit Stonehenge.   *April 1914.*

THOMAS HARDY

*Fife Tune**

(6/8) for Sixth Platoon, 308th I.T.C.

One morning in spring
We marched from Devizes
All shapes and all sizes
Like beads on a string,
But yet with a swing
We trod the bluemetal
And full of high fettle
We started to sing.

She ran down the stair
A twelve-year-old darling
And laughing and calling
She tossed her bright hair;
Then silent to stare
At the men flowing past her —
There were all she could master
Adoring her there.

It's seldom I'll see
A sweeter or prettier;
I doubt we'll forget her
In two years or three.
And lucky he'll be
She takes for a lover
While we are far over
The treacherous sea.

JOHN MANIFOLD

When the Troops Were Returning from Milan

(D. G. Rosetti's translation, somewhat altered by Robert Beloof)

If you could see, fair brother, how dead beat
   The fellows look who come through Rome today, —
   Black yellow smoke-dried visages, — you'd say
They thought their haste at going a strange heat.
Their empty victual-waggons up the street
   Over the bridge hollowly sound and sway;
   Their eyes, as hanged men's, turning the wrong way;
And nothing on their backs, or heads, or feet.
One sees the ribs and all the skeletons
   Of their gaunt horses; and a sorry sight
Are the torn saddles, crammed with straw and stones.
   Shame and hunger order their ragged flight
And send them stumbling on their marrowbones
   Like barrels rolling, jolting, through the night.
Their arms all gone, not even their swords are saved;
And each as silent as a man being shaved.

Niccolo Degli Abizzi

CHAPTER NINE

Figurative Language

That, *Enargia*, or *cleereness of representation*, required in absolute Poems is *not* the perspicuous delivery of a lowe invention; but high, & hearty invention exprest in most *significant* & unaffected phrase; it serves not a skilful Painters turne, to draw the figure of a face onely to make knowne who it represents; but hee must lymn, give *luster, shaddow, & heightening;* which though ignorants will esteeme spic'd & too curious, yet such as have the judicial perspective, will see it hath, *motion, spirit* & life. . . . Obscuritie in affection of words, & *undigested* concets, is pedanticall & childish; but where it shroudeth it selfe in the hart of his subject, uttered with *fitness* of figure, & *expressive* Epithetes; with that darkness will I still labor to be shaddowed. . . .

GEORGE CHAPMAN

We began the last chapter by saying that the central purpose of creative writing is to describe: "the writer wants to tell how certain things seem to him." Yet because he is a writer his work cannot lead to a measurable description, a quantitative end like a chemist's. The writer's description must have as its ultimate purpose the creation of tone, which I take to mean to the literary person what wisdom, as opposed to knowledge, means to the philosopher. That is, tone implies the whole man's experience — his brain, his hands, his organs, his past, his present — set down in such a marvelous way that another, if he has not been castrated by the mind or frontal-lobotomized by the body, may recreate that tone out of his own disciplined and experienced eagerness for life. Tone is, of course, served by every technique and every technical relationship available to the writer. Sometimes a given technique or device may be entirely absent from a work as dialogue may be absent from a descriptive essay, and by its very absence may have a great deal to do with the tone of the piece. In other cases a given device may be but a minor thread in the general pattern. One element which is almost always present and is often of central significance is figurative language.

Figurative language is somewhere near the primitive basis of all knowledge. Man describes, and he learns from that description, by *comparison*. All things in the world are unique, yet all things are related; this paradoxical truth lies behind mankind's ability to differentiate and to see similarities — in short to make comparisons. The scientist may make his comparisons in different ways and with aims different from those of the artist, but they both meet here at this root level, in the comparative process. And because figurative language is *overtly* comparative in its method, it is likely to be especially revealing. Only the author's vision can see the "form-in-the-large" which he is creating, and hence determine that a given comparison is suited to illuminate a certain detail of it. In fact, only his genius can see that "form-in-the-large," which is, in itself, a figure, a whole, that the reader will read and compare with life.

Nowhere in the experiencing of literature is the demand on the reader greater than in his approach to figurative language. For even in the simplest figures of speech, the reader must reconstruct, out of his own experience, the connection aimed at in the comparison. Thus, with the phrase "Jane's hair is black," there is no overt comparison, only a simple visual *image*. But if the phrase is "Jane's hair is coal," then a comparison is made. What is its purpose? That is the question the reader must answer in his reconstruction of the author's intent. Did he mean it is combustible? Did he mean it is hard and dirty? Costs so much per pound? Such possibilities arise from the fact that most objects or actions have an infinite range of possible relationships, attendant feelings, qualities, histories. Thus one might visualize as an infinite line the range of sensibilities attached to coal.

–labor–combustibility–cost–uses–hardness–purity–color–sheen–

infinity   COAL   infinity

Such a line for hair might also be drawn. In short, each word carries a potential for evoking a virtually infinite range of feeling and sensory response. However, placed in the formula, "Jane's hair is coal," the reader perceives almost instinctively that what "hair" and "coal" really have in common in this context is color. Much as a navigator gets a "fix," the reader is brought to see the *particular* similarity or contrast between the two words.

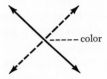

But what is gained over the formulation, "Jane's hair is black"? In this case, relatively little, so simple is the figure used; yet something, as we see when we take the formulation a step further.

Mary's hair is jet, but Jane's hair is black.
Mary's hair is jet, but Jane's hair is coal.

The first sentence is virtually meaningless because it is not really a comparison. Since jet is black, there is no "but" about it, no distinction is possible. On the other hand, as soon as one makes the further comparison of "coal" to "jet," one sees that along with the color comparison given in the hair-coal combination, minor connotations related to quality of surface and of sheen are brought out by the further comparison. Jet is smooth and highly polished. Coal is rough, with the light reflected in broken highlights. Thus, in the second sentence there are two primary comparisons, Jane's hair with coal, Mary's with jet. These comparisons are for the purpose of finding a *similarity* — in each case, color. Then a further comparison is made, one between Jane's hair and Mary's hair. But the purpose of this last comparison is not to find a similarity, but to identify a *difference*. Thus the reader is invited to project the dots on our graphs which represent the crossings of hair–jet and hair–coal, to enlarge these dots, as it were, till he sees that similarity of color in more detail, so that he may see the differences in these blacks.

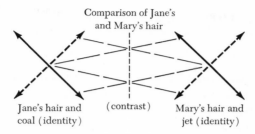

With incredible modulations of this comparative process, the creative writer controls the range of qualities, of overtones, to achieve his more accurate artistic communication.

All this schematizing of art is of little use beyond the simply illustrative, but it might be well to put it in a different mathematic metaphor before moving on. If all knowledge is gained by comparison, it must be remembered that there must always be known factors to help one arrive at an unknown. "X" remains meaningless without a juxtaposition of known factors which define it. The man who discovered the efficacy of penicillin had (1) a germ culture whose normal qualities were known and (2) an unprecedented death of germs on the slide in the presence of a certain mold. These known facts were the basis for the discovery (x) that a certain substance in that mold was deadly to bacteria. Similarly in a figure of speech the reader moves from known facts (the color of coal and of jet) to the unknown (the particular color of hair).

It should be remembered that there is little possibility of profit in attempting to transfer into mathematical symbols or graphs the rich substance of emotional overtones. Learning to recognize those overtones, to feel them when they are called into being by a poem, is one of the achievements of the accomplished reader, and it is in working toward an accurate embodiment of those overtones that oral training and reading has some of its most fruitful moments. For comparisons by means of figurative language are not all made in the same way, any more than scientific comparisons are made through identical experimental situations. Different methods of comparison have been recognized and variously subdivided and named in complex systems of identification for many centuries. However, it is possible to group them under certain simple, if unhistoric, headings which may help to clarify their method of comparison as encountered in reading.

THE CONCEPTUAL FIGURES

Though nearly all figures, in their essential comparisons, invoke sensual responses, certain ones, which we will call the conceptual figures, may have as their aim a primarily intellectual response. In the chapter called *Tone* (suggesting as it did that the problem of comprehending literature might, finally, be tonal) we discussed two of these figures, irony and paradox. We contrasted the primarily lingual, intellectual base of such tones with tones based on such biological responses as happiness, illness, discomfort. Obviously it is of great significance to the oral reader to be aware of these conceptual figures, since this awareness will affect his voice as well as his bodily involvement and facial expression.

The conceptual figures compare a tone given in the story or poem with a tone which the reader recognizes in his imagination would be more appropriate. Irony and paradox are conceptual figures so frequently met with and (particularly irony) so generally used that it seemed best to discuss them while dealing with the central elements of tone. At least two other conceptual figures should be recognized, each partaking, in my opinion, of some of the qualities of irony. These are *hyperbole* and *understatement*.

Understatement is perhaps most vividly defined by a Thurber cartoon in which two fencers are pictured, the one just completing a pass with his saber, the other's head just parting from his body, with "Touche" the caption underneath. A Frenchman's *mot* that marriage is an institution of many joys and few pleasures was prefigured perhaps in this plaintive little poem of understatement by some anonymous Elizabethan:

> Ye Gods, you gave to me a wife,
> Out of your wonted favor,
> To be the comfort of my life,
> And I was glad to have her:
> But if your providence divine
> For something else design her
> To obey your will at any time
> I'm ready to resign her.

When Othello breaks up a duel saying, "Keep up your bright swords, for the dew will rust them," we have a line whose poetic overtones and relationships are so complex as to be almost endless; but throughout, the main impact is one of understatement. The main levels of understatement come, perhaps, from the implied metaphor, dew — blood, and in the more subtle implication by which rust is made to stand for the deaths of the men.

Hyperbole, which is simply overstatement, occurs in such frequently predictable places as the compliments of lovers, the speeches of politicians, advertisements, and humor. That there is a reason for overstatement, or hyperbole, as well as for understatement, might be discovered by examining the difference between the large glossy automobile, by which some men talk big, and their income tax report, in which they may talk small.

This predictable recurrence of hyperbole in certain situations in real life is reflected in art, but with a difference. For though each individual wooer in real life can tell his listener, with some hope of sounding convincing, that she "means more than life itself," poets cannot keep doing so forever in their poems without becoming trite. The use of hyperbole in writing, perhaps more conspicuously than other figures, demands (1) convincing originality, or (2) ironic treatment. Otherwise one comes quickly to agree with the anonymous Elizabethan who, a bit nauseated, one imagines, by floods of hyperbolic sonnets all using the same figures of speech, wrote:

> Your shining eyes and golden hair,
> Your lily-rosèd lips most fair,
> Your other beauties that excel,
> Men cannot choose but like them well;
> But when for them they say they'll die,
> Believe them not, they do but lie.

In this poem the hyperboles in the first two lines we recognize as clichés, figures of speech which have lost their ability to convey in writing a sense of powerful personal conviction, and the third line lumps together and thus dismisses all the other descriptive clichés of lovers. The tonal structure of the poem thus moves to an overt pointing, in the last part of the poem, to the ironic use of hyperbole in the first part. This poem demonstrates perhaps the simplest, most straightforward sort of ironic use of hyperbole.

If hyperboles are not handled with conscious irony, then they must carry conviction of a powerful and deep vision. In Melville's "Two Sides to a Tortoise" we are prepared for the acceptance of hyperbole by Melville's telling us that five months at sea was "a period amply sufficient to make all things of the land wear a fabulous hue to the dreamy mind." The words "fabulous" and "dreamy" lead the reader to expect an extraordinarily sensitized state on the part of the sailor, as he goes on to say that such was his condition that if he had seen three ordinary Spanish custom house officers coming aboard he would have treated them with as much curiosity as savages do civilized guests.

Even so, he begins with figures of speech not really hyperbolic, but heightened by including items of rich emotional impact, such as that the turtles are "black as widower's weeds, heavy as chests of plate." Then comes the first exaggeration in the word "vast." Now, given the necessity for hyperbole to strike the reader with a sense of originality, where is the originality in likening a turtle-shell to a shield? It must surely have been done many times. But the mere determination of whether or not a figure has been used before is not the only, is not even the important, aspect of determining a figure's originality. The term "original" is not so simple as that. Possibilities of new contexts, new attitudes, new details are all potentially available to make new an old figure of speech. In this case, the basis of originality lies in the fact that the comparison is not made casually, but is extended until the details convince one that here is a personal, powerful vision, a vision capped by the mystical reference to the sea. The climax of this first group of hyperboles comes when he sees them first as "Roman Coliseums in magnificent decay" and as "Walled towns" of which he asks the "freedom," that is, the right to enter into the spirit represented by the tortoise. He continues the theme of their ancient age, and its effect upon himself psychologically, till he himself seems like an ancient geologist studying the tracks of extinct life on earth. Then he turns to their chief characteristic, a refusal to turn aside for any impediment; and his question as to whether or not they are victims of a diabolical enchanter leads to a climactic series of hyperboles in which he places them back on their island, which he envisions as a kind of hell, "an isle full of metallic ravines and gulches, sunk bottomlessly into the hearts of splintered mountains . . . ," until, so fully has he entered their "walled towns" sympathetically that he, transformed into a Brahmin, joins them in their eternal labor of supporting the earth. This series of hyperboles, brought forward with perfect conviction in a psychologically profound development, is then followed abruptly by the statement that it was a "wild nightmare," and the feeling of mystic sympathy is shattered by the simple acts of eating the tortoises and making artifacts out of their shells. As suggested elsewhere, this turn is not only prepared for, but is thematically essential.

It is interesting to observe that "Two Sides to a Tortoise" has somewhat the same sort of emotive structure as the anonymous Elizabethan joke-poem: an early flourish of hyperboles, concluding with the flat statement of a contrasting reality. Yet Melville uses this structure with a difference; his final flat statement does not invalidate or render an absolutely negative judgment on the hyperbolic part. Rather each part renders the other ironic. Each delimits the nature and value of the other. While being hyperbolic, the writer is able to extend his emotional awareness enormously, to suffer vicariously, to demonstrate what one might well call a reverence for life, if also a somber view of it. When he turns from hyperbole to "reality," he is free to feast, to fill his belly, to be gay, to create gay objects out of life, but these things are ironically and perhaps paradoxically purchased at the cost of empathy, of caring, and hence of variety and imagination. For, after all, the most that he can say of the soup tureen and the salvers which he has fashioned from the shells is uttered in two unrelieved clichés, "fanciful" and "gorgeous."

This essay is an especially valuable piece of writing to study because the shift in tone of the last paragraph offers an unusually clear example of the relationship between tone and figurative usage. The shift is so striking that, in reading the piece aloud, one quite untrained in vocal expression feels under instinctive compulsion to make some change in voice and face to indicate the flattening out, the objectifying, the simplification, of the final response.

But if the voice becomes flatter, the body, surely, becomes more free. In the bulk of the story, the speaker is lying immobile in his bunk, the wild hyperbolic structure is one of abstract thought initiated by his recollection of the astonishing appearance of the beasts and by their noises on the deck over his head. Surely the body here is quiescent, the eyes, as it were, looking beyond the darkness into a world of imagination. It is the voice that must carry the baroque gestures of this introspective world. In contrast, the last paragraph is delivered with a free body and a thinner voice reflecting the lack of depth of the perceiving mind.

TWO OBJECTS COMPARED (ONE THING STANDING FOR ANOTHER)

A *metaphor* is a comparison of two objects or qualities made in the form of an identity. Thus, earlier in this chapter, "Jane's hair is coal" is a metaphor. Metaphor puts this burden upon the reader, that he is expected not only to figure out just how these two things are alike, but also to recognize that it is a limited comparison in spite of its formulation. To the writer, the advantage of the metaphor is that given an intelligent reader, it is a quick, compact, economical way of stating an essential likeness. It requires, grammatically, fewer motions than its nearest relative among figures of speech, the *simile*, and is therefore useful in, though not confined to, situations where qualities of power and definiteness are desired in the tone. For the simile requires the formula "like" or "as," in short, an overt statement that these two things are not truly identical, but only similar: "Jane's hair is *like* (or black *as*) coal." Thus in one sense a simile is a metaphor with the likeness pointed to by the writer. In fact, it is possible to see all figurative language, since all figurative language is a comparison, as varieties of metaphor. That is why in common usage one hears "figurative language" and "metaphoric language" used as synonyms. However that may be, there are still values in using the word "metaphor" in its more technical sense, along with simile, as a way of distinguishing the basic methods of comparing two more or less equally emphasized objects or qualities.

The first paragraph of "An Experiment in Misery" ends with this sentence: "There were only squads of well-dressed Brooklyn people who swarmed towards the bridge." A metaphoric word here is "squads," which brings with it the military comparison by means of which is emphasized the orderliness, the purposefulness to which these citizens adhere, as opposed to the prior description of the slack and wandering young man and the description that follows, the "aimless men strewn in front of saloons and lodging houses," and is an example of how even so casual and small a figure must function as part of a larger pattern.

The *allusion* is a specific and narrowly defined kind of comparison, a comparison between something in the poem or story and an event, a person, or thing in history or art. Thus when Melville says, "They seemed the identical tortoises whereon the Hindoo plants this total sphere," he is comparing his impression of the tortoises to an element of Hindu mythology, making such an allusion to reinforce his feeling of awe at their exoticism, their venerableness, their endurance. Allusion may be made to any event, person, or thing knowledge of which a community of minds may be expected to share. Certain poets, Milton and Ezra Pound, to pick notable examples, have made a highly complex network of allusion the chief figurative principle of much of their poetry.

It is well to be aware of how the allusion may make its appearance in the work of these authors and of others. One technique very much used by T. S. Eliot consists in the use of quotations from earlier writings, given verbatim in juxtaposition with some modern scene, saying, or other contemporary emotional cue, or with some modern alteration of the old quotation. Examples of both varieties of this technique may be seen in "The Waste Land." In Section III, the Fire Sermon, there is a quotation from a lovely poem by Spenser, the Elizabethan poet, "Sweet Thames, run softly till I end my song." This quotation, meant to recall the Thames River in heroic Elizabethan days when it was still clean and beautiful, precedes a description invoking the modern Thames.

> Sweet Thames, run softly, till I end my song.
> The river bears no empty bottles, sandwich papers,
> Silk handkerchiefs, cardboard boxes, cigarette ends
> Or other testimony of summer nights. The nymphs are departed,
> And their friends, the loitering heirs of city directors;
> Departed, have left no addresses.°

The final stanza of Section II, "A Game of Chess," from the same poem, is a good example of the altered quotation, the allusion this time being to Enobarbus' speech in Shakespeare's *Antony and Cleopatra*.

ELIOT

The Chair she sat in, like a burnished throne,
Glowed on the marble, where the glass
Held up by standards wrought with fruited vines
From which a golden Cupidon peeped out
(Another hid his eyes behind his wing) . . .

SHAKESPEARE

The barge she sat in, like a burnished throne
Burn'd on the water: the poop was beaten gold;
Purple the sails, and so perfumed that
The winds were love-sick with them; the oars were silver,
Which to the tune of flutes kept stroke and made
The water which they beat to follow faster,
As amorous of their strokes.

All such allusions in T. S. Eliot make the modern look shabby. In the first example the technique, a bold montage, is obvious. One must come to see, however, in the second example, the rich sensuality of the Shakespeare passage contrasted to the mildly decorative effect of the "wrought with fruited vines," and the coy sentimentality of the pose of the Cupidons as described, in order to feel the impact of the decadence.

Though Ezra Pound also uses allusion in this way, his are quite commonly of a very personal nature — recollections of conversations with acquaintances, or events clustering around special enthusiasms of his — enthusiasms literary, lingual, and historical. Thus in the poem, "Sienna Mi Fe'; Disfecemi Maremma" (a section of a long poem entitled "Hugh Selwyn Mauberley"), Mr. Verog is a fictitious name for one Victor Gustave Plarr, who had known the poet Lionel Johnson and Johnson's friends of the Rhymers' Club, and with whom Pound discussed that literary group out of his (Pound's) interest in Johnson's poetry. The "pickled phoetuses and bottled bones" refer to the fact that Mr. Plarr was Librarian of the Royal College of Surgeons. Allusions are many, including the names Headlam and Image, men mentioned in Plarr's writings about the group.

Just why writers plague their readers with allusions at all is worth giving some thought to, since it is a truism that all great works of art are founded in contemporaneity — deeply involved in the world the author sees and touches and hears. If the writer wants to define the importance of a thing, or to place an event in a subtle scale of values, one way he can accomplish his purpose is to liken that event to one in the past whose meaning and significance is established and widely known. For obviously, the passage of time arbitrates importance, in ways unexpected and devious. To read the poet Dante, one must learn something about Italian persons of the poet's time, who no longer have any other importance. A contemporary Roman would have named a hundred things as more important than Jesus' crucifixion and would, in his terms, have been right.

A poet, then, may use for his allusion a person or event or thing of such great importance in his personal life that he is driven to allude to it in such a way as to make its significance for him a general and relatively timeless thing (Dante's Beatrice is an example). Or he may turn to a world already nearly timeless in its importance, a world of dates, places, scenes, characters, carried and valued in certain specific ways in the remembering heart of his contemporaries. It is a world where the child's mind is as important as a war, where everything is important simply because it has survived, a world, among other things, of the Bible, Shakespeare, Homer, Aesop's Fables, General Grant, Lao Tse, Alice in Wonderland, and the Leaning Tower of Pisa. These objects, persons, places are used as allusions because they stand for a more or less fixed realm of experience, evaluated in widely accepted ways, and can therefore be counted on to intensify or illuminate that heretofore unevaluated matter to which it is compared.

Metaphor, simile, and *allusion,* the three figures of speech just discussed, may all be found working in the following poem.

> There is a Garden in her face,
> Where Roses and white Lilies grow;
> A heav'nly paradice is that place,
> Wherein all pleasant fruits doe flow.
> There Cherries grow, which none may buy
> Till "cherry-ripe" themselves doe cry.
>
> Those Cherries fayrely doe enclose
> Of Orient Pearle a double rowe;
> Which when her lovely laughter showes,
> They look like Rosebuds filled with snow.
> Yet them no Peer nor Prince can buy,
> Till "cherry-ripe" themselves doe cry.
>
> Her Eyes like Angels watch them still;
> Her Browes like bended bowes doe stand,
> Threatning with piercing frownes to kill
> All that attempt with eye or hand
> Those sacred Cherries to come nigh,
> Till "cherry-ripe" themselves doe cry.
>
> THOMAS CAMPION

In the first line a metaphor is stated which turns into hyperbole, then by suggestion becomes an allusion and develops as the basic figure of speech in the poem. The metaphor compares part of her face to a garden. The second line of the poem develops the metaphor by suggesting that roses and white lilies grow there. This is the initial reference in the poem to a red-and-white duality that the poet sees as existing in her face, colors which have, especially in the forms of roses and lilies, ancient histories as symbolizing the life of passion on the one hand and the life of purity on the other.

The poet then heightens the basic figure to hyperbole, by stating that the garden is a "heav'nly paradise." This is the first hint of the allusion which is so much dwelt on later. Next comes another metaphor, in which fruits of the garden are said to "flow." This suggestion of a stream intensifies the sense of a never-ceasing phenomenon and makes the reader wonder whether he might not take the "pleasant fruits" as not only literally apples and cherries, but as an endless procession of pleasant acts, events, expressions, beauties. However, the next line tells that these pleasant fruits are not available until they themselves declare their readiness. The last line is the perfect case of a reference which was contemporary to the author and familiar to all his contemporaries in London, but must now be resurrected by a footnote. A common part of the daily life in Elizabethan London was the parade of vendors walking the streets crying their wares, and here no doubt is the call, or part of the call, sung out by those selling this fruit. (By the way, here is a good example of how some solid sense of the *poem in Time* [see Chapter six] can directly affect the oral reading. Once one is aware of this historical background of the phrase "cherry-ripe," that it was the cry of a vendor, there is little doubt that this will affect the oral performance in the direction of some light echo of that street-cry).

In the next line the metaphor likening her lips to cherries is made more vivid by seeing them as the settings for her teeth, which, in a further metaphoric step, are given as "Orient Pearle." These lips and teeth, seen as cherries and pearls, are likened in a simile to "Rosebuds filled with snow." The switch to a simile here has served, in a passage dense with figures, to keep them from getting hopelessly confused. Thus while making a further comparison the poet is able to maintain the basic metaphor by saying, in effect, "when she laughs, these lips and teeth, which are cherries and pearls, look *like* rosebuds filled with snow." (Note the continuation of the red–white parallel.) The next two lines repeat and, through the use of "Prince" and "Peer" as figures for power, intensify the fact that the fruit is forbidden.

The next lines return to the first stanza and pick up the hint given in the phrase, "heav'nly paradise," and make of it, if we haven't got the hint yet, a specific allusion to Genesis.

And Jehovah God said, "Behold, the man is become as one of us, to know good and evil; and now, lest he put forth his hand, and take also of the tree of life, and eat, and live forever . . . ," there fore Jehovah God sent him forth from the garden of Eden, to till the earth from whence he was taken. So he drove out the man; and he placed at the east of the garden of Eden, the Cherubim, and the flame of a sword which turned every way, to keep the way of the tree of life.

GENESIS III, 22–24

In short, the garden in her face is seen as Eden, and in two similes, (perhaps the fact that the objects being compared have only abstract or metaphysical similarity rather than such a physical likeness as color explains why the comparisons are developed as similes), her eyes are likened to the angels guarding Eden with bows (rather than the Biblical sword), and her frowns to arrows. And this whole aspect of the "heav'nly" garden, Eden, is brought to a focus by calling them "sacred" cherries. As is frequent with allusion, much of the original is either ignored or altered. (The substitution of bows for a sword we have mentioned, and the whole notion of man having been driven out is not referred to.)

But it must be remembered that it is the reader's job to see what the likenesses or contrasts are. Despite having to ignore all or part of his source of allusion, Campion found in Eden an extremely valuable symbol of perfection because it was one to which everyone could respond in the particular way the poet wanted. Specifically, it was a perfection forbidden to man. But this point he also gives an original turn, in that not only is her face the garden, but also the purity of that garden is its own protection. In other words, the miraculous quality of the garden of Eden, structurally the most important figure, sustains and justifies the figure which is the most important thematically and emotionally; namely, the simile (this simile is also a paradox) of rosebuds filled with snow.

For here at the central point of the poem is the visual and symbolic bodying forth of the poet's peculiar vision, his seeing in her the simultaneous existence of the perfect beauty of carnality and the perfect beauty of virtue. This figure is the core of the created and sustained tension of the poem. It is a figure which makes doubly meaningful the allusion. Recall that it was the tree of life which was guarded against man by the cherubim. Thus the poet is able to suggest that her lips are the fruit of that forbidden tree and that he who wins them will gain eternal life. This final intensification brings to a climax the two rhetorical purposes of the poet: first, to praise both her beauty and her virtue; and second, to show how these create a paradox that serves at once to entice and exclude the speaker, along with all men.

It is interesting that the originality in this poem is not in the comparisons themselves, which were standard, ornate ones used by Elizabethan poets and versifiers. Rather, the originality is in the new relationship of the images, in the fine control of their relationship within the overarching structure of the poem, and the twisting of the cliché, "her lips are rosebuds," into a powerful paradox, "rosebuds filled with snow," at the crucial point.

Since trite figures have been mentioned several times, it might be well to note the difference between those which have an artificial, "unnatural" tone from the first, such as the exaggerated praise in this poem, and those which seem not only natural but almost inevitable, such as the initial figure in the story, "Eveline": "She sat at the window watching the evening invade the avenue." In this second type of trite figure, the comparison attracts so little attention, its purpose is so modest, that it requires very little immediate effort by the reader to make it acceptable and usable. The first type, on the other hand, announces its qualities, attracts immediate, special attention, and will disgust all the more readily if not treated in some strikingly enhanced manner. In short, the successful use of each is a different sort of triumph. Thus, the artificialities of the above poem, requiring to be read aloud in a light, delicate tone, do not in any way reduce the importance of the emotional dilemma which is at the center of the poem. It is this complexity of tone which is the mark of this poet's revivifying of his material.

A THING OR IDEA COMPARED TO ITS OWN PARTS AND RELATIONS

The figure of speech which we shall call metonymy (sometimes subdivided to include synecdoche) is a comparison of a thing or idea to its own parts or relations. One kind of metonymy is very simple and lets a part stand for the whole or the whole for the part. Thus when we say, "two sail are arriving," we know entire ships are referred to. Similarly, a "skirt" is a girl; if a girl "has her diamond," she is engaged; if she is "pinned," she is close to engagement. A man "at the wheel" is driving a car. We speak of "head" of cattle. "Hands" are sailors, or cowboys, or farm help; also we can say "give me a hand." We refer to the "horsey" set, the "commuter communities," the "two-car family." These are daily examples of figures in which a part stands for the whole. The reverse, the whole for the part, is perhaps less common, but it is encountered often enough. It sounds strange to us when, in Shakespeare's plays, the various kings are called by the names of their countries; thus the King of England, referring to the King of France, calls him "our brother France." Yet we do not find it strange when, at a national political convention, the Chairman asks, "Is Kansas here?" or "Has New York voted?" And it is still true that the head of a Scottish clan is called "the MacGregor" or "the Douglas." We may say casually that "the car has broken down," when in reality no total collapse has occurred. And, of course, when New York beats Boston in the ninth inning nothing of the sort has really happened, except as we allow the whole to stand figuratively for a very small part.

Those metonymies in which a closely related idea or thing is allowed to stand for the thing or idea itself are even more difficult to recognize. Let us look at several of the images already mentioned. If a sailor is called a "hand," for instance, this is a part for the whole. But if he is called a "salt," it is clear that the salt is not a part of the sailor, but only a closely related thing which is allowed to stand for the sailor. The same is true of calling a girl a "skirt," which is a part, as against calling her a "doll," which is a closely related object. If we call a freshman, or any beginner, "green," it is because green things are related strongly to the spring of the year — an idea that seems closely enough related to serve.

In the following poem, a number of metonymies function.

Unpopular Song*

When the rain falls, don't you cry
The earth is thirsty, so am I;
Wait until the sun breaks thro',
Remember that I'm loving you.

Loving you thro' fine and wet,
Thick and thin since first we met;
Therefore wipe away those tears,
You'll never wipe away the years

That stain your luscious, peachy cheek
And wrinkle it slow week by week.
Come to bed and stop your whining:
Every shroud has a chilly lining.

VERNON SCANNELL

First, the rain might be seen as a closely related idea standing for sad times, and the sun for bright, happy times. Though the sun and rain figures might be given another name, there is certainly a duality of closely related ideas which is continued in "fine and wet" and given variety in "thick and thin." "Years" is the whole standing for all the events that have occurred in them, while the shroud is a part of death standing for the whole. The metonymies, of course, are all reversals and twists of very clichéd ones from popular songs and proverbs.

* Reprinted by permission of the author.

A TANGIBLE SIGN OF SOMETHING INTANGIBLE

A *symbol* is the most common method of rendering the intangible concrete. To symbolize would seem to be a universal way of suggesting the nature of something too indefinable to describe otherwise. It might be helpful in defining the *symbol* to distinguish between the *symbol* and the *emblem,* though in specific cases it is sometimes difficult to do so.

Fundamentally a symbol bears little or no physical resemblance to that thing or idea for which it stands, and therefore must sometimes be placed in a specific pose or context to indicate that it is a symbol and to clarify what it symbolizes. Thus, depending on context, the eagle may *symbolize* either something as abstract as courage or ferocity or something as specific yet indefinable as the United States. On the other hand, the emblem bears some physical resemblance to that for which it stands. The geographical outline of the state of Texas is often used as an emblem of that state. Context can sometimes become very important in distinguishing whether a given figure is a symbol or an emblem. For instance, a cross may be a symbol of sacrifice, but an emblem of the crucifixion.

It is important to realize that neither the symbol nor the emblem is an inferior version of the other, as Donald Davie has pointed out. Indicating the basically emblematic nature of the poetry of Robert Graves, Mr. Davie quotes Grave's poem:

Love Without Hope*

Love without hope, as when the young bird-catcher
Swept off his tall hat to the Squire's own daughter,
So let the imprisoned larks escape and fly
Singing about her head, as she rode by.

ROBERT GRAVES

Having quoted the poem Mr. Davie comments,[1] "The fullness and explicitness, the dry sharp unshadowed silhouette, the lack of resonance and overtone — these are the virtues of this emblematic writing; and the air of fabrication, even of contrivance (but not labored contrivance), the evidence of forethought, plan and design — these will displease only the reader who comes to this verse for what it never offered to supply." In this same way one can see the growing detail and explicitness in the basic

---

* From *Collected Poems* by Robert Graves, published by Doubleday & Co., Inc., and Cassell & Co. Ltd. Reprinted by permission of International Authors N.V.

[1] Review in *Listen,* vol. 3, nos. 3 and 4, *Spring* 1960, p. 33.

figure of Richard Wilbur's "Driftwood," until the poet names the nature of the figure exactly in the poem, "these emblems / Royally sane."

The less specific, more suggestive nature of the symbol may be seen in Melville's "Two Sides to a Tortoise," where the general theme "may one be gay upon the Encantadas" is developed with the dark shell of the tortoise symbolizing the "dark" side of life, the bright shell the opposite. It is this initial establishing of the symbol which prepares the way for our acceptance of his later metaphysical ponderings about the turtles and for his tremendous hyperboles, since from the beginning we are brought to see the turtle as in some way symbolizing the total range of life.

Sometimes, as in "Two Sides to a Tortoise," in Wallace Stevens' "Anecdote of a Jar," or in Wilbur's "Driftwood," a poem or story develops its own symbols or emblems as it goes along. In others, such as Keats' "Ode to a Nightingale," the writer takes on a basic symbol whose meaning is already culturally established. In the second case, of course, the reader must recognize the reference, the allusion, and must be alert not only to its original meaning, but also to unique developments and permutations in the new use.

But there is a third method of developing a symbol or emblem, a method which by the way can become most vexing for the reader. This technique ignores the communicative advantages of the culturally established figure, and refuses to develop the meaning of its figure clearly and firmly as it goes along. This third device is generally limited to certain poets, prominent among them William Blake and William Butler Yeats, who develop a highly personal *system* of symbols which no one poem will adequately reveal and which can be reconstructed only by reading *all* the poems and, perhaps, a key book or books outside the canon of poems. If such a poet is unimportant, he will effectively have reduced his audience. If he is a fine poet, like Blake or Yeats, a little study of that private symbology will amply reward any reader.

Having discussed the methods of developing the symbol or emblem, perhaps we are ready to face the problem which the symbol often raises for the reader, the problem of just how far to take it. Given its rather shadowy nature, how far is one justified in extending implications? A symbol is likely to cut vertically through many layers of experience, many levels of intensity and profundity. Yet surely each symbol must have its limitations beyond which it does not even hint. It is clear that the figures on the urn in Keats' poem (p. 228) are meant to symbolize the abstract, unchanging world created in art by artists, to symbolize in a further sense a certain kind of eternity. It is clear that Buffalo Bill (p. 242) stands for a kind of physical perfection. In these two cases the firm centers of the symbolic meaning limit the direction and extension of implication.

But it is not quite so easy to see what is precisely the area of experience symbolized in the following poem:

The Sick Rose

O Rose, thou art sick!
The invisible worm
That flies in the night,
In the howling storm,

Has found out thy bed
Of crimson joy,
And his dark secret love
Does thy life destroy.

WILLIAM BLAKE

In the major symbols, the crimson rose and the worm, the poet uses two standard poetic symbols, the one standing for passion, for earthly fleshly love, the second for death, corruption of the flesh. But these simple symbols are set in a dramatic context which makes them difficult to delimit. Actually the rose seems to retain its usual meaning without much increment or loss, except that mention of its "bed" brings the major action of the poem nearer to an overt sexual metaphor. But the worm's meanings increase almost to the point where its central meaning fuzzes out of control. It is not only death. It is clearly some kind of sexual symbol, yet evidently a symbol of abnormal or dark sexuality, since the rose must stand for a clear, open kind of sexuality of which the author approves — a "crimson bed" which is good, but which is destroyed by the worm. One hint as to what is the nature of the worm's evil is in the word "secret," which word immediately, and no doubt erroneously, turns the modern mind to thoughts of Freud's relatively narrow concept of repression. Though such connections may to a degree be clarifying they are, one suspects, only a part of what is meant by "dark secret love," a phrase which seems to reach deeper levels of response than any pseudo-scientific term. But the symbols that raise the overtones almost past the point of central tonal control are in the third and fourth lines. "Night" is traditionally connected with "black," "dark," and other images of death and evil, but the "howling storm" is harder to define. Is it simply life? Such an interpretation would seem to be too broad, for the storm is grammatically given as a parallel to "night," so that it seems to be a further attempt to define the same condition as the word "night." Perhaps it is simply the opposite of peaceful. Perhaps it is meant to define the area of life made up of senseless violence;

certainly the "howling" has animalistic overtones. In an attempt to paraphrase these various symbols, one might say that the openly beautiful sexual life is destroyed by a sexual life that arises from secret sources, arrives in darkness and violence, and fastens itself on the rose. But immediately we would have to qualify that interpretation by admitting that a narrowly sexual construction of the symbolism is nowhere insisted upon. Indeed the poem may be intended as something no more specific than an expression of an archetypal human experience: the destruction of something beautiful by something secret and malignant. Yet one can hardly keep more specific applications from entering his head. And perhaps he should not try to keep them out.

Personification is the bodying forth of abstract qualities, such as love, hate, death, into a human form or personality. Thus, in this little poem we have personification not only of the heart, standing as symbol of the emotional center of man, but also of someone called the Inquisitor, who appears to represent some such concept as time or life.

> The Heart asks Pleasure — first —
> And then — Excuse from Pain —
> And then — those little Anodynes
> That deaden suffering —
> And then — to go to sleep —
> And then — if it should be
> The will of its Inquisitor
> The privilege to die —

> EMILY DICKINSON*

Notice in this poem that a little drama is enacted, the heart asking favors of a person who turns out to be an enemy, a progression of requests based, until the very last, on a naive misconception of the nature of the Inquisitor. Notice how the poet has left the nature of the addressee till the last, letting the reader share the discovery with the heart. The depth of that discovery is to be seen in the irony of the word "privilege." This little drama is an example of that type of figurative narration called an *allegory*. Since the characters in an allegory are often types or personifications, it is well to consider personification and allegory together. The allegory, as this little poem exemplifies, is a story or narrative whose disguised meaning is implied figuratively rather than stated expressly. Not only are the charac-

*Reprinted by permission of the publishers and the Trustees of Amherst College from *The Poems of Emily Dickinson*, Thomas Johnson, Editor (Cambridge, Mass.: the Belknap Press of Harvard University Press), Copyright, 1951, 1955, by The President and Fellows of Harvard College.

ters figurative (types or personifications), but the action is symbolic, overtly so.

Some stories and poems seem to border on the allegorical, so that they share in some of the suggestiveness of allegory without offering the usual complete story. Is not "Two Sides to a Tortoise" in this sense an allegorical action demonstrating man's moments of profound observation of the world as those moments alternate with his times of unthinking physical joy and exploitation of the world? And yet it is not a "tale" in any standard sense. The following poem by Edward Thomas is perhaps another such. The various animals certainly seem to personify various human types — the elusive, quiet one "with all his family," the criminal, as well as the gregarious, extroverted talker and maker. Is the Keeper, time? We can see it all applies to humans, but is it a direct allegory? Perhaps it is a special kind of allegory whose rhythmic pattern of repetition serves as much to delineate its meaning as the usual "progression" of fictive event.

The Gallows*

There was a weasel lived in the sun
With all his family,
Till a keeper shot him with his gun
And hung him up on a tree,
Where he swings in the wind and rain,
In the sun and in the snow,
Without pleasure, without pain,
On the dead oak tree bough.

There was a crow who was no sleeper,
But a thief and a murderer
Till a very late hour; and this keeper
Made of him one of the things that were,
To hang and flap in rain and wind
In the sun and in the snow.
There are no more sins to be sinned
On the dead oak tree bough.

There was a magpie, too,
Had a long tongue and a long tail;
He could both talk and do —
But what did that avail?
He, too, flaps in the wind and rain
Alongside weasel and crow,
Without pleasure, without pain,
On the dead oak tree bough.

* Reprinted by permission of the author's widow, Mrs. Helen Thomas.

And many other beasts
And birds, skin, bone and feather,
Have been taken from their feasts
And hung up there together,
To swing and have endless leisure
In the sun and in the snow,
Without pain, without pleasure,
On the dead oak tree bough.

EDWARD THOMAS

E. E. Cummings has written in the following poem an allegory with a fuller narrative development.

anyone lived in a pretty how town
(with up so floating many bells down)
spring summer autumn winter
he sang his didn't he danced his did.

Women and men (both little and small)
cared for anyone not at all
they sowed their isn't they reaped their same
sun moon stars rain

children guessed (but only a few
and down they forgot as up they grew
autumn winter spring summer)
that noone loved him more by more

when by now and tree by leaf
she laughed his joy she cried his grief
bird by snow and stir by still
anyone's any was all to her

someones married their everyones
laughed their cryings and did their dance
(sleep wake hope and then) they
said their nevers they slept their dream

stars rain sun moon
(and only the snow can begin to explain
how children are apt to forget to remember
with up so floating many bells down)

one day anyone died i guess
(and noone stooped to kiss his face)
busy folk buried them side by side
little by little and was by was

all by all and deep by deep
and more by more they dream their sleep
noone and anyone earth by april
wish by spirit and if by yes.

Women and men (both dong and ding)
summer autumn winter spring
reaped their sowing and went their came
sun moon stars rain

E. E. CUMMINGS*

One of the new turns given to the allegory in this poem is the nature of the personifications. Personifications traditionally are likely to be abstractions such as truth, honor, hope, sin. However, in Cummings's poem, rather than simple nouns, the kind of combination or portmanteau word that was used in naming the allegorical play, "Everyman," is carried systematically forward. One might say that the whole quality of the poem arises from the unorthodox lumping of an adjective or adverb with a noun to create the generalized types of the story. First, there are the three great collectives of mankind, women, men, and children. Second, there are the characters called "anyone," "noone," "someones," "everyones." "Anyone" is the hero of the allegory, and he lives in a "how town." One wonders if there is an echo of "cow town" to emphasize the smallness, the commonness of the community. In any case, a town may indeed be seen as a collection of human and mechanical means of production and consumption. In that sense, all towns are "how" towns. This is not a city, however, and is therefore neither grandly beautiful nor ugly, but rather the more limited "pretty." Further, as in many small towns, with churches and schools and clocks in town halls, there is a general impression of bells, and it is interesting to see how the poet, by delaying the word "down," creates a rhythm remindful of the bells as they seem to hang for a moment at the upward end of their swing. Of "anyone" himself we learn that "he sang his didn't he danced his did." "Didn't" and "did" might be taken as a sort of metonymy for all the actions and all the quietnesses of one's life, and the significant thing about "anyone" is that he didn't just do them, he celebrated them. Whatever he did was like a dance, lovely and meaningful, and his moments of inaction were like songs. Note that one cannot paraphrase exactly what the line of poetry, with its density of suggestion, is saying. But perhaps even a partial paraphrase justifies itself if it sets the imagination going in the right direction. Perhaps "anyone" is simply *any one*, the opposite of the so-called and non-existent average man, a unique unduplicatable human being. On the other hand, "Women and men" are collectives; they are described as both little and small, a conceptual repetition which leads us to think something both physical and spiritual is described. They are indifferent to "anyone"; they "sowed their isn't" and they "reaped their same," grammatical constructions obviously intended to remind of "he sang his didn't, he danced his did," as well as to make allusion to the Biblical saying "As ye sow so shall ye reap." Perhaps these comments are enough to start the imagination toward an exploration of this fine allegory, as well as toward some interesting speculations on the curious and ever-shifting integration between the new and the old, the convention and the original perception.

IMPLIED COMPARISONS

Perhaps in this chapter we have dealt too much with categories. Certainly it is much less important to name, to classify, a figure of speech than it is to recognize that a comparison has been made and to determine what its purpose is. To be able to feel along the thread of the likeness and catch accurately its denotation and its main connotations is the central concern. Seeing the comparison and understanding how it functions are necessities and it follows that those figures which are merely suggested but not overtly stated may involve the reader in his most serious misunderstandings in dealing with figurative language. He may misinterpret a figure, but there is always hope he will correct his error. But if the figure is never seen, there is much less hope for a correction of a misreading. Sometimes these implied comparisons are not really very specific. For instance, one may be reminded of a hospital room by the description of Duffy's room in "A Painful Case," so frequent are the images of white and of bareness. And certainly thinking of such a connection does reinforce certain feelings of illness, sterility, and transiency which one gets from the story. Still, the reader must remember that the comparison is *not* made directly and that, therefore, he must regard this suggestion as only implied, if he is to understand the description properly.

Usually, however, the image is a good deal more definite than a mere suggestion. Look at the scene in which Hamlet and his friend Horatio come to the graveyard. A gravedigger at work there sings a song that has three stanzas. The middle stanza, all that is important to the present purpose, goes

> But Age with his stealing step
> Hath clawed me in his clutch
> And shipped me intil the land
> As if I had never been such.

What is obvious is that Age is personified as someone who seizes the speaker in the poem. What is less obvious is that the major emotional impact of the stanza depends upon an implied comparison with the ancient method of getting sailors by "shanghaiing" or by "impressing" when none were to be had by decent means. Men who were by no means always unattached sailors were simply seized secretly, put aboard ship, and, in short, made to vanish "as if they had never been such." The poem is simply about dying, but by implication it also emotionally characterizes death (the word "shipped" is the key to the figure) as a sudden, secret violence, whose effect is to make one vanish as mysteriously as did those involuntary sailors from their friends and relatives.

Any kind of figure may be obvious or obscure, but any whose elements are not made obvious may be called an implied comparison. Thus, briefly, in a two-line poem Ezra Pound implies a comparison between the faces strung along a subway station and the petals strung along a bough.

In a Station of the Metro*

The apparition of these faces in the crowd;
Petals on a wet, black bough.

Or the implied comparison may be developed more extensively, as in William Carlos Williams' poem, "The Yachts." To say just exactly what the yachts are to be compared with would be perhaps as perilous as to say what the worm symbolizes in Blake's poem, "O Rose, thou art sick." There is this difference, however, that the worm and rose are ancient symbols with accepted meanings clustering around them, whereas the yachts are of the order of those symbols whose significance develops within the poem itself. Still, there can be little doubt that the poem implies other levels of meaning than simply the fascination of the struggle between yacht and yacht and between yachts and sea. Basic to the readers' understanding of the poem is the realization that the contention between the yachts is only a game, a sport, and that the real struggle is between the yachts and the sea.

The Yachts†

contend in a sea which the land partly encloses
shielding them from the too heavy blows
of an ungoverned ocean which when it chooses

tortures the biggest hulls, the best man knows
to pit against its beatings, and sinks them pitilessly.
Mothlike in mists, scintillant in the minute

brilliance of cloudless days, with broad bellying sails
they glide to the wind tossing green water
from their sharp prows while over them the crew crawls

ant like, solicitously grooming them, releasing,
making fast as they turn, lean far over and having
caught the wind again, side by side, head for the mark.

In a well guarded arena of open water surrounded by
lesser and greater craft which, sycophant, lumbering
and flittering follow them, they appear youthful, rare

as the light of a happy eye, live with the grace
of all that in the mind is fleckless, free and
naturally to be desired. Now the sea which holds them

is moody, lapping their glossy sides, as if feeling
for some slightest flaw but fails completely.
Today no race. Then the wind comes again. The yachts

move, jockeying for a start, the signal is set and they
are off. Now the waves strike at them but they are too
well made, they slip through, though they take in canvas.

Arms with hands grasping seek to clutch at the prows.
Bodies thrown recklessly in the way are cut aside.
It is a sea of faces about them in agony, in despair

until the horror of the race dawns staggering the mind,
the whole sea become an entanglement of watery bodies
lost to the world bearing what they cannot hold. Broken,

beaten, desolate, reaching from the dead to be taken up
they cry out, failing, failing! their cries arising
in waves still as the skillful yachts pass over.

WILLIAM CARLOS WILLIAMS

At the very beginning we are told that the yachts cannot stand up to
the beating of the open sea; they must be sheltered partly by the land.
Within that shelter they are both superbly beautiful and triumphant. They
are realized ideals in fact, youthful, graceful, free. One might almost say

there seems something artificial about this absence of the usual marks of age, for besides being youthful, graceful, free, they are also described as "glossy," "well made," "skillful." So far as structural time is concerned, it is interesting that the characterizing of the yachts is the chief concern of the first six stanzas, whereas the last five concern themselves chiefly with characterizing the sea. Immediately following the climactic description of the yachts (perhaps the sharpest image of which is in the simile "rare as the light of a happy eye") the first clear step is taken toward a more limited and meaningful image of the sea, when it is described as "moody." Of course, persons, not seas, are moody, and this giving to an animal or an inanimate object a human emotion is called a "pathetic fallacy." Properly used, the pathetic fallacy is a valuable device for sympathetic intensification, and here is a very good example of such use. The poet begins his characterizing with the modest adjective "moody." It is in a sense all the more acceptable at this point because it is a bit of a cliché. People have been calling the sea moody for a long time, and the poet needs this little pathetic fallacy that is so easy of acceptance, since he must in a very brief time expand it into a highly original and violent comparison. The hint is enlarged modestly (the use of a simile admits the comparison is limited) with the phrase "as if feeling for some slightest flaw." The race starts, the boats speed up, and now the waves no longer "feel"; rather they "strike at them," but again they fail.

Having got the reader to accept without much question the sea as animated in some kind of human way, the poet is ready to present the full force of the comparison. The sea is suddenly "arms with hands grasping." Then the poet takes another step; the sea becomes "bodies thrown recklessly in the way." Thus the reader is prepared for the final vision of great horror: the lovely, delicate, skillful yachts are driving on and cutting through a weltering sea of bodies, bodies which cry "to be taken up," but which the yachts spurn. So it is that, as the reader comes to the final cataclysmic image, he is made forcibly aware of a very strongly implied comparison between the yacht race and some greater human activity. But what activity? I will make a few tentative suggestions regarding possible directions for further speculation on the comparison's relation to reality.

First, but not necessarily most convincing, is the possibility that the yachts represent the living and the sea represents the dead who desire once more to be living, but to whose desires the living are indifferent. Some things work out fairly well in this comparison. The living *do*, in a sense, ride on the achievements of the dead. And they survive under protected circumstances. (The fact of the yachts needing enclosed water for survival must be a first and vital key to any interpretation.) Against this interpretation, perhaps, is the sense that the bodies and hands in the sea are a commingling of dead and living, with the living trying but failing to catch the yachts in order to be taken up.

A second implication might be a sociological one. The poem might be seen as a description of the beauty and skill of a wealthy class, of a privileged group as it maintains itself above the mass of people and at their expense. This interpretation also fits the first requirement (their protection from the anarchic sea), for a privileged class, whether landed or capitalistic or communist bureaucratic, survives because certain customs and laws that order the society as a whole operate to protect its privileged position.

A third possibility is a philosophical or religious one. In this interpretation the yachts might be seen as the carefully rationalized religions or philosophic systems that ride over the welter of life and death, apparently immune to vicissitudes, while those persons incapable of understanding or accepting such systems cry out their ambiguous hatred and envy, their enmity for the yachts, yet their desire for order and perhaps for faith. In this sense the enclosing land might be those initial postulates which any religion or philosophic system needs in order to become self-contained and to explain existence according to its own elaboration. An instance might be the Communists' belief in a certain predetermined history of mankind as the basis on which they erect their arguments; another might be the belief in the special divinity of Christ, from which the ancient Christian dogmas developed their sanction. The implication of the poem would be then that these beliefs, placed outside the protection of their culture and their own arbitrary postulates, could not survive, but that within the boundaries of that protection they survive brilliantly by a kind of ignoring of the chaos of human needs and situations.

I do not know which, if any, of these implications the poet had in mind. Perhaps none of them; perhaps all of them. Perhaps the best interpretation lies in a different direction altogether. Perhaps the poem is simply a reminder that in the basic and violent conflict inevitable between on the one hand skill, self-certainty, disciplined strength and on the other the chaos, the infinity of desire, hatred, need, that make up human existence, only within a protected area of life can the former in the end win. These symbols may sometimes be so difficult of exact interpretation, as in the Blake poem "The Sick Rose," that one may finally feel nothing more specific than the development of some such archetypal pattern as just described, a pattern occurring again and again in different forms and actualities in human history or in the inner life of an individual. General though these symbols are in "The Yachts," one should nonetheless observe that the poem exists on a specific level — a yacht race — and that tones arising from that level are never in doubt. It is the great advantage of the oral performer's relation to literature that he must perforce deeply understand the implied comparison and share in its whole development, until the full "horror of the race dawns staggering the mind. . . ." He must, for instance, realize that the narrative eye in "The Yachts" at first develops its symbol from far enough away to describe the whole bay "which the land partly encloses," and to see the sails at some distance "mothlike in mists," but finally, with the start of the race, moves in close enough to see the waves striking at the sides of the ships and to hear the "cry" in the last stanza. This point of view will be reinforced by the realization that all the sensory appeals up to the "cry" are visual and by the realization that at this point in the poem the symbolizing of the sea and of the general contest reaches its fulfillment. The oral reader, his body and voice changing appropriately from a response to visual clues to a response to this sharp cry, can create the climactic moment for the listener, immediately to be followed by the denouement of "failing, failing."

PREPARATION FOR PERFORMANCE – "The Windhover"

Figurative Language

This poem is an excellent example of how the figurative language of a work of literature makes demands on the living voice. To begin with, the first figures, "morning's minion" and "kingdom of daylight's dauphin," are a part of that series of object-phrases already discussed in a previous chapter. It was mentioned then that these phrases created a climactic pattern leading to the specific naming of the falcon. The oral reader should be aware of the nature of this progression, which is from the abstract, relatively non-specific, to the concrete.

A "minion" is simply a favorite – servant, minister, paramour. The word's denotation names a very general condition and therefore brings no sharp connotations or sensory impressions to mind. Thus for the oral reader the sharpest impression and emphasis in this first phrase will come from the descriptive "morning morning's" rather than from the figurative word "minion." A "dauphin" on the other hand is a more specific reference. Here the denotation is sharp, bringing rich overtones and sensory impressions to mind. It definitely receives more emphasis than "kingdom of daylight's," and should so be read. A prince is a servant only to a king (figuratively, in this case, God), and mental images suggestive of power arise, which substantially modify the notion of servant. Further, sensory impressions of rich dress, grace, and high rank accompany this term, the appropriateness of which becomes clear as the third and most concrete word "falcon" appears. The build-up to the climactic naming of the poem's subject and central symbol can thus be seen as a progression toward the more and more concrete. The movement is clearly a structural one which the oral reader cannot ignore, though it is a minor one and is soon reduced in the poem's larger movements.

After these first two lines, the sense of figurative denseness slacks off, and the impression of visual description is paramount, with the simile which likens the bird's movement to that of a skate being subservient to a descriptive aim. As the physically static quality of the first two lines gives way to this sense of graceful, free motion, the reader's body and voice will, however subtly, feel the release and express it, coming to a climax with the words "hurl and gliding rebuffed." The author has used these verbs as nouns here; and as often happens he thereby suggests a figurative use, in this case a metonymy in which these two *actions* of the bird stand for the whole falcon, as the "big wind" seems a synecdoche of the whole physical setting. A shift of vocal tone should signify that the figure momentarily shifts from the bird to include the speaker. The "heart" is used in its ordinary figurative sense as symbol of the emotional or moral center of the man, but its symbolic value is carried a bit further. There is some slight characterization of the heart here in a specific sense, as of a frightened creature in his retreat.

The turning point of the poem is marked by a further series of metonymies, each designed to intensify the reader's awareness of one aspect of the falcon by making it stand at that moment for the whole. Each of these metonymies seems to be of equal weight, and to read them aloud as such will inevitably make the word "buckle" climactic. If it is ever possible to say that one word is the key to a poem, then "buckle" is such a word. It has several meanings that are important. Perhaps the simplest way to get at them is to list them.

— to fasten or make fast with a buckle —
— to cause to bend, give way or crumple —
— to equip oneself or make ready for a contest or undertaking by or as if by buckling on armor —

The first meaning is most obvious and direct. The speaker asks the falcon, as symbol of Christ — high, noble, free, beautiful — to fasten onto his lowly heart. But this meaning leads to the next. If Christ is to stoop to the man's heart, He must lower himself, He must relinquish His high, free flight for a lowly fate — He must bend, give way, crumple — and one is reminded of the Crucifixion in which according to Christian belief Jesus accepted death as a criminal in order to point the way to God's love. And this meaning leads yet on to the third. For as Jesus did so lower Himself, did so crumple in death, the speaker sees Him as becoming an armor for the heart; and in this sense the speaker is asking Christ to buckle to his heart as one buckles on armor for a contest or undertaking from which the heart has hitherto been hiding.

This notion of armor leads straight to the third direct figure of the falcon-Christ: "Chevalier." Meanwhile the fire that breaks from the bird as a result of his buckling inevitably reminds one of the blood of Jesus crucified, and this association in turn resolves the paradox of "lovelier" and "dangerous." Two final figures are used to explain this strange thing, that the bird should become more beautiful by buckling to a lowly object. And here one must recall a visual fact. When a falcon "stoops" or falls on its prey, there is not only a heightened sense of drama, there are also flashes of great brilliance when the wings of the bird catch the sun as they open and shut, open and shut, in the burst of controlled falling. This visual fact lies behind the two final figures. The poet takes a mundane, unexciting act like plowing and points to the high polish of the plow and the beautiful colors that appear along the side of the furrow where the earth is pushed into a sheen. Then he takes an ordinary gray thing like a coal and points to the fact that though in falling it hurts itself, breaks itself open, yet in doing so it also creates great beauty. The implication is, then, that if two such common objects and acts, in their breaking, downward motion, can cause beauty, how much greater must be the power and beauty of so great a fall as that of Jesus? It is this "no wonder of it" that informs the vocal tones and bodily attitudes of these last three lines. The poet has given the reader the right start in emphasis by stressing "shéer plód," which would no doubt be uttered somewhere in the upper range, with the rest of the phrase descending as the plow descends the field.

There is an over-all pattern of figures which must be emphasized before we leave the matter. The falcon is directly named in three figures: "minion," "dauphin," "chevalier." It is significant that all three of these have a strongly medieval flavor. Furthermore, the falcon itself, as symbol of Christ, recalls the days when falconry was the sport of kings. There are yet other words that underline this general connotation of the medieval world of knights. "Wimpling" comes from a type of headdress worn by medieval women. "Buckle" has already been discussed in its relation to armor. All these word choices serve both to evoke a world where one man might, through honor, purity, courage, and strength, be another's protector, and to evoke the romance of a world whose more sordid daily aspects have dimmed beside the entrancing image of the beautiful, idealistic, strong, and gallant protector. Perhaps this somewhat submerged, but general, figure of the knight is as much as anything responsible for the purity of the joyful, elevated tone in which the oral reader may read the entire poem.

SELECTIONS

*Home Burial**

He saw her from the bottom of the stairs
Before she saw him. She was starting down,
Looking back over her shoulder at some fear.
She took a doubtful step and then undid it
To raise herself and look again. He spoke
Advancing toward her: "What is it you see
From up there always — for I want to know."
She turned and sank upon her skirts at that,
And her face changed from terrified to dull.
He said to gain time: "What is it you see,"
Mounting until she cowered under him.
"I will find out now — you must tell me, dear."
She, in her place, refused him any help
With the least stiffening of her neck and silence.
She let him look, sure that he wouldn't see,
Blind creature; and a while he didn't see.
But at last he murmured, "Oh," and again, "Oh."

"What is it — what?" she said.

                              "Just that I see."

"You don't," she challenged. "Tell me what it is."

"The wonder is I didn't see at once.
I never noticed it from here before.
I must be wonted to it — that's the reason.
The little graveyard where my people are!
So small the window frames the whole of it.
Not so much larger than a bedroom, is it?
There are three stones of slate and one of marble,
Broad-shouldered little slabs there in the sunlight

On the sidehill. We haven't to mind *those*.
But I understand: it is not the stones,
But the child's mound — "

        "Don't, don't, don't, don't," she cried.

She withdrew shrinking from beneath his arm
That rested on the banister, and slid downstairs;
And turned on him with such a daunting look,
He said twice over before he knew himself:
"Can't a man speak of his own child he's lost?"
"Not you! Oh, where's my hat? Oh, I don't need it!
I must get out of here. I must get air.
I don't know rightly whether any man can."

"Amy! Don't go to someone else this time.
Listen to me. I won't come down the stairs."
He sat and fixed his chin between his fists.
"There's something I should like to ask you, dear."

"You don't know how to ask it."
                            "Help me, then."

Her fingers moved the latch for all reply.

"My words are nearly always an offense.
I don't know how to speak of anything
So as to please you. But I might be taught
I should suppose. I can't say I see how.
A man must partly give up being a man
With women-folk. We could have some arrangement
By which I'd bind myself to keep hands off
Anything special you're a-mind to name.
Though I don't like such things 'twixt those that love.
Two that don't love can't live together without them.
But two that do can't live together with them."
She moved the latch a little. "Don't — don't go.
Don't carry it to someone else this time.
Tell me about it if it's something human.
Let me into your grief. I'm not so much
Unlike other folks as your standing there

Apart would make me out. Give me my chance.
I do think, though, you overdo it a little.
What was it brought you up to think it the thing
To take your mother-loss of a first child
So inconsolably — in the face of love.
You'd think his memory might be satisfied — "

"There you go sneering now!"

                                    "I'm not, I'm not!
You make me angry. I'll come down to you.
God, what a woman! And it's come to this,
A man can't speak of his own child that's dead."

"You can't because you don't know how to speak.
If you had any feelings, you that dug
With your own hand — how could you? — his little grave;
I saw you from that very window there,
Making the gravel leap and leap in air,
Leap up, like that, like that, and land so lightly
And roll back down the mound beside the hole.
I thought, Who is that man? I didn't know you.
And I crept down the stairs and up the stairs
To look again, and still your spade kept lifting.
Then you came in. I heard your rumbling voice
Out in the kitchen, and I don't know why,
But I went near to see with my own eyes.
You could sit there with the stains on your shoes
Of the fresh earth from your own baby's grave
And talk about your everyday concerns.
You had stood the spade up against the wall
Outside there in the entry, for I saw it."

"I shall laugh the worst laugh I ever laughed.
I'm cursed. God, if I don't believe I'm cursed."

"I can repeat the very words you were saying.
'Three foggy mornings and one rainy day
Will rot the best birch fence a man can build.'
Think of it, talk like that at such a time!
What had how long it takes a birch to rot

To do with what was in the darkened parlor.
You *couldn't* care! The nearest friends can go
With anyone to death, comes so far short
They might as well not try to go at all.
No, from the time when one is sick to death,
One is alone, and he dies more alone.
Friends make pretence of following to the grave,
But before one is in it, their minds are turned
And making the best of their way back to life
And living people, and things they understand.
But the world's evil. I won't have grief so
If I can change it. Oh, I won't, I won't!"

"There, you have said it all and you feel better.
You won't go now. You're crying. Close the door.
The heart's gone out of it: why keep it up.
Amy! There's someone coming down the road!"

"*You* — oh, you think the talk is all. I must go —
Somewhere out of this house. How can I make you — "

"If — you — do!" She was opening the door wider.
"Where do you mean to go? First tell me that.
I'll follow and bring you back by force. I *will!* — "

ROBERT FROST

*The Farmer's Bride**

Three Summers since I chose a maid,
Too young maybe — but more's to do
At harvest-time than bide and woo.
    When us was wed she turned afraid
Of love and me and all things human;
Like the shut of a winter's day
Her smile went out, and 'twadn't a woman —
    More like a little frightened fay.
        One night, in the Fall, she runned away.

*Reprinted from *Collected Poems* by Charlotte Mew, by permission of
Gerald Duckworth & Co. Ltd. (London).

"Out 'mong the sheep, her be," they said,
  'Should properly have been abed;
But sure enough she wadn't there
Lying awake with her wide brown stare.
So over seven-acre field and up-along across the down
  We chased her, flying like a hare
  Before our lanterns. To Church-Town
    All in a shiver and a scare
We caught her, fetched her home at last
  And turned the key upon her, fast.

  She does the work about the house
As well as most, but like a mouse:
    Happy enough to chat and play
    With birds and rabbits and such as they,
    So long as men-folk keep away.
"Not near, not near!" her eyes beseech
When one of us comes within reach.
    The women say that beasts in stall
    Look round like children at her call.
    I've hardly heard her speak at all.

  Shy as a leveret, swift as he,
Straight and slight as a young larch tree,
Sweet as the first wild violets, she,
To her wild self. But what to me?

The short days shorten and the oaks are brown,
    The blue smoke rises to the low grey sky,
One leaf in the still air falls slowly down,
    A magpie's spotted feathers lie
On the black earth spread white with rime,
The berries redden up to Christmas-time.
    What's Christmas-time without there be
    Some other in the house than we!

  She sleeps up in the attic there
    Alone, poor maid. 'Tis but a stair
Betwixt us. Oh! my God! the down,
The soft young down of her, the brown,
The brown of her — her eyes, her hair, her hair!

                    CHARLOTTE MEW

*The Rival**

The farmer's wife looked out of the dairy:
She saw her husband in the yard;
She said: "A woman's life is hard,
The chimney smokes, the churn's contrary."
   She said:
"I of all women am the most ill-starred.

"Five sons I've borne and seven daughters,
And the last of them is on my knee.
Finer children you could not see.
Twelve times I've put my neck in the halter:
   You'd think
So much might knit my husband's love to me.

"But no! Though I should serve him double
He keeps another love outdoors,
Who thieves his strength, who drains his stores,
Who haunts his mind with fret and trouble;
   I pray
God's curse may light on such expensive whores.

"I am grown old before my season,
Weather and care have worn me down;
Each year delves deeper in my frown,
I've lost my shape and for good reason:
   But she
Yearly puts on young looks like an Easter gown.

"And year by year she has betrayed him
With blight and mildew, rain and drought,
Smut, scab, and murrain, all the rout;
But he forgets the tricks she's played him
   When first
The fields give a good smell and the leaves put out.

"Aye, come the Spring, and the gulls keening,
Over her strumpet lap he'll ride,
Watching those wasteful fields and wide,
Where the darkened tilth will soon be greening,
    With looks
Fond and severe, as looks the groom on bride."

SYLVIA TOWNSEND WARNER

*Wedding-Wind**

The wind blew all my wedding-day,
And my wedding-night was the night of the high wind;
And a stable door was banging, again and again,
That he must go and shut it, leaving me
Stupid in candlelight, hearing rain,
Seeing my face in the twisted candlestick,
Yet seeing nothing. When he came back
He said the horses were restless, and I was sad
That any man or beast that night should lack
The happiness I had.

                    Now in the day
All's ravelled under the sun by the wind's blowing.
He has gone to look at the floods, and I
Carry a chipped pail to the chicken-run,
Set it down, and stare. All is the wind
Hunting through clouds and forests, thrashing
My apron and the hanging cloths on the line.
Can it be borne, this bodying-forth by wind
Of joy my actions turn on, like a thread
Carrying beads? Shall I be let to sleep
Now this perpetual morning shares my bed?
Can even death dry up
These new delighted lakes, conclude
Our kneeling as cattle by all-generous waters?

PHILIP LARKIN

* Reprinted from *The Less Deceived* by Philip Larkin, by permission of
The Marvell Press, Hessle, Yorkshire, England.

The Passionate Shepherd to His Love

Come live with me, and be my love,
And we will all the pleasures prove,
That valleys, groves, hills and fields,
Woods, or steepy mountain yields.

And we will sit upon the rocks,
Seeing the shepherds feed their flocks
By shallow rivers, to whose falls
Melodious birds sing madrigals.

And I will make thee beds of roses,
And a thousand fragrant poesies,
A cap of flowers, and a kirtle,
Embroidred all with leaves of myrtle.

A gown made of the finest wool,
Which from our pretty lambs we pull,
Fair linéd slippers for the cold,
With buckles of the purest gold.

A belt of straw and ivy buds,
With coral clasps and amber studs,
And if these pleasures may thee move,
Come live with me, and be my love.

The shepherds' swains shall dance and sing
For thy delight each May-morning.
If these delights thy mind may move,
Then live with me, and be my love.

CHRISTOPHER MARLOWE

The Nymph's Reply to the Shepherd

If all the world and love were young,
And truth in every shepherd's tongue,
These pretty pleasures might me move,
To live with thee, and be thy love.

Time drives the flocks from field to fold,
When rivers rage and rocks grow cold,
And Philomel becometh dumb,
The rest complains of care to come.

The flowers do fade, and wanton fields,
To wayward winter reckoning yields,
A honey tongue, a heart of gall,
Is fancy's spring, but sorrow's fall.

Thy gowns, thy shoes, thy beds of roses,
Thy cap, thy kirtle, and thy posies,
Soon break, soon wither, soon forgotten:
In folly ripe, in reason rotten.

Thy belt of straw and ivy buds,
Thy coral clasps and amber studs,
All these in me no means can move,
To come to thee, and be thy love.

But could youth last, and love still breed,
Had joys no date, nor age no need,
Then these delights my mind might move,
To live with thee, and be thy love.

SIR WALTER RALEIGH

The Bait

Come live with mee, and bee my love,
And we will some new pleasures prove
Of golden sands, and christall brookes,
With silken lines, and silver hookes.

There will the river whispering runne
Warm'd by thy eyes, more then the sunne.
And there th'inamor'd fish will stay,
Begging themselves they may betray.

When thou wilt swimme in that live bath,
Each fish, which every channell hath,
Will amorously to thee swimme,
Gladder to catch thee, then thou him.

If thou, to be so seene, beest loath,
By sunne, or moone, thou darknest both,
And if my selfe have leave to see,
I need not their light, having thee.

Let others freeze with angling reeds,
And cut their legges, with shells and weeds,
Or treacherously poore fish beset,
With strangling snare, or windowie net:

Let coarse bold hands, from slimy nest
The bedded fish in banks out-wrest,
Or curious traitors, sleavesilke flies
Bewitch poore fishes wandring eyes.

For thee, thou needst no such deceit,
For thou thy selfe art thine owne bait;
That fish, that is not catch'd thereby,
Alas, is wiser farre then I.

JOHN DONNE

CHAPTER TEN

The Voices in Literature

The whole intricate question of method, in the craft of fiction, I take to be governed by the question of the point-of-view — the question of the relation in which the narrator stands to the story.

PERCY LUBBOCK

Imitations produce pain or pleasure not because they are mistaken for realities, but because they bring realities to mind.

SAMUEL JOHNSON

THE CHARACTER OF THE NARRATOR

The Absence of the Narrator

It should be apparent that the character of the narrator of a fiction poses a primary problem for the oral reader. The influences deriving from the character of the narrator touch every aspect of the work of art, great and small, and bear both immediately and eventually on every insight that is to be derived from re-creating the story in the voice and body.

Though it is not altogether necessary to have the voice of the narrator tell a story or poem, such is the more usual method. In the little poem on p. 150, the Scots rivers Tweed and Till hold a conversation. But it is not a conversation which can be understood without help. The fact that the occurrence is being narrated to the reader is made clear in the two phrases, "Says Tweed to Till" and "Says Till to Tweed," by means of which some unidentified voice introduces the participants. This single function served by this particular narrator is essential, for it is difficult to see how the poem could have been written with such great economy and effectiveness had it been necessary for the rivers to introduce themselves somehow in their conversations (though sometimes this necessity can be turned to advantage by giving the reader an unusual sense of immediacy).

The poem "Edward" is an old one. The poem is usually presented as a Scottish popular ballad, though it seems too formally regular to be anything but the largely unaltered work of a specific unknown writer. In any case, the point of view from which the story is told, technically a sophisticated one, is perfectly adhered to (see p. 135 for poem).

The absence of narrator in stories and poems such as "Edward" makes it necessary to use some such device as the first Speaker calling the second Speaker "my son," and of the son responding "mither," as well as the presence of sufficient hints that we can know what is essential about time and locale. However, far from being handicapped, this author has seized on these necessities for exploitation. It becomes clear that this is a tragedy of family, a tale of a strong, hate-filled, ambitious mother and a weak, dominated son. The constant harping on "my son" and "mither" becomes an almost unbearably ironic refrain, while all the references to hawks, horses, towers and hall, on the simplest level giving as much as we need to know of the locale, the class of people, and the time in history, are also used to expose the psychological relationships and motivations which are the core of the tragedy. That this same absence of a narrative voice can be adapted to fiction is demonstrated in "Some Like Them Cold," a short story by Ring Lardner. Lardner has varied the device by using an exchange of correspondence rather than a face-to-face dialogue. In this way the characterizing force of syntax and grammar comes directly at the reader visually in a way that would be harder to accept as accurate were it a narrator's attempt to reconstruct the language of these people.

It should be recognized that the absence of a narrator automatically means the lack of an audience. The characters in "Edward" speak to each other, perfectly indifferent to anyone overhearing them. This absence of an implied audience is what distinguishes such devices from the first-person point of view that will be discussed later. Since the dramatic monologue and the soliloquy are both recognizable varieties of the no-narrator technique, here again there is no implied audience.

We have already observed the dramatic monologue (p. 218) in relation to the story by Dorothy Parker and to the little poem, "Sweet, Let Me Go." This method is a variation of the dialogue situation discussed above, but with one of the speakers simply omitted. The discipline involved is a narrower, more severe one, since we have only the words of one of the two speakers from which to infer the whole situation. The dramatic monologue is often confused with the soliloquy, though for reasons that are important to a proper grasp of the tone it should not be. The dramatic monologue is an interaction between two or more characters but with only one of the characters audible and visible. It is important to remember the total dramatic situation for a proper understanding of the tone, since it means that the one audible, visible speaker is constantly responding to the other characters, getting his cues from their unseen and unheard words and gestures, and shifting his language and attitudes to meet developments.

In a soliloquy, on the other hand, a fictional character is meditating to himself. He may recall many things, and he may be doing anything at the moment. But he is *not* talking with or to anyone. (We must distinguish the soliloquy from the lyric wherever possible, for the lyric is a series of thoughts uttered by a narrator who might be the poet, whereas the soliloquy is spoken by a person fully as fictional as those persons in "Edward" or the woman in "Sweet, Let Me Go.") An excellent example of the soliloquy is this poem.

> it really must
> be Nice, never to
>
> have no imagination) or never
> never to wonder about guys you used to (and them
> slim hot queens with dam next to nothing
>
> on) tangoing
> (while a feller tries
> to hold down the fifty bucks per
> job with one foot and rock a

cradle with the other) it Must be
nice never to have no doubts about why you
put the ring
on (and watching her
face grow old and tired to which

you're married and hands get red washing
things and dishes) and to never, never really wonder i
mean about the smell
of babies and how you

know the dam rent's going to and everything and never, never
Never to stand at no window
because I can't sleep (smoking sawdust

cigarettes in the
middle of the night

                                        E. E. CUMMINGS*

Here are the salient characteristics of the soliloquy: a fictional character whose dramatically essential nature is revealed by his own thoughts, and a situation in which the character's thoughts or words are not directed at any other person in such a way as to involve a response on the part of the other person, but are definitely directed at himself.

Perhaps the differences among these three, the dramatic monologue, the soliloquy, and the lyric, may be seen most vividly if one imagines he is to read them aloud. In the dramatic monologue one would have a fictional character speaking to at least one other fictional character, though the second person could not be seen or heard. To read aloud such a poem with maximum fidelity would necessitate both absorbing the personality of the fictional character and while in that role appearing to hear and to respond to the unheard speaker, in order to account properly for one's own (the heard speaker's) responses. To the audience the situation should appear, though in a conventional way, much like the experience we have when we see and hear one person talking on the telephone and must infer what is being said by the invisible person from the responses of the speaker. In both the soliloquy and the lyric there is no conversation at all, no other speaker, heard or unheard. The speaker we hear may be responding to things in his environment (as in Keats' lyric "Ode to a Nightingale" or in Cummings' soliloquy "it really must"), but there is no dramatic interplay between persons. In each the tension of the poem arises from a conflict in the thoughts and feelings of the one person. The difference between the lyric and the soliloquy lies in the fact that if one were to read the

---

soliloquy aloud, he would have to develop convincingly a fictional character (as in the Cummings poem), whereas in the lyric no such fully objective character can be drawn. The lyric narrator cannot be taken simply as the unfictionalized poet's voice, but is for all that a fictive alter ego quite close to the poet's vision, perhaps a heightened, or intensified, fictionalization of part of his own voice.

These distinctions may at times seem trivial, but they are not. Critics have made serious blunders because they have mistaken the speaking voice in the poem. A proper grasp of tone is impossible without a firm sense of the nature of the speaking situation within the poem and, consequently, of the character of the speaker or narrator. The Cummings poem cannot be read correctly, silently or aloud, if the speaker is mistaken for the poet. Neither the Dorothy Parker story nor "Sweet, Let Me Go" can be read correctly if the reader does not understand at what points and how the other person present is affecting the speaker. You will be misreading "Ode to a Nightingale" if you do not understand that this poem is an ordered, intensified expression of one of the most urgent tensions working within a poet of great capacity.

As I have said, these distinctions are simple ones, but they can be developed with subtle variations that present difficulties in getting the speaking situation clear. The poem "Lessons of the War" (p. 263) is divided into three parts, each involving a different episode and a different "lesson." Taking the cue from that word, remember that a lesson usually implies a teacher and a pupil. Look at the poem, and you discover that there are really two different kinds of language and two different centers of attention. The monotony of the diction in the first lines, "Today we have . . . ," "Yesterday, we had . . . ," "And tomorrow morning we shall have . . . ," compared with the exotic comparison of Japonica to coral which follows casts a doubt that the same person could have said both these things aloud in the same situation. Since there is no indication that the situation alters, there must be two speakers, one the teacher and one the pupil. The attempt to discover everything possible about the first speaker, the teacher, leads to the discovery that much of his language seems formal, stilted, and monotonous, as out of a book of instructions. But also there are revealing moments when he departs a bit too far from the book of instructions and must make his own way. Such moments suggest his level of education, his background, his probable powers of imagination: "you can do it quite easy," instead of the more literary "easily," "the reason being, / Is one which need not delay us," "whatever you do, / Don't call the bleeders *sheep*," "but only on what I might coin a phrase and call. . . ." These clichés and errors in structure and grammar, added to the monotonous repetition of phrases and phrase-patterns, leaves a picture of a British non-com engaged in delivering, over a period of time, a series of lectures and demonstrations so dull that even he is bored at times.

In contrast the second speaker is a person who has a gift for language and who is much more aware of subtleties of situation and response; and the clichés of the first speaker serve only to start in the second speaker a train of probing, painful thought about the war and his own and his fellows' situation in it.

So much for the nature of the two speakers. But is this poem really a dialogue of the same sort as "Edward"? No, for most of the words given to the pupil are obviously suitable only to private thoughts and would never be spoken aloud, especially under the given circumstances. So, while apparently hearing only the teacher's *spoken* words, the reader hears also the pupil's thoughts. But once the reader grasps that he is *in* the pupil's mind, he realizes that *there* is his fixed point of view and that he is actually hearing the instructor from inside the student's mind. There is one, just one, departure from the silence of the student. In the second part, virtually at dead center of the poem, the whole scene is dramatized. The instructor is droning on when he notices that one of his students (the second speaker) is not attending and, by way of waking him up, demands an oral report. The second speaker takes time to make his report in his own way. To himself, he is exact (the trees are elms) and vivid and tender. Then he makes his official report, which uses official terminology (the elms must become poplars, since the instructor had said there were only three kinds of trees), and which, for all its apparent uses of geometry ("to the left of arc"), is really hesitant and inexact. But the important thing is that from the narrative point of view in the soldier-student's mind there need be no quotation marks or other signs of differentiation since both the thought and the spoken word are equally real and visible.

Therefore, since there is no reason to think that the student is a wholly fictional character, we see that we have a lyric which, in its development, has some of the aspects and interest of a dialogue. This example should adequately indicate that naming types and categories of poems and stories is an activity of limited usefulness, and that individual examples usually offer their own subtle variations. Obviously, an oral reader who comprehends the difficulties of the narrative voice in this poem, and can resolve these difficulties through his voice and bodily instrument, will go far toward making this poem truly available to himself and his fellows.

The Story Teller, or the Godlike Narrator

So far I have talked about forms of literature (methods of presenting fictive material) without the intervening presence of a Voice who is the story teller. But it is probably true that the great root of all fiction is this narrative Voice. In the past he may have stood in the public places, a professional already, telling the legends of the culture, or he may have been a grandfather passing on to his grandchild the stories in songs that he had heard from his grandfather. Or he may have been one of the Bardic masters. In any case, he was a story teller, free to take the reader anywhere, as in the epics of Homer, which may have been ordered and established by a poet named Homer, but which had a profound oral tradition. The story teller in these epics moves where he likes. When it pleases him, he sees the Gods at their plots, he sees into the minds of people, and sometimes he stops the action altogether to comment on it. This is the point of view of the godlike narrator, the all-seeing eye that can observe what is happening at two different places at the same time, that can enter into men's minds and see their hidden thoughts. It is the essence of the magic of fiction and because it brazenly announces its lack of realism, has no doubt the widest range of uses and the greatest flexibility of all the points of view from which it is possible to narrate a story.

This point of view is usually called *Third Person Omniscient:* third person because the narrator stands outside the story and refers to all characters in the third-person pronouns "he" or "she," omniscient because of the narrator's total freedom in time and space. The third person omniscient narrative technique is found in both *Sense and Sensibility* and in "Eveline," and a comparison of these two will reveal that there is a difference in degrees of "personality" of this omniscient narrator. In "Eveline" the illusion created is of a faceless, non-evaluative narrator, who is simply recording occurrences without having a personality in his own right. In short the illusion is that the narrator has no personal system of values from which he interprets the occurrences. However, a close examination of the story will show that almost the whole time the narrator is with Eveline's mind, seeing things as she does. There is an exception in the beginning where in three simple sentences, the narrator sets the scene. But the important exception is in the last few sentences. This section has already been discussed in the chapter on description (p. 250), where it was made clear how much the impact of the ending depends on a sudden shifting at the moment of crisis from a point of view from inside her mind, to an external one, in order to emphasize her mindlessness, her surrender to the destructive past, her turning into a "helpless animal." But it is significant that the shift is from her point of view to one that includes her lover's: "Her eyes gave him no sign of love or farewell or recognition." In this way the narrator is able to sustain the illusion of his own objectivity.

On the other hand, in *Sense and Sensibility* the narrator, though omniscient, is nevertheless a real personality and makes no bones about evaluating the various situations and personalities. The person telling the story is obviously a product of the same culture as the characters and is, moreover, a highly witty, unsentimental person. Thus, though the omniscient narrator in this case has not a full "character," she nonetheless has characteristics which must be recognized if the novel is to be adequately comprehended.

The Other Formal Points of View

There are yet other points of view from which to tell a story, but it is well to remember that they are all limited aspects of the omniscient narrator, as any arc is a portion of the full three hundred sixty degrees. Each possible point of view has its own values and potentials, but each develops from deliberate exclusion of other aspects of the complete potential of the time-free, place-free eye.

The *third person limited* is a variation of the third person omniscient in which the narrator deliberately limits his range of viewpoint. This limitation can be of different degrees of severity. A common method of limitation is to be found in "An Experiment in Misery" and in "A Painful Case" where, though free to enter the minds of other characters, the narrator refrains from availing himself of this privilege and follows the thoughts of only one of the characters, seeing the other personae from either the narrator's point of view or from that of the one character. This deliberate restriction not only focuses the primary attention where the author desires, but may serve less obvious purposes. For instance, leaving the reader in ignorance of the depth of Mrs. Sinico's reaction to Duffy's withdrawal from her life not only makes for narrative speed but leaves both the reader and Duffy in the same ignorance, so that the reader has his own shock at the same time Duffy has his, and so that the reader can compare directly with Duffy's his own speculations on her loneliness and dismal end. The death is a surprise for him as well as for Duffy, so that the moment of truth, coming as it does untrammeled by previous information, has its full emotional way with both.

The third person limited can be extremely narrow in its self-imposed restrictions. In "Petrified Man" by Eudora Welty, at no point does the narrator permit entrance into the minds of any of the characters. All thoughts, motivations, reactions, must be inferred from external signs, either of gesture or of word-gesture. Further, the narrator imposes on himself and on the reader a very severe restriction in scope of setting. In fact, all action is restricted not only to the beauty shop, but also to one booth in it. As a result everything learned about Mrs. Pike, one of the three most important characters, is by word of mouth, and the reader receives also by hearsay his impression of such a crucial scene as the identification of the Petrified Man.

Why has the narrator set such limitations on the point of view? After all, since the narrator is not a character in the story, there is no reason why, if the author had desired, the narrator could not have presented Mrs. Pike in the flesh or watched the workings of her mean little mind. But there, perhaps, is the clue. It is indeed a mean little mind; these are indeed, all of them, mean little minds. In fact, when we consider the characterizations in the story, it becomes evident why the author has not titled the story "*The* Petrified Man." For the story is not really about Mr. Petrie, but about a group of people so narrow, so unimaginative, so selfish, and so sterile that they may all be seen as types of humanity petrified. From this point of view the insistence on the one cramped setting of the booth, with its cheap decor, cluttered aspect, and narcissistic purpose, has an effect that might be dissipated by the introduction of other settings and of narrative movement. In the same way, the refusal of the narrator to enter into any of the character's minds serves to place them all on a dead level and, further, serves as more than a hint that there is nothing in those two-dimensional minds that cannot be divined by watching their overt gestures.

Sometimes the type of third person limited that "Petrified Man" represents is called *third person objective,* because the narrator limits himself to describing that which could be described by an actual (though invisible) human being. In short, the narrator can neither tell us what people are thinking nor report on separate but simultaneous events. This technique gives a sense of great objectivity because the narrator is not a character caught up *in* the story and also because the narrator does not know everything, but must, like all of us, judge from externals.

The *first person* is, in a sense, the most realistic of the possible points of view, because the narrator is limited to what he, being in the story, can see with his own eyes, hear with his own ears, and deduce with his own limited knowledge of the situation. The narrator, being himself a character in the story, cannot pretend to the omniscient objectivity of the other points of view. *Tristram Shandy,* as one can see from the fragments given in Chapter two, is a story told by such a narrator. James Thurber's "A Box to Hide In" is another. The advantages of the first person can be several. There is a directness and an intimacy of statement; the narrator is a more rounded, detailed personality than is usually encountered in the third person techniques. As in "A Box to Hide In" the narrator's personality is very often the subject matter of the poem or story. In this story the way in which the man tells his story directly conveys as powerfully as do the incidents themselves his desperate situation. The grim humor, for instance, arises out of the starkness of a narration executed without the elaborations that a godlike narrator might develop, and out of the deadpan seriousness with which the narrator tells us his boring actions and bizarre fantasies.

The simple, repetitive phrases, the limited vocabulary and range of thought express as clearly as do the repetitive and enclosed actions of his day the compulsiveness of his emotional life and the tenuousness of his hold on reality. Only in fantasy is he able to bear any elaboration of experience or to be at all creative. Further, and perhaps most important, one realizes how difficult it would be for a third person narrator to treat such a mental condition humorously, even with such freezing humor as Thurber displays in the present story, without offending the emotional sympathy of the reader. Similarly it would have been difficult for an outside eye to make the delightful *Tristram Shandy* appear anything but a dull lunatic.

There are difficulties in the first person point of view. For one thing the person telling the story must use language appropriate to his character. A mechanic must not talk like a lawyer, nor a teen-ager like a septuagenarian. Further there must be a consistently conceived psychology on the part of the narrator. We must never feel that he has achieved an insight which would in reality not have occurred to him. But perhaps the most difficult problem is the ever-present "I." Nothing is more irritating to a reader than to become aware that the narrator thinks he is a fine fellow and can't help saying so. One might go so far as to put it as axiomatic that, where the narrator is the main character, relating events concerning principally himself, the reader must be allowed to feel some sense of superiority. Perhaps it would be truer to say that the main character in such a situation must display certain personality limitations which the reader is able to discern and evaluate. Such is certainly the case in *Tristram Shandy* and in "A Box to Hide In." Only the incredibly good intentions and fetching whimsicality of Tristram make us love his self-centered garrulity — in spite of our sneaking conviction that we are all Shandys to a certain extent. And we are free to pity Thurber's hero only because he is an inch nearer the fatal edge than we are.

Another method is very often used to make the first person point of view an artistically flexible and unobtrusive technique, and that is for the narrator to be a minor character in the story. This achieves several objectives at once. The narrator is concerned with events that affect primarily others, and the dangerous word "I" can hold a place of becoming modesty. Further, the narrator can be as objective in relating the story as it is possible for a human to be — if objectivity is required. He can be moved nearer or farther from the core of action as the various aesthetic needs dictate.

However, merely because the narrator in such a case is a minor character, the reader is not free to ignore him. On the contrary, it is vitally necessary to make an accurate estimate of his personality and his relationship to other characters in order to evaluate properly his reportage and opinions; and the realization of this necessity leads into what to the reader,

especially the oral reader, is the most important problem among those
attaching to his *tonal* grasp of the narrative perspective.

Realizing the Narrator

Though it is important to recognize that an omniscient third person is
telling a story, or that Chapter One of a novel is third person limited
whereas Chapter Two is first person, nevertheless, such recognitions are,
though important, only rather mechanical ones. Realization of the *character* of the speaking voice must follow. Only words are available from
which to deduce what it is necessary to know of the narrator's nature. In
the process of deducing the character of the narrator the reader must not
deduce too much. We have already mentioned the real but sketchy personality of the story teller of *Sense and Sensibility*. Important as it is to
realize that this speaker has certain definite, if abstract, qualities, it is even
more important that one not exaggerate these sketchy suggestions into a
full character in the story. This degree of non-specificity is carefully retained by the author, for the story is not, after all, focused on the narrator.

It is possible to make a distinction between (1) those speaking voices
which are traditional, representing certain attitudes and poses which have
recurred again and again in literary history; (2) those which are unique to
a given piece of literature; and (3) those which aim at the tone of objective
observer.

It must not be concluded that, because the traditional poses have
been assumed often, they are therefore necessarily clichés. On the contrary, they continue to make appearances because they fill a recurring
need. Simply because they must always come in a matrix of original passion in order to be effective does not alter this fact. We are familiar with,
among others, the prophetic voice, the desperate lover, the elegiaic voice,
and the voice of compliment or praise. Exploring but one of these will
serve as sufficient illustration purpose. On page 172 begins a series of
poems sharing in varying degrees the fictive attitude which we may call
the prophetic voice. Inevitably we begin with the Bible, where this voice
is to be heard in its most deeply moving moments. The passage from
Micah imagines a dialogue between the Lord and one of His people who
seeks a way to atone for his sins. The Lord begins the dialogue by asking
His people what He has done to turn them from Him, reminding them of
His past benefactions. The people's spokesman, perhaps the Prophet, then
asks the rhetorical question as to whether or not rich sacrifices will assuage
the Lord, answering his own question by stating clearly and unmistakably
what it is that the Lord asks. The Lord then speaks again, cataloging the
sins of the city and asking the rhetorical question if these things are to be
forgiven. So much for the simple structure of this section from Micah. But

it is neither the structure nor such wonderfully effective detail as the plain and straightforward desires of the Lord following immediately upon the piled-up exaggerations of "thousands of rams," "rivers of oil," that makes the whole effective. What joins these disparate elements into a meaningful whole is the *truth*, spiritual and physical, a truth as vivid for our people and our cities as it was for those ancient Hebrews, that to do justice, to love kindness, and to walk humbly with God are simple demands which are to be complied with unless we are willing to pay the extravagant price of guilt.

This selection contains the classic ingredients of prophetic writing: the sense of a people's corruption and the appealing to some nobler standard — usually deeds or persons in the past of the culture — as an ideal or corrective. But even more important in creating the work's power is the cry of overt outrage, scorn, despair which, expressed through such means as the catalog, rhetorical question, exclamation, apostrophe, and hyperbole, gives the characteristic tone to this kind of voice: a speech public in nature with a broad sweep of generality.

It is important to be aware of these traditional tones, for to a degree they will be governed by other sorts of originality, and to other sorts of principles, than those we expect either from works that develop a specific personality as speaker or from those which develop from the viewpoint of an objective narrator. To see clearly the difference between the latter two, a comparison of Cotton's "Evening Quatrains" and Swift's "A Description of the Morning" is valuable as a starting point, since some of their details are already familiar from previous discussion.

To begin with the question of point of view, it is clear that in Swift's poem there is an omniscient narrator who can move inside and outside houses and up and down the street. Further, there is little in the language itself and little in the way of overt evaluation of the scene to give the speaker recognizably differentiated qualities. In short, the point of view and the attitude of the narrator present plausibly a diverse range of activity and give the illusion that these events are objectively selected and are representative. This effect is perhaps necessary because the picture presented is not a pleasant one, though it has some of the attraction of a city's energy.

In contrast, as we have already pointed out (p. 214), the language of Cotton's poem presents a problem in range from colloquialism to classical allusion. Further, the scene seems presented from some unified viewpoint as if the speaker, from some elevated focus toward which all the movements of the evening tend, could see and report on these actions as they draw in toward him. Nor is the tone so impersonal as that of the Swift poem. A general but deep affection, which permits him to be both humorous and delicate toward the things he sees, seems to be a characteristic of the speaker. In short it would seem difficult to account for the language, the attitude and the point of view, without creating in our minds a general, if not a completely individual, sense of the speaker. And all these problems are at once resolved if we see the speaker as representative of the best type of English country gentleman of the period: a well-educated man whose love of the classics and of his countryside, of its people and customs, forms in his mind not two conflicting streams, but one broad, continuous view of life, wherein Phoebus is domesticated with an English cart. In fact, the failure to see the nature of the speaker inevitably makes the poem appear an awkward agglomeration of levels of language and levels of tone. However, it is clear that the speaker in Cotton's poem, though given sufficient qualities to delineate him as one of a type of person, is not meant to be seen as an individual. There are, for instance, no references to his appearance or to gestures which might characterize something other than the cast of his mind, which is a typical mind observing a typical scene. In short, the oral reader will find most appropriate to this poem a quiet, self-effacing body — a body mostly engaged through the eyes as they react to the surrounding countryside — and a voice responding to the emotional cues brought to the affectionate mind as the eyes go from object to object.

John Crowe Ransom's poem "The Equilibrists" (p. 60) offers a chance to observe a narrator who is a step nearer to individualization while still having some aspects of the typical. In this poem the narrator is observing the progress of a love affair, one which is, for unspecified reasons involving "honor," never consummated. The first noticeable characteristic of the narrator is his range of vocabulary, which includes words which are not only learned but distinctively seasoned, words of antique, remote association. Despite their remoteness, however, the narrator uses them accurately and in a context that gives a unique reverberation to their echoes of ancient loves and loyalties. Yet (and here is the second characteristic) despite his learning he has nothing but a standard answer to the unique problem of human love which he faces: the lovers must choose — heaven or hell. Still, in this unoriginal response there are individualizing gestures. Facing the unusual, the maddeningly insoluble dilemma, he cries out in anger, not at the couple but at what he takes to be the unreasonableness of their situation. After his angry outburst he tries, with "puddled brow," to arrive at some helpful solution. There is something shallow about a puddle and there is something the opposite of clarifying about one who puddles. This aspect of his character significantly modifies the fact that he is learned. But no sooner has this rather more restricted view of the narrator's character been accepted than a third element is added which complicates and completes the picture. He does not simply give his classic and classical alternatives and withdraw self-righteously from the problem. His love and sympathy keep him watching and puzzling over the lovers' predicament until finally sheer human feeling triumphs over his bookish and categorizing view of life. Thus his final tribute to the lovers marks as much the triumphant expansion of the narrator's wisdom as it does the strange beauty created by the lovers' relationship.

Whatever the degree of individualization, the narrator of a fiction is never the author. The narrator does and says fictive things in a fictive environment. Nonetheless it is a most important step in determining the role of the narrator to discover to what degree he is a spokesman for the author's values. Discovering what point of view the story is told from is merely a first step in making this discrimination between the narrator's and the author's values. For instance, one may discover that the narrator of "Says Tweed to Twill" is third person objective, but one must go on to realize that the attitude of the narrator is unimportant, he is only a functionary to introduce the speakers. The *author's* attitude, of course, is to be reconstructed from the ironies attendant on the speeches of the rivers. As we saw earlier there is in a narrow sense sometimes no narrator at all, and the oral reader may be left with the necessity of making some subtle discriminations in order to determine the character of the speaker(s) in the work as a preliminary to contrasting it with the author's attitudes. In Josephine Miles' poem "Oedipus" there is no intermediary narrator; the reader overhears directly the explanation of a past action. This little poem seems to have qualities both of the dramatic monologue and the soliloquy. The speech is certainly in form an explanation, as if addressed to a listener. Yet absolutely nothing is made of this other person, so that the oral reader would most logically address the poem to the audience, rather than to an imaginary hearer. There is a total absence of setting or scene. Yet the speech seems too externally motivated to be a soliloquy in the strictest sense. In any case, the humor that is such an important element in the tone arises largely out of a discrepancy between the author's point of view and the speaker's character and dramatic situation, however tricky these may be to determine.

How does the reader discover the author's attitudes, if the author has no spokesman? In this poem, we see the author's hand in the impossible fictive situation itself — the straightforward testing of the values of the Greek tragedy against the mind of an "average" modern office worker. Having created this fantasy, related in such workaday words, the oral reader knows that the author's attitude must emerge out of the conflict between the words the author puts in the speaker's mouth and the situation the speaker has been placed in. The author must create believable dia-

logue for this office worker and at the same time he must reveal his own
implied comment. In other words, because of the dramatic situation, the
character of the speaker places limits on the author's approach to his
reader, and these limits provide the oral reader with some of his most significant cues. His reading must never betray that there is anything extraordinary in the American John Doe's talking about Oedipus Rex as if he were
the boss. Yet those ordinary words in such an extraordinary situation must
affect the oral reading, however subtly, for these tones must be projected
to the listener. Thus, the phrase "he had everything" (though the speaker in
the poem is unconscious of it) carries a great weight of irony to the reader
consciously from the author, hence, if the oral reader does his job, to the
audience. What are the ironies of this phrase which the reader must project? To the speaker, the phrase is a cliché. When somebody is rich, in
good health, powerful, we say, "He has everything." But in Oedipus's case,
this "everything" was *too much*. He did not have only a wife; he had a
wife who was also his mother. He did not have only children; he had children who were also his siblings. He was not only proud and strong; his
pride and strength had been part of the crime of patricide. The oral
reader, through an innocence of expression and rather clichéd tonal pattern, might convey the speaker's ignorance of the irony. But he must also
(by perhaps a subtle, exaggerated slowness, perhaps by a pause before
"everything," perhaps by a slightly opaque, not-too-bright look on the face)
convey that the author, hence the oral reader, hence the audience, is aware
of the ironic levels.

Contrast this poem with the soliloquy by E. E. Cummings, "it really
must." Here, though the speaker is another average "Joe," the language less
"educated" than the speaker's in "Oedipus," yet the oral reader has no such
satiric discrepancy between the author's attitude and the speaker's to convey. How does the oral reader know this? Again, by the language which
the author has given to the speaker. We cannot imagine this speaker utter-
ing the flat, trite (and awkward to boot) "which we personally / Should
have liked to receive." His language is direct; it is the language he knows,
and he uses it honestly. He does not speak of experiences he cannot understand. Even the word "imagination" is in itself but a sign that he *has,* in his
own way, imagination. In this poem the difference between the speaker
and author is one not of value, but of distance. One senses the author's
compassion *for* the speaker, which is, of course, what lifts the poem beyond the self-pity of the speaker's limited, if honest vision. Thus, for the
oral reader, something very close to full characterization of the speaker is
demanded here, in order to emphasize the *distance* between the speaker
and the informing intelligence of the author. But this characterization
should be straightforward and sympathetic. Cummings' poem differs from

Miles' in its author's lack of satiric treatment of the speaker. The difference between the author's and the speaker's position in these two poems might be diagrammed thus.

In sum, there are narrators, speakers, and (as will be seen) characters, who are what have been called "reliable," who, though they are *not* the author, are nonetheless truth-sayers, reliably in line with the author's vision. On the other hand there are the "unreliable" narrators, speakers, and characters who tell only limited truths or obvious distortions and who serve as ironic counterpoint to the implied viewpoint of the author.

Perhaps these examples are sufficient to demonstrate both the importance and the difficulty of fixing the exact qualities of the narrator as one finds them in the poem or story. Equally plain, however, should be the fact that nothing is more likely to expose a lack of understanding in this matter than an attempt to read the story aloud. Such an act serves as a check on the overly imaginative as well as on the careless and the obtuse. Critical ingenuity will result in a clever reading, but it is a poor substitute for accurate sympathy, which can come only from developing a reading based on a balanced assessment of the narrative voice.

THE PATTERN OF CHARACTERS

Narratives, both in poetry and prose, consist of action in an appropriate environment. Since the reality of human life might be defined in the same way, it is easy to see how tempting it is to regard narrative writing as essentially an imitation of life. But the importance, in fact the necessity, of artistic selection qualifies quickly any simple use of the word "imitation." Perhaps it is more useful to say that every narrative, in fact every fiction, is in some way a metaphor of life. This definition preserves the truth that the stuff of fiction is taken from life, that the purpose of fiction is an explication, an enlightenment of some part of the chaos of life; at the same time it reminds that fiction is not simply a mirror-image and that, once created, it is in itself a thing existing in reality. It is at once an aspect of reality and a comment on the reality of which it is a part, as a particular elm tree may be a representation of other trees (this elm tree is like other

elm trees), but nonetheless exists in its own right as a particular thing and
not just in its figurative function. The oral reader is so important because, in
his truest moments, he can stand as a paraclete for the dead, one-dimen-
sional words, as the living performer may stand as paraclete for the abstract musical score. He can show us vividly the thing as it exists in its
own right, a living part of a living reality. Though he must be as aware as
any literary historian or critic of the complications of the thing-as-metaphor,
it is he who can most nearly *show* us the life, the existence, of the work. It
should be his greatest aim to show the essential integrity of the whole
work.

Nowhere is this importance of the oral reader more vividly demonstrated than in his re-creation of characters, of the Personae, of the work, for
here the silent reader is handicapped in very meaningful ways. Is his inner
ear for dialect feeble? The oral reader can provide it. Does the rhythm and
style of a character's language elude him? The oral reader can bring it to
him vividly. Does he miss the peculiar combinations of irony and ambiguity in a character's speech? It is the oral reader's duty to resolve these
subtleties into an actual voice. Following are some suggestions toward an
analysis of character that may help the oral reader to comprehend the
characters of a story in their full verbal dimension.

The characters in narratives may not be people at all. The animals in
Aesop's Fables, or Pogo the Possum, or Donald Duck are all examples of
one kind of ancient tradition of storytelling. The Gods of *The Iliad* and the
witches of *Macbeth* are another dimension of this tradition. But in the
main, characters may be said to carry one or all of three basic elements in
ever-new combinations: the realistic, the typic, and the symbolic. And as
one or the other of these aspects predominates, we so classify the character.

The *realistic* character is one in which an individualizing intent on
the part of the author is primary. The author wants us to think of this character chiefly as an individual, as being lifelike. Just as one normally sees a
human being as existing primarily in his own person, so the realistic character makes the reader think of him as unique, not as a bundle of the common characteristics of a party or class or caste.

What I should like to distinguish as the *typic* character shades off on
the one hand into the realistic character and on the other into the symbolic
character. A typic character is one whose principal function is to serve as
an exemplar of caste, class, profession, or other recognizable social group.
Obviously, this kind of character is most usually to be found in narratives
of social comment or satire.

The *symbolic* character usually stands at the other extreme from the
realistic, in that the reader is not primarily to think of the character as an
individual except insofar as he stands as symbol for some larger aspects of

humanity. Remember that in the chapter on figurative language, the discussion of symbol and emblem came under the general heading "A Tangible Sign of Something Intangible." This phrase offers a useful way to think of a symbolic character or of that which is symbolic *in* any character. A special type of symbolic character is found in allegories. What the emblem is to figurative language, the allegorical character is to characterization. Just as the emblem tends to have an *appearance* that bodies forth the tangible thing which is its subject, and tries to create an acceptable physical equivalent of it, so the allegorical character tries to render a quality into some kind of visible likeness. Strict allegorical characters are seldom seen in modern prose fiction, but occur more frequently in drama and poetry. The symbolic character is of far broader use and application.

It is well at once to distinguish two levels in which we commonly use the word "symbolic" in regard to character. In one sense the characters of every work of literary art can be seen as metaphoric, because every such work is, in a way, a metaphor of life. Thus we might say, conversationally, that Mrs. John Dashwood (*Sense and Sensibility*) symbolizes the hard and selfish *kind* of woman who can never see beyond her own comforts and her duties to her most immediate family. But in a second sense the phrase "symbolic character" can be used in a much narrower, much more technical way. This usage refers to a manner of drawing character so as to make it overtly symbolic. It is as hard to draw boundaries around the exact terrain of the symbolic character's implication as it is around the implication of the symbol as figure of speech. What, exactly, does one make of the tortoises in Melville's essay? It is easy to dismiss them as simple symbols, which would be improperly classed as characters. Certainly that is the way Melville first presents them. Yet as the author is more and more caught up in his vision, he addresses them as, "ye oldest inhabitants," and "three ponderous strangers," and particularly at one point endows them with certain human motives and attributes, "I have known them in their journeyings ram themselves heroically against rocks, and long abide there, nudging, wiggling, wedging, in order to displace them, and so hold on their inflexible path. Their crowning curse is their drudging impulse to straightforwardness in a belittered world." The words that particularly tend to humanize the tortoises are "heroically" and "straightforwardness," and it is also principally these words in the passage that give the tortoises their symbolic dimension, however general and indefinite.

The Internal Pattern of a Character

It is common to think of the characters in a story, taken together, as forming a meaningful pattern or patterns. They interact with one another, representing different elements and attitudes, and in so doing create a complex of patterns which may range all the way from the static to the highly volatile. I shall return later to those larger patterns. At the moment, I should like to point to a less obvious pattern — the balance within a given character which may be achieved by the particular inter-involvement of realistic, typic, and symbolic elements.

The critical importance of recognizing this pattern in a character is emphasized if one thinks of reading aloud. Indeed, preparation for an oral reading offers one an optimum situation for seeing not merely the pattern itself, but all its subtleties and permutations. Let us suppose, for instance, that one wished to convey accurately the impression of a basically realistic character. It is vital to realize that such a character (1) moves in a realistic environment, (2) speaks in a realistic language, (3) develops his actions and gestures out of a realistic psychological interplay with other characters and with his environment. The reader's bodily attitudes must then reflect the author's illusion of reality. But first the reader must have an awareness of certain typic qualities. In the scene in which Mr. John Dashwood and his wife decide just how to act upon his deathbed promise to his father, they certainly rehearse a typical human psychological pattern. But the emphasis for the reader is much more on them as individuals, as they work out a solution which is possible for their caste and class, but not necessarily typical of it. But before he can achieve the delineation of the character as a realistic individual, the reader must be aware of certain of the character's aspects that are typic; the character is affected by the general formality of the time, by the clothes he wore which precluded free and easy physical movement and which were status symbols of his wealth and social position. The social respect which his class demanded from inferiors and observed themselves when addressing superiors carried over even into family relations. Though the reader standing before the class is dressed in modern costume, the body must suggest that it is clothed in a manner appropriate to the language, and that its gestures are suitable to the furniture, the rooms, the gardens, the means of transportation, among which and by means of which his character lives, as well as suitable to the modern audience for which the illusion is created. This bodily involvement is not merely necessary to create "a good performance." It is the most direct, economical way for the reader to take into his body the knowledge of these characters. In this way he will come to a fine critical appreciation of the language (of why the wife for instance, even in an intimate discussion, calls her husband "my dear Mr. Dashwood"), of how the style, its diction, rhythm, and figures, emphasizes the character's cultural position. With these typic elements realized, the reader is then free to create the realistic elements, which in this case spring from the revealing psychological interplay of the two characters. In Mr. Dashwood's case the realistic elements are not wholly contra-indicative of the typic elements, and therefore the character may appear more wholly typic than he really is.

There are many cases in which the pattern of typic, realistic, and symbolic elements in a character does contain contra-indications or tensions, and when such is the case they are vital to an understanding in depth. In the first part of "An Experiment in Misery" (p. 186) the young man is dressed in the typical clothes of a tramp. But in himself he still feels his individuality and is miserable in the disparity between the typic role which the children and the rest of the world would cast him in and his own feeling of inappropriateness in that role. By the end of the story he has accepted the psychological as well as the external role of the tramp, has become wholly typic, and it is this change which is really the main dramatic element of the story. And as one comes to be able to rehearse in one's own body some of the gestures, expressions, and intonations appropriate to such a struggle and such an adjustment, he will not only bring this story to a more living reality within his consciousness, he will also be acquiring a vocabulary of total bodily response which will inevitably speed up as well as deepen the silent and oral reading of analogous material.

Of course, it is possible to find characters that are almost purely typic, and these have their own aesthetic nature. If one intends to be able to feel those qualities as realities, he must understand that such a character presents problems, opportunities, and avenues of insight different from the primarily realistic character. The aesthetic delight and knowledge that arise from a realistic character comes from a continuing surprise at the revelation of the character, the deepening knowledge of him. The delight we feel in typic characters and the knowledge we get about them arise from the expected fulfilled astonishingly well and with fuller insight than the reader was previously capable of. In aesthetic effect, the difference between realistic and typic characters lies in the difference between revelation on the one hand and confirmation on the other (seeing brilliantly delineated what we half knew or were subconsciously aware of in our society).

The newspaper account of Mrs. Sinico's death ("A Painful Case") presents a typic group of characters. The doctor, the railway company representative, the husband, the daughter, all become, in the flat reportage of the newspaper, merely vehicles for typical attitudes. This quality makes for a deliberate ironic contrast between the reader's knowledge of the human, real Mrs. Sinico, and of the individual isolation and final agony of Duffy.

Such characters are usually observed externally, as in the instance given above, or, where their thought processes are explored, these reveal

typical patterns of thought and feeling requiring little of the sense of surprise, agony of thought, or paradoxes of feeling that may arise from an experiencing of the inner life of realistic or even symbolic characters.

I have spoken little of the symbolic element in the pattern of a character, or of those characters whose main element is symbolic. The poem
"anyone lived in a pretty how town" (p. 294) is a brief allegory. In this
brief narrative the allegorical aspect of the characters is not, as frequently
happens, delineated by their appearance, but by a few selected actions. As
is common with allegorical characters, the names give clues to the qualities
they are meant to represent. Thus, "anyone" and "noone" are singular,
whereas the others are lumped into collectives. In this way the author emphasizes the fact that "anyone" and "noone" are allegorical figures standing
for the genuine individual, with his own personal loves, successes, and
failures, hence living beings. The "anyones" and "someones" allegorically
stand for those who are really dead, without individual values, and capable only of acting out lifeless routines. This allegorical insight gives the
reader the clue to the proper vocal and bodily directions: on the one hand,
living, joyful, individual tones and actions, and on the other, dull routine,
monotonous ones.

The main character in "A Hunger Artist" (p. 362) is fully symbolic
and has the indefinable boundaries of implication usually attributable to
the symbolic. It is interesting, however, that there is a realistic element in
the pattern of this character. The hunger artist's actions are described realistically. In fact, a great deal of the symbolic meaning arises from the
very complexity of the realistic detail given us about his profession. One
of the simplest of the distinctions that arise from this realistic detail is that
made between the hunger artist and the panther which supplants him in
the public eye. Whereas it takes many paragraphs to describe the hu-
manistically complicated ties and rituals that are involved in the artist-
audience aesthetic experience, it takes only one paragraph to delineate
the panther-audience relationship. This simple contrast in fictive time
makes its comment in much the same way as does the contrast (in "Two
Sides to a Tortoise") between the dark side and the light side of the
tortoise.

How does one identify a character who is primarily symbolic? And
what are the special implications of the symbolic chapter for the oral
reader? Sometimes symbolism is made easy to recognize by borrowing
what one might call a standard symbol to underline its nature. A character
may carry a shepherd's crook. He may wear a uniform with a swastika on
it. However, even where the author has used such symbols they are usually
reinforced by other means which in varying ways achieve an *emphasis*,
and through that emphasis force the reader below the surface characteris-

tics to explore the broader implications of the character. Thus, one of the reasons the reader knows that the hunger artist is meant to symbolize the artist in general is the insistent return to the relation of the hunger artist to the audience and an intense dwelling on the details of the peculiar ironies and ambiguities of their interdependence. Also, the repetition of the problem of the artist's integrity and of the validity of his aims and objectives is a part of the insistence on implications reaching beyond the specific hunger artist. These repeated elements pose, in the symbolic character, special problems for the understanding and the performance of the reader. The curious impersonality of the symbolic character usually combines with an air of broad significance to put some aesthetic distance between the character and the reader. Generally speaking such a character must interest without the usual "feeling-with" which is such a strong element in most tales. The author must bind his reader's emotions by other means, and it is up to the oral interpreter to discover those means. In "A Hunger Artist" our interest is held by an almost fanatic air of factual, meticulous reportage of what is to us now a bizarre profession. In a certain sense this fascination with realistic detail is Kafka's raw substitute for the raw interest we take in more realistic or more typic characters. If one thinks of such stories as Poe's "The Fall of the House of Usher," he can see that in that case there is an elaborate backdrop of melodrama, not only visual but verbal, to catch this raw interest. Whatever the author's solution, the oral interpreter must be aware of it, for it must powerfully affect his environment of gesture.

The External Pattern of Characters

Now that we are aware that we must come to some conscious understanding of the often unique balance that each character contains of the realistic, typic, and symbolic, let us turn to the pattern that characters make in relation to each other. Much that is vital to a story often flows from this pattern and its changes, if any. In Kafka's "A Hunger Artist," for instance, an interesting contrast is set up between the audience's method of proceeding vis-à-vis the hunger artist, its objects of enjoyment, in short, of its character, and of the audience interested in the circus. This pattern is one of simple contrast, for the most part. But this contrasting pattern is there for the purpose of illuminating the key relationship, which is the relationship of the audience to the artist or to what the artist symbolizes of the artistic temperament. First we see the ambivalent feelings of the hunger artist toward his fascinated audience. He wants it there *constantly*. He feels contempt for it, not because it is fascinated by what he does, but because it isn't fascinated enough, is not totally absorbed by his flirtation with death. Yet for all his contempt for it, as the moment comes when no one pays him any attention, when at last he is free to starve as much as he likes, it becomes plain that the audience is essential to him, though not for the same reasons he had expressed. Only the audience's interest, and the discipline of that interest, can transform what is after all only a natural tendency into an art.

Narrative poems develop such patterns in the same way as prose fiction. There is a changing relationship between the man and woman in Frost's "Home Burial," a change which is underlined by their shifting movements. Sometimes a simple diagram will help the reader to visualize the pattern of the characters. In "Home Burial" the two people have been living with some barrier between them. But the situation has been static, and one can see their relationship as two parallel lines.

Then the man sees the secret and begins to move across the distance that separates them.

But she flees from him and the pattern is complete.

One could also draw such a simple linear picture of Mr. Henry Dashwood and his wife to illustrate how his wife slowly persuades him step by step to her own obviously predetermined position. Such simplifications, however, should never become more than a means of clarifying what must lie beyond them as a complex and rich configuration in the mind of the person preparing an oral reading of these or other works of fine literature.

PREPARATION FOR PERFORMANCE — "The Windhover"

The Voices in Literature

Surely this poem must stand among those lyrics whose narrator is very close to being the poet's own voice, separated from it only by the transmutation from spontaneity to the artifice of stylized literary expression. Though such knowledge is not necessary to understand and experience the poem's impact, there can be little doubt that our empathy is increased if we know that the writer was a devout and dedicated Catholic priest. This fact might very well be stated in an introduction if there were reason to think the audience, or part of it, was not aware of the fact.

There are other rather paradoxical facts about this narrator which the oral reader must realize. First of all, the man is a sensualist to the bone. The event which called forth the poem was the sight of a soaring falcon so beautiful in its sensuous appeal that there was for the speaker no equivalent but the corresponding moral beauty of Christ. Then the proof of the great glory of Christ's "buckling" is expressed in images of physical beauty. Throughout the poem, a wealth of brilliant visual images is couched in a poetic music that is densely ornate. So the oral reader must adopt the sensibility of a man who, though devoutly religious, is no gray ascetic rejector of the beauty and glory of the physical world. Indeed it is through that physical world, in its ordinary as well as its extraordinary moments, that he finds a beauty so powerful as to be, for him, a manifestation of his God.

The other presence in the poem is the falcon, a symbolic manifestation of Christ. Birds have been used since ancient times as intermediaries between man and his gods, so there is a traditional symbolic aspect. Nonetheless, the main impression, and the one which the oral reader should convey to his audience, is that of an immediate experience, a literal hawk literally seen that morning, and not, as in Keats' "Ode to the Nightingale," a bird primarily weighted with an ancient symbolism, however literally heard. (It would be interesting to compare these poems, since both have the same central action — a joining of the man with the bird).

A question remains. To whom does the speaker address himself in the octet? Obviously the answer to this question will affect the oral reading considerably. Is there yet a third person to whom he describes the vision of the falcon? One is inclined to think not, for the address to the falcon that immediately follows is too intimate to be exposed to an outsider. It seems more likely that the poet addresses himself, in an internal reminiscence, repeating to himself a vision so powerful he can still hardly credit it.

Such an imagining of the speaker's position would at any rate lend a basic structure to the oral tone of the octet. Certainly the narrator's shift, at the end of the octet, from addressing an unspecified listener to speaking to the falcon itself marks the strongest alteration in the voice of the narrator.

It should be noted in conclusion that the falcon remains unhuman — both a bird and a symbol but never a character whose thoughts or wishes or words are even guessed at.

SELECTIONS

Lament*

When I was a windy boy and a bit
And the black spit of the chapel fold,
(Sighed the old ram rod, dying of women),
I tiptoed shy in the gooseberry wood,
The rude owl cried like a telltale tit,
I skipped in a blush as the big girls rolled
Ninepin down on the donkeys' common,
And on seesaw sunday nights I wooed
Whoever I would with my wicked eyes,
The whole of the moon I could love and leave
All the green leaved little weddings' wives
In the coal black bush and let them grieve.

When I was a gusty man and a half
And the black beast of the beetles' pews,
(Sighed the old ram rod, dying of bitches),
Not a boy and a bit in the wick-
Dipping moon and drunk as a new dropped calf,
I whistled all night in the twisted flues,
Midwives grew in the midnight ditches,
And the sizzling beds of the town cried, Quick! —
Whenever I dove in a breast high shoal,
Wherever I ramped in the clover quilts,
Whatsoever I did in the coal-
Black night, I left my fiery prints.

* From *The Collected Poems of Dylan Thomas*. © 1957 by New Directions. Reprinted by permission of New Directions, Publishers.

When I was a man you could call a man
And the black cross of the holy house,
(Sighed the old ram rod, dying of welcome),
Brandy and ripe in my bright, bass prime,
No springtailed tom in the red hot town
With every simmering woman his mouse
But a hillocky bull in the swelter
Of summer come in his great good time
To the sultry, biding herds, I said,
Oh, time enough when the blood creeps cold,
And I lie down but to sleep in bed,
For my sulking, skulking, coal black soul!

When I was a half of the man I was
And serve me right as the preachers warn,
(Sighed the old ram rod, dying of downfall),
No flailing calf or cat in a flame
Or hickory bull in milky grass
But a black sheep with a crumpled horn,
At last the soul from its foul mousehole
Slunk pouting out when the limp time came;
And I gave my soul a blind, slashed eye,
Gristle and rind, and a roarer's life,
And I shoved it into the coal black sky
To find a woman's soul for a wife.

Now I am a man no more no more
And a black reward for a roaring life,
(Sighed the old ram rod, dying of strangers),
Tidy and cursed in my dove cooed room
I lie down thin and hear the good bells jaw —
For, oh, my soul found a sunday wife
In the coal black sky and she bore angels!
Harpies around me out of her womb!
Chastity prays for me, piety sings,
Innocence blesses my last black breath,
Modesty swaddles my thighs with her wings,
And all the deadly virtues plague my death!

DYLAN THOMAS

My Picture
Left in Scotland

I now think Love is rather deaf than blind,
    For else it could not be
        That she
Whom I adore so much, should so slight me,
    And cast my love behind:
I'm sure my language to her was as sweet,
    And every close did meet
  In sentence, of as subtle feet,
    As hath the youngest he
That sits in shadow of Apollo's tree.
    O, but my conscious fears,
      That fly my thoughts between,
      Tell me that she hath seen
    My hundreds of grey hairs;
    Told seven and and forty years;
Read so much waste, as she cannot embrace
My mountain belly and my rocky face;
And all these through her eyes, have stopped her ears.

BEN JONSON

To an Old Lady*

Ripeness is all; her in her cooling planet
Revere; do not presume to think her wasted.
Project her no projectile, plan nor man it;
Gods cool in turn, by the sun long outlasted.

Our earth alone given no name of god
Gives, too, no hold for such a leap to aid her;
Landing, you break some palace and seem odd;
Bees sting their need, the keeper's queen invader.

No, to your telescope; spy out the land;
Watch while her ritual is still to see,
Still stand her temples emptying in the sand
Whose waves o'erthrew their crumbled tracery;

Still stand uncalled-on her soul's appanage;
Much social detail whose successor fades,
Wit used to run a house and to play Bridge,
And tragic fervour, to dismiss her maids.

Years her precession do not throw from gear.
She reads a compass certain of her pole;
Confident, finds no confines on her sphere,
Whose failing crops are in her sole control.

Stars how much further from me fill my night,
Strange that she too should be inaccessible,
Who shares my sun. He curtains her from sight,
And but in darkness is she visible.

WILLIAM EMPSON

Blessed Be the Hearts that Wish My Sovereign Well

His golden locks time hath to silver turned;
    O Time too swift, O swiftness never ceasing!
His youth 'gainst time and age hath ever spurned,
    But spurned in vain; youth waneth by increasing:
Beauty, strength, youth, are flowers but fading seen;
Duty, faith, love, are roots, and ever green.

His helmet now shall make a hive for bees,
    And, lovers' sonnets turned to Holy Psalms,
A man-at-arms must now serve on his knees,
    And feed on prayers, which are age his alms:
But though from court to cottage he depart,
His saint is sure of his unspotted heart.

And when he saddest sits in homely cell,
    He'll teach his swains this carol for a song,
"Blessed be the hearts that wish my sovereign well,
    Cursed be the souls that think her any wrong!"
Goddess, allow this aged man his right,
To be your beadsman now that was your knight.

GEORGE PEEL

Sonnet #73

From the First Edition, 1609; Copy in the Malone Collection,
Bodleian Library

That time of yeeare thou maist in me behold,
When yellow leaues, or none, or few doe hange
Upon those boughes which shake against the could,
Bare r(ui)n'ed quiers, where late the sweet birds sang.
In me thou seest the twi-light of such day
As after Sun-set fadeth in the West,
Which by and by blacke night doth take away,
Deaths second selfe that seals up all in rest.
In me thou seest the glowing of such fire,
That on the ashes of his youth doth lye,
As the death bed, whereon it must expire,
Consum'd with that which it was nurrisht by.
   This thou perceu'st, which makes thy love more strong,
   To love that well, which thou must leaue ere long.

WILLIAM SHAKESPEARE

*Provide, Provide**

The witch that came (the withered hag)
To wash the steps with pail and rag,
Was once the beauty Abishag,

The picture pride of Hollywood.
Too many fall from great and good
For you to doubt the likelihood.

Die early and avoid the fate.
Or if predestined to die late,
Make up your mind to die in state.

Make the whole stock exchange your own!
If need be occupy a throne,
Where nobody can call *you* crone.

Some have relied on what they knew;
Others on being simply true.
What worked for them might work for you.

No memory of having starred
Atones for later disregard,
Or keeps the end from being hard.

Better to go down dignified
With boughten friendship at your side
Than none at all. Provide, provide!

ROBERT FROST

Sailing to Byzantium*

I

That is no country for old men. The young
In one another's arms, birds in the trees
— Those dying generations — at their song,
The salmon-falls, the mackerel-crowded seas,
Fish, flesh, or fowl, commend all summer long
Whatever is begotten, born, and dies.
Caught in that sensual music all neglect
Monuments of unaging intellect.

II

An aged man is but a paltry thing,
A tattered coat upon a stick, unless
Soul clap its hands and sing, and louder sing
For every tatter in its mortal dress,
Nor is there singing school but studying
Monuments of its own magnificence;
And therefore I have sailed the seas and come
To the holy city of Byzantium.

III

O sages standing in God's holy fire
As in the gold mosaic of a wall,
Come from the holy fire, perne in a gyre,
And be the singing-masters of my soul.
Consume my heart away; sick with desire
And fastened to a dying animal
It knows not what it is; and gather me
Into the artifice of eternity.

IV

Once out of nature I shall never take
My bodily form from any natural thing,
But such a form as Grecian goldsmiths make
Of hammered gold and gold enamelling
To keep a drowsy Emperor awake;
Or set upon a golden bough to sing
To lords and ladies of Byzantium
Of what is past, or passing, or to come.

W. B. YEATS (1927)

An Acre of Grass*

Picture and book remain,
An acre of green grass
For air and exercise,
Now strength of body goes;
Midnight, an old house
Where nothing stirs but a mouse.

My temptation is quiet.
Here at life's end
Neither loose imagination,
Nor the mill of the mind
Consuming its rag and bone,
Can make the truth known.

Grant me an old man's frenzy,
Myself must I remake
Till I am Timon and Lear
Or that William Blake
Who beat upon the wall
Till Truth obeyed his call;

A mind Michael Angelo knew
That can pierce the clouds,
Or inspired by frenzy
Shake the dead in their shrouds;
Forgotten else by mankind,
An old man's eagle mind.

W. B. YEATS

Lullabie

Sing lullabie, as women do,
Wherewith to bring their babes to rest,
And lullabie can I sing to
As womanly as can the best.
With lullabie they still the childe,
And if I be not much beguilde,
Full many wanton babes have I
Which must be stilld with lullabie.

First lullaby my youthfull yeares,
It is now time to go to bed,
For crooked age and hoarie heares,
Have wonne the haven within my head:
With Lullabye then youth be still,
With Lullabye content thy will,
Since courage quayles, and commes behynde,
Goe sleepe, and so beguyle thy mynde.

Next Lullabye my gazing eyes,
Whiche woonted were to glaunce apace:
For every glasse maye nowe suffise,
To shewe the furrowes in my face:
With Lullabye then wynke a whyle,
With Lullabye youre lookes beguyle:
Lette no fayre face, nor beautie bryghte
Entice you efte with vayne delyght.

And Lullabye my wanton will,
Lette reason rule nowe reigne thy thought,
Since all too late I fynde by skill,
Howe deare I have thy fansies bought:
With Lullabye now take thyne ease,
With Lullabye thy doubtes appease:
For trust to this, if thou be still,
My bodie shall obey thy will.

Eke Lullabye my loving boye,
My little Robyn take thy rest,
Since Age is colde, and nothyng coye,
Keepe close thy coyne, for so is beste:
With Lullabye bee thou content,
With Lullabye thy lustes relente,
Lette others paye whiche have mo pence,
Thou arte to poore for suche expense.

Thus Lullabie my youth, myne eyes,
My will, my ware, and all that was,
I can no mo delayes devise,
But welcome payne, lette pleasure passe:
With Lullabye nowe take your leave,
With Lullabye youre dreames deceyve,
And when you rise with waking eye,
Remembre Gascoignes Lullabye.

GEORGE GASCOIGNE

CHAPTER ELEVEN

Structure

The story and the novel, the idea and the form,
are the needle and thread, and I never heard
of a guild of tailors who recommended the use
of the thread without the needle, or the needle
without the thread.

HENRY JAMES

From previous chapters the reader has become aware of many elements of structure, including time, narrative voice, and figure, and he will discover others in subsequent chapters. All of these elements are discussed in this book in appropriate chapters where the student can concentrate on their various functions as they play their inevitable part in fleshing out the fictive structure. Because the basic structural problem of fiction is *to order time*, and because the various elements of fiction are involved in this process of ordering time, they might therefore all be seen as structural elements. But this view of structure would leave us with distinctions so vague as to be relatively useless. In a narrower sense there is a structural principal in all works of fiction, and it is to the recognition of this overall skeleton, and to helping the oral reader come to terms with it, that this chapter is devoted.

The structures of works of fiction are very often crudely divided between those which have as their skeleton a progression of action and those which have some other kind of structure. Thus, in poetry the major division is usually between narrative poetry and all the rest — lyric, philosophic, descriptive. Commonly in prose the distinction is even more forcibly made — on the one hand are the action-structured genres, the novel and the short story, and on the other hand are such non-action genres as the descriptive sketch and the meditative essay.

Leaving for the moment progression of *action*, which I take to be what such terms as *narrative structure* or *narrative form* usually refer to, I think it is further possible to distinguish in fiction, both a progression of logic and a progression of feeling or emotion. These progressions are seldom totally isolated from each other, though much modern experimental writing is no more nor less than an attempt to define quite narrowly the terms of progression — to eliminate a progression, sometimes of action, sometimes of logic, or sometimes of feeling.

Take "naturalism" as an example of such a restrictive theory. "Naturalism" aimed to present a naturalistic "slice of life," without a structurally important beginning, development, and end — with, in short, only a casual progression of action, with no progression of logic, and with only a casual, or accidental, progression of feeling. A famous dramatist once said something to the effect that if someone picks up a gun on the stage, sooner or later that gun must go off. But suppose one writes a play in which the firing of that gun, when it does go off in the third act, is a casual accident and really does not further one's understanding of any of the meaning. If the gun fires and kills someone, but the killing has no motive and no comprehensible results, the original action of picking up the gun in the first act remains disparate, unconnected, meaningless. And this haphazardness is the way of the events of life until *someone's mind orders them*, and to order is automatically to give moral significance, because it means emphasizing certain elements over others.

Thus the extreme structural device of naturalism — simply to show us events as they occur in physical reality — is patently an artistic impossibility, though excellent works have arisen out of practical modifications of the theory. Indeed, the same can be said for its counterpart at the other psychological extreme, the stream-of-consciousness technique. Here the subjectivity of the universe is not only acknowledged but insisted upon, as the author attempts to trace the *thoughts* of persons as they naturally occur, rather than their *actions* as they naturally occur. In these and all other structural methods, selectivity and structuring are inevitably going on all the time — even when the moral point of the author is that there is no moral point to the world. And so one returns to the necessity for an examination of the kinds of progressions, or structures, open to fiction.

PROGRESSION OF EMOTION

The progression of the emotion of speakers, narrators, characters — in sum, of the participants in the actions in a fiction — are not the same as the progression of the implied author's, nor of the reader's. In the story by Eudora Welty ("Petrified Man") the principal change of emotion in the characters is the change from friendship to enmity of Leota and Mrs. Pike, a progression actually accomplished out of sight of the reader. What one actually sees is Leota after the friendship with Mrs. Pike is established and after it is ended. Meanwhile, other emotional attitudes are slowly *revealed*, such as that of the women (Leota, Mrs. Pike, and Mrs. Fletcher) toward their husbands and men in general and toward children. But the emotional relationship of Mrs. Pike and Leota is the only one that actually alters. Then we must ask ourselves what is the significance of this alteration, and we discover it in the reason for their change, in cheap motives, in jealous, greedy minds. The whole story appears extraordinarily naturalistic. Nothing of significance happens, any more than might in an ordinary day. The speech is naturalistic; the setting, though no doubt symbolic, evokes its meaning through naturalistic images; and, as suggested in Chapter 8, the point of view adheres to a naturalistic exclusion of any characterizing or omnipotent narrator. But the story is not unordered, and the triviality of the friendship, its instability, is the point that is made by this one change in emotional ties, a point reinforced by the other, more static emotions and relationships of the story. This use of one shift in emotional pattern highlighted against an unchanging background might be contrasted with Thurber's "A Box to Hide In" where there is no change of emotion in the central character, which lack of change becomes itself a primary part of the meaning of the story. As tends to be true in all lyric poetry, the shifting of the lyric voice's emotion in Keats' "Ode to a Nightingale" p. 375, is the principal structural device of the poem. The poet first envies the nightingale's "immortal" world of song and grows more and more depressed and bitter as he thinks of the evils of mortality. Then, by an effort of imagination, by the aid of poetry, he shares that dark and timeless world. Once there, he is immediately beset by an awareness of what he has sacrificed — the beauties of the temporal world which, though they fade, are poignant and meaningful. Finding in this world of eternal beauty a fatal loss to his humanity, drawn back implacably to his own forlorn mortal world, the poet ruefully admits the limits of fancy ". . . the fancy cannot cheat so well as she is famed to do, ..." And as the whole vision of the other world fades, the poet is left in an emotionally suspended ambivalence: which is the vision, which the dream — or in other words, which life is the ultimate reality? But it is not alone in poetry that this sort of emotional ordering provides the main structural pattern on which the work is based. Melville's "Two Sides to a Tortoise" is so constructed. In this work a sudden change of emotion is the key structural device, a change from the almost mystical awareness of the tragedy and majesty of all things to the active gaiety of the non-reflective life. But in Agee's essay, "Knoxville: Summer of 1915" the whole structure of the work is not so much an abrupt change from one emotion to another as a gradual intensification of nostalgia to the point where at the very last it can become pathos, with the revelation of the author's sense of separateness. Both of these essays demonstrate the slenderness of the dividing line between the essay and what we commonly recognize as the short story. "Two Sides to a Tortoise" is probably as much a fictionalizing of any actual experience as we will meet in, say, "An Experiment in Misery," but we call the one a short story and the other an essay because in the Melville piece the illusion is of the author speaking real thoughts as they really occurred, whereas the form of Crane's story calls upon us to accept the characters as purely fictive. But a close look at the Crane story reveals little actual plot. A young man, a tramp, comes into a town, sleeps in a flophouse overnight, and ends the next morning on a bench with other bums. Indeed, there is no sense of progression in the action or in the logic or form. The only thing that *develops* is the emotion of the young man, a development exposed to us by the author in that moment in which he begins to accept his role, "He confessed himself an outcast, and his eyes from under the lowered rim of his hat began to glance guiltily. . . ." All that has gone before in the story has as its purpose bringing the reader to feel the reality of that emotional change.

Sometimes an artist will risk monotony in a work whose only structural progression rests in his ability either to make the same emotion or emotional pattern, though repeated, gradually more intense or to explore the intensity through repetition. Emily Dickinson's "Twas Like a Maelstrom, with a Notch," presents such a case with remarkable purity. The poem basically poses a situation, then asks a question about it. This progression, *in its essence,* would be accomplished if we were given only the first two stanzas, plus the last two lines of the poem.

> 'Twas like a Maelstrom, with a notch,
> That nearer, every Day,
> Kept narrowing its boiling Wheel
> Until the Agony
>
> Toyed coolly with the final inch
> Of your delirious Hem —
> And you dropt, lost,
> When something broke —
> And let you from a Dream —
>
> .   .   .   .
>
> Which Anguish was the utterest — then —
> To perish, or to live?

There are in fact six stanzas.

414*

> 'Twas like a Maelstrom, with a notch,
> That nearer, every Day,
> Kept narrowing its boiling Wheel
> Until the Agony
>
> Toyed coolly with the final inch
> Of your delirious Hem —
> And you dropt, lost,
> When something broke —
> And let you from a Dream —
>
> As if a Goblin with a Gauge —
> Kept measuring the Hours —
> Until you felt your Second
> Weigh, helpless, in his Paws —

And not a Sinew — stirred — could help,
And sense was setting numb —
When God — remembered — and the Fiend
Let go, then, Overcome —

As if your Sentence stood — pronounced —
And you were frozen led
From Dungeon's luxury of Doubt
To Gibbets, and the Dead —

And when the Film had stitched your eyes
A Creature gasped "Reprieve"!
Which Anguish was the utterest — then —
To perish, or to live?

                    EMILY DICKINSON

The third and fourth stanzas, and again the fifth and half the sixth, present exactly the same problem, but in different figures of speech. Thus, the basic problem is repeated three times, and the basic formal (or rhetorical) pattern is exactly the same — a careful description using each figure, of the approach and presence of death, then the sudden reprieve. The only justification for such a procedure is to be found in an emotion so intense, though static, that only the repetitive insistence can adequately explore it. In short, though there seems to be no reason on grounds of logic or action why the pattern is repeated three times and not a half-dozen, or once, there is an emotional ground for repetition. Everyone has been in a tight corner and has experienced the overwhelming sense of relief when the danger is passed. Everyone has also experienced the ordinary concomitant of such relief: a desire to talk over and over the trouble and the miracle of escape. It is a way of relieving tension, a way of convincing oneself that the bad time is past, a kind of denouement, bridging the time of tension with the time of everyday emotions. This is the groundwork of common emotional experience on which this poem is based, though the poet lifts the experience above the commonplace by her figurative and rhythmic power and by the terrible question with which the poem ends. The *number* of repetitions must be determined by the author's sense of the moment when the intensity will have been properly developed, the final question properly prepared for. These structural considerations are keys to a successful oral reading.

One way in which the sense of repetition, yet of increasing intensity, might be projected is through a stepladder kind of melodic (pitch) pattern in which each two-stanza unit would break downward at the release of tension, with the next two-stanza unit starting at a higher melodic point than the previous one before it broke. This pattern would build to the word "reprieve" which, because of its being a literal cry from a character developed within the figure, demands to be read as climactic. The oral reader must then certainly indicate with a considerable pause that he has come to the end of the long sentence that began with the first word of the poem. And this pause surely presents him with a cue to the shift from a rather frenetic buildup of emotion ("boiling," "delirious," "helpless," "numb," "frozen," "stitched," "gasped") to a grimness centered in the word "anguish," and to the implacable dilemma of the last line.

PROGRESSION OF LOGIC

Some works of art use in their structure a strong sense of logic. That is to say, a premise is stated and developed according to its proper artistic proof, or a contrast is made which either demands of the reader or presents to him a logical synthesis of the contrasted elements. Thus Eliot, when he contrasts the new with the old in his typical usage of allusion (see p. 282), demands that the reader draw the proper logical conclusion.

Sometimes the development of a logical pattern coincides with alterations in the emotion of the speaker, though such alterations may not occur. Thus Austen's *Sense and Sensibility* begins with a logical statement of the novel's central act of folly, the terms of the old man's will, and develops quite logically and with no alteration of the narrator's initial feeling and judgment the events that flowed from that error.

Perhaps a clearer example is to be found in Donne's "A Valediction: Forbidding Mourning" (p. 59). In this poem Donne is trying to console his wife for his departure on a long journey (traveling was perilous in those days and a trip was likely to last months and years). He demonstrates, quite logically, through a series of appropriate figures that their love should be beyond the grief of parting. His own emotional attitude is unchanging throughout the poem as is appropriate to his persuasive purpose.

Quite different from this static attitude is the emotion of Marvell in "To His Coy Mistress" (p. 58), which also employs logic importantly in its structure. In the first stanza Marvell makes the statement that he would like to take ages for this courtship. His reason? She is worthy of it. His attitude is one of wit, sympathetic humor — even of play. In the second stanza he makes his next logical point. They do not have much time; and eternity, for the flesh, is a desert. His attitude here is grim, with an edge of terror perhaps. The wit continues ("The grave's a fine and private place") but now has a touch of horror, of the macabre. In the last section as he draws his logical conclusion from this poetic syllogism, his attitude changes drastically again to one of tender violence, if such a thing can be, of urging, backed by a sense of power and glory.

Sometimes a logical pattern is developed for purposes of irony. In Joyce's "A Painful Case" the newspaper reports the death of Mrs. Sinico, traces the logical efforts of the courts to assess the blame, and concurs (as does Mr. Duffy, in his conscious mind) that "No blame attached to anyone." But the reader has his own evidence and draws rather different conclusions, as would Mr. Duffy if only he could translate into a broader truth his self-centered awareness of aloneness.

In this story, as in all these examples, it should be clear that the perception of these emotional and logical structures arises from the perception of tones of voice. The person who reads "Ode on a Grecian Urn" with comprehension must hear the agony in the voice, in its subtle permutations, whereas the newspaper account of Mrs. Sinico's death can be realized only through a voice whose flat objectivity reveals all too clearly its dehumanization.

NARRATIVE PROGRESSION

I have called these structures "progressions" to emphasize the essential fact that literature moves in *time*. The reader begins at the beginning and reads to the end. Each detail passes his lips in a rigid pattern of word after word which, as Tristram Shandy teaches, cannot be ignored. In this sense a literary work of art is of necessity a progressive structure. It literally *must* move from one thing to another. Many of the terms of literary criticism such as "inflation," "compression," or "repetitiveness," simply express the judgment of the reader that the story or poem has not met in a satisfactory way this imperious commitment to progression. It is imperative that the person who would comprehend the work of art in his own body, i.e., be able to embody its elements in meaningful vocal patterns and bodily tensions, must have a thorough comprehension of these progressions and of their successes and failures.

I shall discuss here more narrowly the progression of gross patterns of action which often provide the larger frame for other lesser progressions. I would say that I intend to discuss *plot*, except that, as we shall see, that "series of motivated incidents" is too narrow in its usual usage to cover the full range of possible ordering of meaningfully sequential action.

"Boy meets girl, boy loses girl, boy finds girl, boy gets girl." Here is a plot, tried and true. Yet it is quite clear that this is not, in itself, a narrative. It is also clear that something is assumed about the *feelings* of the people in the story and about the *feelings* of the reader. What is assumed about the feelings of the people in the story is that the boy *wants* the girl, that the girl *wants* the boy. What is assumed about the reader's feeling is that he *approves* of their getting together, that he desires it. But what if we add an adjective or two to this plot? Suppose we say, "Generous boy meets self-centered girl." *Now* how do you want the plot to go? In short, "boy meets girl" is a summarization of an action — no more and no less. Though it is true that a typical slick-paper magazine story assumes that for any alert, clean-looking, intelligent boy to meet any well-groomed, well-behaved, good-looking girl must inevitably be a desirable thing which ought to lead to marriage, a casual thought about the complexities of life will serve to demonstrate how simple-minded that assumption is, and why such stories are not great writing, not great interpretations of life.

One can say that a story apparently has a structure of *events* or *actions,* but that it evidently also has a structure of *emotion:* the characters not only act, they also feel. But the reader, too, has his feelings. In fact, a common description of the structure of a story — introduction, development, turning point, climax, denouement — equally describes the progression of the reader's emotion. Thus, in the "boy meets girl" plot the two neatly parallel each other.

Action	Boy meets girl	Boy loses girl	Boy finds girl	Boy gets girl
Reader's emotion	Introduction	Complication or Development	Climax	Denouement
		Turning point or crisis		

In this oversimplified schematization, the introduction serves to involve the reader's emotions, the complication or development serves to sustain, suspend, or complicate them, the climax serves to relieve tension, and the denouement serves to bring the reader's emotions back to tranquility, so that he does not leave the story feeling cheated or frustrated.

A poem whose principal structure is that of *action* follows.

Badger

When midnight comes a host of dogs and men
Go out and track the badger to his den,
And put a sack within the hole, and lie
Till the old grunting badger passes by.
He comes and hears — they let the strongest loose.
The old fox hears the noise and drops the goose.
The poacher shoots and hurries from the cry,

And the old hare half wounded buzzes by.
They get a forkèd stick to bear him down
And clap the dogs and take him to the town,
And bait him all the day with many dogs,
And laugh and shout and fright the scampering hogs.
He runs along and bites at all he meets:
They shout and hollo down the noisy streets.

He turns about to face the loud uproar
And drives the rebels to their very door.
The frequent stone is hurled where'er they go;
When badgers fight, then every one's a foe.
The dogs are clapt and urged to join the fray;
The badger turns and drives them all away.
Though scarcely half as big, demure and small,
He fights with dogs for hours and beats them all.
The heavy mastiff, savage in the fray,
Lies down and licks his feet and turns away.
The bulldog knows his match and waxes cold,
The badger grins and never leaves his hold.
He drives the crowd and follows at their heels
And bites them through — the drunkard swears and reels.

The frighted women take the boys away,
The blackguard laughs and hurries on the fray.
He tries to reach the woods, an awkward race,
But sticks and cudgels quickly stop the chase.
He turns agen and drives the noisy crowd
And beats the many dogs in noises loud.
He drives away and beats them everyone,
And then they loose them all and set them on.
He falls as dead and kicked by boys and men,
Then starts and grins and drives the crowd agen;
Till kicked and torn and beaten out he lies
And leaves his hold and cackles, groans, and dies.

JOHN CLARE

One of the first things that strikes the oral reader is the tough, unsentimental swiftness of the narration. The language is never allowed to become "poetic," yet, except for the possible exception of "the frequent stone" there is no sense of cliché. In short, the bareness of the language is a successful means of keeping our attention focused on the action. The author holds our eyes on the badger except at the very beginning, where, before the badger is caught, he quickly sketches in the whole midnight world of the hunter and the hunted. These four lines are absolutely essential to the larger moral meaning of the central action. For though the author wins our admiration for the gutty badger and our hatred for the people, yet we cannot forget that the author has placed the killing of the badger in a world of killers. But he achieves a double purpose, for we notice that, in fact, the killing of the badger is different in kind from the other killings. The goose and the hare are necessary victims for the fox and the poacher, each of whom is killing to sustain life. But the people of the village are killing for sport, and our disgust at them is made more vivid by the contrast. Notice how, after the catching of the badger, the action basically is repetitive. The badger is attacked up and down the street till he dies. The author's problem here is to give us enough of the grim details of the badger's fight to make us see and *feel* his courage, and the length of time the battle goes on, yet to end these details at the precise moment when we have realized these things and boredom might begin. Not the least effective narrative device is the suddenness of the badger's death, grimly accomplished in a couplet. If the reader cannot achieve in his voice the peculiar tonal quality (a kind of hard-won, barely kept objectivity) which these structural elements help give substance to, he has not achieved the power of this poem and is likely to overlook its simplicity as artless.

Here is a true narrative structure, yet one without "plot." There is a beginning, middle, and end to the action, yet there is really no "development," that is, no place where the initial action becomes complicated, and certainly no crisis where the end is in doubt. From the beginning, the badger's death is inevitable. Yet the author grips us by his narrative speed and his ability to make us feel his moral view of the action through the power of his selectivity and skill of presentation. Note there is no dialogue. This method of narration of relating action without dialogue by means of description, is often called *non-dramatized narrative*.

Joyce's story "A Painful Case," for all it is about two middle-aged people, has a plot, is even, I suppose, a variation of "boy meets girl." But these characters are of the flawed stuff of life. A fastidious, sterile man meets a warm, but unloved woman. Here is the introduction. They find they have much in common, and gradually their relationship grows richer and more meaningful. Here is the development. This increasingly intimate relationship leads to the turning point, the moment when any plot so narrows in its possibilities that, in retrospect, one sees it as the fateful moment of the current turning in its final direction, of the first delimiting answer being given to the questions and possibilities present in the introduction. In "A Painful Case" the turning point comes when ". . . Mrs. Sinico caught up his hand passionately and pressed it to her cheek." This action presents Duffy with the necessity either of abandoning his sterile refusal

and giving himself to life or of abandoning the one adult human relationship that has meant anything to him. In other words, it presents him with
a crisis, and some critics use the word "crisis" instead of "turning point" to
describe this movement in a plot. Duffy chooses to protect his isolation,
and the climax comes when he picks up the paper and reads of Mrs. Sinico's
death. The climax of a narrative action may be different from the turning
point or crisis. The turning point is the *logical* hinge of the story. After the
turning point, certain general conclusions or directions are inevitable because the possibilities have narrowed fatally. So it is when Mr. Duffy does
not return Mrs. Sinico's gesture of physical warmth. But it is clear that,
though Duffy has made a *logical* choice, he does not emotionally comprehend what has happened, and there remains the whole sense of unrelieved
suspense, of emotional weight left undischarged. The turning point, then,
has to do with the logical movement of the action, whereas the climax is
the culmination of the emotional impact of the story. For Duffy this climax
comes when he reads of Mrs. Sinico's death and as he goes through the
powerful chain of emotions which leads to the denouement. The denouement is the fulfillment of the pattern. It is the final touch, the last logical
working-out of the plot. And for Duffy it comes in that final sentence, "He
felt that he was alone."

Sometimes part of these elements of plot are not actually given in the
story. In "Petrified Man," for instance, much of the development, as well
as the turning point and climax, are related by Leota. They occur, as it
were, offstage, and we find out they have happened only indirectly. Actually, "Petrified Man" has two elements, the relationship of Leota and Mrs.
Pike and the relationship of Leota and Mrs. Fletcher. One is offstage and
one is onstage. These are not really joined together until the denouement,
which is the final scene with Billy Boy. While the attention is focused offstage on Mrs. Pike and Leota, and the main story seems to be about the
rise and fall of their friendship, many tangential emotional threads are
meanwhile started going, some of which we see and some of which happen
elsewhere and are narrated. Mrs. Fletcher's initial response to her pregnancy is clear enough, but the reader is left wondering what will be her
final adjustment. Also, there is begun an exploration of the offstage emotional relationship of all the women, especially of Mrs. Fletcher, to men.
These seen and unseen threads are brought together in the denouement,
where Billy Boy serves conveniently (compare their attitude toward him
with their talk about the pygmies) as both a male and a child.

Robert Frost's poem "Home Burial" (p. 304) is a narrative in which
the development is virtually finished at the point of the opening of the
narrative, and we are let in on the last moment of development, the crisis,
and the climax. It is curiously, but most effectively, without a denouement.

The denouement is something the reader constructs in his own mind after the poem is cut off abruptly in the midst of the climax. A little reflection is sufficient to convince him of the fact that this relationship has long since been doomed by the woman and that the man is already defeated in his wrestling with the shadow of her fixation.

This poem presents a most interesting relationship of action with emotional sequence. In the beginning the woman is at the top of the stair "Looking back over her shoulder at some fear." From the bottom of the stair, the man sees her gesture and speaks, one presumes, with a mixture of curiosity and insistence. "What is it you see from up there always. . . ." This question is the first hint that this bit of action is but one in a sequence whose beginnings are long in the past. The reader is alerted that, although the structural time of the poem is now beginning, he is actually catching the action sequence somewhere in the middle.

Notice that in the beginning she is physically standing *above* him, and in a certain sense she is also above him in their inner condition. She is superior to him in that she has some knowledge vital to the two of them which he is without. When the man comes high enough to see out the window, she sinks down on the stair and their spatial relationship is described thus, "Mounting until she cowered under him." Though she shrinks from him and thus sinks lower, they are nonetheless at this point at least on a level on the stair, and perhaps her feet are still on a higher stair than his — probably so. She holds her position while she is sure that he will not see. Her emotion has changed "from terrified to dull," and the stiffening of her body along with the facial change gives the reader his second cue to the nature of this relationship. The third cue comes in the fact that she underrates him. She is sure he won't see; but people in love tend to overrate, not underrate, the person they are in love with. The rhythm and syntax tell that the phrase "blind creature" should be defined vocally in tones not of pity, but of contempt.

Then he sees, and his exclamation indicating this fact wrings from her her first speech. She can't believe it, but he tells her what it is, and at the same time drops hints from which the reader can guess something of the development that has gone on before the poem began. But she can't bear that he should know, and the long string of negatives marks something important — either a further complication or the end of the turning point. She then descends the stairs. Note that as their actions have led to a reversal of their physical positions, there is also a reversal of their emotional relationship. Before, she had been in control with her secret. Now he is in the position of knowledge, and she is on the defensive. And it is interesting that in action the rest of the poem is an effort on his part to get her to let him descend to her without her leaving the house. She cannot retreat to her secret, the secret of hate and disgust that has made their living together possible for her. He has usurped that first by seeing it and then by facing the reality of it.

He tries to use his new knowledge to get nearer to her, and does succeed in breaking through her coldness and in getting her to spill out her hate. But here is where the sequence of logic, which the man continues to try to develop, breaks down. Having found her secret, having stood her tirade and come through it still loving her, he believes, with some logic, that now she has got it outside and expressed, she has got rid of it. It is certainly a very real and psychologically valid hope, and such an expression uttered on the day the feeling was born might have freed her of it. But now it has become *her*, her emotional self; her identity is in the certainty of her hatred of life and of him. The logical sequence — his question, his discovery, her response — breaks down on her "You — oh, you think the talk is all," and the sequence of emotion here becomes clear; we see that she will not change and that her string of "Don'ts" on the stair was the turning point, in the sense that her reaction to his new knowledge is fixed irrevocably, and the rest is climax — the working of their emotions toward the inevitable end.

In a good oral reading of this poem, the highly integrated physical and psychological patterns become clear. The deliberate rhythms of the man, a man by no means stupid or insensitive as she must think, but slow, ponderous in his thoughts, and in a certain sense powerful in his search for his wife's feelings; she, elusive, vengeful, catching at his clumsiness to picture him a sneering oaf, fixed in her self-centered grief and defending it as if it were itself her child; those shifting facets of character are framed in the extraordinarily economical structure to offer a verbal work of art of density and power.

A brief discussion such as this can give but the slenderest idea of the possible structural permutations of action-structured fictions — they are indeed as various as the number of great narratives. But perhaps this *can* give some conviction to the potential oral reader's search for the *structure that is there*, rather than for a structure that a narrative ought to have. Certainly without a willingness to believe that a narrative may exist essentially without a development or crisis, he will miss the essential point of any oral reading of "Badger" — the driving, swift, plainness of the narration. Without a willingness to believe that a climax may be completely internal rather than a dramatic acting-out between characters, the oral reader's interpretation of Duffy's long evening will lack the proper development, intensity, and ironic comment on his earlier unconscious aloneness.

PREPARATION FOR PERFORMANCE – "The Windhover"

Structure

Many structural elements have already been discussed in relation to this poem, and each has pointed to the significance of the break between the octet and the sestet. Indeed, as will appear in the discussion of meter and sound, there is not an element in the poem which does not reinforce the reader's sense of this physical break as the turning point of the poem.

In the progression of emotion, the first six lines of the octet are relatively static. It should be remembered they are in the past tense and should therefore not be performed with the loud abandon of a momentary excitement, but rather with the quieter wonder of an ecstatic moment just passed. "My heart in hiding" is not essentially different in tone from these lines, but is a continuation of the same narration of a remembrance, and (even though quieter) is climactic to it. It is, in fact, the remembrance of the bird's power to stir the hiding heart, which leads to the sestet in which the poet asks the falcon to seize his heart completely. Here, then, in the octet, is the essential contrast in *action* as well as emotion. There is the bird – high, free, powerful, beautiful – and here is the poet – lowly, weak, afraid.

Seized by the vividness of this contrast and the remembered power of the bird to stir him, the poet asks the bird to stoop and seize his heart altogether. At this point there is time present, a temporal shift which goes along with the shift in address to underline that here is the turning point of the poem.

The sestet, unlike the octet, has elements of a simple logical development: "if you will seize my heart, then, even though you lower yourself, you will yet be more beautiful, and here are two proofs of why this will be so." This more logical structure would, I should think, lead to a somewhat slower pace in reading aloud. There is yet another significant difference in the sestet. The action of the bird in the octet is high, remote, wide-swinging, and this action is contrasted in a tableau to the lowly, dark, fixed heart. In the sestet this simple contrast is gone, and the actions in these lines are a series of three falling movements: the falcon, the plow, and the embers; and the voice is obviously engaged not only in expressing these, but in seeking out the subtle differences in them. In short, the tableau, rather static, of the first stanza, contrasted with the falling and joining actions of the sestet, gives the rough performance pattern for the whole poem, both as to voice and as to the relevant tensions of the body.

SELECTIONS

A Hunger Artist*

FRANZ KAFKA

During these last decades the interest in professional fasting has markedly diminished. It used to pay very well but today that is quite impossible. We live in a different world now. At one time the whole town took a lively interest in the hunger artist; from day to day of his fast the excitement mounted; everybody wanted to see him at least once a day; there were people who bought season tickets for the last few days and sat from morning till night in front of his small barred cage; even in the nighttime there were visiting hours, when the whole effect was heightened by torch flares; on fine days the cage was set out in the open air, and then it was the children's special treat to see the hunger artist; for their elders he was often just a joke that happened to be in fashion, but the children stood open-mouthed, holding each other's hands for greater security, marveling at him as he sat there pallid in black tights, with his ribs sticking out so prominently, not even on a seat but down among straw on the ground, sometimes giving a courteous nod, answering questions with a constrained smile, or perhaps stretching an arm through the bars so that one might feel how thin it was, and then again withdrawing deep into himself, paying no attention to anyone or anything, not even to the all-important striking of the clock that was the only piece of furniture in his cage, but merely staring into vacancy with half-shut eyes, now and then taking a sip from a tiny glass of water to moisten his lips.

Besides casual onlookers there were also relays of permanent watchers selected by the public, usually butchers, strangely enough, and it was their task to watch the hunger artist day and night, three of them at a time, in case he should have some secret recourse to nourishment. This was nothing but a formality, instituted to reassure the masses, for the initiates knew well enough that during his fast the artist would never in any circumstances, not even under forcible compulsion, swallow the smallest morsel of food; the honor of his profession forbade it. Not every watcher, of course, was capable of understanding this, there were often groups of night watchers who were very lax in carrying out their duties and deliberately huddled together in a retired corner to play cards with great absorption, obviously intending to give the hunger artist the chance of a little refreshment, which they supposed he could draw from some private hoard. Nothing annoyed the artist more than such watchers; they made him miserable; they made his fast seem unendurable; sometimes he mastered his feebleness sufficiently to sing during their watch for as long as he could keep going, to show them how unjust their suspicions were. But that was of little use; they only wondered at his cleverness in being able to fill his mouth even while singing. Much more to his taste were the watchers who sat close up to the bars, who were not content with the dim night lighting of the hall but focused him in the full glare of the electric pocket torch given them by the impresario. The harsh light did not trouble him at all, in any case he could never sleep properly, and he could always drowse a little, whatever the light, at any hour, even when the hall was thronged with noisy onlookers. He was quite happy at the prospect of spending a sleepless night with such watchers; he was ready to exchange jokes with them, to tell them stories out of his nomadic life, anything at all to keep them awake and demonstrate to them again that he had no eatables in his cage and that he was fasting as not one of them could fast. But his happiest moment was when the morning came and an enormous breakfast was brought them, at his expense, on which they flung themselves with the keen appetite of healthy men after a weary night of wakefulness. Of course there were people who argued that this breakfast was an unfair attempt to bribe the watchers, but that was going rather too far, and when they were invited to take on a night's vigil without a breakfast, merely for the sake of the cause, they made themselves scarce, although they stuck stubbornly to their suspicions.

Such suspicions, anyhow, were a necessary accompaniment to the profession of fasting. No one could possibly watch the hunger artist continuously, day and night, and so no one could produce first-hand evidence that the fast had really been rigorous and continuous; only the artist himself could know that, he was therefore bound to be the sole completely satisfied spectator of his own fast. Yet for other reasons he was never satisfied; it was not perhaps mere fasting that had brought him to such skeleton thinness that many people had regretfully to keep away from his exhibitions, because the sight of him was too much for them; perhaps it was dissatisfaction with himself that had worn him down. For he alone knew, what no other initiate knew, how easy it was to fast. It was the easiest thing in the world. He made no secret of this, yet people did not believe him, at the best they set him down as modest, most of them, however, thought he was out for publicity or else was some kind of cheat who found it easy to fast because he had discovered a way of making it easy, and then had the impudence to admit the fact, more or less. He had to put up with all that, and in the course of time had got used to it, but his inner dissatisfaction always rankled, and never yet, after any term of fasting — this must be granted to his credit — had he left the cage of his own free will. The longest period of fasting was fixed by his impresario at forty days, beyond that term he was not allowed to go, not even in great cities, and there was good reason for it, too. Experience had proved that for about forty days the interest of the public could be stimulated by a steadily increasing pressure of advertisement, but after that the town began to lose interest, sympathetic support began notably to fall off; there were of course local variations as between one town and another or one country and another, but as a general rule forty days marked the limit. So on the fortieth day the flower-bedecked cage was opened, enthusiastic spectators filled the hall, a military band played, two doctors entered the cage to measure the results of the fast, which were announced through a megaphone, and finally two young ladies appeared, blissful at having been selected for the honor, to help the hunger artist down the few steps leading to a small table on which was spread a carefully chosen invalid repast. And at this very moment the artist always turned stubborn. True, he would entrust his bony arms to the outstretched helping hands of the ladies bending over him, but stand up he would not. Why stop fasting at this particular moment, after forty days of it? He had held out for a long time, an illimitably long time; why stop now, when he was in his best fasting form, or rather, not yet quite in his best fasting form? Why should he be cheated of the fame he would get for fasting longer, for being not only the record hunger artist of all time, which presumably he was already, but for beating his own record by a performance beyond human imagination, since he felt that there were no limits to his capacity for fasting? His public pretended to admire him so much, why should it have so little patience with him; if he could endure fasting longer, why shouldn't the public endure it? Besides, he was tired, he was comfortable sitting in the straw, and now he was supposed to lift himself to his full height and go down to a meal the very thought of which gave him a nausea that only the presence of the ladies kept him from betraying, and even that with an effort. And he looked up into the eyes of the ladies who were apparently so friendly and in reality so cruel, and shook his head, which felt too heavy on its strengthless neck. But then there happened yet again what always happened. The impresario came forward, without a word — for the band made speech impossible — lifted his arms in the air above the artist, as if inviting Heaven to look down upon its creature here in the straw, this suffering martyr, which indeed he was, although in quite another sense; grasped him round the emaciated waist, with exaggerated caution, so that the frail condition he was in might be appreciated; and committed him to the care of the blenching ladies, not without secretly giving him a shaking so that his legs and body tottered and swayed. The artist now submitted completely; his head lolled on his breast as if it had landed there by chance; his body was hollowed out; his legs in a spasm of self-preservation clung close to each other at the knees, yet scraped on the ground as if it were not really solid ground, as if they were only trying to find solid ground; and the whole weight of his body, a featherweight after all, relapsed onto one of the ladies, who, looking round for help and panting a little — this post of honor was not at all what she had expected it to be — first stretched her neck as far as she could to keep her face at least free from contact with the artist, then finding this impossible, and her more fortunate companion not coming to her aid but merely holding extended on her own trembling hand the little bunch of knucklebones that was the artist's, to the great delight of the spectators burst into tears and had to be replaced by an attendant who had long been stationed in readiness. Then came the food, a little of which the impresario managed to get between the artist's lips, while he sat in a kind of half-fainting trance, to the accompaniment of cheerful patter designed to distract the public's attention from the artist's condition; after that, a toast was drunk to the public, supposedly prompted by a whisper from the artist in the impresario's ear; the band confirmed it with a mighty flourish, the spectators melted away, and no one had any cause to be dissatisfied with the proceedings, no one except the hunger artist himself, he only, as always.

So he lived for many years, with small regular intervals of recuperation, in visible glory, honored by the world, yet in spite of that troubled in spirit, and all the more troubled because no one would take his trouble seriously. What comfort could he possibly need? What more could he possibly wish for? And if some goodnatured person, feeling sorry for him, tried to console him by pointing out that his melancholy was probably caused by fasting, it could happen, especially when he had been fasting for some time, that he reacted with an outburst of fury and to the general alarm began to shake the bars of his cage like a wild animal. Yet the impresario had a way of punishing these outbreaks which he rather enjoyed putting into operation. He would apologize publicly for the artist's behavior, which was only to be excused, he admitted, because of the irritability caused by fasting; a condition hardly to be understood by well-fed people; then by natural transition he went on to mention the artist's equally incomprehensible boast that he could fast for much longer than he was doing; he praised the high ambition, the good will, the great self-

denial undoubtedly implicit in such a statement; and then quite simply
countered it by bringing out photographs, which were also on sale to the
public, showing the artist on the fortieth day of a fast lying in bed almost
dead from exhaustion. This perversion of the truth, familiar to the artist
though it was, always unnerved him afresh and proved too much for him.
What was a consequence of the premature ending of his fast was here
presented as the cause of it! To fight against this lack of understanding,
against a whole world of non-understanding, was impossible. Time and
again in good faith he stood by the bars listening to the impresario, but as
soon as the photographs appeared he always let go and sank with a groan
back on to his straw, and the reassured public could once more come close
and gaze at him.

A few years later when the witnesses of such scenes called them to
mind, they often failed to understand themselves at all. For meanwhile
the aforementioned change in public interest had set in; it seemed to happen almost overnight; there may have been profound causes for it, but
who was going to bother about that; at any rate the pampered hunger
artist suddenly found himself deserted one fine day by the amusement
seekers, who went streaming past him to other more favored attractions.
For the last time the impresario hurried him over half Europe to discover
whether the old interest might still survive here and there; all in vain;
everywhere, as if by secret agreement, a positive revulsion from professional fasting was in evidence. Of course it could not really have sprung
up so suddenly as all that, and many premonitory symptoms which had
not been sufficiently remarked or suppressed during the rush and glitter of
success now came retrospectively to mind, but it was now too late to take
any countermeasures. Fasting would surely come into fashion again at
some future date, yet that was no comfort for those living in the present.
What, then, was the hunger artist to do? He had been applauded by
thousands in his time and could hardly come down to showing himself in
a street booth at village fairs, and as for adopting another profession, he
was not only too old for that but too fanatically devoted to fasting. So he
took leave of the impresario, his partner in an unparalleled career, and
hired himself to a large circus; in order to spare his own feelings he
avoided reading the conditions of his contract.

A large circus with its enormous traffic in replacing and recruiting
men, animals and apparatus can always find a use for people at any time,
even for a hunger artist, provided of course that he does not ask too much,
and in this particular case anyhow it was not only the artist who was
taken on but his famous and long-known name as well, indeed, considering
the peculiar nature of his performance, which was not impaired by advancing age, it could not be objected that here was an artist past his

prime, no longer at the height of his professional skill, seeking a refuge in some quiet corner of a circus; on the contrary, the hunger artist averred that he could fast as well as ever, which was entirely credible; he even alleged that if he were allowed to fast as he liked, and this was at once promised him without more ado, he could astound the world by establishing a record never yet achieved, a statement which certainly provoked a smile among the other professionals, since it left out of account the change in public opinion, which the hunger artist in his zeal conveniently forgot.

He had not, however, actually lost his sense of the real situation and took it as a matter of course that he and his cage should be stationed, not in the middle of the ring as a main attraction, but outside, near the animal cages, on a site that was after all easily accessible. Large and gaily painted placards made a frame for the cage and announced what was to be seen inside it. When the public came thronging out in the intervals to see the animals, they could hardly avoid passing the hunger artist's cage and stopping there for a moment; perhaps they might even have stayed longer had not those pressing behind them in the narrow gangway, who did not understand why they should be held up on their way towards the excitements of the menagerie, made it impossible for anyone to stand gazing quietly for any length of time. And that was the reason why the hunger artist, who had of course been looking forward to these visiting hours as the main achievement of his life, began instead to shrink from them. At first he could hardly wait for the intervals; it was exhilarating to watch the crowds come streaming his way, until only too soon — not even the most obstinate self-deception, clung to almost consciously, could hold out against the fact — the conviction was borne in upon him that these people, most of them, to judge from their actions, again and again, without exception, were all on their way to the menagerie. And the first sight of them from the distance remained the best. For when they reached his cage he was at once deafened by the storm of shouting and abuse that arose from the two contending factions, which renewed themselves continuously, of those who wanted to stop and stare at him — he soon began to dislike them more than the others — not out of real interest but only out of obstinate self-assertiveness, and those who wanted to go straight on to the animals. When the first great rush was past, the stragglers came along, and these, whom nothing could have prevented from stopping to look at him as long as they had breath, raced past with long strides, hardly even glancing at him, in their haste to get to the menagerie in time. And all too rarely did it happen that he had a stroke of luck, when some father of a family fetched up before him with his children, pointed a finger at the hunger artist and explained at length what the phenomenon meant, telling stories of earlier years when he himself had watched similar but much more thrilling performances, and the children, still rather uncomprehending, since neither inside nor outside school had they been sufficiently prepared for this lesson — what did they care about fasting? — yet showed by the brightness of their intent eyes that new and better times might be coming. Perhaps, said the hunger artist to himself many a time, things would be a little better if his cage were set not quite so near the menagerie. That made it too easy for people to make their choice, to say nothing of what he suffered from the stench of the menagerie, the animals' restlessness by night, the carrying past of raw lumps of flesh for the beasts of prey, the roaring at feeding times, which depressed him continually. But he did not dare to lodge a complaint with the management; after all, he had the animals to thank for the troops of people who passed his cage, among whom there might always be one here and there to take an interest in him, and who could tell where they might seclude him if he called attention to his existence and thereby to the fact that, strictly speaking, he was only an impediment on the way to the menagerie.

A small impediment, to be sure, one that grew steadily less. People grew familiar with the strange idea that they could be expected, in times like these, to take an interest in a hunger artist, and with this familiarity the verdict went out against him. He might fast as much as he could, and he did so; but nothing could save him now, people passed him by. Just try to explain to anyone the art of fasting! Anyone who has no feeling for it cannot be made to understand it. The fine placards grew dirty and illegible, they were torn down; the little notice board telling the number of fast days achieved, which at first was changed carefully every day, had long stayed at the same figure, for after the first few weeks even this small task seemed pointless to the staff; and so the artist simply fasted on and on, as he had once dreamed of doing, and it was no trouble to him, just as he had always foretold, but no one counted the days, no one, not even the artist himself, knew what records he was already breaking, and his heart grew heavy. And when once in a time some leisurely passer-by stopped, made merry over the old figure on the board and spoke of swindling, that was in its way the stupidest lie ever invented by indifference and inborn malice, since it was not the hunger artist who was cheating, he was working honestly, but the world was cheating him of his reward.

Many more days went by, however, and that too came to an end. An overseer's eye fell on the cage one day and he asked the attendants why this perfectly good stage should be left standing there unused with dirty straw inside it; nobody knew, until one man, helped out by the notice board, remembered about the hunger artist. They poked into the straw with sticks and found him in it. "Are you still fasting?" asked the overseer, "when on earth do you mean to stop?" "Forgive me, everybody," whispered the hunger artist; only the overseer, who had his ear to the bars, understood him. "Of course," said the overseer, and tapped his forehead with a finger to let the attendants know what state the man was in, "we forgive you." "I always wanted you to admire my fasting," said the hunger artist. "We do admire it," said the overseer, affably. "But you shouldn't admire it," said the hunger artist. "Well then we don't admire it," said the overseer, "but why shouldn't we admire it?" "Because I have to fast, I can't help it," said the hunger artist. "What a fellow you are," said the overseer, "and why can't you help it?" "Because," said the hunger artist, lifting his head a little and speaking, with his lips pursed, as if for a kiss, right into the overseer's ear, so that no syllable might be lost, "because I couldn't find the food I liked. If I had found it, believe me, I should have made no fuss and stuffed myself like you or anyone else." These were his last words, but in his dimming eyes remained the firm though no longer proud persuasion that he was still continuing to fast.

"Well, clear this out now!" said the overseer, and they buried the hunger artist, straw and all. Into the cage they put a young panther. Even the most insensitive felt it refreshing to see this wild creature leaping around the cage that had so long been dreary. The panther was all right. The food he liked was brought him without hesitation by the attendants; he seemed not even to miss his freedom; his noble body, furnished almost to the bursting point with all that it needed, seemed to carry freedom around with it too; somewhere in his jaws it seemed to lurk; and the joy of life streamed with such ardent passion from his throat that for the on-lookers it was not easy to stand the shock of it. But they braced them-selves, crowded round the cage, and did not want ever to move away.

Lapis Lazuli*

(For Harry Clifton)

I have heard that hysterical women say
They are sick of the palette and fiddle-bow,
Of poets that are always gay,
For everybody knows or else should know
That if nothing drastic is done
Aeroplane and Zeppelin will come out,
Pitch like King Billy bomb-balls in
Until the town lie beaten flat.

* Reprinted from *Collected Poems of W. B. Yeats* with permission of The Macmillan Company (N.Y.), the Macmillan Company of Canada Ltd., and Mrs. Yeats. Copyright 1940 by Georgie Yeats.

All perform their tragic play,
There struts Hamlet, there is Lear,
That's Ophelia, that Cordelia;
Yet they, should the last scene be there,
The great stage curtain about to drop,
If worthy their prominent part in the play,
Do not break up their lines to weep.
They know that Hamlet and Lear are gay;
Gaiety transfiguring all that dread.
All men have aimed at, found and lost;
Black out; Heaven blazing into the head:
Tragedy wrought to its uttermost.
Though Hamlet rambles and Lear rages,
And all the drop-scenes drop at once
Upon a hundred thousand stages,
It cannot grow by an inch or an ounce.

On their own feet they came, or on shipboard,
Camel-back, horse-back, ass-back, mule-back,
Old civilisations put to the sword.
Then they and their wisdom went to rack:
No handiwork of Callimachus,
Who handled marble as if it were bronze,
Made draperies that seemed to rise
When sea-wind swept the corner, stands;
His long lamp-chimney shaped like the stem
Of a slender palm, stood but a day;
All things fall and are built again,
And those that build them again are gay.

Two Chinamen, behind them a third,
Are carved in lapis lazuli,
Over them flies a long-legged bird,
A symbol of longevity;
The third, doubtless a serving-man,
Carries a musical instrument.

Every discoloration of the stone,
Every accidental crack or dent,
Seems a water-course or an avalanche,
Or lofty slope where it still snows
Though doubtless plum or cherry-branch
Sweetens the little half-way house

Those Chinamen climb towards, and I
Delight to imagine them seated there;
There, on the mountain and the sky,

On all the tragic scene they stare.
One asks for mournful melodies;
Accomplished fingers begin to play.
Their eyes mid many wrinkles, their eyes,
Their ancient, glittering eyes, are gay.

W. B. YEATS (1938)

His Desire

Give me a man that is not dull
When all the world with rifts is full;
But unamaz'd dares clearly sing,
Whenas the roof's a-tottering;
And, though it falls, continues still
Tickling the citterne with his quill.

ROBERT HERRICK

The Winter Lightning*

For Paul

Over the snow at night,
And while the snow still fell,
A sky torn to the bone
Shattered the ghostly world with light;
As though this were the moon's hell,
A world hard as a stone,
        Cold, and blue-white.

As if the storming sea
Should sunder to its floor,
And all things hidden there
Gleam in the moment silently,
So does the meadow at the door
To split and sudden air
        Show stone and tree.

* Reprinted by permission of Howard Nemerov from *New and Selected Poems,* 1960.

From the drowned world of dark
The sleeping innocence
Surrenders all its seeming;
Under the high, charged carbon arc
Light of the world, a guilty sense
Stiffens the secret dreaming
        Animal park.

So in the camera's glare
The fortunate and famed,
For all their crooked smiles,
Reveal through their regarded stare
How all that's publicly acclaimed
One brutal flash reviles
        For cold despair.

So is the murderer caught
When his lost victim rises
Glaring through dream and light
With icy eyes. That which was thought
In secret, and after wore disguises,
Silts up the drowning sight
        Mind inwrought.

So may the poem dispart
The mirror from the light
Where none can see a seam;
The poet, from his wintry heart
And in the lightning second's sight,
Illuminate this dream
        With a cold art.

HOWARD NEMEROV

The Lover Complaineth the Unkindness of His Love

My lute, awake, perform the last
Labour that thou and I shall waste,
And end that I have now begun;
And when this song is sung and past,
My lute, be still, for I have done.

    As to be heard where ear is none,
As lead to grave in marble stone,
My song may pierce her heart as soon.
Should we then sigh, or sing, or moan?
No, no, my lute, for I have done.

    The rocks do not so cruelly
Repulse the waves continually,
As she my suit and affection;
So that I am past remedy,
Whereby my lute and I have done.

    Proud of the spoil that thou hast got
Of simple hearts, through love's shot;
By whom unkind thou hast them won,
Think not he hath his bow forgot,
Although my lute and I have done.

    Vengeance shall fall on thy disdain,
That makest but game on earnest pain;
Think not alone under the sun
Unquit to cause thy lovers plain,
Although my lute and I have done.

    May chance thee lie withered and old,
In winter nights that are so cold,
Plaining in vain unto the moon;
Thy wishes then dare not be told.
Care then who list, for I have done.

    And then may chance thee to repent
The time that thou hast lost and spent
To cause thy lovers sigh and swoon;
Then shalt thou know beauty but lent,
And wish and want as I have done.

    Now cease, my lute, this is the last
Labour that thou and I shall waste,
And ended is that we begun.
Now is this song both sung and past,
My lute, be still, for I have done.

                                    SIR THOMAS WYATT

Astrophel and Stella

I

Loving in truth, and fain my love in verse to show,
That she, dear she! might take some pleasure of my pain:
Pleasure might cause her read, reading might make her know,
Knowledge might pity win, and pity grace obtain:
    I sought fit words, to paint the blackest face of woe,
Studying inventions fine, her wits to entertain,
Oft turning others' leaves, to see if thence would flow
Some fresh and fruitful shower, upon my sun-burnt brain.
    But words came halting forth, wanting invention's stay,
Invention, Nature's child, fled Stepdame Study's blows,
And others' feet still seemed but strangers in my way,
Thus great with child to speak, and helpless in my throes,
    Biting my truant pen, beating myself for spite,
Fool! said my muse to me, look in thy heart and write.

SIR PHILIP SIDNEY

To the Stone-Cutters*

Stone-cutters fighting time with marble, you foredefeated
Challengers of oblivion
Eat cynical earnings, knowing rock splits, records fall down,
The square-limbed Roman letters
Scale in the thaws, wear in the rain. The poet as well
Builds his monument mockingly;
For man will be blotted out, the blithe earth die, the brave sun
Die blind, his heart blackening:
Yet stones have stood for a thousand years, and pained thoughts found
The honey of peace in old poems.

ROBINSON JEFFERS

Ode to a Nightingale

My heart aches, and a drowsy numbness pains
　My sense, as though of hemlock I had drunk,
Or emptied some dull opiate to the drains
　One minute past, and Lethe-wards had sunk:
'Tis not through envy of thy happy lot,
　But being too happy in thine happiness, —
　　That thou, light-winged Dryad of the trees,
　　　In some melodious plot
　Of beechen green, and shadows numberless,
　　Singest of summer in full-throated ease.

O for a draught of vintage! that hath been
　Cool'd a long age in the deep-delved earth,
Tasting of Flora and the country-green,
　Dance, and Provençal song, and sunburnt mirth!
O for a beaker full of the warm South!
　Full of the true, the blushful Hippocrene,
　　With beaded bubbles winking at the brim,
　　　And purple-stained mouth;
　That I might drink, and leave the world unseen,
　　And with thee fade away into the forest dim:

Fade far away, dissolve, and quite forget
　What thou among the leaves hast never known,
The weariness, the fever, and the fret
　Here, where men sit and hear each other groan;
Where palsy shakes a few, sad, last gray hairs,
　Where youth grows pale, and specter-thin, and dies;
　　Where but to think is to be full of sorrow
　　　And leaden-eyed despairs;
　Where Beauty cannot keep her lustrous eyes,
　　Or new Love pine at them beyond to-morrow.

Away! away! for I will fly to thee,
　Not charioted by Bacchus and his pards,
But on the viewless wings of Poesy,
　Though the dull brain perplexes and retards:
Already with thee! tender is the night,
　And haply the Queen-Moon is on her throne,
　　Cluster'd around by all her starry fays;
　　　But here there is no light,
　Save what from heaven is with the breezes blown
　　Through verdurous glooms and winding mossy ways.

I cannot see what flowers are at my feet,
 Nor what soft incense hangs upon the boughs,
But, in embalmed darkness, guess each sweet
 Wherewith the seasonable month endows
The grass, the thicket, and the fruit-tree wild;
 White hawthorn, and the pastoral eglantine;
  Fast fading violets cover'd up in leaves;
   And mid-May's eldest child,
 The coming musk-rose, full of dewy wine,
  The murmurous haunt of flies on summer eves.

Darkling I listen; and, for many a time
 I have been half in love with easeful Death,
Call'd him soft names in many a mused rhyme,
 To take into the air my quiet breath;
Now more than ever seems it rich to die,
 To cease upon the midnight with no pain,
  While thou art pouring forth thy soul abroad
   In such an ecstasy!
 Still wouldst thou sing, and I have ears in vain —
  To thy high requiem become a sod.

Thou wast not born for death, immortal bird!
 No hungry generations tread thee down;
The voice I hear this passing night was heard
 In ancient days by emperor and clown:
Perhaps the self-same song that found a path
 Through the sad heart of Ruth, when, sick for home,
  She stood in tears amid the alien corn;
   The same that oft-times hath
 Charm'd magic casements, opening on the foam
  Of perilous seas, in faery lands forlorn.

Forlorn! the very word is like a bell
 To toll me back from thee to my sole self!
Adieu! the fancy cannot cheat so well
 As she is famed to do, deceiving elf.
Adieu! adieu! thy plaintive anthem fades
 Past the near meadows, over the still stream,
  Up the hill-side; and now 'tis buried deep
   In the next valley-glades:
 Was it a vision, or a waking dream?
  Fled is that music: — do I wake or sleep?

JOHN KEATS

Nightingales*

Beautiful must be the mountains whence ye come,
And bright in the fruitful valleys the streams wherefrom
        Ye learn your song:
Where are those starry woods? O might I wander there,
    Among the flowers, which in that heavenly air
        Bloom the year long!

Nay, barren are those mountains and spent the streams:
Our song is the voice of desire, that haunts our dreams,
        A throe of the heart,
Whose pining visions dim, forbidden hopes profound,
    No dying cadence nor long sigh can sound,
        For all our art.

Alone, aloud in the raptured ear of men
We pour our dark nocturnal secret; and then,
        As night is withdrawn
From these sweet-springing meads and bursting boughs of May,
    Dream, while the innumerable choir of day
        Welcome the dawn.

                                        ROBERT BRIDGES

Philomela†

Procne, Philomela, and Itylus,
Your names are liquid, your improbable tale
Is recited in the classic numbers of the nightingale.
Ah, but our numbers are not felicitous,
It goes not liquidly for us.

Perched on a Roman ilex, and duly apostrophized,
The nightingale descanted unto Ovid;
She has even appeared to the Teutons, the swilled and gravid;
At Fontainebleau it may be the bird was gallicized;
Never was she baptized.

To England came Philomela with her pain,
Fleeing the hawk her husband; querulous ghost,
She wanders when he sits heavy on his roost,
Utters herself in the original again,
The untranslatable refrain.

Not to these shores she came! this other Thrace,
Environ barbarous to the royal Attic;
How could her delicate dirge run democratic,
Delivered in a cloudless boundless public place
To an inordinate race?

I pernoctated with the Oxford students once,
And in the quadrangles, in the cloisters, on the Cher,
Precociously knocked at antique doors ajar,
Fatuously touched the hems of the hierophants,
Sick of my dissonance.

I went out to Bagley Wood, I climbed the hill;
Even the moon had slanted off in a twinkling,
I heard the sepulchral owl and a few bells tinkling,
There was no more villainous day to unfulfill,
The diuturnity was still.

Up from the darkest wood where Philomela sat,
Her fairy numbers issued. What then ailed me?
My ears are called capacious but they failed me,
Her classics registered a little flat!
I rose, and venomously spat.

Philomela, Philomela, lover of song,
I am in despair if we may make us worthy,
A bantering breed sophistical and swarthy;
Unto more beautiful, persistently more young,
Thy fabulous provinces belong.

                                    JOHN CROWE RANSOM

To the Nightingale

Exert thy voice, sweet harbinger of spring!
    This moment is thy time to sing,
    This moment I attend to praise,
And set my numbers to thy lays.
    Free as thine shall be my song;
    As thy music, short, or long.
Poets, wild as thee, were born,
    Pleasing best when unconfin'd,
    When to please is least design'd,
Soothing but their cares to rest;
    Cares do still their thoughts molest,
    And still th'unhappy poet's breast,
Like thine, when best he sings, is plac'd against a thorn.
She begins, let all be still!
    Muse, thy promise now fulfill!
Sweet, oh! sweet, still sweeter yet
Can thy words such accents fit,
Canst thou syllables refine,
Melt a sense that shall retain
Still some spirit of the brain,
Till with sounds like these it join.
    'Twill not be! then change thy note;
    Let division shake thy throat.
Hark! division now she tries;
Yet as far the Muse outflies.
    Cease then, pr'ythee, cease thy tune;
    Trifler, wilt thou sing till June?
Till thy bus'ness all lies waste,
And the time of building's past!
    Thus we poets that have speech,
Unlike what thy forests teach,
    If a fluent vein be shown
    That's transcendent to our own,
Criticize, reform, or preach,
Or censure what we cannot reach.

ANNE FINCH, COUNTESS OF WINCHILSEA

*In My Craft or Sullen Art**

In my craft or sullen art
Exercised in the still night
When only the moon rages
And the lovers lie abed
With all their griefs in their arms,
I labour by singing light
Not for ambition or bread
Or the strut and trade of charms
On the ivory stages
But for the common wages
Of their most secret heart.

Not for the proud man apart
From the raging moon I write
On these spindrift pages
Not for the towering dead
With their nightingales and psalms
But for the lovers, their arms
Round the griefs of the ages,
Who pay no praise or wages
Nor heed my craft or art.

DYLAN THOMAS

CHAPTER TWELVE

Rhythm

The purpose of rhythm, it has always seemed to me, is to prolong the moment of contemplation, the moment when we are both asleep and awake, which is the one moment of creation, by hushing us with an alluring monotony, while it holds us waking by variety, to keep us in that state of perhaps real trance, in which the mind liberated from the pressure of the will is unfolded in symbols.

W. B. YEATS

Rhythm is of the essence of anything living. It appears that the beginning of life on land is a result of the rhythmic rise and fall of the tides. Certainly the heart beats in rhythm, we walk in a rhythm, and there seems little doubt that talk is rhythmical. What is not done rhythmically is awkward, fragmentary. Thus it would seem a truism to say that so carefully constructed a thing as a fine piece of imaginative writing is an interweaving of various mutually meaningful rhythms.

Because rhythm is such a pervasive and intuitive matter, it is essential to get some sense of the various kinds of possible rhythms, if rhythm is to be talked about at all. And there are no doubt various ways of distinguishing between usages of rhythm. Certainly there are rhythms of time, about which I have perhaps already said enough in the chapter on time. Additionally, one might sensibly distinguish rhythms of action, rhythms of place, and the verbal rhythms. These will be discussed in this chapter. Though some variations of these rhythmic patterns are confined to the larger fictive forms, such as novels and epics, nonetheless as we shall see these large patterns of the novel and the epic have their rhythmic counterpart in smaller works.

But before touching on some examples, it would be well to define the word "rhythm." By rhythm is meant *a regular recurrence of like features.* And it should be immediately observed that the word "like" does not necessarily mean identical, but more usually "similar." One could go further and say that in art, rhythms are not likely to be identical. Thus, though one looks for the meaning of a work of art in part in the repetitions of its likenesses, a good deal of the meaning is likely to be contained in the subtle differences that exist among the like features. It often seems, in fact, that the rhythm is established that these differences may be evoked more vividly against a background of similarity. The emotional basis of a successful artistic rhythm is probably to be found in a psychologically successful interplay of recognition and surprise, integrated in the most useful way with all the other aspects of the artwork.

THE RHYTHM OF ACTION

In writing "A Box to Hide In," James Thurber had a difficult task. To attempt any kind of humor in so pathetic a case is a dangerous thing, and in Chapter ten (p. 322) it has been pointed out how important the point of view is in making the humor acceptable. But perhaps his most difficult task is the initial one of using a mental condition bordering on the psychotic as the center of a story. For the essence of a psychotic person's condition is a boringly repeated pattern of outward action (in some cases violence gives this repetition a melodramatic interest), so that this repetition is certainly the one *required* element in any accurate picture of a deeply disturbed person. Yet the one eternal truth of fiction is that it must not bore. It must hold the interest in one way or another.

Thurber establishes this required rhythm of action by means of three brief scenes, in each of which the protagonist is seeking his box. Thurber solves the problem of boredom (which might arise from repetition of so simple an action) in three ways. First, the story is quite short. Its very brevity both makes the point of the story and keeps the intensity of interest. Second, although there are three recurrences of the box-seeking action, Thurber gets variety in these by treating the second as if it were an extension of the first. That is, he does not repeat the initial question-and-answer pattern, but assuming the introductory question, uses the second grocer to introduce two further questions. The similarity between the two occurrences is reinforced, however, by the similar conclusions: ". . . only cartons that cans come in" and ". . . only some pasteboard cartons that cans come in." Though the third and last request for a box varies in other ways from the first two, its beginning is like the first ("How big a box you want?") and by this return provides a sense of completion for the rhythm of these actions.

His third method of keeping interest is by two brief, introspective statements between the interrogations and, most important, by interrupting the last interview with an extensive reverie which contains the necessary climactic elements of humor and self-pity. This long interruption to the main action, with its tragicomic variations, offers so much more of action than what precedes it, that the reader is perhaps led unconsciously to expect a vigorous ending. The rhythmic reversion at the end to the flat indecisive tone of the first part is thereby made aesthetically more effective.

Rhythms of action may be important without being quite so all-pervading as in "A Box to Hide In." The initial action of "An Experiment in Misery," the trudging of the youth toward "the downtown places" where, once arrived, he "aligns" himself with the human derelicts, is repeated at the end, when he and the "assassin" walk along to City Hall Park to the "little circle of benches sanctified by traditions of their class." This rhythmic return of the initial motif gives a circular quality to these actions which is itself a figure of the dull, routine self-pity of this kind of life. However, the last of these scenes is not entirely like the first. Stephen Crane, who lived for two years among the Bowery tramps and bums of his day, once said that he was trying to show in "Experiment in Misery" that this sort of life was the result of "a kind of cowardice," and we have already pointed out in Chapter eight (p. 249) that beyond the initial scene, where the young man feels apart from society and vaguely menaced by it,

his feelings in the final scene have intensified and so turned in upon themselves that he feels not only a paralysis, but a guilty paralysis.

In the poem "The Gallows," the one action of the poem, the killing of
the birds by the keeper and his hanging their skins out on the dead oak
tree bough, is repeated in each stanza of the poem, yet with such subtle
variation that the inevitability of the action itself becomes the very heart
of the poem's power and accrues force and meaning for the reader in each
succeeding stanza.

THE RHYTHMS OF PLACE

We have mentioned the circular effect of the first and the final actions
in "An Experiment in Misery." Actually, one may see those actions as occurring in places that are similar in important ways. Looking further for
such similarities, one can detect a rhythmic pattern of action and of place
throughout this story: (1) seeking a place apart, (2) joining the place apart,
(3) eating among those apart, (4) sleeping among those apart, (5) eating
among those apart, (6) seeking a place apart, (7) joining a place apart.
Stated thus simply, this pattern makes clear how the reader gets from this
story the illusion of inconclusiveness, for this rhythm of place is designed
to show the endless round of the submerged life. It is in the changed
quality of the boy's reaction to place that the reader may see the story
make its muted conclusion. It is important to notice that, come day,
there is a new need to find the place apart, because with the light comes
new hope, new chances for the attempts of courage. It is this denial of this
new day, the acceptance of the smells and sights of the night, of the continuance, in fact, of the night into the day, "huddled in their old garments,
slumbrously conscious of the march of the hours which for them had no
meaning," it is this new acceptance of his condition which deepens the
young man's feeling of simple apartness into one of apartness with guilt.

In "A Painful Case" we can discover a rough rhythm to the recurrence
of place: (1) lengthy description of Duffy's quarters, with brief description
of his life elsewhere — chiefly dining and recreation places; (2) meeting
with Mrs. Sinico in Rotunda and Earlsfort Terrace; (3) meetings in dark
parlor of Mrs. Sinico's home; (4) description and scene in Duffy's quarters,
restaurant, and pub (see no. (1); (5) courtroom scene of inquest of Mrs.
Sinico's death (see no. (2); (6) scene of Duffy thinking of Mrs. Sinico at
night in the Park and on Magazine Hill (see no. (3).

The relationship between the first and second appearances of Duffy's
room, the restaurant, and the other briefly mentioned places involved in
Duffy's routine is clear. Both are descriptive of the place as scene but
hardly at all as setting. That is, Duffy seems hardly to exist in them, and
so they seem almost bare repetitions of place minus action.

Likewise the relationship between the Rotunda-Earlsfort Terrace meeting places and the courtroom of the newspaper account is obvious. He has his first as well as his last knowledge of her in a public, impersonal place, the latter even more remote because visited only in his imagination by means of a public, impersonal newspaper account.

But the relationship between Mrs. Sinico's parlor and Duffy's final wanderings around Dublin is more subtle and lies as much in the differences as in the similarities. The principal likeness is that both are scenes of darkness. This quality is dwelt on extensively in both: "They spent their evening alone," "many times she allowed the dark to fall on them," "the dark discreet room," and, descriptive of the final scene, "the cheerless evening landscape," "The night was cold and gloomy," "The cold night," are some of the phrases relating to darkness. The most important phrase in this last scene, the one most closely identifying the relationship between the two scenes, no doubt is, "She seemed to be near him in the darkness."

But if the rhythmic reappearance of his room, for instance, is meant to show its unchanged sterility, the recurrence of a place of darkness is intended to make a despairing contrast. The dark of Mrs. Sinico's parlor is humanized, fertile, warmly emotional; it is human companionship given a local habitation. The November night in which he reads of her death is cold, despairing, "gloomy," impersonal; and he wanders through the night "an outcast," and "he felt that he was alone." It should be noted how the rhythm of place in these two scenes of darkness serves to dramatize a contrast in the rhythm of action. In Mrs. Sinico's parlor Duffy is quiet, at peace, "exalted," his mental life "emotionalized." And in this peace, "the music that still vibrated in their ears united them." In the second scene of darkness he is a wanderer, he is apart from the lovers, who wish him gone, and, instead of music, he hears "the laborious drone of the engine reiterating the syllables of her name," and again, when the "rhythm of the engine pounding in his ears" has died away, he enters the final horror, "he could hear nothing: the night was perfectly silent."

THE VERBAL RHYTHMS

One of the general theses of this book is that there is some advantage, in the beginning approach to literature, to an investigation of elements held in common by the various genres of creative writing: short stories, narrative, lyric and philosophic poems, novels, and imaginative essays. Surely the rhythms of time, place, and action might well be considered common territory among the genres as may the purely verbal rhythms (those rhythms which arise from the uses of the words themselves as they are arranged in images, figures of speech, paragraphs, sentences, phrases, syllables, and sounds and pauses). There is a major element of the verbal rhythms, however, which I shall not treat in this chapter: *Meter,* perhaps the only rhythm poetry and fiction do not share, will be reserved for discussion in Chapter thirteen, which is concerned with those elements of fictional technique restricted exclusively to poetry. Also, certain elements of sound repetition, especially the various kinds of rhymes, are used almost exclusively in poetry and will therefore be discussed in Chapter fourteen.

Rhythms of Images and Figures

In "Two Sides to a Tortoise" occurs an example of an image used rhythmically both in detail and as a larger supportive structure. We have already discussed in Chapter eight the theme of this sketch, namely, the possibility of gaiety in a world of gloom. The image used to dramatize this problem is that of light as opposed to darkness. In the first paragraph this duality is firmly established by their rapid rhythmic alternation; the back is "dark and melancholy," but the breastplate is "bright," with a "faint yellowish or golden tinge." Next, one can expose their "bright sides," "Enjoy the bright . . . don't deny the black." It has its "darker" and its "livelier" aspect, and finally for the denouement, "the tortoise is both black and bright." This duality is then developed through the rest of the story in quite an unbalanced way. Dark and gloom is the reiterated image through all the paragraphs right up to the very last, where all is suddenly brightness, merriment, beauty. This irregularity of the larger structural rhythm of light and dark is quite unexpected after the careful balance established in the detail of the first paragraph. But this imbalance supports an interesting contrast of action, for the darkness is intensified and prolonged by contemplation, whereas his merriment is all action and no contemplation. Perhaps it is by using his basic images to heighten this contrast that Melville makes his final profound comment on the nature and source of both melancholy and gaiety.

Important though rhythms of image are likely to be, they are probably seldom developed without the support of figurative language, a generalization which certainly holds true in "Two Sides to a Tortoise." The rhythmic alternation of the black and bright images of the first paragraph comes to its climax in opposed figures which describe the bright on the one hand as like "a great October pumpkin in the sun," while the dark on the other hand is described as an "inky blot."

These figures would seem to make a vivid conclusion to our vision. It is worth noting that the nature of the bright side, particularly, is very much qualified, for it is a brilliance not like the sun itself, but like the subdued orange hue of a vegetable seen in an autumn-weakened sun. These figures of speech are not only a more accurate and powerful visual evocation of the images leading up to them; they also serve as the first thematic statement of the final comment on gaiety and melancholy. Just as melancholy seems a result of contemplation, so the ink spot is quite abstract, capable of many imagined likenesses. And as gaiety seems a result of an intensification of everyday action — of eating, drinking, and labor — so the pumpkin is a thing very much of the flesh. One has only to contrast it to what a white rose, for instance, symbolizes, to see how much a thing of earthy action and growth it is, of homely and simple beauty.

Rhythm of Syllable, Phrase, Sentence

The smallest unit of rhythm in the English language is the rise and fall of stress and slack syllables. It is at this point that the tidy textbook should give a neat description of what constitutes a stress. Unfortunately, linguists disagree on the nature of stress, and it seems to come uncomfortably near to being included among those matters which we know exist, but which we have a good deal of difficulty defining to the satisfaction of all interested parties. However, a stressed syllable in English seems to be one with a relatively striking change of pitch, or one taking a relatively longer time to vocalize, or one demonstrating a combination of these factors. This description seems simple enough and should be helpful even though, as we shall soon see, so many side factors are hidden in that word "relatively" as to give all kinds of difficulty in the lay reader's practical discovery of stress.

A look in the dictionary confirms that virtually every multisyllabic word has at least one syllable more importantly stressed than the others

$$\overset{\prime}{\text{ev}}/ \overset{\times}{\text{er}}, \quad \overset{\times}{\text{to}}/ \overset{\prime}{\text{day}}, \quad \overset{\prime}{\text{im}}/ \overset{\times}{\text{por}}/ \overset{\times}{\text{tant}}/ \overset{\times}{\text{ly}}$$

(ev/ er, to/ day, im/ por/ tant/ ly). Beyond that, when used in phrases, all one-syllable words take a stress or slack depending on, in any given instance, the degree to which their particular contextual importance or unimportance conflicts with or reinforces the everyday common usage. Thus,

$$\overset{\prime}{\text{what}} \ \overset{\times}{\text{do}} \ \overset{\times}{\text{you}} \ \overset{\prime}{\text{see}}$$

receives the reply,

$$\overset{\times}{\text{I}} \ \overset{\prime}{\text{see}} \ \overset{\times}{\text{a}} \ \overset{\prime}{\text{house}}$$

whereas the question

$$\overset{\prime}{\text{what}} \ \overset{\times}{\text{do}} \ \overset{\prime}{\text{you}} \ \overset{\times}{\text{see}}$$

receives the reply

$$\overset{\prime}{\text{I}} \ \overset{\times}{\text{see}} \ \overset{\times}{\text{a}} \ \overset{\prime}{\text{house}}$$

Before going further into the process of learning how to *scan,* (scanning is the process by which one marks off the slack and stress pattern of a given passage), it would be well to look at the difficulties of scansion.

For reasons which will be touched upon later, English presents the difficulty that in most passages of any length there will be a small but very significant number of syllables the degree of whose stress or slack is indefinable. This problem has to some extent been recognized by the dictionaries for a long time in that they show two kinds of stresses for multisyllabic words in their pronunciation guides, a primary and a secondary accent:

pho/ to/ lu/ mi/ nes/ cent, scape/ goat, en/ cy/ clo/ pe/ di/ a.

But these secondary accents, even where definitely discernible, are subject to strengthening and weakening in a given context; and the problem of deciding whether or not they have weakened enough to be a slack or strengthened enough to be a stress must sometimes be left without a firm answer.

Another aspect of the problem of stress is presented by the shift of one-syllable words toward or away from stress, as context demands. In determining the degree of stress of one-syllable words it is helpful to know that regardless of context certain parts of speech are almost always stressed in actual usage: nouns, adjectives, adverbs, and, to a slightly lesser degree, demonstrative pronouns and active verbs. All other parts of speech are a question mark. However, a good formula for their treatment is to say that they are normally slack unless raised by context to a stress. This group includes articles, pronouns, passive verbs, the forms of the connective (auxiliary) verbs "to be" and "to have," and other connectives. A special problem is presented by prepositions. These are usually slack, unless raised by context to a stress; the fact that this rule holds true not only for the one-syllable prepositions but also for the two-syllable ones ("above," "under," "over," etc.) presents a certain difficulty. In the dictionary, each of these words is given a stressed syllable, in keeping with the general rule that all multisyllabic words in English have at least one stress. And if these words are spoken separately the stress is certainly there. But the reality is that in sentences said with conversational speed, the preposition is often so unimportant that its two syllables are sped over in such a way as unmistakably to subordinate them to their surroundings. In actual practice, the stress given these multisyllabic prepositions when they are uttered apart and alone is, in the context of a phrase, often practically eliminated.

I can perhaps put this problem more clearly in another way: at least one source of the trouble seems to be that often English in part seems to orient its stress entirely around a preordained stress on given syllables.

But at other times it simply does not do so. It has been pointed out, for instance, that the rather staccato effect of Spanish seems to arise from the fact that all syllables take approximately the same time to pronounce. In English on the other hand we often are willing enough to compress quite a number of syllables together (and suppress their stresses) for the sake of getting to and emphasizing a much later but more important stress. Professor Kenneth Pike,* who has pointed this fact out to us, thinks that in English we *time stress* rather than syllable stress; that is, we keep the major stressed syllables about an equal temporal distance apart and, in so doing, crush the lesser syllables together. Thus,

He′ is my friend.′

He′ is my very good friend.′

I have already indicated I think English is *sometimes* syllable stressed. I must add a further qualification and say that although English may be sometimes completely (and at other times to a degree) time stressed, this element of time stressing is of very little use in the practical determination of stress by the lay reader. I think it much more important, much more dominating, that English tends to yield its stress to *dramatic* (contextual) considerations, and that the final stressing of a phrase tends to represent a compromise between the (lexical) syllable stress and the dramatic (or contextual) stress. Thus in our phrase above, we all recognize that the word

"very" has, when spoken by itself, a stressed syllable, "very."′ But it is possible to imagine that phrase said rapidly enough that the syllable stress on "very" will yield to the time stress of the important first and last words. But we can modify all that quite easily by *dramatic* considerations.

A. He′ is my friend.′
B. Is he a bad friend?
A. He′ is my very good′ friend.′

A. He′ is my friend.′
B. How good a friend is he?
A. He is my ve′ry good′ friend.′

And, bearing in mind the uncertain stress of the pronoun, notice how easy it is to remove a stress from "he."

A. He′ is my friend.′
B. Is he a good friend or a very good friend?
A. I'm sure′ he is my ve′ry good′ friend.′

* Kenneth Pike, *The Intonation of American English* (Ann Arbor: 1946).

Thus it would seem that in English, on the level of syllable stress, it is difficult to say exactly what constitutes a stress or to determine the exact force of a major or secondary stress. Furthermore, when it occurs in a phrase, this variant syllable stress can be strengthened, weakened, or for practical purposes eliminated by a tendency of English to make time stressing a major element. And beyond that yet, time stress cannot help us determine the stress, for it and syllable stress can and do yield to the over-mastering and fluctuating demands of dramatic stress. It is small wonder that the degree of stress or slack of a given word, pushed relatively this way and relatively that way by these three forces, the syllable stress, the time stress and the dramatic stress, is often difficult to assess. That is why such parts of speech as active verbs, nouns, and, to a slightly lesser degree, adjectives and adverbs, being almost always *dramatically* important, sel-dom yield their syllable stress completely to the exigencies of time stress. Conversely, that is why such oftentimes dramatically unimportant words as pronouns, prepositions, and auxiliary verbs yield their syllable stress so readily to time stress and its attendant patterns of phrasing.

And it must further be added that stress and slack are relative things, that a weak stress in a cluster of four or five slacks will sound like a firm stress, whereas that same weak stress in a cluster of powerful stresses will probably be marked as a slack. Though it is no shock any more to be told that something is relative, such a realization does not comfort one who is in the act of scanning. But it does lead to a very important truth about scansion. This truth is that the average ear must be *trained* to recognize the rhythms of language on a conscious level, insofar as this infinite com-plexity must be reduced to a syllable stress or slack, just as surely as it must be trained to recognize subtleties of musical rhythm insofar as they are to be reduced to a mathematical score. The human ego leads one to presume that, because he can speak with proper accent, he therefore con-sciously knows what he is hearing and that he can write a proper scansion of a phrase automatically. But it is my experience in many years of teach-ing students to scan that, although some students learn the basic skill quickly and pleasurably and others over a longer period of time and with difficulty, nonetheless all must *learn* it. Scholars, by using machines, have discovered not two or three, but many levels of stress; indeed the number of discernible levels seems to be limited only by the sensitivity of the mechanical means of distinguishing them. These nuances may prove useful in many ways, especially in the subtleties of the oral performance. But for our present purposes of scanning, the usefulness of such delicate dis-criminations is nil.

Apart from the question of poetic *intention* — and it is simply common sense that no poet from Anglo-Saxon times up to the present has ever composed poetry based on a system of stress using such fine distinctions consciously — apart from poetic intention, the reader *cannot,* however fine his rhythmic ear may be, translate these distinctions into accurate conscious scansions. But the reader should not despair. Since the human ear is the machine for discriminating stress which is available to both the poet and the reader, the reader is likely to find his ear, if trained, an adequate instrument. Through the history of modern English, readers have been content with grouping the full range of strength of stress, for purposes of scanning, into three groups, the stress, the slack, and something less certain in between. And it has been content with doing so because *that is all on the conscious level that the reader is consistently capable of annotating.* All the other more subtly felicitous variations and rhythmic adjustments are there, are vital, central, but they must be by and large not only unconscious, but they must vary, within certain tolerable limits, from person to person.

Moving on, then, into some brief suggestions as to scansion, let us be content with this simple scheme, which will put one roughly on the right road to find the phrase's rhythm:

x = slack, ′ = stress, ? = that which is in between, or uncertain.

Remember that although scanning is a process of reducing the actual rich variations of vocalized stress into a simplified abstraction of basically three elements — stress, slack, and undetermined — that is not to say that the natural speech rhythms are ignored. I have had students who in previous classes had been instructed that the process of scanning is one of making a decision as to what the basic rhythm is (iambic, for instance) and then proceeding to mark off the syllables mechanically with an unvarying iambic pattern, regardless of how they are spoken.

$$x′ \quad x′ \quad x′ \quad x′$$
$$x′ \quad x′ \quad x′ \quad x′$$
etc.

To mark lines in this mechanical fashion is to negate all conceivable purposes for doing a scansion, for the subtleties of this smallest rhythmic unit of the language, the syllable, rise from constantly shifting combinations of sound created out of the *ordering* of natural speech rhythm, whether that ordering on the part of the writer was conscious or not. Not only is the metronome devoid of rhythm in the aesthetic sense, but it should also be understood that the nearer a rhythm gets to regularity the more important it is to hear the variations that do exist.

Thus, in a passage like this from Whitman,

× ´ × × ´ × ´ × ´ × × ´ × × ´ × × ´ × ´
I think I could turn and live with animals, they are so placid and self-contained
× ´ × ´ × × ´ × ´
I stand and look at them long and long,
´ × × ´ × ´ × × ´ × × ´ ×
They do not sweat and whine about their condition

a syllable scanned wrongly here and there, though perhaps misleading in detail, is not in this poem likely to give a false idea of the basic rhythm, for that rhythm is very irregular, very close to conversation, with the main rhythmic element contained in the balancing of whole phrases.

However in such a passage as this from "Children of Light" by Robert Lowell

× ´ × ´ × ´ × ´ × ´
Our fathers wrung their bread from stocks and stones
× ´ × ´ × ´ × ´ × ´
And fenced their gardens with the Redman's bones

it is absolutely essential to catch accurately the one strong variation from the repeated slack-stress pattern (a type of rhythm usually called "iambic"). It is remarkable how these powerful lines disintegrate if this variation is not caught. The couplet loses snap, the climactic power of "the Redman's bones" to shock is reduced, and the solid march of the beat backed up by percussive sound devices ceases to be something powerful and strong and begins to be something to be regretted. So much does the poet depend upon his reader to *hear*. Naturally, when we read this poem aloud, we shall restore to the abstract scansion full range of subtleties of degree of stress and slack. But the scansion forces us to discover consciously where stress lies and does not lie and, in this sense, helps us both to avoid crude errors of emphasis in our reading and consciously to relate the pattern of rhythmic emphasis to all the other elements leading to a unified awareness of the total meaning of the work.

As there is no substitute for actual conversation in learning to speak a language, so there is no other way to learn to scan than by scanning. Again, in a practical way, it is a great mistake to start scanning too slowly. Rhythm, after all, even at its subtlest, is a flow, an interweaving of sounds at a rate that must in common sense have its minimum and its maximum speeds. In fact, I gave the earlier suggestions as to what parts of speech are usually stressed or slacked with great reluctance. For, once these suggestions are taken as rules, the temptation is to stop and consider, in a conscious way, what part of speech each word is, thus ending any possibility of establishing an inner sense of the rhythm. What are wanted after all are intelligent readers who *hear* the poetry *as they read it* and who can hear it accurately enough to translate it into a living voice. And no reader can so hear the rhythm if each word is a separate, conscious rhythmic problem. Poets do not want scholars of rhythm; they want that great audience (of one person, or of thousands) without which the poem is a sleeping beauty.

In practicing scansion, then, it is far better, particularly in the beginning, to do ten passages in an hour with many mistakes, than to do one in an hour with few mistakes. The thing is to catch the run of the rhythm and to learn to ride it. Don't hop off just because you come to a syllable you are not swiftly certain of. Jot down a question mark and speed on. When you are finished with the passage and have taken full advantage of the moving swing, counterbalances, syncopations of the rhythm, then there is time to return to the question marks and mull them over a bit. This initial scansion should, in fact, be done at as near the normal speaking rate appropriate to the passage as the mechanics of making the marks of scansion will allow.

Although scansion is usually thought of in relation to poetry, the rhythm of syllable is by no means excluded from prose as an important element. Conversely, this most elemental of the rhythms of English is not always the main force either in poetry or in prose, since the central rhythmic power can be carried by phrase, or sentence, or even stanza and paragraph. In neither case is it necessary to chop the rhythm up into "feet" (except in some types of poems where this division seems a part of the author's metric intention [see Chapter thirteen, "Meter"]), for it is extremely doubtful if as much can be seen in that way as by a shrewd discernment of rhythmic *themes* as they occur in context.

Children of Light*

Our fathers wrung their bread from stocks and stones
And fenced their gardens with the Redman's bones;
Embarking from the Nether Land of Holland,
Pilgrims unhouseled by Geneva's night,
They planted here the Serpent's seeds of light;
And here the pivoting searchlights probe to shock
The riotous glass houses built on rock,
And candles gutter by an empty altar,
And light is where the landless blood of Cain
Is burning, burning the unburied grain.

ROBERT LOWELL

* From *Lord Weary's Castle*, copyright, 1944, 1946, by Robert Lowell. Reprinted by permission of Harcourt, Brace & World, Inc.

In this poem there are two primary rhythmic elements. One is the line, which is powerfully reinforced by the solid rhymes, and little modified by the run-on lines and by the two thorn (unrhymed) lines. The second is the syllabic beat, which is either a solid two-part, mostly iambic (slack-stress) rhythm, or a simple but sharp syncopation of the beat. Within that framework, the syncopations — on the whole simple ones — are used to reinforce variations in tone in the development of the over-all statement.

The poem is essentially in two rhetorical parts, the dividing point being the semicolon. In the first part we are told what the pilgrims did. In the second part we are told what the land of their founding is like now. It is interesting to see how little rhythmic variation there is in the first five lines. Only in one line is the strong regularity of rhythm interrupted more than momentarily, and that is the line describing the pilgrims as "unhoused," where the rhythm would seem appropriate to the sense of displacement, of being cast out. Also appropriately, more irregularity is to be observed in the second half, though again this is confined to reinforcing details and does not too much modify the straightforward power of the poem. One notices such lines as the seventh, where the rhythmic syncopations of the "riotous glass houses" snaps abruptly back to the solid rhythm with the statement that they are "built on rock."

Such appropriate handling in syllabic rhythm is, as I have said, not confined to poetry. In "Two Sides to a Tortoise" the only short sentence which is set apart from all the others by making it a complete paragraph, the sentence which is the invocation to spiritual unity with the tortoises, looks like this:

> ′ ′ × × ′ ×× × ′ × ′ × ′ × ′ × ′
> Ye oldest inhabitants of this, or any other isle, said I,
> ′ ′ × × ′ × × × ′ ′ ′
> pray, give me the freedom of your three walled towns.

One may notice the rhythmic balance which reinforces the emotional centrality of this invocation. Observe the rhythmic similarity of the underscored phrases.

> ′ ′ × × ′ × × × ′ , × ′ × ′ × ′ × ′ , ′ , ′ × × ′ × × × ′ ′ ′

In the last paragraph of James Agee's "Knoxville: Summer of 1915," the author combines the movement away from the physical description which has been the main structural as well as emotional thread, with a rhythm which serves to reinforce this purpose as well as to conclude the essay.

    ′ × × ′ × × ×   ′ × ′ ×   ′ × ′   ′   ′
After a little I am taken in and put to bed. Sleep soft
    ′×   ′   × ′ × ×   ×   ′   × ′   ×   ×
smiling, draws me unto her: and those receive me, who
    ′× ×   ′   × × ′   × ′ × ×   ′   × ′   ×
quietly treat me, as one familiar and well-beloved in
    ′   ′   ×   ×   ′ ′   ′   ′   ′   ′   ′
that home: but will not, oh, will not, not now, not
  ′ ×   ×   ′   × ′ ×   ′   ×   ′ × ′
ever; but will not ever tell me who I am.

The sentence, down to the final colon, seems neither to establish a powerful regularity nor irregularity. It is pleasant, without being dull. The
change after the final colon is dramatic, and the long series of hard beats
serves to create a tension, reinforcing the suspense which is the rhetorical
purpose of postponing, by reiterated negatives, our coming to the knowledge of what "they" will not do. After the semicolon, when this knowledge
is finally given, it comes with great relief in a very regular rhythm, which
helps both to emphasize the finality of the sadness and to end the essay
with a release into a hitherto unknown smoothness.

This detection of rhythmic themes which can arise out of scansion
and out of their relationship to the meaning is perhaps more difficult in
poems and prose in which the syllable rhythm is quite irregular, and with,
perhaps, less relevance in detail. Nonetheless, the student should find it an
easy matter, by contrasting, say, *Sense And Sensibility* and "A Box to Hide
In," to see that different treatment of phrase and sentence and paragraph
can produce their own strong sense of individuality. In some authors, both
of prose and poetry, such larger rhythms are generally speaking made
paramount over the rhythm of syllable in conspicuous aesthetic impact.

In comparing "Home Burial" by Robert Frost and "Song of Myself
5," by Walt Whitman, the oral reader should be aware that here are
two poems whose rhythmic impacts do not primarily derive from rhythm
of syllable. Nonetheless, they are essentially different in their rhythmic
nature. It is clear that with Whitman the line is a constantly shifting variable (without fixed length) and that it is the phrase which carries the primary rhythmic impact, for it is the end of the phrase that marks the end
of the line. And this phrase is of a particular nature. It is seldom short, but
it is seldom longer than what can be said in a breath. In sum, a breath
phrase of varying lengths is the central rhythmic fact. This breath phrase,
in addition to gaining variety through differing lengths, is cross-fertilized
by a syllabic rhythm that sometimes comes quite close to regularity, at
other times moves quite far from it.

In "Home Burial," on the other hand, the line is a syllabically rigid
one of ten syllables, and this ten-syllable line is the metrically regular

fact of the poem. However, the syllabic rhythm is *never* regular, is always conversational rather than musical. Some lines are of quite startling and harsh rhythm:

$$\overset{\times}{\text{But}}\ \overset{\times}{\text{the}}\ \overset{\prime}{\text{child's}}\ \overset{\prime}{\text{mound}} \ . \ . \ .$$

$$\overset{\prime}{\text{Don't,}}\ \overset{\prime}{\text{don't,}}\ \overset{\prime}{\text{don't,}}\ \overset{\prime}{\text{don't,}}\ \overset{\times}{\text{she}}\ \overset{\prime}{\text{cried}}$$

This rigid length of line is played off primarily against the sentence. The sentence is primarily a *rational* entity, as opposed to the fragmentary and more emotionally centered phrase, and this rationality would seem in keeping with the objective narrator and the realistic conversation which must be aesthetically appropriate to the narrated sections. On the other hand Whitman the transcendental mystic is concerned not with realistic conversation, but with the rise and slackening of his own vision, so that the phrase, which may be simply an emotional part or whole, in conjunction with an ability to move from irregular to regular syllabic rhythms, would seem to be an appropriate rhythmic vehicle.

The Problem of Pause and Rubato

If it is difficult to mark in a meaningful way the stress and slack syllables, it is truly impossible to measure the length of a pause for purposes of scansion. Yet because pauses are a vital part of the total rhythmic pattern of a poem or story, there have been a number of attempts to devise a system for including them in scansion. Usually these have taken the form of some kind of analogy with a musical score, whereon one sees time relationships so satisfactorily and neatly defined.

But there would seem to be, for any practical, common-sense system, insurmountable difficulties. Even in music, it is never desirable to have in performance a metronomic fidelity to the musical score. In the performance that results between a meeting of the composer's and the performer's geniuses, the score is varied in its time relationships often by as much as one-third. I might say "distorted," except that, instead of an evil, it is just the performer's skill in disciplining and ordering this inevitable and desirable measure of distortion which marks the genius of his interpretation. The musician's name for this variance of rhythm from the mathematically exact score is "rubato." The reader must consider the greater rubato which is an inevitable part of the reading of a poem or a story. In the first place, the writer himself had no more to go on than his own highly developed "feel" of what is rhythmically right. He has set that feeling down in a way which *may* (in some *poetry*), or may not, have been partly formed by the measurement of the number of syllables, or feet, or stresses per line, but which even then attempted no mathematical scoring of the *time* it took to say one word, or one phrase, in relation to another. How, then, if he cannot score the time relationships of words and phrases, can the writer score that much more elusive temporal unit, the pause? Were it possible to make such judgments as that a colon takes twice as long a pause as a semicolon, a semicolon twice as long as a comma, something might be done. But merely suggesting this possibility shows its absurdity. For the pauses we are talking about are not *grammatical* pauses, but rather *dramatic* pauses, though one pause may serve both functions. And it is just in an accurate sense of the *dramatically appropriate length of a pause* that the reader's rubato comes in most powerfully.

It is possible to get on records the same soliloquy from *Hamlet* spoken by John Barrymore, Sir John Gielgud, and Sir Laurence Olivier, surely three of the most successful Shakespearian interpreters of this century. To play them one after another is to receive a sharp lesson in how the length of a pause is related to a *total interpretation,* for one hears quite a range in the handling of a given pause. Yet in none of the three interpretations is one aware of anything inappropriate.

What is at the bottom of these differences is at once crude and subtle. It is not to be expected that a physically powerful actor will interpret this soliloquy in the same way as a physically slender actor, or that one with a magnificent vocal timbre will interpret it in the same way as the actor whose vocal timbre is merely passable. For the actor's, or reader's, instrument is his voice and body, and he must adjust his strengths to his weaknesses, and what he knows and projects must be sufficiently powerful to compensate for what, being human, he inevitably does not know and does not project. These differences, added to differences of birth and background, lead inevitably to different (within an allowable range) projections of the same role. Thus actor A may, as a result of what he is, read a phrase at a medium rate, which may result in a longer pause following it than would be effective with another actor whose greater speed might render a long pause melodramatic. This kind of rubato is the inevitable and natural result, in short, of any reader's individual personality playing on the selection.

The question always must be whether or not we are convinced by the total concept projected by the combination of text and reader. And I do not refer here simply to actors or to persons reading aloud. It is my belief that no silent reader has come to an important living relationship to a text who has not heard, in his own mind, how he himself could say that passage with understanding and conviction. I am sure that the more we learn of human psychology and physiology, the more this theory is substantiated.

But let us turn from such theorizing to the more practical problem of pauses and their place in scansion. It seems advisable, for the various reasons touched upon here, simply to mark the pauses, with no attempt to fix their appropriate temporal duration. In short, pauses exist as a considerable, but generally very relative, element in any literary rhythm.

SELECTIONS

A Modest Proposal

FOR PREVENTING THE CHILDREN OF POOR
PEOPLE IN IRELAND FROM BEING A BURDEN
TO THEIR PARENTS OR COUNTRY, AND FOR
MAKING THEM BENEFICIAL TO THE PUBLIC

JONATHAN SWIFT (1667–1745)

It is a melancholy object to those who walk through this great town, or travel in the country, when they see the streets, the roads, and cabin-doors crowded with beggars of the female sex, followed by three, four, or six children, *all in rags,* and importuning every passenger for an alms. These mothers, instead of being able to work for their honest livelihood, are forced to employ all their time in strolling, to beg sustenance for their helpless infants, who, as they grow up, either turn thieves for want of work, or leave their dear Native Country to fight for the Pretender in Spain, or sell themselves to the Barbadoes.

I think it is agreed by all parties, that this prodigious number of children, in the arms, or on the backs, or at the heels of their mothers, and frequently of their fathers, is in the present deplorable state of the kingdom a very great additional grievance; and therefore whoever could find out a fair, cheap and easy method of making these children sound, useful members of the commonwealth would deserve so well of the public, as to have his statue set up for a preserver of the nation.

But my intention is very far from being confined to provide only for the children of professed beggars, it is of a much greater extent, and shall take in the whole number of infants at a certain age, who are born of parents in effect as little able to support them, as those who demand our charity in the streets.

As to my own part, having turned my thoughts, for many years, upon this important subject, and maturely weighed the several schemes of other projectors, I have always found them grossly mistaken in their computation. It is true a child, just dropped from its dam, may be supported by her milk for a solar year with little other nourishment, at most not above the value of two shillings, which the mother may certainly get, or the value in scraps, by her lawful occupation of begging, and it is exactly at one year old that I propose to provide for them, in such a manner, as, instead of being a charge upon their parents, or the parish, or wanting food and raiment for the rest of their lives, they shall, on the contrary, contribute to the feeding and partly to the clothing of many thousands.

There is likewise another great advantage in my scheme, that it will prevent those voluntary abortions, and that horrid practice of women murdering their bastard children, alas, too frequent among us, sacrificing the poor innocent babes, I doubt, more to avoid the expense, than the shame, which would move tears and pity in the most savage and inhuman breast.

The number of souls in this kingdom being usually reckoned one million and a half, of these I calculate there may be about two hundred thousand couples whose wives are breeders, from which number I subtract thirty thousand couples, who are able to maintain their own children, although I apprehend there cannot be so many under the present distresses of the kingdom, but this being granted, there will remain an hundred and seventy thousand breeders. I again subtract fifty thousand for those women who miscarry, or whose children die by accident, or disease within the year. There only remain an hundred and twenty thousand children of poor parents annually born: the question therefore is, how this number shall be reared, and provided for, which, as I have already said, under the present situation of affairs, is utterly impossible by all the methods hitherto proposed, for we can neither employ them in handicraft, or agriculture; we neither build houses, (I mean in the country) nor cultivate land: they can very seldom pick up a livelihood by stealing till they arrive at six years old, except where they are of towardly parts, although, I confess they learn the rudiments much earlier, during which time, they can however be properly looked upon only as *probationers,* as I have been informed by a principal gentleman in the County of Cavan, who protested to me, that he never knew above one or two instances under the age of six, even in a part of the kingdom so renowned for the quickest proficiency in that art.

I am assured by our merchants, that a boy or a girl, before twelve years old, is no saleable commodity, and even when they come to this age, they will not yield above three pounds, or three pounds and half-a-crown at most on the Exchange, which cannot turn to account either to the parents or kingdom, the charge of nutriment and rags having been at least four times that value.

I shall now therefore humbly propose my own thoughts, which I hope will not be liable to the least objection.

I have been assured by a very knowing American of my acquaintance in London, that a young healthy child well nursed is at a year old a most delicious, nourishing, and wholesome food, whether stewed, roasted, baked, or boiled, and I make no doubt that it will equally serve in a fricassee or a ragout.

I do therefore humbly offer it to public consideration, that of the hundred and twenty thousand children, already computed, twenty thousand may be reserved for breed, whereof only one fourth part to be males, which is more than we allow to sheep, black-cattle, or swine, and my reason is that these children are seldom the fruits of marriage, a circumstance not much regarded by our savages; therefore one male will be sufficient to serve four females. That the remaining hundred thousand may at a year old be offered in sale to the persons of quality, and fortune, through the kingdom, always advising the mother to let them suck plentifully in the last month, so as to render them plump, and fat for a good table. A child will make two dishes at an entertainment for friends, and when the family dines alone, the fore or hind quarter will make a reasonable dish, and seasoned with a little pepper or salt will be very good boiled on the fourth day, especially in winter.

I have reckoned upon a medium, that a child just born will weigh 12 pounds, and in a solar year if tolerably nursed increaseth to 28 pounds.

I grant this food will be somewhat dear, and therefore very proper for landlords, who, as they have already devoured most of the parents, seem to have the best title to the children.

Infants' flesh will be in season throughout the year, but more plentiful in March, and a little before and after, for we are told by a grave author, an eminent French Physician, that fish being a prolific diet, there are more children born in Roman Catholic countries about nine months after Lent, than at any other season; therefore reckoning a year after Lent, the markets will be more glutted than usual, because the number of Popish infants is at least three to one in this kingdom, and therefore it will have one other collateral advantage by lessening the number of Papists among us.

I have already computed the charge of nursing a beggar's child (in which list I reckon all cottagers, labourers, and four-fifths of the farmers) to be about two shillings *per annum,* rags included, and I believe no gentleman would repine to give ten shillings for the carcass of a good fat child, which, as I have said, will make four dishes of excellent nutritive meat, when he hath only some particular friend, or his own family to dine with him. Thus the Squire will learn to be a good landlord, and grow popular among his tenants, the mother will have eight shillings net profit, and be fit for work till she produces another child.

Those who are more thrifty (as I must confess the times require) may flay the carcass; the skin of which, artificially dressed, will make admirable gloves for ladies, and summer boots for fine gentlemen.

As to our City of Dublin, shambles may be appointed for this purpose, in the most convenient parts of it, and butchers we may be assured will not be wanting, although I rather recommend buying the children alive, and dressing them hot from the knife, as we do roasting pigs.

A very worthy person, a true lover of his country, and whose virtues I highly esteem, was lately pleased, in discoursing on this matter, to offer a refinement upon my scheme. He said, that many gentlemen of this kingdom, having of late destroyed their deer, he conceived that the want of venison might be well supplied by the bodies of young lads and maidens, not exceeding fourteen years of age, nor under twelve, so great a number of both sexes in every country being now ready to starve, for want of work and service: and these to be disposed of by their parents if alive, or otherwise by their nearest relations. But with due deference to so excellent a friend, and so deserving a patriot, I cannot be altogether in his sentiments; for as to the males, my American acquaintance assured me from frequent experience, that their flesh was generally tough and lean, like that of our schoolboys, by continual exercise, and their taste disagreeable, and to fatten them would not answer the charge. Then as to the females, it would, I think with humble submission, be a loss to the public, because they soon would become breeders themselves: and besides, it is not improbable that some scrupulous people might be apt to censure such a practice, (although indeed very unjustly) as a little bordering upon cruelty, which, I confess, hath always been with me the strongest objection against any project, however so well intended.

But in order to justify my friend, he confessed that this expedient was put into his head by the famous Psalmanazar, a native of the island Formosa, who came from thence to London, above twenty years ago, and in conversation told my friend, that in his country when any young person happened to be put to death, the executioner sold the carcass to persons of quality, as a prime dainty, and that, in his time, the body of a plump girl of fifteen, who was crucified for an attempt to poison the emperor, was sold to his Imperial Majesty's Prime Minister of State, and other great Mandarins of the Court, in joints from the gibbet, at four hundred crowns. Neither indeed can I deny, that if the same use were made of several plump young girls in this town, who, without one single groat to their fortunes, cannot stir abroad without a chair, and appear at the playhouse, and assemblies in foreign fineries, which they never will pay for, the kingdom would not be the worse.

Some persons of a desponding spirit are in great concern about that vast number of poor people, who are aged, diseased, or maimed, and I have been desired to employ my thoughts what course may be taken, to ease the nation of so grievous an encumbrance. But I am not in the least pain upon that matter, because it is very well known, that they are every day dying, and rotting, by cold, and famine, and filth, and vermin, as fast as can be reasonably expected. And as to the younger labourers they are now in almost as hopeful a condition. They cannot get work, and consequently pine away for want of nourishment, to a degree, that if at any time they are accidentally hired to common labour, they have not strength to perform it; and thus the country and themselves are in a fair way of being soon delivered from the evils to come.

I have too long digressed, and therefore shall return to my subject. I think the advantages by the proposal which I have made are obvious and many, as well as of the highest importance.

For first, as I have already observed, it would greatly lessen the number of Papists, with whom we are yearly over-run, being the principal breeders of the nation, as well as our most dangerous enemies, and who stay at home on purpose with a design to deliver the kingdom to the Pretender, hoping to take their advantage by the absence of so many good Protestants, who have chosen rather to leave their country, than stay at home, and pay tithes against their conscience, to an Episcopal curate.

Secondly, The poorer tenants will have something valuable of their own, which by law may be made liable to distress, and help to pay their landlord's rent, their corn and cattle being already seized, and *money a thing unknown.*

Thirdly, Whereas the maintenance of an hundred thousand children, from two years old, and upwards, cannot be computed at less than ten shillings a piece *per annum*, the nation's stock will be thereby increased fifty thousand pounds *per annum*, besides the profit of a new dish, introduced to the tables of all gentlemen of fortune in the kingdom, who have any refinement in taste, and the money will circulate among ourselves, the goods being entirely of our own growth and manufacture.

Fourthly, The constant breeders, besides the gain of eight shillings sterling *per annum*, by the sale of their children, will be rid of the charge of maintaining them after the first year.

Fifthly, This food would likewise bring great custom to taverns, where the vintners will certainly be so prudent as to procure the best receipts for dressing it to perfection, and consequently have their houses frequented by all the fine gentlemen, who justly value themselves upon their knowledge in good eating; and a skilful cook, who understands how to oblige his guests, will contrive to make it as expensive as they please.

Sixthly, This would be a great inducement to marriage, which all wise nations have either encouraged by rewards, or enforced by laws and penalties. It would increase the care and tenderness of mothers toward their children, when they were sure of a settlement for life, to the poor babes, provided in some sort by the public to their annual profit instead of expense. We should see an honest emulation among the married women, which of them could bring the fattest child to the market; men would become as fond of their wives, during the time of their pregnancy, as they are now of their mares in foal, their cows in calf, or sows when they are ready to farrow, nor offer to beat or kick them (as is too frequent a practice) for fear of a miscarriage.

Many other advantages might be enumerated: For instance, the addition of some thousand carcasses in our exportation of barrelled beef; the propagation of swine's flesh, and improvement in the art of making good bacon, so much wanted among us by the great destruction of pigs, too frequent at our tables, which are no way comparable in taste, or magnificence to a well-grown, fat yearling child, which roasted whole will make a considerable figure at a Lord Mayor's feast, or any other public entertainment. But this, and many others I omit, being studious of brevity.

Supposing that one thousand families in this city, would be constant customers for infants' flesh, beside others who might have it at merry-meetings, particularly weddings and christenings, I compute that Dublin would take off annually about twenty thousand carcasses, and the rest of the kingdom (where probably they will be sold somewhat cheaper) the remaining eighty thousand.

I can think of no one objection, that will probably be raised against this proposal, unless it should be urged that the number of people will be thereby much lessened in the kingdom. This I freely own, and was indeed one principal design in offering it to the world. I desire the reader will observe, that I calculate my remedy *for this one individual Kingdom of Ireland, and for no other that ever was, is, or, I think, ever can be upon earth.* Therefore let no man talk to me of other expedients: *Of taxing our absentees at five shillings a pound: Of using neither clothes, nor household furniture, except what is of our own growth and manufacture: Of utterly rejecting the materials and instruments that promote foreign luxury: Of curing the expensiveness of pride, vanity, idleness, and gaming in our women: Of introducing a vein of parsimony, prudence and temperance: Of learning to love our Country, wherein we differ even from LAP-LANDERS, and the inhabitants of TOPINAMBOO: Of quitting our animosities and factions, nor act any longer like the Jews, who were murdering one another at the very moment their city was taken: Of being a little cautious not to sell our country and consciences for nothing: Of teaching landlords to have at least one degree of mercy toward their tenants. Lastly, of putting a spirit of honesty, industry, and skill into our shopkeepers, who, if a resolution could now be taken to buy our native goods, would immediately unite to cheat and exact upon us in the price, the measure, and the goodness, nor could ever yet be brought to make one fair proposal of just dealing, though often and earnestly invited to it.*

Therefore, I repeat, let no man talk to me of these and the like expedients, till he hath at least some glimpse of hope that there will ever be some hearty and sincere attempt to put them in practice.

But as to myself, having been wearied out for many years with offering vain, idle, visionary thoughts, and at length utterly despairing of success, I fortunately fell upon this proposal, which as it is wholly new, so it hath something solid and real, of no expense and little trouble, full in our own power, and whereby we can incur no danger in *disobliging* ENGLAND. For this kind of commodity will not bear exportation, the flesh being of too tender a consistence, to admit a long continuance in salt, *although perhaps I could name a country, which would be glad to eat up our whole nation without it.*

After all, I am not so violently bent upon my own opinion, as to reject any offer, proposed by wise men, which shall be found equally innocent, cheap, easy and effectual. But before something of that kind shall be advanced in contradiction to my scheme, and offering a better, I desire the author, or authors will be pleased maturely to consider two points. First, as things now stand, how they will be able to find food and raiment for an hundred thousand useless mouths and backs. And secondly, there being a round million of creatures in human figure, throughout this kingdom, whose whole subsistence put into a common stock would leave them in debt two millions of pounds sterling; adding those who are beggars by profession to the bulk of farmers, cottagers, and labourers with their wives and children, who are beggars in effect; I desire those politicians who dislike my overture, and may perhaps be so bold to attempt an answer, that they will first ask the parents of these mortals, whether they would not at this day think it a great happiness to have been sold for food at a year old, in the manner I prescribe, and thereby have avoided such a perpetual scene of misfortunes, as they have since gone through, by the oppression of landlords, the impossibility of paying rent without money or trade, the want of common sustenance, with neither house nor clothes to cover them from the inclemencies of the weather, and the most inevitable prospect of entailing the like, or greater miseries upon their breed for ever.

I profess in the sincerity of my heart that I have not the least personal interest in endeavouring to promote this necessary work, having no other motive than the *public good of my country, by advancing our trade, providing for infants, relieving the poor, and giving some pleasure to the rich.* I have no children, by which I can propose to get a single penny; the youngest being nine years old, and my wife past child-bearing.

"Childe Roland to the Dark Tower Came"
[See Edgar's song in "Lear"]

I

My first thought was, he lied in every word,
  That hoary cripple, with malicious eye
  Askance to watch the working of his lie
On mine, and mouth scarce able to afford
Suppression of the glee, that pursed and scored
  Its edge, at one more victim gained thereby.

II

What else should he be set for, with his staff?
  What, save to waylay with his lies, ensnare
  All travellers who might find him posted there,
And ask the road? I guessed what skull-like laugh
Would break, what crutch 'gin write my epitaph
  For pastime in the dusty thoroughfare,

III

If at his counsel I should turn aside
  Into that ominous tract which, all agree,
  Hides the Dark Tower. Yet acquiescingly
I did turn as he pointed: neither pride
Nor hope rekindling at the end descried,
  So much as gladness that some end might be.

IV

For, what with my whole world-wide wandering,
  What with my search drawn out thro' years, my hope
  Dwindled into a ghost not fit to cope
With that obstreperous joy success would bring, —
I hardly tried now to rebuke the spring
  My heart made, finding failure in its scope.

V

As when a sick man very near to death
  Seems dead indeed, and feels begin and end
  The tears and takes the farewell of each friend,
And hears one bid the other go, draw breath
Freelier outside, ("since all is o'er," he saith,
  "And the blow fallen no grieving can amend;")

VI

While some discuss if near the other graves
   Be room enough for this, and when a day
   Suits best for carrying the corpse away,
With care about the banners, scarves and staves:
And still the man hears all, and only craves
   He may not shame such tender love and stay.

VII

Thus, I had so long suffered in this quest,
   Heard failure prophesied so oft, been writ
   So many times among "The Band" — to wit,
The knights who to the Dark Tower's search addressed
Their steps — that just to fail as they, seemed best,
   And all the doubt was now — should I be fit?

VIII

So, quiet as despair, I turned from him,
   That hateful cripple, out of his highway
   Into the path he pointed. All the day
Had been a dreary one at best, and dim
Was settling to its close, yet shot one grim
   Red leer to see the plain catch its estray.[1]

IX

For mark! no sooner was I fairly found
   Pledged to the plain, after a pace or two,
   Than, pausing to throw backward a last view
O'er the safe road, 'twas gone; grey plain all round:
Nothing but plain to the horizon's bound.
   I might go on; nought else remained to do.

X

So, on I went. I think I never saw
   Such starved ignoble nature; nothing throve:
   For flowers — as well expect a cedar grove!
But cockle, spurge, according to their law
Might propagate their kind, with none to awe,
   You'd think; a burr had been a treasure-trove.

[1] wanderer

XI

No! penury, inertness and grimace,
   In some strange sort, were the land's portion. "See
   Or shut your eyes," said Nature peevishly,
"It nothing skills: I cannot help my case:
'Tis the Last Judgment's fire must cure this place,
   Calcine² its clods and set my prisoners free."

XII

If there pushed any ragged thistle-stalk
   Above its mates, the head was chopped; the bents³
   Were jealous else. What made those holes and rents
In the dock's⁴ harsh swarth leaves, bruised as to baulk
All hope of greenness? 'tis a brute must walk
   Pashing⁵ their life out, with a brute's intents.

XIII

As for the grass, it grew as scant as hair
   In leprosy; thin dry blades pricked the mud
   Which underneath looked kneaded up with blood.
One stiff blind horse, his every bone a-stare,
Stood stupefied, however he came there:
   Thrust out past service from the devil's stud!

XIV

Alive? he might be dead for aught I know,
   With that red gaunt and colloped⁶ neck a-strain,
   And shut eyes underneath the rusty mane;
Seldom went such grotesqueness with such woe;
I never saw a brute I hated so;
   He must be wicked to deserve such pain.

XV

I shut my eyes and turned them on my heart.
   As a man calls for wine before he fights,
   I asked one drought of earlier, happier sights,
Ere fitly I could hope to play my part.
Think first, fight afterwards — the soldier's art:
   One taste of the old time sets all to rights.

² Reduce to powder by heat.   ⁵ crushing
³ coarse grasses   ⁶ ridge-marked
⁴ weed's

XVI

Not it! I fancied Cuthbert's reddening face
  Beneath its garniture of curly gold,
  Dear fellow, till I almost felt him fold
An arm in mine to fix me to the place,
That way he used. Alas, one night's disgrace!
  Out went my heart's new fire and left it cold.

XVII

Giles then, the soul of honour — there he stands
  Frank as ten years ago when knighted first.
  What honest men should dare (he said) he durst.
Good — but the scene shifts — faugh! what hangman's hands
Pin to his breast a parchment? His own bands
  Read it. Poor traitor, spit upon and curst!

XVIII

Better this present than a past like that;
  Back therefore to my darkening path again!
  No sound, no sight as far as eye could strain.
Will the night send a howlet or a bat?
I asked: when something on the dismal flat
  Came to arrest my thoughts and change their train.

XIX

A sudden little river crossed my path
  As unexpected as a serpent comes.
  No sluggish tide congenial to the glooms;
This, as it frothed by, might have been a bath
For the fiend's glowing hoof — to see the wrath
  Of its black eddy bespate with flakes and spumes.

XX

So petty yet so spiteful! all along,
  Low scrubby alders kneeled down over it;
  Drenched willows flung them headlong in a fit
Of mute despair, a suicidal throng:
The river which had done them all the wrong,
  Whate'er that was, rolled by, deterred no whit.

XXI

Which, while I forded, — good saints, how I feared
   To set my foot upon a dead man's cheek,
   Each step, or feel the spear I thrust to seek
For hollows, tangled in his hair or beard!
— It may have been a water-rat I speared,
   But, ugh! it sounded like a baby's shriek.

XXII

Glad was I when I reached the other bank.
   Now for a better country. Vain presage!
   Who were the strugglers, what war did they wage,
Whose savage trample thus could pad the dank
Soil to a plash? Toads in a poisoned tank,
   Or wild cats in a red-hot iron cage —

XXIII

The fight must so have seemed in that fell cirque.
   What penned them there, with all the plain to choose?
   No foot-print leading to that horrid mews,
None out of it. Mad brewage set to work
Their brains, no doubt, like galley-slaves the Turk
   Pits for his pastime, Christians against Jews.

XXIV

And more than that — a furlong on — why, there!
   What bad use was that engine for, that wheel,
   Or brake, not wheel — that harrow fit to reel
Men's bodies out like silk? with all the air
Of Tophet's tool, on earth left unaware,
   Or brought to sharpen its rusty teeth of steel.

XXV

Then came a bit of stubbed ground, once a wood,
   Next a marsh, it would seem, and now mere earth
   Desperate and done with; (so a fool finds mirth,
Makes a thing and then mars it, till his mood
Changes and off he goes!) within a rood —
   Bog, clay and rubble, sand and stark black dearth.

XXVI

Now blotches rankling, coloured gay and grim,
   Now patches where some leanness of the soil's
   Broke into moss or substances like boils;
Then came some palsied oak, a cleft in him
Like a distorted mouth that splits its rim
   Gaping at death, and dies while it recoils.

XXVII

And just as far as ever from the end!
   Nought in the distance but the evening, nought
   To point my footstep further! At the thought,
A great black bird, Apollyon's[7] bosom-friend,
Sailed past, nor beat his wide wing dragon-penned
   That brushed my cap — perchance the guide I sought.

XXVIII

For, looking up, aware I somehow grew,
   'Spite of the dusk, the plain had given place
   All round to mountains — with such name to grace
Mere ugly heights and heaps now stolen in view.
How thus they had surprised me, — solve it, you!
   How to get from them was no clearer case.

XXIX

Yet half I seemed to recognise some trick
   Of mischief happened to me, God knows when —
   In a bad dream perhaps. Here ended, then,
Progress this way. When, in the very nick
Of giving up, one time more, came a click
   As when a trap shuts — you're inside the den!

XXX

Burningly it came on me all at once,
   This was the place! those two hills on the right,
   Crouched like two bulls locked horn in horn in fight;
While to the left, a tall scalped mountain . . . Dunce,
Dotard, a-dozing at the very nonce,
   After a life spent training for the sight!

7 The angel of the bottomless pit; see *Revelation*, ix, 2.

XXXI

What in the midst lay but the Tower itself?
  The round squat turret, blind as the fool's heart,
  Built of brown stone, without a counterpart
In the whole world. The tempest's mocking elf
Points to the shipman thus the unseen shelf
  He strikes on, only when the timbers start.

XXXII

Not see? because of night perhaps? — Why, day
  Came back again for that! before it left,
  The dying sunset kindled through a cleft:
The hills, like giants at a hunting, lay,
Chin upon hand, to see the game at bay, —
  "Now stab and end the creature — to the heft!"

XXXIII

Not hear? when noise was everywhere! it tolled
  Increasing like a bell. Names in my ears,
  Of all the lost adventurers my peers, —
Now such a one was strong, and such was bold,
And such was fortunate, yet each of old
  Lost, lost! one moment knelled the woe of years.

XXXIV

There they stood, ranged along the hillsides, met
  To view the last of me, a living frame
  For one more picture! in a sheet of flame
I saw them and I knew them all. And yet
Dauntless the slug-horn to my lips I set,
  And blew. *"Childe Roland to the Dark Tower came."*

ROBERT BROWNING [1855]

Kubla Khan[8]

In Xanadu did Kubla Khan
A stately pleasure-dome decree:
Where Alph, the sacred river, ran
Through caverns measureless to man
  Down to a sunless sea.
So twice five miles of fertile ground
With walls and towers were girdled round:
And there were gardens bright with sinuous rills,
Where blossomed many an incense-bearing tree;
And here were forests ancient as the hills,
Enfolding sunny spots of greenery.

But oh! that deep romantic chasm which slanted
Down the green hill athwart a cedarn cover!
A savage place! as holy and enchanted
As e'er beneath a waning moon was haunted
By woman wailing for her demon-lover!
And from this chasm, with ceaseless turmoil seething,
As if this earth in fast thick pants were breathing,
A mighty fountain momently was forced:
Amid whose swift half-intermitted burst

---

[8] Written in 1798. Published in 1816. A preface by the author explains the occasion of the composition: "In the summer of the year 1797 [1798], the Author, then in ill health, had retired to a lonely farm-house. . . . In consequence of a slight indisposition, an anodyne had been prescribed, from the effects of which he fell asleep in his chair at the moment that he was reading the following sentence, or words of the same substance, in 'Purchas's Pilgrimage': 'Here the Khan Kubla commanded a palace to be built, and a stately garden thereunto. And thus ten miles of fertile ground were inclosed with a wall.' The Author continued for about three hours in a profound sleep, at least of the external senses, during which time he has the most vivid confidence, that he could not have composed less than from two to three hundred lines; if that indeed can be called composition in which all the images rose up before him as *things*, with a parallel production of the correspondent expressions, without any sensation or consciousness of effort. On awaking he appeared to himself to have a distinct recollection of the whole, and taking his pen, ink, and paper, instantly and eagerly wrote down the lines that are here preserved. At this moment he was unfortunately called out by a person on business from Porlock, and detained by him above an hour, and on his return to his room, found, to his no small surprise and mortification, that though he still retained some vague and dim recollection of the general purport of the vision, yet, with the exception of some eight or ten scattered lines and images, all the rest had passed away like the images on the surface of a stream into which a stone has been cast, but, alas! without the after restoration of the latter!"

Huge fragments vaulted like rebounding hail,
Or chaffy grain beneath the thresher's flail:
And 'mid these dancing rocks at once and ever
It flung up momently the sacred river.
Five miles meandering with a mazy motion
Through wood and dale the sacred river ran,
Then reached the caverns measureless to man,
And sank in tumult to a lifeless ocean:
And 'mid this tumult Kubla heard from far
Ancestral voices prophesying war!

The shadow of the dome of pleasure
Floated midway on the waves;
Where was heard the mingled measure
From the fountain and the caves.
It was a miracle of rare device,
A sunny pleasure dome with caves of ice!

A damsel with a dulcimer
In a vision once I saw:
It was an Abyssinian maid,
And on her dulcimer she played,
Singing of Mount Abora.
Could I revive within me
Her symphony and song,
To such a deep delight 'twould win me,
That with music loud and long,
I would build that dome in air,
That sunny dome! those caves of ice!
And all who heard should see them there,
And all should cry, Beware! Beware!
His flashing eyes, his floating hair!
Weave a circle round him thrice,
And close your eyes with holy dread,
For he on honey-dew hath fed,
And drunk the milk of Paradise.

SAMUEL TAYLOR COLERIDGE

La Belle Dame sans Merci

O what can ail thee, knight-at-arms,
   Alone and palely loitering?
The sedge has withered from the lake,
   And no birds sing.

O what can ail thee, knight-at-arms,
   So haggard and so woe-begone?
The squirrel's granary is full,
   And the harvest's done.

I see a lilly on thy brow
   With anguish moist and fever dew;
And on thy cheeks a fading rose
   Fast withereth too.

I met a lady in the meads,
   Full beautiful — a faery's child,
Her hair was long, her foot was light,
   And her eyes were wild.

I made a garland for her head,
   And bracelets too, and fragrant zone;[9]
She look'd at me as she did love,
   And made sweet moan.

I set her on my pacing steed,
   And nothing else saw all day long,
For sidelong would she bend, and sing
   A faery's song.

She found me roots of relish sweet,
   And honey wild, and manna dew,
And sure in language strange she said,
   "I love thee true!"

She took me to her elfin grot,
   And there she wept and sigh'd full sore,
And there I shut her wild, wild eyes
   With kisses four.

[9] girdle

And there she lulléd me asleep
   And there I dream'd, ah woe betide!
The latest dream I ever dream'd
   On the cold hill side.

I saw pale kings, and princes too,
   Pale warriors, death-pale were they all;
They cried — "La belle Dame sans Merci
   Hath thee in thrall!"

I saw their starved lips in the gloam
   With horrid warning gapéd wide,
And I awoke and found me here
   On the cold hill's side.

And this is why I sojourn here
   Alone and palely loitering,
Though the sedge is wither'd from the lake,
   And no birds sing.

JOHN KEATS

A Lyke-Wake Dirge*

This ae nighte, this ae nighte,
   — *Every nighte and alle,*
Fire and fleet[10] and candle-light,
   And Christe receive thy saule.

When thou from hence away art past,
   — *Every nighte and alle,*
To Whinny-muir thou com'st at last;
   And Christe receive thy saule.

If ever thou gavest hosen and shoon,
   — *Every nighte and alle,*
Sit thee down and put them on;
   And Christe receive thy saule.

* From the Oxford Book of English verse, 1250–1900, ed. Arthur Quiller-Couch, Clarendon Press, Oxford, 1931.

[10] house-room

If hosen and shoon thou ne'er gav'st nane
  — *Every nighte and alle,*
The whinnes sall prick thee to the bare bane;
    And Christe receive thy saule.

From Whinny-muir when thou may'st pass,
  — *Every nighte and alle,*
To Brig o' Dread thou com'st at last;
    And Christe receive thy saule.

From Brig o' Dread when thou may'st pass,
  — *Every nighte and alle,*
To Purgatory fire thou com'st at last;
    And Christe receive thy saule.

If ever thou gavest meat or drink,
  — *Every nighte and alle,*
The fire sall never make thee shrink;
    And Christe receive thy saule.

If meat or drink thou ne'er gav'st nane,
  — *Every nighte and alle,*
The fire will burn thee to the bare bane;
    And Christe receive thy saule.

This ae nighte, this ae nighte,
  — *Every nighte and alle,*
Fire and fleet and candle-lighte,
    And Christe receive thy saule.

                              ANONYMOUS

CHAPTER THIRTEEN

The Nature of Meter in English and American Poetry

Where the boundary between prose and poetry lies, I shall never be able to understand. The question is raised in manuals of style, yet the answer to it lies beyond me. Poetry is verse: prose is not verse. Or else poetry is everything with the exception of business documents and school books.

LEO TOLSTOY

It became clear as the last chapter progressed that a story or poem has many rhythms, that the rhythm of its speech, the stress and slack in the flow of the syllables and their related pauses, may vary greatly in regularity in both poetry and prose. It is possible to find poems as apparently irregular in this respect as most prose, and certainly there are prose rhythms with a high degree — a "poetic" degree of regularity. There is only one kind of rhythm which *some* poetry has that prose does not have and that is meter, which is simply defined as that aspect of the poem which is arithmetically determined. In English this definition usually (but not always) refers to the way in which a poet measures the length of his line. It is perhaps only in historical perspective that we can understand meter and its present uses.

There seems little doubt that metered (i.e., measured) language preceded prose in artistic usage because it was (and is) easier to memorize and to remember. Perhaps the place of poetry in a world without printing can best be understood if we realize that, for most people today, the only body of writing they remember with ease are those nursery rhymes which they encountered before they could read with facility. This is no place to discuss the various oral and mnemonic traditions which kept literature alive from generation to generation; but suffice it to say that from what we know to have been the accomplishments of the Bards of various cultures, not to mention what we know of the memory of the common man for folk-tales and songs, it is certain that the comforting existence of the book in print has minimized the use of a prodigious ability in man for accurate oral transmission of metered language. In the beginning metered language was often, if not always, connected with dance and song, so that, like "anyone" in e. e. cummings' allegory, primitive man celebrated in dance and song the story of his achievements, beliefs, and needs. The specialization of this ability to transmit the history and beliefs of individuals and of a tribe led to the "expert" medicine man, Bard, and so on. The shift from "everybody does it" to the specialist was no doubt a late development, and probably was never complete, in that there always remained certain tales and songs remembered by the common people.

However, we may surmise that this transition led to a more self-conscious art, to a deliberate examination of the various metrical taboos and customs of the tribe, to, in short, a process of increased rationalization which led in rather rapid order to the highly ruled and ordered verse of the type of Pindar and Sappho, or, in another culture, to the Celtic Bardic rhythms. In other arts and other cultures this kind of process led to the high stylization of such so-called primitive art as that of the African mask, which made such an impact on western art in the early part of this century. When we approach the art of another culture, our excitement over it often arises out of a misreading. It often strikes us powerfully as "free" renderings, impressionistic abstractions which we can take as models in the attack which has gone on intermittently for some time now against our Greek-Roman artistic traditions. But of course we are free to see such art as impressionistic only because we are free to ignore the traditions of training, of use, of occasion which made such artifacts classical in the eyes of a native of that culture.

It is impossible, then, to understand how poems in the English language are metered unless one understands the various historical metrical traditions that lie behind present usage.

THE ANGLO-SAXON STRESS METER

The original Old English tongue, Anglo-Saxon, was a Germanic language whose rhythmical base was, as in other Germanic languages, a very strong, unmistakable stress on at least one syllable in each multisyllabic word and on certain monosyllables. Without going unnecessarily into the details, it should be said that the Anglo-Saxons metered their poetry by counting a certain number of stresses per line, which line was divided in a certain way by a caesura, or pause. It did not matter how many syllables to the line there were, so long as the correct number of stresses per line was used. (These stresses were tied to the appearance of a sound device known as alliteration, which we will examine in the following chapter). In short, the poet measured his line by counting the number of stresses. Following is a section of W. H. Auden's long poem "The Age of Anxiety," which is a modern poem written in ancient Anglo-Saxon meter.

QUANT was thinking:

My deuce, my double, my dear image,
Is it lively there, that land of glass
Where song is a grimace, sound logic
A suite of gestures? You seem amused.
How well and witty when you wake up,
How glad and good when you go to bed,
Do you feel, my friend? What flavor has
That liquor you lift with your left hand;
Is it cold by contrast, cool as this
To a soiled soul; does your self like mine
Taste of untruth?

THE CLASSICAL GREEK AND LATIN FOOT METERS

Meters based on the counting of stressed syllables (such as the Anglo-Saxon) are called "qualitative meters" because a stress seems rather a quality than a quantity. Those meters based on length of vowel (such as the classical Greek and Latin) are called quantitative, since the length of syllable seems a matter of quantity. The classical Greek (and the Latin which borrowed from it) meters were based on the fact that in those languages the vowels, hence the syllables, could be perceptibly divided into those which were long, and those which were short, according to the time taken to say them. This variation in length of vowel combined with variations of pitch to create the meter.

When we erroneously speak of long and short vowels in English, we refer to a method of pronunciation, a placement of the organs of the mouth in order to create a certain sound. The Greeks and Romans did not. They meant literally that a *long* "a" or "i" was *held*, was *sounded a longer time than a short* "a" or "i." The Classic poets then took these long syllables (⁻) and these short syllables (˘), put them together in certain basic rhythmic combinations, gave a name to each combination, and called these combinations "feet." Thus,

˘⁻ was an iambic foot
⁻˘ was a trochaic foot
˘˘⁻ was an anapestic foot
⁻˘˘ was a dactylic foot
⁻˘⁻ was an amphimacric foot
˘⁻˘ was an amphibrachic foot
⁻⁻ was a spondaic foot
˘˘ was a pyrrhic foot

There were other feet within the system, but these were the basic ones. The foot was the basis of measurement and the classic prosodies were inclined to be quite rigid not only in the *number* of feet to the line, but in the *arrangement* of the feet within the line. The line, in size the next major metrical unit after the foot, was therefore created by the repetition of a certain number of feet per line, and these lines were called: monometer — one foot; dimeter — two feet; trimeter — three feet; tetrameter — four feet; pentameter — five feet; hexameter — six feet.

THE SYLLABIC METERS

As the Roman Empire declined and disintegrated and the central grammatical authorities disappeared, there arose throughout Europe increasing local variations on the classical Latin tongue, which eventually led to the principal modern Romance languages of France, Italy, and Spain. One of the features of these vulgate Latins was that they tended to lose the ability to distinguish accurately between the long and short vowels. As these vowels lost their firmly fixed quantity, a new metric system arose. In this new meter the poets measured the length of their line by counting the number of syllables in it. This became a highly complicated meter with a variety of means specified, such as elisions (leaving out a vowel, as in the "summ'ry sun") for regularizing the count of syllables. The importance of the syllabic meter as it affected English poetry is that it was the established prosody of Norman French poetry when the Normans conquered England in 1066, and during the following centuries it superseded the local Anglo-Saxon meter.

FREE VERSE

Free verse is poetry written without counting any element, without any mathematical way of determining the length of the line and thus it exists, as a type, only in contrast to metered poetry. Both the practitioners of free verse and those who don't like it are apt to accept the generalization that free verse is a new departure that was begun by Whitman. Such was not the case. There have been repeated interests in non-metrical "poetic" writing for many centuries, perhaps the most notable of which was a fashion for rhymed parallelistic prose, which enjoyed a great vogue in Europe for several centuries during the Middle Ages. In modern English, as it developed from the fusion of Norman French and Anglo-Saxon, the most important document in the development of free verse was without doubt the King James Bible, in which the sections of translated parallelistic Hebrew poetry sound, in English, like poetry, having the intensity of tone and the heightened use of figurative language commonly associated with poetry, yet do not have the lines controlled by meter. In addition to the King James Bible, other occasional examples of works written in free verse show up from time to time, such as *The Thanksgivings* by the seventeenth-century poet Thomas Traherne and, in later times, Christopher Smart's poem "The Cat." This very minor tradition was given heightened interest by the *vers libre* revolution among French poets in the nineteenth century, who began to ignore the extremely rigid rules of syllabic meter and rhyming which had developed during the heyday of Classical French poetry.

However, it should be remembered that except in individual cases — such as Milton, who voluntarily observed strictly the intricate European syllabic rules — poetry in Modern English, though predominantly syllabic, had never been as tightly conventional as French poetry. Shakespeare, for instance, though very conscious of the number of syllables to the line in his early plays, became much more irregular in his later plays, relying more and more on his cultivated instinct for the reach and flow of English spoken rhythms. Even when, for some centuries, the poetry was metered on a count of syllables by virtually all poets, most of them were uninterested in or unaware of the complexity of this meter as developed in Europe and, with a few rules to guide them, made a rather simple and straightforward count of syllables. Thus, metered poetry and free-verse poetry were never so far apart as they were, say, in France. In English and American poetry, irregularities, with a rare and exceptional period or two, have always been looked upon with as much interest as dismay, and small irregularities have scarcely attracted attention. And one cannot overestimate the importance of the example of Shakespeare's late plays with their freedom from rigid syllabic count. It is my belief that the free verse revolt in English and American poetry, as it concerns itself self-consciously with Whitman, was really more preoccupied with subject matter and diction than with meter and that in Whitman's case we are dealing with a man who could write poetry well in no other way. But that problem does not concern us here.

HOW STRESS, SYLLABIC, AND FOOT METERS DEVELOPED IN MODERN ENGLISH

The Norman conquest of England resulted, linguistically, in a situation in which the upper class all spoke Norman French and the lower and commercial classes Anglo-Saxon, with a small but important bilingual group of managers, supervisors, and others whose lives were spent moving between the two lingual groups. It meant the almost immediate end of Anglo-Saxon as the learned language, as the recording language, as the language of poetry addressed to those in power (i.e., all poetry except folk verse). This dual language situation, though it persisted for a couple of centuries, could not long endure, as the Normans in a generation or so became domesticated. Soon they took pride in being English rather than French, both because the base of England gave them greater power than their Norman possessions and because of the natural emotional attachments that grow for the place where one is born. From the point of view of the lower classes, all those who would be anything but the meanest serf must make this lingual adjustment upward toward the seat of power. The result of the meeting of these two languages was what we call *Middle English,* which found its first literary stability and beauty in the poetry of Geoffrey Chaucer. This fusion very quickly underwent some other changes, much slighter, into *Modern English,* the language of Marlowe, Jonson, and Shakespeare, which is essentially the language we still speak.

Whether or not the heavy admixture of the syllable-accentless French-Latin vocabulary had any modifying effect on the heavy Germanic accent of the core Anglo-Saxon words is perhaps now impossible to surmise. However it happened, the important fact is that the English lexical (syllable) accent is, as pointed out in the chapter on rhythm, highly subject to modification by the time accent and the dramatic accent. And whether it was this difficulty of fixing the accent, or other considerations, such as prestige, that led Chaucer to use the French metrical system rather than the Anglo-Saxon, we are not certain. Suffice it to say the French syllabic metric had the advantages of being the system of prosody in the upper-class Norman French and could at the same time ignore the often vexing problem of exactly determining stress and slack. The Anglo-Saxon meter was overshadowed for centuries.

Perhaps Sir Philip Sidney, that man looked to by his Elizabethan contemporaries as the ideal poet, knight, and gentleman, described most succinctly the metric practice that was to be followed in all but a tiny fraction of English poetry till the nineteenth century, when, contrasting contemporary and classical metric usage, he said, "The auncients marked the quantities of each silable, and according to that framed his verse," but that his contemporaries cared for "only number (with some regards of the accent)." What he meant by this description was that the ancients took the quantitative *length* of a syllable as the basis of metering (i.e., counting) the length of their line, but that his contemporaries counted the *number of syllables,* without regard to the syllable's length. The parenthetical comment "(with some regard of the accent)" is a recognition that the *syllabic rhythm* of English (as opposed to the meter, which can be any quality or quantity measured to govern the length of line), springs from its flow of stresses and slacks and their infinite variety of relationships, and that this syllabic rhythm could not be ignored, but rather it must be *effectively ordered,* though not *counted,* within the framework of the syllabic meter. *He thus made a distinction which is too seldom really kept in mind (to the great confusion of us all). He saw clearly that meter and rhythm are two separate things.* As demonstrated in the chapter on rhythm, a story or poem is a complicated texture of all sorts of rhythms, a part of which, and that only in certain kinds of poetry, is the rhythmic recurrence of the length of the line as determined by the *conscious metering* of the poet. I cannot overemphasize this notion of *consciousness* on the part of the poet. It is pointless to make up clever metrical theories for which there is not a shred of historical or textual evidence that they ever were or ever could be used. When a nineteenth-century very minor American poet, Sidney

Lanier, wrote a book attempting to prove that poetic meter should be equated to musical rhythm and that the basic way of metering English poetry was in phrases of ¾ rhythm, he engaged on the one hand in a ludicrous oversimplification of two highly different arts and on the other in either a blind ignorance or blind ignoring of the fact that not one poet before him ever considered it possible to meter English poetry by time-equivalents, as in music.

Several unsuccessful attempts were made in the Renaissance and thereafter, to adapt the classical foot to English, and in this sense it can be said they were attempts to meter a basically qualitative language by quantity. Perhaps most notable in this attempt was the brilliant minor poet Thomas Campion, whose poem "There Is a Garden in Her Face" was observed in Chapter nine (p. 284). That he was also a brilliant musician has made his songs some of the most beautiful ever written. Yet even Campion never imagined that the metering of music and of poetry were similar problems. And as for his attempt to discover long and short vowels in strict existence in English, so that they could be used to form feet as in Greek and Latin poetry, he had to give it up. And in spite of the great fascination felt in the Renaissance period for the classical world, and the Renaissance artist's desire to imitate classical art, every other such attempt was, like Campion's, a failure. Indeed, since we have been able to use recording devices to investigate the nature of sound in language, there is evidence that in English the spoken length of a vowel is strongly correlated to the presence or absence of *stress*.

The kind of meter described by Sir Philip Sidney (see p. 423) continued to be by far the chief meter of English poetry until the nineteenth century. Several things happened during that century to broaden metrical possibilities. The increased usage of free verse has already been noted, in relation to Walt Whitman and the more general interest he excited in unmetered poetry. The long-buried stress prosody of Anglo-Saxon origins (which had also had its occasional near-practitioners, such as Skelton, Blake, Burns, and Chatterton), received a new stimulus when Coleridge, with his great critical and poetic reputation, wrote the poem "Christabel," in the preface to which he claimed for it that it was composed on a "new" principle. He proclaimed that instead of counting syllables to meter the line, he had counted the number of stresses. That Coleridge could claim that his principle was new is difficult to understand, since it is hardly believable that he did not know of the Anglo-Saxon meters and it is not believable that he did not know of certain contemporary German revivals of interest in stress meter. Still, it was true that for centuries no major English poet or critic commanding the attention and respect of the generality of the literary world had attempted to write a major poem in a stress meter. It was not long until the poet Gerard Manley Hopkins began to form his theory of "sprung rhythm," which is essentially a stress meter; and it is fair to say that the interest in stress meter has greatly broadened among modern poets, Auden's attempt to reconstruct the Anglo-Saxon meter entire being perhaps only the most historically self-conscious.

Another direction in meter followed publication of a study by the scholar George Saintsbury in which he pointed out that the rhythms of English as spoken are describable by using the classical names of the feet, only substituting *stress* (′) for the classical long vowel (‾), and the un-stressed, or slack, syllables (×) for the short vowel (˘). He suggested that, given this simple substitution demanded by the basically stressed rhythm of English, one could then refer, perhaps, to an essentially iambic rhythm in English.

It is certainly true that throughout the period of modern English, i.e., for the last four hundred years, there has been a minor but continual awareness of the classical foot meter and occasional attempts to adapt it to English. But all these attempts were the result, like Campion's, of a desire to find a way to determine long and short syllables in English and to base a foot prosody on unchanged classical lines. It was Saintsbury's insight to see that one *could* get something like feet (though certainly *not* the classical foot) in English by substituting stress for long syllables, and slack for short syllables. Since this system presented for the first time a way of achieving a *foot meter* that was not in defiance of the nature of the English language, it is not surprising that the system began to be practiced by a growing number of poets. What *is* surprising is that Saintsbury's system should have been so impressive as to make subsequent writers of textbooks on metric base their entire explanation of metric on the misun-derstanding that throughout the whole history of English poetry poets have *metered* their line along Saintsburian principles.

Under the impact of the growing interest in unmetered free verse on the one hand and of stress meters and foot meters on the other, it looked for a time as if syllabic meter might give way entirely. However, after undergoing a partial eclipse, it has proved to have depths of interest not yet explored; and such diverse poets as Dylan Thomas and Marianne Moore, among others, have seen to it that some of our strongest contem-porary poetry uses this metric.

Thus we may be said to be in an eclectic period, with the personalities of the poets free to seek for appropriateness over the range of unmetered poetry, as well as to try varieties and permutations of the three chief metrical systems: the syllabic, the stress, and the foot.

THE AESTHETIC NATURE AND PROBLEMS OF THE VARIOUS METERS, AND OF FREE VERSE

Syllabic Meter

It is important to keep in mind that, in the syllabic meters, meter and what we may call syllabic rhythm (the rise and fall of stress and slack) are two entirely different things. As Sidney indicated, stress, as a permanent, inherent element of English, must be ordered effectively within the count of syllables, but with most poets, in most of their lines, it is probably an instinctive, or only occasionally conscious ordering, while the count of syllables must be conscious. Although this process of counting syllables may seem "conventional" and arbitrary, and ours is by and large an epoch in man's history in which the word "conventional" is a damning word, it is as well to remember that art *must* operate partially within conventions if for no other reason than that language conventions are necessary for any communication to take place. No matter how daring a sentence, a concept, a figure may be, it must depend for its communicative power on those building-blocks of language, the conventional meanings of words which all accept. In fact, one could go a step further and say that originality could not exist without the concurrent existence of conventionality to serve as measuring stick and contrast.

Of course all sorts of conventionalities are connected with writing, of which meter is only one, and the area in which a given piece of writing may have some of its greatest originality may or may not be in this area. In this sense, it might be interesting to contrast Walt Whitman and Dylan Thomas (see p. 237 and p. 338). Both are very original poets, and Thomas was an admirer of Whitman's work. Yet Walt Whitman's *originality* is almost totally confined to his subject matter, his diction, and to a lesser extent, his prosody. Thomas, on the other hand, is highly conventional in his meters and in his subject matter, but is most original in his figures of speech and diction.

The positive artistic value of the syllabic meters seems to me to center in their ability to set up a regularly recurring rhythmic entity which serves to frame the smaller rhythmic slack and stress unit. This regularly recurring entity is the *line*, which, in the case of such an unvaried one as the ubiquitous English decasyllable (ten-syllable line), quickly becomes a rhythmic unit drummed firmly into one's unconscious. This unit functions, it seems to me, much like the rigid warp of thread laid on a weaving loom, across which the woof of the syllables, with their constantly shifting stress and slack, weaves a pattern of great variety and richness. It thus satisfies the two essentials which all works of art seem to require: (1) the arbitrary frame, setting limits within which aroused expectations can reasonably be satisfied, and (2) the scope for the surprises, variations, creations, of the individual vision, that reordering of life which is the great work of art.

The artistic danger of the syllabic meter (apart from its obvious inappropriateness to certain personalities and visions) is that, like all things firm and conventional in art, it is apt to impose its character on other aspects of the poem, rather than being mastered and used by that which is of the essence of the vision. In this way, as poets discovered in the age of neo-classical poetry, the rigid length of line tended to restrict the patterns of stress rhythms. Because certain stress rhythms went easily and well with the ten-syllable line combined with heroic couplet, for instance, poets tended to rely more and more on those combinations. The clichés of rhythm thus developed are factors in the dullness of the minor poetry of that age as contrasted to that of the Elizabethan period. But no convention should be so rigid that the great artist must discard that miraculous variation which the convention itself has given birth to. Having read that first line in Macbeth's soliloquy which speaks so eloquently in its rhythm of weariness, of enervation, of time-sickness

$$× ´ × \quad × \quad × ´ × \quad × \quad × ´ ×$$
Tomorrow and tomorrow and tomorrow

and having noticed the hauntingly perfect internal stasis of its slack and stress pattern, who would ask Shakespeare to rewrite such a line because it had eleven syllables instead of ten?

The Stress Meter

Modern stress meter is very free compared to Anglo-Saxon usage. A poet may establish a line of any number of stresses, and this consideration of stress is totally unrelated to any other poetic element, in contrast to the recurrence of alliteration to which the stress pattern was tied in Anglo-Saxon times.

Right away it might as well be said that one of the great problems of both stress and foot meters in modern English is the inability, in a small but significant percentage of cases, to determine whether a syllable is slack or stress. Although this problem was discussed in some detail in Chapter 12 and we need not go into it here, it should be recalled that in poems with a highly regular rhythm, a weak stress might be strengthened into a firm stress (or a strong modified to a weak) by the beat that has been established and whose continuance is anticipated by the mind. Thus, in

$$×´ \quad ×´ \quad ×´ \quad ×´ \quad ×´$$
$$×´ \quad ×´ \quad ?´ \quad ×´ \quad ×´$$

the doubtful slack of the middle foot, second line is likely to be depressed to a positive slack by the severely established pattern. In stress prosody, however, such artificially induced stresses (or slacks) should not figure at all, since the kind of stress that is to be counted is the natural stress of natural speech. Because no grouping of stress and slack into preconceived patterns, as in the foot prosody, is conceived by the poet, it is therefore obvious that the poet must rely solely on his trained ear to detect the natural stresses which are the basis of his metering. This complete dependence on distinguishing the natural stress presents him with problems when it comes to determining whether, for instance, a given secondary stress, in the rhythm of the poem, should be counted as a stress or not, or whether a given monosyllable is or is not raised by the sense of the phrase to a stress.

When stress prosody sets up a more or less regular rhythm, it becomes virtually indistinguishable from foot prosody, since it will naturally establish either a basic two-part (iamb or trochee) or a three-part (anapest or dactyl) rhythm. On the other hand, if it allows itself its full theoretical freedom to ignore the number of slacks in the line, and regularize only the number of stresses, it may come to be almost free verse from the point of view of the length of line. Of course so long as something is being measured, the meter is *not* free verse; but in such a case many of the effects of stress prosody, in the ears of the general reader, would be similar.

Gerard Manley Hopkins, one of the principal modern poets and theorists of stress prosody, advanced as his belief that the real power of stress prosody was achieved when it mediated between the extremes represented by a strict foot prosody and free verse. In such cases, a tension is set up between a basic regular rhythm, say the iambic, and variations resulting from the degree to which the rise and fall in the number of slack syllables extend or contract the proximity of the stresses. This tension would function much like a solo instrument playing subtle rhythmic variations over a drum, which sustains the regular beat. But, says Hopkins, because in poetry the poet has only the one line of poetry and the one voice as opposed to the two lines of music for the two instruments, the poet must keep coming back to re-establish his basic rhythm, in order that when he switches to his variations the unconscious rhythmic sense of the reader will keep the beat going. The difficulties of establishing objectively in English what is stress can be demonstrated very well by an attempt to recreate the stresses as Hopkins wanted them in his sprung-rhythm poems. It is often impossible to do so.

Were it not for the modifications and subtlizations of stress which have occurred in our language and which offer the poet those already-mentioned difficulties in measuring his line, and which offer the reader at least equal difficulties in reconstructing with any certainty the poet's metric intentions, I think one would be forced to say that stress meter is in a sense basic to the language, since it chooses to measure what is inevitably the primary, if not always the most important, rhythmic element and avoids what so often seems arbitrary in the count of syllables and in the division of a line into feet. It brings more nearly into unity the meter and a basic natural rhythm of the language.

Foot Meters

The foot meter, if used in conjunction with a highly regular rhythm, closely resembles the syllabic, since, for instance, a succession of five iambic or trochaic feet will come out to ten syllables, which is the old syllabic decasyllable line. On the other hand, where free substitution of two- and three-syllable feet exists and where such shortening devices as the *metrical pause* (where a pause is taken to equal, usually, a half-foot) and initial truncation are used, a line of five feet may vary between nine and perhaps fifteen syllables.

We have previously noted that the classical Greek and Latin poets had very rigid patterns laid down for their use, so that in a given kind of poem a given line might be required to have a specific pattern, such as –⏑–⏑––⏑–⏑. However, when English and American poets first began to think of the possibility of metering the line by counting feet based on slack and stress, they were in no mood to take on a prosody *more* restrictive than the syllabic. Further, given the difficulties encountered with fixing the stress, it is doubtful if they could have imitated the classics had they wanted to. It is true that scholars and theorists have tried to make a number of rules and specifications for execution of the foot meter, but to the poets (and even more so to the lay reader) these have generally proven impractical and have been ignored. In practice, the poet establishes a certain number of feet to the line, he largely ignores the problem of what to do with pauses, and he allows himself free substitution of any kind of foot he wants anywhere. Often the only way one can identify the basic foot is by scanning the whole poem and adding up the number of times the various feet appear. And I have found poems in which the basic foot had no more than a plurality over the others, which will give some idea of the flexibility of the meter as used. Further, I have yet to find a *poet* who makes a meticulous *conscious* division of feet within the line as a part of the act of composition. And in fact often the better as well as the lesser poets have in mind only something as indefinite as, for instance, the creation of a "loose" iambic pentameter line. In practice the modern use of foot prosody might be seen as a compromise between the rigid line of the syllabic meter and the strict count of stress with its looser line. While the line length that develops out of foot prosody is a good deal more restricted in potential variation than that which develops out of the stress metric, yet the foot metric allows far more flexibility in this regard than the syllabic metric. Again, it allows for range in the number of stresses to the line, though probably not the variety that has been used by Milton and others writing in the syllabic meter.

Among the chief disadvantages of the modern use of foot metric is that, mediating as it does between two strong metrical systems (syllabic and stress), its effects are sometimes so similar to one or the other as to make one occasionally wonder at its excuse for being differentiated at all. But perhaps its most serious weakness is that the division of the English poetic line into feet, except as the scholars find it handy in the description of a specific rhythmic pattern, generally seems an arbitrary and questionable procedure. I doubt if one would learn anything more by dividing "tomorrow and tomorrow and tomorrow" into feet, than one knows by observing the rhythmic construct and balance of the whole line.

Free Verse

If one reads a free verse poem aloud, one does not mark the end of the line by a pause for any other reason than that a natural pause of breath or grammar is there or that there is some discernible dramatic reason which has brought the poet to end the line. In metered verse, on the other hand, a line length is measured which in certain cases may have no apparent relationship to grammar or breath or dramatic pauses. The line length may simply mark the end of a certain number of syllables or a certain number of feet, or a certain number of stresses. We call such a line a run-on line; and if the reader looks at the metered poems in this book, he will see that such lines are quite common. Take for instance "Lessons of the War." In the first stanza we have:

> . . . . But today,
> Today we have naming of parts. Japonica
> Glistens like coral in all of the neighboring gardens,

Here the word "Japonica" both ends a line and begins a sentence. In reading this passage aloud, one faces the fact that the problem of vocal pause is not so simple as with free verse. Some persons feel that, because the *metered line* is a specific rhythmic unit always to be acknowledged, then all metered lines, even though run-on, should be noted by a pause, however slight. Others feel that one should be strictly grammatic, and that where no pause is called for by the construction of the sentence one should read through the run-on line like prose. It seems to me that no such doctrinaire approach will do. It is perhaps a good rule of thumb that, where a pause is not really awkward then one should, however slightly, acknowledge the end of the line. But to do so automatically is scarcely to allow that *variety* in the use of any convention which is usually the heart of its power for significance. Why not have faith that the poet will have given the proper indication? In this case, because of the particular rhythmic and grammatic structure of "Japonica / Glistens like coral," it is easy to make a very slight pause; and considering the abrupt switch of subject which has just occurred prior to the word "Japonica," such a pause after that word might be helpful to the audience, as well as to the oral reader. In any case, even though not specifically acknowledged orally in all instances, a measured line is a unit that will usually make itself felt in a reading as a major, though very often most important as a counterpointed, rhythmic element.

In free verse, on the other hand, the possibilities for the line as counterpoint are very limited. The line is, by definition, a rhythmical unit, rather than a metered (counted) unit. Therefore, there can be no counterpoint between rhythmic unit and metered unit. There can only be counterpoint between one rhythmic unit and another (as, for instance, between line and phrase, or line and stanza). And even this use cannot be taken very far. A free verse poem with all or most of the lines run-on would merely look odd, and one would wonder why the poet hadn't broken his lines in the proper places. This absence of run-on lines accounts for the fact that the free verse line is almost always of two kinds (which will be described later).

The arguments that once raged over the use of free verse seem to have died down, but one often wonders if it is not a case of everyone getting weary of it all rather than of anyone being convinced. In the preface to this book it was suggested that energy used in the old discussions over the difference between prose and poetry, and the rather agonized attempts to define one or the other, might better have been spent elsewhere. Clearly the art of writing offers a spread of potential styles, ranging from very plain prose and poetry to lingually ornate prose and lingually ornate metered poetry. Just where in this span the works of a writer may fall depends, I suspect, more on his personality than on any other element, and in his "personality" we must include everything from the literary conventions of his time and his personal reaction to them, to a consideration of the kind and degree of outer discipline which best stimulates his creative originality. This same thing can be said of meter or of free verse, that those who use one or the other do so because of some inner need. We honor Whitman for the high moments of his achievement in free verse, where he showed the world a new vision communicating itself beautifully in its own best terms. But one must not forget that not the least source of Whitman's greatness was his honest appraisal of the dullness of his attempts at metered poetry, an appraisal which we can assume he made from the fact that he did not continue his few attempts into that method, from his constant appreciation of his contemporaries who wrote metered poetry, and from his reiteration that everyone should write the kind of poetry that best suited his needs. These needs may change in time with other changes in the poet. For instance, whereas both Eliot and Pound moved from metered verse to free verse, Marianne Moore and E. E. Cummings have in general moved in the opposite direction, Marianne Moore definitely abandoning free verse, and Cummings' interest in it diminishing substantially. When the drive of personality directs a poet toward free verse, he finds basically two variations of the form available for his use. One is the kind one finds in the Bible and in Whitman, where the line is based on a grammatical or breath phrase and where usually the two are the same. The second kind of free verse occurs where the line is directed by dramatic reasons, where the poet, by breaking the line and maneuvering it as he does, is trying to direct our attention to relationships — to direct us, in short, as to how we should read the passage aloud (hence, silently) to best re-create the poet's meaning. A good example of this type can be seen in Cummings' "Buffalo Bill's" (p. 242).

It seems to me that the difference between these two purposes and techniques is very great. Furthermore it is probably at least as significant artistically as the difference between free verse and metered verse, even though one can sometimes find both kinds in the same poem (particularly in the work of T. S. Eliot, where it should be noted that the switch from one kind to another is very often a principal element in determining the tonal meaning of the poem).

The advantages of free verse have been too often stated by its defenders for me to add a great deal. Still, I should think its greatest value is that, once it is accepted as a legitimate way to write, those people who find free verse necessary to their creative process will not be penalized for writing as they must, any more than one condemns a novelist for not writing sonnets. If the reader has accepted the author's view of the essential community of all fiction, whether "poetic" or "prosaic," he has already seen this point.

However, it is far from true that the simple act of writing in free verse guarantees originality. One is convinced of this fact as he reads the scores of writers who sound like imitation Pounds or Whitmans or Eliots yet who manage to be published. The genuine poetic voice is at least as rare in free verse as it is in metered verse. Further, free verse is as finite in its possibilities as are the meters. As one reads the Whitmanesque free verse based on the breath phrase, one is apt to be reminded of chanting. Further, one is likely to be reminded that there are limits to the appropriate uses of chanting and that, outside those limited areas, a little chanting goes a long way. Where the rhythm of this kind of free verse is *not* heightened enough to remind of chanting, the reader is apt to begin to wonder just *why* bother to break up the poem into lines at all.

Where one encounters the kind of free verse whose line is formed on dramatic purposes, the reader demands a kind of absolute felicity, as in "Buffalo Bill's," or he is very soon led to think that, after all, such poems are written for the sake of an audience hopelessly unable to extract for itself the dramatic essence of a line. The reader is apt to sense crankiness and cussedness in the poet's way of dramatizing the phrasing and to notice how often the poet has "over-directed" the reader, who must, in the final analysis, be permitted the pleasure of individual discovery wherever possible.

HOW TO DETERMINE A POEM'S METER

The following procedure, though offered systematically, is far from a system, and is no more nor less than the result of experience in assisting students to discover the meters of a given poem. It is therefore arbitrary, and there are certainly other ways of going about it. Discovering the meter is only the first step in discovering the degree of appropriateness of a given rhythm, but it is an essential step, for in it one is out to determine insofar as possible what the poet consciously *counted*, not what *rhythms* he unconsciously or consciously created.

The first step is to count syllables, because a strict syllable count in a poem is easy to see. Don't let a line that varies here or there be a disturbance, for most poets have felt that a convention was meant to be broken now and then. Also, there may be some variance between the reader's way of counting syllables and the poet's. The reader may, for instance, have counted "bless(e)d" as one, whereas the poet meant it to be two syllables, "blessèd." But if the reader finds a poem in which lines are with few exceptions confined to a certain number of syllables, he can be sure that this pattern was *not* accidental and that syllables were the elements measured by the poet. A line may be established either as a line repeated throughout the poem, such as a poem made up completely of seven-syllable lines, or it can take the shape of varying line lengths within the stanza, but whose lengths are repeated in the following stanzas. Thus a poem may have a first stanza that looks like this.

Line 1 . . . . 8 syllables
Line 2 . . . . 7 syllables
Line 3 . . . . 8 syllables
Line 4 . . . . 5 syllables

In the usual syllabic poem stanza no. 2 will look exactly the same.

However, if the lines in the same stanzaic position are irregular in number of syllables, one turns to the next step, which is to scan the poem. If the number of syllables per line is *highly* irregular, one is suspicious immediately that one is looking at a free verse poem. But since the poem *may* be metered by count of stress, one scans the poem, then counts the number of stresses per line to see if there is a possibility of regularity there. If the number of stresses does appear to be rather regular, one should immediately consider this information seriously, for it is possible that the few variations of stress are a result of a disagreement between one's ear and the poet's over the degree of stress on certain syllables. If there is *little* apparent regularity of stress, one may assume a free verse poem.

If one finds that the lines of the poem are rather similar in length, varying only from one to five or so syllables, the reader must then take into account the possibility that he has a stress meter, a foot meter, or free verse. A little historical knowledge helps here. For reasons already explained, if the poem was written before the nineteenth century, it is highly likely that it is a syllabic poem; it is highly unlikely to be stress meter, free verse, or foot meter. However, if it is a modern poem, any of these is a possibility. Again, if the number of stresses seem highly regular, it is more likely to be a stress than a foot meter. On the other hand, if the stresses vary a bit (say in a poem whose median syllable count is around ten or eleven syllables, varying between one and three syllables), then quite possibly a foot meter is involved. A *great* variety in the number of stresses per line almost invariably signals a free verse poem (in any case, as one reads more poetry, free verse is usually detectable on sight from its — frequently — long lines, or from the irregularity of its lines and its stanzas).

If one has decided that the number of syllables and stresses is too irregular for those possibilities, and yet one sees that the lines have a certain coherency in length, then the next step is to divide the poem into feet. One should not be too disturbed if some of the divisions seem arbitrary, for they are. The important thing is to see whether or not a consistent number of feet per line can be readily established.

It might be well to see how these suggestions work out in several examples.

An Egyptian Pulled Glass Bottle *in the Shape of a Fish*	*Number* *of syllables*
Here we have thirst	4
And patience, from the first,	6
And art, as in a wave held up for us to see	12
In its essential perpendicularity	12

Not brittle but   4

Intense — the spectrum, that   6

Spectacular and nimble animal the fish,   12

Whose scales turn aside the sun's sword

with their polish.   12

MARIANNE MOORE*

Meter: Syllabic, without variation.

Rhythm: Several problems: is the verb "held" active enough to be stressed in relation to the powerful stresses on each side of it? Is the secondary accent of "y" in "perpendicularity" (so weak normally as to be only potential), lifted by the preceding highly regular rhythm to a stress? And is the pronoun "us" in the third line a stress or a slack?

Relationship of Meter, Rhythm, and Meaning: Apart from these rhythmic problems, several qualities of the rhythm as they reinforce the meaning become visible. The rhythm of the first stanza wavers and balances between a four-part, three-part and a two-part rhythm, building to the first climax of the "wave," with peculiar skill. First there are two slacks between stresses ′ × × ′; then it relaxes to one slack × ′, then it moves up to three × × × ′, and then one again × ′, then climactically leading up to the word "wave," a pause then three slacks × ′, × × × ′. Then the tension of the wave is held with three hard beats ′ ′ ′. The stanza then eases to a normal rhythm, through an increase in repeated iambs × ′, × ′, etc.

The next stanza starts with two sharp blows, as if indeed to test the word "brittle," and the immediate series of three slacks that follow serves to emphasize "intense," and also to set the rhythmic theme, a dexterous alternation of × ′ and × × × ′ which is the rhythmic support here for the adjectives "spectacular" and "nimble." The last line completely abandons the four-part rhythmic theme × × × ′, and turns to a tension built essentially on two-part themes which have their climax in two places: "scales turn" and "sun's sword." The *metrical line* is used very effectively in certain details, as in the way the break in the line throws an emphasis on the word "intense" which emphasis in turn reinforces the emphasis of the stress rhythm; and in the larger sense a tension is set up between the short, tense lines and the long fluid ones which seem to repeat on a broad scale what is happening in detail in rhythm.

	Number of syllables	Number of stresses
Wedding-Wind*		
1 The wind blew all my wedding-day,	8	5
2 And my wedding-night was the night of the		
high wind;	12	5
3 And a stable door was banging, again and again,	13	5
4 That he must go and shut it, leaving me	10	5
5 Stupid in candlelight, hearing rain,	9	5
6 Seeing my face in the twisted candlestick,	11	5
7 Yet seeing nothing. When he came back	9	5
8 He said the horses were restless, and I was sad	12	5
9 That any man or beast that night should lack	10	5 (6)
10 The happiness I had.		
Now in the day	10	5
11 All's ravelled under the sun by the wind's blowing.	12	5
12 He has gone to look at the floods, and I	10	5
13 Carry a chipped pail to the chicken-run,	10	5
14 Set it down, and stare. All is the wind	9	5
15 Hunting through clouds and forests, thrashing	9	5 (4)
16 My apron and the hanging clothes on the line	11	5 (4)
17 Can it be borne, this bodying-forth by wind	10	5
18 Of joy my actions turn on, like a thread	10	5
19 Carrying beads? Shall I be let to sleep	10	5
20 Now this perpetual morning shares my bed?	11	5
21 Can even death dry up	6	5
22 These new delighted lakes, conclude	8	5
23 Our kneeling as cattle by all-generous waters?	13	5

PHILIP LARKIN

* "Wedding-Wind" by Philip Larkin is reprinted from *The Less Deceived* by permission of The Marvell Press, Hessle, Yorkshire, England.

Meter: Stress.

Rhythm: Problems: In the seventh line, the word "yet" might be read without stress; further, the phrase "when he came back" might be scanned as is, or ´ × × ´. Line 9, the second use of "that" might be stressed (in fact here is an excellent example of how usage may change stress in the one-syllable words; there is no question about the first "that" being slack, but because the second points to something specific it may well be stressed without distortion of meaning); Line 11, the word "under" is an excellent example, as used here, of how the two-syllable prepositions can occur without stress in normal speech rhythms, though in this case, because it is surrounded by slacks, there is an ambiguous quality to the syllable "un"; Line 15, the preposition "through" can be read either way. Line 16 seems to me out-an-out irregular, "my" being the only word that might be stressed to make the full count of 5, but I don't see why, in normal speech rhythm, it should be.

Relationship of Meter, Rhythm, and Meaning: It is easy to see why the first line of the poem is short, with its consequent sense of heavier beat. It at once seizes our attention and helps to reinforce the primary sensory impact of the line — that of the force of the wind. The second line moves immediately into a different rhythm, a loose anapest, nicely broken up by an iamb and a spondee, a rhythm which the third line intensifies. Apart from setting up a tension-and-release pattern which is important throughout the poem, this rhythm is also felicitous as a solution to the problem presented by the point of view. The poem is a soliloquy, and the person speaking, a newly married young woman, is likely to speak in rhythms that are those of common speech, yet somewhat heightened in melody because of her situation; and the alternating loose and heavy rhythms enforce not only the sense of informality, but also one abstractly appropriate to both the sense of freedom and the sense of emphatic happiness.

		Number of syllables	Number of stresses	Number of feet
	The Snow Man*			
1	One must/ have a/ mind of/ winter	8	4	4
2	To re/gard the/ frost and/ the boughs	8	3	4
3	Of the/ pine-trees/ crusted/ with snow;	8	4 (3)	4
4	And/ have been/ cold a/ long time	7	4	4
5	To behold/ the junip/ers shag/ged with ice,	10	4	4

* Copyright, 1923, 1951 by Wallace Stevens. Reprinted from *The Collected Poems of Wallace Stevens* by permission of Alfred A. Knopf, Inc.

6	The spru/ces rough/ in the dis/tant glitter	10	4	4
7	Of the Jan/uary sun;/ and not/ to think	11	4	4
8	Of a/ny mise/ry in the soun/d of the wind,	11	4	4
9	In/ the sound/ of a/ few leaves,	7	3	4
10	Which/ is the/ sound of/ the land	7	3 (2)	4
11	Full/ of the/ same wind	5	3	3
12	That is blow/ing in/ the same/ bare place	9	4	4
13	For the list/ener, who list/ens in/ the snow,	10	3	4
14	And,/ nothing/ himself,/ beholds	7	4	4
15	Nothing that/ is not there/ and the			
	no/thing that is.	12	5	4

WALLACE STEVENS

Meter: Foot prosody: iambic tetrameter line. (Frequency of occurrence of important feet: iambic, 15; trochaic, 10)

Rhythm: Problems: Note the lines of seven syllables, lines 4, 9, 10, 14. These may be regularized by a conventional device called "initial truncation," which presumes, if a line is short half a foot, that the initial foot is "truncated." (The problem of allowing a pause to equal a half-foot is a difficult one and is mentioned elsewhere — see p. 429). Only one line is definitely irregular, and that is line 11. There is no possible way of making this a four-foot line. In line 10, the word "which" offers one of the few problems of scansion. Another is "pine-trees" in line 3. The second foot in line 7 is the only four-part foot, as I have divided the poem. However, this division seems the best expression of the rhythm of the line.

Relationship of Meter, Rhythm, and Meaning: One notices two things about the first three lines — the regularity of their syllable count and the importance of the trochee, especially in the first line, whose syllabic regularity is matched nowhere else in the poem. It is as if the first line stated a bareness, a stringency, which is not restated till line 11, and then by the different device of a line short, abrupt. It is notable how the "nothingness," which is the theme of the last line, is rhythmically pointed by the opening out of the whole line into trisyllabic feet. If one identifies, in the last line, the subject of "nothingness" with essentially a three-part rhythm (/ × × × / / × × / × × /) then one can see how the first three lines prepare for this identification, while at the same time, through the strict syllabic count, balancing it with a severity, a certainty, which is perhaps the other major element in the tone of the poem.

SELECTIONS

The Easter Torch

I. L. CARAGIALE

TRANSLATED BY LUCY BYNG

Leiba Zibal, mine host of Podeni, was sitting lost in thought, by a table placed in the shadow in front of the inn; he was awaiting the arrival of the coach which should have come some time ago; it was already an hour behind time.

The story of Zibal's life is a long and cheerless one: when he is taken with one of his feverish attacks it is a diversion for him to analyse one by one the most important events in that life.

Huckster, seller of hardware, jobber, between whiles even rougher work perhaps, seller of old clothes, then tailor, and boot-black in a dingy alley in Jassy; all this had happened to him since the accident whereby he lost his situation as office boy in a big wine-shop. Two porters were carrying a barrel down to a cellar under the supervision of the lad Zibal. A difference arose between them as to the division of their earnings. One of them seized a piece of wood that lay at hand and struck his comrade on the forehead, who fell to the ground covered with blood. At the sight of the wild deed the boy gave a cry of alarm, but the wretch hurried through the yard, and in passing gave the lad a blow. Zibal fell to the ground fainting with fear. After several months in bed he returned to his master, only to find his place filled. Then began a hard struggle for existence, which increased in difficulty after his marriage with Sura. Their hard lot was borne with patience. Sura's brother, the innkeeper of Podeni, died; the inn passed into Zibal's hands, and he carried on the business on his own account.

Here he had been for the last five years. He had saved a good bit of money and collected good wine — a commodity that will always be worth good money — Leiba had escaped from poverty, but they were sickly, the whole three of them, himself, his wife, and his child, all victims of malaria, and men are rough and quarrelsome in Podeni — slanderous, scoffers, revilers, accused of vitriol throwing. And the threats! A threat is very terrible to a character that bends easily beneath every blow. The thought of a threat worked more upon Leiba's nerves than did his attacks of fever.

"Oh, wretched Gentile!" he thought, sighing.

This "wretched" referred to Gheorghe — wherever he might be! — a man between whom and himself a most unpleasant affair had arisen.

Gheorghe came to the inn one autumn morning, tired with his walk; he was just out of the hospital — so he said — and was looking for work.

The innkeeper took him into his service. But Gheorghe showed himself to be a brutal and a sullen man. He swore continually, and muttered to himself alone in the yard. He was a bad servant, lazy and insolent, and he stole. He threatened his mistress one day when she was pregnant, cursing her, and striking her on the stomach. Another time he set a dog on little Strul.

Leiba paid him his wages at once, and dismissed him. But Gheorghe would not go: he asserted with violence that he had been engaged for a year. Then the innkeeper sent to the town hall to get guards to remove him.

Gheorghe put his hand swiftly to his breast, crying:

"Jew!" and began to rail at his master. Unfortunately, a cart full of customers arrived at that moment. Gheorghe began to grin, saying: "What frightened you, Master Leiba? Look, I am going now." Then bending fiercely over the bar towards Leiba, who drew back as far as possible, he whispered: "Expect me on Easter Eve; we'll crack red eggs together, Jew! You will know then what I have done to you, and I will answer for it."

Just then, customers entered the inn.

"May we meet in good health at Easter, Master Leiba!" added Gheorghe as he left.

*   *   *

Leiba went to the town hall, then to the sub-prefecture to denounce the threatener, begging that he might be watched. The sub-prefect was a lively young man; he first accepted Leiba's humble offering, then he began to laugh at the timid Jew, and to make fun of him. Leiba tried hard to make him realize the gravity of the situation, and pointed out how isolated the house stood from the village, and even from the high road. But the sub-prefect, with a more serious air, advised him to be prudent; he must not mention such things, for, truly, it would arouse the desire to do them in a village where men were rough and poor, ready to break the law.

A few days later, an official with two riders came to see him about Gheorghe; he was "wanted" for some crime.

If only Leiba had been able to put up with him until the arrival of these men! In the meanwhile, no one knew the whereabouts of Gheorghe. Although this had happened some time ago, Gheorghe's appearance, the movement as though he would have drawn something from his breast, and the threatening words had all remained deeply impressed upon the mind of the terror-stricken man. How was it that that memory remained so clear?

It was Easter Eve.

From the top of the hill, from the village lying among the lakes about two miles away, came the sound of church bells. One hears in a strange way when one is feverish, now so loud, now so far away. The coming night was the night before Easter, the night of the fulfilment of Gheorghe's promise.

"But perhaps they have caught him by now!"

Moreover, Zibal only meant to stay at Podeni till next quarter-day. With his capital he could open a good business in Jassy. In a town, Leiba would regain his health, he would be near the police station — he could treat the police, the commissionaires, the sergeants. Who pays well gets well guarded.

In a large town, the night brings noise and light, not darkness and silence as in the isolated valley of Podeni. There is an inn in Jassy — there in the corner, just the place for a shop! An inn where girls sing all night long, a Café Chantant. What a gay and rousing life! There, at all hours of the day and night, officials and their girls, and other dirty Christians will need entertainment.

What is the use of bothering oneself here where business keeps falling off, especially since the coming of the railway which only skirts the marshes at some distance?

"Leiba," calls Sura from within, "the coach is coming, one can hear the bells."

The Podeni valley is a ravine enclosed on all sides by wooded hills. In a hollow towards the south lie several deep pools caused by the springs which rise in the hills; above them lie some stretches of ground covered with bush and rushes. Leiba's inn stands in the centre of the valley, between the pools and the more elevated ground to the north; it is an old stone building, strong as a small fortress: although the ground is marshy, the walls and cellars are very dry.

At Sura's voice Leiba raises himself painfully from his chair, stretching his tired limbs; he takes a long look towards the east; not a sign of the diligence.

"It is not coming; you imagined it," he replied to his wife, and sat down again.

Very tired the man crossed his arms on the table, and laid his head upon them, for it was burning. The warmth of the spring sun began to strike the surface of the marshes and a pleasant lassitude enveloped his nerves, and his thoughts began to run riot as a sick man's will, gradually taking on strange forms and colours.

Gheorghe — Easter Eve — burglars — Jassy — the inn in the centre of the town — a gay restaurant doing well — restored health.

And he dozed.

Sura and the child went without a great deal up here.

Leiba went to the door of the inn and looked out on to the road.

On the main road there was a good deal of traffic, an unceasing noise of wheels accompanied by the rhythmic sound of horses' hooves trotting upon the smooth asphalt.

But suddenly the traffic stopped, and from Copou a group of people could be seen approaching, gesticulating and shouting excitedly.

The crowd appeared to be escorting somebody: soldiers, a guard and various members of the public. Curious onlookers appeared at every door of the inn.

"Ah," thought Leiba, "they have laid hands on a thief."

The procession drew nearer. Sura detached herself from the others, and joined Leiba on the steps of the inn.

"What is it, Sura?" he asked.

"A madman escaped from Golia."

"Let us close the inn so that he cannot get at us."

"He is bound now, but a little while ago he escaped. He fought with all the soldiers. A rough Gentile in the crowd pushed a Jew against the madman and he bit him on the cheek."

Leiba could see well from the steps; from the stair below Sura watched with the child in her arms.

It was, in fact, a violent lunatic held on either side by two men: his wrists were tightly bound over each other by a thick cord. He was a man of gigantic stature with a head like a bull, thick black hair, and hard, grizzled beard and whiskers. Through his shirt, which had been torn in the struggle, his broad chest was visible, covered like his head, with a mass of hair. His feet were bare; his mouth was full of blood, and he continually spat out hair which he had bitten from the Jew's beard.

Every one stood still. Why? The guards unbound the lunatic's hands. The crowd drew to one side, leaving a large space around him. The madman looked about him, and his fierce glance rested upon Zibal's doorway; he gnashed his teeth, made a dash for the three steps, and in a flash, seizing the child's head in his right hand and Sura's in his left, he knocked them together with such force that they cracked like so many fresh eggs. A sound was heard, a scrunching impossible to describe, as the two skulls cracked together.

Leiba, with bursting heart, like a man who falls from an immense height, tried to cry out: "The whole world abandons me to the tender mercies of a madman!" But his voice refused to obey him.

"Get up, Jew!" cried some one, beating loudly upon the table with a stick.

"It's a bad joke," said Sura from the doorway of the inn, "thus to frighten the man out of his sleep, you stupid peasant!"

"What has scared you, Jew?" asked the wag, laughing. "You sleep in the afternoon, eh? Get up, customers are coming, the mail coach is arriving."

And, according to his silly habit which greatly irritated the Jew, he tried to take his arm and tickle him.

"Let me alone!" cried the innkeeper, drawing back and pushing him away with all his might. "Can you not see that I am ill? Leave me in peace."

The coach arrived at last, nearly three hours late. There were two passengers who seated themselves together with the driver, whom they had invited to share their table.

The conversation of the travellers threw a light upon recent events. At the highest posting station, a robbery with murder had been committed during the night in the inn of a Jew. The murdered inn-keeper was to have provided a change of horses. The thieves had taken them, and while other horses were being found in the village the curious travellers could examine the scene of the crime at their leisure. Five victims! But the details! From just seeing the ruined house one could believe it to have been some cruel vendetta or the work of some religious fanatic. In stories of sectarian fanaticism one heard occasionally of such extravagant crimes.

Leiba shook with a violent access of fever and listened aghast.

What followed must have undoubtedly filled the driver with respect. The young passengers were two students, one of philosophy, the other of medicine; they were returning to amuse themselves in their native town. They embarked upon a violent academic discussion upon crime and its causes, and, to give him his due, the medical student was better informed than the philosopher.

Atavism; alcoholism and its pathological consequences; defective birth; deformity; Paludism; then nervous disorders! Such and such conquest of modern science — but the case of reversion to type! Darwin, Häckel, Lombroso. At the mention of reversion to type, the driver opened wide his eyes in which shone a profound admiration for the conquests of modern science.

"It is obvious," added the medical student. "The so-called criminal proper, taken as a type, has unusually long arms, and very short feet, a flat and narrow forehead, and a much developed occiput. To the experienced eye his face is characteristically coarse and bestial; he is a rudimentary man: he is, I would say, a beast which has but lately got used to standing on its hind legs only, and to raising its head towards the sky, towards the light."

At the age of twenty, after so much excitement, and after a good repast with wine so well prepared, and so well matured as Leiba's, a phrase with a lyrical touch came well even from a medical student.

Between his studies of Darwin and Lombroso, the enthusiastic youth had found time to imbibe a little Schopenhauer — "towards the sky, towards the light!"

Leiba was far from understanding these "illuminating" ideas. Perhaps for the first time did such grand words and fine subtleties of thought find expression in the damp atmosphere of Podeni. But that which he understood better than anything, much better even than the speaker, was the striking illustration of the theory: the case of reversion type he knew in flesh and blood, it was the portrait of Gheorghe. This portrait, which had just been drawn in broad outline only, he could fill in perfectly in his own mind, down to the most minute details.

❋   ❋   ❋

The coach had gone. Leiba followed it with his eyes until, turning to the left, it was lost to sight round the hill. The sun was setting behind the ridge to the west, and the twilight began to weave soft shapes in the Podeni valley.

The gloomy innkeeper began to turn over in his mind all that he had heard. In the dead of night, lost in the darkness, a man, two women and two young children, torn without warning from the gentle arms of sleep by the hands of beasts with human faces, and sacrificed one after the other, the agonized cries of the children, cut short by the dagger ripping open their bodies, the neck slashed with a hatchet, the dull rattle in the throat with each gush of blood through the wound; and the last victim, half-distraught, in a corner, witness of the scene, and awaiting his turn. A condition far worse than execution was that of the Jew without protection in the hands of the Gentile — skulls too fragile for such fierce hands as those of the madman just now.

Leiba's lips, parched with fever, trembled as they mechanically followed his thoughts. A violent shivering fit seized him; he entered the porch of the inn with tottering steps.

"There is no doubt," thought Sura, "Leiba is not at all well, he is really ill; Leiba has got 'ideas' into his head. Is not that easy to understand after all he has been doing these last days, and especially after what he has done to-day?"

He had had the inn closed before the lights were lit, to remain so until the Sabbath was ended. Three times had some customers knocked at the door, calling to him, in familiar voices, to undo it. He had trembled at each knock and had stood still, whispering softly and with terrified eyes:

"Do not move — I want no Gentiles here."

Then he had passed under the porch, and had listened at the top of the stone steps by the door which was secured with a bar of wood. He shook so that he could scarcely stand, but he would not rest. The most distressing thing of all was that he had answered Sura's persistent questions sharply, and had sent her to bed, ordering her to put out the light at once. She had protested meanwhile, but the man had repeated the order curtly enough, and she had had unwillingly to submit, resigning herself to postponing to a later date any explanation of his conduct.

Sura had put out the lamp, had gone to bed, and now slept by the side of Strul.

The woman was right. Leiba was really ill.

        ✿   ✿   ✿

Night had fallen. For a long time Leiba had been sitting, listening by the doorway which gave on to the passage.

What is that?

Indistinct sounds came from the distance — horses trotting, the noise of heavy blows, mysterious and agitated conversations. The effort of listening intently in the solitude of the night sharpens the sense of hearing: when the eye is disarmed and powerless, the ear seems to struggle to assert its power.

But it was not imagination. From the road leading hither from the main road came the sound of approaching horses. Leiba rose, and tried to get nearer to the big door in the passage. The door was firmly shut by a heavy bar of wood across it, the ends of which ran into holes in the wall. At his first step the sand scrunching under his slippers made an indiscreet noise. He drew his feet from his slippers, and waited in the corner. Then, without a sound that could be heard by an unexpectant ear, he went to the door in the corridor, just as the riders passed in front of it at a walking pace. They were speaking very low to each other, but not so low but that Leiba could quite well catch these words:

"He has gone to bed early."

"Supposing he has gone away?"

"His turn will come; but I should have liked — "

No more was intelligible; the men were already some distance away.

To whom did these words refer? Who had gone to bed or gone away? Whose turn would come another time? Who would have liked something? And what was it he wanted? What did they want on that by-road — a road only used by anyone wishing to find the inn?

An overwhelming sense of fatigue seemed to overcome Leiba.

"Could it be Gheorghe?"

Leiba felt as if his strength was giving way, and he sat down by the door. Confused thoughts chased each other through his head, he could not think clearly or come to any decision.

Terrified, he re-entered the inn, struck a match, and lighted a small petroleum lamp.

It was an apology for a light; the wick was turned so low as to conceal the flame in the brass receiver; only by means of the opening round the receiver could some of the vertical shafts of light penetrate into a gloom that was like the darkness of death — all the same it was sufficient to enable him to see well into the familiar corners of the inn. Ah! How much less is the difference between the sun and the tiniest spark of light than between the latter and the gloom of blindness.

The clock on the wall ticked audibly. The monotonous sound irritated Leiba. He put his hand over the swinging pendulum, and stayed its movement.

His throat was parched. He was thirsty. He washed a small glass in a three-legged tub by the side of the bar and tried to pour some good brandy out of a decanter; but the mouth of the decanter began to clink loudly on the edge of the glass. This noise was still more irritating. A second attempt, in spite of his effort to conquer his weakness, met with no greater success.

Then, giving up the idea of the glass, he left it fall gently into the water, and drank several times out of the decanter. After that he pushed the decanter back into its place; as it touched the shelf it made an alarming clatter. For a moment he waited, appalled by such a catastrophe. Then he took the lamp, and placed it in the niche of the window which lighted the passage: the door, the pavement, and the wall which ran at right angles to the passage, were illuminated by almost imperceptible streaks of light.

He seated himself near the doorway and listened intently.

From the hill came the sound of bells ringing in the Resurrection morning. It meant that midnight was past, day was approaching. Ah! If only the rest of this long night might pass as had the first half!

The sound of sand trodden underfoot! But he was sitting in the corner, and had not stirred; a second noise, followed by many such. There could be no doubt some one was outside, here, quite near. Leiba rose, pressing his hand to his heart, and trying to swallow a suspicious lump in his throat.

There were several people outside — and Gheorghe! Yes, he was there; yes, the bells on the hill had rung the Resurrection.

They spoke softly:

"I tell you he is asleep. I saw when the lights went out."

"Good, we will take the whole nest."

"I will undo the door, I understand how it works. We must cut an opening — the beam runs along here."

He seemed to feel the touch of the men outside as they measured the distance on the wood. A big gimlet could be heard boring its way through the dry bark of the old oak. Leiba felt the need of support; he steadied himself against the door with his left hand while he covered his eyes with the right.

Then, through some inexplicable play of the senses, he heard, from within, quite loud and clear:

"Leiba! Here comes the coach."

It was surely Sura's voice. A warm ray of hope! A moment of joy! It was just another dream! But Leiba drew his left hand quickly back; the point of the tool, piercing the wood at that spot, had pricked the palm of his hand.

Was there any chance of escape? Absurd! In his burning brain the image of the gimlet took inconceivable dimensions. The instrument, turning continually, grew indefinitely, and the opening became larger and larger, large enough at last to enable the monster to step through the round aperture without having to bend. All that surged through such a brain transcends the thoughts of man; life rose to such a pitch of exaltation that everything seen, heard, felt, appeared to be enormous, the sense of proportion became chaotic.

The work outside was continued with method and perseverance. Four times in succession Leiba had seen the sharp steel tooth pierce through to his side and draw back again.

"Now, give me the saw," said Gheorghe.

The narrow end of a saw appeared through the first hole, and started to work with quick, regular movements. The plan was easy to understand; four holes in four corners of one panel; the saw made cuts between them; the gimlet was driven well home in the centre of the panel; when the piece became totally separated from the main body of the wood it was pulled out; through the opening thus made a strong hand inserted itself, seized the bar, pushed it to one side and — Gentiles are in Leiba's house.

In a few moments, this same gimlet would cause the destruction of Leiba and his domestic hearth. The two executioners would hold the victim prostrate on the ground, and Gheorghe, with heel upon his body, would slowly bore the gimlet into the bone of the living breast as he had done into the dead wood, deeper and deeper, till it reached the heart, silencing its wild beatings and pinning it to the spot.

Leiba broke into a cold sweat; the man was overcome by his own imagination, and sank softly to his knees as though life were ebbing from him under the weight of this last horror, overwhelmed by the thought that he must abandon now all hope of saving himself.

"Yes! Pinned to the spot," he said, despairingly. "Yes! Pinned to the spot."

He stayed a moment, staring at the light by the window. For some moments he stood aghast, as though in some other world, then he repeated with quivering eyelids:

"Yes! Pinned to the spot."

Suddenly a strange change took place in him, a complete revulsion of feeling; he ceased to tremble, his despair disappeared, and his face, so discomposed by the prolonged crisis, assumed an air of strange serenity. He straightened himself with the decision of a strong and healthy man who makes for an easy goal.

The line between the two upper punctures of the panel was finished. Leiba went up, curious to see the working of the tool. His confidence became more pronounced. He nodded his head as though to say: "I still have time."

The saw cut the last fibre near the hole towards which it was working, and began to saw between the lower holes.

"There are still three," thought Leiba, and with the caution of the most experienced burglar he softly entered the inn. He searched under the bar, picking up something, and went out again as he entered, hiding the object he had in his hand as though he feared somehow the walls might betray him, and went back on tiptoe to the door.

Something terrible had happened; the work outside had ceased — there was nothing to be heard.

"What is the matter? Has he gone? What has happened?" flashed through the mind of the man inside. He bit his lower lip at such a thought, full of bitter disappointment.

"Ha, ha!" It was an imaginary deception; the work began again, and he followed it with the keenest interest, his heart beating fast. His decision was taken, he was tormented by an incredible desire to see the thing finished.

"Quicker!" he thought, with impatience. "Quicker!"

Again the sound of bells ringing on the hill.

"Hurry up, old fellow, the daylight will catch us!" said a voice outside, as though impelled by the will of the man within.

The work was pushed on rapidly. Only a few more movements and all the punctures in the panel would be united.

At last!

Gently the drill carried out the four-sided piece of wood. A large and supple hand was thrust in; but before it reached the bars it sought two screams were heard, while, with great force, Leiba enclosed it with the free end of the noose, which was round a block fixed to the cellar door.

The trap was ingeniously contrived: a long rope fastened round a block of wood; lengthwise, at the place where the sawn panel had disappeared, was a spring-ring which Leiba held open with his left hand, while at the same time his right hand held the other end taut. At the psychological moment he sprang the ring, and rapidly seizing the free end of the rope with both hands he pulled the whole arm inside by a supreme effort.

In a second the operation was complete. It was accompanied by two cries, one of despair, the other of triumph: the hand was "pinned to the spot." Footsteps were heard retreating rapidly: Gheorghe's companions were abandoning to Leiba the prey so cleverly caught.

The Jew hurried into the inn, took the lamp and with a decided movement turned up the wick as high as it would go: the light concealed by the metal receiver rose gay and victorious, restoring definite outlines to the nebulous forms around.

Zibal went into the passage with the lamp. The burglar groaned terribly; it was obvious from the stiffening of his arm that he had given up the useless struggle. The hand was swollen, the fingers were curved as though they would seize something. The Jew placed the lamp near it — a shudder, the fever is returning. He moved the light quite close, until, trembling, he touched the burglar's hand with the burning chimney; a violent convulsion of the finger was followed by a dull groan. Leiba was startled at the sight of this phenomenon.

Leiba trembled — his eyes betrayed a strange exaltation. He burst into a shout of laughter which shook the empty corridor and resounded in the inn.

Day was breaking.

Sura woke up suddenly — in her sleep she seemed to hear a terrible moaning. Leiba was not in the room. All that had happened previously returned to her mind. Something terrible had taken place. She jumped out of bed and lighted the candle. Leiba's bed had not been disturbed. He had not been to bed at all.

Where was he? The woman glanced out of the window; on the hill in front shone a little group of small bright lights, they flared and jumped, now they died away, now, once more, they soared upwards. They told of the Resurrection. Sura undid the window; then she could hear groans from down the stairs. The corridor was lighted up. As she emerged through the doorway, the woman was astonished by a horrible sight.

Upon a wooden chair, his elbows on his knees, his beard in his hand, sat Leiba. Like a scientist, who, by mixing various elements, hopes to surprise one of nature's subtle secrets which has long escaped and worried him, Leiba kept his eyes fixed upon some hanging object, black and shapeless, under which, upon another chair of convenient height, there burnt a big torch. He watched, without turning a hair, the process of decomposition of the hand which most certainly would not have spared him. He did not hear the groans of the unhappy being outside: he was more interested, at present, in watching than in listening.

He followed with eagerness each contortion, every strange convulsion of the fingers till one by one they became powerless. They were like the legs of a beetle which contract and stretch, waving in agitated movement, vigorously, then slower and slower until they lie paralysed by the play of some cruel child.

It was over. The roasted hand swelled slowly and remained motionless. Sura gave a cry.

"Leiba!"

He made a sign to her not to disturb him. A greasy smell of burnt flesh pervaded the passage: a crackling and small explosions were heard.

"Leiba! What is it?" repeated the woman.

It was broad day. Sura stretched forward and withdrew the bar. The door opened outwards, dragging with it Gheorghe's body, suspended by the right arm. A crowd of villagers, all carrying lighted torches, invaded the premises.

"What is it? What is it?"

They soon understood what had happened. Leiba, who up to now had remained motionless, rose gravely to his feet. He made room for himself to pass, quietly pushing the crowd to one side.

"How did it happen, Jew?" asked some one.

"Leiba Zibal," said the innkeeper in a loud voice, and with a lofty gesture, "goes to Jassy to tell the Rabbi that Leiba Zibal is a Jew no longer. Leiba Zibal is a Christian — for Leiba Zibal has lighted a torch for Christ."[1]

And the man moved slowly up the hill, towards the sunrise, like the prudent traveller who knows that the long journey is not achieved with hasty steps.

Doctor Faustus

Act V, Scene 2

FAUSTUS: Ah, Faustus,
Now hast thou but one bare hour to live,
And then thou must be damn'd perpetually!
Stand still, you ever-moving spheres of heaven,

[1] There is an old Jewish tradition that whoever lights a candle or torch on the night of Easter announces that he has become a Christian.

That time may cease, and midnight never come;
Fair Nature's eye, rise, rise again, and make
Perpetual day; or let this hour be but
A year, a month, a week, a natural day,
That Faustus may repent and save his soul!
O lente, lente currite, noctis equi![2]
The stars move still, time runs, the clock will strike,
The devil will come, and Faustus must be damn'd.
O, I'll leap up to my God! — Who pulls me down? —
See, see, where Christ's blood streams in the firmament!
One drop would save my soul, half a drop: ah, my Christ! —
Ah, rend not my heart for naming of my Christ!
Yet will I call on him: O, spare me, Lucifer! —
Where is it now? 'tis gone: and see, where God
Stretcheth out his arm, and bends his ireful brows!
Mountains and hills, come, come, and fall on me,
And hide me from the heavy wrath of God!
No, no!
Then will I headlong run into the earth:
Earth, gape! O, no, it will not harbour me!
You stars that reign'd at my nativity,
Whose influence hath allotted death and hell,
Now draw up Faustus, like a foggy mist,
Into the entrails of yon lab'ring cloud
That, when you vomit forth into the air,
My limbs may issue from your smoky mouths,
So that my soul may but ascend to heaven!
                    (*The clock strikes the half hour.*
Ah, half the hour is past! 'twill all be passed anon.
O God,
If thou wilt not have mercy on my soul,
Yet for Christ's sake, whose blood hath ransom'd me,
Impose some end to my incessant pain;
Let Faustus live in hell a thousand years,
A hundred thousand, and at last be sav'd!
O, no end is limited to damnèd souls!
Why wert thou not a creature wanting soul?
Or why is this immortal that thou hast?
Ah, Pythagoras' metempsychosis, were that true,

---

[2] Translated by Marlowe himself in his *Ovid's Elegies* as, "Then wouldst thou cry, stay night and runne not thus." It is Ovid's appeal, while Corinna lies in his arms, to the steeds of the night to slow their pace.

This soul should fly from me, and I be changed
Unto some brutish beast! all beasts are happy,
For when they die,
Their souls are soon dissolv'd in elements;
But mine must live still to be plagu'd in hell.
Curs'd be the parents that engender'd me!
No, Faustus, curse thyself, curse Lucifer
That hath depriv'd thee of the joys of heaven.
                              (*The clock striketh twelve*

O, it strikes, it strikes! Now, body, turn to air,
Or Lucifer will bear thee quick to hell!
O soul, be changed into little water-drops,
And fall into the ocean, ne'er be found!
                    Thunder and enter Devils
My God, my God, look not so fierce on me!
Adders and serpents, let me breathe a while!
Ugly hell, gape not! come not, Lucifer!
I'll burn my books! — Ah, Mephistophilis!
                              (*Exeunt with him.*

CHRISTOPHER MARLOWE

God's Grandeur*

The world is charged with the grandeur of God.
It will flame out, like shining from shook foil;
It gathers to a greatness, like the ooze of oil
Crushed. Why do men then now not reck his rod?
Generations have trod, have trod, have trod;
And all is seared with trade; bleared, smeared with toil;
And wears man's smudge and shares man's smell: the soil
Is bare now, nor can foot feel, being shod.

And for all this, nature is never spent;
There lives the dearest freshness deep down things;
And though the last lights off the black West went
Oh, morning, at the brown brink eastward, springs —
Because the Holy Ghost over the bent
World broods with warm breast and with ah! bright wings.

GERARD MANLEY HOPKINS

* Reprinted by permission of the Oxford University Press (London).

*I Wake and Feel the Fell of Dark**

I wake and feel the fell of dark, not day.
What hours, O what black hoürs we have spent
This night! what sights you, heart, saw; ways you went!
And more must, in yet longer light's delay.
   With witness I speak this. But where I say
Hours I mean years, mean life. And my lament
Is cries countless, cries like dead letters sent
To dearest him that lives alas! away.

  I am gall, I am heartburn. God's most deep decree
Bitter would have me taste: my taste was me;
Bones built in me, flesh filled, blood brimmed the curse.
   Selfyeast of spirit a dull dough sours. I see
The lost are like this, and their scourge to be
As I am mine, their sweating selves; but worse.

GERARD MANLEY HOPKINS

In a Dark Time†

I

In a dark time, the eye begins to see:
I meet my shadow in the deepening shade;
I hear my echo in the echoing wood,
A lord of nature weeping to a tree.
I live between the heron and the wren,
Beasts of the hill and serpents of the den.

II

What's madness but nobility of soul
At odds with circumstance? The day's on fire!
I know the purity of pure despair,
My shadow pinned against a sweating wall.
That place among the rocks — is it a cave
Or winding path? The edge is what I have.

* Reprinted by permission of the Oxford University Press (London).
  † "In a Dark Time" copyright © 1960 by Beatrice Roethke as Administratrix of the Estate of Theodore Roethke. From the book, *The Far Field* by Theodore Roethke. Reprinted by permission of Beatrice Roethke.

III

A steady storm of correspondences! —
A night flowing with birds, a ragged moon,
And in broad day the midnight come again!
A man goes far to find out what he is —
Death of the self in a long tearless night,
All natural shapes blazing unnatural light.

IV

Dark, dark my light, and darker my desire.
My soul, like some heat-maddened fly,
Keeps buzzing at the sill. Which I is I?
A fallen man, I climb out of my fear.
The mind enters itself, and God the mind,
And one is One, free in the tearing wind.

                                    THEODORE ROETHKE

Leave Me, O Love Which Reachest

Leave me, O love which reachest but to dust,
And thou, my mind, aspire to higher things;
Grow rich in that which never taketh rust:
Whatever fades, but fading pleasure brings.

Draw in thy beams, and humble all thy might
To that sweet yoke, where lasting freedoms be,
Which breaks the clouds, and opens forth the light,
That doth both shine and give us sight to see.

O take fast hold! let that light be thy guide,
In this small course which birth draws out to death,
And think how evil becometh him to slide,
Who seeketh heav'n, and comes of heav'nly breath.
  Then farewell world, thy uttermost I see;
  Eternal love, maintain thy life in me.

                                    SIR PHILIP SIDNEY

A *Thanksgiving to God for His House*

Lord, Thou hast given me a cell
    Wherein to dwell;
A little house, whose humble roof
    Is weather-proof;
Under the spars of which I lie
    Both soft and dry;
Where Thou my chamber for to ward
    Hast set a guard
Of harmless thoughts, to watch and keep
    Me, while I sleep.
Low is my porch, as is my fate,
    Both void of state;
And yet the threshold of my door
    Is worn by th' poor,
Who thither come, and freely get
    Good words or meat;
Like as my parlour, so my hall
    And kitchen's small;
A little buttery, and therein
    A little bin
Which keeps my little loaf of bread
    Unclipt, unflead.
Some brittle sticks of thorn or briar
    Make me a fire,
Close by whose living coal I sit,
    And glow like it.
Lord, I confess, too, when I dine,
    The pulse is Thine,
And all those other bits, that be
    There placed by Thee;
The worts, the purslain, and the mess
    Of water-cress,
Which of Thy kindness Thou hast sent;
    And my content
Makes those, and my beloved beet,
    To be more sweet.
'Tis Thou that crown'st my glittering hearth
    With guiltless mirth;
And giv'st me wassail bowls to drink,
    Spiced to the brink.

Lord, 'tis Thy plenty-dropping hand,
    That soils my land;
And giv'st me for my bushel sown,
    Twice ten for one.
Thou mak'st my teeming hen to lay
    Her egg each day;
Besides my healthful ewes to bear
    Me twins each year,
The while the conduits of my kine
    Run cream for wine.
All these, and better Thou dost send
    Me, to this end,
That I should render, for my part,
    A thankful heart;
Which, fired with incense, I resign,
    As wholly Thine;
But the acceptance, that must be,
    My Christ, by Thee.

ROBERT HERRICK

Heaven

O WHO will show me those delights on high?
    ECHO. I.
Thou Echo, thou art mortall, all men know.
    ECHO. No.
Wert thou not born among the trees and leaves?
    ECHO. Leaves.
And are there any leaves, that still abide?
    ECHO. Bide.
What leaves are they? impart the matter wholly.
    ECHO. Holy.
Are holy leaves the Echo, then, of blisse?
    ECHO. Yes.
Then tell me, what is that supreme delight?
    ECHO. Light.
Light to the minde: what shall the will enjoy?
    ECHO. Joy.
But are there cares and businesse with the pleasure?
    ECHO. Leisure.
Light, joy, and leisure; but shall they persevere?
    ECHO. Ever.

GEORGE HERBERT

Vertue

Sweet day, so cool, so calm, so bright,
The bridall of the earth and skie:
The dew shall weep thy fall to-night;
    For thou must die.

Sweet rose, whose hue angrie and brave
Bids the rash gazer wipe his eye:
Thy root is ever in its grave,
    And thou must die.

Sweet spring, full of sweet days and roses,
A box where sweets compacted lie;
My musick shows ye have your closes,
    And all must die.

Onely a sweet and vertuous soul,
Like season'd timber, never gives;
But though the whole world turn to coal,
    Then chiefly lives.

GEORGE HERBERT

Holy Sonnet

XIV

Batter my heart, three person'd God; for, you
As yet but knocke, breathe, shine, and seeke to mend;
That I may rise, and stand, o'erthrow mee, and bend
Your force, to breake, blowe, burn and make me new.
I, like an usurpt towne, to another due,
Labour to' admit you, but Oh, to no end.
Reason, your viceroy in mee, mee should defend,
But is captiv'd, and proves weake or untrue.
Yet dearely I love you, and would be loved faine,
But am betroth'd unto your enemie:
Divorce mee, untie, or breake that knot againe,
Take mee to you, imprison mee, for I
Except you enthrall mee, never shall be free,
Nor ever chast, except you ravish mee.

JOHN DONNE

Chorus Sacerdotum

(from Mustapha)

Oh wearisome Condition of Humanity!
Borne under one Law, to another bound:
Vainely begot, and yet forbidden vanity,
Created sicke, commanded to be sound:
What meaneth Nature by these diverse Lawes?
Passion and Reason, selfe-division cause:
Is it the marke, or Majesty of Power
To make offences that it may forgive?
Nature herselfe, doth her owne selfe defloure,
To hate those errors she her selfe doth give.
For how should man thinke that, he may not doe
If Nature did not faile, and punish too?
Tyrant to others, to her selfe unjust,
Onely commands things difficult and hard.
Forbids us all things, which it knowes is lust,
Makes easie paines, unpossible reward.
If Nature did not take delight in blood,
She would have made more easie waies to good.
We that are bound by vowes, and by Promotion,
With pompe of holy Sacrifice and rites,
To teach beleefe in good and still devotion,
To preach of Heavens wonders, and delights:
Yet when each of us, in his owne heart lookes,
He findes the God there, farre unlike his Bookes.

BROOKE, FULKE GREVILLE, BARON

CHAPTER FOURTEEN

Related Aspects of Rhythm and Meter

The best of rules are but as flowers planted
over the graves of prodigious impulses.

LOUIS SULLIVAN

SOUND DEVICES

There is a widespread notion about poetry — and one which seems generally applicable — that it is more rich in sound repetitions and echoes than prose and that it is more likely to use these repetitions and echoes self-consciously to achieve artistic meaning. In general, these sound devices assist in developing the artistic meaning of the poem through (1) emphasis and (2) the process known as association. Certain sudden sound intensities may help the artist call attention to something important, as when the repetition of a sound may point to the relationship between words which contain those sounds. Of course, the opposite can happen also; if a poem hitherto rich in sound echoes becomes suddenly quite plain and devoid of such echoes, that in itself fixes attention. More subtle is the technique (the basic insight of behavioral psychology) by which, during the course of a poem, specific sounds become associated with certain feelings, so that the appearance of the sounds themselves finally begins to call up the desired response.

It is sometimes presumed that certain sounds automatically have certain feelings attached to them, that, for instance, sounds such as "k" and "d" inevitably call up feelings of strength, even harshness. Perhaps in the beginnings of language there might have been some such relationship, and there may still be some echoes of that early simple correspondence. But human language and sensibility have grown infinitely more general, more abstract, till it is not possible to respond to words like "crush" or "kill" or "cadaver" with the same emotions that one responds to such words as to "kiss" and "cuddle" and "caress," even though they exploit much the same sounds. Indeed, if one realizes that all the many thousands of words in the unabridged dictionary are formed by varying combinations of only a few dozen easily distinguishable sounds, it becomes clear that, whatever they were in the lost beginnings of speech, these sounds must now, in themselves, be mostly neutral in feeling, devoid of emotional content, much as the pieces in the game of checkers always remain the same, but their value and meaning shift according to their position on the board. For it is clear that the "k" and "d" in "cadaver" and in "cuddle" not only are, but must be, free to adopt the basic emotional coloration which is radiated by the connotation (and denotations) of each individual word. That is not to say that sounds do not adopt temporary emotional colorations. They certainly do. But these are usually best seen as something acquired temporarily through repetition, in a given poem, in association with those emotions, or even with specific events or characters.

Rhyme

Perhaps the most obvious, if not the most important, use of a sound repetition is *rhyme*. It is not so easy to define rhyme as it might at first seem, for it has many varieties. Indeed the more subtle formulations of rhyme have not even all been named, at least as they occur in English. But the hub from which all the variations radiate, the convention in relation to which, as significant variations, they derive much of their effect, is TRUE RHYME.

Before true rhyme can be defined, it should be mentioned that, in discussing poetry, a line that ends on a slack syllable is said to have a "feminine ending," whereas the line that ends on a stressed syllable has a "masculine ending." Further, it is necessary to recall that a syllable is the next sound unit longer than the letter and that it usually consists of a vowel, sometimes preceded by a consonant, sometimes followed by a consonant, and sometimes both. Thus the word "merry" is a feminine word of two syllables, mĕr ē, the first syllable being consonant-vowel-consonant, the second syllable consisting of only a vowel. The word "above" is a masculine word of two syllables, à bŭv, the first syllable consisting of only a vowel, the second syllable being consonant-vowel-consonant. The word "hardy" is a feminine word of two syllables, här dĭ, the first syllable consisting of consonant-vowel-consonant, the second being consonant-vowel.

Occasionally a syllable is used which has no vowel, but is only consonant-consonant. Such an example as "settle" must be clearly distinguished from a word like "able," where the second syllable uses a vowel phonetically, though not visually; "a bul" is how the word is said. Further, the vowel-less syllables are ignored in discovering rhymes, as we shall see in a moment.

Basically, then, for purposes of rhyme, a syllable consists of a root vowel, which may or may not be preceded or followed or both by a consonant or consonants. With this definition in mind, a *true rhyme* may be defined as the *repetition of two words of masculine ending whose final vowels and any consonant sounds that may follow it are phonetically identical.* It will be noticed that this rhyme (and in fact most varieties of rhyme) demand that the consonant(s) just *preceding* the final vowel shall be phonetically *unlike.* We shall come back to this problem in a moment. Remember that for rhyme the important thing is how the words *sound phonetically,* not how they are spelled visually. Thus "said" and "bed," though the vowels *look* unlike, are nevertheless examples of a true rhyme, because the vowels and following consonants *sound alike.* Conversely "head" and "bead" do not form true rhyme, even though the vowels *look* the same.

Although the *old* rule is that two words must be *masculine* to form a true rhyme, a variation of true rhyme has occurred occasionally from the beginning of modern English poetry and has so grown in favor with modern poets that it must be specifically discussed. That is the use of what we may call *mixed rhyme,* which is the same as true rhyme, except that one of the rhyming words is feminine.

| holy | sing | light | aright | slayer |
| see | wandering | midnight | daylight | spur |

A step beyond mixed rhyme is *feminine rhyme,* wherein *both* rhyming words are feminine.

| tarry | under | extension |
| pony | over | action |

These are all, in a sense, true rhyme, since all require that the final vowels and the consonants that follow them be phonetically identical. One might then speak more accurately of *true masculine rhyme, true feminine rhyme,* and *true mixed rhyme.*

true masculine rhyme	*true feminine rhyme*	*true mixed rhyme*
aloud	any	ahead
proud	lady	seeded

Apart from this group of true rhymes, the most important are the *slant rhymes,* of which there are two principal varieties: the *consonantal* and the *assonantal.* In assonantal rhyme the final vowels must be phonetically identical, and any consonants that follow must be phonetically dissimilar.

assonantal masculine	*assonantal feminine*	*assonantal mixed*
bled	Byron	destroys
wet	wisdom	is álloyed

In *consonantal rhyme* the final vowels must be unlike and all following consonants must be alike phonetically.

consonantal masculine		*consonantal feminine*	*consonantal mixed*
blade	tarn	mental	final
wed	burn	Peekskill	sill

When two or more different types of rhyme are used systematically in one poem, the technique is called *analyzed rhyme.*

	true masculine rhyme	consonantal masculine rhyme
Beneath the *weed*	A	A
A blinkless *bead*	A	A
In an arrow *head*-	B	A
A drop of *dread*.	B	A

Although true rhymes and slant rhymes are the most important, there are other varieties that make their appearance. It was mentioned earlier that the consonant *preceding* the final vowel must be phonetically different in most varieties of rhyme. Where a rhyme *does* occur in which the consonant-vowel-consonant of the final syllable are all phonetically alike, it is called *identical rhyme.*

brede	red	see
breed	(have) read	sea

By and large identical rhymes are avoided by poets, not simply because there is a law, but because such rhymes tend to be flat, overemphatic, and boring. There is yet more complexity to rhyme. Take a rhyme-set like

dread		bleed
tread	or	plead

which are by no means uncommon possibilities in English. The theory of rhyme in English up to this time tends to ignore such rhyming variations. Certainly it cannot be claimed that these are exactly true rhymes, because of the consonantal identity prior to the vowel. Nor are they exactly identical rhyme, since the initial consonant of the final syllable is different. In short, true masculine dead / Ted is quite different in musical impact from dread / tread and different from either one is red / (I have) read. This (dread / tread) type of rhyme where there is some, but not total, phonetic identity of the consonantal pattern preceding the final vowel might well be called consonantal true rhyme. In any case, there are other formulations of rhyme which might well be noted, among them *eye rhyme,* which is not really rhyme at all, but a word-set in which phonetic identity has been abandoned, and visual identity substituted, as in sew / knew, instead / (to) plead, through / dough. Rhymes may, of course, be *multi-syllabic,* as in

edu*cation*	*neatly*	heaven	*attic*
o*ration*	fleetly	seven	demo*cratic.*

And they can be *internal rhyme* (occurring within the line), or *end rhyme* (occurring at the end of line). Rhyme can upon occasion shift from the last syllable to earlier in the word, as in

| deadly | morrow | leader |
| wedding | borrowed | speeded. |

All these rhymes are potentially available to the poet to help him say what he has to say more effectively. There are, of course, many poems, and some among them the greatest, in which rhyme is not appropriate. Though no hard and fast rules can be drawn, these are usually the poems in which interplay of character and incident carry a major thrust. On the other hand, when wit (in the deeper sense as in philosophical or didactic poems) is the method of the poem, or in those lyric poems which are descended from song, rhyme is a source of power seldom ignored by the great poets of the English language.

These various terms (which do not always agree with those used by other writers) clearly come after the fact. Always the reader's aim is not to label, but to see what is there and see how it works with everything else that is there. Terms justify themselves only insofar as they make discussions more convenient and distinctions easier. Actually, the *effects* of rhyme are never quite the same in any two cases, arising as they do out of a changing matrix of rhythm, denotation, density, which taken together form the tone the reader is to *feel with* accurately. But a word about the potential of rhyme in the English language might well precede an examination of its effects in specific examples.

English is a language rich in its number of true rhyme-groups (a rhyme-group consists of all the words in a language that rhyme together in a given way). However, these true-rhyme rhyme-groups, with but few exceptions, do not have very many words in them. This simple fact has very important repercussions in the practical writing of a poem. For instance, up until the advent of the free verse movement in the poetry of France, that country's poetic forms were much more ornate with rhyme than ours, with a single rhyme-group repeating itself stanza after stanza and with very rigid rules governing rhyme. This use of rhyme arose no doubt because there were fewer rhyme-groups than in English, but, more important, the numbers in each rhyme-group averaged very many more words. Of these ornate French forms, few have succeeded in English, probably for the very simple reason that in English any form in which a rhyme-group must be exploited beyond a few words limits the poet to a choice of very few rhyme-groups. Because of this difficulty, which both the reader and poet feel instinctively, most such poems have the aura of a *tour de force,* rather than of triumphant unconsciousness. This shortage of words in a rhyme-group is, perhaps, why even in the periods of English poetry most interested in rhyme, the chief patterns have been the couplet (AABBCC) and the quatrain, usually in one of two main rhyme forms (ABAB or ABBA). This necessity upon English poets to be free to shift from rhyme-group to rhyme-group has from the first, in my belief, made for a poetry based at least as much on variety in its rhyming as on extension and repetition, as much on rhyme as *subordinate* musical element as on rhyme as *major* structural device. The aesthetic handling of rhyme varies enormously from poet to poet, even in English. But the interest in rhyme as a potential for tonal variety as well as structural boundary gained impetus from the very niggardliness of some of our important rhyme-sets.

The popular song rhyme cliché of moon-June-soon-croon-spoon is notorious. Yet the truth is that moon is a word very often connected with lovers, and it is revealing to see how few other words are available in that rhyme-group. Normally the only way out for the poet is to avoid the group altogether. From the beginning, even in periods apparently wholly dedicated to true rhyme, certain important words such as "love" have been permitted slant rhyme, because of the paucity of words in their rhyme-group. In the case mentioned, love-above-dove is about it, unless you think "shove" is likely to be contextually relevant. I believe it is tremendously important to the aesthetic use of rhyme in English that from the beginning of modern English slant rhymes have been occasional necessities, that the rhyme of even a short poem is constantly shifting, and that many of our most important words occur in rhyme-groups so small that their possible rhyme-mates are very soon clichés. It was inevitable therefore that sooner or later the varieties of rhyme, chiefly the slant rhyme, aided by the powerful impetus of such poets as Emily Dickinson and Wilfred Owen, should become at least equal in importance with true rhyme and would create a situation in which the whole catalogue of rhyme-echo is at any given time within the poet's allowable range, as it has been in poetry since 1920.

Alliteration and Other Sound Echoes

After rhyme, alliteration is the most striking of sound repetitions. In old English (Anglo-Saxon) poetry as well as in the poetry of other languages, it once held the place now held by rhyme, as the governing sound pattern to be integrated with the rhythm and with the meter. In modern English it has always been a device used *ad lib.* by the poet for the variety of purposes that may lie behind any sound coloration. Alliteration refers only to the repetition of the initial sounds of words, where those sounds are consonants, "the *b*ad and the *b*eautiful," "*f*ancy *f*ree," "*d*rive to *d*rink."

However, alliteration is but one of the variety of sound echoes, for obviously any sound can be repeated in any position or combination of positions. Usually, where the repetition relates to vowels, the technique is called "assonance," and where a consonant is repeated it is called "consonance," but clearly these are such sketchy terms as to be only vaguely useful in getting at the infinite effects of the infinite possibilities of sound relationships. These possibilities begin with such simple pleasures as "kith and kin," which combines alliteration with assonance and is obviously repeated everywhere for the musical fun of it, since almost no one knows what "kith" means any more. They range on to such subtle musicality as the first line of Coleridge's "Kubla Khan"

consonance

In Zan a d u d i d K u b l a K h a n,

assonance

where the assonance of "a" and "u" beautifully balanced within the alliterations and consonance of "K" and "d" and "n," operates largely for its own pleasure, having very little weight of total meaning to reinforce. And then on to such passages as

> Tomorrow and tomorrow and tomorrow
> Creeps in this petty pace from day to day
> To the last syllable of recorded time

where the whole complex of repetition, alliteration, assonance, and consonance must help the other elements of the passage create a complex tone of endless despair.

Onomatopoeia is the last sound device we shall consider. An onomatopoeic word is one which is formed by imitating the natural sound associated with the object or action involved. There is a tendency among oral readers to find more onomatopoeic words than actually exist. Obviously the occurrence is limited to words whose *meaning* has to do with the creation of a sound, a sharp limitation at the start. For example, *hiss* is onomatopoeic because its formation is based on the sound which is its meaning, while *startle,* which one may feel has some *kinesthetic* relation to its meaning, cannot be onomatopoeic since its meaning is not involved in the creation of a sound. It is possible for a combination of words to be onomatopoeic, though that is a rather rare circumstance. More common is the phrase or line which, through a combination of rhythm and tone coloration, gives one a kinesthetic feeling that in some way relates to its meaning. The line from Shakespeare quoted just above is an excellent example in its ability to create in us a sense of the horror of empty weariness which pervades the sensibility of the character who speaks the lines.

THE VISUAL ASPECTS OF POETIC STRUCTURE

Common sense assumes that before writing was made a reflection of spoken language, there was no such thing as a "poetic line" as distinct from phrase. There were, no doubt, various ways of disciplining the length of phrase: a poetic phrase might last as long as it took for the sound of a chord struck on a stringed instrument to die away; or a phrase might last as long as it took to make a certain number of steps in a dance; or the phrase might last for a certain number of stresses or whatever auditory units might be counted. There may have been all kinds of auditory disciplines now lost or echoing remotely and half guessed at. But once poetry began visibly to be recorded (in writing and later in print), then, just as the discipline of punctuation was bound to develop, so was a discipline of poetic conventions based on writing bound to appear.

Supplemental Use of Vision

Take an important example, so common as to be thought of as perfectly natural to poetry — the run-on line. Clearly, in *oral* poetry the "line" must nearly always be concluded by a pause, related to the dramatic and sense meaning of the poem. Otherwise the sense of the "line" or phrasal unit or rhythmic entity will soon disappear. The run-on line, therefore, where the line is concluded for metrical reasons totally separate from the sense of the phrase, is a device which could be tolerated in any frequency only where the written text adds its own potential to that of the oral aspects. In the first stanza of Wilbur's "Driftwood," the first and third lines, both run-on, depend upon our visual sense to tell us where the line ends. It is interesting that even the phrasal rhythms come at the end of the second and fourth lines, as if further to emphasize that, really, the first and second lines form one oral unit, while the third and fourth form another (a pattern repeated in virtually every stanza of the poem). In this way, the visual discipline gives to the total rhythm a contrapuntal possibility not present where the discipline is purely oral. The slight, almost indefinable, pause (made without dropping the voice or otherwise interrupting the normal speech pattern) which should be given to the end of the run-on line adds a kind of delicate syncopation to the oral phrase. I have already mentioned this syncopation as one positive possibility possessed by the meters, and one may speculate that the metrical line, as such, seen as something apart from the phrase, is probably an offspring of the development of written poetry.

Driftwood*

In greenwoods once these relics must have known
A rapt, gradual growing,
That are cast here like slag of the old
Engine of grief;

Must have affirmed in annual increase
Their close selves, knowing
Their own nature only, and that
Bringing to leaf.

°   °   °   RICHARD WILBUR

In larger aspects, too, aesthetic uses are made of this cleavage between a metrical unit which can be seen and an emotive unit which can
be heard and felt. I have already suggested that significant aesthetic consequences come from the tensions that arise between the line (metrical
unit) and the phrase or sentence (emotive unit). Significant tensions also
rise between the stanza (the larger metrical unit) and the phrase or sentence.
The stanza is to poetry what the paragraph is to prose. However, unlike
the prose paragraph or free verse stanza, the stanza in a metered poem is
usually *metrical* (blank verse is a notable exception). We may consider the
stanza to be the repetition of a certain number and kind of lines in a certain order, and most metered poems in this book will serve as examples.
As a metrical (i.e., measured) unit in itself, the stanza, like the line, may or
may not also coincide with the emotive unit next larger than the sentence.

We have already suggested that in free verse this relationship of the
metrical unit (line, stanza) with the emotive unit (phrase, sentence, paragraph) is almost always simply one-to-one. The phrase or sentence is the
line, and the paragraph is the stanza (see Whitman, p. 237, Cummings,
p. 242, Eliot, p. 100). A close look at these three poets will show that
these metrical and emotive elements develop different appearances in the
hands of different poets, but a one-to-one identity is almost always, in free
verse, their basic aesthetic relationship.

Let us now see how these elements function in the meters. Whether
the line and phrase, the paragraph and stanza coincide is generally important to the total rhythmic impact. This correspondence or lack of it can be
intensified by other factors, especially rhyme, which is usually but not always an important part of the metered stanza. A strong sense of rhyme
can give the metered stanza a very definite sense of being a separate aesthetic unit; and where the conclusion of the grammatical unit and emotive
unit does *not* coincide with the conclusive effect of the stanza's rhyme, a

very sharp syncopation can be created. In a poem where the sense and the stanza seldom or never coincide, this effect can come to seem aesthetically normal, its continual syncopation habitual, and therefore relatively unnoticed (see Browning's "My Last Duchess," p. 139). But the effect can be very sharp where there is a sudden separation of sense or emotive unit from stanza. All we have said of the stanza-paragraph also holds true of the line-phrase dichotomy (the sentence is likely to operate as a third rhythmic element apart from line and phrase, sometimes important in itself, sometimes almost totally subsumed by line or phrase or both). Some poets use the stanza so powerfully as to make it dominate as *rhythmical* unit almost altogether over the line, which in turn would obviously make certain other aesthetic combinations possible. Among these various metrical and emotive relationships the permutations are infinite.

What Is to Be Given*

What is to be given,
Is spirit, yet animal,
Colored, like heaven,
Blue, yellow, beautiful.

The blood is checkered by
So many stains and wishes,
Between it and the sky
You could not choose, for riches.

Yet let me now be careful
Not to give too much
To one so shy and fearful
For like a gun is touch.

DELMORE SCHWARTZ

In the first stanza of this poem the line is dominant. The phrase, we note, sometimes reinforces the line and, at other times, breaks the line into smaller units. (I use the word "phrase" here not in a strictly grammatical sense, but as meaning that which is marked off by a natural pause or by marked intonational patterns so as to form a distinct rhythmical unit.) Yet in this stanza it is the line which exerts the cohesive force.

In the second stanza, the relationship alters. The phrase welds the first two lines together and the last two lines together in such a way as to create a new major rhythmic element. This two-line phrase now dominates the strict line and makes the stanza essentially a two-part unit rather than a four-part unit. The line remains as a minor counter rhythm.

In the third stanza the sentence becomes dominant to the extent that even the possible pause after "fearful" is largely overridden. And this sentence, by coinciding with the stanza, turns the stanza into the major rhythmic element, with both phrase and line subordinate to the longer rhythmic reach of the stanza. So much is clear. It would be interesting for the reader to try to determine the effect of the rhyme in this, and to determine just how this very obvious shift in rhythmic pattern from line to phrase to stanza relates to the tonal meaning.

Next, Please*

Always too eager for the future, we
Pick up bad habits of expectancy.
Something is always approaching; every day
Till then we say,

Watching from a bluff the tiny, clear,
Sparkling armada of promises draw near.
How slow they are! And how much time they waste,
Refusing to make haste!

Yet still they leave us holding wretched stalks
Of disappointment, for, though nothing balks
Each big approach, leaning with brasswork prinked,
Each rope distinct,

Flagged, and the figurehead with golden tits
Arching our way, it never anchors; it's
No sooner present than it turns to past.
Right to the last

We think each one will heave to and unload
All good into our lives, all we are owed
For waiting so devoutly and so long.
But we are wrong:

Only one ship is seeking us, a black-
Sailed unfamiliar, towing at her back
A huge and birdless silence. In her wake
No waters breed or break.

Philip Larkin

In this poem the sentence is very strong, is perhaps the major large rhythmical unit. Sometimes phrase or sentence reinforces the line; at least as often it does not. In only two of the six stanzas can the phrase (not the sentence) be said to assist the stanza as a sense-unit. In general, the stanza

*Reprinted from *The Less Deceived* by Philip Larkin, by permission of The Marvell Press, Hessle, Yorkshire, England.

is strictly a meter-rhyme unit, serving as a syncopation to the dominant reach of the sentence. In such a poem the rhythmic and rhyming quality created in the first two lines arises out of certain rhythmic opportunities which metered poems can create, opportunities for peculiar tensions between the prosaic sentence and the poetic line.

> Always too eager for the future, we
> Pick up bad habits of expectancy.

The ending of the line on "we," immediately following the strong pause of the comma, serves both to emphasize the pronoun and to make especially powerful the run-on line. This focus on the word could only be created by the double device of ending the line with it and by placing it after the pause, for normally a pronoun has no particular stress, and such an ending of a line without the dramatic pause would be a weak, or feminine ending. For instance, in

> Though high we
> May look.

the pronoun has none of the emphasis that it carries in the Larkin poem. This emphasis prepares for the peculiar effect of the minor-key rhyme with the weak secondary accent of "expectancy," which involves a sense of anticlimax much in keeping with the ironic tonal meaning of the poem.

As important as these considerations are, still it is clear from their nature that such visual aspects of poetry as I have been discussing here usually subordinate themselves unobtrusively to the oral disciplines of poetry. I should therefore call them the *supplemental* use of vision. It is true that in such cases as this following we would, without vision, lose all sense of line or phrase as a rhythmic unit. Still I think such visual aids remain by and large subordinate, rendering the dominant oral approach more subtle and various.

Ben Jonson Entertains a Man from Stratford*

> You are a friend then, as I make it out,
> Of our man Shakespeare, who alone of us
> Will put an ass's head in Fairyland
> As he would add a shilling to more shillings,
> All most harmonious — and out of his
> Miraculous inviolable increase
> Fills Ilion, Rome, or any town you like
> Of olden time with timeless Englishmen;

E. A. ROBINSON

Dramatic Use of Vision

The second poetic usage traceable to the visual impact, a usage which I should like to call the *dramatic*, is not so much designed to add subtlety to the oral aspects as to *underline* them, to make them *clear*. So far as I can see, such devices are less a rhythmic development than a further extension of the possibilities of punctuation, by means of which relationships within the poem are more certainly fixed. These *dramatic* uses of vision occur both with free verse (see Cummings' "Buffalo Bill's," p. 242) and with metered poetry. Thus, though Ezra Pound's Cantos in general are free verse in concept, Canto LXXXI is clearly based upon the iambic pentameter line. Only toward the last are there any substantial variations from this meter. In this poem some of the lines drop a space before they continue but the metrical line is not disturbed. This trick of printing is exactly the *dramatic* use of print of which I have spoken.

From "*Canto LXXXI*"*

What thou lovest well remains,
                the rest is dross
What thou lov'st well shall not be reft from thee
What thou lov'st well is thy true heritage
Whose world, or mine or theirs
                or is it of none?
First came the seen, then thus the palpable
      Elysium, though it were in the halls of hell,
What thou lovest well is thy true heritage

The ant's a centaur in his dragon world.
Pull down thy vanity, it is not man
Made courage, or made order, or made grace,
      Pull down thy vanity, I say pull down.
Learn of the green world what can be thy place
In scaled invention or true artistry,
Pull down thy vanity,
                Paquin pull down!
The green casque has outdone your elegance.

"Master thyself, then others shall thee beare"
      Pull down thy vanity
Thou art a beaten dog beneath the hail,
A swollen magpie in a fitful sun,
Half black half white
Nor knowst'ou wing from tail

* From *The Cantos of Ezra Pound.* Copyright 1934, 1948 by Ezra Pound. Reprinted by permission of New Directions, Publishers.

Pull down thy vanity
   How mean thy hates
Fostered in falsity,
   Pull down thy vanity,
Rathe to destroy, niggard in charity,
Pull down thy vanity,
   I say pull down.

But to have done instead of not doing
   this is not vanity
To have, with decency, knocked
That a Blunt should open
   To have gathered from the air a live tradition
or from a fine old eye the unconquered flame
This is not vanity.
   Here error is all in the not done,
all in the diffidence that faltered,

       EZRA POUND

  There is no theoretical difference in purpose between the visual break
with its drop in the middle of the following line, and the exclamation
point that concludes it.

   Pull down thy vanity,
      Paquin pull down!

Both the break and the exclamation point are *dramatic directions* used by
the author to guide the reader. There has been a general trend over the
last several hundred years, both in poetry and in music, for the writer and
composer to use a variety of such signals to direct more and more closely
the performance of his composition. Whether this trend is, in poetry, good
or bad, depends no doubt on individual circumstances. In some cases these
devices seem unnecessary, if not positively restricting, the only excuse for
using them being, perhaps, that the poet feels himself faced with an audience totally unused to rendering the suggestive words on the page into a
living dramatic pattern of human experiences through the living voice, so
that he feels he must guide each step as he might an infant's. It is as if
Shakespeare had not only to write the suggestive words, but, distrustful of
his actors, felt under the necessity to educate them as to how to read his
phrases, by demonstrating the dramatic relationship of his words typo-
graphically. Where this dramatic direction through visual aid is successful,
a harmonious relationship seems to be established with the greater needs
of the poem, so that one feels neither one's imagination unnecessarily
restricted nor his intelligence insulted. *Dramatic* use of visual aid calls in

fact for sensitive instincts on the part of the poet wherever he uses them so extensively as to make them a major aesthetic element. Such poems, no matter how complicated the technique may look and tend to be, like cummings's "Buffalo Bill's" or Eliot's "The Waste Land" and "The Hollow Men," are basically very simple in what they are saying, no doubt because highly complex or ambiguous linguistic patterns are not aided — are in fact probably damaged — by this sort of dramatic clarification.

Emblematic Use of Vision

I have mentioned two ways in which the written word has modified, in poetry, the spoken word: the *supplemental* and the *dramatic*. A third formal use of typography I would like to call the *emblematic*. In this mode, the look of the poem on the page is designed to make some *emblem* or visual insignia related to the subject of the poem. An example is George Herbert's poem "Easter Wings," in subject an Easter prayer, the lines of which conform to the outline of two sets of wings.

Easter Wings

Lord, who createdst man in wealth and store,
Though foolishly he lost the same,
Decaying more and more,
Till he became
Most   poor:
With   Thee
O   let   me   rise
As   larks,   harmoniously,
And   sing   this   day   Thy   victories:
Then shall the fall further the flight in me.

My   tender   age   in   sorrow   did   begin:
And still with sicknesses and shame
Thou did'st so punish sin,
That   I   became
Most   thin.
With   Thee
Let   me   combine
And feel this day Thy victory
For,   if   I   imp   my   wing   on   Thine,
Affliction   shall   advance   the   flight   in   me.

GEORGE HERBERT

It must be noted that between the first two visual aspects, the supplemental and the dramatic, and this third, the *emblematic,* there is an all-important difference. The supplemental and the dramatic had as their aesthetic aims, the first to make more subtle, the second to elucidate, the oral aspects. The emblematic, on the other hand, is something apart, unrelated. In "Easter Wings" the visual aspect does not affect the oral reading, though one must note that Herbert has with great skill matched the phrasal structure with the visual pattern. The poem is written in a syllabic meter. There is no way, listening to the poem, that one could deduce that the poem *looked* like wings. This visual fact is simply an aesthetic bonus, an extra discipline the poet takes on while in the process of signing up for his obligations in composing the poem. It heightens our awe of the poet's skill when we see him write a great poem while fulfilling, not only a rigid metrical and rhyming system, but also a predetermined visual pattern. Still, it is certainly unlikely that we will generally accept such emblematic patterns in lieu of creative excitement in the basic oral elements of the poem.

Pictogram

These are the three major directions developed by the joining of poetry to the written and printed page. But before leaving the subject, I should touch upon a very minor fourth possibility for visual discipline, a direction which I believe only E. E. Cummings, among significant poets in English, has spent much time on, and he has published but a few examples.

I should like to call this minor visual discipline the pictogram. In a pictogram the visual discipline takes over entirely from the oral or auditory. The poem cannot be read aloud in any way that will make its meaning, as developed by the form of the poem, clear. Here is an excellent example.

*ViVa 1**

```
    ,mean-
hum
a)now

(nit
y unb
uria

ble fore(hurry
into
heads are
legs think wrists
```

* Copyright, 1931, renewed, 1959, by E. E. Cummings. Reprinted from his volume, *Poems 1923–1954* by permission of Harcourt, Brace & World, Inc.

argue)short(eyes do
bang hands angle
scoot bulbs marry a become)
ened
(to is

see!so
long door
golf slam bridge train shriek
chewing whistles hugest
to
morrow from smiles sin

k
ingly ele
vator glide pinn
)pu(
acle to

rubber)tres(plants how grin
ho)cen(tel
und
ead the

not stroll
living spawn imitate)ce(re
peat

credo fais do
do neighbours re babies
                   while;

E. E. CUMMINGS

   The first oral impossibility that meets the eye is the split of the word "meanwhile," half of which appears as the first word of the piece, half as the last word. The memory, if the poem were read aloud, would not make the connection. The device must be seen principally as one for the eye, and is used to emphasize the fragmentary minor nature of the experience dealt with in the pictogram. Note also that the poem begins with a comma and ends with a semicolon, punctuation which helps us arrive at the following interpretation: two neighbors in an apartment hotel go for a walk with their infants. The pictogram covers only their accidental meeting at the elevator, their descent, and their parting. Thus the comma at the beginning indicates that this is a secondary episode of the first part of the walk, the preparation, etc., while the semicolon at the end indicates that the main unit of the walk is finished, a major subdivision of the episode is closed.

Parentheses are an important device here. The poem begins in a parenthesis which is never closed and within which lesser parentheses are developed. The word *now* thus stands outside as a kind of comment on the brevity of the whole occurrence, as well as its modernity.

The poem is divided into two parts presented alternately. One part is contained within what, in effect, is a double parenthesis and is, for the most part, the action. The second part stands outside this set of parentheses and is a naming of that which is involved in the action and an evaluative description of it. The two parts, separated, read like this:

1. humanity unburiable foreshortened putrescence
   now
2. hurry into heads are legs think wrists argue eyes do bang
   hands angle scoot bulbs marry a become to is see! so long
   door golf slam bridge train shriek chewing whistles hugest
   tomorrow from smiles sinkingly elevator glide pinnacle to
   rubber plants how grin hotel undead the not stroll living
   spawn imitate repeat credo fais do do neighbours re babies

The key to the pictogram's significance lies in the last two words (excepting the ubiquitous "mean-while"), "re babies." It is this concept which meaningfully unites the two parts in a focus.

The contrast between the adult upper middle-class hotel dwellers and their babies is made more effective by joining the babies' physical view with the writer's moral vision. Thus, in the three words describing this upper middle-class humanity, *unburiable foreshortened putrescence,* the babies' physical relation to the adult is represented by the word *foreshortened* for that is how an adult appears to a child looking upward. But the word has connotations which are curiously appropriate when combined with "putrescence," which one might take as describing something whose future is indeed foreshortened. But it must be remembered that this putrescence only appears "re babies," that it is only when compared to the innocently curious young that the almost insensible decay of the adult becomes manifest.

For the pictogram is primarily contrasting the child's freshness of vision with adulthood's convention-ridden, activity-driven existence. Our principal insight into the knee-level view of the child comes in the second and third stanzas, in which the author assumes the simple diction of a child to describe the action. "Heads are legs think" tells that this is an automatic action, that only the lower reaches of a neural system are involved. With "wrists argue," the legs have *thought* their way into the elevator, and the wrists flash over to punch the button for each desired floor. "Eyes do bang" describes the acknowledgment of two acquaintances who shake hands, "hands angle." The elevator is on its way, and the child's eyes are drawn to the lights flashing the floors: "scoot bulbs marry a become to is see!" The bulbs act as a bridge between the floor that is to come and its existence as it swings before their eyes. Thus, with accurate logic of attention, we are brought to the child's vision of the door, "long door," which is an apt description, since the child comes out of the elevator by the same door that he entered several stories up.

By contrast, we are now presented with a jumbled series of concepts centered around a country-club week-end or some such, which is the gist of the adult conversation. It is interesting that the child's impressions are quite logical. Though odd in expression, they make perfect and often fascinating sense (as the "long door"). A given moment comes; the child sees what its meaning for himself is with unclouded eyes. But as soon as the poet shifts to the adult view of the world, the impressions become chaotic partly because, one imagines, the moment is not sufficient to itself for them since they live for the false but fascinating promise of "hugest tomorrow." It is this attitude toward life, not only the elevator, which makes their "smiles sinkingly" and makes them the "hotel undead," transient creatures neither alive nor buriable.

The poem ends with even less apparent logic, with several languages thrown in to emphasize the foreignness of the words' meaning to the adults: "credo," believe; "fais do do," go to sleep. This last echo from the traditional French lullaby is ironically applied to the "neighbours," the adults, who, "re babies" and their lively observations, are spiritually asleep, "undead."

The contribution of the formal elements to the aesthetic impact of the pictogram is clear. The descriptive evaluation of the "humanity" involved drops down the page bit by bit, clarifying itself slowly as the elevator drops, as the event justifies the judgment, and appears to us rather foreshortened. Sometimes these fragments achieve something incidental, such as the mild pun "rubber)tres(plants," but apart from that they should and do lie well scattered and narrowing.

⁕   ⁕   ⁕

Of these four visual aspects of poetry, the supplemental, the dramatic, the emblematic, and the pictogram, the first two are clearly the most important, being broad in artistic potential as well as actual use. Even at those moments of successful usage, the others seem to suggest more the breathlessness of the stunt superbly brought off than of the miraculous achievement of life reordered.

PREPARATION FOR PERFORMANCE – "The Windhover"

Rhythm, Meter, Sound

One of the difficulties of talking about either the rhythm or the meter of this poem is that it is one of Hopkin's experiments in what he called "sprung rhythm." He describes this rhythm as being essentially based on the count of *stress*. Concerning slack syllables, he says, "any two stresses may either follow one another running or be divided by one, two, or three slack syllables," and again, speaking of two licenses allowed the meter, he says "the other is *hangers* or *outriders*, that is one, two, or three slack syllables added to a foot and not counting in the nominal scanning. They are so called because they seem to hang below the line or ride forward or backward. . . ." In plain language he seems to be after a metric line based on the *count of stress* with an indefinite number of slacks permitted between the stresses.

He made this theory, or tried to make it, a good deal subtler, catching himself in some difficulties and contradictions which the student might some day be interested in exploring for himself. But because one contradiction is of central concern to this poem, we must touch at least lightly upon it. Though at one point he asserts, "Sprung Rhythm cannot be counterpointed," yet only a short while later in enumerating the various occasions when one hears sprung rhythm in use he says, "(4) It arises in common verse when reversed or counterpointed."[1] In short, counterpointed common verse is sprung rhythm. It seems to me that on a subjective level this is the effect he was after – a violently counterpointed rhythm.

Hopkins admired the old Anglo-Saxon poetics in which the line length was flexible since it was measured by a certain number of beats. Hopkins felt, further, that the strict iambic measure had entirely too often come to accompany the strict count of syllables. Hopkins saw the great problem as establishing in the same line at once a sense of meter, and a flexible, usable rhythm of stress which could at times almost break down the sense of meter. He said that, since the poem only had one line, if the dual sense of rhythm was to be accomplished that line had to express the basic rhythm often enough for the mind of the listener to keep it going unconsciously in his head. With the basic rhythm accomplished, the

[1] All quotes taken from *Poems of Gerard Manley Hopkins*, Third Edition, Oxford University Press, N.Y. & London, 1948, pp. 7–10.

counter rhythm theoretically would be free to play its melodic variations over the ground base which was repeating itself in the reader's ear. It was in search of a way of achieving this double voice within the one line that Hopkins turned away from syllabic meters to the stress meters.

With this theoretical background, it is apparent at once that the first line of "The Windhover" is of great significance, for it handles the stress pattern in an iambic mode, without variation. One can, I think, assume that this was the basic *rhythm* which Hopkins wanted the reader to retain in his mind. His *meter*, as we shall see, is five stresses to the line, and his rhythmic variations come by a free interpolation of a variety of slack and semi-slack syllables. For him there was in a rhythmic unit with many slacks something of the sense of time-equivalence which Professor Pike has pointed to — that is, there is a tendency in English to say "dápple Fálcon" and "dápple-dáwn-drawn Fálcon" in much the same length of time, by speeding up and slurring the words in between the stresses. It is by some such process, I suspect, that Hopkins hoped to force onto the oral reader a swiftness of delivery which would be in some sense the musical equivalent of the Falcon's flight.

I must confess that in developing an oral reading of this poem it has become clear to me that in order to force the reader into such a time-equivalent delivery, *it is absolutely essential not to load the speeded-up words with a weight of denotative or connotative meaning.* Take the second line of this poem as an example of such a problem. I have already discussed in a previous chapter the ambiguous possibilities in "dapple-dawn-drawn" and the richness that arises therefrom. Further, Hopkins has used words that alliterate. Now from Anglo-Saxon times it has been obvious that words that are part of a pattern of alliteration have a very strong tendency to be stressed. It is perhaps the strongest underlining of lexical stress available to the poet. Thus a situation arises wherein Hopkins, according to rhythmic patterns in the poem and extrinsic metrical theory, apparently wishes us to read the line thus:

> × × ´ × ´ × ´ × × × ´ × × × ´ ×
> dom of daylight's dauphin, dapple-dawn-drawn Falcon, in his riding

However, he has so loaded the key phrases with overtones and so insisted on each word through the emphasis of sound devices that it is virtually impossible to read the line in any other way but

> × × ´ × ´ × ´ × ´ ´ ´ × × × ´ ×
> dom of daylight's dauphin, dapple-dawn-drawn Falcon, in his riding

(Note that the phrase "Falcon, in his riding" encompasses just as many slack syllables [four] as the phrase in question, but it is really easy to speed over them, for they carry neither weight of meaning nor of music). These lines are excellent examples of the strain put on Hopkin's theory by the practical compositional demands of an art rooted in denotational meaning.

In any case, here is a severe dilemma for the oral reader, revealed by his own particular approach to the poem. I confess that I yield in my interpretation to the exigencies of meaning and the actualities of lingual music, wherever they come into conflict with theory. Line 9 presents this dilemma in a severe form, it seems to me. Each one of these metonymies seems to me important. The only way the line can be read to get five stresses is

> Brute beauty and valour and act, oh, air, pride, plume, here

For my ear, "Brute" must receive a stress, as must "pride" and "plume," since all are as important and weighty as the adjoining words. But here is the poem, with a scansion of the lexical rhythm, with a syllable count, and with a count of stress both as I would read the poem and (in parenthesis) as it would be stressed to get five syllables to the line.

The Windhover:*

To Christ Our Lord

syllables	stress	
10	5	I caught this morning morning's minion, king-
16	7(5)	dom of daylight's dauphin, dapple-dawn-drawn Falcon, in his riding
16	6(5)	Of the rolling level underneath him steady air, and striding
14	6(5)	High there, how he rung upon the rein of a wimpling wing
11	5	In his ecstasy! then off, off forth on swing,
15	8(5)	As a skate's heel sweeps smooth on a bow-bend: the hurl and gliding
10	5	Rebuffed the big wind. My heart in hiding
14	5	Stirred for a bird, — the achieve of, the mastery of the thing!

* Reprinted by permission of the Oxford University Press (London).

13	8(5)	´(×) ´ × × ´ × × ´ × ´ ´(×) ´(×) ´ Brute beauty and valour and act, oh, air, pride, plume, here
13	6(5)	´ × ´ × ´(×) × ´ × × ´ × ´ × Buckle! AND the fire that breaks from thee then, a billion
14	6(5)	´ ´(×) ´ ×× ´(×) ´ × × × × ´ × ´ Times told lovelier, more dangerous, O my chevalier!
12	7(5)	´(×) ´ × × × ´ ´ × ´ ´(×) ´ × No wonder of it: sheer plod makes plough down sillion
9	5	´ × ´ × ´(×) × ´ ´ × ´ Shine, and blue-bleak embers, ah my dear,
10	5	´ ´ × ´(×) × ´ ´ × ´ × Fall, gall themselves, and gash gold-vermilion.

This scansion makes it clear that the rhythm emphasizes the turning point at the end of the octet, along with all the other technical elements so far considered. Simply on the basis of length of line, the octet averages 13.25 syllables per line, and the sestet 11.83, a set of cold statistics made more meaningful when one observes the 14 to 16 syllable lines in the octet and the complete absence of anything above the single 14 syllable line in the sestet. This disparity is particularly significant when one notices that despite the few syllables per line, the sestet has fully as many stresses as the octet. Such facts must indicate a greater feeling of hammering in the sestet, and so one finds it on line-by-line examination. This particular rhythmical alteration would seem to be logically related to the change from the free-wheeling bird to the images of buckling, falling, plodding, and it provides the oral reader with a musical reinforcement of all the other elements that insist on the shift of tone and focus at the turning point.

Nor is rhythm the only musical device that underlines this change. The whole poem is dense with sound patterns. Many of them, such as the frequent near-vowel echoes, are not really capable of being shown on the following chart. But the chart does indicate very clearly that in the ever-present alliteration, there is a strong shift from the softer more liquid consonants of the octet to hard, plosive consonants in the sestet. This change accompanies the shift to a more heavily stressed rhythm. It is interesting to see, too, how the *rhyme* moves at the turning point. All the end-word rhyme in the octet is in one set, the only variation being that there is an *a b b a* pattern in which *a* is a masculine and *b* is a feminine form of the same syllable. In short, "ing" is the rhyme syllable for eight lines. It is dropped abruptly in the lines of the sestet, which are linked by rhyme but in a quite different way. There are two rhyme sets, "here" and "billion." By simple alternation they keep the masculine-feminine balance. The poem begins with a masculine end rhyme and concludes with a feminine rhyme. The following chart will indicate some of the musical patterns which help to create this lovely and powerful poem.

	Alliteration	Assonance	Consonance	Repetition	Echoes and internal rhymes
1.	m (3)		n (2)	morning (2)	morning king
2.	d (6)	dau, daw, draw	n (4)		riding
3.	r (2) st (2)	lev, steady, air. stri	l (3)		rolling air
4.	h (3) r (2) w (2)	high wim, wing			there wimpling wing
5.	s		off, off, forth	off, off	swing
6.	s (4) b (2)		hurl, gli		sweeps
7.	h (2)		rebuff, big		
8.				of, of	stirred bird
9.	b (2) p (2)	Bru, beau, plu		and, and	air, here
10.	b (3) th (4)		then, -ion		
11.	t (2)		l (3) m (3)		
12.	pl (2)	won, of	No, won plod, down		down, sillion
13.	bl (2)		emb-, my		shine
14.	g (3)		l (5) v (2)		fall, gall

SELECTIONS

The Waking*

I wake to sleep, and take my waking slow.
I feel my fate in what I cannot fear.
I learn by going where I have to go.

We think by feeling. What is there to know?
I hear my being dance from ear to ear.
I wake to sleep, and take my waking slow.

Of those so close beside me, which are you?
God bless the Ground! I shall walk softly there,
And learn by going where I have to go.

Light takes the Tree; but who can tell us how?
The lowly worm climbs up a winding stair;
I wake to sleep, and take my waking slow.

Great Nature has another thing to do
To you and me; so take the lively air,
And, lovely, learn by going where to go.

This shaking keeps me steady. I should know.
What falls away is always. And is near.
I wake to sleep, and take my waking slow.
I learn by going where I have to go.

THEODORE ROETHKE

* "The Waking" copyright, 1953 by Theodore Roethke from the book, *Words for the Wind,* by Theodore Roethke. Reprinted by permission of Double-day & Company, Inc.

Missing Dates*

Slowly the poison the whole blood stream fills.
It is not the effort nor the failure tires.
The waste remains, the waste remains and kills.

It is not your system or clear sight that mills
Down small to the consequence a life requires;
Slowly the poison the whole blood stream fills.

They bled an old dog dry yet the exchange rills
Of young dog blood gave but a month's desires;
The waste remains, the waste remains and kills.

It is the Chinese tombs and the slag hills
Usurp the soil, and not the soil retires.
Slowly the poison the whole blood stream fills.

Not to have fire is to be a skin that shrills.
The complete fire is death. From partial fires
The waste remains, the waste remains and kills.

It is the poems you have lost, the ills
From missing dates, at which the heart expires.
Slowly the poison the whole blood stream fills.
The waste remains, the waste remains and kills.

WILLIAM EMPSON

*Do Not Go Gentle into that Good Night**

Do not go gentle into that good night,
Old age should burn and rave at close of day;
Rage, rage against the dying of the light.

Though wise men at their end know dark is right,
Because their words had forked no lightning they
Do not go gentle into that good night.

Good men, the last wave by, crying how bright
Their frail deeds might have danced in a green bay,
Rage, rage against the dying of the light.

Wild men who caught and sang the sun in flight,
And learn, too late, they grieved it on its way,
Do not go gentle into that good night.

Grave men, near death, who see with blinding sight
Blind eyes could blaze like meteors and be gay,
Rage, rage against the dying of the light.

And you, my father, there on the sad height,
Curse, bless, me now with your fierce tears, I pray.
Do not go gentle into that good night.
Rage, rage against the dying of the light.

DYLAN THOMAS

PART THREE

Performance

CHAPTER FIFTEEN

Preparation for Performance

Sentences are not different enough to hold the attention unless they are dramatic. No ingenuity of varying structure will do. All that can save them is the speaking tone of voice somehow entangled in the words and fastened to the page for the ear of the imagination. That is all that can save poetry from sing-song, all that can save prose from itself.

ROBERT FROST

In the presentation of the various elements of literature which must be taken into consideration by the oral reader, we have used divers stories and poems, and parts thereof, as examples. It is inevitable that such a procedure will have left a feeling of disparateness, of chop-chop, whereas there is little doubt that one should try to see a work of art, as well as life, steadily and whole. This sense of fragmentation applies particularly, I should imagine, to those "preparations for performance" which conclude certain previous chapters. An attempt was made there to show how each critical aspect was involved with the oral dimension in a lyric poem. In order to offset the impression left by this earlier piecemeal "preparation" and, further, to give a more coherent view of how the physical response of the reader-performer may be taken as an integral part of seeing the work whole, this chapter will demonstrate a synthesis in which all the critical aspects are considered in the same essay. And since a lyric poem was used earlier, it seemed most useful that the other forms extensively discussed, narrative poetry and the short story, should be represented. I decided these essays should not be any longer than papers a student might be asked to write on a single poem or story, hence they are not models of completion or perfection. If they suggest to the student an approach to other, better preparations for performance, I shall have achieved my aim. Certainly there are many other aspects to an actual preparation for performance before one's classmates, and these have been touched upon at various times, chiefly in the chapters on the voice, the body, and the audience. However, my concern here is to lay the necessary groundwork for those other tasks, by exposing the tonal qualities which the performance must acknowledge and translate into visual and auditory signs.

ANALYSIS IN PREPARATION FOR PERFORMANCE –
"Eros Turannos"

The classical title reminds the reader that the ancients thought of love as the king of gods and men, a tyrant that often drove the victim to his own destruction. Thus, the theme is stated in the title. But beyond stating the theme, the title further prepares the reader for certain qualities of the story which emerge more slowly.

With the beginning phrase, "She fears him," the reader is thrown at once into the emotional core of the drama. Though neither the point of view nor the character of the narrator is yet clear, the story will not be told by one of the main participants. The character of the narrator is not fully revealed until the first line of the last stanza; thus, to the main structure of the poem, which is one of action, is added the emotional unfolding of the role of the narrator. The point of view is fairly complex, though it is easily classified as first person. A part of the complexity arises from the fact that though the story is narrated by a single voice who identifies himself *with* a group, the voice goes much further and speaks to the outsider *for* the group of people, not only echoing their gossip but also commenting on their role in the story. From internal evidence, one takes this group of people to be the townspeople of the small community in which the drama occurred. From knowing that Robinson was a New Englander, as well as from such suggestive phrases as "a sense of ocean and old trees," "tradition, touching all he sees," and "while all the town and harbor side," one can safely assume the story to have occurred in a small New England coastal town. I have used the word "drama" several times. Technically the work is a narrative, not a drama, yet the nature of the narrator cannot help reminding one of Greek tragedy, if the title and some of the early words ("fated," "mask") and the role of the chorus in those plays have not already done so. There, too, the townspeople talked of the tragedy in their midst, and stood for the same "average" non-tragic man, as contrast to the heroes of the drama and their terrible destinies. Obviously these classical implications are key considerations for the person who is trying to catch the tonal qualities in preparation for a performance. The somewhat analytical descriptive language is reasonable in relation to the character of the narrator and the point of view.

The particular point of view raises a question concerning the use of the eyes by the performer. Should he read to the audience, or should he adopt fully the fictional situation and pretend to be speaking at all times to a character, a fictive listener? Which is the convention that will most truly reveal the nature of the poem? Perhaps the answer to this question lies in the fact that there is no real evidence that this is a *dramatic* monologue. That is, the words of the speaker are never, apparently, cued by something he sees on the face or in the attitude of the listener. Only his own thoughts motivate the speaker on to his next words. In short, the listener is never given any character at all beyond the general one of "stranger" or "listener." Since this general one is the audience's role also, it would seem best to read to the audience, taking that collective body as the listener.

Turning to a more intensive look at the language for tonal clues, one notices an absence of eccentric words, of bizarre phrases. The language is intelligent and at times acute ("a blurred sagacity," for instance, though not startling, is subtle in its use of a concrete visual image describing an abstract concept, creating thus a hint of a paradox), but it (the language) never departs from a common vocabulary, a conversational diction.

As one would expect in a poem with the tonal elements so far discussed, the figurative language is neither frequent nor prominent. One pattern of figures is used to emphasize – if not always blindness – at least poor vision and, by figurative extension, poor insight. ". . . engaging mask . . . ," ". . . blurred sagacity . . . ," ". . . doubts . . . are dimmed . . . ," ". . . a place where she can hide . . . ," ". . . we'll have no kindly veil between her visions and those we have seen . . . ," are all phrases scattered through the poem that build and extend this notion of lack of vision.

Water and figures relating to it appear throughout the poem. There is something fateful always about these water images, something deceptive or threatening or both: "foamless weirs," ". . . once had power to sound him . . . ," "a sense of ocean . . . envelops and allures him . . . ," ". . . the pounding wave reverberates . . . ," ". . . like waves breaking . . . ," ". . . a stairway to the sea. . . ." Another group of figures that surrounds these characters is concerned with trees. These are related to a sense both of stability and of passing time, perhaps because though a tree appears quite permanent and stable, it is nonetheless changing in a natural way and is, beyond that, subject to rapid alteration by outside forces. In this way the trees suggest the stability, the tradition, which attracts the man to the woman, ". . . a sense of ocean and old trees envelops and allures him . . . ." Yet this sense of stability is an illusion, for time brings its inevitable disillusionment to her, and she changes, ". . . the falling leaf inaugurates . . . ." These synecdoches, the falling leaf and pounding wave, stand for the whole passage of time and the beating in of the truths that time forces on her. ". . . a changed familiar tree . . ." brings these tree figures to a conclusion.

And finally there is a minor but important series of three figures related to falling: ". . . the downward years . . . ," ". . . the falling leaf . . . ," ". . . like a stairway to the sea where down the blind are driven. . . ."

It is essential to understand the tonal importance of the concluding series of figures. They bring together in a close relationship the threads of tropes (figures) noted above, the images of blindness or blurred vision, of water, of trees, and of falling. The oral reader must have prepared, by subtle bodily recognition of the qualities of these figures as they appear throughout the story, for proper projection of the culminating power of these last lines. Later, when discussing the pattern of characters, I shall suggest the use for the oral reader of the particular grammatical structure in which these figures are couched.

Time is handled in this story in such a way as to leave some elements uncertain. What is clear is that a fictive time of around a year and perhaps more is collapsed into these six stanzas. There is a general feeling that the courtship is concluded in the spring or early summer, and an even stronger suggestion that the beginning of the end, of her disillusionment, occurs in the fall (". . . the falling leaf . . .") and the early winter storms (". . . the pounding wave . . ."). What is left vague is the amount of time she had known him prior to his proving himself a "Judas," and one is not sure how much time has elapsed between the conclusion of the drama and the present moment in the poem — i.e., the moment of the villager narrating the story to the outsider. However, one feels the story to be a recent one, fresh in the narrator's mind. One of the techniques employed by the author that contributes to his vagueness about time is his constant use of the present tense, with no use of the more specific past or perfect tenses. This is, of course, a common colloquial storytelling technique and suits the notion of a story told by an untrained story-teller. We are all familiar with it, as it is used among our friends. "You see, I'm going along minding my own business, when this guy comes up to me . . . ," — all of us are familiar with some such approach to a story. However, I believe in this case it has a specific artistic use. By telling everything in the present tense, a kind of timelessness is given to the tale, thereby enhancing the classical tragic tradition which is such a strong element in the story. Also when one comes right down to it, everything is uncertain, speculative, except the fact of the woman's downfall, and speculation on that event brings up the question of characterization.

There are three characters in the story, the woman (she), the man (he), and the narrator (who identifies himself as part of a collective, "we"). To all these people the setting is of considerable importance. She is evidently of an old family in a New England coastal town, but beyond that the reader has little knowledge about her. Because of the nature of the man, one can fairly safely assume she is of the town aristocracy — perhaps of a wealthy family. Because of her social superiority, not to mention her pride, it is she who does the choosing. But it is a near certainty that, without her social status, this man would not otherwise be interested in her.

In a certain sense the man is the key figure in the drama, for it is his character that is the catalyst for the tragedy. First of all, we are told "she fears him," and the possibility that she fears him, at least to some degree, physically as well as morally is nowhere contradicted. The next description of him is that he has an "engaging mask." Now the word "engaging" when applied to a person favorably is not a very profound compliment. An engaging person may not be a very good or a very wise or a very broad or a very gifted person. In a sense the word in itself contains certain qualities of the superficial, connotations which are given a sinister direction when they modify the word "mask." Even his social charm — a minor virtue — is a mask. Next he is described as a Judas. The story is considerably complicated by this allusion, for the reader sees that this courtship has not proceeded without a forewarning. Somehow, even before she "secures him," he has revealed his nature to her by some kind of betrayal. Since these are lovers it is likely that the betrayal was a sexual one, but just what it was is not important and the little mystery is not clarified. It is sufficient to the story that a betrayal has in fact occurred, that he is in fact a Judas. Finally, the narrator takes us speculatively into the mind of the man at the point at which he knows he has the woman hooked. What attracts him? The sense of timelessness, of stability, of tradition that resides in and around her. And we gather from the attraction these qualities hold for him that he is a stranger to them, that he is an adventurer, a guy on the make, who is playing it very cool, ". . . He sees that he will not be lost / And waits and looks around him. . . ."

Further evidence that he is of another and lower class than the woman lies in her reaction to him. First, the early uncomplicated attraction is over before the story begins. "She fears him," yet she chose him. What was the fate that made her do it? She doesn't know. The narrator speculates that, in balance, a life without him looked more fearful, more full of evil chance, than life with him. So the poem opens with the woman on the knife-edge of her fate — she knows the one thing, and she wills the other. In the twist and torment of this dilemma, her ability to see him clearly blurs, and she is caught between her failing judgment on the one hand, and a love (Eros Turannos) that keeps distorting his image ("that will not let him be / the Judas that she found him"). In this dilemma, her pride almost is sufficient to reassure her (ironically her pride is part of the price of getting him). Finally her doubts "are dimmed" by her daily need of him, "even prejudice delays and fades," her own sense of her moral and class superiority, and we reach the turning point of the narrative with the ironic phrase "she secures him." The ironies here are rich indeed. Beyond the fact that she marries him, she secures him in *his* way too, that is, gives him the position and wealth he has sought. And she secures her own future, tragically, by "securing" his. Finally, the season turns and illusions go; she retreats into a home that has been transformed by her downfall into a refuge from the gossip, triumph, and perhaps even sympathy of neighbors.

So far I have talked very little about the narrator, yet one thing that must strike the reader is this structural peculiarity, that the actual story takes up but two-thirds of the structural time of the narration, leaving the final third dominated by the narrator, who talks at length about his own relation to the tragedy and ends by speculating on how it must be to be in the grip of the tyrant love. It is a rather unorthodox denouement of quite extraordinary length and must have some fictive purpose. This fictive purpose would seem to involve the character of the narrator. The man and woman in the story are essentially characterized in realistic fashion, realistic, with but the two reservations that the realistic data are given second-hand, speculatively, and second, that in acting out their drama they may be identified with tragically love-driven people in countless tales. But the narrator does not emerge as a realistic character at all. Although he is certainly intelligent and articulate and self-aware, perhaps more so than others of the villagers with whom he identifies, and thus to that degree individualized, he is nonetheless a type, a spokesman for a group, sharing their insights and moral position. He represents the last element of the poem's pattern of human blindness. As the man is "beguiled" by the life he aspires to and the woman's insight is distorted by her love, so the narrator, in seeking a meaning for the tragedy, makes mock of his own curiosity, exposes the shallowness of his own observations, and points to the insignificance of such everyday insights as his own to those who are principals in a tragedy. The poem ends with the narrator trying to sum up in a series of three impressionistic images (all, as I have said, prepared for previously throughout the poem) what he imagines it would be like to be one of the fated ones. It would be, he speculates, like being in the smashing power of waves, or like a tree suddenly gone into the barrenness of winter or some other dramatic alteration, or like being blinded and driven down a stairway to drowning and destruction. The rhetorical structure in which this series is couched emphasizes the groping, rather awed, speculative tone of the narrator's mind.

Metrically the poem is syllabic, an eight-line stanza whose second, fourth, and eighth lines are seven syllables; the others, eight. This metric pattern is never varied. The rhyme scheme is an interesting one, and in at least one detail very unusual. It is *a, b, a, b, c, c, c, b*. It is not very common in an eight-line stanza to turn from an *a, b, a, b,* rhyme in the first four lines to a triplet, *c, c, c*. What holds the two groupings of four lines together is that the last line reverts to a rhyme word of the quatrain, *b*. And this return is emphasized in a most unusual way. A casual observation shows that in the first three stanzas, the rhyme *b* is a two-syllable feminine rhyme and is made of two separate words, whereas the *a* and *c* rhymes are true rhymes. Beyond that the identical element of the *b* rhyme (the last syllable) is the *selfsame word throughout the three stanzas*. In the fourth stanza the word "him" is dropped, but the *b* rhyme continues to be a two-syllable feminine rhyme, with the difference that the rhyme is not compounded of separate words. The fifth stanza continues to use two-syllable feminine rhyme, but reverts to the practice of making the rhyme elements out of separate words, with the identical element the word "be." Finally, in the last stanza the *b* rhyme remains two-syllable and feminine, but is compounded of one word, as in the fourth stanza. This rhyme pattern is of

great significance for the oral reader. It must be noted that the repetitive
"him" carries to the turning point of the narration. What happens at the
turning point? "She secures him." Obviously, the key emotional factor of
the narrative is her obsession with "him," and there is no question that this
obsessive quality is heightened by the constant reiteration of "him," in a
terminal or semi-terminal rhyming position. How can the oral reader keep
this repetition of the pronoun from degenerating into simple monotony?
Again, the poet provides the clue. The repetitions are not close together,
but more important is their decided weakness in the rhythmic structure.
It would be a serious error for the reader to give emphasis to any occurrence of this word. Rather, it should recur as a minor, persistent element
whose effect is cumulative, until finally the obsessive concern is climaxed,
"she secures him." Other elements of rhyme and rhythm I will discuss as I
suggest how these elements affect a reading aloud of this poem.

     First of all, it is clear from what has been said of the various elements
radiating from the point of view and character of the narrator that this is
not likely to be a poem of extreme bodily attitude, vocal pattern, or facial
expression. The narrator is too remote from the tragedy and has only the
bystander's interest of curiosity and sympathy. The reader imagines the
dramatic situation: somehow the subject of this woman or this couple has
arisen in the conversation between a native of a New England coastal
town and a stranger. We do not need to know more exactly the dramatic
context. The native, then, is telling the story, and we note from the beginning that he speaks in a relatively regular iambic pattern, that there is a
certain regularity of rhythm which, given the theme and subject of the
poem, may be seen as particularly appropriate to the inexorable progress
and tragic denouement of the woman's fixation. The first rhythmic variation emphasizes the word "always" (line 1) which, together with the next,
"what fated" (line 2), defines quickly the quality of the trap which she
herself wilfully walks into. Line 3 presents a question as to whether or not
the "his" is stress or slack, the answer to which seems to depend on
whether or not one reads the phrase as primarily governed by time-stress
or by dramatic-stress; either seems to produce a reasonable, though in
meaning not identical, reading.

     There is a pause after the word "mask," not a heavy one, but one of
more substance than the almost imperceptible pause that sometimes marks
the end of a run-on line. This pause is in part set up by the rhythmic variation with which line 4 begins and helps the reader identify and subtly emphasize the slight irony and the considerable importance of "mask."
Further, the rhythmic variation of line 4 helps the reader echo the emphatic quality centering in the words "all" and "refuse." The reader now
has a perfectly regular iambic line, which reflects the relative lack of

weighty context and also reflects the rhetorical balance on which the words are constructed. Also, this regularity seems to me to act as the approach to the powerful figure that conveys the first appearance of both the water images and the kinesthetically strong references to falling. It seems to me almost a necessity that the voice reflect here in some appropriate measure this sense of descent.

Stanza 2 continues in much the same tone as the first stanza, perhaps a bit more regular rhythmically, until the dash at the end of the sixth line. This marks a decided shift in narrative focus. The narrator turns from speculating about what goes on in the woman's mind and attempts to delineate the man's thought. This narrative movement must obviously be projected through voice and body. The narrator up to now, within the proper limits of his rather distant perspective, will have to some degree reflected both the woman's fear and her compulsive fretting about the problem presented to her by the man. Perhaps her emotions will have been projected through a tension, a slight leaning forward of the body, a certain aspect of fear and puzzlement in the face and a wide agitation of the voice, restless and probing. Now the reader moves into the man's mind at the moment when his doubts are resolved. Therefore, the pause marked by the dash must be incisive: the body's tension eases; perhaps the reader will straighten and settle back on his heels in a rather easy, complacent pose. The face will be more relaxed, conveying a sense of watchful certainty, and the eyes will obey the injunction ". . . looks around him. . . ." The diction of this line, the negative and the passive side so underlined, is not accidental. It emphasizes the man's essentially passive role in the drama. He has not won, as an active person might win a contest, but "he will not be lost." This passivity is underlined in the next line, "he waits and looks around him." If the body echoes a kind of complacent ease, I think the voice must reflect a trace of suavity and unction through the narrator's reflection of what he thinks of the man. The water and tree figures that are so baneful to the woman, he sees on a superficial, easy level; they envelop him with a sense of security and charm.

The next tonal change in the poem occurs at the end of line 4, stanza 3. Again the narrator shifts focus to the woman, so that the pause between line four and line five must again contain a significant bodily gesture. But the figure "days . . . dimmed" informs the interpreter that he is not to return to the tension and vocal agitation when he was last reporting the woman's thoughts. For now her doubts are not resolved, but dimmed. She has arrived at the stasis of decision. In this the body seems to me somewhat neutral, but because the narrator edges his reportage with more of his own viewpoint, so that the ironies are a bit more pointed and obvious, the voice must be quite active. What are the tones combined here? There is a kind of fateful descent of the voice, I should think, not too dramatic, but firm and tinged with a curious mixture of pity and irony. Certainly it is necessary to make sure the lovely antithesis of "says . . . days," so pointed by one of the poem's few slant rhymes, is adequately expressed. And the vocal structure of the last two lines must catch the irony of ". . . even prejudice . . . ," followed by the fading descent, ending in perhaps the lowest vocal tone of the reading thus far, sounding an ominous note.

Now the pause marking the turning point must be substantial, and the tone that begins the next stanza must catch the regular rhythm, the dirgelike music of destruction which these figures iterate with such compression and economy. In the last four lines of this stanza the climactic word is "vibrate," which the author has placed in a position and a rhythmic juncture where it is easily made the climax of the phrasing. Consider the richness of this word, and it is clear why it not only requires a key phrasal position, but also should be given such vocal coloration as will enhance its meaning. "Vibrate" means "to swing back and forth," thus emphasizing that the talk isn't getting anywhere. Further, a vibration is usually a small, rapid swinging. Contrasting the word with "move," one senses immediately the connotations of shallowness that cling to "vibrate." This stanza is the climax of the poem. The even greater regularity of this stanza is one cue for the reader. Another is the emergence of a rich texture of the deep back vowels in a subtle assonance;

> falling . . . inaugurates . . . reign . . . her . . .
> wave . . . reverberates . . . dirge . . . her

but this assonance is closed, bounded by consonants. Except for the unaccented beginning of "inaugurates," none of the key words begins or ends in vowels; the key consonants, appropriately for the gentle leaf-fall, are "f," "l," and "n" in the first two lines, whereas for the violence of the waves the key consonants are "d," "v," and "p-b." (Contrast these sound values with those of the lines reflecting the man's thoughts, where from the words "a sense" to the words "reassures him" several key words begin in vowels, mostly frontal ones, and the lighter consonant patterns are couched in a less insistent rhythm.)

This point, where the poem turns abruptly from this tone of formidable fatefulness is marked partly by an abrupt shift in sound patterns, to a consonance of "it," a reduction of sonority, a sudden loosening of the rhythm to the most irregular in the poem. Again the pause between stanzas must be marked by a shift in bodily attitude, this time away from tension to a more easy one, perhaps a slight shrug might be appropriate here, as if the narrator were casting off his sombre concentration on the tale to make his comment on himself. Thus, when the reader starts to speak, his changed vocal tone has been prepared for by a change in the body. The voice in this stanza has two subtly different tones that must be unified, each change to the alternate tone being marked by the phrase "as if." Also it is necessary to mark vocally the antithesis of "*her* visions and those we have seen."

The tone of this stanza, reflecting the ironic attitude with which the narrator regards himself and those he represents, continues into the last stanza; therefore the pause between these stanzas is of little significance dramatically. But the tone begins to change from the words "for they," as the narrator turns back to a consideration of the characters of the drama. Having admitted his own limitations, which by their existence must render anything he says suspect and imperfect, he nonetheless makes a last effort to read the condition of the protagonists. And as he does, the tone of tragic wonder, never completely lost in the fifth stanza (particularly in the third, fourth, seventh, and eighth lines) reasserts itself. And the face will, I should think, assume something of a set, grim expression. The eyes might settle on one spot straight ahead to reinforce the sense of certainty. When the voice arrives at the final series of figures (whose importance has already been discussed) with its return to a richer sound pattern and more insistent rhythm, there would probably be a vocal descent in a series of steps to the ultimate unended but certain denouement.

ANALYSIS IN PREPARATION FOR PERFORMANCE —
"A Resumed Identity"

Structurally, the story is divided into three parts, each of which has its own particular tone. A determination of these tones, of their intra- and inter-mural development, will be central to the preparation for performance. I will begin by making some generalizations about the handling of time, point of view and the character of the narrator, and description and characterization. A more detailed discussion of the story, section by section, will follow.

The structural time of this story consists of somewhere around 2,220 words, and each section is approximately a third shorter than the section preceding: section one, approximately 1,080 words; section two, approximately 730 words; section three, approximately 410 words. Thus there is a pattern of diminution or contraction which one might expect to see related by development or contrast to the other aspects of the story and playing its part in its performance. Fictive time is moderately collapsed, less so in Part II than in the first and third parts, so that perhaps an hour or an hour and a half is encompassed by structural time (the time it takes to read the 2,220 words of the story).

The narrator speaks from a point of view which might best be described as third person limited. I say "limited," because though the reader is taken several times into the mind of the man (it cannot therefore be third person objective), the man's thoughts are not followed in detail. Similarly, the narrator limits himself severely to what can be seen by the characters in the story; he does not omnisciently take us before or after the story in time or describe scenes distant from the characters of the story. Further enhancing this "limited" quality, is the fact that though there are two characters in the story, the narrator does not enter both their minds in the scene they have together.

Thus, in Part I the narrator sees essentially what the man sees, though he describes what the man sees in words one is certain are the narrator's rather than words the man would have used. This technique creates a particular balance of objective-subjective qualities. Because he does not have the man's words and phrasing, the reader feels rather detached from him; yet because he sees nothing the man does not see and because he automatically accepts the fact that the narrator is, as it were, translating what the man sees into suggestive and meaningful terms, the reader feels, in his position, tied to and involved with the man.

In Part II the narrator abruptly identifies with the doctor and the reader sees the man and the countryside in the doctor's way, though the reader should note that the narrator's relationship with the doctor's viewpoint is exactly the same distant one that the narrator held toward the man in Part I.

In Part III the narrator returns to seeing the world more or less from the man's viewpoint. However, the reader should note that there is even less of an *identification* with the man than in Part I. Except for a few brief summarizing insights into the man's mind, "He could not account for this . . . ," ". . . with no very definite intent . . . ," there is only one phrase which one feels to be a fairly direct paraphrase of one of the man's specific thoughts, but it is a key one: "How strange! — a mere bullet-stroke and a brief unconsciousness should not make one a physical wreck."

The method of handling the narrative point of view just described has a decided effect on the characterization and the description. The first and third parts reflect vocally the man's changing emotions and describe the world around more or less as the man would see it, with the qualification that those descriptions and emotional changes are given us not direct, but through the narrator's personality which happens to be a somewhat "objective" and distant one. Part II, on the other hand, reflects the doctor's role as spectator and ironic observer, and the tones are cool and crisp, offering strong contrast to the tones of Part I and III.

This quality of objective-subjective tone is reflected in the *means* of description. A study of the figurative language of the story reveals, for instance, that it is virtually barren of tropes, and this absence no doubt contributes to a sense of dispassionate objectivity, a feeling that leads one all the more to accept the story's moods (and there are well-developed moods) as having some objective base. On the whole these moods are developed by images and direct sensory appeal without the heightening effect of figurative language. The sensory appeal of the story is almost totally visual, and the few exceptions are used to underline some visual quality or to direct attention to it.

Essentially Part I has a mood of detachment within which are two distinct parts. In the first part, the description of the scene emphasizes certain qualities, all adding up to a sense of indistinctness, separation, lifelessness, to some vaguely mysterious quality residual in the landscape. Here the absence of other senses than sight is specifically referred to and is used as a means of creating this mood. The moonlight, the reiteration that mist or haze obscured the landscape, that even where seen clearly, trees or soldiers were merely "masses," the fact that the only *sound* is mechanical, thus emphasizing its lifelessness, that an army is marching nearby without making a noise, these qualities at once heighten the sense of dream or vision as opposed to solid reality. This sense is further accentuated by the two first touches of characterization of the man, both hinting at some slight confusion on his part: ". . . what he might not have known otherwise . . . ," and "Endeavoring to orient himself, as a surveyor or navigator might say . . . ," and this sense of disorientation comes to a first minor climax with, "The man could not rightly understand; he thought himself deaf; . . . ." But this first climax of tension, of doubt (and the performer must be careful to realize how minor it is — the first of successive waves of doubt which must be carefully prepared for and developed), this tension is relieved by hearing his own voice and by accounting for the silence of the passing troops by remembering the phenomenon of the "acoustic shadow."

The reason why dramatic irony is one of the most difficult things for the performer to project properly is the same reason why dramatic irony is not only rich, but possible: literature is a temporal art. A character says or feels something which, at the moment, seems natural and even insignificant, yet which later, as the whole story unfolds, comes to carry a rich irony. It is the performer's particular task so to heighten that moment that it is memorable, without in any way betraying what is coming or apparently making more of it than is appropriate at that moment. Since this is a story rich in dramatic irony, this problem of performance will be regularly encountered. For instance, "The man could not rightly understand. . . ." When the reader finishes the story, he sees what a gross understatement that is; and the fact that in the beginning the man understood so little the depth and significance of his confusion strikes the reader with delayed but enhanced impact. Even though the author enriches this statement with ironic details (such as the grimly understated word "disappointed" in connection with what he hears of his own voice), this preparation for a later revelation of irony will present a delicate problem in underlining for the performer.

Easier, perhaps, is the problem of the "acoustic shadow," for the author spends so much time on it that it is much likelier to linger in the mind, until the reader comes to realize the enormous depth and scope of the acoustic shadow in which the man has been living for many years.

Going back a moment to the description of the passing army, we notice with what skill the author combines specific details ". . . the cannoneers riding with folded arms . . ." with a sense of the vague and mysterious (these effects are combined in one image with ". . . dimly gleaming rifles aslant above their shoulders . . .") so as to leave the question of that parade's reality perfectly ambiguous. The performer must strike exactly that tone of ambiguity and must not tip his hand either way.

One thing that is left ambiguous by the vagueness of this army and the color of its uniform leads to the next wave of tension and doubt on the part of the man. Should he flee or not? And here the performer's body for the first time must respond to a specific progression: alertness, fear, retreat. These are the cues which arise with the words "Then came a thought of self — an apprehension — ." This progression is, of course, prepared for by the earlier, but bodily more vague cue, "He was profoundly disquieted. . . ."

I mentioned earlier that Part I is divided into two sections. The first with its mood of mystery and vagueness ends with "The chill of a sudden breeze upon the back of his neck drew his attention to the quarter whence it came, and turning to the east he saw a faint grey light along the horizon — the first sign of returning day." One is free to see this first faint returning light in connection with the sudden galvanizing of his fear, as symbolic of the light that will later shock him into a final darkness, for it is followed by a line rich in irony and portent, "I must get away from here or I shall be discovered and taken," for actually the voice is not simply passive, but grimly active, then passive. He is not "discovered," he "discovers," and is, indeed, "taken."

This "chill breeze" marks the end of a very quiet section. The man is immobile; the narrator surveys the countryside that the man sees; all is motionless. Even the passing army, in its silence and vagueness is somehow paradoxically motionless. All this changes for the performer. The body breaks from quiescence, the ghostly army vanishes, and then suddenly everything freezes again. But this new immobility is on a deeper level with probings still vague but more profound. And here is another of

those richly ironic sentences, "So swift a passing of so slow an army!" And
the big difference after all is the growing light of day which gradually
casts the inner shadow into sharper contrast, ". . . he found no other light
than that of day; his understanding was involved as darkly in doubt as before." One of the few figures of speech is thus used to emphasize his emotional state at this critical point.

And now the narrator's and the man's eyes turn once more to the
broad landscape, now opened up clear by daylight, with motion, song, all
perfectly natural in contrast to the half mysterious images of the previously dark landscapes. Yet ironically, this sun-lit world reveals a greater
mystery than the night. At least the night was full of what he expected, an
army. But now "on every side lay cultivated fields showing no sign of war
and war's ravages." The performer must here reflect both the uncomplicated, everyday quality of the landscape, its motion and sanity, and the
challenge that this scene presents to the man's sanity, who, though jarred
out of his inner questioning of the meaning of the army's disappearance,
looks outward to the landscape only to be shaken and immobilized by the
same question in another form, until finally the reality of his own body
gives him (how ironically) reassurance and he "walked confidently toward
the road." This break in tension is preceded, in the man's gesture of putting his hand to his head, by perhaps the performer's first logical cue for
something like a complete hand gesture. A gesture at this time is justified
not only by the easiness with which it would develop from the text, but if
one considers the text here closely for the emotive progression one notices
how that progression could be clarified by such a gesture. The man is staring stupidly. He puts his hand to his head and passes it through his hair,
one would imagine automatically. Then he attentively considers the palm.
Now this turning of the attention is psychologically important, for it offers
a bridge from the landscape with its puzzle. He looks at his hand, no doubt
in the first place still stupidly, but slowly the reality of that palm, even
though there may be things about it that are odd, brings him out of his
stunned puzzle, so that he is able to turn his back on the landscape and confidently to the road. This transition the performer must develop in his eyes,
face, and body. It should be remembered clearly that the gestures must be
developed, not as if the performer were the man, but rather as the narrator
might sketch in this reaction. Otherwise, the performer will disastrously
lose the point of view.

I have dwelt upon this point because it marks the next break of tension and the one that lasts longest. Since he is finally leaving his isolated
hill and walking toward the sane, public road whereon his perplexities will
surely fade or be resolved, the break marks not merely the break in the
second wave of tension, but also the end of Part I and the apparent turn-

ing point of the story. I say apparent, because as the story goes on we see that there is no turning point, that in the pattern of characters what looks to be a moving away from the mysteries of the dark is in fact a moving toward an intensification of those mysteries, for the public road gives him no answer, only questions. Only a later, final turning to himself gives any answers. And even though, at the climactic moment, the man faces a truth, that truth, though fatal to him, leaves the reader far greater mysteries with which to contend. But I am jumping ahead.

I have pointed out that Part I deals with images of the general setting — with the world around the man and the narrator. Part II turns to humanity — to the man as seen by another human being and to the man's reaction in that human contact. Part II is, in short, a dramatic *scene* in that everyday world toward which the man has turned. One thing would seem to be clear about this scene: structurally, much exposition is developed which is necessary to the reader's understanding of the man's dilemma, information concerning what he was doing, or thought he was doing, prior to finding himself on that hill before dawn. But ironically, the more the reader learns the more he becomes puzzled. And as for the man and *his* questions — who won the battle? Where are the armies? These questions are not answered at all, but the man ironically is asked questions in return by the doctor which he is hard pressed to answer. There is little doubt that in this masterful little scene the author has quite deliberately built this growing subconscious tension over these difficult questions to the explosion of dramatic irony, ". . . Sir, you may go to the devil." One is reminded of Oedipus with Tiresias — of all those times in the record of man when in threatening or denouncing others a man has unconsciously pronounced his own doom.

I need not develop at length the difference in the tones between the doctor and the man which the performer must achieve, but I must mention that, except perhaps for a sharp if understated humor, or a keen though restrained edge of curiosity, the doctor remains essentially static. Not so the man. He begins the scene confidently, sure of himself and of what he wants to know. His walk to the road was direct. But as the Doctor's questions move him first to uncertainty and then anger, which is no doubt a cover for a profound disquiet, he leaves the public road "very much at random." Part II is a third shorter than Part I, its hope lasts but a brief while, yet in that shorter time it has left both the man and the reader with more disturbing questions than did the more apparently mysterious Part I. Further there is beginning to be a divergence between the questions that are bothering the man and the reader.

Part II ends with the man walking away "very much at random." Part III begins by leaving the Doctor and his scientific answers and his public highway and goes on to follow the man into the countryside through which he moves "rather deviously." Of course, the doctor was not loquacious (he talked less than the man), but that the man thought him so is another sign of the effect of the doctor's terse questions.

The man seats himself on a rock and, placing his hand on his knee, he looks at the back of it. Twice before, the assurance of the reality of his own being has given him confidence and, he thought, freed him of delusions. First, that he heard his own voice proved he wasn't deaf, though he was aware the voice was "disappointing." Second, looking at the palm of the hand he has just drawn through his hair, he recovers from the puzzle of a countryside without signs of war. But now a somewhat different pattern emerges. Though in the end the hand offers him a possibility which seems to solve all his personal paradoxes, in the beginning he finds it disturbing; it is "seamed and furrowed," so that for the first time he is forced to puzzle about one of the odd things he has noticed in *himself*, rather than thinking the oddness is in the *landscape*. Trying to account for the hand brings out an automatic answer, "I must have been a long time in hospital." This possibility, brought suddenly in the forefront of his mind makes it possible for him to face another oddity of the landscape — it is summer and the battle was in December — , and the hospital offers a solution which answers many questions. He has been temporarily deranged by his wound, and that disturbance would account for the vision of the army. His stay in the hospital accounts for the change in season and for the peaceful countryside.

This whole business of the hand and the speaking aloud requires very careful handling by the performer to illuminate the exact progression of emotion. Looking at the back of one hand on the lectern and sketching briefly on the back of it with the fingertips of the other hand would offer a chance to underline a structural pattern for the listeners by reminding them of the other hand gesture earlier in the story and of the similar, though less complex, functions of the hand at that time. Also it is important to project the great significance of the pause between ". . . in hospital." and "why what a fool I am!" and of the relief and release of tension that occurs facially and bodily in it.

I mentioned a long time back that not only did the narrator's focus turn back to the man from the doctor in this section, but that there was also a shift in descriptive focus. Part I is the broad landscape, with the man slowly moving into a more important role. Part II is chiefly devoted to the characters as seen somewhat from the doctor's angle, with very little attention to the landscape. Part III turns back to the man's mind, but now the description of the setting is quite different. The world has narrowed. There are no more broad vistas. Now the man and the narrator are focused on the man's body and on two specific objects: the monument and the pool of water. This contraction of the world represents in visual image the narrowing down of the man to the sudden revelation, of the gradual elimination of each hope and each illusion. In this much more specific context the last wave of tension and relaxation is acted out. For these two external objects relate directly to himself; the first suggests a horror, the second reveals it.

History tells some interesting facts about the battle commemorated by the inscription. The battle was the battle of Murfreesboro or Stone's River. The opposing generals were Rosecrans and Bragg. It was a drawn battle, very bloody, a segment of which was called Hell's Half Acre by the soldiers. Wm. B. Hazen's brigade of 1,300 Ohio, Indiana, Illinois, and Kentucky volunteers beat back wave after wave of Confederates, though losing one-third of its men. Sheridan was reported to have greeted Rosecrans after the battle with, "Here we are, all that are left of us." Little of this seems directly relevant. But as one thinks of the causes of amnesia, of the withdrawal of a mind from a horror it cannot bear, the man's return to the battlefield and his sudden recapture of his memory, and of, in a sense, his finally dying on the battlefield and as a result of the battle, these things intensify the ironic interplay.

One could comment also on the richness of irony in the subtitles of the three sections, but the last, though less obviously witty, is the subtlest, for it points specifically to what might otherwise seem far-fetched — the Narcissus legend and its ironic connection with the man's looking into a pool of water. Narcissus looked, saw how beautiful he was, fell in love with himself, and faded away because he could not tear himself away from his own image. The man dies too, but because of the horror he sees, the face of one whose life has already faded away without his knowing it.

One of the rare figures of speech in the story, the personification of time, combines with the allusion of "one with Nineveh and Tyre," and with the last sentence which must, of course, be spoken deliberately, with a weight of sombre strangeness, to point to one of the basic elements of the story. The problem of time reverberates throughout. Constantly the performer is called upon to delineate some problem of time. At first these are simple — "it was near the hour of dawn." But they grow more and more complicated and vexed. What is time? Is time simply a matter of consciousness? What happens to time forgotten? And this problem of time interweaves with the problem of identity to complete the thematic pattern of the story. Who is the man? Which life was the real life? Which life has he lost? At one time the doctor would have to be either a friend or an enemy. Now he is neither. But though he calls himself physician, he cannot, as the subtitle suggests, heal a life that is lost. Who is he to the man but a character out of a folktale? Didn't the man really die in the battle? Did the other man die a little before dawn of this day? Did one or both men die when the soldier saw the other man's aged face? Is identity merely the function of time? Does time give us our identity? Which is the man? When does he die?

These questions and, no doubt, a complexity of others, melodramatic if you will, must more or less emerge in a voice that is never melodramatic. The voice is always in that subjective-objective tone, which has been evolved, if not defined, and reflects a sympathetic, yet objective, realistically limited mind. It is a mind which can relate an occurrence bizarre almost to the point of the supernatural, see the metaphysical richness of this (in mood) strange, remote action, yet never lose the physical and the psychological reality that is the basis of the scene, and, by this realistic base, make the questions posed by the story all the more compelling.

A FINAL WORD

Reading aloud is an art which can lead to wisdom and delight. It leads to wisdom through the ever-enlarging vocabulary of vocal and physical response which the reader brings to the task of translating, whether silently or aloud, the dead words on the page into a living reality. It leads to delight when the aim is not self-display, but the complete and ungrudging reconstruction of the exact intellectual passion of a work of literary art. As with any other art, there are many pitfalls; melodrama, sentimentality, exhibitionism, frigidity, perverse wilfullness, and (in its bad sense) intellectual pride. These are all risks that any creator or performer of any art must run if he is to create. Beyond that, they are the risks of being alive. Welcome to another facet of that awesome process.

Index of Authors, Titles, and First Lines

General Index

Including Authors and Works Discussed in the Text